The Nibelungen Tradition
An Encyclopedia

Edited by
Francis G. Gentry
Winder McConnell
Ulrich Müller
and
Werner Wunderlich

ROUTLEDGE
New York and London

Published in 2002 by
Routledge
29 West 35th Street
New York, NY 10001

Published in Great Britain by
Routledge
11 New Fetter Lane
London EC4P 4EE

Routledge is an imprint of the Taylor & Francis Group.

Frontispiece: Nibelungen-ms. D (Bayerische Staatsbibliothek Muenchen, cgm 31, 14th century), fol.1r: Beginning of the *Nibelungenlied*. Courtesy of Kümmerle, from Otfrid Ehrismann, ed., *Das Nibelungenlied: Abbildungen, Transkriptionen und Materialien zur gesamten handschriftlichen Üeberlieferung der I. und XXX. Aventiure* (Litterae, Göppinger Arbeiten zur Germanistik, edited by Ulrich Müller, Franz Hundsnurscher, Cornelius Sommer, vol. 23). Göppingen: Kümmerle, 1973. Figure 1 courtesy of Ulrich Müller. Figure 2 courtesy of Philipp Reclam jun. GmbH & Co., Stuttgart, from Siegfried Grosse, ed., *Das Nibleungenlied. Mittelhochdeutsch/Neuhochdeutsch*. Stuttgart: Reclam, 1997.

Library of Congress Cataloging-in-Publication Data is available from the Library of Congress.

The Nibelungen tradition: an encyclopedia/edited by Francis G. Gentry, Winder McConnell, Ulrich Müller, Werner Wunderlich
ISBN 0-8153-1785-9

Printed on acid-free, 250-year life paper.
Manufactured in the United States of America.

10 9 8 7 6 5 4 3 2 1

Table of Contents

Vns ist jn alten mæren wunders vil geseit·
von helden lobeberen vo grozzer arbeit· von vreudé vnd hochgeziten· von weinen vnd von chlagen· vo chuiner rechen striten mugt ir wunder hoin sagen·

Es wuchs jnbvrigvndé ein edel magedin· daz jn allen landen nicht schoners mochte sin· Chrimhilt was si geheizen die ward ein schonez wip· Dar vm me mnsten degen vil vliesen den lip·

Der minnechlichen magde treuten wol gezam· Jr mvtten chune rechen niemen was ir gram· Ane mazzen schone so was ir schoner lip· d' iunchfrouwen schone die zirten einR pflagen diev wip· dietz chvnige edel vnd rich

Hvnther vnde Gernot di recken lobelich· Gyselher d' iunge ein vzerwelter degen· die vrouwe was ir swester· die fursten heten si in ir pflegen·

En reiche chvnegnine vrouwe vie ir muter hiez· Jr vater d' hiez Dant wart d' in die erde her sint nach snem lebn ein ellen trucher man· d' ouch msi ner iugent grozzer ern vi te hren gewan·

Si warn milde· von arte hoch geborn· Sir chraft vn mazzen chune· die recken vz erchorn· Da zv den Bv rigvnden so was ir lant ge nant· Si frvmten starchev wunder sint in Etzelemes zu wurmtz bi lant·

Ze dem rine· si woten mit ir chraft· Jn dienste von ir lande vil stoltze ritterschaft· Sur lobelichen ern vntz an ir endes zit· Si storbe iamerlichen sint von zw eier vrouwen nit·

Je driee chvnige warn als ich gesaget han· Von vil hohen ellen in warn vncertan ouch die

Preface

The *Nibelungen Tradition* is the first comprehensive reference work on one of the major themes in Germanic and world literature, and is intended to provide the reader with an extensive overview of the Nibelungen tradition from its origins to the present. For in much the same fashion as another great medieval icon, Arthur, his knights, and the courtly ideals embodied in his tales, have survived the ages to inspire less chivalrous times, so, too, have Siegfried, the Germanic heroes, and the bold virtue of unswerving loyalty and death before dishonor which they incorporate endured the transition from the heroic to the present, decidedly "post-heroic" age.

Departing from the practice that has prevailed in the series, we have not listed entries solely in alphabetical order but rather have divided them up into ten major categories:

1) Primary works in which the Nibelungen topic plays a significant role;
2) Names of all important persons and places in the major literary works of the Middle Ages that contain elements of the Nibelungen theme;
3) Explanations of key words, motifs, themes, and objects related to the story of the Nibelungen;
4) Manuscript collections and literary/historical analogues;

5) Examination of major scholarly questions associated with the topic of the Nibelungen;
6) Literary reception of the Nibelungen theme in German;
7) Literary reception of the Nibelungen theme in languages other than German;
8) Music and composers associated with the Nibelungen theme;
9) Art and artists, film and filmmakers, sculpture and sculptors associated with the Nibelungen theme; and
10) Historians, clerics, politics, the military, propaganda, psychology, education, iconography, and geography.

Although we intended from the onset of the project to be as comprehensive as possible in our selection of entries, it might be argued that certain references are too indirect in nature to deserve inclusion—the many personal names cited from the *Volsunga saga* or the *þiðreks saga,* for example—but a conscious decision was made by the editors to err, if err we did, on the side of generosity and inclusiveness with respect to the Scandinavian analogues. While this volume is clearly not intended as an all-encompassing reference work on all extant Germanic heroic epics, in those instances where primary works in Old Norse did incorporate elements of the Nibelungen tradition, we have taken the liberty of including many of the figures who constitute a vital part of the overall heroic scenery. We cannot, on the other hand, claim to have found every pertinent reference that should be included in a work of this nature.

While the bulk of entries in *The Nibelungen Tradition* are directly related to the Nibelungen theme, with references to the *Nibelungenlied* based on manuscript **B,** unless otherwise stated, the one obvious area that has not been considered in detail is Wagneriana. To be sure, Wagner's *Der Ring des Nibelungen* itself, along with all of its figures, has been included, but only the most standard scholarship has been cited in the bibliography, and no attempt has been made to treat systematically the corpus of works that constitute its literary reception.

There are no individual entries on Nibelungen scholars. The major trends in Nibelungen scholarship from its beginnings to the present have been summarized in Part V of the Encyclopedia.

This encyclopedia, like all works of the genre, is less a finished product than an ongoing enterprise. In the final stages of the book's preparation for publication, several more significant entries came to the attention of one or more of the editors and were subsequently added to the text. Thus we can say with assurance that the work on this project will continue long after it has been published.

There remains the enjoyable task of thanking all those colleagues, editors, and students, some of whom have been involved in the project from the beginning. First and foremost, our heartfelt thanks go to our colleagues, an international team from North America, Europe, and Asia, who willingly and graciously contributed their erudition and effort to accommodate the editors' wishes. Obviously, without their cooperation, this volume would not have progressed beyond the "drawing board." We also wish to thank most sincerely the University of St. Gall for its generous support. That such a project depends in large measure on the knowledge and cooperation of library colleagues goes without saying, and we wish to thank all our colleagues and friends at various university and archival libraries who have so selflessly assisted us. In particular we would like to single out three colleagues, pars pro toto, for special mention, Opritsa Popa, Distinguished Librarian of the University of California, Davis; Doris Überschlag, Bibliothekarin der Kantonsbibliothek Vadiana in St. Gall, Switzerland; and Dr. Gerlinde Weiss (Salzburg), who provided the vast majority of contributions on the Old Norse materials pertaining to the Nibelungen theme. The editors also wish to thank Routledge for including this volume within its series of highly useful and respected encyclopedias.

Finally, the editors would like to stress that this encyclopedia is the happy result of a truly cooperative international editorial undertaking with two editors in the United States, one on each coast, and two in Europe, one in Austria and the other in Switzerland. It is true that the modern aids of e-mail and fax greatly facilitated communication and overcame otherwise daunting logistical problems, but the spirit of the enterprise was present in each editor in full measure.

Francis G. Gentry
Winder McConnell

Ulrich Müller
Werner Wunderlich

List of Contributors

SGA: Samuel G. Armistead
University of California, Davis

RB: Ralph Breyer
Humboldt-Universität zu Berlin

AC: Albrecht Classen
University of Arizona

BC: Beatrice Crockett
University of California, Davis

MD: Monika Deck
Universität Mannheim

ESD: Ernst S. Dick
University of Kansas

AE: Annemarie Eder
Universität Salzburg

OE: Otfrid Ehrismann
Justus-Liebig-Universität Gießen

RHF: Ruth H. Firestone
Fort Hays State College, Kansas

JLF: John Flood
University of London

FGG: Francis G. Gentry
Pennsylvania State University

MEG: Marion Gibbs
University of London

PG: Peter Göhler
Humboldt-Universität zu Berlin

AH: Andreas Härter
Universität St. Gallen

WRH: Will Hasty
University of Florida

BH: Barbara Haupt
*Heinrich-Heine-Universität,
Düsseldorf*

ERH: Edward R. Haymes
Cleveland State University

JH: Joachim Heinzle
Philipps-Universität Marburg

WLH: Wolfgang Hempel
University of Toronto

EH: Ernst Hintz
Fort Hays State College, Kansas

WH: Werner Hoffmann
Universität Mannheim

MH: Margarete Hubrath
Technische Universität Chemnitz

FH: Frank Hugus
University of Massachusetts

SJ: Sibylle Jefferis
University of Pennsylvania

SMJ: Sidney Johnson
Indiana University

RK: Rupert Kalkofen
        Universität St. Gallen

WL: Walter Lenschen
        Université de Lausanne

CM: Catherine MacGillivary
        University of Iowa

SJM: Susannah Martin
        University of California, Davis

KM: Karen McConnell
        Boston College

WM: Winder McConnell
        University of California, Davis

WCM: William C. McDonald
        University of Virginia

JVM: James V. McMahon
        Emory University

UM: Ulrich Müller
        Universität Salzburg

BOM: Brian O. Murdoch
        University of Stirling

AKN: Ann-Katrin Nolte
        Universität Bamberg

BÖ: Bernhard Öhlinger
        *Universität   Salzburg/University
        of Hiroshima*

OP: Opritsa Popa
        University of California, Davis

KQ: Katrin Quisenberry
        University of California, Davis

HR: Hermann Reichert
        University of Vienna

MR: Michael Resler
        Boston College

PS: Peter Schäffer
        University of California, Davis

SSch: Siegrid Schmidt
        Universität Salzburg

SS: So Shitanda
        University of Hiroshima

GCS: Gary Shockey
        University of California, Davis

BS: Britta Simon
        University of Washington

JHS: James H. Spohrer
        University of California, Berkeley

MS: Margarete Springeth
        Universität Salzburg

IS: Inge Stephan
        Humboldt-Universität zu Berlin

ASH: Alexandra Sterling-Hellenbrand
        Goshen College

RGS: Robert Sullivan
        University of Massachusetts

LDT: Lynn D. Thelen
        Ursinus College

VU: Victor Udwin
        University of Tulsa

NV: Norbert Voorwinden
        University of Leiden

RW: Ray Wakefield
        University of Minnesota

JKW: James K. Walter
        Ohio Northern University

GW: Gerlinde Weiss
        Universität Salzburg

WW: Werner Wunderlich
        Universität St. Gallen

List of Contributions

I. PRIMARY WORKS

	Ältere Nibelungennot. See "Scholarship."
BOM	*Atlakviðá* (Lay of Atli)
GW	*Atlamál in groenlenzku* (The Greenlandish Lay of Atli)
GW	*Brot af Sigurðarkviðu* (Fragment of a Sigurd Lay)
GW	*Codex Regius*
JLF	*Das Lied vom Hürnen Seyfried* (The Lay of Seyfrid with the Horny Skin)
RHF	Dietrich Epics
MD	*Diu Klage* (The Lament of the Nibelungen)
GW	*Edda*
GW	*Fáfnismál* (The Lay of Fáfnir)
GW	*Grimhilds Hævn*
BOM	*Grípisspá* (Prophecy of Gripir)
GW	*Guðrúnarhvot* (Gudrun's Lament)
GW	*Guðrúnarkviða (in fyrsta)* (The First Lay of Gudrun)
GW	*Guðrúnarkviða (onnur)* (The Second Lay of Gudrun)
GW	*Guðrúnarkviða (in þridia)* (The Third Lay of Gudrun)
BOM	*Hamðismál* (Lay of Hamðir)
HR	*Heldenschau*
GW	*Helreið Brynhildar* (Brynhild's Ride to Hel)
JLF	*Historia von dem gehörnten Siegfried* (The Story of Siegfried with the Horny Skin)
WW	*Hven Chronicle*
GW	*Hyndluljóð* (The Lay of Hyndla)
UM	*Marner*
WH	*Nibelungenlied*
GW	*Oddrúnargrátr* (Oddrun's Lament)
JKW	*Ragnars saga loðbrókar* (The Saga of Ragnar)
GW	*Reginsmál* (The Lay of Regin)
ESD	*Ritter Löwhardus*
JH	*Rosengarten zu Worms* (Rose Garden at Worms)

GW	*Sigrdrífumál* (The Lay of Sigrdrifa)
GW	*Sigurðarkviða in meiri* (The Longer Lay of Sigurd)
GW	*Sigurðarkviða hin skamma* (The Short Lay of Sigurd)
ERH	*Þiðreks saga af Bern* (Saga of Dietrich of Verona)
JKW	*Volsunga saga*
GW	*Waltari and Hildigund*
BOM	*Waltharius* (*Waltharilied*)

II. PERSONAL AND PLACE NAMES

WM	Adelind
ASH	Aesir
BOM	Aetius, Flavius
WM	Agnar
KQ	Alberich (Albrich)
FH	Aldrian (1) (King of Niflungaland)
FH	Aldrian (2) (Son of Atli)
GW	Aldrian (3) (Hogni's son)
GW	Alfrik (Alpris)
WM	Alsvid (1) (One of two horse pulling sun chariot)
WM	Alsvid (2) (Son of Heimer and friend of Sigurd)
AC	Alzei (Alzeye)
KM	Amelrich
UM/WM	Amelung/Amelungen
UM	Amelungelant
WM	Andvari
GW	Apulia/púl(l)
GCS	Arabia
WW	Arminius
NV	Arras
WM	Arvak

JKW	Aslaug
FH	Aspilian
NV	Astolt
BOM	Athanagild
GW	Atli
BOM	Attila
GW	Auða
FH	Aventrod
RGS	Azagouc
GCS	Bavaria
NV	Bavarians
WM	Bekkhild
JLF/SMJ	Bern (Verona)
FH	Bertangaland
WM	Bikki
GW	Biturulf
BOM	Bleda
WM	Bloedel (in)
WM	Borghild
WM	Botelung
WM	Boymunt (Bohemond)
WM	Bragi
WM	Bredi
BÖ	Brünhild
BOM	Brunhild (Brunichildis; Visigoth, wife of Sigibert)
GW	Brynhild
BC	Buda
SSch	Budapest
WM	Budli
WW/WM	Burgundians
WW	Burgundy
KM	Chaplain
BOM	Chilperich
WM	Conrad

AC	Gran	BS	Haki
GW	Grani/Grane	BS	Hakon
WM	Granmar	BS	Half
WM	Grimhild (1) (Wife of King Gjuki, mother of Gunnar, Hogni, Guttorm, and Gudrun)	WM	Hamdir
		WM	Hamund
		GW	Hartwin
FH	Grimhild (2) (Daughter of Aldrian, sister to Gunnar et. al., Hogni's half sister)	WM	Heimburg
		GW	Heime/Heimir
UM	Grimhilde	WM	Heimir
WM	Gripir	WM	Hel
NV	Grossmehring	JVM	Helche
GW	Guðrún	WM	Helgi
GW	Gullrond	WM	Helmnot
BOM	Gundahari	WM	Helpfrich
BOM	Gundomar	GW	Herborg
GW	Gunnar	FH	Herbrand
JHS	Gunther	GW	Herkja
WM	Gunther jr.	WM	Herlind
BOM	Gunthram (Guntramm)	WM	Herman of Poland
FH	Guthilinda (1) (Eldest daughter of King Drusian of Drekanfils)	GW	Hermann
		GW	Herraland
FH	Guthilinda (2) (Sister to Duke Nauthung and wife of Rothingeir)	BS	Herrat (Herad)
		GW	Hertnit/Hertnid
		WM	Hessen
FH	Guthorm	JKW	Hildebrand
UM	Gutrune	WM	Hildeburg
JHS	Gutthorm (Guttormr Gjukasson)	FH	Hildibrand
		BOM	Hildico
JLF	Gybich	GW	Hildigund
JLF	Gyrnot	WM	Hindarfell
WM	Hadeburg	WM	Hjalli
WM	Hagbard I	WM	Hjalmgunnar
WM	Hagbard II	WM	Hjalprek
WM	Hagen	WM	Hjordis
JLF	Hagenwald	WM	Hjorvard
NV/SSch	Hainburg		

WM	Hljod	WM	Jarisleif
GW	Hniflung	GW	Jarizkár
WM	Hnikar	WM	Jonakr
WM	Hodbrodd	JLF	Jorcus
GW	Hognar, Hognir, or Hegnir	WM	Jormunrek
GW	Hogni	SMJ	Kiewe
WM	Holkvir	GW	Knefrod
GW	Holmgard	NV	Konrad
WM	Hoenir	JHS	Kostbera (also Bera)
KM	Hornboge	WM	Kriechen
GW	Hornbogi	FGG	Kriemhild
GW	Hrauðung	JLF	Kuperan
WM	Hreidmar	FGG/WM	Liudegast and Liudeger
WM	Hrimnir	WM	Liudeger (King of France)
WM	Hropt	SMJ	Lochheim
GW	Húnaland, or Hunland	SMJ	Lofnheid
WM	Hunding	JVM	Loge
KM	Hunold	JKW	Loki
JKW	Huns	NV	Lorraine (or Lotharingia)
FH	Ilias	NV	Lorsch
WM	Indîâ	WM	Lybîâ/Lybîân
NV	Inn	GW	Lyngheid
WM	Iring	WM	Lyngvi
WM	Irnfrid	WM	Machazin and Machmet
WM	Irung (1) (Warrior and king of Nibelungenland)	FH	Maeri
		NV	Main
WM	Irung (2) (Old Norse counterpart to Iring in *Nibelungenlied*)	WM	Marroch
		NV	Mautern
		SSch	Melk
WM	Isalde	NV	Metz
WM	Isenstein	GW	Mime
ASH	Island	JVM	Mimir
FH	Isung (1) (King of Bertangaland)	WM	Misenburg
		WM	Moeringen
FH	Isung (2) (Juggler, musician, and companion of Thettleif)	GW	Myrkheim

III. THEMES, MOTIFS, OBJECTS, AND KEY WORDS

IV. MANUSCRIPT COLLECTIONS AND LITERARY/HISTORICAL ANALOGUES

V. SCHOLARSHIP

VI. THE LITERARY RECEPTION OF THE NIBELUNGEN THEME IN GERMANY, AUSTRIA, AND SWITZERLAND

VII. THE LITERARY RECEPTION OF THE NIBELUNGEN THEME IN NON-GERMAN-SPEAKING COUNTRIES

UM	Sattler, Josef		BOM	Gregor of Tours
WW	Schleef, Einar		WM	Hagen Offensive
UM	Schmoll von Eisenwerth, Karl		WW	Hohenems
UM	Schnorr von Carolsfeld, Julian		WM	Irish Siegfried
UM	Schumacher, Carl Georg Christian		WLH	Jordanes
			WM	Jung, Carl Gustav
UM	Schwanthaler, Ludwig		JVM	Kéza, Simon
UM	Schwegerle, Hans		WM	Nibelungen-Brücke
UM	Sinding, Stephan		WM	Nibelungen Division
UM	Slevogt, Max		SSch	Nibelungengau
UM	Staeger, Ferdinand		MR/UM	Nibelungenhalle (Passau)
UM	Stassen, Franz		WM	*Nibelungenlied* Postage Stamps
UM	Stuck, Franz von			
UM	Tàpies, Antoni		SMJ	Nibelungenstädte
UM	Thoma, Hans		MR	Nibelungenstrasse
UM	Tieck, Friedrich		WW	Nibelungentreue
UM	Trillhaase, Adalbert		WM/OP	Nibelungen Verlag
UM	Wagner, Ferdinand		WM	Nibelungenwerke
UM	Wartburg		UM	Nordic Stones
UM	Wrubel, Michail		UM	Norwegian Churches
			JVM	Olah, Nicolaus

X. MISCELLANEOUS: HISTORIANS, CLERICS, POLITICS, THE MILITARY, PROPAGANDA, PSYCHOLOGY, EDUCATION, ICONOGRAPHY, AND GEOGRAPHY

			WW	Pedagogy
			BOM	Poeta Saxo
			BOM	Priscus of Panium
			HR	Psychology
JVM	Callimachus Experiens		WM	Rosenberg, Alfred
MEG	Carlyle, Thomas		SSch	Sachbücher
UM	Compact Discs—German		UM	Sanguesa
SMJ	Der Lindelbrunnen der Gemeinde Mossautal		JKW	Saxo Grammaticus
			UM	Siegfried Iconography
WW	Dolchstosslegende		WM	Siegfried Line
UM/AE	Faeroe Islands		IS	Spielrein, Sabina (Siegfried Phantasy)
BOM	Fredegar(ius)			
WW	Göring, Hermann		WM	Unternehmen Nibelungen
SMJ	Grasellenbach		WM	Unternehmen Walküre

PART I

Primary Works

ÄLTERE NIBELUNGENÔT (Elder Nibelungenot). Given the hypothetical nature of this work, see under PART V: SCHOLARSHIP.

ATLAKVIÐA (Lay of Atli), a poem in the *Elder Edda* combining the fall of the Burgundians with the death of Attila and the collapse of the Hun empire. The Burgundian brothers Gunnar and Hogni are invited to the court of Atli and, in spite of warnings from their sister Guðrún, now Atli's wife, Gunnar makes the decision to go to the court accompanied only by a select band of warriors. Their departure is mourned, and on arrival Guðrún curses them for coming. After a brave struggle against the avaricious Huns Gunnar and Hogni are taken prisoner. Then, in a reversal of the situation that prevails at the end of the *Nibelungenlied,* Gunnar refuses to reveal the whereabouts of their treasure until he knows that his brother Hogni is dead. After an attempt to trick him with the heart of another warrior, which Gunnar knows cannot be Hogni's because it is trembling, Hogni is killed and his heart is brought to Gunnar. Gunnar then refuses once more to reveal where the treasure is hidden and dies defiantly in a snake pit, singing a song of triumph. He is praised by the poet for behaving as a king should and for defending his gold against his enemies. The treasure, now lost to all, is referred to as the "metal of strife." Guðrún then exacts revenge for the death of her brother by killing the drunken Atli and burning the hall. Gunnar is here more heroic than Gunther, to whom he corresponds in the *Nibelungenlied,* and he takes the dominant role, while his sister Guðrún is more violent than the sister Kriemhild in the *Nibelungenlied.*

[BOM]

Bibliography

Dronke, Ursula, ed. and trans. *The Poetic Edda.* Vol. 1 of *Heroic Poems.* Oxford: Clarendon, 1969, pp. 1–74.

Gottzmann, Carola L. *Das alte Atlilied.* Heidelberg: Winter, 1973.

Murdoch, Brian. *The Germanic Hero.* London: Hambledon, 1996, pp. 46–52.

ATLAMÁL IN GROENLENZKU (The Greenlandish Lay of Atli) is one of the most recent lays of the *Poetic Edda* and it is the longest one (105 stanzas in *málaháttr;* this meter is only used here in an Eddic poem, being more typical of scaldic poetry). It was written during the twelfth or the thirteenth century (Icelandic scholars suggest a much earlier date, 1050–1150). The title indicates that the lay was written in Greenland, and the work corresponds to the poet's inclination to describe everyday life in modest circumstances. There is also the presence of the *hvítabjorn* (white bear), the polar bear, in stanza 18, further pointing to Greenland as a place of the lay's origin, although this animal was known to Icelanders as well. The rural atmosphere described in the poem is typical of wide areas in Scandinavia. Thus while scholars suspect that the lay was written in Greenland, its origin cannot be proven definitively.

The lay relates the same story as the *Atlakviða* in a broader and more descriptive style. The poet included new persons and new scenes, foreboding dreams, and many events in retrospect. He is more interested in the mental and emotional state of his figures, especially in Gudrun's cruelty to her children, than in action and events. According to the story, Atli invites Gunnar and Hogni, the sons of the Rhenish King Gjuki, to his court. Gudrun tries to warn her brothers of the treachery planned by her husband, but her warning runes are subtly altered by Vingi, a treacherous messenger, and her intended message does not get through. The Hunnish envoys are received very kindly by Hogni and Gunnar, yet their wives, Kostbera and Glaumvor, have dreams that foretell a catastrophe. The husbands interpret the dreams as being harmless and depart together with Snäwar and Solar, Hogni's sons, and Orkning, Kostbera's brother. They row their boat so violently that they ruin it and leave it untied (stanza 37; cf. *Nibelungenlied* **B**, 1581). When Vingi admits that he has deceived Gunnar and Hogni, they kill him. The two are later joined by their sister in the battle that takes place in the hall. Snäwar, Solar, and Orkning are killed and Hogni is taken prisoner. Beiti, Atli's master of ceremonies, advises the Huns to kill Hjalli instead of Hogni and cut his heart out of his breast. Hjalli is such a coward that he is spared at Hogni's request, and Hogni is killed. Gunnar ends up in a snake pit playing the harp with his toes. (According to the *Volsunga saga* his hands are bound together. The scene of Gunnar playing the harp with his toes is depicted on the portals of the Norwegian churches of Hyllestad and Ostad.) Atli tries to reconcile with Gudrun, but she does not accept his presents. She is intent on revenge. She gives him so much beer that he becomes completely drunk. Meanwhile, in a tender scene, Gudrun says goodbye to her and Atli's boys and then cuts their throats. She has drinking vessels made out of their skulls, and Atli drinks beer mixed with the children's blood

out of them and consumes their roasted hearts. A long dialogue between Gudrun and the dying Atli closes the poem. Gudrun and Hniflung (he is not mentioned before), Hogni's son, finally strike Atli dead.

[GW]

Bibliography

Andersson, Theodore M. "Atlamál in groenlenzku." In *Dictionary of the Middle Ages,* edited by Joseph R. Strayer. Vol.1. New York: Scribner, 1982.

_____. "Did the Poet of *Atlamál* Know *Atlakviða?*" In *Edda: A Collection of Essays,* edited by Robert J. Glendinning and Haraldur Bessason. Winnipeg: University of Manitoba Press, 1983, pp. 243–257.

de Vries, Jan. *Altnordische Literaturgeschichte.* Vol. 2. 2nd ed. Grundriss der germanischen Philologie 15. Berlin: de Gruyter, 1967, pp. 150–154.

Dronke, Ursula, ed. and trans. *The Poetic Edda.* Vol. 1 of *Heroic Poems.* Oxford: Clarendon Press, 1969, pp. 77–141.

Finch, R. G. *"Atlakviða, Atlamál,* and *Volsunga Saga:* A Study in Combination and Integration." In *Speculum Norroenum: Norse Studies in Memory of Gabriel Turville-Petre,* edited by Ursula Dronke et al. Odense: Odense University Press, 1981, pp. 123–138.

Gering, Hugo, and B. Sijmons. *Kommentar zu den Liedern der Edda.* 2. Hälfte: *Heldenlieder.* Germanistische Handbibliothek VII 3,2. Halle (Saale): Buchhandlung des Waisenhauses (Francke), 1931, pp. 364–410.

Haymes, Edward R., and Susann T. Samples. *Heroic Legends of the North: An Introduction to the Nibelung and Dietrich Cycles.* New York: Garland, 1996, pp. 124f.

Simek, Rudolf, and Hermann Pálsson. *Lexikon der altnordischen Literatur.* Stuttgart: Kröner, 1987, pp. 24, 240.

BROT AF SIGURÐARKVIÐU (Fragment of a Sigurd Lay). The beginning of this Eddic lay is lost in the lacuna of the *Codex Regius.* Only nineteen stanzas in *fornyrðislag* exist. Obviously the scribe did not know the end of the poem, and so he used a prose bridge about Sigurd's death to the *Guðrúnarkviða in fyrsta.* Andreas Heusler called the lay *Sigurðarkviða in forna* (The Old Lay of Sigurd) and believed it to be the oldest and shortest of the Sigurd lays. Although parts of the lay are missing, we can reconstruct those parts of the story from the *Volsunga saga.*

The background of the story is that Sigurd arrives at the court of Rhenish King Gjuki's sons, Gunnar, Hogni, and Gutthorm. He marries Gudrun, their sister, and becomes blood brother to Gunnar and Hogni. Sigurd agrees to help Gunnar win the valkyrie-like queen Brynhild, and, drawing on his magical powers, exchanges shapes with him, because Gunnar cannot pass through the *Waberlohe* (wall of flame) around her hall. He spends three nights with Brynhild with a drawn sword between them. Later, while bathing in a river, Gudrun and Brynhild quarrel about their husbands, and Brynhild finds out she has been deceived by Sigurd. She then claims that Sigurd had betrayed Gunnar while they slept together and that she does not want to be the wife of two men. At that moment the lay begins. Gunnar learns of his own supposed deception and wants Sigurd to be killed, but Hogni opposes the murder. Finally Gutthorm, who is not bound by an oath, kills Sigurd in the forest. The deed itself is not depicted in the lay. The kings return home, and Hogni tells Gudrun that they have murdered her husband. During the night and after a drinking spree, Brynhild tells Gunnar the truth: she had lied to them, Sigurd never broke his oath, and as a result they were treacherous in their murderous deed. The final prose passage discusses the different versions of Sigurd's death. The original conclusion probably told of Brynhild's suicide and her joining Sigurd on his funeral pyre.

The lay closely mirrors the German tradition: Sigurd/Siegfried is killed in the forest "south of the Rhine," not in his bed or at the *Thing,* the Old Norse assemby. His death is already connected with the fall of the Niflungs/Nibelungs. The Hunnish king Atli will avenge Sigurd's death on Gunnar and Hogni (contrary to the *Atlakviða,* in which Atli invites the brothers because of his greed for Sigurd's gold). The lay is very heterogeneous in its language and its narrative style. Some scholars suggest it may be very old (ninth and tenth centuries), although most of them believe it was written between the eleventh and twelfth century.

[GW]

Bibliography

Andersson, Theodore M. "The Lays in the Lacuna of Codex Regius." In *Speculum Norroenum: Norse Studies in Memory of Gabriel Turville-Petre,* edited by Ursula Dronke et al. Odense: Odense University Press, 1981, pp. 6–26.

de Vries, Jan. *Altnordische Literaturgeschichte.* Vol. 1. 2nd ed. Grundriss der germanischen Philologie 15. Berlin: de Gruyter, 1964, pp. 299–303.

Gering, Hugo, and B. Sijmons. *Kommentar zu den Liedern der Edda.* 2. Hälfte: *Heldenlieder.* Germanistische Handbibliothek VII 3,2. Halle (Saale): Buchhandlung des Waisenhauses (Francke), 1931, pp. 223–233.

Haymes, Edward R., and Susann T. Samples. *Heroic Legends of the North: An Introduction to the Nibelung and Dietrich Cycles.* New York: Garland, 1996, p. 122.

Heusler, Andreas. "Die Lieder der Lücke im Codex Regius." In *Germanistische Abhandlungen Hermann Paul dargebracht.* Strassburg: Trübner, 1902, pp. 1–98.

Schier, Kurt. "Brot af Sigurðarkviðu." In vol. 18 of *Kindlers neues Literaturlexikon,* edited by Walter Jens. Munich: Kindler, 1992, pp. 340–341.

See, Klaus von. "Die Werbung um Brynhild." *ZfdA* 88 (1957/1958): 1–20.

Simek, Rudolf, and Hermann Pálsson. *Lexikon der altnordischen Literatur.* Stuttgart: Kröner, 1987, p. 48.

BRYNNHILDA TÁTTUR. see PART X: FAEROE ISLANDS

CODEX REGIUS is the name given to the main vellum manuscript of the *Poetic Edda* (Icelandic: *Konungsbók eddukvæða*), written in the second half of the thirteenth century and preserved since 1662 in the Royal library Copenhagen (Gl.kgl.sml.2365 4to). In April 1971 the *Codex Regius* was returned to Iceland as the first of a series of Old Icelandic manuscripts and is now preserved in the Icelandic Foundation for Manuscripts (Stofnun Árna Magnússonar á Islándi). Formerly it had belonged to the Icelandic bishop Brynjólfr Sveinsson at Skálholt (1605–1675), who gave it the title *Edda Saemundi multiscii* (Edda of Saemund the Learned), thereby demonstrating that he believed it to be the work of the Icelandic historian Sæmundr Sigfússon inn fróði (Saemund Sigfusson the Wise, 1056–1133). It is clear, however, that the book was compiled at a much later period than that of Saemund, probably in the 1270s, and written in a single hand, although some of the poetry contained in it is among the oldest preserved in a Scandinavian language. The scribal and linguistic evidence of the manuscript indicates that all the poems now preserved in the *Codex Regius* must have existed in written form before 1240. We do not know where in Iceland the codex was written. There is also no record of the manuscript before it came into the possession of Bishop Brynjólfr Sveinsson in 1643. Already at that date it had lost the original fifth gathering, probably of eight leaves. This lacuna concerns poems about Sigurd, mainly the *Brot af Sigurðarkviðu*. In 1662 the manuscript was sent as a gift by the bishop to King Frederick III of Denmark, and so it later became part of the "Old Royal Collection."

The codex contains forty-five leaves in six gatherings, five of which consist of eight leaves, and the last one of five leaves. It also includes eleven mythological poems, sixteen heroic poems preserved in their entirety, two heroic poems in fragmentary form, and two short prose parts. The poems in the last two gatherings all deal with the legends of Sigurd and Brynhild, the Niflungar and their descendants.

[GW]

Bibliography
Codex Regius of the Elder Edda. MS No. 2365 4to in the Royal Collection in the Royal Library in Copenhagen. With an introduction by Andreas Heusler. Corpus Codicum Islandicorum Medii Aevi 10. Copenhagen: Levin & Munksgaard, 1937.
Schier, Kurt. "Edda, Ältere." In *Reallexikon der germanischen Altertumskunde*, edited by Johannes Hoops. 2nd ed. Berlin: de Gruyter, 1986, pp. 355–394.

DAS LIED VOM HÜRNEN SEYFRID (The Lay of Seyfrid with the Horny Skin), this poem, first known from a Nuremberg edition of about 1530, is a clumsy compilation from different sources. Though devoid of merit in purely literary and poetic terms, it is of interest for the light it throws on narrative traditions and popular beliefs around 1500. The lay consists of 179 strophes in the *Hildebrandston* (Hildebrand's melody), of which strophes 16–172 focus on Seyfrid's rescue of Krimhilt, daughter of King Gybich of Worms, from a dragon who has abducted her. Strophes 1–15 give a laconic account

of Seyfrid's adventures largely as found in Scandinavian sources, telling how he acquired a horny skin. Strophes 173–179 represent an attempt to relate the story of Seyfrid's rescue of Krimhilt from the dragon to the story known from the *Nibelungenlied:* Seyfrid returns to Worms with Krimhilt after having thrown the treasure he has won from the dwarfs into the Rhine to avoid envy. His behavior gives rise to hatred in Krimhilt's brothers, Günther, Gyrnot and Hagen, who murder him broadly speaking in the manner recounted in the *Nibelungenlied*.

The importance of the *LhS* lies in the fact that it contains material found in Scandinavian sources (Eddic lays, *Volsunga saga*, *Þiðreks saga* (especially chapters 163–168) but which are otherwise only uncertainly attested in Germany, for example in *Rosengarten* (see Golther, p. xxx). It is not clear whether the *LhS* as known to us was composed only in the sixteenth century (see the diagram in King, p. 90) or whether it is a derivative of a much earlier (thirteenth-century) version which has not survived.

Humble work though it is, the *LHS* was able to inspire further versions. It was the chief source of Hans Sachs's seven-act "tragedy" of 1557 and also influenced the Dutch *Historie van den Reus Gilias*. It was revitalized in the mid-seventeenth century when it was turned into prose as the *Historia von dem gehörnten Siegfried*.

[JLF]

Bibliography
Golther, W. *Das Lied vom hürnen Seyfrid.* Neudrucke deutscher Literaturwerke des 16. u. 17. Jhs. 81/82. 2nd ed. Halle: Niemeyer, 1911.
King, K. C. *Das Lied vom hürnen Seyfrid.* Manchester: Manchester University Press, 1958.
Brunner, H. "Hürnen Seyfrid." In vol. 4 of *Die deutsche Literatur des Mittelalters. Verfasserlexikon.* 2nd ed., edited by Kurt Ruh et al. Berlin: de Gruyter, 1977ff, cols. 317–326.
Flood, John L., and Jürgen Beyer. "Siegfried in Livland? Ein handschriftliches Fragment des 'Liedes vom Hürnen Seyfrid' aus dem Baltikum." In *Jahrbuch für Volksliedforschung.* Forthcoming.
Lecouteux, C. "Seyfrid, Kuperan et le dragon." *Etudes Germaniques* 49 (1994): 257–266.

DIETRICH EPICS, a collective term for twelve late Middle High German narratives connected through the presence of the character Dietrich von Bern. There are also two related ballads, *Koninc Ermenrikes Dot* (King Ermenrich's Death) and the *Jüngere Hildebrandslied* (The Later Lay of Hildebrand); the prose summary of the *Heldenbuch;* the Norse *Þiðreks saga,* adapted from German sources; and two fragments. Although the epics as we have them were all composed in response to the *Nibelungenlied,* their authors drew upon the same orally transmitted and written stories of Dietrich and his men that were available to the Nibelungen poet. On the basis of content (and, to some extent, transmission), the epics fall into three groups, the "historical" Dietrich epics, the *âventiurenhaft* or "questlike" epics, and epics that parody the *Nibelungenlied.* There are three "historical" Dietrich epics, so called because some of the characters are named after historical figures. The central conflict of these epics is military-political, and like the *Nibelungenlied* this body of works serves as the vehicle for contemporary, thirteenth-century social criticism. Among the historical characters, Dietrich is named after Theoderich the Great (d. 526 a.d.), Ermenrich after Eormenrich (d. ca. 375), and Etzel after Attila (d. 453). The central conflict in all three "historical" epics is between Dietrich and Ermenrich: Ermenrich invades Dietrich's territories and Dietrich attempts to defend them. The first two narratives were composed in the second half of the thirteenth century. The *Rabenschlacht* (Battle of Ravenna, written in a unique, six-line strophe) probably antedates the *Buch von Bern* (Book of Verona), also called *Dietrichs Flucht* (Dietrich's Flight, written in the rhymed couplets of chronicles and courtly romances). A man named Heinrich der Vogelære (after King Heinrich I, "the fowler") identifies himself in the *Buch von Bern,* but the nature and extent of his contribution to its composition is unclear. Their sequel, *Alpharts Tod* (Alphart's Death, about half of which is in Nibelungen strophes, the rest in *Hildebrandston*), was composed later in the thirteenth century. The *Buch von Bern* and the *Rabenschlacht* are transmitted together in this order in all complete manuscripts, showing that the Austrian nobles for whom they were compiled interpreted them according to similarities in content as a double epic. *Alpharts Tod,* a long fragment, is found only in a fifteenth-century

manuscript from Hanau, but it is probably based on a late thirteenth-century Alemannic source. If, as seems likely, the *Alpharts Tod* manuscript and manuscript **n** of the *Nibelungenlied* are one and the same, *Alpharts Tod* was once followed by the second part of the *Nibelungenlied* (an abridgement of the **C** version).

The *Buch von Bern* and *the Rabenschlacht* are both set in an earlier time than the *Nibelungenlied* and they attempt to resolve positively the ambiguities of Dietrich's character as it is depicted there, most strikingly in his relationship to his men, his continuing exile, and his lack of enthusiasm for his marriage with Herrat. Due probably to tempering and moralizing clerical influence on the heroic tradition, he is doomed to misfortune. His every effort to make good results only in personal and political tragedy.

The clergy knew that Theoderich the Great was an Arian heretic, the murderer of Boethius and others. Narratives like the *Kaiserchronik* depict his bad end, which is also mentioned in the *Þiðreks saga* and the prose summary of the *Heldenbuch.* As in the *Nibelungenlied,* Hildebrand serves as Dietrich's aide and mentor, and Wolfhart plays the role of undisciplined and impudent warrior. In the *Buch von Bern,* which protests unjust treatment of nobles by princes, Dietrich's concern for his men at the expense of his own political and personal well-being is seen positively as the mark of a responsible leader. In that story Dietrich's army defeats the enemy, but a few of his men are taken hostage, so Dietrich chooses to go into exile at Etzel's court rather than sacrifice their lives. With Etzel's help, Dietrich tries to recover his lands. He wins the first battle but loses Ravenna when Witege, left in charge of the city, defects to Ermenrich. Etzel and Helche (his wife) then set marriage to Helche's niece Herrat as the condition for further aid. Dietrich reluctantly agrees and then wins the last battle, but Ermenrich escapes. Afterward Dietrich buries the fallen on both sides, thus paving the way to eventual reconciliation, and returns to exile. The *Rabenschlacht* (with an "editorial bent" that reeks of the cloister) deplores revenge. If Dietrich refused to let his men fight in the *Nibelungenlied* out of lack of confidence in the goodness of the divine order, here his tragedy is the result of overpermissiveness based on overconfidence. The *Rabenschlacht* begins where the *Buch von Bern* ended, with Dietrich lamenting for the dead. Helche, hoping to relieve his depression, arranges for him to marry her niece, Herrat. After, Dietrich obtains Etzel's aid for a new campaign. He becomes overconfident that he will win, and mistakenly thinks God will help him avenge Ermenrich's depredations because he is in the right. But all is lost from the outset. Just as Wolfhart promotes tragedy in the *Nibelungenlied* by persuading Hildebrand to let all of Dietrich's men accompany him to negotiations with the Burgundians, the two young sons of Helche and Etzel beg to go to Verona with Dietrich. Dietrich, believing that he can protect them, persuades their very reluctant parents to let them go. The boys and Dietrich's younger brother are then left in the care of the elderly warrior Elsan. They are forbidden to leave Verona, but they run off, lose their way in a fog, and are killed in unequal combat by the disloyal Witege. Dietrich's campaign thus ends in tragedy despite the defeat of Ermenrich's forces. Then, as if to refute accusations of heresy, Dietrich confesses his sins in the narrative and afterward survives a duel with Siegfried because he is wearing relics. Having repented his overconfidence, he now despairs that Helche and Etzel will not forgive him. Rüdiger persuades Helche that the deaths were not treachery on Dietrich's part. She and Etzel then reluctantly forgive him.

Alpharts Tod takes place at an earlier time than the *Buch von Bern* or the *Rabenschlacht*. The conflict is depicted on a less personal level than that between Dietrich and the emperor, Ermenrich, who lays claim to Dietrich's hereditary territories, and here Dietrich is depicted as in the right. He is deeply concerned for the welfare of his men and they, in turn, serve him loyally and well. A catalogue of Dietrich's warriors foreshadows the tragedy of *Alpharts Tod* as well as that of the *Nibelungenlied* by underscoring the presence of Nuodung, said in the *Nibelungenlied* to have been slain by Witege (1699, 3–4). As in the other two narratives, Ermenrich attacks Dietrich. Against everyone's advice, Dietrich's counselor and warrior, Alphart, who is also Hildebrand's nephew and Wolfhart's younger brother, insists upon going on watch alone. After proving his mettle by vanquishing Hildebrand in a duel, he is killed in unequal combat (here, in mirror image to the *Rabenschlacht,* two against

one) by Witege and Heime, formerly Dietrich's men but now serving Ermenrich. In this narrative the poet underscores the fact that their disloyalty is not Dietrich's fault. Dietrich and his men avenge Alphart's death and prevent Ermenrich from taking Verona, but Ermenrich, Witege, and Heime all escape. There is no mention of exile, which might be an effort on the part of the poet and/or compiler of the manuscript to avoid redundancy in connection with *Nibelungenlied* **n.**

The Dietrich epics of the second and largest group are now named according to their structure, *âventiurenhaft* (like a chivalric quest). Earlier they were named *märchenhaft* (like a folktale), after Dietrich's opponents, many of whom are dwarfs or giants. Several were anthologized in manuscript and printed as *Heldenbücher* (large anthologies and/or anthologies containing heroic narratives) and were circulated widely among nobles and burghers alike from the late thirteenth to the late sixteenth century. All of the works constituting this second group criticize heroic and courtly literature. Dietrich's character is drawn as if in answer to the *Nibelungenlied:* he is naive with regard to love and chivalry, is frequently accused of cowardice because he refuses to fight without just cause, but exonerates himself by acting for the good of all. Three of these narratives are named after Dietrich's opponents—the *Eckenlied* (Song of Ecke; a giant), *Goldemar* (a dwarf), and *Sigenot* (a giant)—and are written in a thirteen-line strophe called *Bernerton* (Strophe of Verona) or *Eckenstrophe* (Ecke's strophe). Another narrative written in the thirteen-line strophe is *Virginal,* sometimes called *Dietrichs erste Ausfahrt* ("Dietrich's first quest") or *Dietrich und seine Gesellen* ("Dietrich and his companions"). Virginal is a queen in distress whom Dietrich helps and, in two of three versions, marries. Albrecht von Kemenaten names himself as author in the fragmentary *Goldemar.* He was long thought to have written all four of these thirteen-line-strophe narratives, but differences in dialect and transmission have disproved this theory. In contrast to *Goldemar,* only nine strophes of which remain, *Eckenlied* (which probably originated as an etiological explanation for the name of Dietrich's sword, *Eckesachs* [sharp blade]) enjoyed long-term popularity throughout the German-speaking area. It is the earliest of all Dietrich epics to be documented. One strophe is found in the early thirteenth-century Bavarian *Carmina Burana,* and there is also an Ecca episode in the *Þiðreks saga.* In addition, the *Eckenlied* is one of the latest printed of the Dietrich epics, the latest edition appearing in Cologne in 1590. The elder *Sigenot,* an abbreviated version, exists in only one manuscript as an introduction to the *Eckenlied.* Like "Ecke the younger," *Sigenot* and *Virginal* were very popular. Other Dietrich epics of this group include *Laurin* (a dwarf). *Laurin,* which was also very popular, is sometimes called *Der kleine Rosengarten* (The Small Rose Garden) to distinguish it from *Der große Rosengarten zu Worms* (The Large Rose Garden at Worms; see Heinzle's article). In *Laurin,* Dietrich trespasses on Laurin's rose garden then fights him to rescue the sister of his friend Dietleib. A sequel, *Walberan,* named after Laurin's uncle, follows one version of *Laurin.* Walberan comes to Verona to rescue Laurin, who, converted to Christianity, is no longer in need of rescue. Last, but not least, there is the popular *Wunderer* (A Monster), which survives in three complete and numerous fragmentary versions. Some, including a Shrovetide play, are composed in rhymed couplets, others in *Heunenweise* strophes. The work derives much of its humor in reaction to the *Nibelungenlied.* Moreover it is the only narrative of the questlike group that depicts Dietrich at Etzel's court, not as an exile, but as a youth being educated there. At a feast a princess asks for protection against the Wunderer, a giant who is threatening to eat her because she has not accepted his marriage proposal. Etzel, who in reality fears the giant, refuses to help because his rank is too high. Rüdiger cannot help because his station is too low. Only Dietrich can protect her. He defeats the Wunderer in a duel and beheads him. The princess then identifies herself as "Fraw Seld" (Lady Luck), which might refer obliquely to Dietrich's lamentation at his lack of good fortune in the *Nibelungenlied.*

Three more epics are usually classified as Dietrich epics, but at least two of them might well be viewed instead as Nibelungen parodies. The two are *Biterolf und Dietleib* and *Der große Rosengarten zu Worms* (see Heinzle's article for further discussion). *Biterolf,* in rhymed couplets, is preserved only in the sixteenth-century *Ambras Codex* but probably was composed in the third quarter of the thirteenth century for nobles in Styria. Dietrich plays only a subordinate role. Biterolf and Dietleib are father and son. Young Dietleib, seeking his father, is on his way to Etzel's court when he encounters Gunther, Hagen, and Gernot returning from the Saxon war. Dietleib, only a squire, has disguised himself as a knight. The Burgundians challenge him when he refuses to identify himself. He defeats each one in a duel (Gunther hopes he will surrender to him without a fight because he is a king). Even though Dietleib is victorious, he thinks the Burgundians have insulted him by assuming he was a knight, and he refuses to accept knighthood at Etzel's court until this insult has been avenged. This motivation for revenge is as trivial as Kriemhild's was great, but it underlies the largest part of the epic: a journey and battle that are the reverse of that of the *Nibelungenlied.* Etzel's troops, allied with many others, among them Dietrich and his men, march to Worms. Dietrich is afraid to fight Siegfried, but a duel with Hildebrand restores his confidence. Wolfhart is overeager to fight in a tournament but is soon benched for breaking the rules, whereupon the allies negotiate to have the tournament changed to a real battle. Rüdiger acts as liaison between the allies and the Burgundians. His interactions with Kriemhild and Brünhild ironically foreshadow the events of the *Nibelungenlied.* The battle/tournament ends in reconciliation. Upon returning to Etzel's country, Biterolf and Dietleib are given Styria as a fief, but there is no further mention of Dietleib's knighthood. The fragmentary narrative *Dietrich und Wenezlan* (also composed in rhymed couplets) is preserved on two mid-thirteenth-century leaves used as part of a book cover. It resembles *Biterolf* more closely than it does any other Dietrich epic, though it combines elements of all groups. Dietrich is in exile. He and Etzel are on their way to a military encounter, because they are encamped with an army somewhere near the Salzach river. Wolfhart brings Dietrich a challenge from Wenezlan of Poland: he and Hildebrand are Wenezlan's hostages. Wenezlan will have them killed if Dietrich refuses to duel with him. Dietrich at first refuses to help, but, when Wolfhart accuses him of cowardice, he agrees to the duel, saying his refusal was only a joke. The duel takes place the next day and is still in progress as the fragment ends.

[RHF]

Bibliography

Curschmann, Michael. "Zu Struktur und Thematik des Buchs von Bern." *BGDSL* 98 (1976): 357–383.

———. "*Biterolf und Dietleib:* A Play upon Heroic Themes." In *Germanic Studies in Honor of Otto Springer,* edited by Stephen J. Kaplowitt. Pittsburgh: K & S Enterprises, 1978, pp. 77–91.

Firestone, Ruth H. "An Investigation of the Ethical Meaning of Dietrich von Bern in the *Nibelungenlied, Rabenschlacht,* and *Buch von Bern.*" In *"In hohem Prise:" A Festschrift in Honor of Ernst S. Dick,* edited by Winder McConnell. GAG 480. Göppingen: Kümmerle, 1989, pp. 61–82.

———. "The Literary Classification of *Dietrich und Wenezlan:* A Reevaluation." *German Studies Review* 5 (1982): 9–20.

Heinzle, Joachim. *Mittelhochdeutsche Dietrichepik: Untersuchungen zur Tradierungsweise, Überlieferungskritik und Gattungsgeschichte später Heldendichtung.* MTU 62. Zurich: Artemis, 1978.

Jänicke, Oskar, ed. *Laurin-Walberan* and *Biterolf und Dietleib.* Deutsches Heldenbuch, I, 2nd. ed. 1866. Reprint, Berlin: Weidmann, 1963.

Martin, Ernst, ed. *Alpharts Tod, Dietrichs Flucht,* and *Rabenschlacht.* Deutsches Heldenbuch, II, 2nd ed. 1866. Reprint, Dublin: Weidmann, 1967.

Röhrich, Lutz. *Erzählungen des späten Mittelalters und ihr Weiterleben in Literatur und Volksdichtung bis zur Gegenwart.* Vol. 2. Berne: Francke, 1967.

Schnyder, Andre, ed. *Biterolf und Dietleib.* Sprache und Dichtung 31. Berne: Haupt, 1980.

Wisniewski, Roswitha. Mittelalterliche Dietrichdichtung. Sammlung Metzler 205. Stuttgart: Metzler, 1986.

Zatloukal, Klaus, ed. *2. Pöchlarner Heldenliedgespräch: Die historische Dietrichepik.* Philologica Germanica 13. Vienna: Fassbaender, 1992.

Zimmer, Uwe. *Studien zu "Alpharts Tod" nebst einem verbesserten Abdruck der Handschrift.* GAG 67. Göppingen: Kümmerle, 1972.

Zupitza, Julius, ed. *Virginal, Goldemar, Sigenot, Eckenlied, Dietrich und Wenezlan.* Deutsches Heldenbuch, V. 1870. Reprint, Dublin: Weidmann, 1968.

DIU KLAGE (The Lament of the Nibelungen). Most of the intact manuscripts of the *Nibelun-* *genlied* also contain the *Klage,* the length of which ranges from 4360 to 4425 verses, depending on the specific version of the text. Based on the classification of the script variants, two main texts, **B** and **C,** can be differentiated, to which the closely related versions **J** and **D** must also be attributed. The *Klage,* whose author remains anonymous, can be divided into four main narrative segments. The first part (**B,** 1–586) consists of a summary, mainly of the events described in the second section of the *Nibelungenlied,* the content of which is assumed to be already known. The question of who is to be made responsible for the tragic events at Etzel's court figures prominently and Kriemhild is effectively absolved of all guilt. Her revenge for Siegfrid's death is justified by her true loyalty (*triuwe*) towards her first husband. Etzel's mourning for the slain opens the second part of the epic. The discovery, the final journey, and burial of the dead of all parties—Kriemhild and Ortlieb, the Burgundian and Hunnish heroes, as well as the Amelungs—involved in the conflict are described in great detail (**B,** 587–2496). The discovery of the dead bodies is "complemented" by the desolation of the survivors. The life and times of the deceased and their role in the bloody conflict are then outlined in short biographies.

The minstrel Swemmel's journey introduces a new, more animated segment of the plot (**B,** 2497–4999). Swemmel brings the news of the tragic events to the court of Duchess Isolde of Vienna, to Rüdiger's family in Bechelaren, and to Bishop Pilgrim in Passau, uncle of Kriemhild and Gunther. Wherever the message is received, it evokes immeasurable anguish, ultimately even at Swemmel's final destination, Worms, where the minstrel's report to the prince's household summarizes once again the course of the battle. Queen Ute, who undertakes for this reason a journey from her residence in Lorsch to Worms, dies of grief. Urged by Brünhild's followers, the advice of Bishop Pilgrim to crown the prince is heeded at last: dynastic continuity is assured by the much-celebrated coronation of the Queen's adolescent son. In the fourth and last part of the text (**B,** 4100–4360), Dietrich's departure from Etzel's court is described. According to the text, Dietrich and his wife, Herrat, visit Rüdiger's daughter, Dietlind, on their way to Dietrich's kingdom. They give Dietlind all the support they can, for her mother has just died of grief over Rüdiger's death. Afterwards the poet describes how Pilgrim has the story of the fall of Burgundy written down in Latin by his scribe, Master Conrad. This story is called *Diu chlage* (**B**, 4322) and has been widely read in the German language ever since. The thirty-eight verses which complement version **B** of the *Klage* document (in an extremely verbose fashion) underscore the fact that nothing is known of Etzel's life after Dietrich's departure.

Although the *Klage* summarizes, adds to, and recounts the *Nibelungenlied* (if sometimes in a slightly deviant manner), it differs from its great predecessor with regard to its form and its way of dealing with the material. The exclusive use of rhymed couplets, the meter of the courtly epic, combined with a more descriptive narrative style, contrasts with the narrative flow of the *Nibelungenlied*, which is written in strophes, each of which concludes with a *Langzeile* (extended verse). Furthermore the heroic stance of the *Nibelungenlied* provides a sharp contrast to the *Klage*'s exclusively Christian perspective. While the author of the *Nibelungenlied* accentuates the inherent dynamism of the fall of Burgundy by a near total omission of (Christian) values, the writer of the *Klage* detects the cause of the avoidable catastrophe in the false moral judgment of the main protagonists. This tendency to moralize is obvious in the schematic "black and white" portrayal of the characters: the author of the *Nibelungenlied* is able to show Hagen both as a coldly calculating executor of an unavoidable destiny, while at the same time calling him his master's loyal follower. In the same way it is also possible to portray Kriemhild's revenge as a legitimate consequence of her loyalty towards her husband while calling the cruelty resulting from her revenge the work of a she-devil. This refined, but at the same time impartial, depiction of the characters is lost entirely on the writer of the *Klage*, for whom Hagen alone is seen as the embodiment of the mortal sin of *superbia* (*übermuot*/vanity) and who is made responsible for all the suffering experienced by the guests taking part in the feast at Etzel's court. On the other hand Kriemhild is declared free of all guilt and made to appear as the loyal wife who behaves according to Christian principles and whose place in heaven is assured. Therefore the

Klage is not simply a continuation of the *Nibelungenlied*, but also acts as a commentary and an interpretation of that epic tale. Its origins most probably lie in the contemporary reader's perplexity, brought about by the bloodthirsty conclusion of the *Nibelungenlied*. The catastrophe described in the *Nibelungenlied* is overcome emotionally by the description of the lamentation for, and the burial of, the fallen heroes and brought to an adequate conclusion from a Christian point of view. In addition the coronation of Gunther's son (Siegfried) and the subsequent joyful celebration justify a positive outlook on the future. This perspective supports the Christian view of medieval history, which could not accept the cessation of all dynastic continuity, as exemplified by the fall of the kings of Burgundy in the *Nibelungenlied*, as being a valid ending to a well-rounded heroic epic. After all, according to Augustine, God created history as a whole, having both a beginning and an end. The fact that the *Nibelungenlied* and the *Klage* have for the most part been passed on as one entity (except for the *Wiener Piaristenhandschrift* **k** [Viennese Piarist Manuscript **k**], the *Klage* is missing only in the more recent manuscript **n**) demonstrates that the medieval recipients of the epic thought that both works belonged together, regardless of their formal differences and their disparate contents. The historical and literary importance of the *Klage*, therefore, also lies in its function as the earliest evidence of the *Nibelungenlied*'s reception in medieval times. The Christian perspective of the fall of the Nibelungs makes the assumption likely that the author of the *Klage* was himself a clergyman, whose place of activity was possibly the cathedral town of Passau in Bavaria.

The *Klage*'s thoroughly autonomous approach to the contents of the *Nibelungenlied* has repeatedly brought up the question as to the relation of both epics to one another, to what extent each is influenced by the other, and/or whether they were both written as more or less separate entities. Even though there is no agreement on the matter of its origins, it must be accepted as likely that the *Klage* was influenced by the *Nibelungenlied*, which was already available in book form. Version **C** of the *Nibelungenlied*, which presents a similar assessment of events from a Christian point of view as well as the question of the guilt and the exoneration of Kriemhild, illustrates that the *Klage*'s antiheroic basis soon altered the face of the heroic epic (i.e., the *Nibelungenlied*). One of the central clues that helps to date the *Klage* is provided by some of the themes contained therein, which, it can be said with some certainty, were taken from Wolfram von Eschenbach's later work *Willehalm* (probably written between 1210 and 1220). Such is the case with the unusual metaphor of death as a pair of scales. Verses 2829–2936 of the *Klage* manuscript **C** read as follows: "ouch liezen si da hinder in, [. . .] ir vil liben mage/in des todes wage" (There they left behind them, too, [. . .] their beloved kin on the scales of death), and in *Willehalm* 80,25ff. one finds: "dune gultes mine mage/mit des todes wage" (You cannot atone for [the deaths of] my kin, unless it be on the scales of death [i.e., unless you die]). If the author of the *Klage* had really drawn upon Wolfram's work, his text could not possibly have been written before 1220, about twenty years after the composition of the earliest version of the *Nibelungenlied*.

It was mainly the reference to the exaltation of the *Nibelungen* material upon the initiative of Bishop Pilgrim that created a stir in contemporary research, since it is possible on the one hand to use the passage concerning Master Conrad's Latin manuscript as proof that someone had tampered with source material in order to convince readers of the narrative's authenticity. Fictional references to source material of that kind were widespread in medieval epics: a clerical or worldly authority testified to the fact that the narrated events were true and had the tale written down in Latin, the respected language of medieval sciences. In *Herzog Ernst,* for example, possible doubts as to the authenticity of the hero's fantastic escapades are dispelled by mentioning a Latin adaptation of that very story written down by a "master" in Bamberg upon the initiative of the emperor, who himself owes his knowledge to Ernst. On the other hand Conrad's Latin text may be regarded as one of the first written versions of the *Nibelungenlied,* set down in the tenth century at the court of the historical Bishop Pilgrim (971–991), a distant "relative" of the *Nibelungenlied* we know today. If such a text ever existed in Latin, then it must have been written in the form of a *chronique scandaleuse*. It must, however, be considered that no other text has survived besides the *Klage* which confirms the existence of such a document.

Less convincing is the view that the source material mentioned by the *Klage* is a hidden eulogy of Bishop Wolfger of Passau. The historical bishop of Passau appears as the patron and initiator of the canonization of the *Nibelungenlied:* thus Wolfger, who supposedly had the epic written down, is insinuated by the appearance of the character Pilgrim. If this is the case, then Conrad's Latin text would refer to the *Nibelungenlied* itself. Ultimately the achievements of contemporary research, which consider the *Nibelungenlied* and the *Klage* mainly in their literary context, have downplayed theories of oral formulaic composition. At the same time, the view that both epics are only textual representations of the same material but in different oral traditions has been discarded. Earlier it was believed that oral fragments of the material and autonomous single scenes were woven into the story line, whereby the *Klage* was even thought of as the older of the two epics. In addition it was seen as a wholly separate poem, which could be understood without reference to the *Nibelungenlied*. Even the possibility that the *Nibelungenlied* itself was influenced by the *Klage* was considered. However this new evaluation of the dependency of the poems on each other does not allow a basic demarcation: even if the *Nibelungenlied* and the *Klage* are only different descriptions of one oral version of the epic, that oral version must have been remarkably fixed in substance as well as in subject matter by 1200. The impracticality of this thesis lies in the fact that its advocates expect the interaction between *Lied* and *Klage* to be evident as early as the time of their written composition, which then would ultimately lead to the aforementioned form of the *Klage* as a continuation of and a commentary to the *Nibelungenlied*.

[MD]

Bibliography

Bartsch, Karl, ed. *Diu Klage. Mit den Lesarten sämtlicher Handschriften.* 1875. Reprint, Darmstadt: Wissenschaftliche Buchgesellschaft, 1964.

Bumke, Joachim. *Die vier Fassungen der "Nibelungenklage."* Untersuchungen zur Überlieferungsgeschichte und Textkritik der höfischen Epik im

13. Jahrhundert. Quellen und Forschungen zur Literatur- und Kulturgeschichte. Berlin: de Gruyter, 1996.

———, ed. *Die Nibelungenklage. Synoptische Ausgabe aller vier Fassungen.* Berlin and New York: de Gruyter, 1999.

Classen, Albrecht. "Diu Klage: A Modern Text from the Middle Ages." *Neuphilologische Mitteilungen* 96 (1995): 315–329.

———, trans. *Diu Klage. Mittelhochdeutsch– Neuhochdeutsch.* GAG 647. Göppingen: Kümmerle, 1997.

Curschmann, Michael. "'Nibelungenlied' und 'Klage.'" In *Die deutsche Literatur des Mittelalters. Verfasserlexikon.* 2nd rev. ed., edited by Kurt Ruh. Vol. 6 of *Lieferung* 3/4. Berlin: de Gruyter, 1987, cols. 926–969.

———. "'Nibelungenlied' und 'Nibelungenklage': Über Mündlichkeit und Schriftlichkeit im Prozeß der Episierung." In *Deutsche Literatur im Mittelalter: Kontakte und Perspektiven. Hugo Kuhn zum Gedenken,* edited by Christoph Cormeau. Stuttgart: Metzler, 1979, pp. 85–115.

Deck, Monika. *Die Nibelungenklage in der Forschung. Bericht und Kritik.* Europäische Hochschulschriften. Reihe 1: Deutsche Sprache und Literatur 1564. Frankfurt a. M.: Lang, 1996.

Gillespie, G. T. "'Die Klage' as a commentary on 'Das Nibelungenlied.'" In *Probleme mittelhochdeutscher Erzählformen. Marburger Colloquium 1969,* edited by Peter F. Ganz and Werner Schröder. Berlin: Erich Schmidt, 1972, pp. 153–177.

Günzburger, Angelika. *Studien zur Nibelungenklage. Forschungsbericht, Bauform der Klage, Personendarstellung.* Europäische Hochschulschriften. Reihe 1: Deutsche Sprache und Literatur 685. Frankfurt a. M.: Lang, 1983.

Hoffmann, Werner. *Das Nibelungenlied.* 6th ed. Sammlung Metzler 7. Stuttgart: Metzler, 1992, pp. 126–140.

Kühebacher, Egon. *Deutsche Heldenepik in Tirol: König Laurin und Dietrich von Bern in der Dichtung des Mittelalters.* Schriftenreihe des südtiroler Kulturinstitutes 7. Bolzano: Athesia, 1979.

Lachmann, Karl. *Der Nibelunge Noth und die Klage nach der ältesten Überlieferung mit Bezeichnung der unechten und mit Abweichungen der gemeinen Lesart.* 5th ed. Berlin: G. Reimer, 1878.

Lienert, Elisabeth. "Intertextualität in der Heldendichtung. Zu Nibelungenlied und 'Klage.'" In *Neue Wege der Mittelalter-Philologie: Landshuter Kolloquium 1996,* edited by Joachim Heinzle. Wolfram-Studien 15. Berlin: Erich Schmidt, 1998, pp. 276–298.

———. trans. Die Nibelungenklage: Mittelhochdeutscher Text nach der Ausgabe von Karl Bartsch. Schöninghs mediävistische Editionen, vol. 5. Paderborn: Schöningh, 2000.

McConnell, Winder, trans. *The Lament of the Nibelungen (Diu Chlage).* Translations from Medieval Literature, edited by Evelyn S. Firchow. Columbia, SC: Camden House, 1994.

———. "The Problem of Continuity in *The Klage.*" *Neophilologus* 70 (1986): 248–255.

Ranft, Brigitte, ed. "Diu Klage. Kritische Ausgabe der Bearbeitung *C.*" Diss., Marburg/Lahn, 1971.

Schröder, Werner. *Wolfram von Eschenbach, 'Das Nibelungenlied' und 'Die Klage.'* Akademie der Wissenschaften und der Literatur. Abhandlungen der Geistes- und Sozialwissenschaftlichen Klasse 5. Mainz: Akademie der Wissenschaften und der Literatur; Stuttgart: Steiner, 1989.

Szklenar, Hans. "Die literarische Gattung der *Nibelungenklage* und das Ende 'alter maere.'" *Poetica* 9 (1977): 41–61.

Voorwinden, Norbert. "Nibelungenklage und Nibelungenlied." In *Hohenemser Studien zum Nibelungenlied,* edited by Irmtraud Albrecht and Achim Masser. Dornbirn: Vorarlberger Verlagsanstalt, 1981, pp. 276–287.

Wachinger, Burkhard. "Die Klage und das Nibelungenlied." In *Hohenemser Studien zum Nibelungenlied,* edited by Irmtraud Albrecht and Achim Masser. Dornbirn: Vorarlberger Verlagsanstalt, 1981, pp. 264–275.

Wehrli, Max. "Die 'Klage' und der Untergang der Nibelungen." In *Zeiten und Formen in Sprache und Dichtung. Festschrift Fritz Tschirch.* Cologne: Böhlau, 1992, pp. 96–112.

EDDA. The name is given to two books written in Iceland in the thirteenth century: The *Prose Edda* and the *Poetic Edda.* The name *Edda* was applied first to the *Prose Edda* and belonged originally to that book alone. The *Prose Edda* is also called the *Younger Edda* or *Snorri's Edda,* because it was written by Snorri Sturluson (1178/79–1241), the most important and prominent Icelandic author and historian, probably during the years 1222 to 1223. The meaning of the name *Edda* is not quite clear and many interpretations have been offered. The Icelandic word *edda* means *great-grandmother,* as a title possibly referring to a collection of ancient tales. Perhaps *Edda* is derived from óðr (poetry). If so, then the title means *poetics,* and in fact, the *Prose Edda* is a handbook of poetics. Another interpretation connects *Edda* with Oddi, the name of the farm where Snorri was brought up and educated. An equally plausible explanation is that *Edda* is derived from Latin *edo,* "I proclaim," according to medieval etymology.

The *Prose Edda* is divided into four sections: Prologue, Gylfaginning, Skáldskaparmál, Háttatal. The short Prologue stands apart. Its contents show historical interest: the Norse gods are traced from heroes of Greece and ultimately from Adam. The Háttatal (List of Verse Forms) presents one hundred different verse forms in 102 stanzas. The Skáldskaparmál (Speech of Poetry) contains Snorri's explanations of the poetry of skalds (poets, especially court poets). Skaldic poetry is quite unlike Anglo-Saxon and early Germanic poetry. It differs from the poetry of the *Poetic Edda* in meter, in syntax, and choice of expression. For, example the skalds use *kennings* (periphrases) of such complexity that their poems often read like riddles. The various types of kennings are illustrated with examples from the works of poets who lived between the ninth and twelfth century. In some chapters of the Skáldskaparmál, Snorri retells legends of Sigurd, Brynhild, the Burgundian kings, Hogni, and the Norse gods. The Gylfaginning (Beguiling of Gylfi) is an account of the Norse gods written in the form of dialogue between Gylfi and three gods. Snorri wrote it to inform skalds about the mythological concepts a writer had to know in order to understand kennings. He chiefly used lays about the gods, many of which are preserved in the *Poetic Edda*. Snorri was educated as a Christian and he wrote his *Edda* more than two centuries after Iceland had been converted to Christianity. Therefore the value of the book as a record of mythology has been questioned.

The *Poetic Edda* is also called *Elder Edda* or *Saemund's Edda*. It is a collection of lays preserved in the vellum manuscript *Codex Regius,* which formerly belonged to the Icelandic bishop Brynjólfr Sveinsson (1605–1675), who believed it to be the work of the Icelandic historian Sæmundr Sigfússon inn fróði (Saemund Sigfusson the Wise, 1056–1133). But the book was compiled at a much later period than that of Saemund. Some Eddic lays are handed down in other manuscripts, for example in *Snorri's Edda* or in the *Flateyjarbók* (Book of Flatey). All these lays were passed down anonymously.

The poetry of the *Edda* falls into two groups, the mythological and the heroic lays. Among the mythological poems are narrative lays and didactic lays. The most famous one is the *Voluspá* (Sibyl's Prophecy), a narrative lay about the story of the world and of the gods from the beginning until the end of the world and the doom or twilight of the gods. The *Hyndluljód* (The Lay of Hyndla), a didactic lay, is the only mythological lay that concerns the Nibelungs.

Nearly all the heroic lays in the *Edda* are associated in some way with the story of Sigurd; only the *Volundarkviða* (The Lay of Wayland) is totally separated from his story, and the three Helgi lays (*Helgakviða Hjorvarðssonar, Helgakviða Hundingsbana I, II*) have only a distant relationship with him. Many of the legends upon which the heroic lays are based originated in continental Germania. Some of the heroes in these lays appear in Old English and Middle High German literature, especially in the *Nibelungenlied*. A group of lays is concerned with Sigurd and Brynhild: *Grípisspá* (The Prophecy of Gripir; the most recent heroic lay, believed to have been set in writing no earlier than about the thirteenth century), *Sigurðarkviða hin skamma* (The Short Lay of Sigurd), *Brot af Sigurðarkviðu* (Fragment of a Sigurd Lay), and *Sigurðarkviða in meiri* (The Longer Lay of Sigurd). The last one is completely lost in a lacuna of the *Codex Regius* and can only be reconstructed from a prose version in the *Volsunga saga*. The deeds of young Sigurd are told in the *Fáfnismál* (The Lay of Fafnir), the *Reginsmál* (The Lay of Regin), and the *Sigrdrífumál* (The Lay of Sigrdrifa). One lay is devoted to Brynhild's death: *Helreið Brynhildar* (Brynhild's Ride to Hel). Two lays are concerned with Atli (Attila) and the downfall of the Burgundians: *Atlakviða* (The Lay of Atli) and *Atlamál in groenlendzku* (The Greenlandish Lay of Atli). They contain memories of events that took place in western Germany in the fifth century, when Gundicarius (Gunnar), the Burgundian king, was defeated by a Hunnish army. The *Oddrúnargrátr* (The Plaint of Oddrun) is connected with the story of Gunnar's life. The spiritual conflicts of Gudrun, Gunnar's sister, are described with great pathos in four lays: *Guðrúnarhvot* (Gudrun's Lament) and *Guðrúnarkviða I-III* (The Lay of Gudrun I-III). The *Hamdismál* (The Lay of Hamdir), perhaps the oldest lay in the maunscript (earlier than 1000), relates the story of Svanhild, Gudrun's daughter.

Many of the poems, both mythological and heroic, have prologue, narrative links, and epilogue in prose to explain the background and action of the verses. Three alliterative meters are commonly distinguished in Eddic poetry: the *fornyrðislag* (meter for old sagas/poems), a four-syllable, two-footed line, about eight lines forming one stanza; the *málaháttr* (quotation tone), a five-syllable, two-footed line, about eight lines forming one stanza; and the *ljóðaháttr* (tune/ melody of songs), a stanza consisting of two four-syllable, two-footed lines forming one long line, and a single three-footed full line without a caesura. Most of the narrative poems are in the *fornyrðislag,* which resembles the measure used by Anglo-Saxon and early Germanic poets.

The *Poetic Edda* contains only a small proportion of the heroic poetry known in Iceland in the early Middle Ages. Much has been lost, but fragments of ancient lays are found in prose sagas of the thirteenth and fourteenth century.
[GW]

Bibliography

Beck, Heinrich, ed. *Heldensage und Heldendichtung im Germanischen.* Reallexikon der germanischen Altertumskunde: Ergänzungsband 2. Berlin: de Gruyter 1988.

Bellows, Henry Adams, trans. *The Poetic Edda.* 1923. Reprint, New York: The American-Scandinavian Foundation, 1969.

———, trans. *The Poetic Edda.* Lewiston, NY: Mellen, 1991.

Boklund-Schlagbauer, Ragnhild. *Vergleichende Studien zu Erzählstrukturen im Nibelungenlied und in nordischen Fassungen des Nibelungenstoffes.* GAG 626. Göppingen: Kümmerle, 1996.

de Vries, Jan. *Altgermanische Religionsgeschichte.* 2 vols. 2nd ed. Grundriss der germanischen Philologie 12/I, 12/II. Berlin: de Gruyter, 1956–1957.

———. *Altnordische Literaturgeschichte.* 2 vols. 2nd ed. Grundriss der germanischen Philologie 15, 16. Berlin: de Gruyter, 1964–1967.

Dronke, Ursula, "Eddic Poetry as a Source for the History of Germanic Religion." In *Germanische Religionsgeschichte: Quellen und Quellenprobleme,* edited by Heinrich Beck. Reallexikon der germanischen Altertumskunde: Ergänzungsband 5. Berlin: de Gruyter, 1992, pp. 656–684.

———, ed. and trans. *The Poetic Edda.* Vol. 1 of *Heroic Poems.* Oxford: Clarendon Press, 1969.

Glendinning, Robert J. and Haraldur Bessason, eds. *Edda: A Collection of Essays.* Winnipeg: University of Manitoba Press, 1983.

Harris, Joseph. "Eddic Poetry." In *Old Norse-Icelandic Literature: A Critical Guide,* edited by Carol J. Clover and John Lindow. Islandica 45. Ithaca: Cornell University Press, 1985, pp. 68–156.

Hauck, Karl, ed. *Zur germanisch-deutschen Heldensage.* Wege der Forschung 14. Darmstadt: Wissenschaftliche Buchgesellschaft, 1965.

Haymes, Edward R. and Susann T. Samples. *Heroic Legends of the North: An Introduction to the Nibelung and Dietrich Cycles.* New York: Garland, 1996.

Hollander, Lee Milton, trans. *The Poetic Edda.* 2nd ed. Austin: University of Texas Press, 1962.

Hoops, Johannes, ed. *Reallexikon der germanischen Altertumskunde.* Vol. 6. 2nd ed. Berlin and New York: de Gruyter, 1986. See articles by Kurt Schier, *Edda, Ältere.* pp. 355–394; Gerd Wolfgang Weber, *Edda, Jüngere,* pp. 395–412; Heinrich Beck, *Eddische Dichtung,* pp. 413–425; Heinrich Beck, *Eddische Preislieder,* pp. 425f.

Jónsson, Finnur, ed. *Edda Snorra Sturlusonar.* Copenhagen: Gyldendalske boghandel, 1931.

Kellogg, Robert L. "The Prehistory of Eddic Poetry." In *Poetry in the Scandinavian Middle Ages: The Seventh International Saga Conference,* edited by Teresa Pároli. Spoleto: Presso la sede del Centro Studia, 1990, pp. 187–199.

Klingenberg, Heinz. *Edda: Sammlung und Dichtung.* Beiträge zur nordischen Philologie 3. Basel and Stuttgart, 1974.

Neckel, Gustav, and Felix Neidner, trans. *Die jüngere Edda mit dem sogenannten ersten grammatischen Traktat.* Sammlung Thule 20. Darmstadt: Wissenschaftliche Buchgesellschaft, 1966.

Neckel, Gustav, and Hans Kuhn, eds. *Edda: Die Lieder des Codex Regius nebst verwandten Denkmälern.* 5th ed. Heidelberg: Winter, 1983.

Reichert, Hermann, and Günter Zimmermann, eds. *Helden und Heldensage. Otto Gschwantler zum 60. Geburtstag.* Philologica Germanica 11. Vienna: Fassbaender, 1990.

Schier, Kurt. "Edda." In vol. 18 of *Kindlers neues Literaturlexikon,* edited by Walter Jens. Munich: Kindler, 1992, pp. 512–519.

———. "Snorri Sturluson: Edda." In vol. 15 of *Kindlers neues Literaturlexikon,* edited by Walter Jens. Munich: Kindler, 1991, pp. 646–648.

Simek, Rudolf, and Hermann Pálsson. *Lexikon der altnordischen Literatur.* Stuttgart: Kröner, 1987.

Sturluson, Snorri. *Edda: Prologue and Gylfaginning,* edited by Anthony Faulkes. Oxford: Clarendon Press, 1982.

———. *Gylfaginning.* Texte, Übersetzung, Kommentar von Gottfried Lorenz. Texte zur Forschung 48. Darmstadt: Wissenschaftliche Buchgesellschaft, 1984.

———. *Edda: Háttatal,* edited by Anthony Faulkes. Oxford: Oxford University Press, 1991.

Terry, Patricia. *Poems of the Elder Edda.* Philadelphia: University of Pennsylvania Press, 1990.

FÁFNISMÁL (The Lay of Fáfnir). In the *Codex Regius* of the *Poetic Edda* this heroic lay is not separated from the *Reginsmál* and the *Sigrdrífumál.* The title was taken from the more recent paper manuscripts.

The lay relates an event of Sigurd's youth and is composed in verse (forty-four stanzas) with prose bridges. The metrical form is not homogeneous. Some passages are composed in the epic *fornyrðislag,* with others in *ljóðaháttr.* Andreas Heusler called the poem an "einseitiges Ereignislied" (one-sided lay relating an event).

Regin covets Fafnir's gold. His brother Fafnir has turned himself into a dragon, and now he guards a hoard of gold on the Gnitaheide. Regin provokes Sigurd into killing the dragon. Sigurd digs a pit, jumps into it, and when Fafnir creeps over it, he stabs the dragon in the heart with his sword. In a dialogue the mortally wounded dragon addresses his killer (stanzas 1–22). He asks for Sigurd's name, which Sigurd does not reveal at first, calling himself "gofuct dýr" (wonderful animal). Fafnir wants to know why Sigurd has killed him. He warns him that the treasure he has won will bring him an early end. He also warns him of the curse on the gold and of the treacherous Regin. Within this section, stanzas 12–15 contain mythological wisdom that has nothing to do with Sigurd.

The second part of the lay begins with a dialogue between Regin and Sigurd (stanzas 23–29). Regin clearly expects to share the spoils of Sigurd's victory. Two stanzas (30, 31) follow that depict the character of a warrior, his boldness, his fearlessness, and his good spirits. The story is continued in prose. Sigurd roasts the dragon's heart and, upon tasting the blood, burns his fin-ger, puts it into his mouth, and is able to understand the language of the birds. Seven titmice warn him (according to the *Volsunga saga,* there are six birds, and in the *Þiðreks saga* two birds warn him; the motif does not exist in the German tradition) that Regin plans to kill him to avenge his brother's death. The birds advise him to kill Regin, who is here called a giant (contrary to the *Reginsmál,* in which Regin is a dwarf). The scene of Sigurd roasting Fafnir's heart and listening to the birds was often depicted in wood or stone in Norway, Sweden, and England, and the motif may be Irish in origin (stanzas 32–38).

In a further prose bridge, we are informed that Sigurd decapitates Regin, eats Fafnir's heart, and drinks Fafnir's and Regin's blood. In stanzas 40–44 the titmice talk to him again. They foretell that he will marry Gjuki's daughter and that he will find a sleeping warrior maiden (the *Volsunga saga* calls her Brynhild) on a high hill. The story relates that Odin had pricked her with a thorn and now she waits for her liberator. In a prose passage that finishes the lay, Sigurd fills two boxes with gold, puts them on Grani's (his horse's) back, takes Fafnir's helmet, a golden suit of armor, Fafnir's sword, Hrotti, and other treasures and rides away.

The most significant difference between this lay and the *Nibelungenlied,* the *Þiðreks saga,* and the *Lied vom Hürnen Seyfrid* is the combination of the dragon fight and the winning of the hoard. But this linking of the two motifs is an old pattern of heroic poetry, as shown in Sigmund's dragon fight in *Beowulf.* Andreas Heusler tried to rearrange the stanzas of the *Reginsmál* and those of the *Fáfnismál* in order to arrive at two more homogeneous poems: a *Lied vom Drachenhort* (Lay of the Dragon's Hoard), written in *ljóðaháttr,* and a *Lied von Sigurds Vaterrache* (Lay of Sigurd's Revenge for His Father) written mainly in *fornyrðislag,* but including Hnikar's advice for Sigurd in *ljóðaháttr.* Poems about Young Sigurd's deeds are usually more recent than those retelling old continental tales. Perhaps these events were only told in prose at the beginning of the tenth century. Therefore the "Lay of Regin" is frequently dated between 1000 and 1150. Icelandic scholars suggest that it may have been written earlier than 1000.

[GW]

Bibliography

Andersson, Theodore M. "Reginsmál and Fáfnismál." In vol. 10 of *Dictionary of the Middle Ages,* edited by Joseph R. Strayer. New York: Scribner, 1988, pp. 290f.

Beck, Heinrich. "Fáfnismál." In vol. 18 of *Kindlers neues Literaturlexikon,* edited by Walter Jens. Munich: Kindler 1992, pp. 564–565.

Cathey, J. E. "Fáfnismál." In vol. 4 of *Dictionary of the Middle Ages,* edited by Joseph R. Strayer. New York: Scribner 1984, pp. 581f.

de Vries, Jan. *Altnordische Literaturgeschichte.* 2 vols. 2nd ed. Grundriss der germanischen Philologie 15, 16. Berlin: de Gruyter, 1964, 1967.

Gering, Hugo, and B. Sijmons. *Kommentar zu den Liedern der Edda.* 2. Hälfte: *Heldenlieder.* Germanistische Handbibliothek VII 3,2. Halle (Saale): Buchhandlung des Waisenhauses (Francke), 1931, pp. 184–204.

Haymes, Edward R., and Susann T. Samples. *Heroic Legends of the North: An Introduction to the Nibelung and Dietrich Cycles.* New York: Garland, 1996, pp. 115, 121.

Heusler, Andreas. "Altnordische Dichtung und Prosa von Jung Sigurd." 1919. Reprint in *Kleine Schriften.* Berlin: de Gruyter, 1943, pp. 26–64.

Simek, Rudolf, and Hermann Pálsson. *Lexikon der altnordischen Literatur.* Stuttgart: Kröner, 1987, p. 288.

Tuppa, Gerlinde. "Die Bedeutung der Tiere und der Tiermotive in der germanischen Heldensage." Diss., Vienna, 1965, pp. 433–442.

GRIMILDS HÆVEN (Grimild's Revenge).

In the Danish ballad *Grimilds Hævn,* the demise of the Nibelungs is retold. Kremold (= Kriemhild) extends an invitation to Gynter (= Gunther), Gierlo (= Gernot), Falquor Spilmand (= Volker), and Helled Hagen (= Hagen). She cannot forget that Hagen killed her husband Seifrid (= Siegfried). Hagen's mother, Buodel, has dreamed about dead birds and tries, therefore, to warn her son, but her efforts are in vain. On his way to Kremold, Hagen is warned again by a mermaid, whom he decapitates. A ferryman also warns the Nibelungs, when he is offered gold by Hagen to transport them across the sound. Hagen kills him and throws his body into the water. The heroes then cross the sound alone during a storm. Their oars break. When they reach the castle, they receive yet another warning from a guard. Kremold immediately accuses Hagen of Seifrid's murder. King Kanselin (= Etzel or Blödelin) invites the Niflungs to a tournament, and the fighting breaks out on the spot. In the end all of the knights are dead, including King Kanselin. According to a longer version of the ballad, Hagen is able to escape and gains Huenild's favor. Later she gives birth to Hagen's son, Rancke, who subsequently avenges the death of his father. In this version of the ballad Obbe Jern appears in the last two stanzas. Hagen fights bravely, he even drinks his men's blood, but finally loses his sword. Young Obbe Jern gives him his own weapon, which once belonged to his brother. Obbe Jern corresponds to Rüdiger in the *Nibelungenlied.* Perhaps elements of Eckewart's role are of importance, too. This ballad is one of the best known *folkeviser.* It associates the Norse tradition (*Edda,* Faeroese ballads) with texts of German origin (*Nibelungenlied, Þiðreks saga, Ermenrikes Dot*) and the Danish *Hven Chronicle,* but the exact connections between these texts are not quite clear. It is certain, nonetheless, that German and Scandinavian sources mingle in *Grimilds Hævn.* The ballad belongs to the so-called oral poetry of the thirteenth or fourteenth century. It was written down by Anders Sørensen Vedel (1524–1616), who changed the text (albeit to an unknown extent) in accordance with his knowledge of Old Norse poetry.

[GW]

Bibliography

de Vries, Jan. *Altnordische Literaturgeschichte.* Vol. 2. 2nd ed. Grundriss der Germanischen Philologie 16. Berlin: de Gruyter, 1967, pp. 129f.

Holzapfel, Otto. *Die dänischen Nibelungenballaden: Texte und Kommentare.* Göppingen: Kümmerle, 1974, pp. 111–166.

Kralik, Dietrich. *Die dänische Ballade von Grimhilds Rache und die Vorgeschichte des Nibelungenliedes. Nach dem Vortrag in der Sitzung am 23. April 1958 aus dem Nachlass herausgegeben.* Sitzungsberichte der österreichischen Akademie der Wissenschaften. Phil. hist.Kl. 241/1. Vienna: Böhlau, 1962.

Schneider, Hermann. *Germanische Heldensage.* Vol. 1. 2nd ed. Grundriss der germanischen Philologie 10/I. Berlin: de Gruyter, 1962, p. 111.

GRÍPISSPÁ (Prophecy of Gripir),

a poem in the Elder *Edda* giving the entire history of the Norse

Sigurd (Sigurðr) in the form of a prophecy, which strongly underlines the fate aspect of the story. Although late in composition (first part of the thirteenth century), it is the first of the Sigurd poems in the *Codex Regius*. In the poem, Sigurd asks the seer Gripir to outline his future. He is told that he will kill dragons and will become betrothed to Brynhild, but will be trapped by magic into marrying Guðrun, daughter of Grimhild. Gripir is reluctant to tell Sigurd the whole story, but reveals eventually that the hero will help Gunnar win Brynhild, but then will be murdered at her instigation by Gunnar, Hogni, and Guðorm. Sigurd seeks assurance throughout that he will himself be blameless, and that heroic songs will be sung about him. Gripir tells him that songs about his deeds will be used as battle-inspiration as long as the world lives. Thus reassured, Sigurd accepts his fate and rides out to meet it.

[BOM]

Bibliography

Neckel, Gustav, ed. *Edda: Die Lieder des Codex Regius.*4th ed. Revised by Hans Kuhn. Heidelberg: Winter, 1962.

Terry, Patricia. *Poems of the Vikings*. New York: Bobbs-Merrill, 1969, pp. 140–149.

Murdoch, Brian. *The Germanic Hero*. London: Hambledon, 1996, pp. 17–20.

GUÐRÚNARHVOT (Gudrun's Lament, or Gudrun's Goading). This Eddic title literally translated means "Gudrun's Provocation" and can be easily explained by the first part of the poem. The English title "Gudrun's Lament" is self-evident for the second half of the poem. The lay consists of twenty-one stanzas mainly in *fornyrðislag*. After the *Atlamál in groenlenzku* there follows a prose section about Gudrun's further lot, according to which we learn that she and Hniflung, Hogni's son, killed Atli. Then she tries to drown herself in the sea, but the waves bring her to Jonaker's land. Gudrun marries the king and bears him three boys, Sorli, Erp, and Hamdir. The boys grow up with Svanhild, Sigurd's posthumously born daughter. Svanhild is killed by King Jormunrek because his counselor, Bikki, had slandered her. The story of Svanhild is also told in the *Hamðismál* (Lay of Hamdir).

Guðrúnarhvot starts at the moment when Gudrun provokes her sons to take revenge on Jormunrek for their sister's murder. She is even willing to sacrifice her own flesh to accomplish this act of revenge. She laughs as she arms her sons and weeps after their departure because both she and her sons know that they will never meet again. In stanza 8 Gudrun starts to relate her hard and bitter fate in a retrospective elegiac lay (*Rückblickslied;* Andreas Heusler). She had been married three times but now she has lost all hope of domestic joy. She speaks about the horror of her brothers' deaths and about the murder of Sigurd. Gudrun is totally alone now and passionately calls for death. She hopes that Sigurd will ride back from Hel, the world of the dead, to meet his wife, who is still grieving for her dead husband. She made a vow with Sigurd that death would never part them. Now they will lie on their funeral pyre together. This manner of Gudrun's death is only told here. Perhaps it is influenced by poems relating of Brynhild's death on a pyre. The contents of the lay are also related in the *Volsunga saga*. The poem must be late in the tradition of heroic verse, and the echoes of the *Atlamál* suggest that it was composed towards the end of the twelfth century. Some Icelandic scholars suggest an earlier date: 1050–1150. In any case Gudrun's provocation (*hvot*) of her sons may be a very old literary motif.

[GW]

Bibliography

Dronke, Ursula, ed. and trans. *The Poetic Edda*. Vol. 1 of *Heroic Poems*. Oxford: Clarendon, 1969, pp. 143–157.

de Boor, Helmut. "Die nordische Schwanhilddichtung." In *Erbe der Vergangenheit. Festgabe für Karl Helm zum 80. Geburtstage*. Tübingen: Niemeyer, 1951, pp. 47–63.

de Vries, Jan. *Altnordische Literaturgeschichte*. Vol. 2. 2nd ed. Berlin: de Gruyter, 1967, pp. 140–142.

Gering, Hugo, and B. Sijmons. *Kommentar zu den Liedern der Edda*. 2. Hälfte: *Heldenlieder*. Halle (Saale): Buchhandlung des Waisenhauses (Francke), 1931, pp. 411–424.

Harris, Joseph. "Guðrúnarhvot."In vol. 6 of *Dictionary of the Middle Ages,* edited by Joseph R. Strayer. New York: Scribner, 1985.

Heusler, Andreas. *Die altergermanische Dichtung.* 2nd ed. Potsdam: Athenaion, 1941, pp. 183ff.

Schröder, Franz Rolf. "Die Eingangsszene von Guðrúnarhvot und *Hamðismál.*" *PBB* (Tübingen) 98 (1976): 430–436.

See, Klaus von. "Guðrúnarhvot und *Hamðismál.*" *PBB* (Tübingen) 99 (1977): 241–249.

Zeller, Rose. *Die Gudrunlieder der Edda.* Tübinger germanistische Arbeiten 26. Stuttgart: Kohlhammer, 1939.

GUÐRÚNARKVIÐA (IN FYRSTA) (The First Lay of Gudrun).

This Eddic lay consists of twenty-seven stanzas in *fornyrðislag.* It closes with a short prose epilogue, giving us information taken from the *Guðrúnarkviða (onnor)* (The Second Lay of Gudrun). Therefore we know that this Second Lay of Gudrun must have been composed earlier than the first one. We do not know when the lay was written. Icelandic scholars tend to suggest an earlier date (about 1050–1150) than other scholars (second half of the 12th/13th century). In any case the lay belongs to the group of younger Eddic lays. It is a *Standortlied* (A. Heusler), which is a lay set in one place or position, because it does not relate heroic events, but rather informs us in the tone of an elegy about the feelings and reactions of Gudrun and Brynhild shortly after Sigurd's murder. Gudrun is mourning for Sigurd and cannot weep. Clever dukes (*jarlar*) and noble women try to comfort her by telling of their ill fate but without success. Three women are mentioned by name: Gjaflaug, Herborg, and Gullrond. When Gullrond unveils Sigurd's dead body, Gudrun is able to weep. She now praises her outstanding husband, whom her brothers have killed for Fafnir's gold, and she predicts Gunnar's death. Brynhild scolds Gullrond for having caused this outburst, but Gullrond asks her to be quiet because she blames the disaster on Brynhild. Yet according to Brynhild, it is all Atli's (her brother's) fault because he forced her into a marriage with Gunnar. She loved Sigurd and could not bear to see her hero married to Gudrun. The final prose tells us that Gudrun vanished into the woods and went on until she came to Denmark. There she lived with Hakon's daughter Thora for seven years. Brynhild did not want to live any longer without Sigurd and fatally injures herself in order to be cremated with Sigurd as is related in the *Sigurðarkviða in skamma* (The Short Lay of

Sigurd). The origin of this lay of Gudrun might be a Danish-German cycle of poems.

[GW]

Bibliography

Beck, Heinrich. "Guðrúnarkviða I" In vol. 18 of *Kindlers neues Literaturlexikon,* edited by Walter Jens. Munich: Kindler, 1992, pp. 677ff.

de Vries, Jan. *Altnordische Literaturgeschichte.* Vol. 2. 2nd ed. Grundriss der germanischen Philologie 16. Berlin: de Gruyter, 1967, pp. 135–138.

Gering, Hugo, and B. Sijmons. *Kommentar zu den Liedern der Edda.* 2. Hälfte: *Heldenlieder.* Halle (Saale): Buchhandlung des Waisenhauses (Francke), 1931, pp. 235–243.

Harris Joseph. "Guðrúnarkviða I." In vol. 6 of *Dictionary of the Middle Ages,* edited by Joseph R. Strayer. New York: Scribner, 1985, pp. 36f.

Haymes, Edward R., and Susann T. Samples. *Heroic Legends of the North: An Introduction to the Nibelung and Dietrich Cycles.* New York: Garland, 1996, p. 123.

Zeller, Rose. *Die Gudrunlieder der Edda.* Tübinger germanistische Arbeiten 26. Stuttgart: Kohlhammer, 1939.

GUÐRÚNARKVIÐA (ONNUR) (The Second Lay of Gudrun).

This Eddic lay is called *Guðrúnarkviða in forna* (The Old Lay of Gudrun) in the final prose section of the *Brot af Sigurðarkviðu: Frá dauða Sigurðar* (Fragment of a Sigurd Lay: About the Murder of Sigurd). In *Nornagests þáttr* (The Story of Nornagest; early fourteenth century) it is called *Guðrúnarræða* (The Speech of Gudrun). There are references to the lay in the *Volsunga saga.*

The lay consists of forty-four stanzas in *fornyrðislag,* partly written as a monologue by Gudrun in the tone of sentimental retrospection. We can distinguish three scenes: The first (twelve stanzas) relates Gudrun's life up to Sigurd's murder, assuming a version of his death that is mentioned otherwise only in *Nornagests þáttr:* Gunnar and his brothers had ridden with Sigurd to a *Thing* (assembly) and Sigurd was fatally wounded there by Gunnar's brother Gutthorm, who is in turn slain by the dying Sigurd. Gudrun is forced to wander through the woods in search of his body. The second scene (up to the thirty-fifth stanza) tells us that she finally arrives at the Danish court. There she spends three-and-a-half years with Thora, the daughter of King

Half, doing needlework. The best earls woo her, but she cannot forget Sigurd. Finally Grimhild, her mother, prepares a potion of forgetfulness and asks her to accept compensation and to marry Atli. Gudrun resists remarriage, particularly because Atli is Brynhild's brother. Apparently under the influence of the potion, she relents and leaves the Danish court in order to marry Atli. The last scene is written as a dialogue between Gudrun and Atli. Heavy dreams weigh upon Atli's mind. Gudrun interprets them ambiguously, hinting at the dreadful events that will follow.

The elegiac poem is very heterogeneous in language and style and is partly dependent on late German-Danish ballads. The lay may even be fragmentary because it breaks off with stanza forty-four. Most likely its time of origin is the second half of the twelfth century, although Icelandic scholars suggest that, as the first lay, it was also written between 1050 and 1150.

[GW]

Bibliography

Beck, Heinrich. "Guðrúnarkviða II." In vol. 18 of *Kindlers neues Literaturlexikon,* edited by Walter Jens. Munich: Kindler, 1992, pp. 677ff.

de Vries, Jan. *Altnordische Literaturgeschichte.* Vol. 2. 2nd ed. Grundriss der germanischen Philologie 16. Berlin: de Gruyter, 1967. pp. 131–135.

––––––. "Das 'Zweite Gudrunlied.'" *ZfdP* 77 (1958): 176–199.

Gering, Hugo, and B. Sijmons. *Kommentar zu den Liedern der Edda.* 2. Hälfte: *Heldenlieder.* Germanistische Handbibliothek VII 3,2. Halle (Saale): Buchhandlung des Waisenhauses (Francke), 1931, pp. 290–316.

Glendinning, Robert J. "Guðrúnarqviða forna. A Reconstruction and Interpretation." In *Edda: A Collection of Essays,* edited by Robert J. Glendinning and Haraldur Bessason. Winnipeg: University of Manitoba Press, 1983, pp. 258–282.

Harris Joseph. "Guðrúnarkviða II." In vol. 6 of *Dictionary of the Middle Ages,* edited by Joseph R. Strayer. New York: Scribner 1985, pp. 36f.

Haymes, Edward R., and Susann T. Samples. *Heroic Legends of the North: An Introduction to the Nibelung and Dietrich Cycles.* New York: Garland, 1996, pp. 123f.

Zeller, Rose. *Die Gudrunlieder der Edda.* Tübinger germanistische Arbeiten 26. Stuttgart: Kohlhammer, 1939.

GUÐRÚNARKVIÐA (IN THRIDIA) (The Third Lay of Gudrun). This short Eddic lay (eleven stanzas) is written in the *fornyrðislag* meter. The lay was not used by the scribe of the *Volsunga saga.* The episode is related partly as a report, partly in direct speech called a *doppelseitiges Ereignislied* (double-sided lay relating an event) by Andreas Heusler.

Gudrun is married to Atli, who has a concubine, Herkja. Herkja tells Atli that his wife has committed adultery with Thjodrek, Thjodmar's son. Gudrun swears on the holy white stone that she is innocent and that she never embraced Thjodrek, yet she confesses that they have talked about their bitter fate. Thjodrek lost his thirty brave men who came with him to Atli's court, and she herself lost her brothers Gunnar and Hogni because of Atli. An ordeal for her is planned, and she asks Atli to send for Saxi, who is capable of consecrating the boiling kettle used in the ordeal. Seven hundred men witness the ordeal, in which Gudrun takes bright stones out of the boiling kettle without burning her hand. Atli is very pleased to see that Gudrun does not get burned and forces Herkja to reach into the boiling water. Herkja burns her hand and is sentenced to death and sunk in a fen.

The events of this poem take place after the death of Hogni and Gunnar and before Atli's death, but the Eddic lays depict Gudrun's revenge on Atli immediately after the death of her brothers, so that there is no time left during which this ordeal might have taken place.

The lay shows features of the German tradition about the Nibelungs and Dietrich of Bern, son of Dietmar, the historical Theodemer, at the court of Etzel. It is interesting that the poet combined Christian and heathen elements to prove Gudrun's innocence. The ordeal of the boiling kettle, introduced in Norway at the time of Olaf the Holy (Olaf II Haraldsson, 995–1030), out of which Gudrun has to take bright stones, is Christian, but her oath on a holy white stone (on which a person's foot was placed during the swearing of the oath) and Herkja's death in the fen are heathen.

The text resembles more a ballad than a heroic Eddic lay, its tone is elegiac, typical of later lays, written during the second half of the twelfth century. According to Icelandic scholars, the poem might have been composed earlier, about 1150.

[GW]

Bibliography

Andersson, Theodore M. "Guðrúnarkviða III." In vol. 6 of Dictionary of the Middle Ages, edited by Joseph R. Strayer. New York: Scribner, 1985, p. 38.

Beck, Heinrich. "Guðrúnarkviða III." In vol. 18 of Kindlers neues Literaturlexikon, edited by Walter Jens. Munich: Kindler, 1992, pp. 677ff.

Gering, Hugo, and B. Sijmons. Kommentar zu den Liedern der Edda. 2. Hälfte: Heldenlieder. Germanistische Handbibliothek VII 3,2. Halle (Saale): Buchhandlung des Waisenhauses (Francke), 1931, pp. 317–323.

Haymes, Edward R. and Susann T. Samples. Heroic Legends of the North: An Introduction to the Nibelung and Dietrich Cycles. New York: Garland, 1996, p. 124.

Heusler, Andreas. Die altgermanische Dichtung. 2nd ed. Potsdam: Athenaion, 1947, pp. 154ff.

Simek, Rudolf, and Hermann Pálsson. "Guðrúnarkviða III." In Lexikon der altnordischen Literatur. Stuttgart: Kröner, 1987, p.125.

Zeller, Rose. Die Gudrunlieder der Edda. Tübinger germanistische Arbeiten 26. Stuttgart: Kohlhammer, 1939.

HAMÐISMÁL (Lay of Hamðir), one of the earlier poems in the elder Edda (with some confusing lines and gaps in the train of thought). Gudrun urges her last surviving sons Hamðir and Sorli to avenge the death of their sister Svanhild, who has been killed by being trampled to death by horses (an echo of the actual death of the historical Brunhild) on the orders of Jormunrek, king of the Goths. Their bastard half brother Erp offers to help but is killed by them in an act of hubris, which they later regret since without him they are defeated. They cut Jormunrek down, but without Erp, who might have cut off his head, the king can still call out for assistance.

There are references earlier in the poem to the death of Gudrun's husband Sigurd, who in this version was dragged from his bed and killed by Hogni, and to Gudrun's own killing of Atli's children, Erp and Eitill. The latter incident is a closer match with the Nibelungenlied than the former. There is also a close relationship between this piece (sometimes with identical stanzas) and the later Edda poem Guðrúnarhvot (Gudrun's Chain of Woes).

[BOM]

Bibliography

Dronke, Ursula, ed. The Poetic Edda. Vol. 1 of Heroic Poems. Oxford: Clarendon, 1969, pp. 159–242.

HELDENSCHAU is the modern name of a central part of the Þiðreks saga, that relates of the following events. After a period of peace, which corresponds to the one before King Arthur's feast in Geoffrey of Monmouth's Historia Regum Britanniae, Thidrek decides to invite the most outstanding heroes to his court. The twelve bravest men sit together with Thidrek on one bench. The Niflungar Gunnar and Hogni are mentioned as guests, and the other ten are Hildibrand, Hornbogi, Vidga, Aumlung, Thetleif, Fasolt, Sistram, Vildiver, Herbrand, and Heime. In these twelve one can find an obvious parallel to the twelve "Pairs of France" in Geoffrey's Historia, which later became the model for the Round Table. These heroes and two more who are not present (Sigurd and Sifka) are consistently described according to a particular pattern: usually their appearance (color of hair, form of face, size), habits, and weapons. After the feast they decide to test their skill in single combat against the thirteen warriors of King Isung of Brittany, Arthur's successor (twelve sons and Young Sigurd). The combat scenes are subsequently described in a manner similar to what is found in the Rosengarten epics in Germany.

The Heldenschau shows clear signs of having been inserted into the context of the banquet scene, as after it the statement that the heroes were all sitting on one bench has to be repeated for the sake of coherence. The Volsunga saga took the description of Sigurd from a manuscript of the Þiðreks saga contained within the family of the Icelandic manuscript **A**, which assists in the dating of the former.

[HR]

Bibliography

Reichert, Hermann. Heldensage und Rekonstruktion. Untersuchungen zur Thidrekssaga. Vienna: Fassbaender, 1992.

HELREIÐ BRYNHILDAR (Brynhild's Ride to Hel). This Eddic lay is recorded in the Codex

Regius, in the *Flateyjarbók* (Book of Flatey) and in the *Olafs saga Tryggvasonar* (*Nornagests tháttr* = Story of Nornagest). The lay consists of fourteen stanzas (only stanza seven is to be found in the *Codex Regius*), written in *fornyrðislag*. It is a *Rückblickslied* (A. Heusler), a "retrospective lay," and its place in the *Poetic Edda* falls after those poems that relate the glory and the final disaster of Sigurd's life. The events are told by a first-person narrator, Brynhild. The following Eddic lays take place at Atli's court.

The story begins with a short prose passage: Brynhild killed herself in order to be cremated together with Sigurd. Two funeral pyres were built. Sigurd was cremated first. Now it is Brynhild, lying on a cart covered with a carpet, who rides to Hel, the underworld. At this point the lay begins. Brynhild arrives at the farm of a giantess and talks to her. The giantess does not allow Brynhild to enter because she thinks Brynhild is responsible for the catastrophes that have been inflicted on Sigurd or will be inflicted on Gunnar and his brothers, Gjuki's sons. Brynhild repudiates the reproach: she lived in Hlymdalir with her foster father Heimir (his name is not mentioned here). There she was called *Hild und hjalmi* (Hild under the helmet). When she was twelve years old, Odin granted the victory in single combat to Hjalmgunnar, yet Brynhild was forced to help Agnar, Auda's brother, because Agnar had taken away the swanshirts of Brynhild and her seven maidens, and so she had to swear oaths to him. Odin punished her and shut her up in *Skatalund* (royal grove). There she fell asleep, protected by a wall of shields and a fire burning around the hall. Only the best hero would be able to awaken her, and this man would have to bring her Fafnir's gold. When a hero on Grani's back rode to her, she stayed with him for eight nights, believing he was Gunnar, but like brother and sister. Later Gudrun accused her of having slept in Sigurd's arms. She realized that she had been deceived during the bridal courtship: it had been Sigurd in Gunnar's shape who had awakened her. Therefore she decides to go to Hel with Sigurd, the hero with whom she had not been able to live. Brynhild tells the giantess to return to the underworld.

[GW]

Bibliography

Andersson, Theodore M. "Helreið Brynhildar." In vol. 6 of *Dictionary of the Middle Ages,* edited by Joseph R. Strayer. New York: Scribner, 1985.

———. *The Legend of Brynhild.* Ithaca: Cornell University Press, 1980.

Beck, Heinrich. "Helreið Brynhildar." In vol. 3 of *Kindlers Literaturlexikon.* Zurich: Kindler, 1967, col. 1620.

de Vries, Jan. *Altnordische Literaturgeschichte.* Vol. 2. 2nd ed. Grundriss der germanischen Philologie 16. Berlin: de Gruyter, 1967, pp. 146f.

Gering, Hugo, and B. Sijmons. *Kommentar zu den Liedern der Edda.* 2. Hälfte: *Heldenlieder.* Germanistische Handbibliothek VII 3,2. Halle (Saale): Buchhandlung des Waisenhauses (Francke), 1931, pp. 279–286.

Haymes, Edward R., and Susann T. Samples. *Heroic Legends of the North: An Introduction to the Nibelung and Dietrich Cycles.* New York: Garland, 1996, p. 122.

Heusler, Andreas. *Die altgermanische Dichtung.* 2nd ed. Postsdam: Arhenaion, 1941, 183ff.

Simek, Rudolf, and Hermann Pálsson. *Lexikon der altnordischen Literatur.* Stuttgart: Kröner, 1987, p. 162.

HISTORIA VON DEM GEHÖRNTEN SIEGFRIED (The Story of Siegfried with the Horny Skin), the prose adaptation of the *Lied vom Hürnen Seyfrid.* At least thirty-seven editions are known from the mid-seventeenth to the mid-nineteenth century. Though the earliest surviving edition was published at Braunschweig and Leipzig in 1726, in *Ritter Löwhardus* it is clearly stated that there was an edition printed at Hamburg in 1657. Both the *Historia* and *Ritter Löwhardus* seem to have been written by the same author, a view supported by the fact that both works reveal some evidence of the influence of Sir Philip Sidney's *Arcadia.* Sowden has suggested that the author may have been Andreas Heinrich Buchholtz (1607–1671), author of *Herkules und Valiska* (1659), though the stylistic parallels adduced are not fully persuasive. He was, however, certainly a North German and a Protestant, as in shown by the replacement of Krimhilt's appeal to the Virgin Mary (*LHS,* 30) by phrases from Luther's catechism (Golther, p. 67).

The names of the characters are changed: Seyfrid becomes Siegfried (described here as a

Cavallier who is eventually slain with a *Rappier*) and Krimhilt is now Florigunda. King Gybich and his sons Günther, Hagen, and Gyrnot become Gibaldus, Ehrenbertus, Hagenwald and Walbertus. Eugleyne/Eugel the dwarf and Kuperan the giant become Egwaldus and Wulffgrambähr respectively. The story itself, on the other hand, follows that of the *Lied vom Hürnen Seyfrid* quite closely, indeed in parts almost verbatim, though certain details are embroidered. Thus whereas *LHS* (32) tells how Gybich dispatches messengers to enlist help in the search for his daughter, in the *Historia* when the foreign kings arrive to offer Gibaldus their condolences he turns the occasion into a colorful tournament at which Siegfried outshines all others. Then after Siegfried has slain the last of the dragons, Siegfried's recovery from his exertions and his growing love for Florigunda are described in a series of Hollywoodesque clichés (Golther, pp. 85–87, corresponding to *LHS* 155). Strophes 170–172 of the *LHS* describe the return of Seyfrid and Krimhilt and their marriage in Worms. This segment is also developed in the *Historia,* and the comic fight between the cowardly Jorcus and Zivelles is totally new (Golther, pp. 92–97). According to this version, Hagenwald (= Hagen) is slain in his sleep by Zivelles.

The author seems to have been familiar with some heroic material other than his immediate source, for he mentions a story of a battle, unleashed by greed for the treasure, from which only Hildebrand and Dietrich emerged unscathed (Golther, p. 89), and at the end Florigunda and her son are said to have gone to the Netherlands to live with her father-in-law (Golther, p. 98; cf. *Nibelungenlied* 1073), a detail not mentioned in *LHS.*

[JLF]

Bibliography

Conrady K. O., ed. *Deutsche Volksbücher.* Rowohlts Klassiker. Deutsche Literatur 24. Reinbek: Rowohlt Taschenbuch Verlag, 1968.

Golther, Wolfgang, ed. *Das Lied vom hürnen Seyfrid.* Neudrucke deutscher Literaturwerke des 16. u. 17. Jhs. 81/82. 2nd ed. Halle: Niemeyer, 1911, pp. 61–99.

Jantz, Harold. "The Last Branch of the Nibelungen Tree." *MLN* 80 (1965): 433–440.

Sowden, J. K. "Andreas Heinrich Buchholtz and the Siegfried Chapbook." *GLL,* n.s., 24 (1970–71): 32–42.

Suchsland, P., ed. *Deutsche Volksbücher in drei Bänden.* Vol. 1. Bibliothek deutscher Klassiker. Berlin: Aufbau-Verlag, 1968, pp. 241–88.

HØGNA TÁTTUR. (see Part X: Faeroe Islands).

HVEN CHRONICLE. A prose rendition of the demise of the Nibelungen on the island of Hven in the Oere Sound. It was originally composed in Latin in the sixteenth century and is extant today solely in a Danish translation dating from the beginning of the seventeenth century.

[WW]

HYNDLULJÓÐ (The Lay of Hyndla). The lay is a very young Eddic poem consisting of fifty stanzas, written perhaps during the thirteenth century. It belongs more to the mythological poems than to the heroic lays, although its framework is not truly mythological. It is partly a poem of wisdom, relating the historical and pseudohistorical genealogy of Norwegian generations, offering a catalogue of about seventy names of heroes, beginning with the mythic past and the age of the great migrations of Germanic peoples, the *Völkerwanderung,* to the period of the Vikings. In the middle of the lay (stanzas 29–44), a mythological poem is inserted as an independent part. Snorri Sturluson (1178/79–1241), the renowned Icelandic author/historian, cites stanza 33 of this poem in his *Voluspá in skamma* (The Short Voluspa) in the *Snorra Edda.*

Perhaps the *Hyndluljóð* was written for a Norwegian (possibly from the family of Óttarr, a favorite of King Sigurdr Jórsalfari, see Gering/Sijmons, p. 375) by a learned man, who knew the *Hákonarmál* (a poem of the skald Eyvindr Skáldaspillir, written about 960), the two heroic lays about *Helgi Hundingsbani* and tales about Jormunrek, Eylimi, Hraudung, Hjordis, Sigurd, Fafnir, Gunnar, Hogni, Gjuki, Gudrun, and Gutthorm (stanzas 25–27). The lay is not part of the *Poetic Edda,* it is only recorded in the *Flateyjarbók* (Book of Flatey), an important compilation of texts written about 1380–1390.

[GW]

Bibliography

Beck, Heinrich. "Hyndluljód." In vol. 3 of *Kindlers Literatur-Lexikon.* Zurich: Kindler, 1965, cols. 2307–2308.

de Vries, Jan. *Altnordische Literaturgeschichte.* Vol. 2. 2nd ed. Grundriss der germanischen Philologie 16. Berlin: de Gruyter, 1967, pp. 369–398.

Gering, Hugo and B. Sijmons. *Kommentar zu den Liedern der Edda: Götterlieder.* Germanistische Handbibliothek VII, 3, 1. Halle (Saale): Buchhandlung des Waisenhauses (Hermann Francke), 1927, pp. 369–398.

Klingenberg, Heinz. *Edda: Sammlung und Dichtung.* Beiträge zur nordischen Philologie 3. Basel: Helbing & Lichtenhahn, 1974, pp. 9–36.

Simek, Rudolf, and Hermann Pálsson. *Lexikon der altnordischen Literatur.* Stuttgart: Kröner, 1987, p. 186.

MARNER, a Middle High German poet and minstrel of the thirteenth century. In two stanzas (XV 14 and 16) he indicates which stories he can relate as an epic singer and, in particular, what all his public have wished to hear from him (XV 14). He refers to the "Nibelungen hoard," a term which was clearly in vogue at the time and also indicates that the public was especially interested in the stories that related the way in which Kriemhild was betrayed and Siegfried's death.

[UM]

Bibliography

Strauch, Philipp, ed. *Der Marner.* 1876. Reprint, with an afterword, index, and bibliography by Helmut Brackert, Berlin: de Gruyter, 1965.

NIBELUNGENLIED. The *Nibelungenlied* is not only the first but also the most significant heroic epic of Middle High German literature. Around 1200, at the time courtly culture and courtly literature were developing, an unknown author set down in epic form the poetic work about the Nibelungen, which was Germanic in origin and which up until that time had been passed on orally. He thus provided an example for the conceptualization of a large epic and also for the written form of other works dealing with heroic material, such as the very popular tales associated with Dietrich von Bern. His poetic work was a great success, as demonstrated by the legacy of more than thirty manuscripts produced of it from the early thirteenth to the beginning of the sixteenth century. While the number of manuscripts may be considerably fewer than what we have for Wolfram von Eschenbach's *Parzival* and *Willehalm,* it is nevertheless greater than those which we have, for instance, for Hartmann von Aue's *Iwein* or Gottfried von Straßburg's *Tristan.* Very soon after the appearance of the *Nibelungenlied,* a discussion must have ensued regarding the interpretation of the cataclysmic events of the epic, as well as an evaluation of its main figures. This is evident not only in the manner in which the work was altered and adapted by succeeding redactors, but also in the appearance two decades later, possibly even directly after its appearance, of a special poetic piece that was appended to it, the *Klage.* This has justifiably been regarded as the first contemporary interpretation of the *Nibelungenlied,* and it is included in almost every complete manuscript of the epic. The only exceptions are manuscript **k** of the Piarists from the second half of the fifteenth century and manuscript **n** from 1449, which was not discovered until 1976 and which cannot be included without reservation among the complete manuscripts.

The continuing dispute as to which version represents the presumed original *Nibelungenlied* and which are later revisions is, nowadays, more or less decided. It should be mentioned, however, that not all scholars are of the opinion that the St. Gall manuscript **B** and, apart from a few deviations, the Hohenems-Munich manuscript **A,** come closest to the original, while the Hohenems-Laßberg or Donaueschingen manuscript **C** clearly represents a systematically revised version. It is nonetheless from the latter that the epic derives its name, in accordance with the last verse: "hie hât daz maere ein ende: daz ist der Nibelunge liet" (here the story comes to an end: this is the song of the Nibelungs; 2440,4). In comparison, the same passage in manuscripts **B** and **A** reads: "hie hât daz maere ein ende: daz ist der Nibelunge nôt" (**B** verse 2379,4; **A** verse 2316,4). On the basis of these final verses one distinguishes between the *nôt*-version and the *liet*-version of the epic. The Middle High German word *nôt* conveys the meaning *battle* as well as *difficulty, need, suffering,* and *misery,* and can even be understood as *downfall* in this context. The Middle High German *liet* means primarily *strophe;* its secondary meaning is a poem written in strophic form. More precisely it can be understood as a song as well as a narrative poem. Finally it is also used to designate a larger poem not written in strophes.

The Nibelungs, who are mentioned again at the end of the epic, are the Burgundians (*Burgonden* in the *Nibelungenlied* manuscripts), the name used from the beginning of the text. But in line 1523,1 (according to **B,** without a corresponding reference in **C**) the synonymous name *Nibelunge* is mentioned for the first time in the formulation "die Nibelunges helde" (the heroes of [King] Nibelung), which is actually not at all correct. They are not Nibelung's men, as the latter is only mentioned within a time framework that precedes the events of the *Nibelungenlied,* nor are they Siegfried's, in whose service they later stand. The attentive author of version *C probably left the line out for precisely this reason. In **B** strophes 1526 and 1527 (**C** 1562 and 1563), the name "Nibelung" applies both to the people and its clan of kings. No satisfactory answer has been found to explain why the change of name occurred at precisely this point. The following commentary is based principally on the *nôt*-version The characteristic differences between the latter and the *liet*-version require a separate discussion because, according to the manuscripts, the *liet*-version was more widely known during the Middle Ages. One can say from the outset that the differences do not involve the narrative framework as such and even most of the details correspond in both the *liet*- and *nôt*-versions. This provides strong support for the opinion that the different manuscripts— and both of the versions represented by them— are based on a formulated written concept and composition of the epic, such as can only be attributed to a single poet and not to a number of different epic singers. His poetic achievement occasioned such a high obligation towards the representation of the subject matter that, on the one hand, there are different versions but, on the other, no really different Nibelungen poems, as is the case, for instance, with the *Wolfdietrich* materials.

The *Nibelungenlied* is divided into two parts with different origins: the Siegfried-Kriemhild-Brünhild-plot (*âventiuren* 1–19), and the story of the downfall of the Burgundians or Kriemhild's revenge (*âventiuren* 20–39). Version *C has one *âventiure* fewer in the second part, as the thirty-third and the thirty-fourth *âventiuren* are combined to form the thirty-third *âventiure*. The second part of the epic is almost 100 strophes longer in version *B and more than 100 strophes longer in version *C. The two sections are connected through the presence of the Burgundian princess, Kriemhild. She is the central figure and it is quite revealing that in two manuscripts the epic is named after her: in manuscript **D** (the second Munich manuscript, dating from the first third of the fourteenth century), "Daz ist das Buch Chriemhilden" (This is the book of Kriemhild); and in manuscript **d** (the famous *Ambraser Heldenbuch,* written during the years 1504 to 1515/16 by Hans Ried on behalf of Emperor Maximilian I), "Ditz Puech heysset Chrimhilt" (This book is called Kriemhild). This is quite understandable, given the fact that medieval writers often entitled a work of literature according to the first proper name that appears in the text.

In the epic Kriemhild is the inordinately beautiful sister of the Burgundian kings Gunther, Gernot, and Giselher, who reside in Worms on the Rhine. She dreams of taming a falcon that is torn apart by two eagles. Her mother, Ute, interprets the falcon as a symbolic representation of a nobleman, leading Kriemhild to reject every thought of love in an effort to escape the sorrow resulting from it. The reputation of Kriemhild's beauty leads Siegfried, the son of King Siegmund, who resides in Xanten on the Lower Rhine, to Worms. At first the Burgundians in Worms do not realize who the visitor is. But Hagen von Tronege, a relative and vassal of the kings and their most important adviser, identifies the newcomer as Siegfried and he reports in strophes 87–100 how the young hero won the hoard of the Nibelungs, killing not only both sons of King Nibelung, but also twelve giants and seven hundred of their warriors. Siegfried had already received the sword Balmung from the two princes. He subsequently won the cloak of invisibility from the dwarf Alberich, the guardian of the hoard in the land of the Nibelungs. This cloak not only makes its wearer invisible, it also gives him the strength of twelve men. In another adventure the young Siegfried slays a dragon and, by bathing in its blood, causes his skin to become invulnerable to weapons. Upon his arrival in Worms, Siegfried behaves aggressively and demands that Gunther duel with him to determine who will rule over the Burgundian empire. He is subsequently persuaded to calm down and stays for a whole year at the court without ever setting eyes on Kriemhild. She, on the other hand, catches sight of him frequently and secretly. She gives the resplendent young man (who emerges victorious from every tourney) her loving attention, forgetting the warning provided by the falcon dream. When the Saxons and the Danes declare war on the Burgundians, it is Siegfried who gains the victory for his hosts and at the subsequent celebration he is allowed to see Kriemhild for the first time face to face.

The marriage between the two, however, is only possible after Siegfried has conquered the powerful Queen Brünhild of *Islant* (not the Iceland of today) for Gunther. Siegfried and Gunther agree on a contract which establishes that Gunther will only give his sister to Siegfried if the latter will help him to court Brünhild. Brünhild is only willing to marry the man who is able to beat her in three warrior games (javelin-throwing, stone-hurling, and long jump). Those men whom she defeats in the three tests, and there have been quite a few, forfeit their lives. Siegfried, who introduces himself to Brünhild as Gunther's *man* (vassal), obviously so as not to be considered a contestant for the proud queen, succeeds in passing the tests with the help of his cloak of invisibility. The splendid wedding of the two couples takes place in Worms, although Siegfried has to remind the Burgundian king of his promise. When Brünhild sees that the sister of her husband has been given to Siegfried as his wife and so, as he himself had intimated to her in *Islant,* to a nonequal, whom she furthermore considers to be a serf, she breaks out in tears and refuses to consummate her marriage to Gunther because he is unable to give her a satisfactory explanation regarding Siegfried's status. Brünhild rejects Gunther's advances and demonstrates her superior strength by tying him up with her girdle and hanging him from a nail in her chamber until morning. The next day Gunther complains to his brother-in-law about what has happened to him and Siegfried immediately is willing to help him a second time. The following night, with the help of his cloak of invisibility, Siegfried is able to break Brünhild's

strength without violating her sexually. Before leaving the bedroom, he takes Brünhild's ring and girdle, which he later gives to Kriemhild. Siegfried then returns with his wife to his native land, where Siegmund entrusts him with the power of kingship.

Ten years later Kriemhild and Brünhild each give birth to a son. Brünhild is still mulling over the inexplicable fact that Siegfried, the supposed vassal, has been allowed to marry the sister of the Burgundian kings and that he has never fulfilled his vassal duty in all these years. She persuades Gunther to invite his sister and his brother-in-law to journey to Worms for a festival, during which, however, a violent quarrel ensues between the two queens over the respective priority status of their husbands. The tension escalates; at first it is confined to an exchange of words between just the two of them, but this develops into a public confrontation. Brünhild's assertion that Kriemhild's husband is a serf is countered by Kriemhild's retort that her sister-in-law is the mistress of Siegfried, that it was he who deflowered her, and she provides "evidence" for her claim by showing Brünhild the ring and girdle. Gunther is quite willing to forget what has happened once Siegfried demonstrates his readiness to swear an oath that he did not brag about what Kriemhild had stated publicly. But Hagen is absolutely determined to avenge the insult to his Queen by killing Siegfried. He is able to draw Gunther into the plot, despite the latter's initial reluctance to consider such a move. Hagen makes up a story that the Saxons and the Danes have again declared war on the Burgundians and has absolutely no difficulty convincing Kriemhild to reveal to him the location of Siegfried's sole vulnerable spot, supposedly so that he can better protect him during the anticipated battle. (When Siegfried was bathing in the blood of the slain dragon, the leaf of a lime tree had fallen onto his shoulder and this is the only place where he is not protected.) Kriemhild marks the spot by sewing a cross onto Siegfried's clothing. The supposed declaration of war is subsequently "dropped," and instead of marching off to war, the Burgundian knights, without the younger brothers Gernot and Giselher, go on a hunt in the *Waskenwalt* (the Vosges Mountains; in manuscript **C,** more accurately in the Odenwald [line 919, 3]). Ominous dreams, which Kriemhild relates to her husband, fail to hinder him from participating in the hunt. Hagen deliberately leaves behind the wine intended for the feast of the hunt. As Siegfried quenches his thirst by drinking from a nearby spring, Hagen treacherously stabs him from behind with a spear in the spot that had been marked by Kriemhild. He then has the dead body placed in front of Kriemhild's chamber. She knows immediately who the murderer is and Hagen's guilt is apparent in the judgment of God as manifested through the *Bahrprobe:* as Hagen walks beside the stretcher on which Siegfried's corpse is laid out, his wounds begin to bleed. Yet this has no legal consequences for Hagen. Kriemhild remains in Worms. After three and a half years a reconciliation is effected between her and her brothers which is not, however, extended to Hagen, although he had been the individual primarily responsible for bringing it about. Shortly after that, Kriemhild is persuaded to have the gigantic hoard of the Nibelungs brought to Worms. When she begins to use her wealth to recruit men loyal to her, Hagen recognizes the danger and, following Gernot's advice, sinks the treasure in the Rhine. In the meantime the kings have left the country so that they can pretend to be innocent. A decade passes without any further noteworthy events.

With the beginning of the second part of the *Nibelungenlied* (strophe **B** 1143; **C** 1166), the plot shifts to a new geographical setting, to Hungary, the land of the Huns. Etzel, the king of the Huns, is a widower and, following the advice of relatives and friends, he decides to court Kriemhild. Margrave Rüdiger von Bechlarn is given the task of acting as his emissary in conveying the marriage suit. While Kriemhild's brothers approve of the marriage of their sister, Hagen is in total disagreement. At first Kriemhild herself refuses to accept Etzel's courtship, but she has a change of mind when Rüdiger solemnly swears to avenge any harm done to her. While he is thinking of possible future harm, she is thinking of the suffering already caused her by Hagen. The wedding ceremony is performed in Vienna. Kriemhild gains high esteem in the subsequent years in the country of the Huns and, after seven years, gives birth to a son, Ortlieb, who is baptized according to Kriemhild's wishes.

It is not difficult for Kriemhild to convince Etzel to invite her relatives to Hungary. She is motivated solely by her desire to take revenge on Hagen for the murder of Siegfried. Etzel does not have the slightest idea of her intentions. Hagen perceives the danger and opposes the invitation, but again the kings do not follow his advice. However he manages to convince them to set out on the journey with a large and heavily armed army. When they reach the flooded Danube, they cannot find a ferryman to take them across. While searching for ferrymen, Hagen comes across bathing water nymphs, one of whom makes a catastrophic prediction: none of the Burgundians, except for their chaplain, will return to the Rhine. After killing the ferryman, whom he had finally found but who, in self-defense, refused to take the Burgundians across the river, Hagen himself rows the entire army across the Danube. To test the truth of the prophecy, he hurls the chaplain into the waters of the Danube. Although the chaplain cannot swim, he reaches the riverbank with the help of God. Following a nocturnal skirmish with the Bavarian earls Else and Gelpfrat, both of whom had wished to avenge the death of the ferryman, and a short sojourn with the Bishop Pilgrim of Passau, the brother of the Queen Mother Ute, the Burgundians pay a visit to the generous Rüdiger. Here, on the advice of Hagen, Giselher is married to Rüdiger's daughter. Even before the Burgundians arrive at the court of the Huns, they are warned of Kriemhild's intentions by Dietrich von Bern, who lives there in exile. That she has not ceased to suffer is demonstrated by the fact that of all her relatives she only welcomes her favorite brother Giselher. A verbal clash ensues between her and Hagen in which the latter proves to be the more sharp-tongued of the two. Also, before the official reception of the guests by Etzel, Kriemhild, with the crown of the Huns upon her head, goes to Hagen and accuses him of having murdered Siegfried, which he then openly admits. But she does not succeed in convincing the four hundred Huns that are accompanying her to attack him. A night attack on the Nibelungs by Hunnish soldiers is also unsuccessful because of the *Schildwacht* (guard duty) undertaken by Hagen and his friend Volker.

The atmosphere is extremely tense the following morning. The hospitable and impartial

Etzel is able to prevent an armed clash that Volker tries to provoke. Etzel's brother, Bloedelin, enticed by Kriemhild's promise of a high reward, attacks the Burgundian squires who had been housed separately from their masters. All the attackers and the squires are wiped out, precipitating the outbreak of hostilities between Huns and Burgundians in the Great Hall of Etzel. Hagen's beheading of Ortlieb, son of Kriemhild and Etzel, provides the immediate catalyst. Owing to his reputation, Dietrich is not only able to obtain the withdrawal from the hall for himself and his men, but also for the Hunnish royal couple. Rüdiger is also allowed to leave the hall with his vassals. The fighting is costly for both sides. Finally, during the night, Kriemhild orders the hall to be set on fire. But at least six hundred Nibelungs manage to survive the inferno. The next morning Kriemhild appeals to Rüdiger to fulfill the oath he had sworn when he had initially presented the wedding suit, and Etzel also urges him to observe his feudal duty. After a torturous battle with his conscience, Rüdiger gives in. He and all his men lose their lives, Rüdiger by the hand of Gernot, whom he, in turn, kills with the last stroke of his sword. The Amelungs' request that the Burgundians hand over Rüdiger's corpse leads to the final mass battle. The only survivors among the Burgundians are Gunther and Hagen and, on the side of the Amelungs, Hildebrand, Dietrich's old sword master. Now it is Dietrich's turn to demand satisfaction for the wrong done to him, but this is refused by Hagen. Dietrich overcomes both Gunther and Hagen in individual combat and hands them over to Kriemhild. She demands that Hagen return the treasure hoard of the Nibelungs. He answers that he has sworn not to betray its whereabouts as long as one of his masters is alive. Kriemhild thereupon has her brother Gunther beheaded. Hagen, however, is accorded the final triumph over his enemy by declaring that now only he and God know where the treasure lies hidden. Kriemhild kills Hagen with Siegfried's sword, only to lose her own life seconds later at the hand of Hildebrand. Dietrich and Etzel, the only princes to have survived the bloodbath, are left to mourn the countless dead.

It is clear that the two parts of the *Nibelungenlied* are causally connected: the central event of the first part, the murder of Siegfried, is the prerequisite for the events in the second part, Kriemhild's revenge, which leads to the destruction of all the Nibelungs at the court of the Huns. This was not always consistent with tradition. The circle of legends to which the two parts of the epic can be traced back were not originally connected. If one accepts the premise that heroic legend and heroic epic basically have a historic foundation, then the historic substratum for the decline of the Burgundians can be clearly detected; that being the crushing defeat of this Germanic people under King Gundahar (Gunther) in the year 437, when they tried to extend their power into Roman Gaul. The Huns were involved in the battle as Roman reserve units, but were not led by Attila (Etzel). The historic foundations for the first part of the *Nibelungenlied* are less clear but might be located in the Merovingian history of the sixth century, which offers us the topics of rivalry between women, the murder of kings, revenge, as well as such names as Sigibert and Brunichild (Brunhild), even though the figures themselves did not share the same relationship as their namesakes in the *Nibelungenlied.* Although the Austrasian King Sigibert, who was murdered in 575, could be the historic "model" for Siegfried, the character of the latter seems to be rooted in mythology as well as he is the personification of the youthful, mythical hero. In the *Nibelungenlied* this mythical layer is totally ignored or rather transformed into the burlesque.

Regardless of the actual origins of these two groups of legends, they remained separated for centuries as is the case in the songs of the *Edda,* which obviously represents an older developmental stage of the subject matter of the Nibelungs. Beyond the thematic historicity it is interesting to note that in the *Edda,* Gudrun (the Nordic name for the Middle High German name Kriemhild) exacts vengeance for her brothers on Atli (Middle High German Etzel), who had had them killed to satisfy his greed for gold. The female protagonist thus supports her clan, in contrast to the Middle High German epic, in which she avenges Siegfried through actions taken against her clan. Marriage, which was preceded by romantic love in the *Nibelungenlied,* not dynastic considerations, is valued higher than relationships based on blood. That these have not, however, become meaningless, can be seen in the fact that the dying Siegfried commends Kriemhild to the care of her brother Gunther, who had, after all, agreed to his murder and been a part of the intrigue (**B** 996,2–997,2 = **C** 1006,2–1007,2) and in the fact that Siegfried fears that his little son will forever be stigmatized by the unfaithful and underhanded crime committed against him by Kriemhild's relatives (**B** 995 = **C** 1004).

It is not clear when the two groups of legends were joined into one cycle. According to Andreas Heusler, it was the author of the *Nibelungenlied* who first connected them around 1200. In addition he also expanded the events surrounding Siegfried and Brünhild, which until then had merely existed in heroic songs, into epic breadth, whereas the so-called *Ältere Not* (older *Not*) already had epic dimensions in 1160/1170, although not as extensively as in the *Nibelungenlied.* This opinion has not gone unchallenged. It is quite possible that the two groups of legends were joined together earlier, perhaps in the first third of the twelfth century.

The fact that the poet gives the love between Siegfried and Kriemhild such high status in an epic indebted to heroic tradition is not surprising at a time when *minne* (courtly love) had become a central topic of narrative works of literature as well as poetry; a time in which the relationship between the sexes acquired such a new dimension—the erotic—that one could speak of the "discovery of love during the High Middle Ages" (Peter Dinzelbacher, 1981). Friedrich Panzer called the relationship between Siegfried and Kriemhild "from its budding to its fulfillment . . . by far the most beautiful and intimate love story in a medieval German work of literature" (1955, p. 465). It is the kind of love that survives the death of the beloved husband and does not come to an end through the marriage of Kriemhild and Etzel. Indeed Kriemhild only agrees to this second marriage because it provides her with the opportunity to demonstrate her absolute loyalty to Siegfried after his murder through an act of revenge that is similarly absolute. But it is precisely this loyalty that leads Kriemhild to precipitate a tremendous blood bath, which even engulfs the innocent, and finally, with the sword of her *holden vriedel* (beloved husband), to behead Hagen herself and thereby definitively transgress the role of women

during the Middle Ages. At the conclusion of the work, she does, therefore, appear to be the dehumanized *vâlandinne* (she-devil) described by Dietrich von Bern (**B** 1748,4 = **C** 1789,4) and Hagen (**B** 2371,4 = **C** 2431,4). This certainly corresponds to point of view expressed by the poet, who withdraws the sympathy he had earlier displayed for the loving and suffering Kriemhild and which he had tried to instill within his listeners. This is very revealing and anticipates what actually does ensue, namely, that the poet himself associates Kriemhild's actions with the devil in strophe **B** 1394 (not in the *liet* version) and that he speaks of the *argen willen* (bad will) of the Queen (**B** 1399,4 = **C** 1426,4). However it would be imprudent to interpret as a foreshadowing of impending disaster the fact that Etzel's courtship of the widowed Kriemhild, and therefore also their marriage, takes place thirteen years after the death of Siegfried (**B** 1142), or that, thirteen years after having married Etzel, Kriemhild prepares to take her revenge (**B** 1390). The number thirteen was probably not an unlucky number during the Middle Ages. It is noteworthy, nonetheless, that the author of version **C* (who sees Kriemhild in a somewhat more positive light) replaces the number both times with the more common number twelve (**C** 1157 and 1417).

As early as in the first part of the *Nibelungenlied,* the poet has shown with the figure of Siegfried that *minne,* and the actions resulting from it, are contradictory. In order to win the beloved virgin, Siegfried has no scruples about lying and deceiving and then procuring Brünhild for a man who is not her equal. His uncompromising adherence to his role as Gunther's *man* (vassal) in *Islant,* his taming of Brünhild during the wedding night and, finally, the removal of Brünhild's ring and girdle and his thoughtless presentation of both of them to the woman he loves, Kriemhild, lay the foundation for his own destruction. In this way *minne* in the *Nibelungenlied* is depicted as being rather ambiguous. Of course Siegfried himself is not conscious of the inherent danger in the double betrayal of Brünhild and, therefore, of the possible results of his actions. This accords with his characteristic naïveté and his unawareness of what is happening around him when the events have a "political" dimension as, for instance, the (supposed) disclosure of the concubinal status of the Burgundian Queen during the argument between the sisters-in-law. Hagen, on the other hand, recognizes immediately that this is an explosive political issue. Love and marriage between kings and queens is never merely personal and the poet has made this very clear by showing the results of the fervent love between Kriemhild and Siegfried. The extreme counterpart to Siegfried's excessive trust and blindness (compare strophe **B** 923 = **C** 931) is Hagen's matter-of-fact and cold, but correct, assessment of people, his thinking and planning ahead and his calculated, reasoned actions. Can it be a mere coincidence that Hagen—diametrically opposed to Siegfried—is never touched, let alone overcome, by *minne,* so that his actions are never influenced by it? It can certainly be seen that the "most beautiful and intimate love story" of medieval German literature is much more problematic than might be assumed from the aforementioned formulation by Friedrich Panzer, apart from the fact that the *Nibelungenlied* is more than just a romance about *minne* or Kriemhild. At the same time the *Nibelungen nôt* emphasized in the last strophe of the epic, as far as it arises from the relationships and conflicts of the characters, is ultimately a consequence of Siegfried and Kriemhild's love.

The untold suffering, into which all happiness and also the joy of love are transformed, is brought about step by step by the actions of the people and not through some disaster hovering over them, an inevitable destiny. Though the characters normally act in accordance with the dictates of a specific code of behavior, they have internalized this behavior to such an extent that their nature, their "character," is entirely ruled by it and they really do not have any freedom of choice. Most of all the consequences of an initial action develop their own dynamic to the point that they can have ramifications that extend considerably beyond the original intentions of the people involved. This is, for instance, the case with Kriemhild's revenge. With his matter-of-fact outlook on reality, the poet shows, time and time again, the ambivalence of values and virtues. This not only holds true for *minne,* but also for *triuwe* (loyalty): Kriemhild's excessive revenge is the consequence of her absolute loyalty to Siegfried. The bonds of loyalty, defined according to the laws of the feudal system, between

the Burgundian kings and Hagen make it impossible for Gunther and his brothers to turn their vassal over to Kriemhild at the court of Etzel, thereby possibly ending the terrible bloodshed. Hagen himself—although there certainly is no consensus on this point among the interpreters of the *Nibelungenlied*—acted in accordance with the interests of the Burgundian state when he killed Siegfried; at least his personal motives are the same. But in the second part of the epic the man who has been called "Burgundy's political conscience" (Otfrid Ehrismann, 1987, p. 129) decides, despite his insight and contrary to all common sense, to take part in the expedition into the country of the Huns. As the leader of the Burgundians—it is not King Gunther—it is Hagen who makes their voyage irreversible because he knows for certain, at least since the crossing of the Danube, that none of them will survive. The hero of Troneck makes the decision to ride along because his *êre* (honor) is at stake, and the threat to it (compare the strophes **B** 1462 and 1463 = **C** 1490 and 1491) is as deadly to the aristocratic warrior as physical death. Moreover, unlike death, it would be a disgrace for him to remain at home without honor. Overcoming his own self is as impossible for Hagen as it is for Kriemhild, who never even considers the Christian commandment of forgiveness, at least not in association with her deadly enemy Hagen, even though she attends church assiduously. On the whole Christianity appears in the *Nibelungenlied* as something merely superficial and formal (if one disregards the figure of Rüdiger, who appears to be the only one in the work concerned with his soul). As Gottfried Weber (1963) and others have stressed, Christianity in the *Nibelungenlied* is a *Taufscheinchristentum* (Christianity only on paper, on the baptismal certificate), without any real Christian ethics.

Hagen shares his knowledge of imminent death with the Burgundians (**B** 1587–1589 = **C** 1627–1629) and the *snellen helde* (courageous heroes) turn pale when they consider the *herten tôt* (bitter death) that awaits them. However, when they are finally drawn into battle, none of them loses heart for a moment, rather they display exemplary heroism in the face of death. The poet, who has created an almost apocalyptic work of literature and has demonstrated the consequences of human fallibility in his plot, does not deny the courageous and fearless warriors respect; he sometimes even seems to be reporting their deeds with some admiration (compare strophe **B** 1970 = **C** 2023 devoted to Giselher and the narrative comments in lines **B** 2210,4 and 2283,2–4 = **C** 2268,4 and 2342, 2–4). Very revealing, in this context, is what the dying Wolfhart, a hot-headed young vassal of Dietrich von Bern, says to his uncle Hildebrand:

> Unde ob mich mîne mâge   nâch tôde wellen klagen,
> den naehsten unt den besten   den sult ir von mir sagen,
> daz si nâch mir niht weinen;   daz ist âne nôt.
> vor eines küneges handen   lige ich hie hêrlîchen tôt.
> (**B** 2302 = **C** 2362)

[And if my kinsmen wish to lament me when I am dead, tell those who are nearest and dearest not to weep for me, there is no need. I die a magnificent death, slain by the hand of a king.]

In his perception of himself it is an honor to have lost his life in battle with a king (Giselher) whom he then killed with the last stroke of his sword, just as Rüdiger had killed Giselher's brother Gernot (compare also lines **B** 2303,3–4 = **C** 2363,3–4). One should not simply interpret passages such as these as the poet's attempt to glorify a heroic attitude and propagate heroic death, as these statements are embedded in a narrative context in which the consequences of absolute egotism are developed, of which pride to the point of arrogance, *êre,* and fame are integral components. One should also not overlook the fact that the poet lets another warrior, who is no less driven by *êre,* express a reaction toward his death that stands in marked contrast to that demonstrated by Wolfhart. The Dane Iring, who lives at Etzel's court and to whom the poet dedicates a whole *âventiure* (the thirty-fifth) and whom he repeatedly calls *helt* (hero), is fatally wounded by Hagen. His final words do not exude a sense of pride in his deeds but rather contain a warning to the Danes and the Thuringians not to let Kriemhild entice them with gifts into participating in the battle and therefore into death (**B** 2068,2–4 = **C** 2124,2–4), but it is not enough to stop them from joining the fray. This certainly is a relativization, by an apparently sympathetic

poet, of Wolfhart's heroic attitude, which ultimately culminates in his death.

The conclusion of the *Nibelungenlied* is dominated by sorrow and grief without a single positive perspective for the future, such as that later added by the poet of the *Klage.* With its pessimistic and tragic outlook, the work fundamentally differs from the optimistic and utopian atmosphere of the contemporary courtly romance. Grief is experienced in courtly (Arthurian) romance, but it is never complete and always transitory. Sorrow and disharmony are overcome and transformed into all-embracing joy and harmony at the conclusion, which usually finds its expression in a huge feast. By contrast in the *Nibelungenlied* the catastrophe evolves from the feast which Kriemhild organizes with the ulterior motive of using it as a springboard for her revenge. The two major exceptions to the optimistic and joyful atmosphere of the courtly romance—Gottfried's *Tristan* and Wolfram's *Willehalm*—were written later than the epic of *der Nibelungen nôt,* so that the poet of the *Nibelungenlied* was the first to give literary form to a position that ran counter to that encountered in courtly romance. Ursula Schulze has quite correctly pointed out that Arthurian romance and the *Nibelungenlied* are complementary literary models within the same social frame: "The Arthurian romance demonstrates the path to joy and happiness by means of an idealized conception; the *Nibelungenlied* underscores the path of human mortality with the help of an historically related tale" (1988, p. 273). One could also say it shows the world consigned to a state of hopelessness. The question is whether the vision of the world so described is only to be found within literary discourse. This is unlikely. The statements might be a matter of fiction, as far as literary theory goes, but they are not made without desired and recognizable reference, according to the author's intention as well as the understanding of a contemporary audience, to the reality of contemporaries. The perspective from which the poet presents the events of the *Nibelungenlied*—regardless of whether one labels it pessimistic, resigned, skeptical, or simply astute—would therefore mirror the perspective from which he judged the history of his time. He might have anticipated, in a quasi-visionary manner, the decline of the power of the magnificent Hohenstaufen dynasty, which would not have been such a far-fetched reason for anxiety at that time, considering the early death of Emperor Henry VI in 1197 and the ensuing election of two kings (Philipp of Swabia and the Guelph Otto IV) in 1198 which subsequently led to civil war in Germany. Even without this concrete realization of the Christian perspective of mortality it is clear that the *Nibelungenlied* is not just a new account of *alte maere* (old tales) for the sake of recounting *alte maere,* but that the poet associated it with a message to contemporary aristocratic courtly society. Of course we do not know whether the audience decoded the message in accordance with the author or in another way. It is very probable, however, that the reaction from the audience was not uniform.

Who was the anonymous poet who expounded the terrible consequences of values and patterns of behavior in the first heroic epic to be written in the German language, values which not only typified heroism, but which were also retained, at least in part, in medieval knighthood (e.g., *êre, triuwe*)? All attempts, even in more recent times, to determine who he was have not borne fruit. There is no doubt, however, that he was an educated man who, to a certain degree, was familiar with classical and French literature and with the more recent literary developments in Germany. This points to a cleric,which does not necessarily mean a priest; perhaps one in the administrative service of a large court, most likely that of Bishop Wolfger von Passau (1191–1204). There are quite a number of indicators that speak in favor of Passau as the *Nibelungenlied's* place of origin.

The *Nibelungenlied* is undoubtedly based on a narrative concept that has been accorded careful consideration, and the author alludes to the tragic ending at every phase of the story through his ominous predictions. On the other hand he often focuses so intensively on the particular *âventiure* (or scene) that a number of inconsistencies, incongruities, and contradictions result. The reader notices these more than the listener, who was never exposed to the epic as a whole but only to numerous oral performances stretched out over a couple of days. (The Viennese musician and singer Eberhard Kummer, who sang the entire *Nibelungenlied* for the first time in 1988, required a total of thirty-three hours over a period of five days.) It is quite likely that during the Middle Ages just parts, rather than the whole epic, were recited. In addition the poet is clearly not capable of telling his story with the same linguistic agility as, for instance, his contemporary Hartmann von Aue, with his *Iwein.* His vocabulary, which definitely exhibits modern courtly words borrowed from French, is limited, especially where rhymes are concerned. For the 9516 rhymes in the *nôt* version, there are only 796 rhyming words, of which forty are used more than fifty times and some of these even more than a hundred times (*man, lant, hant, lîp, wîp,* etc.). Most are pure rhymes, as had been the case in German narrative works of literature since Heinrich von Veldeke; deviations with respect to quantity (*man: getân, dan: stân,* etc.) remain within the framework of what is also customary with Wolfram von Eschenbach. Only the proper name *Hagene* forces the poet to use very inexact rhyming pairs (e.g., *Hagene: degene*). The stereotypical character of the language is inherited from the oral tradition of the subject matter of the Nibelungs. The high percentage of formulaic and stereotypical expressions is not to be interpreted as the *Nibelungenlied's* dependence on oral composition with respect to its origins. It is not a product of the oral tradition, but rather of the written word, while containing distinct traces of a century-old oral tradition. The pseudo-oral formulae, which have become elements of style, can sometimes evoke monotony among modern readers as, for instance, when the poet consistently uses the same formulae to introduce direct quotations: *Dô sprach der künec rîche* (Thus spoke the noble king), *Dô sprach der künec Gunther* (Thus spoke King Gunther), *Dô sprach aber Etzel* (Then Etzel spoke once again), *Dô sprach der kuchenmeister* (Thus spoke the master of the kitchen), and so on. Yet this rather monotonous tendency to use linguistic stereotypes does not preclude, even in our own time, the emerging certainty that one is reading an important and deeply moving work of literature. As Arthur T. Hatto so accurately put it: "It is marvelous that the Nibelung-poet can say so much so well with so wretched an epic diction" (1980, p. 191).

The undeniable artistic weaknesses of the *Nibelungenlied* are countered by the masterly shaping of expressive and powerful images in which gestures and actions combine in striking symbolism: in the seventh *âventiure,* when Siegfried leads and holds Gunther's horse by the reins; when Hagen destroys the only boat after having crossed the Danube in the twenty-fifth *âventiure;* when Kriemhild welcomes only Giselher with a kiss in the twenty-eighth *âventiure,* which Hagen then answers with a gesture that is just as expressive by binding his helmet tighter; when Hagen and Volker refuse to get up from their seats in honor of the deceptive Queen Kriemhild in the twenty-ninth *âventiure.* Likewise the poet demonstrates considerable talent in his depiction of particular scenes. The events of the epic often seem to be taking place on a stage, which gives this work of literature, together with its frequent dialogues, an intensely dramatic character. Instances of such events include the arrival of the four suitors in Islant (beginning of the seventh *âventiure*); the quarrel of the queens in the fourteenth *âventiure,* particularly the segment that transpires in front of the Cathedral of Worms; the beginning of the thirty-third *âventiure* with the very theatrical "entrance" by Dancwart; and, last but not least, the highly dramatic final encounter between Kriemhild and Hagen in the thirty-ninth *âventiure.* It is this scene, in particular, that demonstrates how far the epic poet can let himself be drawn into the individual scenes, even to the point that the narrative context is neglected. After Kriemhild has cut off the head of Hagen, her mortal enemy, Etzel, Dietrich, and Hildebrand are suddenly present with no explanation from the poet as to where they have come from or where they were during the final encounter between the major protagonists. **B** 2373,4 = **C** 2433,4 could be taken as an indication that Etzel, at least, enters the room at the very moment Kriemhild kills Hagen. Certain questions remain unanswered that might be asked by a reader who approaches fiction in a very rational manner and who pays attention to a strict logic of action. They are, however, unimportant when compared to the succinct, dramatic force with which the concluding section of the epic is described.

If one can deduce the intention and the artistic achievement of the poet of the *Nibelungenlied* primarily from version *****B,** one should not forget that obviously not all contemporary and later audiences were in agreement with his representation of the subject. Apart from the murder of Siegfried by Hagen, the poet throughout the epic clearly refrains from explicitly judging the events he describes. He also avoids painting Kriemhild and Hagen in crude black-and-white terms; he also tends to refrain from categorizing people's actions as a sign of guilt. The author of version *****C** offers a clear shift of emphasis. The date of origin is a matter of some uncertainty. Some scholars assume that it immediately succeeded version *****B,** therefore having already existed in 1205/1206 or earlier; others date its emergence to the second decade of the thirteenth century. The adaptation is diverse but hardly ever completely consistent (Werner Hoffmann, 1967). It has the function, for instance, of smoothing the metrics of the text, of heightening the linguistic melodiousness, of clarifying the formulations, of eliminating inconsistencies and contradictions. The author of this adaptation turns out to be someone who is very concerned with clarity and transparency even to the point of small-mindedness and pedantry. With regard to the content of the work, it is illuminating that he makes an attempt to be more specific with his recriminations, and this corresponds to a medieval understanding of human behavior influenced by Christianity. It is absolutely correct to suggest that the author of the *liet*-version was interested in having Kriemhild appear in a more flattering light and, at the same time, degrading and discrediting Hagen. The omission of strophes 698/699 in the *nôt*-version is typical of this tendency. After her marriage to Siegfried, Kriemhild wishes to exercise her right to bring back to Xanten those Burgundian vassals to whose services she is entitled. In these two strophes she calls upon Hagen, the most powerful vassal at the court in Worms and the chief pillar of the Burgundian kingdom, as well as his nephew Ortwin, to follow her, which Hagen emphatically refuses to do. This incident is part of the reason for Hagen's unrelenting resentment of Kriemhild and it finally leads to the overt enmity between the two. In the *liet*-version Kriemhild does not give Hagen any such cause for complaint. The author of this adaptation inserts two strophes (**C** 821/822) just before the altercation between the queens, depicting Brünhild as deliberately having caused it by following the blandishments of the devil (822,1). He thereby reduces Kriemhild's role in the disastrous events that ensue. In one of the most famous strophes of the *Nibelungenlied* (**B** 1912), the omniscient narrator claims that Kriemhild deliberately exposed her little son, Ortliep, to danger and sacrificed him so that she could finally have her revenge. The narrator condemns her for this to a degree that far exceeds what might be legitimately justified: "wie kunde ein wîp durch râche immer vreislîcher tuon?" (How could a woman ever do a more dreadful thing in pursuit of revenge? 1912,4). In version ***C*** this strophe has been entirely reworked to favor Kriemhild; the condemnation of the woman, which goes back to an older stage of the *Nibelungenlied,* has been eliminated (1963). The additional strophes **C** 1882, 1947, and 2143 stress, whether through figures of speech or omniscient interjections, Kriemhild's intention to hurt no one but Hagen (she explicitly orders that none of the Burgundians are to be harmed), and clearly function as an exoneration of Kriemhild. The wider dimensions of the plot, in the course of which Kriemhild becomes the purveyor of ever more injustice, almost turning into a Fury, have, of course, not been changed in the adapted version. In the additional strophes **C** 1153 and 2428, the character of Hagen is downgraded. In both these strophes he is accused of having demonstrated *untriuwe* (disloyalty): in the first passage, in which it is insinuated that he has a craving for gold, toward the Burgundian kings in general; and in the second passage, explicitly toward his lord Gunther. The author of this version claims that Hagen deliberately chose the words that inevitably led to Gunther's death (**B** 2368 = **C** 2427) because he was afraid that Kriemhild might spare her brother's life and let him return to Worms, while killing Hagen. The tendency (and it is no more than that) to express more explicit and judgmental recriminations or exonerations anticipates the *Klage,* which far outdoes version ***C*** of the epic in this aspect. It offers an understandable, but more shallow interpretation, of the horrible events of the *Nibelungenlied,* for which there was, however, obviously a need.

[WH]

Bibliography

Andersson, Theodore M. *A Preface to the Nibelungenlied.* Stanford: Stanford University Press, 1987.

Batts, Michael S. "The Nibelungenlied." In *The Middle Ages and the Renaissance,* vol. 1 of *European Writers,* edited by W. T. H. Jackson. New York: Scribner, 1983, pp. 211–236.

———, ed. *Das Nibelungenlied: Paralleldruck der Handschriften A, B, und C nebst Lesarten der übrigen Handschriften.* Tübingen: Niemeyer, 1971.

Buschinger, Danielle, and Wolfgang Spiewok, eds. *La Chanson des Nibelungen hier et aujourd'hui. Actes du colloque Amiens 12 et 13 janvier 1991.* Amiens: Université de Picardie, 1991.

Curschmann, Michael. "Nibelungenlied und 'Klage.'" In vol. 6 of *Die deutsche Literatur des Mittelalters. Verfasserlexikon,* 2nd ed., edited by Kurt Ruh. Berlin: de Gruyter, 1987, cols. 926–969.

de Boor, Helmut, ed. *Das Nibelungenlied,* after the edition by Karl Bartsch. 22nd ed. by Roswitha Wisniewski. Mannheim: Brockhaus, 1988. Manuscript **B.**

Dinzelbacher, Peter. "Über die Entdeckung der Liebe im Hochmittelalter." *Saeculum* 32 (1981): 185–208.

Ehrismann, Otfrid. *Das Nibelungenlied: Epoche, Werk, Wirkung.* Munich: Beck, 1987.

Gentry, Francis G. "'*Mort*' oder '*untriuwe*'? *Nibelungenliet* und *Nibelungennôt.*" In *Ergebnisse und Aufgaben der Germanistik am Ende des 20. Jahrhunderts. Ludwig Erich Schmitt zum 80. Geburtstag,* edited by Elisabeth Feldbusch. Hildesheim: Olms-Weidmann, 1989, pp. 302–316.

Göhler, Peter. *Das Nibelungenlied. Erzählweise, Figuren, Weltanschauung, literaturgeschichtliches Umfeld.* Berlin: Akademie-Verlag, 1989.

Hatto, A. T. "Medieval German." In *The Traditions,* vol. 1 of *Traditions of Heroic and Epic Poetry,* edited by A. T. Hatto. London: Modern Humanities Research Association, 1980, pp. 165–195.

Haymes, Edward R. *The Nibelungenlied: History and Interpretation.* Illinois Medieval Monographs 2. Urbana and Chicago: University of Illinois Press, 1986. See also German version; Munich: Fink, 1999.

Heinzle, Joachim. *Das Nibelungenlied: Eine Einführung.* Munich: Artemis, 1987; Frankfurt a. M.: Fischer Taschenbuch Verlag, 1994.

Hennig, Ursula, ed. *Das Nibelungenlied nach der Handschrift C.* Altdeutsche Textbibliothek 83. Tübingen: Niemeyer, 1977.

Heusler, Andreas. *Nibelungensage und Nibelungenlied: Die Stoffgeschichte des deutschen*

Heldenepos. 6th ed. 1965. Reprint, Dortmund: Ruhfus, 1991.

Hoffmann, Werner. *Das Nibelungenlied.* Frankfurt a. M.: Diesterweg, 1987.

——. *Das Nibelungenlied.* 6th ed. Sammlung Metzler 7. Stuttgart and Weimar: Metzler, 1992.

——. "Die Fassung *C des Nibelungenliedes und die 'Klage.'" In *Festschrift Gottfried Weber,* edited by Heinz Otto Burger and Klaus von See. Bad Homburg v. d. H.: Gehlen, 1967, pp. 109–143.

Jaeger, C. Stephen. "The Nibelungen Poet and the Clerical Rebellion against Courtesy." In *Spectrum medii aevi. Essays in Early German Literature in Honor of George Fenwick Jones,* edited by William C. McDonald. Göppingen: Kümmerle, 1983, pp. 177–205.

Knapp, Fritz Peter, ed. *Nibelungenlied und Klage: Sage und Geschichte, Struktur und Gattung. Passauer Nibelungengespräche 1985.* Heidelberg: Winter, 1987.

Masser, Achim, ed. *Hohenemser Studien zum Nibelungenlied.* Dornbirn: Vorarlberger Verlagsanstalt, 1981.

McConnell, Winder. *The Nibelungenlied.* Twayne's World Authors Series 712. Boston: G. K. Hall, 1984.

——, ed. *A Companion to the Nibelungenlied.* Columbia, SC: Camden House, 1998.

Moser, Dietz Rüdiger, and Marianne Sammer, eds. *Nibelungenlied und Klage. Ursprung, Funktion, Bedeutung. Symposium Kloster Andechs 1995.* Munich: Institut Bayerische Literaturgeschichte der Universität München, 1998.

Müller, Jan-Dirk. *Spielregeln für den Untergang: Die Welt des Nibelungenliedes.* Tübingen: Niemeyer, 1998.

Nagel, Bert. *Das Nibelungenlied: Stoff, Form, Ethos.* Frankfurt a. M.: Hirschgraben, 1965; 2nd ed., 1970.

Panzer, Friedrich. *Das Nibelungenlied: Entstehung und Gestalt.* Stuttgart: Kohlhammer, 1955.

Rupp, Heinz, ed. *Nibelungenlied und Kudrun.* Wege der Forschung 54. Darmstadt: Wissenschaftliche Buchgesellschaft, 1976.

Schröder, Werner. *Nibelungenlied-Studien.* Stuttgart: Metzler, 1968.

Schulze, Ursula. *Das Nibelungenlied.* Literaturstudium. Stuttgart: Reclam, 1997. With extensive bibliography, pp. 299–325.

——. "Nibelungenlied." In *Deutsche Literatur: Eine Sozialgeschichte,* edited by Horst Albert Glaser. Vol. 1, *Aus der Mündlichkeit in die Schriftlichkeit: Höfische und andere Literatur,* edited by Ursula Liebertz-Grün. Reinbek bei Hamburg: Rowohlt, 1988, pp. 264–278.

Thomas, Heinz. "Die Staufer im Nibelungenlied." *ZfdPh* 109 (1990): 321–354.

Weber, Gottfried. *Das Nibelungenlied: Problem und Idee.* Stuttgart: Metzler, 1963.

Wolf, Alois. *Heldensage und Epos: Zur Konstituierung einer mittelalterlichen volkssprachlichen Gattung im Spannungsfeld von Mündlichkeit und Schriftlichkeit.* Tübingen: Narr, 1995.

Wunderlich, Werner, and Ulrich Müller, eds. *"Waz sider da geschach." American-German Studies on the Nibelungenlied.* Göppingen: Kümmerle, 1992. *With bibliography 1980–1990/91.*

Zatloukal, Klaus, ed. *Pöchlarner Heldenliedgespräch: Das Nibelungenlied und der mittlere Donauraum.* Philologica Germanica 12. Vienna: Fassbaender, 1990.

——, ed. *3. Pöchlarner Heldenliedgespräch: Die Rezeption des Nibelungenliedes.* Philologica Germanica 16. Vienna: Fassbaender, 1995.

——, ed. *4. Pöchlarner Heldenliedgespräch. 1000 Jahre Österreich: Heldendichtung in Österreich, Österreich in der Heldendichtung.* Philologica Germanica 20. Vienna: Fassbaender, 1997.

ODDRÚNARGRÁTR (Oddrun's Lament), an Eddic lay recorded in the *Codex Regius.* The title comes from the more recent paper manuscripts. The lay consists of thirty-four stanzas in *fornyrðislag* and begins with a prose part providing background material. After the poem there also follows a prose passage about Atli's death. Oddrun is also mentioned in the *Sigurðarkviða in skamma* and in one of the prose bridges, *Dráp Niflunga,* (The Murder of the Niflungs) and in the *Volsunga saga.*

Borgny, the daughter of King Heidrek, had a lover called Vilmund. She could not give birth to her child until Oddrun, Atli's and Brynhild's sister, came to her assistance. Oddrun had been the beloved of Gunnar, Gjuki's son. Here the poetic part begins. At the beginning it once again tells us about Borgny's plight. Then Oddrun sings magic tunes for the sick woman. Borgny gives birth to a boy and a girl and wants to thank Oddrun, but the latter rejects her thanks brusquely, because once Borgny had blamed her for her illegal love of Gunnar. She had only come because she had promised to help all the poor and needy.

The second part of the lay is really Oddrun's lament. She grew up happily in a king's palace. Her dying father Budli betrothed her to Gunnar, but her sister Brynhild was destined to become a valkyrie. Brynhild's castle was taken by Gunnar, yet he was unable to win her, so Sigurd exchanged shapes with him, and successfully wooed her. This betrayal of trust led to a number of cataclysmic events that culminated in Sigurd's and Brynhild's death.

Oddrun fell in love with Gunnar, but her brother Atli did not approve of their good relations. He even rejected Sigurd's gold when Gunnar sought her hand. Gunnar and Oddrun met secretly but were discovered by Atli's men. Atli invited Gunnar and Hogni to his court. When Hogni was killed (his heart was cut out of his breast) and Gunnar was put into the snake pit, Oddrun heard her lover play the harp and set out to save him, but she was too late, because she had been brewing beer for Geirmund at Hlesey at that time. Atli's mother, in the form of a serpent, had already killed Gunnar. Now she could only weep and lament for her dead beloved.

The author of the poem aimed to retell an old tale about the fall of the Niflungs from a different point of view. He invented Oddrun and made her Atli's sister. Gunnar's and Hogni's deaths are seen as a cruel punishment because Atli condemned the secret love between Gunnar and Oddrun. The elegiac tone of Oddrun's retrospective monologue is typical of the more recent Eddic lays (second half of the twelfth century/ thirteenth century; Icelandic scholars suggest 1050–1150).

[GW]

Bibliography

Beck, Heinrich. "Oddrúnargrátr." In vol. 5 of *Kindlers Literaturlexikon.* Zürich: Kindler, 1964, cols. 785f.

de Vries, Jan. *Altnordische Literaturgeschichte.* Vol. 2. 2nd ed. Grundriss der germanischen Philologie 16. Berlin: de Gruyter, 1967, pp. 143–145.

Gering, Hugo, and B. Sijmons. *Kommentar zu den Liedern der Edda.* 2. Hälfte: *Heldenlieder.* Germanistische Handbibliothek VII 3,2. Halle (Saale): Buchhandlung des Waisenhauses (Francke), 1931, pp. 324–338.

Haymes, Edward R., and Susann T. Samples. *Heroic Legends of the North: An Introduction to the Nibelung and Dietrich Cycles.* New York: Garland, 1996, p. 124.

Mohr, Wolfgang. "Wortschatz und Motive der jüngeren Eddalieder mit südgermanischem Stoff." *ZfdA* 76 (1939), 149–217.

Simek, Rudolf, and Hermann Pálsson. *Lexikon der altnordischen Literatur.* Stuttgart: Kröner, 1987, p. 263.

RAGNARS SAGA LOÐBRÓKAR, the tale of Ragnar Loðbrók, along with his wife Aslaug and his sons. The saga is found in the same manuscript (Ny kgl. saml. 1824b, 4to.) as the *Volsunga saga,* which it follows without interruption, only a small space having been left for the new title. Schlauch believes that the first chapter may actually have belonged to the *Volsunga saga. Ragnars saga* is not the invention of the *Volsunga saga* compiler, however; it has its own sources, among them Adam of Bremen and Saxo Grammaticus.

The saga opens with Heimir, the foster father of Aslaug, hiding Aslaug in a harp. Aslaug is the daughter of Sigurd and Brynhild. Heimir takes her to Norway where he is murdered and Aslaug is found and raised by a peasant couple who name her Kraka. We are then introduced to Ragnar Loðbrók, who kills a dragon in order to win Thora, the daughter of Herraud. Thora and Ragnar have two children, Erik and Agnar. After Thora's death, Ragnar finds and weds Aslaug. She bears him five sons: Ivar the Boneless, Bjorn, Hvitserk, Rognvald, and Sigurd Snake-Eye. When Thora's sons Erik and Agnar are killed in battle against Eystein, king of Sweden, and his divine cow Sibilia, Aslaug urges her sons to avenge their deaths and accompanies them to battle in Sweden under the name Randalin. Ivar kills Sibilia, Eystein is slain, and the Swedes are defeated. After this Ragnar's sons win fame in countless battles as they attack and destroy a number of famous fortified towns. Ragnar desires to cultivate his own fame and consequently launches a poorly planned attack on the English. He is defeated by the English king Ella, captured, and cast into a snake pit, where he dies (note also Gunnar's fate in the *Volsunga saga* and *Atlakviða*). Ella sends messengers to Denmark to inform Ragnar's sons, and except for Ivar, who has other plans, they set out for England, where they, too, are defeated. Ivar demands from Ella only an ox hide's worth of land as compensation for his father's death. He then stretches and cuts the ox hide so that it covers a large tract of land where he builds a mighty fortress. Ivar uses his position to buy off many

English warriors, and when his brothers return to fight, they are victorious and Ella is captured and executed. After this the line of Sigurd Snake-Eye is detailed: his daughter Ragnhild will be the mother of Harald of Norway, the first monarch to unite the country. Ivar rules England until his death. Later, when William the Conqueror opens his grave mound, he finds Ivar's body uncorrupted and burns him on a pyre.

The saga's chief function would seem to be as a "sequel" of sorts to the *Volsunga saga,* a bridge between the legends of Sigurd and Brynhild and actual history of the ninth through eleventh centuries. The Norwegian royal house receives a mythological ancestor (Sigurd) on which to base claims of superiority, and the ninth century establishment of the Danelaw in England is related to the same lineage in the person of Ivar. (An English chronicle cites Ingvar as the slayer of King Aella in 866.)

The exploits of Ragnar and his sons also take up much of Book IX of Saxo Grammaticus' *Gesta Danorum.* Many parts of the saga can be read in Saxo, including Ragnar's winning of Thora as bride and the origin of his nickname; Ragnar's subsequent marriage to Swanloga (Aslaug?); the deeds of Ragnar's sons, particularly the deeds of Iwar (Ivar), who gained so much land in England with the ox hide, and those of Siward (Sigurd Snake-Eye), whose nickname is explained in quite a different way. Ragnar's own wars in England against Ella and his death in the snake pit are also recounted there.

[JKW]

Bibliography

Olsen, Magnus, ed. *Volsunga saga ok Ragnars saga loðbrókar.* Copenhagen: Møller, 1906–1908.

Schlauch, Margaret, trans. *The Saga of the Volsungs; The Saga of Ragnar Loðbrók together with the Lay of Kraka.* New York: AMS Press, 1978.

REGINSMÁL (The Lay of Regin). In the *Codex Regius* of the *Poetic Edda,* this heroic lay is not separated from the *Fáfnismál* and the *Sigrdrífumál.* The title has become customary since Sophus Bugge's edition in 1867. Older editions call the lay *Sigurðarqviða Fáfnisbana onnor* (The Second Lay of Sigurd, the Killer of Fafnir). It contains an event of Sigurd's youth. The lay is written in the form of a dialogue in twenty-six

stanzas in *ljóðaháttr.* A longer prose passage at the beginning is followed by the poem about Sigurd acquiring the treasure. The same story is told in the *Volsunga saga,* some parts following this lay word for word.

Regin, a dwarf magician and a smith, has two brothers, Otr and Fafnir. Otr has the habit of spending his time in the shape of an otter and likes to fish in a waterfall that is the home of the dwarf Andvari, who possesses a great hoard of gold. The gods, Odin, Hoenir, and Loki, meet Otr, and Loki kills him with a stone. Afterwards they seek shelter with Otr's father, Hreidmar. The father demands compensation for his son. The gods are forced by Regin, Fafnir, and Hreidmar to fill the flayed skin of the otter with gold and to cover it completely with gold. Loki is therefore compelled to seek the gold they need. He goes back to the waterfall and catches Andvari with a net, for the dwarf has turned into a pike. Loki forces Andvari to hand over all the gold, including a ring that would have allowed the dwarf to build up his treasure again. Andvari curses the gold. He prophesies that two brothers (Fafnir and Regin) will be killed and eight earls (Sigurd, Gutthorm, Gunnar, Hogni, Atli, Erp, Sorli, and Hamdir) will start to quarrel about the treasure. Hreidmar is compensated, but he does not want to share the gold with his sons. Fafnir therefore kills his father, takes the gold, turns himself into a dragon, and guards the gold on the Gnitaheide.

Later Sigurd is raised by Regin, who now wants Sigurd to kill the dragon and gives him the excellent sword Gram for this deed. Sigurd agrees to do so, but only after he has avenged his own father. In a bloody battle, Sigurd kills Lyngvi and his brothers, the sons of Hunding. On his journey Hnikar (another name for Odin) enters Sigurd's ship and tells him about good and bad omens.

The lay is very heterogeneous in form and content, and the prose bridges relate more of the story than the dialogues. In this lay the continental tale of Sigurd is connected to the Northern tale of Helgi Hundingsbani (Helgi, the killer of Hunding) by making Sigurd a stepbrother to Helgi. Both are the sons of King Sigmund and come from the Volsung family.

Andreas Heusler tried to rearrange the stanzas of the *Reginsmál* and those of the *Fáfnis-*

mál in order to get two more homogeneous poems, the *Lied vom Drachenhort* (Lay of the Dragon's Hoard), written in *ljóðaháttr;* and the *Lied von Sigurds Vaterrache* (Lay of Sigurd's Revenge for His Father) written mainly in *fornyrðislag,* but including Hnikar's advice to Sigurd in *ljóðaháttr.* Poems about young Sigurd's deeds are usually more recent than those retelling old continental tales. Perhaps these events were only told in prose at the beginning of the tenth century. Therefore the *Lay of Regin* is frequently dated between 1000 and 1150. Icelandic scholars suggest it may have been written earlier than 1000.

[GW]

Bibliography

Andersson, Theodore M. "Reginsmál and Fáfnismál." In vol. 10 of *Dictionary of the Middle Ages,* edited by Joseph R. Strayer. New York: Scribner, 1988, pp. 290f.

Beck, Heinrich. "Reginsmál." In vol. 19 of *Kindlers neues Literaturlexikon,* edited by Walter Jens. Munich: Kindler, 1992, pp. 499–500.

Bugge, Sophus, ed. *Norrøn fornævk di: islandsk samling af folkelige oldtidsdigte om Nordens guder og heroer almindelig kaldet Sæmundar Edda hins Fróda.* Christiana: P.T. Malling, 1867.

de Vries, Jan. *Altnordische Literaturgeschichte.* 2 vols. 2nd ed. Grundriss der germanischen Philologie 15, 16. Berlin: de Gruyter, 1964, 1967.

Gering, Hugo, and B. Sijmons. *Kommentar zu den Liedern der Edda.* 2. Hälfte: *Heldenlieder.* Germanistische Handbibliothek VII 3,2. Halle (Saale): Buchhandlung des Waisenhauses (Francke), 1931, pp. 160–183.

Haymes, Edward R., and Susann T. Samples. *Heroic Legends of the North: An Introduction to the Nibelung and Dietrich Cycles.* New York: Garland, 1996, pp. 115, 121.

Heusler, Andreas. "Altnordische Dichtung und Prosa von Jung Sigurd" (1919). Reprint in *Kleine Schriften.* Berlin: de Gruyter, 1943, pp. 26–64.

Simek, Rudolf, and Hermann Pálsson. *Lexikon der altnordischen Literatur.* Stuttgart: Kröner, 1987, p. 288.

RITTER LÖWHARDUS. The seventeenth-century "History of Ritter Löwhardus" is the latest account of the living tradition of the Nibelungen legend. It is the first and only story of Siegfried's son, the story of a hero who never had a story before. Like the name of his mother, which changed from Kriemhild in the *Nibelungenlied* to Florigunda in the folk book of Siegfried (the *Gehörnte Siegfried*), the son's name also changed from Gunther to Löwhardus. The book about Löwhardus is already mentioned by the author of the *Gehörnte Siegfried,* but there was no record of its existence until Harold Jantz rediscovered it and presented his findings several decades ago. The only extant copy of the book is the one in the Jantz collection housed at Duke University. It was published in Erfurt around the middle of the seventeenth century. With its 216 pages, it is considerably longer than the prose book about Siegfried, which obviously served as its model, but it almost appears to have been written by the same author. Departing from the heroic core of the Siegfried legend like its predecessor, the new folk book embraces the notion of an open-ended family saga to be continued from one sequel to the next. Consequently the story of Löwhardus is in turn to be followed by a book about his oldest son, Artaxant, king of Sicily.

The Erfurt print of *Ritter Löwhardus* shows no date of publication. But the text contains an important reference to the publication of the *Gehörnte Siegfried,* namely, "zu Hamburg Anno 57" (N 6 r). This is the only source for an earlier date of the Siegfried book than that of the earliest preserved edition (1726). At the same time it suggests a time frame for the dating of *Ritter Löwhardus.* A conflicting reference to Erfurt as "recent" place of publication for the *Gehörnte Siegfried* (Preface, A 2 v) suggests a possible reprint of an original North German text. Jantz concludes that probably both books first appeared in Hamburg and were subsequently reprinted in Erfurt by Martha Hertz. Since the author of the *Siegfried* book seems completely familiar with the *Löwhardus* book, it is reasonable to expect its appearance in print to be not too far removed from the date of the Hamburg *Siegfried.* This argues for a date of the *Löwhardus* book somewhere between 1657 and the early 1660s. Such a time frame is, as Jantz suggests, also in keeping with the typographical evidence.

Nothing is known about the author's identity. Judging from his interest in military events in North Germany and his reference to a Pomeranian chronicle in particular, he was likely someone steeped in military history and closely related to the coastal region of northeastern Germany, somewhere in the area of Stralsund and Greifswald. His extensive knowledge of a great variety of earlier narrative materials also suggests someone of considerable erudition with specialized knowledge in regional history.

The type of story told in *Ritter Löwhardus* resembles less a traditional heroic tale than a *Ritterroman*. At the same time the folk book accommodates the narrative content of Late Hellenistic family romance. In an innovative two-part structure, the book combines the bride-quest scheme patterned on the Siegfried story with an adventurous separation and reunion plot based on the journey scheme of Greek romance. Most of the action takes place in the area of the Mediterranean and the Orient, with Sicily functioning as a pivotal point. The book title gives the following synopsis of the plot: " . . . Eine vortreffliche wunderschöne History . . . von eines Königes Sohn aus Niederland/wie derselbe die schöne und tapffere Heldin Sicilianen/des Königes in Sicilien Tochter durch seine Heroische Männliche Thaten überkommen/und wie diese Liebpaar/nach viel und grosser ausgestandener Gefahr und Wunder/endlich zur gewünschten Ruhe gelanget . . . ." [A splendid and marvelous tale of a king's son from the Netherlands and a beautiful and brave heroine, Siciliana, whom he won over from the king of Sicily through his heroic and manly deeds, and how this love pair, after enduring much danger and fantastic adventure, finally reach a much desired state of peace.] Surprisingly, the return of the couple constitutes the entire second part, thus forming a narrative entity in its own right. The preview given in the *Gehörnte Siegfried,* which simply concluded with the winning of the bride in Sicily, did apparently not foresee the addition of a second part. The seemingly endless trials of the couple, which include the bride's apparent death and revival, a period of Babylonian captivity, repeated shipwrecks, separations and reunions, single combat between husband and wife, captivity in an Egyptian brothel and on the island of a pirate prince, up to a final gigantic sea battle against the Turks off the Dutch coast, all this is hardly related to the Nibelungen tradition. Its origins are closer to the type of romance of late antiquity, such as Heliodor's *Aithiopica.* A new story called for new narrative resources.

The composition is strikingly syncretistic. The title announces that the story has been gleaned from "many ancient writers." The sources include Old and New Testament materials; narrative schemes from Greek romance; elements from popular narrative in fables, legends, and anecdotes; central motifs from medieval romance and contemporary folk books; and even episodes from regional chronicles. Examples of how these many sources manifest themselves in the story include the bride quest sequence of the first part, which leans strongly on Tristan's dragon strategy in winning Isolde, and in the second part the rescue operation on the island of the pirate prince, a scene that suggests basic motifs of the Korntin episode in *Wigalois.* The very name of the hero, Löwhardus, supported by his status as a knight with a lion, reflects the biblical lion of the Samson story as well as the legendary lion healed by a hero—the "grateful lion" of medieval romance. The most extensive borrowing of an entire narrative sequence occurs in the second part, where the separation and reunion of the hero and his wife follows closely the popular story of Apollonius von Tyrus, of which a folk book was available in Steinhöwel's translation of 1461. It has been shown that nearly all of the major episodes relating to the fates of Löwhardus and Siciliana after their departure from Sicily match the calamities of Apollonius and Cleopatra after their marriage (see Dick 61f.).

Owing to the systematic adaptation of the Apollonius romance, the story of *Ritter Löwhardus* has outgrown the traditional narrative mold of the Siegfried story. It results in a translation of the heroic subject matter to the medium of romance. The hero figure becomes a courtly knight, and instead of an early tragic death he is rewarded for his sufferings by a happy fairy-tale end with infinite prospects of continuation. The transformation involves the names as well as the setting of the story in time and place, but above all a fundamental change in the narrative paradigm of the folk book genre. In its new format the *Löwhardus* book differs from the *Siegfried* book in that it represents a new form of fiction, a hero figure that undergoes a spiritual crisis. It also shows a shift from the Nibelungen tradition to the fantastic realm of the earliest form of European romance merged with a seventeenth-century penchant for the popularized fiction of medieval chivalry.

[ESD]

Bibliography

German Baroque Literature: A Descriptive Catalogue of the Collection of Harold Jantz. 2 vols. No. 3274, reel 592. New Haven: Research Publications, 1974.

Dick, Ernst S. "Ritter Löwhardus: The Folk Book of Siegfried's Son." *Monatshefte* 78 (1986), 54–68, esp. 61f.

Jantz, Harold. "The Last Branch of the Nibelungen Tree." *MLN* 80 (1965), 433–440.

Steinhöwel, Heinrich. Apollonius von Tyrus. 1461; reprint Hildesheim: Olms 1975.

ROSENGARTEN ZU WORMS (Rose Garden at Worms), Middle High German epic poem in the metric form of the *Hildebrandslied*. It may have originated in the first half of the thirteenth century and is today extant in twenty manuscripts (dating from ca. 1300 to ca. 1500) and six printed versions (1479 to 1590). Author and place of origin are unknown (earlier scholars suggested Austria). At least five versions can be distinguished, which deviate from each other in some parts substantially in the details of the narrative plot; the most important versions are **A** and **DP,** as they are the most widespread. According to version **A,** Kriemhild tends a gorgeous rose garden at Worms, which is guarded by twelve heroes, among them her father Gibeche, her brothers Gunther and Gernot, her fiancé Siegfried, and also Hagen. She wishes to see Siegfried fight Dietrich von Bern and lets the latter be challenged. Siegfried travels with his heroes to Worms. Each one of Dietrich's heroes is individually pitted in a contest against a guardian of the rose garden. Dietrich's men are victorious, only the fight between Dietleib (on Dietrich's side) and Walther ends in a tie. Each of the winners receives a kiss from Kriemhild and a rosary. In the last contest, Siegfried and Dietrich von Bern confront each other as the twelfth pair, but Kriemhild intercedes in the fight, preventing Dietrich from killing Siegfried. Following the regular battles, the monk Ilsan challenges fifty-two more opponents, defeats all of them, and wins fifty-two rosaries for his fellow monks and fifty-two kisses from Kriemhild; as punishment

for her arrogance (she thinks that nobody measures up to the guardians of the rose garden) and bloodthirstiness, he scratches her face bloody with his beard, declaring "this is the way I will kiss a treacherous young lady." In version **DP,** Gibeche appears as the lord of the garden. He has publicly proclaimed that he will subject himself to the man who defeats the guardian of the garden. Thereupon the king of the Huns, Etzel, and Dietrich von Bern, who is being challenged personally by Kriemhild, travel to Worms. Rüdiger presents Etzel's and Dietrich's challenges for battle to Kriemhild. The heroes from Worms are defeated here as well except for Walther, whose fight again ends in a tie (this time against Hartnit). Dietrich spews fire at Siegfried during their fight, which causes the hero's horny skin to melt. Kriemhild is also mocked by Brünhild, who is already living at the court of Worms, and is scolded by Hagen ("queen Kriemhild cooked up the murderous fighting;" strophe **D** 604). Comparable to **A,** Gibeche at the end has to take his own land in feudal tenure from the winners.

The characterization of figures in the *Rosengarten* allows it to be closely linked to the reception of the *Nibelungenlied*. As an attempt to interpret the ambiguous figure of Kriemhild of the *Nibelungenlied* it follows in the tracks of the *Nibelungenlied* version *C** and the *Klage*. But while these emphasize the positive image of Kriemhild as the loyal and faithful widow and exculpate the avenger as much as possible, the *Rosengarten* already presents the young Kriemhild as a *vâlandinnne* ("she-devil," as she is also called in the second part of the *Nibelungenlied*). Since the *Klage* has been handed down regularly together with other versions of the *Nibelungenlied* and consequently guides their reception and interpretation in its own sense, the positive Kriemhild image must be seen as the generally accepted one in the *Nibelungenlied* tradition. That the rival Kriemhild characterization of the *Rosengarten* was no less popular is evidenced by the widespread transmission of the text and by the fact that "übeliu Kriemhilt" (wicked Kriemhild) was a common term of abuse in the later Middle Ages.

Apparently all through the Middle Ages there was (besides the *Nibelungenlied*) a strong and lively narrative tradition (probably predominantly oral) about the Nibelungs. Therefore, it does not come as a surprise that the *Rosengarten* has absorbed elements from the Nibelungen tale that are absent in the *Nibelungenlied*. Thus Kriemhild's father bears his original name Gibeche (which in the *Nibelungenlied,* except in the late manuscript **k,** is replaced by "Dancrat"). There are also allusions to Siegfried's youth with a smith (strophe **A** 331) and his slaying in strophe **A** 329 of a dragon "ûf eime steine" (on a crag). The dragon fight probably involved the liberation of Kriemhild as is related in the *Lay of Hürnen Seyfried* and mentioned in manuscript **n,** and to which the version of manuscript **m** of the *Nibelungenlied* (which is lost except for the listing of chapter headings) devotes three *âventiuren.*

[JH]

Bibliography

Holz, Georg, ed. *Die Gedichte vom Rosengarten zu Worms.* Halle: Niemeyer, 1893.

Heinzle, Joachim. "Konstanten der Nibelungenrezeption im Mittelalter und Neuzeit." In *3. Pöchlarner Heldenliedgespräch. Die Rezeption des Nibelungenliedes,* edited by Klaus Zatloukal, Philologica Germanica 16. Vienna: Fassbaender, 1995, pp. 81–107.

———. *Mittelhochdeutsche Dietrichepik. Untersuchungen zur Tradierungsweise, Überlieferungskritik und Gattungsgeschichte später Heldendichtung,* MTU 62. Munich: Artemis, 1978.

———. "Rosengarten." In vol. 8 of *Die deutsche Literatur des Mittelalters. Verfasserlexikon,* 2nd ed., edited by Kurt Ruh et al. Berlin: de Gruyter, 1992, cols. 187–192.

SIGRDRÍFUMÁL (The Lay of Sigrdrifa) is a heroic poem in the *Poetic Edda.* It is not presented as a poem separate from the *Reginsmál* and the *Fáfnismál* in the *Codex Regius.* Only in the more recent paper manuscripts is it an independent poem, also called *Brynhildarljóð.* The lay consists of thirty-seven stanzas but only seven of them concern an event of Sigurd's youth. The stanzas are written partly in *fornyrðislag,* partly in *ljóðaháttr.* The metrical inconsistencies correspond to inconsistencies found in the order of the stanzas, and the poem includes includes parts that do not fit together. But the lay is embedded in narrative prose to guarantee the understanding of the events.

Sigurd, Sigmund's son, rides to the Hindarfjall. He sees a bright light on top of the hill and finds a person asleep in full armor. When he removes the metal covering, he discovers that it is a woman. She calls herself Sigrdrifa, greets the day and the world, and asks who has awakened her. She tells Sigurd that Odin had punished her for disobedience. Her transgression occurred when she helped Agnar, Auda's brother, to win in combat against Hjalmgunnar, to whom Odin had promised victory. Odin thus pricked her with a thorn of sleep (*svefnþorn;* cf. the fairy tale about Sleeping Beauty). At this point Sigrdrifa is no longer a valkyrie and is compelled to marry, but she states that she would never marry a timid man. Most of the subsequent text is occupied with general advice concerning magic runes and then with proper and wise behavior. In the middle there is a short passage which suggests that Sigurd and Sigrdrifa swear to marry, even if they thereby choose death. The original conclusion of the poem is lost because of the lacuna in the *Codex Regius.* The lay was used by the scribe of the *Volsunga saga.* Although there is no suggestion in the poem that Sigrdrifa is Brynhild, the author of the saga and the late paper manuscripts intimate that she was.

[GW]

Bibliography

Andersson, Theodore M. "Sigrdrífumál." In vol. 11 of *Dictionary of the Middle Ages,* edited by Joseph R. Strayer. New York: Scribner, 1988, pp. 288f.

Beck, Heinrich. "Sigrdrífumál." In vol. 19 of *Kindlers neues Literaturlexikon,* edited by Walter Jens. Munich: Kindler, 1992, pp. 499–500.

de Vries, Jan. *Altnordische Literaturgeschichte.* 2 vols. 2nd ed. Grundriss der germanischen Philologie 15, 16. Berlin: de Gruyter, 1964, 1967.

Gering, Hugo, and B. Sijmons. *Kommentar zu den Liedern der Edda.* 2. Hälfte: *Heldenlieder.* Germanistische Handbibliothek VII 3,2. Halle (Saale): Buchhandlung des Waisenhauses (Francke), 1931, pp. 205–222.

Haymes, Edward R., and Susann T. Samples. *Heroic Legends of the North: An Introduction to the Nibelung and Dietrich Cycles.* New York: Garland, 1996, p. 121.

Simek, Rudolf, and Hermann Pálsson. *Lexikon der altnordischen Literatur.* Stuttgart: Kröner, 1987, pp. 308f.

SIGURÐARKVIÐA IN MEIRI (The Longer Lay of Sigurd).

This lay is completely lost in the lacuna of the *Codex Regius.* We can only reconstruct the contents from chapters 25 to 32 in the *Volsunga saga.* The name was given to it by Andreas Heusler, who thought the lay may have had about 160 stanzas. As far as we know, the story resembled that of the *Sigurðarkviða in skamma,* but its metrical and stylistic form was different. It was more courtly in diction, and the details of its plot may have been more similar to the *Nibelungenlied* than to the other Eddic lays. Therefore, the poem was likely one of the most recent Sigurd lays. In 1902 Heusler reconstructed three Eddic lays that had been completely lost: the *Meiri;* a *Traumlied* (Dream Lay), which corresponds to Kriemhild's dream about the falcon or hawk (*Volsunga saga,* ch. 26–27); and a *Falkenlied* (Hawk Lay), a recent lay about Sigurd wooing Brynhild (*Volsunga saga,* ch. 24–25). The beginning of the *Brot af Sigurðarkviða* and the end of the *Sigrdrífumál* are also lost in the lacuna. This gap has occasioned a vast amount of speculation about the contents of the missing lays. Some scholars think that only one lay may be missing, the *Meiri,* which must have been very extensive and substantial. Theodore M. Andersson suggests: "If we assume that this gathering was largely filled with the *Long Lay of Sigurd,* we may suppose that it was borrowed for the specific purpose of consulting this latest, longest, and perhaps at the time most fashionable version of the tale of Sigurd and Brynhild. We may regret that the borrower never returned the gathering, but his delinquency has done nothing to detract from the fascination of the piece."

[GW]

Bibliography

Andersson, Theodore M. "The Lays in the Lacuna of Codex Regius." In *Speculum Norroenum: Norse Studies in Memory of Gabriel Turville-Petre,* edited by Ursula Dronke et al. Odense: Odense University Press, 1981, pp. 6–26.

———. "Beyond Epic and Romance: *Sigurðarkviða in Meiri*". In *Sagnaskemmtun: Studies in Honour of Hermann Pálsson,* edited by Rudolf Simek, Jónas Kristjánsson, and Hans Bekker-Nielsen. Vienna: Böhlau, 1986, pp. 1–12.

Beck, Heinrich. "Eddaliedforschung heute: Bemerkungen zur Heldenlied-Diskussion." In *Helden und Heldensage: Otto Gschwantler zum 60.Geburtstag,* edited by Hermann Reichert and Günter Zimmermann. Vienna: Fassbaender, 1990, pp. 1–24.

de Vries, Jan. *Altnordische Literaturgeschichte.* Vol. 2. 2nd ed. Grundriss der germanischen Philologie 16. Berlin: de Gruyter, 1967, p. 150.

Heusler, Andreas. "Die Lieder der Lücke im Codex Regius." In *Germanistische Abhandlungen Hermann Paul dargebracht.* Strassburg: Trübner, 1902, pp. 1–98.

Simek, Rudolf, and Hermann Pálsson. *Lexikon der altnordischen Literatur.* Stuttgart: Kröner, 1987, pp. 228, 315.

SIGURÐARKVIÐA IN SKAMMA (The Short Lay of Sigurd)

is a later version, hence also referred to as *The Younger Lay of Sigurd,* of the story told in the older *Brot af Sigurðarkviða.* It consists of seventy-one stanzas in *fornyrðislag.* Its place in the *Codex Regius* is between *Guðrúnarkviða in fyrsta* and the *Helreið Brynhildar.* It was probably created between the second half of the twelfth century and the beginning of the thirteenth century. Yet Icelandic scholars suggest an earlier date: 1050–1150. The poem is not particularly unified in composition and integrates allusions to other poems into its verses, sometimes combining lines of relative insignificance. In comparison to the *Brot,* it is noteworthy that the poet is greatly interested in Brynhild's feelings and emotions. Her soliloquies are accorded considerable space, but only two lines are concerned with Sigurd's murder. The middle of the poem occurs in Brynhild's statement: "Hafa scal ec Sigurð/—eða þó svelti!—/mog frumungan,/mér á armi!" (I will hold Sigurd, the young hero, in my arm—or I must die! stanza 6).

The lay begins with Sigurd's arrival at Gjuki's court. Gjuki's sons, Gunnar and Hogni, become blood brothers with Sigurd, and Sigurd marries Gudrun. Later Gunnar decides to win Brynhild with Sigurd's help. Sigurd spends three nights with Brynhild, but the hero lays a sword between them. From that moment on Brynhild knows that an evil, unalterable fate is working against them. She does not get the man she loves. Therefore she now demands that Gunnar kill

Sigurd. Hogni advises Gunnar against murdering their brother-in-law, but finally Gutthorm, who is not bound by oaths, murders Sigurd in his bed. Gudrun wakes up lying in Sigurd's blood. The dying Sigurd entrusts his wife to her brothers and avenges himself by throwing his sword at his attacker. (This is the only difference between this work and the *Brot,* in which Sigurd dies in the woods.) Gudrun cries bitterly, but Brynhild laughs and elects to die with Sigurd. Neither Hogni nor Gunnar can prevent her suicide and she kills herself with a sword. Dying, she forsees the future: Gunnar will be murdered at Atli's court, and Gudrun will lead an unhappy life with her husbands, Atli and Jonaker. Her last wish is to lie on a funeral pyre next to Sigurd.

[GW]

Bibliography

Andersson, Theodore M. "Sigurðarkviða in skamma." In vol. 11 of *Dictionary of the Middle Ages,* edited by Joseph R. Strayer. New York: Scribner, 1988, p. 293.

Beck, Heinrich. "Sigurðarkviða in scamma." In vol. 19 of *Kindlers neues Literaturlexikon,* edited by Walter Jens. Munich: Kindler, 1992, pp. 500–501.

de Vries, Jan. *Altnordische Literaturgeschichte.* Vol. 2. 2nd ed. Grundriss der germanischen Philologie 15. Berlin: de Gruyter, 1967, pp. 147–150.

Gering, Hugo, and B. Sijmons. *Kommentar zu den Liedern der Edda.* 2. Hälfte: *Heldenlieder.* Germanistische Handbibliothek VII 3,2. Halle (Saale): Buchhandlung des Waisenhauses (Francke), 1931, pp. 244–278.

Haymes, Edward R., and Susann T. Samples. *Heroic Legends of the North: An Introduction to the Nibelung and Dietrich Cycles.* New York: Garland, 1996, p. 122.

Simek, Rudolf, and Hermann Pálsson. *Lexikon der altnordischen Literatur.* Stuttgart: Kröner, 1987, p. 315.

SJURÐARKVAEÐI see PART X: FAEROE ISLANDS.

ÞIÐREKS SAGA AF BERN (Saga of Dietrich of Verona; Thidrekssaga) assembles most of the known heroic legends of Germany around the life of Thidrek, a legendary figure based on the historical Ostrogothic king Theoderic the Great, who reigned over Italy from 493 to 526. A considerable part of the saga is devoted to the Nibe-

lung legend and it is this part of the saga that has received the most scrutiny in Germanistic scholarship.

According to statements made within the saga, this compendium was assembled from the stories and songs of German men. The single medieval manuscript is Norwegian and is usually dated to the middle of the thirteenth century. This circumstantial evidence leads us to place the work at the court of King Hakon the Old of Norway in Bergen, where a number of other Norse retellings of continental materials were produced. The earliest and best known of these is the *Tristrams saga ok Isönd,* done in Norse by a certain Brother Robert in 1226. There are also Norse adaptations of romances by Chrétien de Troyes, the lais of Marie de France, and several chansons de geste of the Charlemagne cycle. It is clear that Hakon's court was most interested in continental European literature and that there were men at the court who were able to prepare Norse versions of that literature. The *Þiðreks saga* is the only work of this group with German sources.

Theodore Andersson has argued that the saga represents a German prose compilation that was simply translated into Norse. He offers no evidence for this thesis that would justify ignoring the claims made by the saga's compilers themselves that their saga was made from stories and songs heard from German men. The presence of a mixture of German and Norse name forms and a few motifs from Norse versions of the sagas make a literal translation from a German source even more unlikely. The presence of German loan words in the text does not affect the argument either way since they could have been borrowed from German oral sources or from a written text with equal ease. Some parts of the saga do seem to have an extensive written source. We will discuss one of these in more detail when we turn to the *Niflunga saga.* There is a Swedish version of the saga from the fourteenth century and the relatively free handling of the materials there suggests the possibility that it may be derived from a source of the surviving saga, rather than from that text itself.

When one speaks of the *Þiðreks saga,* it is usually the text contained in the Norwegian manuscript mentioned above that is meant. This manuscript lacks the opening pages and the conclusion, but these can be supplied from Icelandic paper manuscripts from the seventeenth century that seem to be derived in a reasonably straight line from the Norwegian parchment. There is evidence of a large-scale revision affecting the first half of the Norwegian manuscript. Sections have been clearly moved from one part of the manuscript to another and new bridge passages have been composed to cover the changes. These revisions were part of the process that produced the manuscript in the thirteenth century and cannot be blamed on post-medieval "revisors."

The saga begins with a narrative about an otherwise unknown grandfather of Thidrek's named Samson. Samson violates the trust of his lord to gain the latter's daughter in what can only be called a kidnapping. Samson is able to fight off the forces of his lord and later of his lord's brother, the king. He is finally able to establish himself as king in their place. His sons Erminrek and Thetmar divide the inheritance unequally and Thetmar passes his holdings on to his son Thidrek. The next major portion of the saga tells the stories of the youthful adventures of the heroes of Germanic legend, most of whom eventually become retainers of Thidrek in a sort of Germanic Round Table. The conclusion of this process is marked by a great feast followed by a tournament/battle with King Isung and his sons in Bertangaland (Brittany).

In the second major portion of the saga, the heroes are engaged in a series of bride winning, seduction, and rape stories that begins with the deception and rape of Brynhild by Young Sigurd and Gunnar and concludes with the rape of Sifka's queen by his king, Erminrek. This last act leads directly to the expulsion of Thidrek from his lands and his thirty-year exile at the court of Atli.

The last third of the saga includes many tragic heroic tales, including the story of the Niflungs and their destruction at Atli's court. This section concludes with Thidrek's return home and his reinstallation over the lands formerly held by Erminrek and Sifka. This return story includes the encounter between Hildibrand and his son Alibrand in a form very similar to the *Younger Hildebrandslied*. The saga concludes with an epilog in which Thidrek, after carrying out the dragon fight and bride winning told of Wolfdietrich in Germany, observes the end of the age of heroes and is finally spirited off to Hel by a mysterious horse that appears to him while he is bathing in a river.

Students of the Nibelung legend will find the treatment of Sigurd particularly interesting because it follows neither the Norse version we know from the *Volsunga saga* and the *Eddas* nor the South German version we know from the *Nibelungenlied*. King Sigmund of Tarlungaland (perhaps a corruption of Karlungaland—the land of the Carolingians) woos Sisibe, the daughter of King Nidung of Spain. After he brings her home he is called away to support his brother-in-law in a military campaign, leaving his pregnant wife at home. During his absence a courtier attempts to force his attentions on the queen and when she refuses him, the courtier rides to meet the king before he can see his wife and tells him that she is pregnant with another man's child. Sigmund orders her to be abandoned in the forest. There she gives birth to Sigurd, whom she places in a glass container and sets adrift in a river. Later the container washes ashore and the infant is suckled by a hind in the forest. He is later adopted by a smith named Mimir, who has a brother in dragon form named Regin. Because of Sigurd's unruly behavior, Mimir sends him into the forest, expecting that he will be killed by Regin. Sigurd kills Regin instead and, upon tasting the monster's blood, is able to understand the birds who tell him to kill Mimir as well, since he will want revenge for his brother. Sigurd returns home and Mimir gives him excellent armor and a sword, which Sigurd promptly uses to dispatch his foster father. He then journeys to Brynhild, the daughter of Budli, who tells him of his true parentage. She also gives him the horse Grani. He then goes and joins the court of King Isung.

There is a brief chapter introducing the court of King Aldrian of Niflungaland. His queen is ravished while she sleeps by a supernatural being. She later gives birth to Hogni. Her children by Aldrian are Gunnar, Gernoz, Gislher, and their sister Grimhild. Later the saga returns to Niflungaland and tells of the arrival of Young Sigurd who marries Grimhild and agrees to help Gunnar win Brynhild as his bride. Brynhild is enraged when she hears about this because she and Sigurd had sworn to marry each other on his earlier visit. She refuses herself to Gunnar and Sigurd has to take his place in the marriage bed to tame the supernatural woman. A fight between the two queens takes place over seating rights in the hall. Grimhild reveals that Sigurd was the man who had taken Brynhild's virginity. Brynhild then forces Gunnar to have Sigurd killed. Hogni kills him with a spear in the back at a stream in the forest where the men lie down to drink. The men bring his body back and throw it into the bed with Grimhild, who accuses Hogni of the deed, although the men claim he was killed by a boar.

The widow Grimhild is married to Atli. She tells him of the Niflung treasure and he invites the Niflungs to his court with the idea of gaining it. Queen Oda, the mother of the Niflung kings, advises against the journey, but the men set out. At the Rhine Hogni is told by some mermaids how he is to cross the Rhine and that he will never return. Hogni ferries the army across, killing the ferryman. The men approach the land of Markgraf Rodingeir and Hogni, who goes ahead of the men finds a sleeping watchman named Ekkivard, who leads them to Rodingeir's castle. The host's daughter is betrothed to young Gislher and Hogni receives a shield that had belonged to Naudung.

The Niflungs ride to Atli in Susa (Soest) where they take part in a great feast until Grimhild is able to convince Irung to break the peace and begin the battle. While the latter is killing the squires, Grimhild incites her little son to strike Hogni, who beheads the boy and throws the head at the queen. The battle then breaks out in earnest and hundreds are killed. Gunnar is captured and ends his life in a snake pit. Gislher kills Rodingeir, an act that brings Thidrek into the battle. The final duel is between Hogni and Thidrek and it is decided when Thidrek breathes fire at Hogni, who is forced to tear off his heated byrnie and surrender. Hogni asks for and is granted a woman on whom to sire an heir in his last night before dying of his wounds. Grimhild goes about with a torch trying to determine who is dead. She sticks the brand into the mouth of the still-living Giselher, who dies of the mistreatment. Thidrek asks permission to slay the "she-devil."

The close similarity of events in this *Niflunga saga* to those narrated in the second half of the *Nibelungenlied* makes it highly probable that both works had a common source.

Friedrich Panzer argued that the *Þiðreks saga* had simply made use of the *Nibelungenlied* itself, but most scholars feel that the source was a relatively extensive telling of the fall of the Burgundians in written German verse. The great differences in events before the *Niflunga saga* makes the *Nibelungenlied* itself unlikely as a source. Following Andreas Heusler, scholars have called this common source the *ältere Not*.

[ERH]

Bibliography

Andersson, Theodore M. *A Preface to the Nibelungenlied.* Stanford: Stanford University Press, 1987. (Contains translations of the Nibelungen portions of the saga.)

Andersson, Theodore M. "An Interpretation of Thidreks saga." In *Structure and Meaning in Old Norse Literature,* edited by John Lindow, Lars Loennroth, and Gerd Wolfgang Weber. Odense: Odense University Press, 1986, pp. 347–377.

_____. "The Epic Source of Niflunga saga and the Nibelungenlied." *Arkiv for nordisk filologi* 88 (1973), 1–54.

Bertelsen, Henrik, ed. *Thidreks Saga af Bern.* 2 vols. Copenhagen: Møller, 1905–1911.

Curschmann, Michael. "The Prologue of Thidreks Saga: Thirteenth-Century Reflections on Oral Traditional Literature." *Scandinavian Studies* 56 (1984), 140–151.

Haymes, Edward R. "The Bridewinning, Seduction, and Rape Sequence in Thidrekssaga." In *In hôhem Prîse: A Festschrift in Honor of Ernst S. Dick on the Occasion of his 60th Birthday, April 7, 1989,* edited by Winder McConnell. Göppingen: Kümmerle, 1989, pp. 145–152.

_____, trans. *The Saga of Thidrek of Bern.* Garland Library of Medieval Literature 56, Series B. New York: Garland, 1988.

_____, and Susann T. Samples. *Heroic Legends of the North: An Introduction to the Nibelung and Dietrich Cycles.* Garland Reference Library of the Humanities 1403. New York: Garland, 1996.

Kralik, Dietrich von. *Die Überlieferung und Entstehung der Thidrekssaga.* Halle: Niemeyer, 1931.

Reichert, Hermann. *Heldensage und Rekonstruktion: Untersuchungen zur Thidrekssaga.* Philologica Germanica 14. Vienna: Fassbaender, 1992.

Wyss, Ulrich. "Struktur der Thidrekssaga." *Acta Germanica* 13 (1980), 69–86.

VOLSUNGA SAGA is the ambitious project of an anonymous twelfth-century author, who, in this work and in the *Ragnars saga loðbrókar* which follows in the manuscript, retells in prose saga form the legends of the Volsungs and their ancestors, of Sigurd the dragon slayer, of the fall of the Burgundians (Gjukungs), and of the fate of Gudrun's children. In the *Ragnars saga* these are connected to the fate of Sigurd's daughter, Aslaug, the role of her husband Ragnar and her sons in the Danish settlement of England in the eighth and ninth centuries, and their place among the ancestors of Norway's first king, Harald Fairhair. Accordingly Harald can count Sigmund and Sigurd, the greatest of Scandinavian heroes, among his ancestors. The composite work weaves together Germanic legend, fairy-tale motifs, historical sagas, *Edda* verse, and Scandinavian myth. The identity of the author-compiler is unknown; though some have argued for a Norwegian author, most scholars see here the work of an Icelander who wrote the saga in the thirteenth century, most likely during the reign of Norwegian king Hakon Hakonarson (1217–1263).

The *Volsunga saga* (which as mentioned is immediately followed by *Ragnars saga loðbrókar,* as well as the related *Lay of Kraka*) exists in a single vellum manuscript (Ny. kgl. saml. 1824b 4to), written about 1400, and in twenty-one paper manuscripts, from the seventeenth through the nineteenth centuries, all of which are based on the vellum. The traditional chapter divisions are found in the vellum manuscript, and there is some reason to believe they reflect the author's intent.

Besides stories and native material, the origins of which remain untraceable, it is clear that the author borrowed material from a number of sources, primarily found in the *Poetic Edda:* the *Lay of Atli,* the *Greenlandish Lay of Atli,* the *Lay of Fafnir,* the *Old Lay of Gudrun, Gudrun's Inciting,* the *Prophecy of Gripir,* the *First Lay of Helgi Hunding's Bane,* the *Lay of Hamdir,* the *Lay of Regin,* the *Lay of Sigrdrifa,* the *Short Lay of Sigurd,* the prose tale *About the Death of Sinfjotli,* and the *Þiðreks saga.* The missing sections of the *Poetic Edda* must have contained a *Sigurds saga* (fragments of which are extant) from which much of the compiler's material was borrowed. Finch's study of the saga showed that the author-compiler, in borrowing from poetic sources, sought to eliminate all traces of poetic

diction, particularly unusual words, poetic circumlocution, and kennings. The compiler also demythologized the material, removing all but the most necessary references to the actions of Scandinavian deities.

While the relationship of the *Volsunga saga* to the Middle High German *Nibelungenlied* is clear, particularly in that in both works the legends of Sigurd/Siegfried are connected to the downfall of the Burgundians, the Scandinavian work reflects the undoubtedly older version of the Burgundians' destruction by the Huns: Gudrun, the royal sister, does not seek to avenge her husband's death, instead she attempts to warn them, fights alongside them in battle, and later exacts bitter revenge on Attila. Sigurd's youthful adventures, merely alluded to in the *Nibelungenlied,* take up a significant part of the saga. The saga writer's desire to create a prose saga which ultimately connects with Danish and Norwegian history, as well as Scandinavia's distance from the courtly societies of Western Europe, account for major differences in artistry and focus between these two most important works of the Siegfried/Sigurd-Burgundian cycle.

The *Volsunga saga* can be neatly divided into five sections, each of which (except for the opening chapter) is marked by the introduction of a king, according to the formula: "N. hefir konungr heitit" or "N. hét konungr." Chapters 1 and 2, which have no known sources, introduce the kinship between the god Odin and the Volsung kings. The outlaw Sigi becomes a great king. After he is killed by his wife's brothers, his son Rerir inherits his lands and avenges his father's death. Through Odin's intervention, Rerir's otherwise barren wife is able to conceive a child. The child, Volsung, must be cut from the dying woman. Later Volsung marries Hljod, with whom he has a daughter, Signy, and ten sons, the oldest of whom is Sigmund.

Chapters 3 through 10 can be seen as a *Saga of Sigmund and Sinfjotli,* wherein Sigurd's ancestry is revealed. There are few known sources for this material, though the prose tale *About the Death of Sinfjotli* and the *Lay of Helgi Hundingsbane* underlie chapters 8 through 10. King Siggeir of Gautland asks for Signy in marriage, and the request is granted. At the banquet in Volsung's hall, Odin appears and thrusts a sword into the center tree, promising it to whoever can pull it out. Only Sigmund is able to do so and thus keeps the sword. Siggeir offers to buy it, but his offer is met with insult. He takes Signy home, and in three months' time invites Volsung to visit him. Upon his arrival in Gautland, Volsung is warned by Signy of Siggeir's plot to kill him. He is killed in battle, and his sons are captured. The brothers are then executed one-by-one by a she-wolf. Sigmund, however, kills the wolf with Signy's help and escapes to the forest. Signy has Sigmund test the courage of Siggeir's two sons, and when they fail, she allows him to kill them. She then exchanges appearances with a sorceress and sleeps with Sigmund, from which union Sinfjotli is born. Sinfjotli passes Sigmund's test and the two live as marauders in the forest. When they go to Siggeir's hall for revenge, they are discovered by his two young children, whom they kill. For their treacherous act Siggeir buries Sigmund and Siggeir alive in a mound, but Signy sneaks Sigmund's sword into the mound and the two men cut their way out, burn down Siggeir's hall, and kill the king. Signy refuses to leave the burning hall, informs Sigmund that Sinfjotli is his son, and dies with her husband. Sigmund returns home, marries Borghild and has two sons, Helgi and Hamund. Helgi fights a war in which he wins Sigrun as wife. Sinfjotli, who has killed Borghild's brother, is poisoned to death by his stepmother.

Chapters 11 through 25 form a "Lay of Sigurd the Dragon Slayer," their material derived from the "Death of Sinfjotli," the *Lay of Regin,* the *Lay of Fafnir,* and the *Lay of Sigrdrifa,* along with the *Prophecy of Gripir* (a summary of which makes up chapter 16), and chapter 291 of the *Þiðreks saga* (the basis of chapter 23). The final three chapters of this section (23–25), wherein the hero's worthiness and his relationship to Brynhild are emphasized, differ in style and vocabulary from the preceding chapters, reflecting courtly interests of Western Europe in the twelfth and thirteenth centuries. They conclude the youthful adventures of Sigurd and form a transition to his adventures among the Burgundians. Sigmund, having driven away Borghild, marries Hjordis. He is then killed in battle when Odin appears and breaks his sword. The pregnant Hjordis is later taken as wife by King Alf. Hjordis gives birth to Sigurd, and Regin becomes his foster father. Sigurd soon acquires Grani, his horse. Regin urges him to kill Fafnir the dragon in order to recover a treasure hoard. Regin recites the story of how Fafnir got his treasure, and reforges Sigmund's broken sword, whereupon the boy raises an army and kills his father's slayers. After this, Sigurd kills Fafnir and takes his treasure. Regin drinks Fafnir's blood and asks Sigurd to roast the heart for him. As Sigurd follows Regin's request, he burns his finger on the heart and puts the burnt finger into his mouth, whereupon he can understand the singing of some nearby birds. The birds tell him to eat the heart himself and to kill Regin. Sigurd does so and rides away with Fafnir's treasure. As has been foretold, Sigurd finds Brynhild tied to a slab of stone in the middle of a fire. He releases her, and she gives him lessons in traditional lore; the two pledge to marry one another. Later Sigurd goes to stay with Heimir, Brynhild's uncle, where he sees Brynhild again and they renew their oaths.

In chapters 26 through 41, the author, working from what must have been a complete Sigurd lay attested to by fragments found in the *Edda,* as well as from the *Old Lay of Gudrun,* the *Lay of Atli* and the *Greenlandish Lay of Atli,* takes up the story of the fall of the Burgundians, the sons of Gjuki. In the story King Gjuki and his wife Grimhild are the parents of three sons, Gunnar, Högni and Guttorm, and a daughter Gudrun. Gudrun has two dreams, which Brynhild interprets for her; namely, that she will have a life full of loss and sorrow. When Sigurd comes to the Gjukungs, Grimhild gives him a drink which causes him to forget Brynhild. He now swears a pact of brotherhood with Gunnar and his brothers and marries Gudrun. He then urges Gunnar to seek Brynhild in marriage. She lives in a house surrounded by fire (the motif is repeated), and will only marry the man who rides through the flames to her. Sigurd exchanges shapes with Gunnar, rides to Brynhild and spends three nights with her, his sword between them. He gives her treasures from Fafnir's hoard, but takes back the ring he had given her earlier. This ring he now gives to Gudrun. Only after he and Gunnar have returned to their actual forms, and Gunnar has married Brynhild, does he remember his oaths to Brynhild. While bathing in the river, Brynhild and Gudrun argue over their husbands' status. Gudrun shows Brynhild the ring that Sigurd gave her, and Brynhild is stricken with grief. Sigurd goes to her but she will not be consoled, saying at last to Gunnar: "This shall be Sigurd's death or yours or mine." While Gunnar and Hogni have sworn friendship to Sigurd and cannot kill him, they persuade Guttorm to commit the act. Guttorm kills Sigurd as he lies in bed, and the dying Sigurd kills his attacker. Brynhild then commits suicide and is burned on Sigurd's funeral pyre. Gudrun subsequently flees to Denmark, where Grimhild finds her and persuades her to marry King Atli. Atli covets the Gjukungs' treasure and so arranges a feast at his court where he hopes to force them to yield him their wealth. Gudrun's attempts to warn her brothers about the danger of the invitation fail. Hogni's and Gunnar's wives have warning dreams, but the brothers still disregard them, and ride to Atli's court where they meet a hostile reception. The Gjukungs fight well. Gudrun fights alongside her brothers, but in the end Gunnar and Hogni are captured. When they refuse to reveal the whereabouts of the treasure, Atli has Hogni's heart cut out. Gunnar dies bravely in a snake pit. To avenge the death of her brothers, Gudrun kills Atli's sons and feeds him their hearts and blood at his victory feast. Later Hogni's son Niflung gives Gudrun a sword with which she kills Atli. She then fires his hall and all his retainers die with him. Gudrun attempts suicide by throwing herself into the sea but is carried by the waves to King Jonakr. Her daughter with Sigurd, Svanhild, is raised there, and she has three sons with Jonakr.

The final three chapters tell of Gudrun's children, using material from *Gudrun's Inciting* and the *Lay of Hamdir*. Svanhild is married to King Jormunrek, but sleeps with Jormunrek's son, Randver. The couple is betrayed, and as a result Randver is hanged and Svanhild is trampled to death by horses. Gudrun urges her sons to avenge their half sister. One of the sons, Erp, is killed by his brothers on the way to Jormunrek's land, but the other two attack Jormunrek, cutting off his hands and feet. Protected by their mother's magic, they cannot be killed by iron, but through the advice of an old man (Odin), they are killed by stoning instead. The *Ragnars saga loðbrókar* follows immediately; in fact some editors have chosen to number its first chapter as chapter 45 of the *Volsunga saga*. The *Volsunga*

saga was the principal source used by Richard Wagner for his *Ring* cycle.

[JKW]

Bibliography

Byock, Jesse L. *The Saga of the Volsungs.* Berkeley: University of California Press, 1990.

Finch, R. G., ed., trans. *The Saga of the Volsungs.* London: Thomas Nelson, 1965.

Finch, R. G. "The Treatment of Poetic Sources by the Compiler of the Volsunga Saga." In *Saga Book of the Viking Society for Northern Research* 16 (1965): 315–353.

Olsen, Magnus. *Völsunga saga ok Ragnars saga loðbrókar.* Copenhagen: Møller, 1906–1908.

WALTARI AND HILDIGUND. The story of Waltari and Hildigund in the *Þiðreks saga* follows the tale of the establishment of Attila as the king of Húnaland. It stands alone in the middle of the second major section of the saga that is devoted to a series of bride-winning stories, without any connection to the story of Thidrek. Attila, king of Susa, and Erminrek, son of King Samson of Salerni, have become friends. King Erminrek sends Waltari of Waskastein, his sister's son, and twelve knights as noble hostages, whereas King Attila sends his relative Osid and twelve knights to secure the peace. Two years later Hildigund, daughter of Jarl Ilias of Greece, is sent as a hostage to the Hunnish court. Hildigund and Waltari grow up together at Attila's court and fall in love. Now they try to escape together and to return to his homeland. Hildigund collects Attila's treasures at the court and they ride away. When Attila finds out that they have fled, he sends out twelve knights, among them Hogni, King Aldrian's son, in order to get back the treasures, he even orders that Waltari be killed by the Hunnish knights. Despite the odds, Waltari is effectively able to fight off eleven knights. Only Hogni is able to escape during the battle. Waltari, although himself wounded, takes care of Hildigund and roasts the thigh of a boar for her and himself. At that moment Hogni ambushes him. Waltari hurls the big bone of the boar at him, and the blow cuts out Hogni's eye and wounds him badly on the cheek. Hogni then flees and returns to Attila. Waltari and Hildigund arrive at Erminrek's court and, concerned about relations with Attila, Erminrek decides to give a great of deal money to the king as a pledge of further peace.

There were at least four medieval versions of the story including that in the *Þiðreks saga.* The most important difference between the above-mentioned story and the other versions is the fact that Gunnar/Gunther is not included. The oldest written version is a Latin poem called *Waltharius manu fortis* (about 930). Two brief fragments of an Old English version exist which must have belonged to a poem of considerable length. Finally we have a few fragments of a Middle High German epic poem, written in stanzas very much like those used in the *Nibelungenlied,* and the story is also mentioned in that epic. The gist of the story seems to have been a battle over treasure. Originally it was Gunther who was filled with avarice and who tried to procure Walter and Hildegund's gold. In contrast, in the *Þiðreks saga* the emphasis is on the bride-winning story. There are also allusions to the tale of Waltari and Hildigund in the German heroic epics *Biterolf und Dietleib,* the *Rosengarten,* and elsewhere. Even Walther von der Vogelweide must have known it, because he calls his beloved lady Hildegunde ("Die mir in dem winter fröide hânt benommen . . ." [Those who have taken away my joy in winter] **L** 74,19). The story is continued and related differently in the *Chronicle of Novalesa* (based on the Latin *Waltharius,* eleventh century) and in a Polish tale (thirteenth century). It is also mentioned in the Middle High German poem "Von einem übelen wîbe" (Regarding a terrible woman).

[GW]

Bibliography

Haymes, Edward R., and Susann T. Samples. *Heroic Legends of the North: An Introduction to the Nibelung and Dietrich Cycles.* New York: Garland, 1996, pp. 60–63, 69.

Schneider, Hermann. *Germanische Heldensage.* Vol. 1. 2nd ed. Grundriss der germanischen Philologie 10/I. Berlin: de Gruyter, 1962, pp. 331–344.

WALTHARIUS (WALTHARILIED),

a Latin poem of nearly 1500 hexameters, variously attributed to Ekkehart I of St Gall (d. 973) or to an otherwise unknown German monk, Gæraldus, perhaps writing in the ninth century. The latter name is attached to a prologue found in several of the major manuscripts. The poet claims to be a novice, and his work contains frequent echoes of Vergil. The story (versions of which are also known in other languages, including the Anglo-Saxon fragment *Waldere,* Norse analogues, and a Polish text) opens with the Huns threatening the Germanic tribes in Western Europe (Franks, Visigoths of Aquitaine, and Burgundians), who elect to pay tribute and to send hostages to Attila. The king of the Franks is Gibicho (Gibica) and his infant son is Guntharius (Gundahari), in whose place Hagen, a noble youth, is sent, together with Walthari, prince of the Visigoths, and his betrothed, Hiltgund (Hildegunda), a Burgundian princess. That the Burgundian names are here applied to Franks reflects the later Frankish takeover (well established by the time of the poem) of what were originally Burgundian territories. Attila treats the hostages well, and the two young men are brought up as warriors, becoming firm friends. However, when Gibicho dies, Guntharius ceases to pay tribute, and Hagen is forced to flee. Walthari organizes a feast, and while Attila is drunk, Walthari and Hiltgund escape with a large amount of treasure. That none of the Huns will pursue them is a milder version of the decline of the Hunnish empire attributed to Attila's drunkenness, which is given a far more violent twist in texts like the *Atlakviða.*

When the fugitives arrive in the land of the Franks, Guntharius hears of them and decides to take the treasure, claiming it to be his own. Hagen advises against an attack on Waltharius but is overruled by the king (to whom the word *superbus* [arrogant] is applied in the work). Waltharius then takes up a defensive position in the Vosges mountains (Waskenstein) and kills most of Guntharius's twelve warriors in single or multiple combat. Guntharius himself is severely wounded. In a final battle he fights his former friend Hagen, who has so far refused to fight. He agrees to do so only at the last moment with some reluctance, pressured by feelings of loyalty to his king and to his nephew, one of those already killed by Waltharius. Waltharius has lost a hand and Hagen an eye by the time the battle, which has reached a stalemate, is called off. Hiltgund tends the wounds, and the poet summarizes that "this is how the gold arm rings of the Huns were shared."

Walthari and Hiltgund return to Aquitaine and rule for thirty years. The quasi-happy ending (which has biblical echoes) may have been supplied by the poet to replace an earlier outcome, which perhaps called for the death of one or both of the warriors. The arrogant figure of Guntharius matches Gunther in some respects, and the role of Hagen as chief adviser, who has detailed knowledge of the unknown, but fierce, warrior with the treasure, is a parallel with Hagen of Tronje, even though in the *Nibelungenlied,* Hagen is in favor of obtaining the treasure. The exile at his court of Hagen and Walter of Spain (that is, of the Visigoth territory, Aquitaine in the Latin poem) is referred to by Etzel, who speaks of having sent Hagen back, while Walther ran away with Hildegund. Hildebrant refers at the end of the German epic to the encounter between Hagen and Walther at the Waskenstein, implying that Hagen hesitated while others fought. Such references clearly identify the Hagen of this poem with that in the *Nibelungenlied.* In line 555 of the Latin poem, too, when Walthari sees the Franks coming toward them (he is afraid at first that they are Huns in pursuit), he refers to them as *nebulones* (probably Nibelungs), yet another echo of the Nibelungenlied.

[BOM]

Bibliography

Gregoire, Henri. "La patrie des Nibelungen," *Byzantion* 9 (1934): 1–39.

Kratz, Dennis M., trans. *Waltharius and Ruodlieb.* New York: Garland, 1984, pp. 1–71.

Learned, Marion Dexter. *The Saga of Walther of Aquitaine.* Latin text with texts of all the analogues. 1892; repr. Westport, Conn.: Greenwood, 1970.

Murdoch, Brian, trans. *Walthari.* Glasgow: SPIGS, 1989.

Strecker, Karl. *Waltharius.* Text and German trans. by Peter Vossen. Berlin: Weidmann, 1947.

PART II

Personal and Place Names

ADELIND, in the *Klage,* a countess and the daughter of Sintram, a nobleman who resides in the Marches of Hungary at a place called Püten. Adelind had earlier been one of a number of women whom Helche, first wife of Etzel, had raised. She arrives at the court of Etzel after the massacre.

[WM]

AESIR, the chief deities in Old Norse mythology. They play a large role in the *Edda* and the *Snorra Edda,* both of which provided some of the material upon which the story of the Middle High German *Nibelungenlied* is based. However, the *Nibelungenlied* is a work written from the perspective of a predominately Christian society, and the warrior gods of the Norse pantheon do not figure prominently in the poem.

[ASH]

Bibliography

Auty, Robert, et al., eds. "Asen." In vol. 1 of *Lexikon des Mittelalters,* Munich: Artemis, 1991, cols. 1104–1106.

Munch, Peter Andreas. *Norse Mythology, Legends of Gods and Heroes,* translated by Sigurd Bernhard Hustvedt. Detroit: Singing Tree Press, 1968.

Simek, Rudolf. *Lexikon der germanischen Mythologie.* Stuttgart: Kröner, 1984.

AETIUS, FLAVIUS, a Western Roman military leader, killed in 454 by the emperor Valentinian III. He defeated the Burgundians under Gundahari in 435–436 with the aid of Hunnish auxiliaries (not, however, led by Attila), who in 436–437 destroyed them. With the Visigoths, Aetius defeated Attila's Huns near Troyes in 451, and thus provides a historical link between the fall of the Burgundians and Attila (see BURGUNDY).

[BOM]

AGNAR (also called **AUÐABRODIR**), is the name of a king mentioned by Brynhild in the *Volsunga saga.* Agnar had fought against another, older king, Hjalmgunnar, to whom Odin had promised victory. When Brynhild elects to assist Agnar by striking down Hjalmgunnar, she is stabbed by the god Odin with a sleeping thorn. It is in this state, lying asleep in full armor, that Sigurd finds Brynhild.

[WM]

ALBERICH (ALBRICH), in the *Nibelungenlied,* dwarf and keeper of the hoard of the Nibelungs. After Schilbung and Nibelung are killed by Siegfried, Alberich seeks to avenge his masters' deaths and attacks Siegfried but is also overpowered. Alberich then swears allegiance to Siegfried, who is now the new master of the hoard and the land of the Nibelungs. At this point Alberich once again finds himself designated treasurer (*kameraere*) of the hoard. Siegfried needs troops to garrison Island (as a consequence of the successful wooing mission aimed at procuring Brünhild for Gunther), and he arrives unannounced in Nibelungeland to obtain reinforcements. The dwarf, not recognizing his king and master, who disguises himself in his magic hood, attacks him and is almost killed. Siegfried restrains himself, however, and reveals his identity. Alberich reaffirms his allegiance to the master. Alberich is last mentioned in the *Nibelungenlied* when Kriemhild sends her brothers, Gernot and Giselher, to obtain the hoard, which had been given to her by Siegfried as a morning gift (*Morgengabe*). Although Alberich does not refuse to deliver the hoard, he does lament the loss it signifies for Nibelungeland and claims the treasure would never have been lost if Siegfried had left the magic hood (tarnhut) behind. In another story, the German epic *Ortnit,* the hero Ortnit has a dwarf father Alberich, but he looks like a beautiful child and is not an old, gray man like Alberich in the *Nibelungenlied.* In Wagner's *Ring* cycle, Alberich is Wotan's rival and the brother of Mime. He forged the Ring that accords its owner power over the entire world.

[KQ]

ALDRIAN (1), king of Niflungaland in the *Þiðreks saga.* With his wife he fathers Gunnar, Gernoz, Gislher, and Grimhild. Hogni, although called the son of Aldrian the King, is actually the son of Aldrian's queen and an elf. When Aldrian dies, Gunnar becomes king of Niflungaland. In another scribal tradition of the *Þiðreks saga,* King Irung and Queen Oda replace Aldrian and his unnamed queen as rulers of Niflungaland and parents of Gunnar and the others.

[FH]

ALDRIAN (2), in the *Þiðreks saga,* the young son of King Atli and Queen Grimhild, and nephew to Gunnar, Hogni, Gernoz, and Gislher. At a banquet in Atli's hall for the visiting Niflungs, Grimhild urges Aldrian to show the bravery of his kin and slap Hogni in the face. Aldrian does so. Hogni draws his sword and beheads Aldrian and throws the child's head at Grimhild's breast. The unwitting Aldrian is thus the direct cause of the final battle between the Huns and the Niflungs.

[FH]

ALDRIAN (3), Hogni's son, according to the *Þiðreks saga.* Hogni is taken prisoner by Thidrek, King of Verona. He is mortally wounded. Nevertheless, Thidrek allows a woman to spend the night with Hogni, who tells her that she will give birth to a boy, whom she shall name Aldrian. Hogni hands her the key to Siegfried's cellar, in which the Niflungs' treasure is stored. Then Hogni dies of wounds sustained in combat against Thidrek. The boy grows up at King Atli's court, and Atli loves him dearly. When the boy is twelve years old, he tempts Atli with tales of Siegfried's treasure. He brings Atli to a mountain, opens three doors there and leads him into the cellar of treasure. While the Hunnish king enjoys the sight of the gold, Aldrian runs out and shuts the doors. Three days later he returns and tells Atli that the king has to starve in front of the gold he always has desired so much. Aldrian puts stones and grass over the doors and leaves the place. He rides to Brynhild and tells her what has happened. She is so pleased with him that she gives him a kingdom as big as that of Gunnar's and Hogni's together. Thus Aldrian avenged the death of his relatives, the Niflungs, and Atli and the Niflungs' treasure disappeared forever.

[GW]

ALFRIK (ALPRIS) is the name of a dwarf in the *Þiðreks saga.* The name of the figure corresponds to Alberich in the *Nibelungenlied.* Here Alberich is a dwarf and the treasurer of the kings of Nibelungeland, from whom Siegfried wins his sword Balmunc and his hoard of treasure. Siegfried also wins Alberich's *Tarnkappe,* a cloak that allows its wearer to become invisible and gives him the strength of twelve men. Alberich and his men are forced to swear an oath to him, and they have to serve Siegfried, who has killed their liege lords. This story is related in a similar way in *Biterolf und Dietleib,* and the events surrounding the dwarf king Eugel in *Das Lied vom Hürnen Seyfrid* are also comparable to this tale. However, the *Þiðreks saga* does not tell us anything about Sigurd's acquisition of the hoard of treasure. Therefore, Alfrik has no place in the tale of Young Sigurd. But the author knew a story about this dwarf and told it in connection with Thidrek af Bern. According to the story, Thidrek catches Alfrik, a cunning dwarf and a thief, during a deer hunt. Alfrik promises Thidrek the sword Nagelring, which Alfrik has forged himself, if Thidrek will set him free. This sword will help Thidrek to get much gold and silver, and many precious stones. After the dwarf swears to be true and faithful to Thidrek, he is set free. He brings the sword and disappears. Later Thidrek and Hildibrand fight against giants and win their treasure.

[GW]

Bibliography

Grimm, Wilhelm. *Die deutsche Heldensage.* 4th ed. Darmstadt: Wissenschaftliche Buchgesellschaft, 1957, pp. 85–92.

Haymes, Edward R., and Susann T. Samples. *Heroic Legends of the North: An Introduction to the Nibelung and Dietrich Cycles.* New York: Garland, 1996, pp. 133, 145, 154.

Schneider, Hermann. *Germanische Heldensage.* Vol. 1. 2nd ed. Grundriss der germanischen Philologie 10/I. Berlin: de Gruyter, 1962, pp. 352–353.

ALSVID (1), one of two horses (the other being Arvak) charged with pulling the sun chariot across the heavens in the *Volsunga saga.* Brynhild informs Sigurd in verse that "mind runes," associated with wisdom, were cut into the head of the horse.

[WM]

ALSVID (2), son of Heimir and friend of Sigurd in the *Volsunga saga.* A good companion to Sigurd, Alsvid advises him to stay away from women and that Brynhild is beyond his reach. It is advice that Sigurd elects not to follow.

[WM]

ALZEI (ALZEYE), on the Rhine is first referred to in the *Nibelungenlied* in connection with Volker, Hagen's friend and powerful companion (9,4). The *Klage* poet has Hildebrand, Dietrich's liege man, explain to King Attila that Volker was born in Alzeye and owned land near the Rhine (1355–1363). Alzei appears to have

originally been settled by Celts about 400 B.C. Later the Romans established a fortress on the site, which was destroyed in 406 A.D. by Visigoths and Burgundians. In the fifth century Alzei was founded again by Franks. It acquired its city privilege in 1277. Today, Alzei is a town situated northwest of Worms in Rhineland-Westphalia.

[AC]

AMELRICH, in the *Nibelungenlied,* the name of the Danube ferryman's brother, not present in the work, but who Hagen pretends to be when leading the Burgundians to Hungary. Hagen is forewarned by water sprites that the river they must cross is impassable due to a pugilistic ferryman who is unwilling to assist travelers. Following the sprites' advice, Hagen calls himself Amelrich, deceiving the ferryman, who believes that it is his long-missing brother who had departed following a dispute.

[KM]

AMELUNG/AMELUNGEN (MHG *Amelunc;* pl. *Amelunge*), family and clan name, Old Norse equivalent *Amelungr, Aumlungr.* In heroic epic the name applies to the "Amelung" Dietrich von Bern (Old Norse Thidrekr), his relatives, and heroes. A genealogy is provided in the late MHG epic *Dietrichs Flucht (Buch von Bern,* vv. 2297ff.). Amelung is the only son of Hugedietrich and grandson of Wolfdietrich; Amelung's three sons are Ermich, Diether, and Dietmar. Dietmar is the father of two sons, another Diether and Dietrich von Bern. Karl Simrock called his collection of heroic German epics the *Amelungenlied* (Lay of the Amelungs). In the *Þiðreks saga* Amelung is first mentioned as a separate individual in chapter 107 as the son of Jarl Hornboge, who joins his family at the court of Dietrich and who enjoys a reputation as a perfect knight (chapter 158). He later jousts with Sigfrid, to whom he is related, in an attempt to reclaim a horse taken by the latter as tribute to his lord Isung. He is unseated, but once Sigfrid has established Amelung's identity, he returns his horse to him and sends him back to Dietrich along with his own horse, shield, and spear. After a successful battle against Isung, Amelung receives the latter's daughter, Fallborg, as his bride. Amelung is later defeated in battle by Hildebrand, but his life is spared.

[UM/WM]

AMELUNGENLANT, the kingdom of the Amelungs, which Dietrich von Bern/Thidrek(r) had sought to establish in Northern Italy.

[UM]

ANDVARI, a dwarf mentioned in the *Volsunga saga.* Regin tells Sigurd about Andvari, who lives in Andvari's Fall in the shape of a pike. Loki captures Andvari in his effort to procure the dwarf's treasure so that he and the other Aesir (Odin and Hoenir) can offer it to Hreidmar as ransom for his son, Otr, whom Loki has killed and skinned. Andvari claims that Odin was his father, but it is assumed that the actual name of his father was Oin, a dwarf who is referred to by Andvari in "The Lay of Regin." Andvari is forced to hand over his gold, but prior to doing so he places a curse on the gold ring, Andvaranaut.

[WM]

APULIA/PÚL(L) is mentioned three times in the *Þiðreks saga.* In the prologue to the saga the reader is informed that the story will start in Apulia. In that part of Italy, King Samson and his son Erminrek rule in Salerno, its capital. From here Erminrek extends his empire.

[GW]

ARABIA, alluded to several times in the *Nibelungenlied* to designate the origin of fine gold or garments: "Die arâbîschen sîden wîz alsô der snê" (Arabian silks as white as snow, 362,1); "Ûz arâbîschem golde vil gesteines scein" (gleam of many stones [set] in Arabian gold, 366,1); "von pfelle ûz Arabî" (brocade from Arabia, 576,3); "die truogen liehte pfelle geworht in Arâbîn" (They wore bright brocade fashioned in Arabia, 833,2); "und manec bettedach/von arâbîschen sîden, die beste mohten sîn" (And many a coverlet of Arabian silk, the best that could be [had], 1825,2–3). The display of Arabian products underscored the affluence and prestige of the owners, and the poet is cognizant of the splendor of the products he is describing.

[GCS]

Bibliography

Bäuml, Franz H. and Eva-Marie Fallone. *A Concordance to the "Nibelungenlied."* Leeds: W. S. Maney and Son Ltd., 1976.

Labib, S. Y. "Araber." In vol. 1, pt. 5 of *Lexikon des Mittelalters,* edited by Robert Auty et al. Munich: Artemis, 1979, col. 847.

ARMINIUS (German *Herman*), ruler of the Germanic tribe called the Cheruskans. He was a Roman citizen and warrior who probably commanded a group of Roman auxiliaries made up of Cheruskans. During a revolt against Roman rule, Arminius defeated the entire army of the Roman governor Varus in 9 A.D. in the Teutoburg Forest. This victory halted the Roman advance through Germania on the left side of the Rhine. After defeating Marbod, king of the Markomanns and an ally of Rome, in 19 A.D., Arminius was killed by his own relatives who had become fearful of the power he had acquired. In his *Annales* Tacitus alludes to Arminius as the liberator of Germania. The German unification movement in the nineteenth century subsequently praised him as a symbol of a united Germany. In literature the intermeshed characters of Siegfried and Arminius represented the personification of the German desire for unification. In Carl Friedrich Eichhorn's tragedy *Chriemhildens Rache* (1824), Herman's battle in the Teutoburg Forest is depicted with Siegfried assuming the role of Arminius and Hagen that of Varus. In the twentieth century, Paul Albrecht's novel *Arminius-Sigurfrid* (1935) and Bodo Ernst's epic *Sigfried-Armin* (1935) glorify the racism of National Socialism through the characters of Arminius and Siegfried, who are depicted as the heroic protagonists of German liberation from foreign domination and the Nordic ancestors of a new Aryan race.

[WW]

Bibliography

Beneke, Arnold. *Siegfried ist Armin!* Dortmund: Ruhfuhs, 1911.

Ernst, Bodo. *Siegfried-Armin. Der Mythos vom deutschen Menschen.* Breslau: Nickisch, 1935.

ARRAS (MHG *Arraz*), a town in northern France, mentioned once in the *Nibelungenlied* (1825,1) as the place where fabric (MHG *pfellel*) of extremely good quality is produced. Arras was part of Flanders until the end of the twelfth century, when it became part of Artois. During the Middle Ages it was famous for its manufacture of fine woolens and tapestries.

[NV]

ARVAK, one of two horses (the other being Alsvid) in the *Volsunga saga* that are charged with pulling the sun chariot across the sky. Both horses had runes cut on their heads, in the case of Arvak, on its ears.

[WM]

ASLAUG, the daughter of Sigurd and Brynhild in the *Volsunga saga*. In the *Ragnars saga loðbrókar,* she is left with Heimir, Brynhild's foster father, after the death of her parents. Heimir hides her inside a harp and takes her to Norway, where he is given shelter and then murdered by a peasant couple. They find Aslaug and raise her, calling her Kraka. As Ragnar Loðbrók's second wife, Aslaug bears several sons, including Ivar the Boneless and Sigurd Snake-Eye. Under the name Randalin she fights alongside her sons against Eystein of Sweden. Through her the saga writer establishes the blood relationship between Sigurd of legend and the historical Norwegian king Harald Fairhair.

[JKW]

ASPILIAN, in the *Þiðreks saga,* one of King Nordian's four giant sons. When Nordian dies, Osantrix makes Aspilian king of his father's lands. Aspilian takes part in Osantrix's victorious campaign against King Milias. Later Aspilian supports Osantrix in his battle against Attila but is forced to flee to Austriki. Near the end of the *Þiðreks saga,* after Heimir, the son of Studas, has entered a monastery in Lungbarthaland (also called Lungbardi), Aspilian steals an estate from the monks and challenges them to find a champion to fight him for possession of it. Heimir, known to the monks only as Lothvigr, accepts the giant's challenge and meets Aspilian on an island where he kills him.

[FH]

ASTOLT, mentioned in the *Nibelungenlied* (1329,1) as lord of Melk, a small town ten kilometers east of Pöchlarn on the right bank of the Danube. He welcomes Kriemhild and her company on their journey to the land of the Huns and directs them towards Mautern into Austria. In the poems *Biterolf und Dietleib* and the *Rabenschlacht,* Astolt is lord of Mautern; in these poems he is less hospitable than in the *Nibelungenlied.*

[NV]

ATHANAGILD, a king of the Visigoths in Spain from 555 to 567 and father of Gailswintha and Brunhild, who married the Frankish kings Sigibert and Chilperic. The large dowry he provided for Brunhild is a possible source for the Nibelung treasure.

[BOM]

ATLI, in the Norse tradition, corresponds to Etzel in the *Nibelungenlied*. Atli, the Hunnish ruler, is Budli's son and Brynhild and Oddrun's brother. He has four siblings, with whom he becomes involved in a feud. He forces Brynhild to marry Gunnar; thus his sister later can accuse him of being the real cause of the disaster at the end of her life. After Brynhild commits suicide, Atli tries to blame the Gjukungs, claiming in chapter 38 of the *Volsunga saga* that they had contrived Brynhild's death. In order to reconcile Atli with them, Gunnar forces his sister, Gudrun, to marry Atli. Erp and Eitill are Gudrun and Atli's sons. In another episode that does not correspond to the entire course of events in Atli's life, Gunnar seeks Oddrun's hand after Brynhild's death but is refused by Atli. The lovers meet secretly but are discovered by Atli's men. When Gunnar is cast into a snake pit, Oddrun tries to save him. Gunnar plays the harp to calm down the snakes, but Atli's mother, in the form of a serpent, kills him.

Atli had lured the Nibelungs to his court because he could not tolerate the affair between his sister Oddrun and Gunnar. Gunnar was, in his view, already responsible for Brynhild's death, and Atli is not particularly happy about "losing" another sister to him. When Atli invites Gunnar and Hogni, Gudrun sends a warning to the latter, but he and Gunnar nonetheless decide to accept the invitation. When the Gjukungs arrive at Atli's court, the Hunnish ruler is giving a banquet. Gudrun tries to warn her brothers again. Atli arms himself and his men, and the fight begins. Gudrun tries to help Hogni and Gunnar and even kills two of Atli's brothers, but finally her own brothers are killed. Gudrun curses Atli and reproaches him with having murdered not only her brothers but also her mother and her female cousin. Atli offers her money in order to placate her. At a feast in honor of his dead, Atli misses his two sons. Gudrun informs her husband that she has already taken her revenge on him by killing his sons, Erp and Eitill, and that Atli has drunk out of their skulls and devoured their roasted hearts, and now she is going to destroy him. Atli is so drunk that he is unable to ward off Gudrun. According to *Atlakviða,* his wife kills him in his bed and sets the hall on fire. Originally the Norse tradition might have had Gudrun die in the flames at the side of her husband. According to *Atlamál,* however, the leader of the Huns is killed by Gudrun and Hniflung, Hogni's son. Gudrun outlives her husband and purchases a ship and a coffin for Atli's burial.

The episode dealing with Herkja, Atli's concubine, does not correspond to Atli's life story because both *Atlakviða* and *Atlamál* tell us that Gudrun took revenge on Atli immediately after the death of her brothers. Herkja slanders Gudrun, and Atli forces both women to submit to a trial by ordeal. Gudrun proves to be innocent, but Herkja is sentenced to death.

Different versions of Atli's death are recorded in the *Þiðreks saga* and in *Hogna táttur.* In the *Þiðreks saga* Attila invites the Burgundian brothers out of avarice, a motif that also occurs in the *Atlakviða* but not in the *Atlamál.* This greed for gold causes Attila's death. Hogni's son, here called Aldrian, lures Attila into Sigurd's cellar, in which the Niflungs' gold is stored and shuts the doors behind him. Attila has to starve in front of the gold he had always desired so much. In *Hogna táttur,* both Artala (Atli) and Gudrun meet their deaths this way.

In contrast to the *Nibelungenlied,* the Norse versions are not only interested in the fall of the Niflungs at the Hunnish court, but also describe the end of Atli's life. Atli's portrayal differs widely from that of the *Nibelungenlied.* He is not a passive, peace-loving king, but rather the murderer of the Niflungs, the enemy of his in-laws, and a powerful and greedy man, who ultimately receives just punishment.

[GW]

Bibliography

Andersson, Theodore M. "Did the Poet of Atlamál Know Atlaqviða?" In *Edda: A Collection of Essays,* edited by Robert J. Glendinning and Haraldur Bessason. Winnipeg: University of Manitoba Press, 1983, pp. 243–257.

Finch, R. G. "Atlakviða, Atlamál, and Volsunga Saga: A Study in Combination and Integration." In *Speculum Norroenum: Norse Studies in Memory of Gabriel Turville-Petre,* edited by Ursula Dronke et al. Odense: Odense University Press, 1981, pp. 123–138.

Haymes, Edward R., and Susann T. Samples. *Heroic Legends of the North: An Introduction to the Nibelung and Dietrich Cycles.* New York: Garland, 1996, pp. 124f.

Schneider, Hermann. *Germanische Heldensage.* Vol. 1. 2nd ed. Berlin: de Gruyter, 1962, pp. 197ff.

ATTILA, ruler of the Huns until his death in 453, son of Mundiuch or Mondzucas (the name varies) and initially co-ruler with Bleda until he had him killed in 444/445. Defeated by Aetius near Troyes in 451, he died in 453. According to the historian Priscus, he died on the night of his wedding to Hildico, of a hemorrhage brought on by excessive drinking. In later sources he is said to have been stabbed by a woman (sometimes Hildico).

[BOM]

Bibliography

de Boor, Helmut. *Das Attilabild.* 1932. Reprint, Darmstadt: Wissenschaftliche Buchgesellschaft, 1963.

Gordon, C. D. *The Age of Attila.* 1960. Reprint, New York: Dorset, 1992.

Howarth, Patrick. *Attila, King of the Huns.* London: Constable, 1994.

Thompson, E. A. *The History of Attila and the Huns.* Oxford: Clarendon, 1948.

AUÐA is Agnar's sister. Her brother is Brynhild's protégé whom she helps against Odin. She is mentioned twice in the *Poetic Edda,* in *Sigrdrífumál,* and in *Helreið Brynhildar,* and in chapter 21 of the *Volsunga saga* (see AGNAR).

[GW]

AVENTROD, in the *Þiðreks saga,* one of King Nordian's four giant sons. He participates in Osantrix's victory over King Milias. When King Attila attacks Osantrix's land, Aventrod fights on the side of Vilkinaland but is forced to flee to join Osantrix. Aventrod is later killed by Vildifer.

[FH]

AZAGOUC. In the *Nibelungenlied* Brünhild arrives for the contest with Gunther in Island wearing over her armor a surcoat of silk from Azagouc, an imaginary place name whose linguistic form suggests Arabic origins and thus the exotic Orient (439,2). The name appears otherwise to be unknown, with the exception of its occurrence three times in Wolfram's *Parzival* (234,5; 750,19; 770,27; in the last two instances, coupled with the place name Zazamanc, a name also unique to *Parzival* and the *Nibelungenlied* [362, 2]). If the word was borrowed from Wolfram, as has been sometimes argued, then it offers a fairly secure terminus post quem for the *Nibelungenlied* of 1204/1205.

[RGS]

BAVARIA. The term "der Bei(y)er lant" occurs once in the *Nibelungenlied* (1174,3). The verse imparts a sense of territoriality and a certain knowledge of the people. "Beier" and "beierisch," according to Lexer, are sometimes used in a pejorative sense; Buesching and von der Hagen underscore "eine die Beiern im mittelalter auszeichnende rohheit . . ." (a crudeness characterizing the Bavarians in the Middle Ages). Magoun views this as a "conscious disparagement on the part of the poet" (92). See also the *Nibelungenlied,* 1302,3–4). Since 1180 Bavaria had been under the control of the first Wittelsbacher, Otto v. Wittelsbach (1180–1255). His son Ludwig I (1183–1231) determined the political course of events; feuds with rivals (the bishop of Regensburg and Archbishop of Salzburg) led to chaotic conditions within Bavaria, which undoubtedly prompted the *Nibelungenlied* poet's commentaries.

[GCS]

Bibliography

Hagen, Friedrich Heinrich von der, and J. G. Buesching, eds. *Deutsche Gedichte des Mittelalters,* 2 vols. Berlin: Realschulbuchhandlung, 1808. See vol. 2.

Lexer, Matthias. *Mittelhochdeutsches Handwörterbuch,* 3 vols. Leipzig: Hirzel, 1872. Vol. 1, col. 159: "Beier, beierisch."

Magoun, Jr., Francis P. "Geographical and Ethnic Names in the *Nibelungenlied.*" *Mediaeval Studies* 7 (1945): 85–138.

Schwertl, G. "Bayern." In vol. 1, pt. 9. of *Lexikon des Mittelalters,* edited by Robert Auty et al. Munich: Artemis, 1980, cols. 1704–1709.

BAVARIANS, inhabitants of Bavaria, according to the *Nibelungenlied* the region south of the Danube, west of the Inn River and east of Swabia; more accurate data are not provided. The Bavarians (MHG *Beier, Beyer, Peyer*) are mentioned in the epic on several occasions. According to the story, Rüdiger travels through Bavaria twice, accompanied by five hundred knights (1174 and 1295–1302) to avoid trouble with the Bavarians, and Etzel's messengers travel safely through the country because the Bavarians fear the king's (Etzel's?) anger (1427–1429). The region is also mentioned in the section concerning the Burgundians' crossing of the Danube to fight Gelpfrat and Else, margraves of Bavaria (1600–1619). In addition, every time a journey through Bavaria is described, the narrator stresses that the travelers are not being robbed, which is apparently quite exceptional in Bavaria. This negative image of the Bavarians, which can also be found in the *Klage* (3490–3492), could be due to an aversion of the poet, who probably lived in neighboring Passau.

[NV]

BEKKHILD, in the *Volsunga saga,* she is the daughter of Budli, sister of Brynhild, the wife of Heimir, and the mother of Alsvid. The first component of her name, *bekk-*, means *bench* in Old Norse. In contrast to her sister, Bekkhild was the epitome of domesticity, particularly well known for her needlework.

[WM]

BERN, not Bern/Berne in Switzerland, but Verona (occasionally called Dietrichsbern in German in earlier times), located about 100 kilometers west of Venice in Italy. Although Ravenna was his capital, Dietrich is named in the *Nibelungenlied* and elsewhere as Dietrich von Bern because in MHG heroic poetry Bern was regarded as the capital of his rightful territory. Hence in the *Nibelungenlied* he is called "der vogt von Berne" (1730,1), "der fürste von Berne" (1804,1), "der herzoge ûz Berne"

(2258,1), and "der Bernaere" (2312,1). The connection has an historical basis. Dietrich is modeled after the historical Theodoric, the king of the Ostrogoths. In 489 Theodoric drove his adversary Odoacer (Otacher in the OHG *Hildebrandslied*, Octaher in the MHG *Eckenlied*) out of Verona, forcing him to seek refuge in the then impregnable fortress of Ravenna (MHG "Raben," cf. *Die Rabenschlacht* [The Battle of Ravenna]).

[JLF/SMJ]

BERTANGALAND, in the *Þiðreks saga,* also called Bertanga, is possibly the historical province of Brittany in NW France (Fr. Bretagne). It is ruled originally by King Artus. After Artus's death King Isung and his eleven sons capture Bertangaland from the sons of Artus. Before fighting Ekka, who guards the castle of Drekanfils, the young Thidrek of Bern identifies himself as Heimir, the son of Studas of Bertangaland. King Osantrix sends the giant Ethgeir to King Isung of Bertangaland who sets Ethgeir up in a forest at the edge of Bertangaland to defend his borders. After encountering Brynhild and receiving Grani, Sigurd proceeds to Bertangaland and becomes Isung's counselor and standard-bearer. Thidrek and his twelve champions ride to Bertangaland where they challenge Isung, his eleven sons, and Sigurd. Thidrek sends his nephew Herburt to Bertangaland to ask for the hand of Artus's daughter Hildr (who elopes with Herburt). Hertnith, King of Vilkinaland, invades Bertangaland and kills Isung.

[FH]

BIKKI, he appears in the *Volsunga saga* as a malevolent and inept adviser to King Jormunrek (Ermanaric), king of the Goths. Brynhild appears to trust in his counsel, for as she dies, she refers to the latter in conjunction with the later death of Svanhild, Jormunrek's bride. Bikki is a dark figure who encourages Randver, Jormunrek's son, to take Svanhild for himself. When Randver and Svanhild act on this advice, Bikki betrays them to Jormunrek, who has both his son and his bride put to death.

[WM]

BITURULF, a Danish nobleman on Skane, according to the *Þiðreks saga.* He lives in Tum-

mathorp. His wife is Oda, the daughter of an Earl of Saxland (Saxony). Their son is Thetleif. The *Þiðreks saga* tells us the story of Thetleif's first adventures. This story is also told in a very different way in *Biterolf und Dietleib* (thirteenth century): Biterolf lives in Toledo (Spain), his wife is Dietlinde, the daughter of Diether the Old, a relative of Ermanerich. Perhaps his roots are to be sought in Denmark, because Biterolf calls himself Fruote of Denmark when he comes in secret to Etzel's court.

[GW]

Bibliography
Haupt, Waldemar. *Zur niederdeutschen Dietrichsage: Untersuchungen.* Palaestra 129. New York: Johnson, 1970, pp. 1–82.

BLEDA, the brother of Attila, joint ruler of the Huns until Attila had him killed in 444/445. He appears as Etzel's brother Bloedel(in) in the *Nibelungenlied,* where his fall is also swift.

[BOM]

BLOEDEL(IN), the brother of Etzel in both the *Nibelungenlied* and the *Klage.* He allows himself to be bribed by Kriemhild to attack the Burgundian squires. In the thirty-second *aventiure* of the *Nibelungenlied,* he leads one thousand men against the Burgundians but is killed early on in the fighting by Hagen's brother, Dancwart. In Robinson Jeffers's poem, "At the Birth of an Age," he appears as Blada, a Hunnish nobleman, but not as brother of Attila, and is killed by a dying Hoegni through a dagger blow to the head.

[WM]

BORGHILD. In the *Volsunga saga,* the first wife of King Sigmund, mother of Helgi and Hamund.

[WM]

BOTELUNG, the father of Etzel and Bloedel in both the *Nibelungenlied* and the *Klage.* He is deceased by the time the action described in both works takes place. In the *Nibelungenlied* his name occurs only in reference to his son, Etzel, in the formulation *Botelunges kint* (Botelung's child), whereas in the *Klage* he is referred to directly early on as the father of Etzel, to whom he has bequeathed considerable power.

[WM]

BOYMUNT (BOHEMOND), the name of Rüdiger's horse as recorded in the *Klage* (v. 2855), which tends to run off when it does not see its master. It is reported as being sad upon returning to Pöchlarn after the death of Rüdiger.

[WM]

BRAGI, the god of poetry in Norse mythology. He is alluded to by Brynhild in the *Volsunga saga,* as are the runes that were cut on his tongue.

[WM]

BREDI, the name of a thrall, owned by Skadi, who is mentioned in the opening lines of the *Volsunga saga.* He proves to be a better hunter than Sigi, son of Odin, and is killed by the latter out of jealousy. As a consequence, Sigi is forced to flee the land and become an outlaw.

[WM]

BRÜNHILD (see also BRUNHILD [BRUNI-CHILDIS] and BRYNHILD). In Nordic mythology Brynhild was known as a valkyrie and the daughter of Odin, and in Wagner's *Ring* tetralogy, which, in the aggregate, is more oriented towards the Old Norse analogues than the *Nibelungenlied,* she appears as the daughter of Wotan. With the waning of Germanic influence and the integration of Christian elements, the figure of Brünhild appears to have lost some significance. The Middle High German work no longer contains the motif of the jilted lover and avenger, based on a previous passionate encounter with Siegfried that had culminated in their betrothal. Gone is the hate-love relationship to Siegfried, which had manifested itself quite strikingly in the hysterical laughter and shriek that comes from Brünhild when Siegfried is murdered. If Brünhild's origins in the Nordic tradition had been divine, the *Nibelungenlied,* already influenced by Christianity, portrays her, given her enormous strength and power, as a scion of the devil. On the other hand she also appears in line with Christian imagery as the ideal embodiment of the militant virgin. Brünhild is most certainly an enigma, and not without cause did Hebbel have her appear in his dramatic trilogy *Die Nibelungen* with a rune carved into her face.

In the Nordic analogues Brünhild loves Siegfried (Sigurd) and dies when he is killed.

The *Nibelungenlied* poet, however, depicts her as motivated solely by her wounded pride and her loss of power. After the murder of Siegfried, which in the *Nibelungenlied* is to be traced more to Hagen's zeal than to Brünhild's instigation, she disappears into history. In the *Klage,* however, we are told that she temporarily assumes power for Gunther's son in Worms.

Hebbel and Wagner, the two most significant adapters of the Brünhild figure in the nineteenth century, ignored the motif of the love-death and the love passion that bordered on insanity. Hebbel, for example, incorporated the hysterical shriek of laughter after Siegfried's death and Wagner has Brünnhilde die through self-immolation, similar to an Indian widow. It remains an open question why the author of the *Nibelungenlied* lent such emphasis to Kriemhild's revenge while completely avoiding such a motif in the case of Brünhild. It is regrettable that, in the process, various poetic elements and details were lost in the Middle High German version which were then partly reconstituted in the nineteenth century, including, for example, the idea that the northern lights could be traced back to the shine on Brünhild's shield, or the fact that she teaches Siegfried the runes and that the two of them swear oaths to one another. In addition one might cite Brünhild's prophecy of an unhappy love and, above all, the motif of love that has turned to hate. That a figure such as Brünhild lends itself to a broad spectrum of possibilities was recognized by both Germanic mythology and the *Nibelungenlied.* At a time when people still believed in gods or at least enjoyed hearing tales about them, Brünhild appeared as the invulnerable, immortal valkyrie, riding about on her horse, a woman who freed many warriors from their fear of death through the belief that many of them had been chosen by her to be taken to Valhalla. Once Christianity was already well established and courtly culture was at its height, Brünhild, as a relatively domesticated and secularized figure, gave concrete substance to the idea of the unapproachable virgin, implanting in both the feminine and masculine psyche the image of a chaste and distant mistress of love. Such an image came to assume ever more precise forms at least from the time that *Minnesang* came into being and was disseminated.

[BÖ]

Bibliography

Steger, Priska. "Brünhild." In *Herrscher, Helden, Heilige,* edited by Ulrich Müller and Werner Wunderlich. Mittelalter-Mythen 1. St. Gall: Universitäts-Verlag Konstanz, 1996, pp. 341–366.

BRUNHILD (BRUNICHILDIS), a Visigothic princess, wife of Sigibert, king of the Franks. Her sister Gailswintha, wife of Sigibert's half-brother Chilperic, was strangled at the instigation of Chiperic's concubine Fredegund, on whose orders Sigibert was himself murdered in 575. In spite of the name, Brunhild is a part-source for Kriemhild. After Sigibert's death Brunhild remained in conflict with Chilperic and succeeded as ruler of Burgundy on the death in 592 of another brother of Sigibert, Gunthram. She was killed in 613 by a group of Frankish nobles.

[BOM]

BRYNHILD. The most complete account of her life is told in the *Volsunga saga* and in the *Poetic Edda.* Here she is the sister of Atli (also in the *Þiðreks saga*) and Oddrun. She and her foster father Heimir live in Hlymdalir (*Þiðreks saga:* Saegard). There she is called *Hildr und hjalmi* (Hild under the helmet) and has a happy childhood. Her father Budli prepares her to become a valkyrie. Her horse is called Vingskornir. When she is twelve years old, King Agnar takes away the swanshirts of Brynhild and her seven maidens, and so she is forced to swear oaths to him. She helps Agnar to defeat Hjalmgunnar, contrary to Odin's wishes. Odin punishes her and sends her to Hindarfjall, where she falls asleep protected by a ring of fire (the *Waberlohe*)—according to the *Volsunga saga,* the sleeping beauty lies inside a rampart of shining shields—and only the best warrior is able to ride through the flames. Odin does not allow her to be a valkyrie any longer; she has to marry. She swears that she will never wed a timid man. When Sigurd arrives at Hindarfjall and awakens her, she and Sigurd promise to marry each other. In the *Ragnars saga loðbrókar,* the two sleep together, and later Brynhild gives birth to a daughter called Aslaug, who grows up in Hlymdalir under Heimir's protection.

Sigurd leaves Brynhild and arrives at Gunnar's court. Gunnar's mother gives him a magic potion, an ale of forgetfulness, and he forgets his oaths. In the shape of Gunnar he rides through the flames for a second time and woos Brynhild for Gunnar. He sleeps with Brynhild for three (or eight) nights disguised as Gunnar, keeping a drawn sword between them. Brynhild's marriage takes place on the same day as Sigurd's marriage to Gudrun. Brynhild leads an unhappy married life and seeks revenge as soon as she finds out that she has been deceived. She demands that Gunnar and the Gjukungs kill Sigurd and even his little son. When she is informed about Sigurd's death, she laughs and congratulates the Gjukungs on their murder. Then she prophesies that the Gjukungs will die because they have killed Sigurd, who never broke an oath. She gives her treasures to her serfs and asks to be burned on a funeral pyre together with Sigurd. After she has killed herself, two piles of wood are built, one for Sigurd, the other for Brynhild. Eventually she arrives in Hel ("the underworld") and hopes that some day she will be united with Sigurd forever.

There may be an echo of Brynhild's supernatural powers as a valkyrie in the extraordinary powers she displays in the *Nibelungenlied* as the Queen of Isenstein (Island). In both narratives, Sigurd/Siegfried is only able to defeat Brynhild by a combination of magic and treachery. Her loss of virginity signals her loss of power. In the German heroic epics Brünhild does not commit suicide, yet she is of no relevance for the plot after Siegfried's murder in the *Nibelungenlied.* The *Klage,* however, relates that when she is informed about the catastrophe at Etzel's court, she confesses to having had Siegfried killed. She weeps bitterly over Gunther's death, but she knows that she has to be a mother of good and noble character when her son is crowned king of Burgundy. In the German version of *Biterolf und Dietleib,* she is portrayed as a perfect social hostess in a knightly-courtly milieu.

[GW]

Bibliography

Andersson, Theodore M. *The Legend of Brynhild.* Ithaca: Cornell University Press, 1980.

Classen, Albrecht. "The Defeat of the Matriarch Brünhild in the Nibelungenlied, with Some

Thoughts on Matriarchy as Evinced in Literary Texts." In *"Waz sider da geschach." American-German Studies on the Nibelungenlied,* edited by Werner Wunderlich and Ulrich Müller. GAG 564. Göppingen: Kümmerle, 1992, pp. 89–110.

Ehrismann, Otfrid. "Die Fremde am Hof. Brünhild und die Philosophie der Geschichte." In *Begegnung mit dem "Fremden." Grenzen, Traditionen, Vergleiche. Akten des VIII. Internationalen Germanisten-Kongresses,* edited by Ejiro Iwasaki. Munich: Iudicium, 1991, pp. 320–331.

Gunzburger, Angelika. *Studien zur Nibelungenklage: Forschungsbericht, Bauform der Klage, Personendarstellung.* Europäische Hochschulschriften: Reihe 1, Deutsche Sprache und Literatur 685. Frankfurt a. M.: Lang, 1983, pp. 228–233.

Haymes, Edward R., and Susann T. Samples. *Heroic Legends of the North: An Introduction to the Nibelung and Dietrich Cycles.* New York: Garland, 1996, pp. 146f.

Heinrichs, Anne. "Brynhild als Typ der prä-patriarchalen Frau." In *Arbeiten zur Skandinavistik,* edited by Heinrich Beck. Frankfurt a. M.: Lang, 1985, pp. 45–66.

Newmann, Gail. "The Two Brünhilds?" *ABäG* 16 (1981): 69–78.

Reichert, Hermann. "Die Brynhild-Lieder der Edda im europäischen Kontext." In *Poetry in the Scandinavian Middle Ages. The Seventh International Saga Conference,* edited by Teresa Pároli. Spoleto: Presso la sede del Centro Studia, 1990, pp. 71–95.

See, Klaus von. "Die Werbung um Brünhild." *ZfdA* 88 (1957): 1–20.

Toman, Lore. "Der Aufstand der Frauen: Ein strukturalistischer Blick auf die Brünhild-Sage." *Literatur und Kritik* 131 (1979): 25–32.

BUDA, in the *Klage,* is the childhood home of Duchess Adelinde, the daughter of "brave Sintram" (who is not mentioned elsewhere in either the *Nibelungenlied* or the *Klage*). Adelinde is one of the group of mourning women at Etzelnburg following the massacre. Buda is described only as "a house located in the Marches of Hungary which also has the name Püten." Historically it was a hilly area on the bank of the Danube that was developed and settled as early as the Neolithic era. It was later the site of the Roman capital Aquincum, which was destroyed by the Mongols in 1241. King Bela IV built a hill fortress named Buda on the site. Emperor Sigismund added a palace for Hungarian rulers and Buda became the capital of Hungary

in 1361. In 1875 Buda, Obuda, and Pest were united to create the modern city of Budapest on both banks of the Danube.

[BC]

BUDAPEST. According to one fifteenth-century writer, it was a "ain stat" on the Danube where Etzel had built a "slos." At that time it was called Etzelnburg, established in the vicinity of an old Roman town called Aquincum. Later it was renamed Buda, and eventually became connected with the town of Pest to form Budapest. It is the place where Etzel and Kriemhild resided as king and queen and where the Burgundians met their demise.

[SSch]

BUDLI, in the *Volsunga saga,* he is the father of both Brynhild and Atli. While he consents to give Brynhild's hand to Gunnar in marriage, his daughter will later claim that she was forced into the union. Brynhild appears to enjoy a much closer relationship to her foster father, Heimir, than to Budli, as she elects to have Aslaug, her child by Sigurd, raised by the former.

[WM]

BURGUNDIANS, in the first part of the *Nibelungenlied,* the narrator refers to the nobles at Worms and to King Gunther's men as the Burgundians. Later, after Hagen has sunk the cursed treasure of the Nibelungs in the Rhine, the Burgundians assume the name Nibelungs. The designation Nibelungs for this sworn confraternity makes it clear that they are all destined for calamity and destruction; it may also be a reflection of the very ancient custom that the victor assumes the name of the vanquished. Historical examples are the Roman generals Germanicus and Britannicus, while a literary example is Parzival, named the Red Knight after having killed Ither, who because of his red armor, was formerly known by this appellative.

[WW/WM]

BURGUNDY. In the *Nibelungenlied* Burgundy is a Middle Rhenish kingdom with its main city of Worms. Originally from the area around the mouth of the Vistula, the Ostrogothic tribe of the Burgundians reached the Main and Rhine rivers in the fourth century. Beginning in 406, King Gundahar proceeded to bring areas and territories on the left bank of the Rhine under his control. As result of these campaigns, the Burgundian kingdom, with its royal seat in Borbetomagus (Worms), came into existence in 413. However, further Burgundian expansion to the west ended in 436/437 with their defeat at the hands of the West Roman general Aetius, whose Hunnish mercenaries annihilated most of the Burgundians as well as their king, Gundahar. The survivors were resettled in Sapaudia (Savoy) as subjects of the Roman Empire. Before Lugdunum (Lyons) became the capitol in 461, the first royal residence of the new Burgundians was Genava (Geneva). The Hunnish leader who defeated the Burgundians in 436 was not Attila. Not until 451, in the Battle of the Catalaunian Fields, in which Aetius defeated the Huns under Attila, did Burgundians fight on both sides. It was, in fact, the eighth-century historian, Paulus Diaconus (Paul the Deacon), who reset the annihiliation of the Burgundians from 436/437 to 451, thus making Attila responsible for the downfall of the Burgundian kingdom. Before 516 during the reign of King Gundobad, the *Lex Burgundionum* (Burgundian Code) was drawn up. In this document the kings Gibica, Gundomar, Gislahar, and Gundahar, all of whom have since become part of the legendary and literary tradition of the Nibelungs, are named as Gundobad's ancestors. In the northern (i.e., Scandinavian) heroic tradition, Gibica, named either Gjuki or Gibiche, is the father of the three royal brothers, while in the *Nibelungenlied* he is called Dancrat. Gundomar is Guthorm or Gernot, Gislahar is Giselher, and Gundahar is Gunnar or Gunther. In 534 the Franks overran the Burgundian kingdom and assimilated it within their empire. In 843 Burgundy was, for the most part, allotted to the Frankish Middle Empire of Lothar I. In 879 Count Bosco of Vienne founded the kingdom of Lower Burgundy on the Rhône. In 950 Upper and Lower Burgundy were joined to form the kingdom of Arelat, which in turn became part of the German Empire in 1032. At the end of the ninth century Bosco's brother, Richard the Just, founded the Duchy of Burgundy west of the Saône. In the fourteenth and fifteenth centuries Burgundy played a significant political and cultural role in Europe. Because of the expansion plans of Duke Charles the Bold, the years 1474 to 1477 are marked by war between the Burgundians and the Swiss Confederation under the leadership of Berne. After the defeat and death of Charles the Bold in the Battle of Nancy (1477), the Burgundian territories were ceded to the Habsburgs and to France.

[WW]

Bibliography

Beyerle, Franz, ed. *Gesetze der Burgunden.* Germanenrechte. Texte und Übersetzungen 10. Weimar: H. Böhlaus Nachf., 1936.

Hoffmann, Werner. *Das Nibelungenlied.* 6th ed. Sammlung Metzler 7. Stuttgart: Metzler, 1992, pp. 41ff.

CHAPLAIN, in the *Nibelungenlied,* the religious escort of the Burgundians on their journey to Etzel's (but, more importantly, Kriemhild's) Hungary. While on the journey, Hagen encounters a group of water sprites and then, believing them to be endowed with the second sight, steals their clothes in order to hear their visions of the future. The first sprite named Hadeburg lies, promising good fortune, but the second, Sigelind, offers a more ominous prediction, telling of the encounter with a ferryman and revealing that if the Burgundians continue towards Hungary, all will be killed except the chaplain. Perhaps to test whether or not this is indeed the Burgundians' fate, Hagen throws the unfortunate chaplain over the side of the ferry while crossing the Danube. Despite the protests of his fellow travelers (although no one makes any effort to restrain him), Hagen attempts to hold him down under the water and drown him, but the chaplain manages to swim safely back to shore. For Hagen this is proof positive of the catastrophic destiny predicted for him and the Burgundians by Sigelind.

[KM]

CHILPERIC, a Frankish king of Neustria (ruling from Tournai, Soissons) from 561 to 584. After his half-brother Sigibert married Gailswintha's sister Brunhild, he married Gailswintha, but his longtime concubine, Fredegund, had her murdered and took her place. His name (in the form Helferich) is assigned to one of Dietrich's men.

[BOM]

Bibliography
Lasko, Peter. *The Kingdom of the Franks.* London: Thames and Hudson, 1971, pp. 63–65.

CONRAD, a clerk in the *Klage,* who, in the service of Bishop Pilgrim, was charged with writing down in Latin an account of the catastrophe at Etzel's court based on information provided by the minstrel Swemmel.

[WM]

DANCRAT, in the *Nibelungenlied,* king of the Burgundians, husband of Ute, and father of Kriemhild, Gunther, Gernot, and Giselher. In his youth he is reported to have garnered much honor. Dancrat is already deceased by the time that the action of the *Nibelungenlied* begins. He is also mentioned briefly in the *Klage* as having left considerable holdings to his sons and to his wife, Ute.

[WM]

DANCWART, in both the *Nibelungenlied* and the *Klage,* Hagen's brother and Gunther's marshal at court. In the *Nibelungenlied* (342,3) he is picked by Siegfried as a participant in the wooing expedition to Island. Dancwart plays no role in the murder of Siegfried. On the way to the land of the Huns, he saves his hard-pressed brother from being overcome by the Bavarian count Gelpfrat by dealing the latter a fatal blow (1614,2). In the fighting in Etzel's Great Hall, he is killed by Helpfrich. In the *Klage* Dancwart is the first Burgundian warrior among the dead to be found by Dietrich.

[WM]

DANES (MHG *Tenen* or *Tenelender*), inhabitants of Denmark, frequently mentioned in the *Nibelungenlied.* In the fourth *âventiure* a combined army of Saxons and Danes fights a war against the Burgundians but it is defeated through Siegfried's intervention. In the second part of the poem, an exiled king, Hawart of Denmark (1345,1), and his liege man, Margrave Irinc (2028,1), are mentioned as living at King Etzel's court. Here the Danes seem to be closely associated with the Thuringians, because they always appear in the company of an exiled king, Irnfrit von Düringen.

[NV]

DANPR is the Dnieper. This name occurs in *Atlakviða,* stanza 5. Atli promises Gunnar and Hogni valuable gifts, among them also the *staði Danpar,* the shores of the Dnieper. This curious line seems to come from the *Hlodskviða* (The Lay of Hlod), a very old heroic Eddic lay preserved in the *Hervarar saga ok Heidreks konungs.* This lay contains the story of a battle between the Huns and the Goths. A reflection of this line also appears in the mythological Eddic lay *Rigsþula* (Song of Rig), preserved in the prose *Edda.*

[GW]

Bibliography
de Vries, Jan. *Altnordische Literaturgeschichte.* Vol. 1. 2nd ed. Grundriss der germanischen Philologie 15. Berlin: de Gruyter, 1964, pp. 69ff.
Gering, Hugo, and B. Sijmons. *Kommentar zu den Liedern der Edda.* 1. Hälfte: *Götterlieder.* Halle (Saale): Buchhandlung des Waisenhauses (Francke), 1927, p. 367.
———. *Kommentar zu den Liedern der Edda.* 2. Hälfte: *Heldenlieder.* Halle (Saale): Buchhandlung des Waisenhauses (Francke), 1931, p. 343.
Simek, Rudolf, and Hermann Pálsson. *Lexikon der altnordischen Literatur.* Stuttgart: Kröner, 1987, p. 169.

DANUBE (MHG *Tuonouwe*), river rising from the eastern slopes of the Black Forest, flowing first northeast to Ratisbon, then southeast through Austria and Hungary, where it turns south near Esztergom, continuing through Serbia and Rumania to the Black Sea. It is mentioned or referred to in the *Nibelungenlied* many times in connection with the two journeys from Worms on the Rhine to Etzel's residence in Hungary, which are described at great length. Four southern tributaries of the Danube are mentioned (Inn, Traun, Enns, and Traisen) and fifteen towns (from west to east): Grossmehring and Pförring on the left bank, Plattling (only in **C**), Passau, Efferding, Enns, Pöchlarn, Melk, Mautern, Traismauer (only in **C**, other manuscripts have Zeiselmauer), Tulln, Vienna, Hainburg, Wieselburg and Gran or Etzelnburc (Etzelnburg) on the right bank. It is remarkable that neither the most important town on the Danube, Ratisbon, nor the only stone bridge across it, built there in 1146, is mentioned. The Danube is always crossed by ferries, not only in the *Nibelungenlied* but also in *Biterolf und Dietleib*.

[NV]

DENMARK (MHG *Tenemarke* or *Tenelant*), in the *Nibelungenlied* mentioned as the region beyond (i.e., north of) Saxony, ruled by King Liudegast, brother of King Liudeger of Saxony. It can be reached on horseback (220,1 and 311,2), which means that the name Denmark already includes Jutland, a situation which is attested since about 700 a.d. In the second part of the *Nibelungenlied* and in the *Klage* (400 and 2372), Denmark is mentioned as the homeland of an exiled king living at King Etzel's court. In the first part of the poem the country is usually called "Tenemarke" (140,3), in the second part, "Tenelant" (2058,1). This could be reminiscent of the distinction made in tenth-century sources between *marca vel regnum Danorum,* indicating the existence of a borderland (*mark*) between the rivers Eider and Schlei, which was inhabited by Danes but part of the German Empire, and a kingdom of Denmark north of it. Danish heroes appear in most of the Middle High German heroic poems.

[NV]

Bibliography

Johannes Hoops, ed. *Reallexikon der germanischen Altertumskunde.* 2nd ed., edited by Herbert Jankuhn et al. Vol. 5. Berlin: de Gruyter, 1984, pp. 175–177.

DIETLINDE, daughter of Gotelind and Rüdiger, niece of Dietrich. In the *Nibelungenlied* her name is not mentioned. When Kriemhild travels through Pöchlarn, Dietlinde receives twelve golden bracelets from her and expresses the wish to become one of her ladies in Etzelnburg in order to learn courtly manners. When she meets the Burgundians, she appears to be so intimidated by Hagen's appearance that she does not want to receive him with a courtly kiss. She becomes engaged to Giselher, and they are supposed to be married on the Burgundians' return from Etzelnburg. In the *Klage* Dietlinde dreams of her father's death prior to the arrival of the messengers who inform her of his demise. She strongly grieves for Rüdiger but tells the messengers to send her love to Brünhild. She

also sends a message to Ute, informing her of her engagement to Giselher (who kills Wolfhart but also dies by his hand in the fighting in Etzel's Great Hall) and of Gernot's slaying her father. After Gotelind's death, Dietrich promises to find Dietlinde a husband able to take care of her land and entrusts her to the care of Rüdiger's retinue. Dietlinde subsequently proves to be a successful ruler.

[BS]

DIETRICH VON BERN, who is first mentioned in the *Nibelungenlied* (1347,1), plays a subsidiary, yet significant role in the events that unfold at the court of Etzel where he lives in exile. In chapter 38 he becomes involved in the fighting between the Huns and the Burgundians through the death of Rüdiger and loses all his men except Hildebrant. He captures Gunther and Hagen, and watches in distress as Kriemhild beheads Hagen and then as she in turn is slain by Hildebrant. In the *Klage* Dietrich organizes the burial of the dead and sends messengers to the bereaved before departing with his wife, Herrat, and Hildebrant to his own kingdom.

How Dietrich comes to be at Etzel's court is not explained in the *Nibelungenlied,* but from other MHG heroic poems about him we may deduce that he is exiled from his own lands in Italy, which have been usurped by Ermanaric. In *Dietrichs Flucht* Dietrich and Rüdiger are both exiles with Etzel, and in *Die Rabenschlacht* Rüdiger acts as mediator between Dietrich and Etzel after the death of Etzel's sons in the battle. His sojourn at Etzel's court is thus involuntary. The link between Dietrich and the Hunnish court is a reminiscence of the Ostrogoths' historical contacts with the Huns in the fifth century, and in particular these poems reflect, however inaccurately, events surrounding the reign of Theodoric the Great in northern Italy in the period from 488 to 526.

The nature of his character in the *Nibelungenlied* has been much debated. Whereas Bert Nagel and Gottfried Weber, among others, have argued that he represents the ideal of Christian chivalry, Blanka Horacek has maintained that he evades the need to act and allows himself to be guided by his own interests, thus displaying signs of weakness. Carola Gottzmann has pursued indications of implicit criticism of Dietrich in the historical Dietrich poems themselves. To some extent the image of Dietrich seems to have been influenced by the figure of the weak king that is so widespread in medieval European literature (King Arthur, King Marke in Gottfried von Strassburg's *Tristan,* and Gunther and Etzel in the *Nibelungenlied* itself, for example.)

Dietrich's exploits were related in a large number of texts throughout the Middle Ages. There are two principal kinds of poems about him (1) those that have a rather nebulous historical foundation, like *Dietrichs Flucht, Rabenschlacht,* and *Alpharts Tod;* and (2) those in which he is matched against giants, as in the *Eckenlied* (see Ecke and Fasold) and *Sigenot,* dwarfs (as in *Laurin*), and other unnatural beings (as in *Wunderer*). From Ecke he acquires his sword Eckesahs (though this name does not occur in the *Nibelungenlied*). In all these poems, and indeed as far back as the OHG *Hildebrandslied,* Dietrich's inseparable companion and mentor is Hildebrant. As depicted in the *Nibelungenlied,* Dietrich does not overtly display any of the traits with which he is characterized in other parts of literary and extra-literary tradition (e.g., youthful inexperience, breathing fire in battle, and diabolical birth and death).

Given the popularity of stories about Dietrich and about Siegfried in the Middle Ages, it is not surprising that poems were composed in which the Dietrich and Nibelungen strands were brought together. In the *Rosengarten* complex of poems, Dietrich is associated with the characters who appear in the *Nibelungenlied.* Kriemhild or her father Gibica challenge Dietrich and his men to fight against the twelve warriors who guard Kriemhild's rose garden at Worms. Dietrich has to fight Siegfried and overcomes him. There is also a fight between Dietrich and Siegfried in *Die Rabenschlacht,* and the motif is borrowed from the *Rosengarten* by *Biterolf und Dietleib,* probably composed in Styria between 1250 and 1275.

Of all the Germanic heroes in the Middle Ages, Dietrich von Bern was arguably the best-known and the best-loved. That today he is largely forgotten is due to two principal factors. The first was the rediscovery of the *Nibelungenlied* in the eighteenth century and the subsequent recognition that it is a work of literature qualitatively far superior to any of the Dietrich poems.

The second is the popularity of Richard Wagner's refurbishment of the Siegfried story in the *Ring* cycle, contrasting with the lack of any comparable artistic recreation of the Dietrich stories. (see also THIDREK)

[JLF]

Bibliography

Flood, J. L. "Dietrich von Bern." In *Mittelalter-Mythen I: Herrscher, Helden, Heilige,* edited by Ulrich Müller and Werner Wunderlich. St. Gall: UVK, Fachbuchverlag für Wissenschaft und Studium, 1996, pp. 287–304.

Gottzmann, Carola L. *Heldendichtung des 13. Jahrhunderts. Siegfried, Dietrich, Ortnit.* Frankfurt a. M.: Lang, 1987, pp. 109–136.

Haymes, Edward R. Haymes. "Dietrich von Bern im Nibelungenlied." *ZfdA* 114 (1985): 159–165.

Horacek, Blanka. "Der Charakter Dietrichs von Bern im Nibelungenlied." In *Festgabe für Otto Höfler zum 75. Geburtstag,* edited by Helmut Birkhan. Vienna: Braumüller, 1976, pp. 297–336.

Nagel, Bert. "Das Dietrichbild des Nibelungenliedes." *ZfdPh* 78 (1959): 258–268; and 79 (1960): 28–57.

———. *Das Nibelungenlied. Stoff, Form, Ethos.* Frankfurt a. M.: Hirschgraben-Verlag, 1965, pp. 250–272.

Weber, Gottfried. *Das Nibelungenlied: Problem und Idee.* Stuttgart: Metzler, 1963, pp. 161–170.

Wisniewski, Roswitha. *Mittelalterliche Dietrichdichtung.* Sammlung Metzler 205. Stuttgart: Metzler, 1986.

DRASOLF. In the *Þiðreks saga,* Drasolf is married to Sigmund's sister, Signy. When he starts a campaign against Poland, Sigmund joins him with many knights, leaving his wife, Sisibe, under the protection of his two advisors, Hartwin and Hermann. Drasolf is a brave knight and successful in his campaign. The figure is not mentioned anywhere else.

[GW]

DÜRNSTEIN, a small town on the Danube that became famous as the place where Richard the Lionheart, king of England, was held for ransom in the twelfth century. Bishop Wolfger of Passau, who appears to have had a connection to the *Nibelungenlied,* was also involved in the negotiations to free Richard. There is mention in the *Nibelungenlied* of the high arches and walls in

Dürnstein, which are passed by the Burgundians on their way to Etzel's court.

[SSch]

EAST FRANCONIA (MHG *Ostervranken*), in the ninth century the name of the whole German-speaking part of the Carolingian Empire. After the partition of the empire the name was used to indicate the region north and south of the river Main, east of Rhenish Franconia (MHG "Rînvranken"), which is mentioned as the home-land of the Burgundians in the *Klage* (303). East Franconia is separated from Rhenish Franconia by the Taunus, Spessart, and Odenwald hills. It is mentioned in the *Nibelungenlied* (1524,2 and 1525,1) as the region through which the Burgundians march on their way from Worms to the land of the Huns. In the poem *Biterolf und Dietleib,* it has the same function. In *Dietrichs Flucht* and *Rabenschlacht* it is mentioned as the homeland of a Duke Hermann.

[NV]

ECKE, in the *Eckenlied,* a giant, brother of Fasold. Ecke enjoys considerable fame as a war-rior. Dietrich of Bern (Verona) receives the sword Eckesahs from him. Ecke is ultimately killed by Dietrich after intense hand-to-hand combat, but Dietrich regards his victory over Ecke as shameful (see *Eckenlied,* 146, 12–13). In the *Þiðreks saga,* Ecke's brother Fasold be-lieves that Ecke has been killed in his sleep by Dietrich.

[WM]

ECKEWART, a margrave of the Burgundian kings in the *Nibelungenlied.* He is Kriemhild's treasurer and swears to be true and faithful to her throughout his life. He accompanies Kriemhild to the Netherlands and later to Etzel. At night he is found asleep on the border of Rüdiger's march. When Hagen takes off his sword, Eckewart is full of despair because he has not guarded the border well, a fact that only makes sense if it is Kriemhild who tries to warn her brothers of her husband. Hagen takes pity on him and returns the sword to him and gives him some golden arm-lets. Eckewart warns the Burgundians that they should be on their guard with the Huns as there is still animosity towards them as a result of Sieg-fried's death. Finally he leads the knights to

Rüdiger's castle in Bechelaren. He is mentioned several times in *Dietrichs Flucht.* The *Þiðreks saga* knows Ekkivard as one of Rodingeir's men. The event at the border is told exactly in the same way as in the *Nibelungenlied,* but that is the only similarity involving Ekkivard.

[GW]

Bibliography
Schneider, Hermann. *Germanische Heldensage.* Vol.1. 2nd ed. Grundriss der germanischen Philo-logie 10/I. Berlin: de Gruyter, 1962, pp. 90, 194f.

EFFERDING (MHG *Everdingen*), a town on the Danube mentioned in the *Nibelungenlied* and through which Kriemhild passes (1302,1) on her way to the land of the Huns.

[WM]

EGWALDUS, also Egwald, is the dwarf king in the *Historia von dem gehörnten Siegfried.* He corresponds to Eugel in the *Lied vom Hürnen Seyfrid.*

[JLF]

EHRENBERTUS, one of the sons of Gibaldus in the *Historia von dem gehörnten Siegfried* who corresponds to Gunther in the *Nibelungenlied.*

[JLF]

EITELL, son of Gudrun and Atli in the *At-lakviða.* After Atli has murdered Gudrun's brothers Gunnar and Hogni in his futile quest for the Nibelungen hoard, Gudrun exacts a most fearful revenge on her husband. Part of her plan involves the slaying of Eitell and his brother Erp, cooking their hearts, and serving them in honey to Atli: "Now has the sword-wielder eaten his sons'/gory hearts made sweet with honey!" (37,1–2).

[FGG]

Bibliography
Terry, Patricia, trans. "The Lay of Atli." In *Poems of the Vikings: The Elder Edda.* Indianapolis and New York: Bobbs-Merrill, 1969, pp. 210–216.

EKKIHARTH, a figure in the *Þiðreks saga,* the most accomplished of the smith Mimir's twelve apprentices. When Sigfreth (Sigurth/Sigurd), whom Mimir is rearing, is nine years old, Ekkiharth hits him on the ear with his tongs. Sigfreth grabs Ekkiharth by the hair and, pursued by the other apprentices, drags him out of the smithy to Mimir. Sigfreth's treatment of Ekkiharth causes Mimir to put the unruly Sigfreth to work and goad him to attempt to kill the dragon, Reginn. Ekkiharth is the first person to see Sigfreth returning with Reginn's head. He warns Mimir and the other apprentices to flee before the angry young Sigfreth. (Wilhelm Grimm identified Eckewart in *Dietrichs Flucht* with Ekkiharth, although it appears much more likely that the former is derived from the Eckewart of the *Nibelungenlied*.)

[FH]

ELBE. The river Elbe is referred to once in the *Nibelungenlied*, namely, by Giselher, when pointing out to Kriemhild (1244,2) that from the Rhone to the Rhine, and from the Elbe to the sea, there is no king more powerful than Etzel, i.e., that he would be an excellent match for her and she would be happy as his queen.

[WM]

ELEVEN SONS OF ISUNG. According to the *Þiðreks saga*, Isung, king of Bertangaland (Bretagne), has eleven sons. When King Thidrek decides to test his best twelve knights, King Isung, his eleven sons, and Young Sigurd are their opponents in single combat. Thidrek's liegemen and friends are Heime, Herbrand, Wildifer, Sintram, Fasold, Amlung, Hornbogi, Hogni, Thetleif, Hildibrand, Gunnar, and Widga. Isung's sons win eight fights, and Isung himself is victorious over Gunnar. Yet the most interesting single combat is between Sigurd and Thidrek, which Sigurd is able to win because Widga gives him his excellent sword, Mimung. In the end nobody is killed and Thidrek and Sigurd become friends. Isung and his sons (later the youngest one is called Lorantin) die in a fierce battle against Hertnit, son of Osantrix, because of the magic power of Hertnit's wife, Ostacia. This story is also told in the *Rabenschlacht*, in *Biterolf und Dietleib*, and in the *Rosengarten*, but there are many differences between each of the plots.

[GW]

Bibliography

Schneider, Hermann. *Germanische Heldensage.* Vol. 1. 2nd ed. Grundriss der germanischen Philologie 10/I. Berlin: de Gruyter, 1962, pp. 286–310.

ELSE, appears in the *Nibelungenlied* as the margrave of a Bavarian march on the right bank of the Danube (1545,4). He is the brother of the margrave Gelpfrat, whose ferryman is decapitated by Hagen, and who is killed himself by Dancwart in a confrontation with the Burgundians. Else eventually retreats, after being wounded and having lost eighty of his men (1615).

[WM]

ELSUNG in the *Þiðreks saga* corresponds to Else, brother of Gelpfrat, in the *Nibelungenlied*. When the Burgundians travel to Atli's court, Hogni wants to cross the Danube (at the confluence of the Rhine and Danube) in the march of Jarl Elsung the Young. In order to avoid a fight, he pretends to be Jarl Elsung's man. He offers a golden armlet to the ferryman, who accepts the bribe and ferries the Burgundians over the river. Later, when Thidrek, Herrad, and Hildibrand return home after the death of the Burgundian kings, Elsung the Young remembers that years ago Samson and his sons, Erminrek and Thetmar (Thidrek's father), killed his blood relative Jarl Elsung of Bern the Old. He determines that now is a propitious time to take revenge. He leaves his castle Babilon together with thirty-one knights, among them Amlung, who is married to Elsung's sister. They meet Thidrek and Hildibrand. Half of Elsung's men are killed, and Thidrek himself kills Elsung. Hildibrand overcomes Amlung but does not kill him. This story is not told in any German heroic epic. Only in *Biterolf und Dietleib* is Young Else called "des alten Elsen kint." Perhaps the story reflects a fight between the Niflungs and Jarl Elsung's knights in an older version of the story about the ferryman (see *Nibelungenlied*, twenty-sixth *âventiure*). The *Þiðreks saga* also mentions that Thetmar is married to Odilia, Jarl Elsung's daughter. In *Dietrichs Flucht* Dietmar is married to the daughter of a king called Desen.

[GW]

Bibliography
Schneider, Hermann. *Germanische Heldensage.* Vol. 1. 2nd ed. Grundriss der germanischen Philologie 10/I. Berlin: de Gruyter, 1962, pp. 97f.

ENNS (MHG *Ense*), a small town on the Enns, a southern tributary of the Danube, about 15 kilometers east of the Traun. Town and river are both mentioned only once in the *Nibelungenlied* (1301,2 and 1304,1). Kriemhild and her retinue stay there overnight on their journey to the land of the Huns. The Enns was the western border of the Margraviate of Austria until 1156. In the *Nibelungenlied* it is considered to be the western border of Rüdiger's land. Gotelind rides there to meet Kriemhild and her company.

[NV]

ERKA, (see also HELCHE and HERKJA) in the *Þiðreks saga,* the daughter of Osantrix and Oda (the daughter of Milias). She is sequestered by her father in a castle that no man may enter. Both Northung, king of Svavaland, and Attila ask for her hand. Although Osantrix is favorably disposed to Northung's suit, Attila's emissary, Rotholf, contrives to enter Erka's castle and persuades Erka (who has prayed to God to become Queen of Húnaland) to go with him to Húnaland. Attila and Erka marry and have two sons, Erp and Ortvin. Later, while Attila is away hunting, Erka releases her wounded and imprisoned kinsman, Thidrek Valdimarsson, against Attila's wishes and nurses him back to health. Thidrek Valdimarsson then escapes from Susa, despite Erka's pleas that this will cost her her head. Erka begs a badly wounded Thidrek of Bern to capture his namesake. When Thidrek of Bern returns to Susa with his opponent's head, Erka mistakes him for her kinsman. Thidrek of Bern throws Thidrek Valdimarsson's head at her feet. Erka laments that so many kinsmen lose their lives for her sake. Later Thidrek of Bern appeals to Erka for help in regaining his kingdom. Erka conveys his request to Attila with elegance and tact. Attila and Erka provide Thidrek with men and arms; Erka entrusts her sons, Erp and Ortvin, to Thidrek. She weeps when she learns that her sons have been slain but, after reassuring herself that they died as warriors, she reconciles Thidrek to Attila. On her deathbed Erka gives Thidrek and Hildibrand gifts and tells Attila that he will remarry but warns him not to take a wife from Niflungaland or from Aldrian's line; otherwise, great misfortune will result.

[FH]

ERMANARIC (ERMANARICH, ERMEN-RICH, ERMENRIK), king of the Ostrogoths, from the line of the Amals (a name perpetuated in the *Nibelungenlied* when Dietrich von Bern and his men are referred to as "der künec der Amelunge" [*Nibelungenlied* 1981,3], and "Amelunge" [*Nibelungenlied* 1721,2] respectively). Ermanaric committed suicide in 376 when the Huns and Alans invaded. Already by the sixth century his deeds and his death had become legendary (see Jordanes, *De origine actibusque Getarum*). He becomes a major, if shadowy, figure in MHG heroic poetry where, taking over the role of the historical Odoacer, he becomes the principal adversary of Dietrich von Bern, his nephew, whom he ousts from his homeland. It is because of this that Dietrich lives as an exile at the court of Etzel.

[JLF]

Bibliography
Beck, H. and W. Herwig. "Ermanarich." In vol. 7 of *Reallexikon der germanischen Altertumskunde.* 2nd ed., edited by Herbert Jahkuhn et al. Berlin: de Gruyter, 1989, pp. 510–15.
Brady, C. *The Legends of Ermanaric.* Berkeley: University of California Press, 1943.
Holder, Alfred, ed. *Iordanis De origine actibusque Getarum.* Freiberg i.B.: Mohr, 1895.
Zink, G. *Les Légendes héroiques de Dietrich et d'Ermrich dans les littératures germaniques.* Lyon: IAC, 1950.

ERP (1), see EITELL.

ERP (2), the half brother of Hamdir and Sorli in the *Hamðismál* (Lay of Hamdir). Incited by their mother Gudrun to avenge the death of their sister, Svanhild, on the latter's husband, Jormunrek (Ermanaric), Hamdir and Sorli ride off to beard the king of the Goths in his lair. On the way they meet Erp, who has also traveled to stand with his half brothers in the coming battle. An unclear exchange ensues in which Erp, a bastard, is accused of being cowardly and is slain by the brothers. Hamdir and Sorli manage to slay many

Goths and cut off Jormunrek's hands and feet before they are overwhelmed and killed. Sorli realizes at the end the folly of having killed their half brother:

The king's head would be off if Erp were alive,
the great warrior we killed on our way,
courageous as he was—the Norns compelled
me—
our own brother whose blood we shed. (27)

[FGG]

Bibliography
Terry, Patricia, trans. "The Lay of Hamdir." In *Poems of the Vikings: The Elder Edda.* Indianapolis: Bobbs-Merrill, 1969, pp. 237–241.

ESZTERGOM, a town in Hungary, about 150 kilometers east of Wieselburg and about 60 kilometers upstream from Budapest. Mentioned in the *Nibelungenlied* under the name of Etzelnburg (1379,1) or Gran (1497,2) as the residence of Etzel. Esztergom (from Latin *Istrogranum*) was the cradle of Christianity in Hungary and the birthplace of King Stephen I, the patron saint of Hungary. It was the capital of Hungary until 1361 and the see of an archbishop from 1001 on. The identification of Esztergom as Etzel's residence has been disputed.

[NV]

ETHGEIR, in the *Þiðreks saga,* one of Nordian's four giant sons, Ethgeir accompanies Osantrix against King Milias. When Attila routs Osantrix's forces, Ethgeir flees to Austriki with Aspilian. Osantrix later sends Ethgeir to King Isung who puts the giant into a forest to guard the borders of Bertangaland. When Thidrek and his twelve champions approach Bertangaland, Vithga (Ethgeir's kinsman) advances into the forest, wakes the sleeping giant, and challenges him, chiding him for sleeping while on watch. Ethgeir advises Vithga to leave, saying that he would not want to trouble himself to stand up and kill him. He goes back to sleep. Vithga kicks him again, breaking two ribs. Ethgeir leaps to his feet and throws his halberd at Vithga but misses his mark. Vithga wounds the giant who pleads for his life, promising to redeem himself with gold

and silver. Ethgeir then leads Vithga to an underground room. Reasoning that the giant will try to trap him underground, Vithga orders Ethgeir to enter first and cuts off the giant's head as he does so.

[FH]

ETZEL, in the *Nibelungenlied,* he is the son of Botelung, and the brother of Bloedelin. He is king of the Huns and a heathen in both the *Nibelungenlied* and the *Klage.* Based loosely and in many respects improbably on the historical figure of Attila the Hun (d. a.d. 453), Etzel is portrayed as a noble character whose great wealth and power place him in a position of superiority over the Burgundian kings, who provide the chief intrigue in the first half of the *Nibelungenlied.*

Etzel appears first in the twentieth *âventiure.* At his court in Etzelnburg many great heroes such as Dietrich of Verona, Irnfrid of Thuringia, Hawart of Denmark, and King Gibeche, are members of his retinue. After his first wife Helche dies, he sends his vassal Rüdiger of Pöchlarn to Worms bearing his marriage suit to Kriemhild, despite initial misgivings regarding their religious differences. Etzel and Kriemhild get married in Vienna during Pentecost and take up residence in Gran (Etzelnburg). They have a son, Ortlieb. In accord with Kriemhild's repeated requests, Etzel invites the Burgundians to a courtly feast in Gran, not knowing that she still grieves for Siegfried and seeks revenge for his death (and the loss of the Nibelungen hoard), although Dietrich and Eckewart are aware of her state of mind. He welcomes the Burgundians in a courtly manner and does not know that his men later attempt to attack the Burgundians at night. Kriemhild contrives to pit Etzel against his guests, yet for a time he refuses to be aggressive toward them out of respect for the rules of hospitality. Although the Burgundians refuse to attend Mass without their weapons on the following day, Etzel does not suspect that anything is afoot. When Volker kills one of Etzel's garish knights in a tournament, Etzel commands his angry men not to attack the Burgundians. After Bloedelin's attack on the Burgundian squires and the ensuing fight in the hall, Etzel leaves the hall under Dietrich's protection. Roused to action by the murder of his and Kriemhild's son Ortlieb, he sets loose the forces in a battle which will ultimately culminate in the destruction of the Burgundians, Kriemhild's death, and the decimation of his own warrior vassals. Yet he is the only man who does not participate in the fight. When Etzel faces the corpses of his men killed by the Burgundians, he wants to join the fighting and has to be prevented by his men from rushing into the hall. He and Kriemhild manipulate Rüdiger into fighting the Burgundians by kneeling in front of him and thus reversing their vassalage relationship. When the fight in the hall is over, Etzel laments Rüdiger's death; he also laments Hagen's inappropriate death at the hands of a woman—his spouse, Kriemhild—as well as Kriemhild's death at the hand of Hildebrand. In the *Klage,* Etzel is portrayed lamenting in an immoderate, dishonorable manner while attending the recovery of the dead from the ruins, their corporeal reconstruction when they are placed upon biers, and afterwards their burial. Etzel is frequently admonished by Dietrich to moderate his grief over losing his power, his worldly fame, his retinue, and his family. On Hildebrand's advice, Etzel gathers together the clothes and weapons of the highest-born dead warriors and sends them with his messengers to their families, along with a pledge to continue to attend to them with affection and material assistance. When Dietrich, Lady Herrat, his spouse, and Hildebrand leave Etzelnburg, Etzel loses his mind due to his suffering. The narrator of the *Klage* ironically laments the fact that Etzel's subsequent life is unknown. He might have been killed, he might have simply disappeared, he might have gone up into the air, been buried alive, carried up to heaven, dropped out of his skin, slipped away into the holes of stone walls, fallen into hell, or have been devoured by the devil.

Etzel's portrait in the *Nibelungenlied* is at odds in many respects with that presented by the Gothic historian Jordanes, who depicts him as a crude and ruthless plunderer rather than the august lord of a sumptuous and noble court. In contrast in the *Nibelungenlied* Etzel cuts a royal figure as a noble heathen whose warrior instincts are nonetheless far more courtly and nuanced than the blind and bloodthirsty quest for revenge that motivates Kriemhild.

[BS/JHS]

Bibliography
de Boor, Helmut. *Das Attilabild in Geschichte, Legende, und heroischer Dichtung.* 2nd ed. Darmstadt: Wissenschaftliche Buchgesellschaft, 1963.

ETZELNBURG, in the *Nibelungenlied,* is identified as the chief residence of Etzel. Alternately, Etzel's city is on one occasion called Gran (1497). Both are identical with one another and refer doubtless to present-day Esztergom in Hungary, situated close to the confluence of the Hron and the Danube, roughly twenty-five miles northwest of Budapest. Well known as a grain market, Esztergom was also the residence of the early Arpád kings. The connection with the German *Nibelungenlied* may well lie in the fact that in 1189, while on his way to the crusades, the German emperor Friedrich Barbarossa stopped at Esztergom where he was cordially received and sumptuously feted by the Hungarian king Bela III. The city was sacked by the Mongols in 1242.

[FGG]

EUGEL (also **EUGLEYNE,**) a dwarf in the *Lied vom Hürnen Seyfried* and Hans Sachs's *Tragödie von dem hürnen Seyfrid* who brings Seyfrid to the "Trachenstain" where Krimhilt has been imprisoned by Fafnir.

[WM]

EYLIMI, a king in the *Volsunga saga* who is visited by Sigmund with the purpose of marrying his daughter, Hjordis. Following the marriage ceremony, Eylimi returns with Sigmund to the land of the Volsungs. Together with his son-in-law, Eylimi engages in a fierce battle against a rival suitor, Lyngvi, but both are killed, ostensibly because of the intervention of Odin on the side of Lyngvi.

[WM]

EYMOD, a figure in the *Volsunga saga* who occurs briefly in chapter 34 and is described as one of the renowned warriors who is to accompany Grimhild, Gunnar, and his brothers on their expedition to Gudrun to seek reconciliation for the death of Sigurd and Gudrun's three-year-old son, whom Brynhild ordered killed.

[WM]

FAFNIR, in the Norse *Edda,* the brothers Fafnir and Regin kill their father Hreidmar to obtain his treasure. Fafnir turns himself into a dragon and guards the treasure, refusing to share it with his brother. Regin goes as a smith to persuade Sigurd to kill the dragon, which he does by piercing Fafnir's belly from below; hence he is called Sigurðr Fafnisbani, "Sigurd the slayer of Fafnir." The dragon's blood gives Sigurd the ability to understand the language of birds, which reveal to him that Regin is plotting his death. Sigurd kills Regin and takes possession of the treasure. In the German tradition (*Nibelungenlied, Lied vom Hürnen Seyfrid*) the dragon does not bear a name. In Wagner's *Ring* cycle Fafner and his brother Fasolt are two giants who build Wotan's fortress Walhall. Fasolt is murdered by his brother who afterwards turns into a dragon.

[JLF]

FALKA, in the *Þiðreks saga,* Thidrek's horse; its brothers are Velent's and Vithga's horse Skemming, Heimir's mount Rispa, and Sigurd's Grani. Heimir selects Falka as a three-year-old foal from the stud of his father, Studas, and presents Falka to Thidrek. Falka twice breaks free of its reins to come to Thidrek's aid: when Ekka has Thidrek pinned to the ground, Falka breaks Ekka's back with his hooves; shortly thereafter, when the "elefans" has likewise pressed Thidrek to the ground, Falka pushes it away from Thidrek. Thettleif pawns Falka to procure gold to supply his men at Erminrek's festival. Thidrek lends Falka to Ulfrath so that Ulfrath can ride from the castle that is besieged by King Valdimar's army to alert Rothingeir. After he is crowned in Rome, Thidrek has a copper statue made of himself and Falka.

[FH]

FALLBORG, daughter of King Isung in the *Þiðreks saga.* After the contest between the champions of Thidrek and Isung, when Thidrek has defeated Sigurd in single combat, Sigurd suggests that Isung marry Fallborg to Omlung, one of Thidrek's twelve champions. Fallborg accompanies her husband Omlung from Bertangaland to Vindland.

[FH]

FASOLD (FASOLT, VÂSOLT), a long-haired giant, brother of Ecke, opponent of Dietrich von Bern in the *Eckenlied* and in the *Þiðreks saga.* In Tyrolean folk-myth, which seems strongly to have influenced the *Eckenlied,* Fasold was possibly originally a storm demon. In the *Eckenlied* Dietrich rescues a maiden from him in the forest, but Vâsolt threatens to hang them both. Dietrich overcomes him in battle, and Vâsolt swears loyalty to him, until he discovers that Dietrich has already slain Ecke. In the *Dresdner Heldenbuch* version of the *Eckenlied* and in Hans Sachs's *Tragödie von dem hürnen Seyfrid* (830), Dietrich is said to have slain Fasolt. In the *Þiðreks saga* Fasold accuses Thidrek of having slain Ekka in his sleep. Thidrek defeats him and Fasold joins Thidrek's band of warriors. He eventually dies at the hands of Hertnit, son of Osantrix. [JLF]

FENG. In the *Volsunga saga* Sigurd sets out to avenge his father Sigmund and takes on board his ship an old man who tells him that he is variously named Hnikar, Feng, or Fjolnir. He is, in fact, Odin. When the ship reaches land, Feng disappears.

[WM]

FJOLNIR, one of the names that Odin uses in the *Volsunga saga* (chapter 17) when, on the journey to the sons of Hunding, Sigurd is hailed by an old man on a craggy rock who asks that he be taken along on the trip. (see also FENG)

[WM]

FJORNIR. In the *Volsunga saga,* Gunnar's wife, Glaumvor, relates ominous dreams which she believes augur ill for her husband. The next day Gunnar has Fjornir, his cup bearer, serve him and his men generous quantities of wine, suggesting that this may in fact be the last banquet they celebrate together.

[WM]

FLORIGUNDA, in the *Historia vom dem gehörnten Siegfried,* is the name of the woman whom Siegfried rescues from a dragon. She corresponds to Krimhilt in the *Lied vom Hürnen Seyfrid.* The new name in itself indicates that the story has to some extent been revised in the spirit of the heroic novel of the Baroque age.

[JLF]

FOLKHER, in the *Þiðreks saga,* Hogni's kinsman and Gunnar's man. In the *Nibelungenlied* he appears as Volker. Folkher is not mentioned until an angry Hogni goes to tell him that he must accompany the Niflungs on their fateful journey to Attila's court. Like Hogni, Folkher adopts a belligerent attitude toward Grimhild. During the battle between the Huns and Niflungs, Folkher fights his way to the wounded Hogni. Thithrek kills Folkher, cutting off his head as Folkher stands guarding the doorway to the castle into which Hogni, Gislher, Gernoz, and Folkher have retreated.

[FH]

FREDEGUND(A), concubine of the Frankish king Chilperic, queen after murdering Gailswintha, sister of Brunhild. She had Sigibert, king of the Austrasian Franks, murdered in 575. Her original status and her role in the death of Sigibert are clearly sources for the later *Nibelungenlied,* although she has taken on the name of her rival in the poem.

[BOM]

FREY, in Scandinavian myth, one of three principal male deities, the god of fertility, sun, rain, and the harvest; the male counterpart of the fertility goddess Freyja. According to Saxo Grammaticus, the Swedes regarded Frey as the founder of their race and there was a temple built for him at Uppsala, where he was said to preside over sacrificial rites. In a motif later found in the *Volsunga saga,* Frey's servant Skirnir (probably an aspect of Frey himself) rides through a curtain of flame on horseback in a bid to woo Gerd (*Skirnismál*).

[JKW]

FREYA (variously **FREYJA, FRAIA**), a Scandinavian goddess whose name most likely means "the Lady," and who is the most important female deity in the *Edda.* Freya is the goddess of love, sexuality, and fertility, and is often portrayed as being promiscuous. She has also been connected with war, riding to battle in a chariot drawn by two cats, and with the world of the dead. In addition, Freya is said to have taught the gods witchcraft. In the *Lay of Hyndla,* Freya's human lover, Ottar, is told that he is a

kinsman both of Sigurd and of the Gjukungs (Burgundians).

[JKW]

FRICKA, the form of the name Frigg used by Richard Wagner in the *Ring des Nibelungen,* the goddess of love and marriage and the wife of Wotan. In *Das Rheingold* Fricka's pleas lead to the release of her sister Freia from Fasolt and Fafner the giants. In *Die Walküre* she acts as an advocate for the sanctity of marriage and is opposed to the adulterous love of Siegmund and Siegelinde; she subsequently convinces Wotan to abandon Siegmund.

[JKW]

FRIGG, a Scandinavian goddess who is Odin's wife and overseer of other goddesses who are often described as her maidservants. Frigg is a maternal figure, an image reinforced by her identity as the slain Balder's weeping mother, and was often invoked by women in labor. In the *Volsunga saga,* she hears the prayers of Rerir and his wife for a child and carries their request to Odin, who intervenes to bring about the birth of Volsung.

[JKW]

GA(I)LSWINTH(A), daughter of Athanagild, king of the Visigoths, and sister of Brunhild. Married to the Frankish king Chilperic and strangled at the instigation of his mistress Fredegund.

[BOM]

GELPFRAT, in the *Nibelungenlied,* margrave in Bavaria and brother of Else. He proves to be more than a match for Hagen in the twenty-sixth *âventiure* and the latter has to call to Dancwart, his brother for help. Gelpfrat falls by Dancwart's sword.

[WM]

GERBART, in the *Nibelungenlied,* one of Dietrich's men. Along with Ritschart, Helpfrich, and Wichart, he is mentioned in 2281 as a remarkable fighter, not given to sparing himself in battle. Dietrich also laments his death in 2323. The *Klage* indicates that he was killed by Giselher.

[WM]

GERE, in the *Nibelungenlied,* margrave and relative of the Burgundians. He is dispatched with the ill-fated invitation that brings Siegfried and Kriemhild back to Burgundy, and Siegfried, ultimately, to his death. Ordered by Gunther to serve Kriemhild after Siegfried's murder, Gere delivers the news that King Etzel of Hungary wishes to marry her and accompanies Kriemhild on her journey to the land of the Huns.

[KM]

GERNOT. In the *Nibelungenlied* and in the *Klage,* the brother of Gunther, Giselher, and Kriemhild, second son of Ute and Dancrat. In the highly charged first encounter between Siegfried and the Burgundians at Worms in the third *âventiure* of the *Nibelungenlied,* it is Gernot who shows restraint and courtly decorum and who attempts to diffuse a situation that is particularly volatile. His initial efforts are met with a considerable degree of arrogance by Siegfried, who provokes Hagen. He appears to be at odds with Hagen with respect to Siegfried's murder and the theft of the Nibelungen treasure from Kriemhild, but he never undertakes anything to address the problem. Like the other Burgundian kings, Gernot's behavior is, at best, ambivalent. He is a stalwart warrior, courageous, resolute, and can be counted upon during the final conflagration at the court of Etzel, but he never impresses the reader as a particularly unique individual. He dies at the hands of Rüdiger, while carrying the same sword that Rüdiger had presented to him earlier at Bechelaren.

[WM]

GERNOZ, in the *Þiðreks saga,* Gernoz is either the middle son (between Gunnar and Gislher) of Aldrian or the third son of King Irung and Oda. Gernoz is usually found in the presence of Gunnar and Hogni and takes part in their decision making. Although his role in Sigurth's death is not explicitly mentioned, he is present when Hogni murders Sigurth. Gernoz is one of the leaders of the Niflungs on their journey to Attila's court, and he shows great fighting ability against the Huns. Gernoz urges Thithrek to fight on the side of the Niflungs. After Gunnar's death Gernoz assumes leadership of the Niflungs. He slays Blothlin, one of Attila's men. One of the last of the Niflungs to fall (only Gislher and Hogni survive him), Gernoz is slain by Hildibrand. Grimhild thrusts a burning brand into his mouth to make certain that he is dead.

[FH]

GEVA LANGA (Geva the Long) is a figure in the Faeroese ballad *Hogna táttur.* In the final battle between the Niflungs and the Huns, a man called Geva the Long is ordered to come to Gudrun, Gjuki's daughter. She asks him to kill Hogni, who has murdered her little son. Geva is not successful, however, and Hogni's sword goes right through him. Geva is not mentioned anywhere else.

[GW]

Bibliography
Fuss, Klaus. *Die faröischen Lieder der Nibelungensage: Text, Lesarten, und Übersetzung.* Vol. 3: *Hoegni.* Göppingen: Kümmerle, 1987, p. 90.
Schneider, Hermann. *Germanische Heldensage.* Vol. 1. 2nd ed. Grundriss der germanischen Philologie 10/I. Berlin: de Gruyter, 1962, p. 112.

GIBALDUS, in the *Historia von dem gehörnten Siegfried,* Gibaldus or Gilbaldus in some early editions (Gybich in the *Lied vom Hürnen Seyfrid*), is the father of Florigunda. When Gibaldus learns of the murder of Siegfried, he dies of a broken heart; his wife then also succumbs after lying in fever for four days.

[JLF]

GIBECHE, exiled king at King Etzel's court, mentioned in the *Nibelungenlied* (1343,4; 1352,2; 1880,1). Gibeche always appears together with Ramunc von Vlachen and Hornboge, two of King Etzel's vassals. The same three men are also mentioned together in one scene in *Biterolf und Dietleib.* In *Dietrichs Flucht* the name is given to a counsellor at King Ermrich's court: Gibeche von Galaber (i.e., Calabria).

[NV]

GIBICA, first of the Burgundian kings named in the *Lex Burgundionum* and there associated with Gundahari. He is king of the Franks at Worms and the father of Guntharius in the *Waltharius,* king of the Burgundians in Anglo-Saxon writings, and father of Kriemhild in the Dietrich epics. In the *Edda* his equivalent, Gjuki, is the father of Gunnar, Hogni, and Gudrun. In the *Nibelungenlied* Dancrat is Gunther's father in most manuscripts, but he is named Gibîche in one late ms. (**k**). Gibeche is also a king in exile with Etzel.

[BOM]

GISELHER, in the *Nibelungenlied,* the youngest son of Dancrat (already deceased) and Ute, brother of Gunther, Gernot, and Kriemhild, who remains relatively well disposed towards him even following Siegfried's murder. Giselher expresses outrage over Hagen's plan to deprive Kriemhild of the Nibelung treasure, but does nothing to assist his sister when she appeals to him directly following the theft. This is not altogether surprising, as he had conveniently "left town" with his brothers, allowing Hagen to act on Gernot's suggestion that the hoard be sunk in the Rhine. On the way to Etzel's court in the second part of the *Nibelungenlied*, Giselher—at Hagen's instigation—is betrothed to Rüdiger's daughter during a short sojourn at Bechlarn. In the course of the fighting in the Great Hall of Etzel, Giselher advises the Burgundians/Nibelungs to eject the dead and wounded Huns; his reference to his own resolve (2011,4) earns him immediate praise from Hagen. A short while later, he and Wolfhart, one of Dietrich's men, kill each other in single combat. In the *Klage* Giselher is depicted as being greatly distressed over the death of his betrothed's father, Rüdiger, and his own death is viewed by the narrator as the worst loss sustained by the Burgundians. He is also absolved of any guilt with respect to the fate that befell Siegfried. In the *Þiðreks saga* he is the youngest son of King Aldrian. He defies his mother's (Ute's) wish to keep him at home while his brothers accept Attila's invitation to come to the land of the Huns. Margrave Rodinger presents him with two gifts: his daughter and the sword Gram, which had previously belonged to Sigfrid. It is with this sword that Gislher kills Rodinger in the subsequent fighting. Despite Hogni's efforts to have Grimhild grant him safe passage home, a defiant Gislher attacks Hildebrand and is killed by the old warrior.

[WM]

GISLAHARI, a Burgundian king named in the *Lex Burgundionum;* there is no indication that he is the brother of Gundahari, whom he precedes in the list, though the names equate to Giselher and Gunther.

[BOM]

GJAFLAUG, Gjuki's sister. She is mentioned in *Guðrúnarkviða in fyrsta* (first lay of Gudrun). She tries to comfort Gudrun, who is mourning for Sigurd but is unable to weep. She tells Gudrun that she has lost five husbands and eight brothers, yet she has to go on living. Stories of multiple widowhood are related several times in the sagas, and even Gudrun marries three times. According to the Eddic lays and the *Volsunga saga*, Gjaflaug's husbands are Sigurd, Atli, and Jonakr. Gjaflaug is an invention of the poet and her name is only mentioned here.

[GW]

Bibliography
de Vries, Jan. *Altnordische Literaturgeschichte.* Vol. 2. 2nd ed. Grundriss der germanischen Philologie 16. Berlin: de Gruyter, 1967, pp. 135–138.
Gering, Hugo, and B. Sijmons. *Kommentar zu den Liedern der Edda.* 2. Hälfte: *Heldenlieder.* Halle (Saale): Buchhandlung des Waisenhauses (Francke), 1931, p. 235.
Simek, Rudolf, and Hermann Pálsson. *Lexikon der altnordischen Literatur.* Stuttgart: Kröner, 1987, pp. 124f.

GJUKI (Old Norse *Giuka*), a southern Rhenish king, ruler of the Gjukungs and husband of the magically gifted Grimhild. He appears in the *Volsunga saga* and repeatedly throughout the *Edda*, particularly in conjunction with his hall or his daughter (*Hyndluljóð, Grípisspá, Fáfnismál, Brot af Sigurþarkviðu, Guðrúnarkviða I*). He is the father of Gunnar, Hogni, and Guttorm, as well as a daughter, Gudrun. In the *Volsunga saga*, he greets Sigurd in a most friendly manner, and Gjuki treats him like one of his sons. Gjuki is persuaded by Grimhild to offer Gudrun in marriage to Sigurd. In the *Hyndluljóð,* however, Guttorm is portrayed as Gjuki's stepson.

[WM]

GJUKUNGS, the name used to describe the people and descendants of Gjuki in the *Volsunga saga.* Their kingdom, located south of the Rhine, is said to have flourished as a result of the prowess of Gjuki's children. They later fight against King Atli and his troops but are defeated. From a structural point of view, they are analogous to the Burgundians in the *Nibelungenlied.*

[WM]

GLAUM, Atli's charger, referred to in the thirty-second stanza of the *Atlakviða.*

[WM]

GLAUMVOR, Gunnar's wife in the *Volsunga saga,* "a woman of noble character," who has prophetic powers. She and Kostbera serve Gunnar and Hogni the drink that inebriates them and causes them to succumb to Vingi's ruse to lure them to Atli's camp. Her dream presaging Gunnar's death is not heeded by her husband.

[JHS]

GNITAHEATH, in the *Volsunga saga,* the heath where the serpent/dragon Fafnir, according to his brother Regin, has his lair and watches over his hoard. Gunnar and Hogni eventually acquire all of the gold there. The Gnitaheath is also alluded to in the *Grípisspá, Reginsmál, Fáfnismál,* and the *Atlakviða.*

[WM]

GOLNIR, a giant in the *Volsunga saga.* Sinfjotli insults Granmar by telling him that he was Golnir's goatherd.

[BS]

GOLDRUN, in the *Klage,* Goldrun is the daughter of King Liudeger of France, one of the eighty-six ladies at Etzel's court, raised and educated by Helche.

[BS]

GOTELIND. In the *Nibelungenlied,* Gotelind is the courtly wife of Rüdiger and the generous hostess in Pöchlarn where she receives Kriemhild on her way to Etzelnburg. She later receives Etzel's messengers Wärbel and Swemmel on their way to Worms, and then hosts the Burgundians on their way to Etzelnburg when she gives Hagen the shield of Nuodung as a gift. In the *Þiðreks saga,* Nuodung is identified as her dead brother. In the *Klage,* Gotelind has dreams portending Rüdiger's death before Etzel's mes-

sengers bring her the news. Struck by grief, she is no longer able to function as a hostess to the messengers. She dies of grief three days before Dietrich, Herrat, and Hildebrand reach Pöchlarn.

[BS]

GOTHS. Germanic tribe, migrated in the first century from Scandinavia to the area around the lower Vistula, where they then expanded their territory to include the plains north of the Black Sea. In the fourth century two tribes can be distinguished: Visigoths and Ostrogoths. About 375 a.d. both tribes were forced by the Huns either to flee or to subject themselves. The Visigoths moved as far as Spain, where their kingdom was finally destroyed by the Moors in 711. The Ostrogoths occupied Hungary and Italy, where they were defeated by the Byzantines in 555. Reminders of the relationship between the Huns and subjected elements among the Goths can be found in the *Nibelungenlied* and in other heroic poems, in which the ruler of the Huns, Attila (MHG *Etzel*), appears as the protector of the exiled Ostrogothic king, Theodoric the Great (MHG *Dietrich von Bern*). The name of the Goths, however, never appears in these poems.

[NV]

GOTI, the name of the horse ridden by Gunnar in the *Volsunga saga* during his expedition to woo Brynhild. The horse balks when Gunnar attempts to urge it through the ring of fire that surrounds her hall.

[WM]

GRAN (Latin *Strigonium*), mentioned in the *Nibelungenlied* (1497,2) and in *Dietrichs Flucht* (4545) is located near Ofen, Hungary, on the banks of the Danube across from the estuary of the Gran River. King Geza (970–997) made Gran the capital of the Arpad dukedom. In 1001 King Stephan I was born in Gran, which from then on became the site of the royal coronations in Hungary and also the seat of an archbishop. The *Nibelungenlied* poet describes Gran as a city in the center of which is a formidable castle, the residence of the Hunnish King Etzel or Attila (1497). It is also in Gran where the final, pitched battle between the Burgundians and Kriemhild's forces takes place and where the Burgundians are decimated. The *Klage* poet discusses in great detail the extensive mourning and burial of the dead at Gran.

[AC]

Bibliography

Schünemann, K. *Die Entstehung des Städtewesens in Südost-Europa.* Breslau-Oppeln: Priebatsch, 1929.

GRANI/GRANE is Sigurd's horse in the *Þiðreks saga.* The blacksmith Mime advises Sigurd to ask for this horse at Brynhild's stud farm and he receives the stallion as a present during his first visit to Brynhild. Grani is the brother of Falka, Skemming, and Rispa, yet he is the best of all these horses. The lays of the *Edda* and the *Volsunga saga* tell us a somewhat different story: Grani is bred on Hjalprek's stud farm. Sigurd chooses the horse himself. A bearded man (Odin) drives Hjalprek's horses into a river. All the animals except Grani quickly swim out of the water, and so Sigurd chooses this young, grey, and strong stallion. Nobody has hitherto ridden the horse. Sigurd is informed by Odin that Grani is a brother of Sleipnir, Odin's horse. Only Sigurd is able to ride Grani, and so it is Sigurd on Grani's back who is able to ride through the wall of flames of the *vafrlogi.* Grani has a human mind and therefore can mourn for Sigurd after his death, and Gudrun can talk to him at that time. According to the *Þiðreks saga,* Gunnar gives the horse to Thidrek after Sigurd's murder.

[GW]

Bibliography

Tuppa, Gerlinde. "Die Bedeutung der Tiere und der Tiermotive in der germanischen Heldensage." Diss., Vienna, 1965, pp. 270ff.

GRANMAR, the father of King Hodbrodd in the *Volsunga saga.* He is also referred to, however, as Hodbrodd's brother. Granmar engages in a taunting scene with Sinfjotli, but nothing is reported of his fate in the ensuing battle between the Volsungs and the forces of King Hodbrodd.

[WM]

GRIMHILD (1), in the *Volsunga saga,* the wife of King Gjuki and mother of Gunnar, Hogni, Guttorm, and Gudrun. Grimhild is gifted in the art of magic. In a number of instances she is also the person chiefly responsible for the events that lead to the death of Sigurd. In accordance with Brynhild's prophecy Grimhild provides Sigurd with a potion that causes him to forget Brynhild and is instrumental in arranging the marriage between Sigurd and Gudrun. She prompts Gunnar to woo Brynhild and is also responsible for urging Guttorm to murder Sigurd. Further, Grimhild engineers the reconciliation between Gudrun and her brothers, once again through the use of a magic drink that causes her daughter to forget what has happened, and recommends that Gudrun marry the Hun, Atli. In *Guðrúnarkviða II* (The Second Lay of Gudrun), Gudrun relates how her mother, Grimhild, attempted to determine if her brothers were willing to make amends for the killing of Sigurd and his son, Sigmund. Grimhild is also reported here to have provided her daughter with a goblet filled with a potion of forgetfulness, which does not, however, appear to have been particularly effective.

[WM]

GRIMHILD (2), in the *Þiðreks saga,* the strong-willed daughter of Aldrian and his queen and sister to Gunnar, Gernoz, Gislher (or in a variant scribal tradition, daughter of Irung and Oda and sister to Gunnar, Guthorm, Gernoz, and Gislher). She is Hogni's half sister. After Thidrek has defeated Sigurd in the contest between Thidrek's and Isung's champions, Thidrek, his men, and Sigurd ride to Niflungaland. There Sigurd is married to Grimhild and receives one half of Gunnar's kingdom. Grimhild's quarrel with Brynhild over which of them is preeminent leads to Brynhild's humiliation and results in Sigurd's murder by Grimhild's brothers. Following Sigurd's death, Grimhild agrees to marry Atli but weeps for Sigurd daily. After seven winters in Húnaland she convinces Atli to invite her brothers to Susa. Grimhild gathers a great force of men. As she welcomes her brothers, she weeps for Sigurd and asks for his treasure. Grimhild attempts to enlist the aid of Thidrek, Blodlin, Atli, and Irung to avenge Sigurd, but all refuse except Irung. Grimhild precipitates later hostilities by urging her son, Aldrian, to strike Hogni in the face. Hogni beheads Aldrian and flings the child's head at Grimhild's breast. During the ensuing battle Grimhild distributes weapons and promises gold and silver to all who will fight the Niflungs. She has her captured brother Gunnar cast into a snake pit and has the Huns set fire to the hall in which the rest of the Niflungs have taken refuge. To assure herself that her brothers Gernoz and Gislher are dead, she thrusts a burning brand into their mouths. Atli orders Thidrek to kill her, and Thidrek does so by cutting her in half.

[FH]

GRIMHILDE, the mother of Gunther and Hagen in Wagner's *Ring des Nibelungen.* Grimhilde and King Gibich are the parents of Gunther, the legitimate heir to the Burgundian throne. Alberich uses his wealth to persuade Grimhilde to bear him a son (Hagen). Thus, as in the *Þiðreks saga,* Wagner's Gunther and Hagen are stepbrothers; everything else is Wagner's invention.

[UM]

GRIÞIR, Sigurd's maternal uncle in the *Volsunga saga.* Renowned for his ability as a soothsayer, he is sought out by his nephew and, although reluctant to do so, foretells Sigurd's future.

[WM]

GROSSMEHRING (MHG *Moeringen*), a small town on the left bank of the Danube, about 15 kilometers east of Ingolstadt in Bavaria, where the Burgundians cross the river on their way to the land of the Huns. In the *Nibelungenlied* it is mentioned only once (1591,1). It is the place where the water sprites predict to Hagen that none of the Burgundians shall return, where Hagen slays the ferryman, and where he flings the chaplain overboard.

[NV]

GUÐRÚN (*Gudrun*). In the Norse versions of the Nibelung cycle (*Edda, Volsunga saga*), Kriemhild appears as Gudrun. The *Þiðreks saga* uses both names, more frequently Grimhild (corresponding to the Low German version) but occasionally also Gudrun. Her name alliterates even better than Kriemhild with her brother's name Gunnar/Gunther, for both names contain *gunnr/guþr,* which means *battle* or *fight.* In the Norse version the name Grimhild is given to

Gudrun's mother, who is called Uote in the *Nibelungenlied.*

Gudrun is a very popular name in Norway and Iceland, yet we do not know why the best-known female figure in medieval Germanic literature was given a new name in the Norse tales. There seems to be no connection to the heroine of the South German epic *Kudrun.* Gudrun, the daughter of King Gjuki and his wife Grimhild, has three brothers: Gunnar, Hogni, and Guthorm (according to the *Hyndluljóð* Guthorm is only her stepbrother) and one sister, Gullrond. After a happy youth she marries Sigurd, whom she loves dearly. She gives birth to two children, Sigmund and Svanhild. Brynhild, Atli's sister, and Gudrun's brothers envy her. When Gudrun accuses Brynhild of having given herself to Sigurd, Sigurd is killed by the Niflungs. Most of the versions say he is killed while lying in bed beside Gudrun. Even Gudrun's little son, Sigmund, is murdered. When Gudrun wakes up lying in Sigurd's blood, her dying husband tries to comfort her. She is so full of grief that she cannot weep. Only when her sister Gullrond unveils Sigurd's dead body, does Gudrun burst into tears. She cries so bitterly that the geese begin to chatter loudly and Brynhild wakes up and begins to laugh in triumph. Gudrun tells Gunnar that the possession of Sigurd's hoard will cause his downfall and she curses Brynhild. Only Hogni confesses to the murder. Gudrun hopes that Hogni's heart will be torn apart by ravens, but Hogni answers that she will be even more unhappy if her curses are realized.

Gudrun leaves her home and spends three and a half years in Denmark doing needlework together with Thora, King Hakon's daughter. Grimhild finds out where Gudrun lives and arranges for the brothers to pay a fine to their sister. It is Grimhild together with her sons, who decides that Gudrun should marry Atli. When Atli sends his messengers, Grimhild brews a draught of forgetfulness. As a result, Gudrun accepts compensation and marries Atli, with whom she later has two sons, Erp and Eitil, but they do not lead a happy married life.

Atli tries secretly to send messengers to Gunnar and Hogni to invite them to his court with the intent of procuring their treasure. Gudrun finds out and tries to warn her brothers. She sends them a ring with a wolf's hair woven into it and uses runes to convey her message, but these signals are altered by Atli's messenger. Kostbera, Hogni's wife, recognizes that Gudrun's information has been distorted, but Gunnar and Hogni cannot be persuaded not to risk the journey. When Gudrun hears that her brothers are already engaged in fighting with the Huns she takes off her jewelery and joins them. When she does not succeed in making peace between the opponents, she herself takes up a sword, cuts off the leg of Atli's brother, and kills a second Hun. Atli is furious and accuses her of being the cause of Brynhild's death, an allusion to the initial quarrel between the two queens that set the chain of events in motion that lead to Brynhild's suicide. Gudrun reminds her husband that he murdered her mother because of her treasures and that he starved her cousin in a cave (details which are only mentioned in the *Atlamál*). Full of hate for his wife, Atli orders the murder of Gunnar and Hogni.

The episode involving Herkja, Atli's concubine, who slanders Gudrun and is forced by Atli into a trial by ordeal that culminates in her being sentenced to death, does not correspond to Gudrun's life story because the main sources (*Atlakviða* and *Atlamál*) tell us that she took revenge on Atli immediately after her brothers' deaths. Gudrun persuades her sons Erp and Eitill to follow her, cuts their throats, and turns their skulls into goblets which she fills with a drink blending it with their blood. Atli is forced to drink this mixture and eat the roasted hearts of his sons. Atli threatens to have Gudrun stoned and then cremated on a pyre but she knows that her life will continue. Finally she kills Atli with the help of Hniflung, Hogni's son. In the *Atlakviða* Gudrun burns Atli in his hall. In the *Atlamál* Gudrun buys a ship (a pagan motif) and a coffin (a Christian motif) for Atli's burial. Ship burials and grave chambers were commonly used during the Viking Age, but there is no evidence that the corpse was ever placed inside a coffin in the funeral ship. According to this older tradition, Gudrun appears to be the avenger of her brothers. She is not responsible for her brothers' deaths, as Kriemhild is in the *Nibelungenlied*. After the murder of Atli, Gudrun tries to drown herself but she is washed ashore alive in Jonakr's territory. She marries King Jonakr and bears him three sons, Sorli, Hamdir, and Erp

(according to the *Hamðismál,* Erp is Jonakr's son but not Gudrun's). Svanhild, Sigurd's daughter, grows up at Jonakr's court. Gudrun loves her dearly and marries her off to the Gothic king Jormunrek. Svanhild is slandered by Bikki, Jormunrek's advisor, and is sentenced to death. Gudrun provokes her sons, Hamdir and Sorli, the last Niflungs, to avenge their sister. The two kill their (step)brother Erp, whose help they disdain. Eventually both are killed in Jormunrek's court. Gudrun is now completely unhappy and without friends. She wants Sigurd to return from Hel and take her with him into the kingdom of the dead.

Different versions of Gudrun's death are told in the *Hven Chronicle* and in the Faroese ballad *Hogna táttur.* The *Hven Chronicle* tells us that Gudrun/Kriemhild is starved to death by Hogni's son. In the *Hogna táttur* both Artala (Atli) and Gudrun meet their deaths in this way.

[GW]

Bibliography

Haymes, Edward R., and Susann T. Samples. *Heroic Legends of the North: An Introduction to the Nibelung and Dietrich Cycles.* New York: Garland, 1996, pp. 152f.

Vestergaard, Elisabeth. "Gudrun/Kriemhild—soster eller husfru?" *Arkiv för nordisk filologi* 99 (1984): 63–78.

Zeller, Rose. *Die Gudrunlieder der Edda.* Stuttgart: Kohlhammer, 1939.

GULLROND. In *Guðrúnarkviða in fyrsta* (First Lay of Gudrun) Gullrond is the name of a woman who tries to comfort Gudrun, who is mourning for Sigurd and is unable to weep. She is called Gjuki's daughter and therefore she must be Gudrun's sister. She unveils Sigurd's dead body and asks Gudrun to kiss him on his mouth, and so she makes Gudrun weep for her husband. Then she praises the deep love between Sigurd and Gudrun. Only now can Gudrun talk about her great loss. When Brynhild gets angry about Gullrond having caused this outbreak, Gullrond asks her to be quiet because she blames the disaster of Sigurd's death on Brynhild. The figure is an invention of the poet of this Eddic lay. Her name is only mentioned once more in the *Flateyjarbók: Aettartala frá Hoð* (Book of Flatey: family tree of Hod). Its author must have known this lay.

[GW]

Bibliography

Gering, Hugo, and B. Sijmons. *Kommentar zu den Liedern der Edda.* 2. Hälfte: *Heldenlieder.* Halle (Saale): Buchhandlung des Waisenhauses (Francke), 1931, pp. 237ff.

de Vries, Jan. *Altnordische Literaturgeschichte.* Vol. 2. 2nd ed. Grundriss der germanischen Philologie 16. Berlin: de Gruyter, 1967, pp. 135–138.

Simek, Rudolf, and Hermann Pálsson. *Lexikon der altnordischen Literatur.* Stuttgart: Kröner, 1987, pp. 124f.

GUNDAHARI (GUNTHARIUS), named in the *Lex Burgundionum* and, according to the historian Prosper of Aquitaine, king of the Burgundians when they were defeated by Aetius and a force of Hunnish auxiliaries in 435/437. One of the allies of Gundahari was the khan or khagan Goar of the Alans, who may have served as a model for the figure of Hagen. In the *Waltharius* Guntharius is the king of the Franks.

[BOM]

GUNDOMAR, a Burgundian king listed in the *Lex Burgundionum,* perhaps linked with the Norse Guþorm, half brother of Gunnar and Hogni in the *Edda* and the *Þiðreks saga.* The Frankish name Gernot has replaced this Burgundian one as the third brother of Gunther.

[BOM]

GUNNAR of the *Poetic Edda,* the *Volsunga saga,* and the *Þiðreks saga* corresponds to Gunther in the *Nibelungenlied.* Gunnar, king of the Burgundians, is the son of Gjuki and Grimhild, the brother of Hogni, of Guthorm (sometimes Guthorm is his stepbrother), of Gudrun, and of Gullrond. When Sigurd marries Gudrun, he becomes Gunnar's brother-in-law, and he is his blood brother. On Grimhild's advice Gunnar woos Brynhild. On his journey he is accompanied by Sigurd and even exchanges shapes with him, because he is unable to pass through the wall of flame around her hall. He marries Brynhild on the same day as Sigurd marries Gudrun. Brynhild cannot forget Sigurd, whom she met before on Hindarfell, and therefore she leads an unhappy married life with Gunnar. Gunnar listens to his wife when she slanders Sigurd, pretending he broke his oath. She provokes Gunnar into murdering Sigurd by threatening to leave him. Gunnar is very upset about her rude remarks, but he does not have any solution for his difficulties. He would rather die than lose Brynhild and her treasures. He consults Hogni about their concerted actions against Sigurd. They decide that Guthorm should kill Sigurd, because their younger brother did not swear an oath to Sigurd. After Sigurd's death, Gunnar is unable to speak to Gudrun. She calls him a murderer and curses him. When Grimhild wants him to fine Gudrun heavily, he is willing to do so. Gunnar scolds Brynhild for laughing about Sigurd's death and threatens to murder Atli, Brynhild's brother. But Brynhild knows that Atli will live much longer than Gunnar and his brothers. Gunnar cannot prevent his wife from committing suicide. The dying Brynhild predicts his future for him. Gunnar and Hogni take possession of Sigurd's gold.

Gunnar marries Glaumvor. When Atli extends an invitation to Gunnar and Hogni, Gudrun, now Atli's wife, tries in vain to warn her brothers. Glaumvor's troubling dreams do not hinder Gunnar, although he understands their warning. When he arrives at Atli's court, Gudrun warns him once again that Atli will betray him and cast him into the snake yard or snake pit (according to the *Þiðreks saga,* the dungeon is a snake tower in the middle of Susa). Gunnar and Hogni are helped by Gudrun in the final battle against the Huns. Although Gunnar defends himself bravely, he is taken prisoner. (The *Þiðreks saga* relates a different story: Gunnar is the first one of the Niflungs who is taken prisoner during the breakout from Holmgard.) He is asked whether he will give gold in order to be released, but before he consents to this he wants to see Hogni's heart as proof of his death. The Huns bring him the heart of the serf Hjalli, which trembles so much that it cannot be Hogni's heart. Now the Huns kill Hogni and eventually Gunnar is the only one left who knows where Sigurd's treasure is sunk in the Rhine. Atli will never possess the gold, so he orders that Gunnar be cast into the snake pit. There he plays the harp that Gudrun has sent to him, either with his hands or with his toes, stilling the serpents until one of them eventually kills him. According to the *Nornagests þáttr* Gunnar sings a minstrel lay (*Gunnarsslagr*), probably a fierce lament over the wrong done to him. Gudrun mourns deeply over the loss of her brother. Ragnar Loðbrok's death in a snake pit reflects the end of Gunnar's life (note *Ragnars saga loðbrókar*) in a thoughtless manner.

One episode of Gunnar's life does not fit into this story. It is the episode concerning Oddrun, the sister of Brynhild and Atli. After Brynhild's death Gunnar seeks Oddrun's hand but is refused by Atli. The lovers meet secretly but are discovered by Atli's men. When Gunnar is cast into the snake pit, Oddrun tries to save him. Although Gunnar plays the harp to calm the snakes, Oddrun is too late: Atli's mother, in form of a serpent, has already killed him. This death scene is very impressive, because it transforms Gunnar into a Christ-Orpheus figure, calming the evil serpents by his playing of the harp. In comparison to the *Nibelungenlied* Gunnar is given a role of the greatest importance in the confrontation with Atli in the *Poetic Edda* and in the *Volsunga saga*. The secondary role he plays in the *Nibelungenlied* is reflected in the *Þiðreks saga*, in the *Rosengarten*, and in *Biterolf und Dietleib*. In the *Nibelungenlied* his parents are called Dancrat and Ute. His brothers are Gernot and Giselher, and his sister is Kriemhild. Hagen is not his brother, he is his loyal vassal. At Etzel's court he is defeated in single combat by Dietrich von Bern. Eventually he is beheaded on Kriemhild's orders. According to the *Þiðreks saga*, Hogni is a half brother to Gunnar, Gernoz, and Gislher, and his sister is called Grimhild or Gudrun. His father is an elf, a supernatural being who appeared to his mother during the king's absence. His mother is Oda, who is married to Aldrian (or Irung) of Niflungaland.

Gunnar also appears in different versions of the Walther story (see *Waltharilied*) as an avaricious and greedy king who tries to rob Walther and Hildegund of their treasure. In a fierce fight Walther strikes off King Gunnar's leg.

[GW]

Bibliography

Harris, Joseph. "Guðrúnarbrögð and the Saxon Lay of Grimhild's Perfidy." *Mediaeval Scandinavia* 9 (1976): 173–180.

Haymes, Edward R., and Susann T. Samples. *Heroic Legends of the North: An Introduction to the Nibelung and Dietrich Cycles*. New York: Garland, 1996, p. 149.

McTurk, Rory. "The Relationship of Ragnars Saga Loðbrókar to Þiðreks saga af Bern." In vol. 2 of *Sjötíu Ritgerðir helgaðir Jakobi Benediktsyni 20 juli 1977*, edited by Einar G. Péttursson and Jónas Kristjánsson. Reykjavík: Stofnun Arna Magnússonar, 1977, pp. 568–585.

Schneider, Hermann. *Germanische Heldensage*. Vol. 1. 2nd ed. Grundriss der germanischen Philologie 10/I. Berlin: de Gruyter, 1962, pp. 129ff.

GUNTHER, brother of Kriemhild and one of the three Burgundian kings (with Giselher and Gernot) in the *Nibelungenlied*. Gunther at first welcomes Siegfried as a potential ally when the latter comes to Worms, and his courtesy is rewarded when Siegfried defends the Burgundians against a Saxon/Danish invasion. Siegfried offers his assistance when Gunther seeks the hand of Brünhild, although he declares in strophe 388 that he does not agree to help Gunther out of any friendship towards the Burgundian king, but rather on account of his sister, Kriemhild. It is clear that by himself or with his brothers, Gunther would have been unequal to the task of wooing the Icelandic queen and would doubtless have lost his life in pursuit of her. Persuading Gunther to overcome his fear in his contests with Brünhild, it is Siegfried who dons the *tarnkappe* that renders him invisible and assists the Burgundian king in defeating the queen and in therefore winning her hand for Gunther.

Likewise in Gunther's attempt to consummate his union with Brünhild, it is Siegfried who must step in to tame the maiden, whose superhuman strength he alone could overcome. Although at first Gunther does not resent the superior strength of Siegfried, and indeed seems genuinely grateful to his Netherlandic friend for his help, it is not long before the rivalry between Kriemhild and Brünhild leads him to become ambivalent in his attitude towards his sister's husband. Despite Siegfried's solemn denial of the charge of having taken Brünhild's maidenhood, Gunther eventually acquiesces in Hagen's plan to murder him, although his motivations for doing so appear to be multidimensional.

Following Siegfried's death and Kriemhild's period of mourning, Gunther wins Kriemhild's confidence again so that she will have the Nibelungen hoard, her dowry from Siegfried, brought to the Burgundian kingdom.

However, Gunther again betrays his sister, by allowing Hagen to seize the treasure and sink it in the Rhine.

Although Gunther is presented on these occasions as being persuaded by Hagen to undertake or authorize treachery towards his sister and brother-in-law, rather than as the instigator of these nefarious deeds, on two instances he does go against the counsel of his advisor. The first occurs when Etzel sends Rüdiger with a proposal of marriage to Kriemhild. Hagen warns that by marrying the powerful Hunnish ruler (by all accounts in the *Nibelungenlied,* a much more powerful figure than Gunther himself) Kriemhild will ultimately gain the means to wreak her revenge on the Burgundians. Despite the warning, Gunther overrules Hagen and thus provides Kriemhild with the opportunity to seek her revenge on her brothers and, in particular, on Hagen. When, after consolidating her position in Etzel's court as a worthy successor to Queen Helche, Kriemhild persuades Etzel to invite the Burgundians to a festival in his court, Gunther again dismisses Hagen's premonitions of disaster. Gunther's failure to heed Hagen's warning ultimately leads to the destruction of the entire body of Burgundians when they travel to Etzel's court in Hungary and are greeted with the full fury of Kriemhild's revenge.

It is in the journey to Hungary and the battle scenes at Etzel's court that we see the full measure of Gunther's character: despite the multiplying portents of disaster and his increasing realization that Kriemhild's anger has not abated even after the passage of so many years, Gunther pushes forward relentlessly as if unable to recoil from the danger in which he has placed himself and his entourage. His pride and his sense of honor prevent him from turning back from the impending disaster. During the series of skirmishes at Etzel's court, which form the climax of the poem, and in particular in the scene in which his erstwhile friend Rüdiger enters the fray on Etzel's behalf, Gunther demonstrates both a magisterial courtliness and a savage fury in battle that are characteristic of the medieval warrior-king. Although his exploits in these final battles are somewhat overshadowed by those of Hagen, he nonetheless demonstrates his fierceness and bravery time after time during the siege by Etzel's forces. After his and Hagen's capture at the hands of Dietrich, Hagen refuses to reveal the location of the hidden Nibelungen treasure to Kriemhild, declaring that he has sworn to keep its location secret as long as any one of his lords is still alive. Kriemhild commands that Gunther be killed and has his severed head brought before his liegeman Hagen, whose prophecy of the downfall of the Burgundians Gunther had ignored.

[JHS]

GUNTHER JR. In the *Nibelungenlied* Siegfried and Kriemhild have one child, a son, whom they name Gunther, "nâch sînem oeheim" (after his uncle, 716,2). Following the murder of Siegfried, Kriemhild entrusts the raising of young Gunther entirely to his grandparents in Xanten and never again lays eyes on him.

[WM]

GUNTHRAM (GUNTRAMM), Frankish king of Burgundy and brother of Sigibert, who aided him against the Saxons in 572. On his death in 592 his lands were ruled by Sigibert's widow, Brunhild. His name is linked with Guthorm in the *Edda,* though some of his character and history may be sources for Gunther.

[BOM]

GUTHILINDA (1), appears in the *Þiðreks saga* as the eldest of the nine daughters of the late King Drusian of Drekanfils. Thidrek, Fasold, and Thetleif ride to Drekanfils and ask for the three eldest daughters in marriage. During a nine-day wedding feast, Thidrek marries Guthilinda, who returns with him to Bern.

[FH]

GUTHILINDA (2), in the *Þiðreks saga,* sister to Duke Naudung and wife of Rothingeir. She receives Thidrek courteously when he rides to Rothingeir's castle after having escaped Erminrek. When the Niflungs stop at Bakalar on their ill-fated journey to Húnaland, Guthilinda welcomes them and agrees that Rothingeir marry their daughter to Gislher. She weeps when Rothingeir presents the late Naudung's shield to Hogni. When Rothingeir sets out to accompany the Niflungs to Húnaland, he asks Guthilinda to rule his land well until they meet again.

[FH]

GUTHORM (Norse *Guþorm*), in the *Þiðreks saga,* the second son of Irung (doubtless a scribal error for Aldrian) and Oda. He is the brother of Gunnar, Gernoz, Gislher, and Grimhild, the half brother of Hogni. Guthorm is the only one of the brothers who is not specifically mentioned as having made the journey to Atli's court. His role in the *Þiðreks saga* is a secondary one. In Eddic poetry however, Guthorm is a more prominent figure. This is particularly true of the many references to him in the so-called *Poetic Edda*. In *Sigurþarkviða hin skamma* (The Short Lay of Sigurd), Guthorm is the killer of Sigurd, having been egged on by his brothers, and is himself slain by the dying Sigurd. In *Guðrúnarkviða onnur* (The Second Lay of Gudrun), Hogni tells Gudrun that Sigurd, the slayer of Guthorm, has been killed. *Gripisspá* (Gripir's Prophecy) implicates Guthorm in Sigurd's death. *Brot af Sigurþarkviðu* (Fragment of a Sigurd Lay) implies that Guthorm was one of several killers of Sigurd. In *Hyndluljód* (The Lay of Hyndla), however, Guthorm is said only to be the brother of Gunnar, Hogni, and Gudrun, but not of the line of Gjuki. In the *Skaldskaparmál* (Poetic Diction) section of *Edda Snorra Sturlusonar* (The Edda of Snorri Sturluson), Guthorm is Gjuki's stepson and the brother of Gunnar and Hogni who goad Guthorm into killing Sigurd. Guthorm stabs a sleeping Sigurd who awakens and flings his sword Gram at the retreating Guthorm, cutting him in half.

[FH]

GUTRUNE, sister of Gunther and wife of Siegfried in Wagner's *Ring des Nibelungen.* Wagner depicts her, in contrast to Kriemhild in the *Nibelungenlied,* as a woman who becomes Siegfried's wife only through a fraud conceived by Hagen.

[UM]

GUTTORM (GUTTORMR GJUKASSON see also GUTHORM), one of King Gjuki's three sons in the *Volsunga saga* (the others being Gunnar and Hogni). Through sorcery and the promise of wealth, his brothers incite him to murder the sleeping Sigurd. After stabbing him, the fleeing Guttorm is killed by the dying Sigurd, who throws his sword Gram across the room, cutting the murderer in two. Guttorm's remains are cremated along with those of Sigurd and Brynhild on a single pyre.

[JHS]

GYBICH, in the *Lied vom Hürnen Seyfrid* (strophe 16) and Hans Sachs's *Der hürnen Seufrid,* king at Worms and father of Krimhilt, Günther, Hagen and Gyrnot. Similarly in *Waltharius* and the *Rosengarten* poems where he is called Gibicho and Gibeche respectively. The name Gibica already appears among the ancestors of the Burgundian king Gundobad in the *Lex Burgundionum* of 516. In Norse tradition the father of Gunnar, Hogni and Gudrun is named Gjuki. In the *Nibelungenlied* (7,2) Gunther's father is called Dancrat, but the name Gibeche is given to an exiled king at Etzel's court (*Nibelungenlied* 1343,4).

[JLF]

GYRNOT, in the *Lied vom Hürnen Seyfrid* (str. 176) and Hans Sachs's *Der hürnen Seufrid* (l. 1003), Gyrnot is one of the sons of Gybich, corresponding to Gernot in the *Nibelungenlied.*

[JLF]

HADEBURG, the first of two water sprites encountered by Hagen in the twenty-fifth *âventiure* of the *Nibelungenlied* while leading the Burgundians to the land of the Huns. In an effort to have Hagen return the clothes he has stolen from her and her sister, Sigelind, Hadeburg predicts that the Burgundians will fare well in Hungary (1537), a blatant lie that is, however, countered by Sigelind's accurate prediction of their fate (1539f.).

[WM]

HAGBARD I, mentioned briefly in chapter 9 of the *Volsunga saga* as the son of Hunding who is killed in battle against Helgi.

[WM]

HAGBARD II, a king in the *Volsunga saga.* When Gudrun asks Brynhild who she considers to be the greatest kings, she names Hagbard and his brother Haki, sons of Hamund, and renowned for their prowess in battle. Gudrun is not impressed, however, referring to any lack of initiative aimed at avenging the abduction of one of their one sisters and the murder of another by Sigar.

[WM]

HAGEN (see also HOGNI), one of the major figures in the Nibelungen tradition. He is the son of Aldrian, the brother of Dancwart, and hence uncle to Gunther, Gernot, Giselher, and Kriemhild. In his youth he was a hostage, together with Walther of Spain and Hildegund, at the court of Etzel the Hun. In the *Nibelungenlied* he is not only a relative of the Burgundian royal family, but also serves them as a vassal. Hagen has knowledge of the otherworld and it is he who, in the third *âventiure,* informs Gunther of Siegfried's adventures in that sphere. His attitude toward Siegfried is strained somewhat from the outset owing to the arrogant behavior of the latter on his arrival in Worms. He becomes an adversary of Siegfried and it is clear that the two will never enjoy a close relationship as fellow warriors. Hagen's efforts are directed towards the utilization of Siegfried's skills in the interest of Worms, first in the campaign against the Danes and the Saxons, and then in the endeavor to procure Brünhild as a bride for Gunther. His primary motivation, however, appears to be the enhancement of Burgundian power and prestige, although it is conceivable that he derives a certain degree of personal satisfaction in having Siegfried perform a variety of tasks, including some he may deem somewhat menial (e.g., serving as an envoy), in the hope of eventually obtaining Kriemhild as his bride. Hagen is primarily clan oriented, as is evident in his reaction to Kriemhild's request that he and other Burgundians accompany her back to Siegfried's home in Xanten. Infuriated at the suggestion that he leave Worms, Hagen makes it unmistakably clear that his family, the Tronecks, have always served the Burgundian kings at Worms, and that Gunther himself cannot simply transfer his service to another. Hagen's stature is such that Kriemhild's request is immediately dropped.

While there are reasons why Hagen would have been less than favorably disposed towards Siegfried prior to the embarrassment caused to the Burgundian court through the public argument of Brünhild and Kriemhild before the Worms Cathedral, the "revelation" that Siegfried appears to have robbed Brünhild of her maidenhood provides the immediate impetus for his promise to Brünhild that Siegfried will pay for the deed (note 864). Although he encounters initial opposition from the Burgundian kings to the idea of killing Siegfried, Hagen is ultimately successful in winning over Gunther, among other things by showing how his power will increase yet further with Siegfried gone. The king may also be swayed by the growing discontent of his own people over the manner in which Siegfried's knights behave (note 871). The darker side of Hagen is particularly reflected in the manner in which he goes about obtaining information on Siegfried's vulnerable spot from Kriemhild. The murder itself appears to be condemned by all and sundry, including the narrator. There is little that can change the patently negative image of Hagen spearing Siegfried from behind because Siegfried was, after all, a guest at the Burgundian court. At the same time, however, Hagen was powerless to act against the near invulnerable hero in any other way. A fair contest of arms was out of the question. Considerable insight into Hagen's state of mind at this point is provided by strophe 993, in which he attempts to counter Gunther's somewhat belated remorse over the act:

Dô sprach der grimme Hagene: "jane weiz ich, waz ir kleit.
ez hât nu allez ende   unser sorge unt unser leit.
wir vinden ir vil wênic, die getürren uns bestân.
wol mich, deich sîner hêrschaft hân ze râte getân."

[Then fierce Hagen spoke: "Well, I don't know why you are lamenting. All of our worries and sorrows are over and done with. We will not find anyone who will dare attack us now. I'm quite happy that I have put an end to his supremacy."]

Hagen may well have more in mind than just the immediate problems visited upon them by Siegfried's indiscretion (in revealing anything about the "bedroom" struggle with Brünhild to Kriemhild) when he refers to "unser sorge unt unser leit." Siegfried was always a potential threat to Burgundian society, given his knowledge of the circumstances of Gunther's courtship of Brünhild, but in a more general sense because of his unpredictability and spontaneity, which had become all too apparent upon his initial arrival at Worms. There is also the power factor, in which Hagen has always been interested. No one is likely to challenge those who have acquired the reputation of having killed Siegfried. Finally, Hagen takes a certain personal satisfaction in having been the one to have dealt the death blow, and it is more than likely that a long-standing, pent-up animosity he has felt toward Siegfried is at the root of this comment.

From this point on much of the action of the *Nibelungenlied* revolves around the adversarial polarity between Hagen and Kriemhild. Not only has Hagen murdered Kriemhild's spouse after having tricked her into revealing his one vulnerable spot, he also places the body in front of her chamber. This may be seen as a deliberate move on Hagen's part to drive home to Kriemhild the imprudence of her own behavior concerning the manner in which she turned her back on the best interests of her own clan from the moment she met Siegfried. The robbing and sinking of the Nibelungen treasure in the Rhine is undertaken by Hagen the pragmatist, who sees only too clearly that it represents a danger in Kriemhild's hands, as she will use it to buy allies in her efforts to avenge Siegfried's death. Hagen remains at all times fully aware of the breach that has developed between Kriemhild and her clan and is never convinced that a reconciliation is possible, hence his reluctance to accept the invitation brought by the Hunnish envoys to visit Etzel's court. When, however, Giselher suggests in strophe 1463 that Hagen remain at home, for fear of what might transpire in Etzelnburg, Hagen's honor demands that he accompany the Burgundians. The signs are, of course, ominous: Rumold, the master of the kitchen, also fears that the journey to Hungary is ill-advised; Ute, mother of Kriemhild, has a dream in which she sees all of the birds of the land dead; and a water sprite later intimates that all, save one, are doomed on this trip. Hagen finds this prophecy confirmed when the chaplain whom he tries to drown, testing the sprite's prediction, escapes and reaches the river bank safely. Noteworthy throughout this section of the *Nibelungenlied* is the fact that it is Hagen who becomes the de facto leader of the Burgundians on their travels into what is, for all intents and purposes, a land of the dead, something that seems underscored by the bloody ferryman incident at the Danube and the violent encounter with Else and Gelphrat on the right bank of the Danube during which Hagen almost loses his life.

Hagen was earlier reviled as the murderer of Siegfried. Clearly, however, the image of the man presented in the second half of the epic stands in contrast to what we encounter in the first part. He is welcomed in a most friendly manner by Rüdiger and his family at Bechelarn (Pöchlarn), and Dietrich warns him of Kriemhild's state of mind. The image that prevails of him throughout the second half of the *Nibelungenlied* is devoid of any lasting taint as Siegfried's killer. It is only Kriemhild who is obsessed with having him pay for the deed, even more than two decades after the fact. Time appears to have ameliorated for everyone else the significance of the murder in the sixteenth *âventiure,* while for Kriemhild the passage of time has served solely to turn her desire for revenge into an obsession. Hagen serves as both the physical and spiritual "protector" (*trôst*) of the Burgundians/Nibelungs during their last days in the land of Huns. He is the one who, before anyone else, knows how things will eventually end, and his comportment in the face of death is exemplary heroic behavior.

On the other hand it may be argued that his death—decapitation by Kriemhild—is anything but heroic. Even Etzel, Kriemhild's spouse, finds his wife's act abhorrent because it is perpetrated by a woman against a defenseless warrior, regardless of the fact that this same warrior took the life of his only son, Ortlieb, only a few hours earlier. Hagen may also be seen as the "murderer" of his liege lord, Gunther, whose death on Kriemhild's orders he has manipulated to insure that she never does get her hands on the Nibelungen treasure. It is also possible to see him as a failure, as his raison d'être was to serve and enhance the stature of the Burgundian royal family. Such a perspective is probably too modern and too harsh. Part of the Germanic warrior's world is the acceptance of inexorable fate, and Hagen's obligation is to ensure that the Burgundians die with honor. The circumstances of his own death are less a reflection of his disgrace than they are of Kriemhild's. At the same time it should be noted that the status of Hagen as a hero warrior was anything but the unanimous opinion of the *Nibelungenlied*'s contemporaries. The anonymous poet of the *Klage,* as well as figures in that work such as Rumold, have nothing but disdain for the hero of Troneck who, in the poet's opinion, bears the heavy and principal guilt for the tragedy that ensues at Etzelnburg.

In Wagner's Ring cycle Hagen is the son of Alberich and Gunther's stepbrother and is portrayed as an unequivocally dark figure.

[WM]

Bibliography

Backenköhler, Gerd. "Untersuchungen zur Gestalt Hagens von Tronje in den mittelalterlichen Nibelungendichtungen." Diss., Bonn, 1961.

Gentry, Francis G. "Hagen and the Problem of Individuality in the Nibelungenlied." *Monatshefte* 68 (1976): 5–12.

Homann, Holger. "The Hagen Figure in the Nibelungenlied: Know Him by His Lies." *MLN* 97 (1982): 759–769.

Mahlendorf, Ursula R., and Frank J. Tobin. "Hagen: A Reappraisal." *Monatshefte* 63 (1971): 125–140.

Salmon, P. B. "Why Does Hagen Die?" *GLL* 17 (1963–64): 3–13.

Sonnenfeld, Marion. "The Figure of Hagen in Germanic Heroic Poetry and in Modern German Literature." Ph.d. diss., Yale, 1955.

Stout, J. *Und ouch Hagene.* Groningen: Wolters, 1963

HAGENWALD, in the *Historia von dem gehörnten Siegfried* one of the sons of Gibaldus, who corresponds to Hagen in the *Nibelungenlied.* He slays Siegfried with his rapier, and in the campaign that Siegfried's father mounts to avenge his son, Hagenwald is killed in his sleep by Zivelles, in a similar way to how Hagen slays Seufrid in Hans Sachs's *Der hürnen Seufrid* (ll. 1068ff.).

[JLF]

HAINBURG (MHG *Heimburc*), a town on the right bank of the Danube near the Hungarian border. In the *Nibelungenlied* it is mentioned only once (1376,1). Kriemhild and Etzel stay there overnight on their way from Vienna to Gran. This town is chosen instead of the nearby and more important fortress of Bratislava either because the Austrian poet preferred an Austrian town for the last overnight stay before entering the land of the Huns or because the whole journey took place on the right bank of the Danube

after the crossing at Pförring. During the 1980s there were attempts to rebuild Bratislava and a performance of the *Nibelungenlied* was staged there by the inhabitants of Hainburg.

[NV/SSch]

HAKI, son of Hamund in the *Volsunga saga.* Brynhild considers him and his brother Hagbard the foremost of kings because of their warrior skills. However, Gudrun disagrees with her since Haki and Hagbard did not take revenge on Sigar for abducting one of their sisters and burning another one in her house. For the complete account, see Saxo Grammaticus, *The History of the Danes,* Book 7.

[BS]

HAKON, in the *Volsunga saga* and *Guðrúnarkviða onnor,* Hakon is the father of Thora, the woman Gudrun stays with in Half's hall for three and a half years after Sigurd's murder. In the *Heimskringla,* Snorri gives a detailed account of the deeds of Hakon, king of Norway, son of Harald Hairfair and foster son of Athelstan.

[BS]

HALF, king of Denmark. In the *Volsunga saga* Gudrun leaves Gunnar after Sigurd's murder and stays for three and a half years with Thora in Half's hall.

[BS]

HAMDIR, in the *Volsunga saga,* a son of Gudrun by her third husband, Jonaker (the other two being Sorli and Erp).

[WM]

HAMUND, in the *Volsunga saga,* one of two sons King Sigmund has by Borghild.

[WM]

HARTWIN is, according to the *Þiðreks saga,* one of the advisors of King Sigmund. During Sigmund's campaign in Poland, Hartwin is regent of the empire and protector of Sigmund's wife, Sisibe. Hoping to become king himself, he tries in vain to seduce the queen. His friend, Hermann, wants to support him, but both are unsuccessful. When King Sigmund returns from Poland, Hartwin and Hermann slander the queen. Hartwin even tries to kill Sisibe but is prevented from doing so by Hermann, who cuts off Hartwin's head.

[GW]

HEIME/HEIMIR. In the *Þiðreks saga* Heime/Heimir is introduced in a somewhat strange context. In the story of Studas we are told that Studas had a son, named Studas after his father, who lost his name, because he looked as grim and ferocious as a dragon called Heimir (which he had killed, according to German versions). The Northmen called him Heimir. Middle High German epics of the *Dietrich Cycle* refer to his father as Adelger or Madelger of Lamparten, and Heime is either a duke or a giant who has three or four hands or elbows, a distinguishing feature for giants also known to the Swedish version of the *Þiðreks saga.* Heime is an able warrior, who rides the famous horse Rispa. His sword Blodgang is one of the best weapons ever fashioned. Heime leaves his father when he is seventeen years old, resolved to fight against Thidrek, who is only twelve years old at that time. He reaches Bern and provokes Thidrek to single combat. Heime's sword breaks into pieces but Thidrek does not kill him, and Heime becomes his liegeman. Thidrek even gives him his excellent sword Nagelring, when he himself wins the sword Eckesachs. The German epics relate that Heime is a treacherous man who left Thidrek and is frequently allied with Ermenrich, who obviously gave him much gold for his change of allegiance. The saga does not mention this fact, although it does tells us that he and his comrade in arms, Widga, are Erminrek's men. Hama (Heime) and Wudga (Widga) are mentioned together in *WidsiÞ,* and Hama is also mentioned in *Beowulf.* Heime is among Thidrek's twelve men who fight against Isung and his eleven sons. In the German epic *Alpharts Tod* Heime rescues Witege (Widga) from Alphart, a young kinsman of Hildebrand. Heime and Witege kill Alphart in an uncourtly fashion by simultaneously engaging him in combat at the same time. At the end of the *Þiðreks saga,* we are told that Heime spends some of his last years in a monastery where he goes by the name of Ludwig. When the monastery is threatened by the giant Aspilian, he feels himself to be a warrior again. He gets back his weapons and his old horse and finally

kills the giant. He attempts to return to his monastic life but fails in this endeavor as Thidrek appears to call him back to a warrior's life. Again Heime returns to the monastery in order to demand high taxes. When the monks do not meet his demand he robs them, kills the abbot and all the monks, and burns down the monastery. He then has to fight against another giant, but this time he fails and is killed. King Thidrek takes revenge on the giant and kills him. German sources say that Heime is buried in the monastery of Wilten near Innsbruck (Austria). The figure has nothing in common with Heimir, Brynhild's foster father, who is mentioned in the *Gripísspá,* in the *Helreið Brynhildar,* and in the *Volsunga saga.*

[GW]

Bibliography
Haymes, Edward R., and Susann T. Samples. *Heroic Legends of the North: An Introduction to the Nibelung and Dietrich Cycles.* New York: Garland, 1996, p. 151.
Schneider, Hermann. *Germanische Heldensage.* Vol. 1. 2nd ed. Grundriss der germanischen Philologie 10/I. Berlin: de Gruyter, 1962, pp. 322–324.

HEIMIR, a ruler in the *Volsunga saga* whose home is at Hlymdale and who is married to Bekkhild, Brynhild's sister. He is the father of Alsvid, who welcomes Sigurd to the estate and generously offers him whatever he wishes. (This situation stands in marked contrast to the third *âventiure* in the *Nibelungenlied,* in which Siegfried arrives at the Burgundian court of Worms and demands that the Burgundians turn over all their lands to him.) Sigurd appears to enjoy a particularly warm relationship to both Heimir and Alsvid. His advice is sought by Gunnar when he elects to woo Brynhild, and Heimir informs them that Brynhild would most likely only marry the man who was successful in his attempt to break through a ring of fire that surrounds her hall.

[WM]

HEL, in Norse mythology, the goddess who is associated with the realm of the dead, which bears the same name. In the *Volsunga saga* the dragon Fafnir is sent to Hel by Sigurd, and the latter also assures Gudrun when they consummate their relationship that he will later visit her from Hel and also wait for her to join him there.

[WM]

HELCHE, in the *Nibelungenlied,* the first wife of Etzel, and the aunt of Herrat, noted for her beauty and her generosity with her husband's wealth. After Helche's death Kriemhild marries Etzel partly because she hopes to have the same kind of wealth-based power that Helche had. In the Dietrich stories Helche is Dietrich's advocate at the court of Attila, and she reconciles Dietrich with Attila after the death of Attila's sons and Dietrich's brother in the battle to regain Dietrich's kingdom. In the *Rabenschlacht* a detailed picture is painted of a resplendent Helche as Etzel's wife and mistress of the Hunnish court who is plagued by dreams of a dragon that carries off her two sons. Her name varies greatly in different sources: Priscus calls her Kreka, and Nicolaus Olah calls her Herrichis; she is Erka in the *þiðreks saga;* in the Dietrich stories she is Helche, Herche, Herriche, or Heillig; in the Third Lay of Gudrun in the *Poetic Edda* she appears as a former concubine of Atli named Herkja.

[JVM]

Bibliography
Martin, Ernst, ed. *Alpharts Tod, Dietrichs Flucht,* and *Rabenschlacht.* Pt. 2 of Deutsches Heldenbuch. Berlin: Weidmann, 1866, esp. pp. 227ff.

HELGI, one of two sons King Sigmund has by Borghild in the *Volsunga saga.* He becomes renowned for his military accomplishments at an early age and was highly respected by his people, the Volsungs. His defeat of a powerful king, Hunding, increases his stature as a warrior. Helgi subsequently proves victorious in battle against Hunding's sons. In order to prevent the marriage of Sigrun to Hodbrodd, Helgi engages him in a furious battle at Frekastein, kills the king, and marries Sigrun.

[WM]

HELMNOT, a warrior in the service of Dietrich in the *Nibelungenlied.* He is mentioned only once, (2261,1), lamenting the death of Rüdiger

with Wolfbrand and Helpfrich and the other Amelungs.

[WM]

HELPFRICH, in the *Nibelungenlied,* one of Dietrich's men who, in the thirty-eighth *âventiure,* is sent by the Veronese to inquire about the cause of the great lamentation that has been emanating from the area around Etzel's Great Hall. He returns to Dietrich bringing news of the death of Rüdiger. In the subsequent battle against the Burgundians/Nibelungs, he kills Dancwart, brother of Hagen. Although no details are provided, he also dies in the fighting. In the *Klage* he is mentioned only once (1347) when Hildebrand pays tribute to him for having saved his life by separating him from the minstrel Volker. He appears throughout the Dietrich epics as an ally of Dietrich in the latter's attempt to retake the lands ravaged and stolen from him by his uncle Ermenrich.

[WM]

HERBORG, the name of a Hunnish queen who is the foster mother of Gullrond Gjukadottir in the *Guðrúnarkviða in fyrsta.* She tries to comfort Gudrun, who is mourning for Sigurd but is unable to weep. She tells Gudrun about her own hard fate: She lost seven sons and her husband in a battle in the South; she lost her father, her mother and four brothers in a shipwreck; and she had to bury them herself. She was taken prisoner and had to serve a nobleman, who seemed to love her, but his wife was jealous of her and made her work hard and even beat her. We get no information about Herborg's relationship to the Hunnish royal family (perhaps *Húnalanz drótning* refers to a German princess) or why she is at King Gunnar's court. The figure is an invention of the poet of this Eddic lay and is only mentioned here. The story strongly corresponds to a part in the German heroic epic *Kudrun* and to the ballads of Südeli known in Germany and Scandinavia.

[GW]

Bibliography
de Vries, Jan. *Altnordische Literaturgeschichte.* Vol. 2. 2nd ed. Grundriss der germanischen Philologie 16. Berlin: de Gruyter, 1967, pp. 135–138.

Gering, Hugo, and B. Sijmons. *Kommentar zu den Liedern der Edda*. 2. Hälfte: *Heldenlieder*. Halle (Saale): Buchhandlung des Waisenhauses (Francke), 1931, p. 236.

Simek, Rudolf, and Hermann Pálsson. *Lexikon der altnordischen Literatur*. Stuttgart: Kröner, 1987, pp. 124f.

HERBRAND, one of Thidrek's champions in the *Þiðreks saga*. Widely traveled, wise and very knowledgeable, he becomes Thidrek's standard-bearer and counselor. In Attila's battle against Osantrix, Herbrand acquits himself well. Herbrand cautions a boastful Thidrek that Isung of Bertangaland and his sons are a match for Thidrek and his champions. Herbrand then leads Thidrek and his champions to Bertangaland. In the contest of the two kings' champions, Herbrand is defeated and bound by Isung's second son. After Thidrek's triumph over Sigurd in the concluding contest and the reconciliation of Isung and Thidrek, Herbrand returns to his own realm.

[FH]

HERKJA is only mentioned in the Eddic lay *Guðrúnarkviða in thridia* (Third Lay of Gudrun). The same person is called Erka in the *Þiðreks saga* and Herche or Helche in the German heroic epics. She is Attila's first wife, whom Priscus of Panium calls Kreka in his *History*. Priscus had visited Attila's headquarters in Walachia in the company of a Roman embassy in 449. In the *Guðrúnarkviða in thridia* Herkja is not Atli's legal wife, but simply his concubine. She slanders Gudrun, Atli's wife, and is forced by Atli into a trial by ordeal, namely, an ordeal by fire (a boiling kettle). Whereas Gudrun passes the ordeal, Herkja burns her hand and is sentenced to death and sunk in a fen.

[GW]

HERLIND, in the *Klage,* a Greek noblewoman at Etzel's court who is a companion to Goldrun, daughter of King Liudeger of France.

[WM]

HERMAN OF POLAND, mentioned in the *Klage* (345f.), but not in the *Nibelungenlied*. He is a duke who willingly places himself at the disposal of Kriemhild in the fight against the Nibelungs. He and all his men are killed in the slaughter at Etzel's court.

[WM]

HERMANN is, according to the *Þiðreks saga,* one of the advisors of King Sigmund and the friend of Hartwin. He shares in the guilt for Sisibe's death in the woods, buries her corpse, and rides back to the king, hoping that Sigmund will show mercy to him, but he is instead driven out of the realm.

[GW]

HERRALAND is only mentioned once in the *Þiðreks saga;* it is the country of Osid (2), the son of Attila's brother Otnid. Perhaps Friesland in Lower Saxony is meant.

[GW]

HERRAT (HERAD), in the *Nibelungenlied,* Herrat is the daughter of Näntwin, raised and educated by her aunt Helche in Etzelnburg. She is Dietrich's fiancée, and chief representative of the courtly ladies in Etzelnburg, where she teaches Kriemhild the customs of Etzel's court. In the *Klage* she leaves Etzelnburg with Dietrich and Hildebrand after the dead are buried. On their way through Pöchlarn she tries to console Dietlinde. In the *Þiðreks saga* Herad then travels with Thidrek/Dietrich to Verona, where she reaches old age and dies soon after Hildebrand, lamented by many men.

[BS]

HERTNIT/HERTNID. This name is attached to at least two figures in the *Þiðreks saga,* one of whom is an unlucky king married to a witch. In the *Niflunga saga* Mime tells Sigurd that he has forged a helmet, a shield, and a suit of armor for Hertnid in Holmgard (Novgorod), the best armor to be found far and wide. Now Sigurd is to take it as a conciliatory gift because Mime did not treat him well. This Hertnid might be the same person about whom the scribes tell us stories similar to those attributed to Ortnit in the German heroic epic *Ortnit* and who is called Hertnit, king of Russia, in the *Þiðreks saga.* Ortnit is especially famous for his golden armor, which the dwarf

Alberich had forged and which is later possessed by Dietrich von Bern. Some of the Middle High German epics also tell of a man called Hertnid von Reussen (of Russia).

[GW]

Bibliography

Grimm, Wilhelm. *Die deutsche Heldensage.* 4th ed. Darmstadt: Wissenschaftliche Buchgesellschaft, 1957, pp. 242f.

Schneider, Hermann. *Germanische Heldensage.* Vol. 1. 2nd ed. Grundriss der germanischen Philologie 10/I. Berlin: de Gruyter, 1962, pp. 351ff.

HESSEN. Mentioned once in the *Nibelungenlied* as a land through which Siegfried and the Burgundians ride (176,1) on their way to do battle with the Saxons and Danes.

[WM]

HILDEBRAND (usually Master Hildebrand), appears in the Middle High German works of the Dietrich cycle and in the *Þiðreks saga,* where he is Dietrich's/Thidrek's older, wiser, loyal retainer and counselor. Having abandoned his wife and son years earlier, this skilled warrior has been at his lord's side ever since. In an episode of the *Þiðreks saga* called "King Thidrek's Feast," we are told that Hildebrand is superior to other warriors in that he knows how to deliver a swordblow against which no one can defend himself, and so normally gains victory over opponents with a single stroke. The stories about Hildebrand originated in the period of migrations. He is best known for the single combat against his son Hadubrand, the theme of the Old High German *Hildebrandslied,* retold in the Norse *Asmundrsaga Kappabana.* Another later tradition reflected in the *Þiðreks saga* and the *Younger Lay of Hildebrand* gave this story a happier ending. Hildebrand is depicted as a warrior reluctant to begin fighting, but who takes up the task with skill once fighting is forced upon him, a treatment that may well have colored his characterization in Dietrich epics.

In the *Nibelungenlied* Hildebrand is first encountered in the twenty-eighth *âventiure,* where he is, as always, at Dietrich's side. In the thirty-first *âventiure,* Hildebrand supports Dietrich's refusal to become involved in the fighting. Later, in the thirty-eighth *âventiure,* Hildebrand goes with Dietrich's men to recover the body of the slain Rüdiger. In line with his traditional character he seeks to avoid conflict but is forced by the impetuous actions of his nephew, Wolfhart, to take up the fight; when forced to engage in combat, he shows his skill and ferocity, attacking Hagen, then killing Volker. The ensuing combat between Hagen and Hildebrand has more than the usual dramatic force, for each man has lost a dear friend or close relative to the other (Volker is Hagen's close companion; Wolfhart was Hildebrand's beloved nephew). Hildebrand is wounded and flees, and will thus be the only survivor among Dietrich's men. In the final *âventiure,* Hildebrand, outraged at the death of his former opponent, strikes down Kriemhild after she beheads the captured Hagen.

Hildebrand is also a major character in the thematically related *Klage,* where, as one of the survivors of the fight at Etzel's court, he sorts through the many slain warriors from both sides and laments their deaths. The wound he received from Hagen in battle weakens him, and he is not able to carry the body of Rüdiger out for burial.

Hildebrand's actions in the *Nibelungenlied* set him up for a medieval audience's disapproval in that he violates the code of behavior normally expected of praiseworthy heroes in epic lore: first he runs from a fight and then he kills a woman. That Hildebrand's reputation has been harmed by the first act may be seen in the rebuke given him by Dietrich (2345) after he and Hagen insult one another's honor. Regarding the second offense, however, both the *Nibelungenlied* poet and the scribe of the *Klage* may wish to excuse Hildebrand. In the view of the first poet, Hagen is unjustly and most unceremoniously killed by Kriemhild, an act to which Hildebrand understandably reacts in a fit of rage (2376). In the *Klage* we are told that Hildebrand has acted (line 366) *in unsinne* (out of madness) and (line 261) *durch sinen herzegrimmen zorn* (out of his heartfelt fierce anger).

These issues do not surface for the Hildebrand of the *Þiðreks saga* in the episode "Saga of the Niflungar." Though he is, of course, at Thidrek's side in the fight at Attila's court, he is not the killer of Folker (instead, he kills Gislher), he does not engage in combat with Hogni, and finally it is Thidrek, not Hildebrand, who kills Grimhild.

[JKW]

HILDEBURG, a Norman noblewoman at the court of Etzel in the *Klage.* She is a companion to Goldrun. There is no mention of her in the *Nibelungenlied.*

[WM]

HILDIBRAND, the son of Duke Reginbald of Fenidi and Svava in the *þiðreks saga.* He is knighted by his father at the age of twelve. At 30 he leaves home to seek out Thettmar in Bern and becomes the foster father to the five-year-old Thidrek. For the rest of his long life Hildibrand accompanies Thidrek on all but a handful of his forays as his counselor and standard-bearer. Protective of Thidrek, he nonetheless allows Vithga to best his swaggering young foster son in order to teach him proper knightly behavior. Hildibrand is overcome by Isung's tenth son in the contest of the kings' champions. When Thidrek is forced to leave Bern, Hildibrand follows him into exile in Húnaland. After taking part in the battle between Attila and Valdimar and being obliged to retreat, Hildibrand complains to Thidrek that Attila is a coward. On her deathbed Attila's wife Erka gives Hildibrand her best gold ring as a sign of the deep friendship between them. In the battle between the Niflungs and the Huns at Attila's court, Hildibrand slays Gernoz and Gislher. When a very old man, Hildibrand sets out with Thidrek and Herath to regain Bern. He is compelled to fight his own son, Alibrand, who now rules Bern. Hildibrand overcomes his son despite Alibrand's treachery. When Alibrand learns that Hildibrand is his father, the two are reconciled. After Thidrek defeats an army led by Sifka, King Ermenrich's treasurer and counselor, Hildibrand bestows on him Ermenrich's crown. When Hildibrand dies, he is said to be either 150 or 200 years old, and Thidrek weeps for him.

[FH]

HILDICO, a Germanic princess married to Attila, who died on their wedding night in 453 of a hemorrhage. Later historians accuse Hildico of having stabbed her husband. Part of her name may echo Kriemhild.

[BOM]

HILDIGUND is the beloved wife of Waltari, according to the *þiðreks saga.* Like Waltari, she is a noble hostage at Attila's court. Her father is Jarl Ilias of Greece. In the Middle High German version, her father is Herrich of Burgundy or she is called Princess of Arragon. Waltari and Hildigund had been betrothed by their parents and are growing up together at the Hunnish court. Hildigund falls in love with Waltari and agrees to run away with him. When they do so, they take along large amounts of treasure. In a more recent Polish version Hildigund is wooed by Prince Wislaus, while her husband Walter wages war. The lovers escape, but Walter later finds the adulterous couple and kills them.

[GW]

Bibliography
Raszmann, August. *Die Sagen von den Wölsungen und Niflungen, den Wilcen und König Thidrek von Bern in der Thidrekssaga.* 2nd ed. Hanover: Rümpler, 1863, pp. 289–297.
Schneider, Hermann. *Germanische Heldensage.* Vol. 1. 2nd ed. Grundriss der germanischen Philologie 10/I. Berlin: de Gruyter, 1962, pp. 331–344.

HINDARFELL, the name given to Brynhild's "sleeping place," which is a mountain in the *Volsunga saga.* It is in this place that Sigurd finds Brynhild and awakens her.

[WM]

HJALLI, a thrall who appears in the *Volsunga saga.* A counselor in the camp of King Atli proposes that Hjalli, who he considers to be an unrelenting troublemaker, ought to be put to death instead of Hogni. When Atli's men prepare to kill Hjalli, however, Hogni intercedes on his behalf and the thrall is spared for the time being. When Gunnar refuses to reveal the site of his treasure and maintains that he would rather see his brother's heart cut out than divulge its whereabouts, Hjalli is seized again and killed. When his heart is brought before Gunnar, the king declares that its quaking is a sure sign that it could not be the heart of Hogni, but rather had to be that of the cowardly Hjalli. Hogni is subsequently killed by the Huns and his heart shown to Gunnar, who correctly identifies it as that of his brother.

[WM]

HJALMGUNNAR, an old king referred to by Brynhild in the *Volsunga saga.* Odin sides with him in his battle against Agnar, but he is killed nonetheless by Brynhild. His death is avenged by Odin who sticks a sleep thorn into Brynhild.

[WM]

HJALPREK, king of Denmark and father of Alf in the *Volsunga saga.* He assumes the chief responsibility for raising Sigurd, son of Hjordis and Sigmund, after Hjordis has been brought back to Denmark following the death of her husband in battle.

[WM]

HJORDIS, the daughter of King Eylimi in the *Volsunga saga.* She marries Sigmund, but he is killed, along with her father, in battle against a rival suitor, Lyngvi. Her dying husband exhorts her to raise their unborn son well and to watch over the pieces of his broken sword, from which Gram will later be fashioned and wielded by their son. She and her bondswoman are discovered by the Viking Alf, son of King Hjalprek of Denmark, and brought back to his land. Alf then weds Hjordis. She gives birth to Sigurd (Sigmund's son), who becomes renowned among men for his strength and exploits.

[WM]

HJORVARD, son of King Hunding and brother of Lyngvi in the *Volsunga saga.* He is killed by Sigurd during the campaign waged by the latter to avenge his father, Volsung.

[WM]

HLJOD, daughter of the giant Hrimnir in the *Volsunga saga.* She serves Odin at his command, and in the guise of a crow, she brings an apple to King Rerir, son of Odin's son Sigi. The powers of the apple are directly responsible for the subsequent pregnancy of Rerir's hitherto barren wife.

[WM]

HNIFLUNG is the son of Hogni and the grandson of Gjuki, according to the *Atlamál.* His stepbrothers are Saewar and Solar. Strangely enough he is reared at Atli's court. He hates Atli because the king has killed his father. He speaks about his hatred to Gudrun and the two ally against Atli and kill him. In the *Volsunga saga* Hogni's son is called Niflung. Here Atli is killed when he is asleep. The two take a sword and thrust it through the king's breast.

In those literary works which represent the Low German version of the Nibelung cycle, Hogni's posthumously born son is either called Aldrian (*Þiðreks saga*), Ranche/Rancke (*Hven Chronicle;* the Danish ballad *Grimilds Haevn* [Grimild's Revenge]), or Hogni (Faroese ballad *Hogna táttur*). In the *Hogna táttur,* the *Hven Chronicle,* and in *Grimilds Haevn,* an elaborate reason is given for the fact that Hogni's son lives at Atli's court: the child's mother Helvik/ Huenild suspects that Gudrun harbors malicious intentions against young Hogni and exchanges her child and Gudrun's in their cradles. Gudrun then cuts off the head of the child she supposes to be Hogni's and rears the other as her own. Later on in the work, Hogni's son is able to lure Artala (Atli) to his death.

[GW]

Bibliography

Dronke, Ursula, ed. and trans. *The Poetic Edda.* Vol. 1 of *Heroic Poems.* Oxford: Clarendon Press, 1969, pp. 104f.

Fuss, Klaus. *Die faröischen Lieder der Nibelungensage. Text, Lesarten, und Übersetzung.* Vol. 3 of *Hoegni.* Göppingen: Kümmerle, 1987.

Gering, Hugo, and B. Sijmons. *Kommentar zu den Liedern der Edda.* 2. Hälfte: *Heldenlieder.* Germanistische Handbibliothek VII 3,2. Halle (Saale): Buchhandlung des Waisenhauses (Francke), 1931, p. 402.

Holzapfel, Otto. *Die dänischen Nibelungenballaden. Texte und Kommentare.* Göppingen: Kümmerle, 1974, pp. 158f.

HNIKAR, one of Odin's several bynames in the *Volsunga saga.* The god himself refers to it in a strophe contained within chapter 17 when he comes on board one of the ships commanded by Sigurd.

[WM]

HODBRODD, in the *Volsunga saga,* the son (who is also depicted as brother) of King Granmar. He is engaged to be married to Sigrun who, unhappy at the prospect, convinces Helgi to prevent the match. Hodbrodd dies in battle against Helgi at a place called Frekastein.

[WM]

HOENIR, appears in chapter 14 of the *Volsunga saga,* a companion of Odin and Loki when they come to Andvari's Fall, where Otr, one of Hreid-mar's sons, is killed by the irascible Loki.

[WM]

HOGNAR, HOGNIR, or HEGNIR are forms of the name Hogni in the *Hogna táttur*. They are cognate with Hagen in the *Nibelungenlied* (Hoegnar Júkason) and with Hogni's son (Heg-nir ungi or Hoegni Hoegnason; cf. Hniflung).

[GW]

Bibliography

Fuss, Klaus. *Die faröischen Lieder der Nibelun-gensage. Text, Lesarten, und Übersetzung.* Vol. 3 of *Hoegni.* Göppingen: Kümmerle, 1987.

HOGNI corresponds to Hagen of Tronege in the *Nibelungenlied*. The Scandinavian traditions re-late the following: Hogni is the son of King Gjuki and Grimhild, the brother of Gunnar and Gutthorm (or Gutthorm's stepbrother). His sis-ters are Gudrun and Gullrond. He is married to Kostbera, and his sons are Solar, Snaewar, Gjuki, and Hniflung. He possesses the horse Holkvir. He is brother-in-law to Sigurd and becomes his blood brother. When Brynhild provokes Gunnar into murdering Sigurd and confiscating his hoard, Hogni reminds him of their sworn oaths. So the Gjukungs decide to provoke Gutthorm to murder because he is not under oath (in some versions Hogni himself is involved in the mur-der). It is Hogni who informs Gudrun about her husband's murder; and he does not fear her curs-ing. When Brynhild decides to commit suicide, Gunnar takes Hogni's advice to let her do as she pleases. Gunnar and Hogni take possession of Sigurd's treasure, and Hogni is willing to offer Gudrun monetary compensation for the murder. When Atli invites Gunnar and Hogni to his court, Gudrun, now married to Atli, sends a warning to Hogni. Hogni explains to Gunnar that their sister is trying to warn them, but they decide to accept the invitation. One of Hogni's sons wishes them good luck when they depart. During the fighting at Atli's court, Hogni proves to be one of the bravest warriors and kills eight Huns. When Gunnar is taken prisoner and is asked whether he would offer gold in order to save his life, he answers that he wishes to see Hogni's bleeding heart in his hands. At first the serf Hjalli is killed,

but his heart trembles when cut out, and so Gun-nar knows that Hogni is still alive. Then Hogni himself is killed, and Gunnar is the only one who knows where Sigurd's treasure is hidden.

According to another Scandinavian version, it is Hogni's wife, Kostbera, who cautions the brothers about accepting Atli's invitation be-cause she understands Gudrun's warning. She had ominous dreams that made her fear disaster. Nevertheless Gunnar and Hogni depart, taking Hogni's sons Snaevar and Solar and his brother-in-law Orkning along with them. When Hogni is taken prisoner at Atli's court he intercedes with the Huns for Hjalli. Hjalli is saved and Hogni's heart is cut out. Gudrun is overcome with pain at Hogni's death and does not want to accept com-pensation from Atli. When Herkja accuses her of adultery, she complains that Hogni can no longer help her. She eventually provokes Hogni's son Hniflung into avenging his father and with his help she kills Atli. According to the *Þiðreks saga*, Hogni of Troia is taken prisoner by Thidrek and is fatally wounded. Herrad ban-dages his wounds. Thidrek allows a woman to spend the night with Hogni. On the next day the warrior dies. Later the woman gives birth to Hogni's son, Aldrian, who avenges his father's death on Attila.

In the *Nibelungenlied* Hagen of Tronege is not the brother of the Burgundian kings, but rather their loyal vassal and kinsman. He is also the royal advisor and therefore a powerful man. According to stanza 1753 of the *Nibelungenlied* **B** and to the *Þiðreks saga,* his father's name is Aldrian and his brother is Dancwart. In the saga Hogni's mother is called Oda. During the night in which Hogni was fathered, an elf, a supernatural being, came to her in Aldrian's shape while the king was absent. Thus Hogni is a half brother to Gunnar, Gernoz, Gislher, and Gudrun or Grimhild. In the *Nibelungenlied* Hagen is the slayer of Siegfried/Sigurd and the destroyer of the treasure and thus Kriemhild/Gudrun's arch-antagonist, not her beloved brother for whom she mourns. Hagen is even slain by Kriemhild. In other Middle High German epics (e.g., *Rosen-garten, and Biterolf und Dietleib*), Hagen is shown as a brave, courageous, and fearless war-rior. Hagen/Hagano also plays a major role in the Waltari legend (*Waltharilied*). A warrior king with the same name Hogni/Hagen appears in the Eddic lays *Helgakviða Hundingsbana in fyrri* and *Helgakviða Hundingsbana onnur* as well as in the Middle High German epic *Kudrun.*

[GW]

Bibliography

Backenköhler, Gerd. "Untersuchungen zur Gestalt Hagens von Tronje in den mittelalterlichen Nibelungendichtungen." Diss., Bonn 1961.

Dickerson, Jr., Harold D. "Hagen: A Negative View." *Semasia* 2 (1975): 43–59.

Gentry Francis G. "Hagen and the Problem of Individuality in the Nibelungenlied." *Monatshefte* 68 (1976): 5–12.

Haymes, Edward R. "A Rhetorical Reading of the 'Hortforderungszene' in the Nibelungenlied." In *"Waz sider da geschach." American-German Studies on the Nibelungenlied,* edited by Werner Wunderlich and Ulrich Müller. Göppingen: Kümmerle, 1992, pp. 81–88.

———— "Hagen the Hero." *Southern Folklore Quarterly* 43 (1979): 149–155.

Haymes, Edward R., and Susann T. Samples. *Heroic Legends of the North: An Introduction to the Nibelung and Dietrich Cycles.* New York: Garland, 1996, p. 150.

Homann, Holger. "The Hagen Figure in the Nibelungenlied: Know Him by His Lies." *MLN* 97 (1982): 759–769.

Schneider, Hermann. *Germanische Heldensage.* Vol. 1. 2nd ed. Grundriss der germanischen Philologie 10/I. Berlin: de Gruyter, 1962, pp. 190ff.

Stout, Jacob. *Und ouch Hagene.* Groningen: Walters, 1963.

Wapnewski, Peter. "Hagen: ein Gegenspieler?" In *Gegenspieler,* edited by Thomas Cramer and Werner Dahlhem. Munich: Hanser, 1993, pp. 62–73.

HOLKVIR, the name of the horse ridden by Hogni in the *Volsunga saga* when he accompanies Gunnar on his attempt to woo Brynhild.

[WM]

HOLMGARD, the name of two different places in the *Þiðreks saga.* **Holmgard** (1) is the garden in which Attila gives the banquet for the Niflungar. The name means *battleground,* and it is here that the hostilities between the Niflungar and the Huns begin. During the breakout from Holmgard, Gunnar is taken prisoner by Osid and is finally killed, whereas all the other Niflungar survive. This detail about Gunnar's life does not correspond to the *Nibelungenlied,* yet it is similar to the *Atlakviða* and the *Volsunga saga:* in these texts Gunnar is the first among the Niflungar who is taken prisoner, but the heroes have to fight in a hall (as in the *Nibelungenlied*), not in a garden with a wall around it. **Holmgard** (2) is the name of Novgorod or Russia with Novgorod as its capital. It belongs to Attila's empire. According to the *Vilzina saga* the following areas belong to Attila: Vilcinaland (i.e., Scandinavia and the adjoining areas), Holmgard, Brandinaborg (Brandenburg), Bavaria (with Bakalar/Bechelaren as its center), and Húnaland (Lower Germany) with the capital Susa(t) (i.e., Soest in Westphalia). The fact that Etzel possesses an enormous empire is also related in the *Nibelungenlied* (twenty-second *âventiure*). In the German heroic epic *Biterolf und Dietleib* and in the *Klage,* we are also informed about the area that Etzel controls, but his royal capital is always called Etzelnburg.

[GW]

HORNBOGE. In the *Nibelungenlied* one of Etzel's vassals. He arrives at Etzel's court in order to participate in the festivities with the Burgundians, which soon turn deadly. His appearance there, together with Schrutan, Gibech, and Ramung, immediately precedes Volker's attack upon the dandified Hun.

[KM]

HORNBOGI. Jarl Hornbogi is one of Thidrek's best men, according to the *Þiðreks saga.* His son is Amlung. Hornbogi is a brave knight and can ride a horse as swiftly as a hawk can fly. He is among those warriors who fight against Isung and his eleven sons. He finally loses in single combat, but he is not killed. Later he and his son return to their country Win(d)land. Perhaps Jarl Hornbogi is identical to "Hoerning with his horn bow" in *Ermenrikes Dot.* In the Danish ballad *Kong Diderik og hans Kæmper,* he is called Humlung Jersing, and his son is Humlung. Jarl Hornbogi cannot be "Hornboge der snelle" in the *Nibelungenlied* because that knightly character is Etzel's vassal.

[GW]

Bibliography

Holzapfel, Otto. *Die dänischen Nibelungenballaden: Texte und Kommentare.* Göppingen: Kümmerle, 1974, pp. 167ff.

Raszmann, August. *Die Sagen von den Wölsungen und Niflungen, den Wilcinen und König Thidrek von Bern in der Thidrekssaga.* 2nd ed. Hanover: Rümpler, 1863, pp. 466, 512f.

HRAUÐUNG is an ancestor of Hjordis, according to the *Hyndluljóð;* perhaps he is the father of Hjordis's mother.

[GW]

Bibliography

Gering, Hugo, and B. Sijmons. *Kommentar zu den Liedern der Edda.* 1. Hälfte: *Götterlieder.* Germanistische Handbibliothek VII 3,1. Halle (Saale): Buchhandlung des Waisenhauses (Francke), 1927, pp. 387ff.

HREIDMAR, father of Regin, Fafnir, and Otr in the *Volsunga saga.* He is visited by the Aesir (Odin, Loki, and Honir) after they have killed Otr and skinned him. As a ransom, the Aesir are required to pay a great treasure (Andvari's gold) equivalent to the amount that will fit into Otr's skin. The treasure is cursed by Loki, however, and Hreidmar is afterwards killed by his son Fafnir.

[WM]

HRIMNIR, in the *Volsunga saga* is a giant whose daughter Hljod brings the apple of fertility to King Rerir and his wife, allowing the latter to conceive a son, Volsung.

[WM]

HROPT, a name used for Odin in the *Volsunga saga.* Brynhild refers to the god by this name as she instructs Sigurd in rune lore. Hropt/Odin is associated with "mind runes," which can make a man wiser than all other men.

[WM]

HÚNALAND or **HUNLAND.** According to *Guðrúnarkviða in fyrsta* and to *Oddrúnargrátr* Húnaland is the land of the Huns. In the *Þiðreks saga* Húnaland is clearly Attila's realm. But it is strange that Sigurd's ancestors in the *Volsunga saga*—Sigi, Volsung, and Sigmund—are said to rule Húnaland. In addition, Sigurd is often called *inn húnski,* (Hunnish; cf. *Sigurðarkviða in*

skamma and *Atlamál*). Perhaps the word only implies that Sigurd is of southern origin. Otto Höfler suggested a link between Húnaland and Westphalia and regarded the epithet *inn húnski* as a relic of historical fact (cf. Susat/Soest).

[GW]

Bibliography

Dronke, Ursula, ed. and trans. *The Poetic Edda.* Vol. 1 of *Heroic Poems.* Oxford: Clarendon Press, 1969, p. 140.

Höfler, Otto. *Siegfried, Arminius, und die Symbolik.* Heidelberg: Winter, 1961, pp. 104ff.

HUNDING, a king in the *Volsunga saga* who is killed, along with his sons Alf, Eyjolf, Hervard, and Hagbard, in battle against the forces of Helgi. He is the father of Lyngvi and Hjorvard, who are killed by Sigurd.

[WM]

HUNOLD, a vassal and Lord Chamberlain of Gunther's court in the *Nibelungenlied.* He participated with acclaim in the Burgundian battle, which was led by Siegfried against the intruding kings of Denmark and Saxony, Liudegast, and Liudeger.

[KM]

HUNS, a nomadic/pastoral people with origins in the Altai Mountains or the Hsiung-Nu, against whom, in part, the Chinese built the Great Wall. By about the year 375, they had appeared on the Russian steppes, defeating the Ostrogoths and Visigoths and forcing them into Roman territories. The Huns then settled on the plains of present-day Hungary.

After 430 the Huns began to move westward. In 436 Hunnish mercenaries (without Attila) took part in a Roman-orchestrated offensive that decimated the Burgundians near Worms. This battle forms the historical basis of the "Fall of the Burgundians" legends. Attila led a Hunnish invasion of Roman Gaul in 451 and was defeated. His empire then broke apart after his death in 453 due to quarreling among his heirs. After a major defeat in 454 by an alliance of subjugated peoples, the Huns began to decline in importance, and after 550 they are no longer mentioned. Modern Hungarians (Magyars) are not descended from them.

In the *Nibelungenlied* the Huns are a non-German, non-Christian people whose lands lie east of Austria. Despite this foreignness, Attila's court is praised for its religious tolerance and the nobility of its warriors. The presence at this court of many Germanic warriors reflects the historical reality of the Huns' reliance on warriors drawn from the ranks of conquered peoples. Very few of the Huns themselves have names: Etzel, son of Botelunc, is their king; Ortlieb is his son and Helche is his first wife; his brother is Bloedel; and Swemmel and Waerbel are his messengers. The Scandinavian versions, on the other hand, depict the Huns as a Germanic people. In the *Volsunga saga* Sigi, founder of the Volsung dynasty, is a ruler of "Hunland" (as are Sigmund and Sigurd), and Atli is Brynhild's brother. In the *Þiðreks saga* Attila is a Frisian prince who later seizes power in "Hunland," which is located in Northern Germany; Attila's city (Susa) is equated with modern Soest.

Despite the *Nibelungenlied*'s positive view of Etzel, all the versions of the legend treat the Huns, rather stereotypically, as a sinister, faceless, numerically superior horde that does not perform well in battle, often engaging in cowardly behavior and suffering casualties in far greater proportion than do their outnumbered victims.

[JKW]

ILIAS, in the *Þiðreks saga,* third son by a concubine of King Hertnith of Holmgarth (Novgorod), later of Vilkinaland, and younger brother of Osantrix. Hertnith sets Ilias up as earl of Greece. Ilias's two sons are Hertnith and Hirthir.

[FH]

INDÎÂ. A land identified as the origin of fine gems in the *Nibelungenlied* and referred to in connection with the gems worn by Hagen and Dancwart on their arrival in Island during the wooing of Brünhild (403,1).

[WM]

INN (MHG *daz In*), southern tributary of the Danube, forming a boundary between Germany (Bavaria) and Austria, mentioned in the *Nibelungenlied* (1295,4) as the site of Passau: "where the Inn flows with a strong current into the Danube."

The *Klage* contains the same topographical reference (3292) and also alludes to messengers who ride across the Inn, which seems to imply the presence of a bridge (3305).

[NV]

IRING, a particularly courageous warrior in the *Nibelungenlied* (the entire thirty-fifth *âventiure* is devoted to a description of his single-handed assaults on the Burgundians), who is also referred to in the *Klage*. He is a liege man to Hawart of Denmark. He fights alone against various Burgundians at Etzel's court, is wounded by Giselher, recovers and wounds Hagen, and returns to his men. In a second round, however, he is wounded by Hagen who ultimately kills him with a spear through the head as he attempts to retreat. In the *Klage* he is described as having come from Lorraine. Here, too, he dies from a spear thrown by Hagen.

[WM]

IRNFRID, appears in both the *Nibelungenlied* and the *Klage* as the (former) Landgrave of Thuringia. In the *Nibelungenlied* Irnfrid has taken up residence with Etzel and is later killed by Volker in the fighting. In the *Klage* he is renowned for his bravery, but, together with Hawart and Iring, has become an outlaw because of transgressions committed against the Roman emperor. As a result of the excellent treatment he receives from Etzel and Kriemhild, Irnfrid is more than willing to serve them against the Burgundians and dies in the subsequent battle.

[WM]

IRUNG (1), in the *Þiðreks saga,* a mighty warrior and king of Nibelungenland (chapter 151). Irung's wife, Oda (Ute), has sexual intercourse (albeit without her knowledge) with a stranger during her husband's absence and subsequently gives birth to the elf Hogni. Irung and Oda have four sons and one daughter of their own: Grimhild, Gunnar, Guthorm, Gernot, and Gislher.

[WM]

IRUNG (2), the second figure with this name to appear in the *Þiðreks saga* (chapter 352). He is most likely the Old Norse counterpart to Iring in the *Nibelungenlied* and the *Klage*. He is described as being above other knights who serve Grimhild and to whom she appeals to avenge the wrong done her through the death of Sigurd. While he is impressed by her promise of a shield filled with gold in return for his services, Irung is more concerned about retaining Grimhild's friendship. In the fighting that ensues in Atli's camp, Irung and his 300 men fell many of the Niflungs (Nibelungs). Spurred on by Grimhild to attack Hogni and bring her his head, Irung manages to wound him in the first encounter. In the second, however, he is killed by Hogni.

[WM]

ISALDE, an affluent duchess in the *Klage* whose residence is in Vienna. She invites the Hunnish envoys bearing news of the catastrophe at Etzel's court to stay in her house.

[WM]

ISENSTEIN is the name given to Brünhild's castle/fortress in Island in the *Nibelungenlied* (note 382,3; 384,3; 476,3). The name itself (with its components *îsen* = "iron" + *stein* = "stone") may have been intended to convey a sense of the cold, foreboding nature of the realm over which Brünhild holds sway.

[WM]

ISLAND, the name given to Brünhild's kingdom, according to the *Nibelungenlied.* Associations with the historical Iceland illustrate a connection with strands of the *Nibelungenlied* taken from the tales of Atli and Sigurd in the *Poetic Edda.* The "Island" of the *Nibelungenlied,* however, actually has little to do with the real geographic location of Iceland, except perhaps for the fact that it is an island located far from the Burgundian realm. More frequently referred to as *Prünhilde lant* (Brünhild's land; e.g., *Nibelungenlied,* 344,2**b** and 382,3b), this land lies twelve days' journey by boat from Worms (*Nibelungenlied,* 381,1–4), thus placing Brünhild and her fortress Isenstein outside of the courtly world, in stark contrast to Kriemhild. Brünhild's location in Island emphasizes not only her otherness but also her attractiveness for Gunther, who stands to gain both land and a famous, attractive spouse if the wooing mission is successful.

[ASH]

ISUNG (1), king of Bertangaland in the *Þiðreks saga.* After slaying the dragon Regin and receiving Grani from Brynhild, young Sigurd becomes Isung's counselor and standard-bearer. Isung, his eleven sons, and Sigurd combat Thidrek and his twelve champions (Heime, Herbrand, Wildifer, Sintram, Fasold, Amlung, Hornbogi, Hogni, Thetleif, Hildibrand, Gunnar, Widga). Isung defeats Gunnar. At the conclusion of the contest, Isung and Thidrek assure each other of their friendship. Isung marries his daughter, Fallborg, to Omlung, one of Thidrek's champions. Hertnit, son of Ilias, attacks Bertangaland to avenge the death of his uncle Osantrix. Isung and all his sons are killed because of the sorcery of Ostasia, Hertnit's wife. Variations of this story are to be found in the *Rabenschlacht, Biterolf und Dietleib,* and the *Rosengarten.*

[FH]

Bibliography
Schneider, Hermann. *Germanische Heldensage.* Vol. 1. 2nd ed. Grundriss der germanischen Philologie 10/I. Berlin: de Gruyter, 1962, pp. 286–310.

ISUNG (2), in the *Þiðreks saga,* a skilled juggler and musician and companion of Thetleif. When Vithga is captured by Osantrix, Isung aids Vildifer in freeing him from captivity.

[FH]

JARISLEIF, a highly renowned warrior in the *Volsunga saga* who is in Gunnar and Grimhild's entourage when they set out to visit and attempt a reconciliation with Gudrun (chapter 34) subsequent to the murder of Sigurd.

[WM]

JARIZKÁR. According to the *Guðrúnarkviða onnur* (the *Volsunga saga* does not mention him), Jarizkár is among those knights whom Gunnar and Hogni ask to come to King Half's hall. The knights offer Gudrun precious gifts in order to compensate her for the death of her sons and Sigurd. Gudrun, however, trusts none of them. It is not certain whether Jarizkár is meant to be a Danish or a Slavic knight (cf. Jarizleif = the Russian Jaroslav); he may be Atli's vassal.

[GW]

Bibliography

Gering, Hugo, and B. Sijmons. *Kommentar zu den Liedern der Edda.* 2. Hälfte: *Heldenlieder.* Germanistische Handbibliothek VII 3,2. Halle (Saale): Buchhandlung des Waisenhauses (Francke), 1931, pp. 300ff.

JONAKR, a powerful king in the *Volsunga saga* and Gudrun's second husband, a union that was earlier prophesied by Brynhild. They have three sons: Hamdir, Sorli, and Erp. Jonakr is fully supportive of King Jormunrek's intention to marry Svanhild, Gudrun's daughter by Sigurd, but it turns out to be a less than fortuitous choice for Svanhild, who is later accused of adultery with Jormunrek's son, Randver, and is executed by being trampled by horses.

[WM]

JORCUS, as part of the entertainment at the wedding feast of Siegfried and Florigunda in the penultimate chapter of the *Historia von dem gehörnten Siegfried,* a nobleman persuades Florigunda's father, Gibaldus, to allow him to instigate a fight between two notorious cowards, Jorcus, Gibaldus's overseer of his cattle, and Zivelles, a faint-hearted soldier in the retinue of Sieghardus, Siegfried's father. A slapstick joust takes place, and the encounter concludes with Jorcus being declared the victor just as he proposes to cut Zivelles's throat with his butcher's knife, an action which, we are told, would not have been consonant with the chivalric code. The whole episode is adapted from the 1593 version of Sir Philip Sidney's *Arcadia,* as translated into German by Valentin Theokritus von Hirschberg in 1629 and revised by Martin Opitz in 1639. At the end of the *Historia* we learn that Jorcus died during the war that Sieghardus unleashed to avenge Siegfried's death.

[JLF]

JORMUNREK, first mentioned in the *Volsunga saga* in chapter 32 in Brynhild's deathbed prophecy: the daughter of Gudrun and Sigurd (Svanhild) will marry Jormunrek, king of the Goths. The union is arranged, but Bikki, Jormunrek's counselor, suggests to Jormunrek's son, Randver, that he would be a more suitable match for the young woman than his aging father. However, when Randver and Svanhild act on Bikki's advice, the counselor betrays them to Jormunrek. The king has his son hanged and Svanhild trampled to death by horses. Gudrun avenges Svanhild through her sons, Hamdir and Sorli, who cut off Jormunrek's hands and feet, but under Odin's advice the king's men stone Hamdir and Sorli to death.

[WM]

KIEWE (Kiev). Among the knights from many countries and regions who accompany Etzel as he rides to meet Kriemhild in the twenty-second *âventiure* are many from the "land" of Kiev (the Russian city): "Von dem lande ze Kiewen reit da vil manic degen" (Many a warrior-knight from the land of Kiev was riding there; 1340,1).

[SMJ]

KNEFROD is mentioned in the *Atlakviða.* He is Atli's messenger, who invites Gunnar and Hogni to the Hunnish court. He offers them weapons, horses, and precious goods. However, he speaks in such a cold voice that the Gjukungs suspect trouble. The same role is played by Wingi in the *Atlamál* (cf. the prose part *Dráp Niflunga*).

[GW]

Bibliography

Gering, Hugo, and B. Sijmons. *Kommentar zu den Liedern der Edda.* 2. Hälfte: *Heldenlieder.* Germanistische Handbibliothek VII 3,2. Halle (Saale): Buchhandlung des Waisenhauses (Francke), 1931, pp. 288, 338f.

KONRAD. In the epilogue of the *Klage* (4315) a scribe named Konrad is mentioned to whom Bishop Pilgrim of Passau gave the order to write down the eyewitness account of the defeat and death of the Burgundians. The account was said to have been given by Swemmelin, King Etzel's messenger. According to the poem, the report was written in Latin and translated into German verses many times afterwards. This information has led to speculation that a Latin *Nibelungenlied,* the so-called *Nibelungias,* existed. However, no trace of such a poem has ever been found. It is probably best interpreted as a reference to a fictitious source. In the past, scholars have uncovered evidence of a scribe called Konrad who was employed at the chancery of the bishop of Passau from 1216 until 1224 and at the chancery of the duke of Austria between 1226 and 1232. It is not evident, however, that the text refers to this particular Konrad, as the name was one of the most common in use at the time.

[NV]

Bibliography

Meves, Uwe. "Bischof Wolfger von Passau, *sîn schrîber, meister Kuonrât* und die Nibelungenüberlieferung." *Monfort* 32 (3/4): 246–263 (1980).

KOSTBERA (also **BERA**), Hogni's wife, "the most fair of women," in the *Volsunga saga*. It is she who discovers that the runes sent by Gudrun warning of Atli's treachery have been falsified by Vingi. She recounts to her husband her dreams, which presage the perfidy of Atli.

[JHS]

KRIECHEN (Greeks). In the *Nibelungenlied* Etzel's court is a veritable melting pot of nationalities, including a number of Greek warriors alluded to in 1339,1.

[WM]

KRIEMHILD, in the *Nibelungenlied,* Burgundian princess, daughter of Dancrat and Ute, sister of Gunther, Gernot, and Giselher. Kriemhild married Siegfried and after his death remained a widow for many years. Later she married Etzel, king of the Huns. Although it is clear that the *Nibelungenlied* is the tale of the downfall of a society due, paradoxically, to the traditionally rightful actions of its individuals, for many the epic has always been the story of Kriemhild. Indeed Bodmer's 1757 publication of a section of manuscript **C** appeared under the title of *Chriemhilden Rache und die Klage: Zwei Heldengedichte aus dem Schwäbischen Zeitpuncte* (Kriemhild's Revenge and the Lament: Two Heroic Poems from the Swabian Epoch). Kriemhild is certainly the most passionate character in the work, moving with disturbing ease from tender lover to avenging fury, from faithful spouse to unnatural mother. Although she is a woman in what is very much a man's world and is thus subject to the customs of her brothers' court (e.g., congress mainly with the other women and formal appearances at court at the request of her brothers, as well as acquiescence to marriage arrangements made on her behalf), it is in her interaction with the males of

the story that she demonstrates her true character. Far from being the sweet woman forced by circumstances and the machinations of men, principally Hagen, to do terrible things totally out of character (a mantra of most scholars from the *Klage* on), Kriemhild demonstrates from the beginning of the epic a sharp sense of self-awareness and a determination to assert herself as much as possible in her world. In the first *âventiure* Kriemhild the sweet maiden is introduced. But even at this early point she demonstrates her independent thinking. In response to her mother's interpretation of the dream in which two eagles attack and kill a falcon as portending Kriemhild's marriage, she states that she has no intention of marrying:

> "Waz saget ir mir von manne,   vil liebiu muoter mîn?
> âne recken minne   sô wil ich immer sîn.
> sus scoen' ich wil belîben   unz an mînen tôt.
> daz ich von mannes minne   sol gewinnen
>   nimmer nôt." (15)

[Why are you speaking to me of a man, my dear mother; I intend to remain without a warrior's love and, thus remain beautiful until I die without reaping sorrow from a man's love.]

While Kriemhild's view of the value of marriage to a woman is doubtless correct, it would hardly be realistic for a princess of the royal family to expect a life without an arranged marriage. Indeed this is what happens when Gunther agrees to give Kriemhild to Siegfried in exchange for the latter's assistance in winning Brünhild for Gunther. The poet, however, goes out of his way to portray the union as a love match. There are several encounters with much blushing and coquettishness, and their wedding night is a much happier affair, as the poet coyly tells us, than that of Gunther and Brünhild. Although Kriemhild appears to be a contented mate to Siegfried, she nonetheless once again shows her self-awareness when she and her husband are about to take leave of Gunther and journey to Xanten. Before they go, Kriemhild insists that her brothers divide the kingdom and provide her with her part, a statement that irritates Siegfried: "leit was ez Sîfride, do erz an Kriemhilt ervant" (It troubled Siegfried that he discovered this [trait] in Kriemhild; 691,4). Later, when Gislher makes the proposal to divide the kingdom, Siegfried peremptorily rejects the offer. Kriemhild responds that even if he feels free to dispose of her inheritance, it will not be so easy for him to reject her demand for Burgundian knights to accompany her to her new home. Taking knights from one's home to her husband's country was a prudent move for any new bride. Although it is not the case in the *Nibelungenlied,* a young bride's life at her new husband's court was not always happy or secure. It was a necessity to have armed retainers upon whom one could depend absolutely. But here, too, Kriemhild oversteps her bounds as a woman and insists that Hagen and Ortwin accompany her to Xanten. To request that the chief vassal of her brothers accompany her is a heedless demand and is a clear sign of Kriemhild's own overweening status consciousness. Hagen angrily rejects the possibility, and Kriemhild makes other choices. It is clear that Kriemhild has a well-developed sense of her own status in the world and intends to preserve as much of it as she can. This all becomes unraveled in the fourteenth *âventiure* when Brünhild and Kriemhild argue about the respective worth of their husbands. And it is here that Kriemhild declares that Brünhild's allegations about Siegfried's status, and by implication her own, cannot be true because she is *adelvrî* (free and noble.) It is, of course, well known what transpires afterward. The important point, however, is not that the dispute was about their husbands, but rather about themselves and their status. Because of their stubbornness and pride, the women have, in the opinion of the poet, brought chaos into an otherwise orderly male world, something to which he alludes in the first *âventiure* when he says: "si sturben sît jæmerlîche von zweier edelen frouwen nît" (They [the Burgundians] all later died because of the envy of two women; 6,4). This particular epic foreshadowing is repeated several times so that there can be no doubt that the attitude found in the text represents a male point-of-view. Assertive women are dangerous because they can upset the social order. Docile women are the ideal, and if they are not docile to begin with, their husbands should see to it that they become so, as Siegfried makes clear to Gunther after the dispute between the queens:

> "Man sol sô vrouwen ziehen,"   sprach Sîfrit der degen,
> "daz si üppeclîche sprüche   lâzen under wegen.
> verbiut ez dînem wîbe,   der mînen tuon ich sam.
> ir grôzen ungefüege   ich mich wærlîche scham."
> (862)

["One must discipline such women," spoke Siegfried the bold, "so that they put an end to such impertinent tattle. You chastise your wife, and I will do the same to mine. Truly, her outrageous conduct shames me."]

Later we learn of the nature of Siegfried's "chastisement," when Kriemhild speaks to Hagen: "Daz hât mich sît gerouwen," sprach daz edel wîp./ "ouch hât er sô zerblouwen dar umbe mînen lîp" (I have since greatly regretted [my argument with Brünhild] . . . He [Siegfried] beat me soundly all over my body; 894,1–2).

   Siegfried's murder dashes all hopes of a reconciliation, and Kriemhild withdraws using Siegfried's treasure to attract many foreign knights to her service, so much so that Hagen becomes uneasy and presses Gunther to steal the Nibelungen treasure from Kriemhild. Aside from Hagen's disquiet about the treasure, there is no overt indication that Kriemhild is planning revenge at this time. Indeed the poet still refers to her as "diu getriuwe" (the loyal one [to Siegfried]). But with the last of her treasure gone, either robbed by Hagen or given away, and as she prepares to depart with Rüdiger for Gran to become the wife of Etzel, king of the Huns, so, too, is the last mention of her "fidelity" (1281).

   The second half of the *Nibelungenlied* is taken up with the carrying out of Kriemhild's revenge. No longer the loyal woman, she is, instead, listening to the counsels of the devil (1394). Indeed she is herself demonic, a *vâlandinne* (she-devil; note 1748,4 and 2371,4). At the end of the tale Kriemhild's image is monstrous. The poet describes her swaggering before an unarmed and bound Hagen carrying the head of her brother Gunther by the hair, demanding that Hagen tell her where her treasure is. When he refuses, she kills him. This is too much for Etzel and the doughty old warrior Hildebrand. Etzel exclaims:

> "Wâfen, . . .   wie ist nu tôt gelegen
> von eines wîbes handen   der aller beste degen,

der ie kom ze sturme   oder ie schilt getruoc!"
  (2374,1–3)

[Alas and woe, here lies slain by a woman's hand,
the best warrior who ever went to battle or bore a
shield.]

Hildebrand vows to avenge Hagen's death and
kills Kriemhild in a particularly brutal way by
hacking her to pieces. No one criticizes Hildebrand, and the end is one of unremitting sorrow
and lamenting.

Far from undergoing an absolute character
change after the murder of Siegfried, Kriemhild
has simply developed to an extreme degree that
aspect of her personality that has been present
from the beginning, awareness of her status and a
desire to maintain it and assert it, come what
may. Of course, most do not view Kriemhild as
an arrogant, self-serving figure, but rather as a
victim. Certainly the *Klage* and the **C** poet consider her to be the victim of Hagen and lay all
blame for every misfortune squarely at his feet,
even if that involves altering descriptions found
in the **B** text, such as removing the designation of
Kriemhild as a *vâlandinne* (she-devil). If
Kriemhild is a victim, then it is not as an individual but rather as a product of her time. As long as
she was the obedient wife, she could have the
little fantasies that probably made her life more
pleasant. But the minute those fantasies threatened to intrude upon the world of men and the
moment she took on the prerogatives of men
herself, she was condemned as a devil and was
worthy of a gruesome death.

          [FGG]

Bibliography

Ehrismann, Otfrid. "'Ze stücken was gehouwen dô daz
    edele wîp:' The Reception of Kriemhild." In *A
    Companion to the Nibelungenlied,* edited by
    Winder McConnell. Columbia, SC: Camden
    House, 1998, pp. 18–41.
Schröder, Werner. "Die Tragödie Kriemhilts im Nibe-
    lungenlied." *ZfdA* 90 (1960/61): 41–80, 123–
    160. Reprinted in W. S. *Nibelungenlied-Studien.*
    Stuttgart: Metzler, 1968, pp. 48–156.

KUPERAN, in the *Lied vom Hürnen Seyfrid* and
in Hans Sachs's *Tragödie von dem hürnen
Seyfrid,* a giant who rules a thousand dwarfs. (In
some editions of the poem he is called Ruperan,

owing to confusion of **K** and **R** in gothic types. In
the *Historia von dem gehörnten Siegfried* the
giant is named Wulffgrambähr.) He is in the service of the dragon (Fafnir) who has imprisoned
Krimhilt on the *Trachenstain* (dragon's stone).
Brought here by the dwarf Eugleyne/Eugel,
Seyfrid defeats Kuperan and forces him to free
Krimhilt. Inside a cave Kuperan shows Seyfrid
the sword (Balmunc) with which the dragon can
be killed. Kuperan then attacks Seyfrid again,
but he is hurled from the mountain to his death.

          [JLF]

LIUDEGAST (King of the Danes) and
LIUDEGER (King of the Saxons), are brothers
in the *Nibelungenlied* who wage war on the Burgundians. Both are defeated and captured by
Siegfried. The tale of the war against the two
invaders takes up the fourth *âventiure,* titled
"How He [Siegfried] Fought against the
Saxons." It is significant because this episode
provides the only opportunity for Siegfried to
demonstrate his heroic warrior qualities actively.
It was obviously considered important by the
poet that the hero substantiate his great reputation by deeds and not merely by report or hearsay. In the fifteenth *âventiure* a fictitious declaration of hostilities by Liudegast and Liudeger is
used as the pretext to set the planned betrayal and
murder of Siegfried into motion. Liudeger and
Liudegast are also listed in *Dietrichs Flucht*
(5899–5900; 8629; 8631), where they first appear among the warriors sent by Helche, Etzel's
wife, to help Dietrich hold Verona, which
Dietrich's man Amelolt recaptured from Ermenrich. They later are portrayed, along with
such other *Nibelungenlied* characters as Gunther
and Gernot, as allies of Ermenrich, a role they are
also accorded in the *Rabenschlacht* (734–735).
In the *Klage* Liudeger is portrayed as the king of
France and father of Lady Goldrun.

          [FGG/WM]

LOCHEIM (LOCHE). After Siegfried's death
Kriemhild had the entire hoard of the Nibelungen brought to Worms and showered on the rich
and poor alike until Hagen began to fear that she
was recruiting forces against the Burgundians.
Over the objections of King Gunther and
Giselher, Hagen took the treasure and, at the

suggestion of Gernot, had it sunk in the Rhine so that no one would have it so long as any of them lived. The place where Hagen had it sunk was "da ze Loche" (at the hole; 1137,3a). This is thought to refer to Locheim, a town that was located between Mainz and Worms and washed away by a great flood in the thirteenth century.

[SMJ]

Bibliography
Huber, Werner. *Auf der Suche nach den Nibelungen: Städte und Stätten, die der Dichter des Nibelungenliedes beschrieb.* With photographs by Michael Göock. Gütersloh: Praesentverlag, 1981, pp. 52–55.

LOFNHEID, is mentioned briefly as the sister of Fafnir in the Old Norse Eddic poem *Reginsmál.* Fafnir had killed his father Hreidmar to get a treasure and took all the gold for himself. It was Fafnir's brother, Regin, who tried unsuccessfully to get his share. He made Sigurd the sword called Gram and asked him to kill Fafnir. The *Reginsmál* gives evidence of the story of the earlier life of Siegfried in the *Nibelungenlied* and quite possibly points to his acquiring the Nibelungen treasure.

[SMJ]

Bibliography
Terry, Patricia, trans. *Poems of the Elder Edda.* With an introduction by Charles W. Dunn. Philadelphia: University of Philadelphia Press, 1990.

LOGE, Wagner's variation on the name Loki. In *The Ring of the Nibelung* Loge persuades the giants to accept the Rheingold instead of Freia as their payment for building Valhall, and then obtains the gold from Alberich by trickery. Wagner plays on the derivation of the name *Loge* from a word meaning *fire.*

[JVM]

LOKI, a Norse deity, the son of two giants, and Odin's half brother. He embodies unpredictability and introduces the element of change into the necessarily fixed order over which the gods rule. Loki frequently involves the gods in difficult situations and must use deceit to extricate them from trouble. By the later Eddic myths

Loki has been transformed into a purely evil character, causing the death of Baldur and unleashing the forces of destruction at the world's end. Loki's essential character is reflected in the *Volsunga saga,* in which he murders Otr, then captures Andvari and seizes his gold so that the gods can pay compensation for Otr's death. Andvari's curse on the treasure leads to its owners' deaths, including Sigurd's and the Burgundians'.

[JKW]

LORRAINE (or **LOTHARINGIA,** MHG *Luthringe*), the middle part of the Carolingian Empire after the partition in 843 (Treaty of Verdun), extending from the Low Countries to Italy; the latter was separated from Lotharingia in 855. In 925 it was united with the eastern part of the Empire as the duchy of Lotharingia, one of the five great tribal duchies of Germany. It is mentioned twice in the *Klage* as the homeland of the courageous warrior Iring, who was slain by Hagen. According to the *Nibelungenlied,* however, Iring was from Denmark. In the poem *Dietrichs Flucht,* Lotharingia is the homeland of Helpfrich; in *Biterolf und Dietleib,* the people of Lotharingia are the allies of the Burgundian king Gunther, but one of them, Iring, is living as an exile at King Etzel's court.

[NV]

LORSCH (MHG *ze Lôrse*), small town, about 15 kilometers east of Worms on the right bank of the Rhine. In the Middle Ages, Lorsch was dominated by a mighty Benedictine monastery, first mentioned in a charter of 764. According to manuscript **C** of the *Nibelungenlied,* Kriemhild stayed there with her mother Ute for twelve years after Siegfried's death (strophes 1158–1165). In the *Klage* Ute is still living at Lorsch when she receives word of the death of her children (3682); she dies from grief within a week and is buried there (3959). According to popular belief, a large sarcophagus in the chapel of Lorsch Abbey is Siegfried's coffin.

[NV]

LYBÎÂ/LYBÎÂN (Lybia), a country renowned for its fine silks during the Middle Ages. In the

Nibelungenlied Kriemhild and thirty of her ladies-in-waiting prepare fine clothes from Lybian silk (364,1) for Gunther, Siegfried, Hagen, and Dancwart in preparation for their wooing expedition to Island. Brünhild herself wears silk from Lybia under her battledress (429,3).

[WM]

LYNGHEID. According to the *Reginsmál,* Lyngheid is Hreidmar's daughter and Lofnheid's sister. Her brothers are Regin, Otr, and Fafnir. When Hreidmar is mortally wounded by Fafnir, he hopes that his daughter will avenge him. Lyngheid replies that a sister is not allowed to take revenge on her brother. Hreidmar predicts that she will give birth to a daughter whose son will avenge the killing. In the end the hero who kills Fafnir is Sigurd. If Hreidmar's prediction were true, then Lyngheid would be Sigurd's grandmother and her husband would be Eylimi (the name of his wife is mentioned nowhere). She also would not only have had a daughter (Hjodis), but also a son (Gripir). This genealogy is not very plausible, because if it were so, Sigurd would be a relative of Fafnir and such an allusion does not exist in any source. Later Regin asks Lyngheid how he ought to deal with Fafnir. She advises him to be friendly towards him, because a brother should not demand his share of the hoard with a sword in his hand.

[GW]

LYNGVI, a rival suitor for the hand of Hjordis, daughter of King Eylimi in the *Volsunga saga.* Although he loses out to Sigmund, Lyngvi, with the assistance of Odin, subsequently defeats both Sigmund and Eylimi in battle, albeit with no success in his attempt to gain Hjordis. Sigurd later kills Lyngvi during a campaign to avenge his father.

[WM]

MACHAZIN AND MACHMET, two pagan gods mentioned together in the *Klage* (965) in whom Etzel once trusted, but in whom he loses faith following the great slaughter in his camp.

[WM]

MAERI, in the *Þiðreks saga,* a lake located near the confluence of the rivers "Duna ok Rin"

(Danube and Rhine). During his night watch Hogni searches for a boat to ferry the Niflungs across the Rhine on their journey to Atli's court. He discovers two mermaids in the lake. By threatening to keep their clothing, he compels the older mermaid to foretell the fate of the Niflungs. When the mermaid reveals that the Niflungs will cross the river but will not return, Hogni kills both mermaids.

[FH]

MAIN (MHG "Meun"), the main eastern tributary of the Rhine, arises near Bayreuth and meanders westward, dividing Spessart and Odenwald (both mentioned in the *Nibelungenlied*) before it flows into the Rhine near Mainz, about sixty kilometers north of Worms. It is mentioned in the *Nibelungenlied* (1524,1), when the Burgundians start their journey to the land of the Huns along the Main through eastern Franconia. The same route from Worms to Hungary is mentioned in *Biterolf und Dietleib.*

[NV]

MARROCH (Morocco), as with Lybia, also famous in the *Nibelungenlied* for its silks (364,1), the best of which are used by Kriemhild and her ladies-in-waiting to prepare fine clothes for the participants of the wooing expedition to Island.

[WM]

MAUTERN (MHG *Mûtâren*), a small town in Austria on the right bank of the Danube, about 40 kilometers downstream from Melk. It is mentioned in the *Nibelungenlied* (1329,3) as the place to which Kriemhild's uncle, Bishop Pilgrim of Passau, accompanies his niece. It was not the eastern border, but only one of the key points of the diocese of Passau in this area. In the poems *Biterolf und Dietleib* and the *Rabenschlacht,* Mautern is mentioned as the residence of Astolt, who is lord of Melk in the *Nibelungenlied.* Another reference to Mautern can be found in *Alpharts Tod.*

[NV]

MELK (MHG *Medelicke*), the first residence of the Babenbergers, the first Austrian monarchs. Leopold I had a fortress built there after 976. In the *Nibelungenlied* Kriemhild journeyed through Melk following her stay in Pöchlarn. Today it is the site of a large Benedictine monastery and the most recent discovery of a *Nibelungenlied* fragment.

[SSch]

METZ (MHG *Metze*), town in Lorraine (France) on the Moselle River. From 879 until 1552 Metz was part of the German empire and a bishop's see since the fourth century. Under the reign of the emperors, the bishop of Metz had the additional status of a burgrave. Metz occurs eight times in the *Nibelungenlied,* but only as an epithet linked to the name of Ortwin, Hagen's maternal nephew, who is steward of Burgundy and lord of Metz. In the poem *Waltharius* a governor ("metropolitanus" and "praefectus") of Metz appears, while in *Biterolf und Dietleib,* Metz is mentioned as a town on the route from Spain and Paris to Worms.

[NV]

MIME is the brother of Regin according to the *Þiðreks saga.* He is the foster father of young Sigurd and a blacksmith in Hunaland. Young Sigurd finally kills Mime with Gram, a sword Mime had given to him. Mime takes on the role of Regin in the *Edda.* In the mythological lays of the *Edda,* Mime or Mimir is a wise water spirit. In German epic poetry a blacksmith named *Mime der alte* is only mentioned in *Biterolf and Dietleib* (cf., *Dietrich Epics*). Here he forges the sword Schrit for Biterolf. In Wagner's *Ring* cycle Mime is Alberich's brother and the creator of the magic cape.

[GW]

MIMIR, according to the *Prose Edda,* Mimir is master of the well that lies beneath that root of the ash tree called Yggdrasil which reaches toward the land of the frost giants. He is very wise because he drinks regularly from this well. Odin is one-eyed because he once asked for a drink from the well, giving his eye as a pledge that he would drink only one mouthful. He then drank his fill, making him very wise, but causing him to forfeit the pledged eye. There is also a Mimir whose story is told in *Heimskringla.* He, too, was very wise, and was sent by the Aesir to live with the Vanir in an exchange of hostages. The Vanir

beheaded him and sent the head back to the Aesir. Odin preserved the head and gave it magic powers so that he could get advice from it.

[JVM]

MISENBURG In the *Nibelungenlied* the last town through which Kriemhild passes on her journey to the land of the Huns before arriving at Etzelnburg. She and her entourage board ships here for the last segment of the trip down the Danube.

[WM]

MOERINGEN (Mering), a town on the Danube and the site in the *Nibelungenlied* where the ill-fated Burgundians are ferried across the river by a Charon-like Hagen (1591,1).

[WM]

MYRKHEIM (World of Darkness), according to the *Atlakviða,* the place in Atli's realm where Gunnar is killed in the snake pit. Myrkheim can hardly have been a common place name. The term reminds us of *Niðavellir* (Valleys of Darkness) and the *Niðafjoll* (Mountains of Darkness) in the mythological Eddic lay *Voluspá.* Snakes also live in these regions, and it is in this world of the dead that Loki is tormented by snakes. Thus it is likely that the poet of the *Atlakviða* deliberately portrayed Gunnar's death against a mythological background.

[GW]

Bibliography

Dronke, Ursula, ed. and trans. *The Poetic Edda.* Vol. 1 of *Heroic Poems.* Oxford: Clarendon Press, 1969, p. 65f.

MYRKVIÐ (Black Forest) is a barrier between the land of the Huns and Gunnar's realm in the *Atlakviða.* In the eleventh century Thietmar von Merseburg calls the Erzgebirge *Miriquidui.* Indeed a messenger riding from the Danube to the Rhine would have to cross these mountains. Myrkvið is also the border between one land and another in the first lay of Helgi Hundingsbani (*Helgakviða Hundingsbana in fyrri*) and in the lay of Velent (*Volundarkviða*). In the Norse poetic tradition "crossing the Black Forest" came to signify penetrating the barriers between one world and another, especially between the world of the gods and the world of fire, where Surt lives (cf. *Lokasenna* and *Voluspá* in the *Poetic Edda*).

[GW]

Bibliography
de Vries, Jan. *Altgermanische Religionsgeschichte.* Vol. 2. 2nd ed. Grundriss der germanischen Philologie 12/II. Berlin: de Gruyter, 1957, pp. 397, 402.
Dronke, Ursula, ed. and trans. *The Poetic Edda.* Vol. 1 of *Heroic Poems.* Oxford: Clarendon Press, 1969, pp. 47f.
Gering, Hugo, and B. Sijmons. *Kommentar zu den Liedern der Edda.* 1. Hälfte: *Götterlieder.* Germanistische Handbibliothek VII 3,1. Halle (Saale): Buchhandlung des Waisenhauses (Francke), 1927, p. 298.

NÄNTWIN, mentioned in passing in the *Nibelungenlied* (1381,4), he is the father of Herrat. His wife is the sister of Helche.

[MEG]

NAUÐUNG, duke of Valkaborg in the *Þiðreks saga,* corresponds to Nuodung in the *Nibelungenlied.* He is mentioned when Margrave Rodingeir gives presents to the Niflungar at Bakalar (Pöchlarn). Hogni asks for Naudung's blue shield. Rodingeir is pleased to hear this and explains that Duke Naudung wore this shield when he fought bravely against Witege (Widga) and his famous sword Mimung. Finally, Naudung died decapitated in the battle against Witege. Rodingeir's wife, Gudelinda, begins to weep bitter tears over the death of her brother, Naudung. The story of that tragic fight is told in earlier chapters of the saga: Naudung fought together with Atli's sons against Erminrek in support of Thidrek at Gransport, situated on the Moselle River near the sea. During the fight he carried the banner of Thether, who is Thidrek's brother. In the course of the battle Witege found him, smashed the pole of the banner to pieces, and cut off Naudung's head with Mimung. These events correspond in part to the German heroic epic *Rabenschlacht.* Here Nuodung is among Etzel's heroes, but he only fights against Fruot of Denmark. His fight against Witege is totally forgotten. The *Þiðreks saga* has preserved an older version.

[GW]

Bibliography
Grimm, Wilhelm. *Die deutsche Heldensage.* 4th ed. Darmstadt: Wissenschaftliche Buchgesellschaft, 1957, pp. 111ff., 233.
Schneider, Hermann. *Germanische Heldensage.* Vol. 1. 2nd ed. Grundriss der germanischen Philologie 10/I. Berlin: de Gruyter, 1962, pp. 219ff.

NER, in the *Klage,* the father of Wolfwin, one of Dietrich's Amelungs who is killed in the fighting against the Burgundians.

[WM]

NIBELUNG, mentioned in Hagen's cautionary description of Siegfried in the third *âventiure* of the *Nibelungenlied* which deals with Siegfried's arrival in Burgundy. He and his brother, Schilbung, sons of the elder Nibelung (who established their dynasty), are rulers of the otherworldly Nibelungenland and the possessors of the vast Nibelung treasure. He initially welcomes Siegfried with graciousness, but conflict arises when Siegfried is unable to divide these riches, a service for which the brothers had unwisely given Siegfried Nibelung's sword, Balmung. In the ensuing battle twelve giants, seven hundred warriors, and the unfortunate Nibelung and Schilbung themselves are killed, prompting their devoted dwarf Alberich to contemplate revenge upon Siegfried, something which, given Siegfried's strength, proves impossible. This story is told not only to provide evidence of Siegfried's physical strength and prowess, which was clearly significant even prior to his encounter with the dragon, but also as a warning to the Burgundians to be wary of Siegfried's capabilities, Nibelung and his brother Schilbung having been hitherto strong and undefeated princes. Note also the reference to him in the epic *Walberan* (139).

[KM]

NIBELUNGS, the inhabitants of the (geographically undefined) realm conquered by Siegfried in the *Nibelungenlied* prior to his arrival in Worms and who are likely named after King Nibelung, father of the two princes, Schilbung and Nibelung. The treasure associated with the family, which Siegfried acquires, along with Balmung and the cloak of invisibility, was also known as the *Nibelungenhort*. The name *Nibelungs* is transferred to the Burgundians in the second part of the epic (see 1523,1), albeit without an explanation. In Wagner's *Ring* cycle the Nibelungs are dwarfs living in caves of the earth; they were forced to dig for gold by Alberich using the power of his magic ring.

[KM]

NIDERLANT, with its variants *Niderland* (occurring six times in the *Nibelungenlied*), *Niderlanden* (one time), and *Niderlant* (nineteen times), the Netherlands represent a significant place in the epic tale. There is a strong relationship between Siegfried and Niderlant; it is the place of his birth and the country of which he becomes king (in addition to Nibelungenland). Niderlant may have been a term associated with the Lower Rhine, and perhaps Xanten (Santen) functioned as a regional center of territorial accretion.

[GCS]

Bibliography

Alberts, Wybe Jappe. "Die Reisen der deutschen Könige in die Niederlande im Mittelalter." In *Niederlande und Nordwestdeutschland: Studien zur Regional- und Stadtgeschichte Nordwestkontinentaleuropas im Mittelalter und in der Neuzeit,* edited by Wilfried Ehbrecht and Heinz Schilling. Cologne: Böhlau, 1983, pp. 18–40.

Bäuml, Franz H., and Eva-Maria Fallone. *A Concordance to the "Nibelungenlied."* Leeds: Maney, 1976.

Magoun, Jr., Francis P. "Geographical and Ethnic Names in the *Nibelungenlied.*" *Mediaeval Studies* 7 (1945): 109ff.

NIFLHEIM, one of nine worlds of Norse cosmology, found on the lower third level and characterized by bitter cold and unending night. Hel, guarded by a fierce and hideous female monster, is in Niflheim (sometimes called Niflhel). It is the realm of the dead, though heroes in battle are taken to Valholl. The only clear relationship between Niflheim and the Nibelungs is etymological: they share a root meaning fog or mist (cf. Old High German *nebul*). The word *Nibelung* may have been applied originally to a race of treasure-guarding dwarves in a misty, gloomy homeland. In the *Nibelungenlied* neither

Hagen's description of how Siegfried took the Nibelung treasure (third *âventiure*), nor the depiction of Siegfried's journey to Nibelungenland to get warriors for Gunther (eighth *âventiure*) offers any real connection to Niflheim. In the *Þiðreks saga, Niflaland* simply refers to the land of the Burgundians.

[JKW]

NIFLUNG, son of Hogni in the *Volsunga saga.* He hates Atli for having killed his father and conspires with Gudrun to avenge the death of Hogni and Gunnar and the other Gjukungs. While he is reported to have helped Gudrun kill Atli, only Gudrun is actually depicted thrusting a sword into the chest of the sleeping monarch.

[WM]

NIFLUNG/AR (Nibelungen) is the name given to Gunnar, his brothers, and their liege men in the prologue of the *Þiðreks saga* and throughout the whole of its *Niflunga saga.* The scribes never use the name Burgundians for them, a name which frequently occurs in the *Nibelungenlied* and is also mentioned in the Eddic lay *Atlakviða* and the second *Waldere* fragment, an Anglo-Saxon poem in alliterative verse (cf. *Waltharilied*).

[GW]

Bibliography

Schneider, Hermann. *Germanische Heldensage.* Vol. 1. 2nd ed. Grundriss der germanischen Philologie 10/I. Berlin: de Gruyter, 1962, pp. 205ff.

NIFLUNGALAND, according to the *Þiðreks saga,* the Burgundian area, ruled by Gunnar and his brothers, the Niflungar. Their kingdom is never called Burgundy in this saga. The capital of Niflungaland is Verniza on the Rhine (i.e., Worms).

[GW]

NINNIVÊ. Mentioned once in the *Nibelungenlied* (850,1) as a land from which fine silks are imported. In the particular context referred to above, the splendor of Kriemhild's attire combined with her proud comportment serves further to distress Brünhild after Kriemhild has produced her belt and ring to underpin her claim that

Siegfried had bedded the queen of Iceland prior to Gunther.

[WM]

NITGER, mentioned in the *Klage* (v. 1543) as one of Dietrich's warriors killed by Giselher during the fighting in Etzel's Great Hall.

[WM]

NITHUNG (1), king of Spain and father of Sisibe in the *Þiðreks saga.* Sigmund of Tarlungaland sends messengers to ask for Sisibe's hand. Nithung receives Sigmund's emissaries well but is reluctant to marry his daughter to Sigmund. Sigmund himself then travels to Spain to request her in marriage. Nithung greets Sigmund honorably, marries Sisibe to Sigmund, and gives them half his empire. The other half he gives to his son, Ortvangis, and because he is a feeble old man, Nithung makes Ortvangis king.

[FH]

NITHUNG (2), in the *Þiðreks saga,* king of Jutland; he has three sons and one daughter. Velent's tree-trunk vessel floats to his shores, and Nithung grants Velent permission to remain in his realm and serve him. Velent eventually becomes Nithung's smith. On a military campaign Nithung promises one half of his empire as well as his daughter to the man who will bring him his "victory stone" before the sun rises the following day. None of his men is willing to risk this venture, and Nithung asks Velent to retrieve his stone. Velent succeeds but upon his return is confronted by Nithung's steward who demands the stone. Velent refuses and kills the steward, for which Nithung banishes him. After Nithung defeats the Vikings, Velent returns in disguise and attempts to poison the king and his daughter, but Nithung hamstrings Velent and forces him to work as his smith. When Egill, Velent's brother, comes to Nithung's court, the king tests him by making him shoot an apple from his son's head. Velent kills Nithung's two youngest sons and rapes his daughter. He then reveals his deeds to Nithung as he hovers above the king and Egill on wings that he has crafted. When the king orders Egill, known as an expert archer, to kill Velent, Egill shoots an arrow into a bladder filled with blood that Velent has placed beneath his arm, and

Velent escapes. Nithung dies and is succeeded by his only remaining son, Otvin.

[FH]

NORDIAN (1), in the *Þiðreks saga,* the huntsman of Iron, earl of Brandinaborg. He accompanies Iron on his hunting expeditions. Not willing to abandon his lord when all of Iron's other men flee, Nordian is captured with Iron by King Salamon. Salamon sends Nordian to Isolde, Iron's wife, to procure ransom for Iron. After Iron has been slain by Aki Omlungatrausti, Nordian and three other men of the late earl ride to Hunaland to tell Atli the news.

[FH]

NORDIAN (2), in the *Þiðreks saga,* the second son of King Vilkinus of Vilkinaland (and half brother to Vathi). After Vilkinus's death, Nordian becomes king of Vilkinaland. A less able ruler than his father, he is attacked by Hertnit, who had paid tribute to Vilkinus but who now refuses to do so to Nordian. Nordian's force is smaller, and Nordian is defeated and flees. He appeals to Hertnit for mercy. Hertnit complies and makes Nordian ruler of "Svithjoth" (= Sweden), later called "Sjoland." When Osantrix succeeds to the throne of Vilkinaland, Nordian becomes his man. Nordian has four sons, Ethgeir, Aventrod, Vitholf, and Aspilian, all of them giants. After Nordian's death, Osantrix makes Aspilian king of Sjoland.

[FH]

NORWAY is mentioned in the *Nibelungenlied* as the country where the Nibelungs reside and have their castle (739,3).

[AC]

NUODUNG, a magnificent warrior mentioned throughout the Dietrich epics as an ally of Dietrich. It is most likely his wife whom Kriemhild promises to Bloedel in the *Nibelungenlied* in her attempt to have the latter avenge Siegfried's death by attacking Hagen. His name also occurs in Heinrich Wittenwiler's *Ring.*

[WM]

NUODUNG'S WIFE, the bribe offered Bloedel by Kriemhild in the *Nibelungenlied* to induce the former to attack the Nibelungs and avenge her husband, Siegfried. After failing to convince others to undertake the task, Kriemhild promises Bloedel, Etzel's brother, the riches, lands, and castles of the deceased Nuodung (see also *Alpharts Tod* 78f.) and, most importantly, his bride, whose beauty is Bloedel's greatest temptation. However, Bloedel is never in a position to enjoy these prizes, as he is slain by Hagen's brother, Dancwart.

[KM]

NYBLING, an old dwarf king mentioned in the story of the *Hürnen Seyfrid* (14,1; 14,6; 134,1; 134,5; 156,7; 168,4). He is the father of the dwarf Eugel and his two brothers. In the *Hürnen Seyfrid* he is the original owner of the Nibelungen treasure. In the later printed editions the sons exile their father, while in the earlier, more authentic editions, the sons simply push the treasure of Nybling into a hollow in order to hide it (135,1). Nybling dies of grief. His name corresponds to the dwarf Nibelunc in the *Nibelungenlied* (87,3), but in the *Hürnen Seyfrid,* it is not used in a general way to refer to a collective group.

[RB]

OBBE JERN, a figure in the Danish ballad *Grimilds Hævn,* who toward the conclusion of the work offers a swordless Hagen his own weapon. He displays traits that are reminiscent of both Rüdiger and Eckewart in the *Nibelungenlied.*

[GW]

ODA (1), in the *Þiðreks saga,* Hildibrand's wife, not mentioned until almost the conclusion of the work, when Thidrek and Hildibrand return from their long exile. Oda weeps when she sees her wounded son Alibrand ride into Bern with Hilbrand after their father-son battle but rejoices when she learns that her long-absent husband has returned. She welcomes Hildibrand and binds Alibrand's wound.

[FH]

ODA (2), in the *Þiðreks saga,* wife of Irung, king of Niflungaland. When Irung is absent from the realm, an elf sleeps with Oda. Their child is Hogni. With Irung, Oda bears Grimhild, Gunnar, Guthorm, Gernoz, and Gislher. When her sons receive the invitation to visit Atli's court, she relates a dream to them, in which she saw in Húnaland so many dead birds that all the land was bereft of the creatures. She predicts great misfortune for the Niflungs and the Huns if her sons travel to Húnaland and asks them not to go.

[FH]

ODA (3), daughter of Milias, king of Húnaland in the *Þiðreks saga.* She is courted by kings and earls, but Milias loves her so much that he does not wish to marry her to any man. Osantrix sends messengers to ask for her hand and later appears in disguise before Milias to repeat his request. He is refused despite Oda's pleas to the contrary. Later, having defeated Milias, a still disguised Osantrix tells Oda that he will take her to Osantrix. He sets her on his knee and slips a silver and gold shoe onto her feet. He then reveals his identity to her, marries her, and reconciles himself with Milias. Their daughter is Erka.

[FH]

ODA (4), in the *Þiðreks saga,* the daughter of the earl of Saxland, wife of Biturulf of Skani in Denmark and mother of Thetleif.

[FH]

ODDRUN, Atli's sister in the *Volsunga saga.* As she dies, Brynhild prophesies Gunnar's love affair with Oddrun, which Atli has forbidden, and which leads to the downfall of the royal lines of both Gjuki and Atli.

[JHS]

ODENHEIM, a town in the Kraichgau, about 25 kilometers almost due south of Heidelberg and 30 kilometers west of Heilbronn, is mentioned at the end of the sixteenth *âventiure* in manuscript **C** of the *Nibelungenlied* as the location of the spring where Siegfried was killed: "Von dem selben brunnen, da Sivrit wart erslagn,/sult ir div rehten mære von mir hoern sagen./vor dem Otenwalde ein dorf lit, Otenheim;/da vliuzet noch der brunne, des ist zwifel dechein" (You shall hear me tell the right tale about that very spring where Siegfried was slain. A town called Odenheim is located before the Odenwald; there the spring is still flowing, of that there is no doubt; 1030). The spring itself is outside the town at the foot of a wooded mountain slope. A stone with the inscription "Siegfried Brunnen" arches over the water gushing out into a pool and above it is a stone tablet showing Hagen throwing his spear at Siegfried kneeling at the spring. This is one of three Siegfried springs (see also Grasellenbach and the Lindelbrunnen).

[SMJ]

Bibliography

Huber, Werner. *Auf der Suche nach den Nibelungen: Städte und Stätten, die der Dichter des Nibelungenliedes beschrieb.* With photographs by Michael Göock. Gütersloh: Präsentverlag, 1981, pp. 34–37.

ODENWALD, the name of the forest (MS. **C,** 919,3; MS. **B,** 911,3: "Waskenwald") in which Siegfried goes hunting with the Burgundians and in which he is killed at a spring by Hagen. Scholars hold diverse opinions regarding the actual place of the killing. [see: Vosges]

[SSch]

ODIN (also **HNIKAR, FENG, FJOLNIR,** and **HROPT**), the chief Norse deity, appears on several occasions under different names in the *Volsunga saga.* He is the father of Sigi and assists in his escape after the latter has murdered the thrall, Bredi. Odin provides Rerir, son of Sigi, with an apple of fertility. He is the one who sets the challenge of the sword set in a tree trunk which leads to the battle between Siggeir and Volsung; he transports Sinfjotli's body into the realm of the dead. Odin intervenes in the battle between Sigmund and Lyngvi by causing Sigmund's sword to break and bringing about his demise. Regin informs Sigurd how Odin, Loki, and Hoenir came upon Otr at the waterfall of the dwarf Andvari and how Loki killed Otr with a stone. The act forced the gods to pay Hreidmar, Otr's father, Andvari's gold as ransom, including the cursed ring, Andvaranaut. Later, in the guise of an old man, he instructs Sigurd in the most effective manner to kill the dragon Fafnir. When Brynhild kills Hjalmgunnar in battle, to whom Odin had promised victory in combat against Agnar, the god causes her to fall into a deep sleep, be robbed of future victories, and intimates that she should marry. As Hnikar, he joins the tumultuous voyage undertaken by Sigurd to avenge the Volsungs. He disappears as soon as

Sigurd and his men land in the realm of the Hundings. As Hropt, Odin is also the creator of mind runes.

[WM]

OMLUNG (1), in the *Þiðreks saga,* the nephew of Elsung. As Thidrek, Hildibrand, and Herath approach Bern, they are confronted by a vengeful Elsung and his warriors. Omlung brashly challenges Hildibrand who overcomes him. During a brief battle Elsung is slain, but Omlung surrenders to Thidrek and is reconciled with him. Omlung tells Thidrek that Erminrek is near death because of Sifka's treachery. He returns to Babilon (Elsung's castle) with Elsung's armor and twelve survivors and relates that Thidrek and Hildibrand have slain Elsung and fourteen of his men.

[FH]

OMLUNG (2), the son of Hornbogi in the *Þiðreks saga.* When Thidrek and his champions approach Bertangaland to challenge Isung and his champions, Sigurd rides out to meet them demanding tribute to Isung. Thidrek consents, and the lot falls to Omlung to relinquish his horse and shield. Angered, Omlung wants to ride after Sigurd to retrieve his property. He asks his father to lend him his horse, but Hornbogi refuses. Omlung is able to borrow a horse from Vithga, son of Velent the smith, only after he has pledged his lands and inheritance as security. Once he has the horse he overtakes Sigurd, and challenges him. Suspecting that Omlung is his kinsman, Sigurd proposes a joust and unhorses Omlung. Then, sympathizing with Omlung's plight, Sigurd reveals his identity to Omlung who acknowledges their kinship. Sigurd then gives Omlung his two horses, tells Omlung to tie him to a tree and ride back to Thidrek with Sigurd's spear, horse, and shield. Vithga suspects that Omlung's opponent was Sigurd and that Sigurd must have given Omlung his possessions voluntarily. As Vithga rides into the forest to find out the truth, Sigurd breaks free and flees, and Vithga believes Omlung's story. During the combat of the champions, Omlung, seeing the first five of Thidrek's men defeated and bound, vows not to suffer their fate. He overcomes Isung's sixth son and compels the release of Thidrek's five companions. After his defeat by Thidrek,

Sigurd gives Hornbogi and Omlung great gifts. At Sigurd's request, Isung marries his daughter Fallborg to Omlung. Hornbogi, Omlung, and Fallborg accompany Thidrek to Bern and from there to Hornbogi's realm, Vindland.

[FH]

ORKNING, in the *Volsunga saga,* he is mentioned briefly as the brother of (Kost)Bera, Hogni's wife. He is one of the few warriors who accompany Hogni and Gunnar to Atli's camp.

[WM]

ORTLIEB, Kriemhild and Etzel's son in the *Nibelungenlied.* He is murdered by Hagen when the latter hears of the attack on the Burgundian squires by the Huns. His imminent death is hinted at in an earlier remark by Hagen (1918,3–4), when he voices his doubts regarding Ortlieb's future. When Dancwart enters Etzel's Great Hall after the attack on himself and the Burgundian squires, Hagen decapitates Ortlieb in the presence of both Etzel and Kriemhild, unleashing the terrible battle that ultimately culminates in the mass destruction of Burgundians, Huns, and Amelungs.

[KM]

ORTVANGIS, mentioned in the *Þiðreks saga,* is the son of King Nidung of Hispania and the brother of Sisibe, the mother of Young Sigurd (Sigurð svein). King Nidung gives most of his possessions to Sisibe and his son-in-law, Sigmund, and only very little to his son Ortvangis. Ortvangis is not mentioned anywhere else.

[GW]

ORTWIN VON METZE (Ortwin of Metz), on the Moselle, is mentioned in the first *âventiure* of the *Nibelungenlied* along with the other significant figures at the Burgundian court. He is the king's steward (*truhsæze,* 11,2) and the nephew of Hagen and Dancwart. He appears as a hothead who is angry at the proposed conciliation with Siegfried (116) and calls for swords (119), a situation that is defused by Gernot. Although frequently mentioned early in the poem, and described as *der degen* (the warrior) and as *küen* (bold), he fades out of the action, does not go on the journey to Isenstein, and more significantly, takes no apparent part in the expedition to Etzel's court.

[MEG]

OSANTRIX, a figure in the *Þiðreks saga,* the eldest son of King Hertnit of Vilkinaland. The aged Hertnit makes Osantrix king of Vilkinaland with Nordian as his tributary king. When Osantrix's queen dies, he asks for the hand of Oda, daughter of King Milias of Húnaland. Milias imprisons Osantrix's emissaries. Osantrix then travels to Húnaland in disguise; with him are Aspilian, Aventrod, Ethgeir, and Vitholf. He asks Milias for sanctuary, claiming to be at odds with Osantrix. Milias refuses his requests and after the third refusal, Aspilian knocks Milias unconscious. Osantrix and his men then attack, forcing Milias to flee. Osantrix marries Oda and is later reconciled with Milias. Their daughter is Erka. When Milias dies, Atli annexes Húnaland. Osantrix attempts unsuccessfully to regain Oda's patrimony. Atli sends proxy wooers to Osantrix asking for Erka's hand, but Osantrix refuses them all. Atli attacks Vilkinaland and routs Osantrix's forces, retreating before Osantrix can counterattack. Osantrix then pursues Atli to the border between Denmark and Húnaland. After a brief nighttime skirmish, Osantrix returns to Vilkinaland and Atli to Susa. Atli's man, Rotholf, disguises himself and rides to Osantrix's court, where he remains for two winters. Rotholf convinces Erka to flee to Susa with him and become Atli's wife. Osantrix pursues them and corners them in a castle in Falstrskog but retreats as Atli advances. Enmity between Osantrix and Atli continues. As Osantrix ages, his disposition becomes harsher and more despotic. He is guarded constantly by the giants, Vitholf and Aventrod. After Osantrix rejects an overture of peace from Atli, Atli and Thidrek of Bern attack Vilkinaland, and Osantrix flees. He throws the captured Vithga into a dungeon. Vildifer and Isung the juggler free Vithga, and Vildifer beheads Osantrix.

In a variant tradition of Osantrix's death, Osantrix has captured Brandinaborg, which is then surrounded by Atli's forces. When Osantrix rides out of the castle to attack the besiegers, he is killed by Ulfrath, the nephew of Thidrek of Bern.

[FH]

OSID. Three different men are accorded this name in the *þiðreks saga:* **Osid** (1) is king of Friesland and Atli's father. In the German heroic epics Etzel's father is called Botelung; in the lays of the *Edda* his name is Budli. In history his name was Mundzuck. King Osid has two sons, Otnid and Atli. When he dies he gives Friesland to his son Otnid, who has a son called Osid. **Osid** (2), son of Otnid, is brought up at Atli's court and becomes one of Atli's bravest knights. Atli sends him out together with Rodolf to woo Erka, daughter of Osantrix, yet Osid is unsuccessful in his task. Therefore Atli attacks Osantrix and his Vilkinamen and wins his wife Erka. Osid demonstrates considerable courage in these fights. Later he is sent to woo Grimhild for Atli, adopting a function of Rüdiger von Bechelaren in the *Nibelungenlied.* During the last banquet of the Niflungar at Atli's court, Duke Osid sits to Atli's left side next to King Thidrek and Rodingeir. In the final fight, King Gunnar is defeated by Osid (contrary to the *Nibelungenlied,* here Gunnar is tied up by Dietrich von Bern). We do not get any information about Osid's death, although only Atli, Thidrek, and Hildibrand survive, according to the saga. **Osid** (3). Hirdir, son of Jarl Ilias, brother of Hertnit, is called Osid in a single sentence. Here, however, Osid might be a slip of the pen.

[GW]

Bibliography
Kralik, Dietrich von. *Die Überlieferung und Entstehung der Thidrekssaga.* Halle (Saale): Niemeyer, 1931, pp. 58f., 68ff.

ÓSKÓPNIR. In *Fáfnismál,* Óskópnir (The Ugly, Deformed) is the name of the island where the gods and the demons, especially Surt, fight their last battle at the end of the world. According to a different tradition, this battlefield is called *Vígríðr* (The Field Where the Battle Rages).

[GW]

Bibliography
de Vries, Jan. *Altgermanische Religionsgeschichte.* Vol. 2. 2nd ed. Grundriss der germanischen Philologie 12/II. Berlin: de Gruyter, 1957, p. 397.
Gering, Hugo, and B. Sijmons. *Kommentar zu den Liedern der Edda.* 2. Hälfte: *Heldenlieder.* Germanistische Handbibliothek VII 3,2. Halle (Saale): Buchhandlung des Waisenhauses (Francke), 1931, p. 191.

OSTERLANT, OSTERRÎCHE (Austria), as used in the *Nibelungenlied* designates the area between Mautern and Hainburg. While the author tells us nothing about the passage of the Burgundians from Pöchlarn to the castle of Etzel, the journey of Kriemhild and her entourage through Austria is described in great detail. As told shows them "die strâze in das Osterlant/ gegen Mûtâren die Tuonouwe nider" (the way to Austria toward Mautern down the Danube; 1329,3–6). Rüdiger escorts Kriemhild first of all to Traismauer (*Treisenmûre*) or Zeiselmauer (*Zeizenmûre*), where Helche, Etzel's first wife, is supposed to have held court. References to Traismauer can only be found in manuscripts **C, D, a** (1332,2) and **C, R, a** (1336,1), but the local designation *bî der Treisem,* as well as the fact that Zeiselmauer is east of the travelers' next station Tulln, have convinced most scholars that the other manuscripts are corrupt in this respect. Kriemhild remains in Traismauer for four days, while Etzel and his knights are already on their way through Austria in order to welcome her (1336). The first encounter between Etzel and Kriemhild takes place in Tulln, *ein stat bî Tuonouwe lît in Osterlant* (a town in Austria situated on the Danube), which is so overcrowded by all those who have come to honor Kriemhild that Rüdiger's companions have to seek lodging in the countryside (1363). Finally, the marriage between Kriemhild and Etzel takes place *in der stat ze Wiene* (in the town of Vienna; 1365) and is followed by seventeen days of festivities. According to the author of the *Nibelungenlied,* when Etzel and his wife arrive at Hainburg, which was historically the last German town and is situated at the "Porta Hungarica," they have already reached Etzel's home country, *daz hiunische lant* (the Hunnish land).

[MH]

Bibliography
Brunner, Karl. "Ein 'Land' den 'Nibelungen.'" In *Helden und Heldensage. Otto Gschwantler zum 60. Geburtstag,* edited by Hermann Reichert and Günther Zimmermann. Philologica Germanica 11. Vienna: Fassbaender, 1990, pp. 45–56.

Hansen, Walter. *Die Spur des Sängers. Das Nibelungenlied und sein Dichter.* Bergisch Gladbach: Lübbe 1987.

————. *Wo Siegfried starb und Kriemhild lebte: Die Schauplätze des Nibelungenliedes.* Vienna: Ueberreuter, 1997.

OTR (Otter), one of Hreidmar's three sons in the *Volsunga saga.* He assumes the shape of an otter during the day and is an accomplished fisherman. He had the reputation of being something of a loner, as he would come home late in the day and eat alone with his eyes closed because he could not bear to see his food disappear. A kenning for gold is otter payment. One day, as Odin, Loki, and Hoenir were exploring the world, they saw Otr, who was dozing over a salmon he had caught in Andvari's Fall. Loki hit the otter with a stone and killed him. His father Hreidmar and brothers Fafnir and Regin bound the gods and demanded as penalty enough gold to fill the otter's skin and then cover it completely. The gods obtained this gold from Alberich. It was later taken by Fafnir and came to belong to Sigurd when he slew Fafnir and Regin.

[WM/JVM]

ÓTTAR, the son of Innstein and Hlédís, and the protégé of Freyja, according to the *Hydluljóð.* He is engaged with Angantýr in a lawsuit concerning his inheritance. The giantess Hyndla informs him about his ancestors in order to help him. Among the names cited are heroic figures of the Nibelung cycle, for example Sigurd and Gunnar. Perhaps the poet wished to connect a Norwegian family with these heroes so as to sing their praises. It is suggested that Óttar may be Óttarr birtingr, a protégé of the Norwegian king Sigurd Jórsalfari (1090–1130).

[GW]

Bibliography

Gering, Hugo, and B. Sijmons. *Kommentar zu den Liedern der Edda.* 1. Hälfte: *Götterlieder.* Germanische Handbibliothek VII 3,1. Halle (Saale): Buchhandlung des Waisenhauses (Francke), 1927, p. 375.

PASSAU, a city situated on the Danube at the Austro-German border, a station on the journey of the Nibelungs/Burgundians. The *Nibelungenlied* mentions both a monastery as well as the Inn River, which also runs through the city. A third river is called the Ilz, a place where the Burgundians are said to have camped. The connection of Passau to the *Nibelungenlied* goes beyond geography. It has been suggested that the epic was written in Passau about 1200. The Archbishop Pilgrim of Passau in the *Nibelungenlied* is portrayed as the brother of Ute, the uncle of Kriemhild and her brothers. In reality, his reign was from 971–991. The archbishop at the time of the *Nibelungenlied*'s conception was Wolfger. With Pilgrim he shared a love of literature, art, and music. Ferdinand Wagner, a nineteenth-century artist, created a large painting of Pilgrim and Kriemhild riding into the city and this can be seen today in the city hall of Passau.

[SSch]

PETSCHENÆRE (Petschenegen). A Finnic-Ugrian people and one of the many groups of nationalities in the *Nibelungenlied* who are subjects of Etzel. The epithet used to describe them in 1340,2 is "wild," although they are also reputed to be particularly skilled archers.

[WM]

PFÖRRING (MHG *Vergen*), a small town on the left bank of the Danube, about thirty-five kilometers east of Ingolstadt (Bavaria). It is mentioned only once in the *Nibelungenlied* (1291,1) as the place to which Gernot and Giselher accompany their sister and where Kriemhild and her retinue cross the river on their way to the land of the Huns. The identification of Vergen with Pförring is not undisputed because the word means "at the ferryman's," which could be anywhere along the river. Moreover, the equivalent of MHG "Vergen" should be Pföring and not Pförring.

[NV]

PILGRIM. In the *Nibelungenlied* and the *Klage,* the Bishop of Passau, brother of Ute and uncle to Gunther, Gernot, Giselher, and Kriemhild. In the *Klage* he is adamant about having the events that have transpired at Etzel's court written down for posterity, based on the account provided by the minstrel Swemmel. See also PASSAU.

[WM]

PLATTLING (MHG *Pledelingen*), a small town on the River Isar near its confluence with the Danube, halfway between Ratisbon and Passau. It is only mentioned in the **C** version of the *Nibelungenlied* (**C**, 1324,1) as a place where Kriemhild and her company stay overnight during their journey to the land of the Huns. Here Kriemhild meets her uncle, Bishop Pilgrim of Passau. The town was probably added by the adapter of the **C** version to indicate the western boundary of the diocese of Passau.

[NV]

PÖCHLARN (MHG *Bechelaren*), one of the oldest cities in Austria. Rüdiger, the earl of Bechelaren on the Danube, is host to Kriemhild during her journey to the land of the Huns. Later on the Burgundians also stop there and Giselher becomes engaged to Rüdiger's daughter, Dietlinde (named in the *Klage*, but not in the *Nibelungenlied*). Rüdiger presents Gernot with his sword, while his wife, Gotelind, passes on to Hagen the shield of her relative, Nuodung, who was killed in battle against Witege. Pöchlarn is the main city in the Nibelungengau and the site of annual performances of scenes lifted from the *Nibelungenlied*.

[SSch]

POELÂN (Poles) are also numbered among the many nationalities serving Etzel at his court in the *Nibelungenlied* (1339,2).

[WM]

RAGNAR LOÐBRÓK, the main character of the saga bearing his name, where he fathers six sons famed for raiding and making war. Loðbrók refers to the "hairy breeches" Ragnar wears in order to defeat the dragon and win the hand of Thora, his first wife. After Thora's death, he marries Aslaug, the daughter of Sigurd and Brynhild. He is captured on an ill-conceived raid against the English, and, in a manner reminiscent of Gunnar in the *Volsunga saga,* put to death in a snake pit by the English king Ella. The saga thus connects Ragnar and his sons with the English *Aella* and the Danish raids on England in the mid-ninth century. He is also (with Aslaug) made to be an ancestor of the Norwegian king Harald Fairhair. Ragnar's verses, his death speech in the snake pit, make up the whole of the *Lay of Kraki.*

They are perhaps most remarkable in their expression of a warrior ethic and pagan religious fervor. Ragnar is also a major figure in Book IX of Saxo Grammaticus's *Gesta Danorum.*

[JKW]

RAMUNG OF WALLACHIA, in the *Nibelungenlied* he is identified as a duke from Wallachia who is invited to the court of Etzel to celebrate the wedding between the king and Kriemhild. He brings along seven hundred men, who are described as "flying birds" as they make their way into the land of the Huns.

[WM]

RANDVER, son of King Jormunrek in the *Volsunga saga.* His father sends him and the counselor Bikki to woo for him Svanhild, Gudrun's daughter. Bikki suggests to Randver that he would be a more suitable husband for Svanhild than his father, and Randver (as well as Svanhild) appear to agree. They are betrayed, however, by the malevolent Bikki to Jormunrek, who has his son hanged and Svanhild trampled to death by horses.

[WM]

REGIN, a wise, skillful, cunning dwarf and magician. It is principally the *Reginsmál* and the *Fáfnismál* that tell us something about this character. He is the son of Hreidmar and the brother of Fafnir and Otr, his sisters are Lyngheid and Lofnheid. He helps his father to take Odin, Hoenir, and Loki into custody because these gods have killed Otr. When the Aesir (the gods) have paid the fine, his father does not give him his share. After Fafnir has killed Hreidmar, Regin demands his heritage, but in vain. His sister Lyngheid advises him not to raise a weapon against his brother. Regin comes to King Hjalprek, the foster father of Sigurd, and becomes Sigurd's teacher. He knows that Sigurd will be a brave hero and tells him the story of Fafnir, who guards an immense treasure on the Gnitaheath. He even forges the sword Gram, with which Sigurd splits the anvil, and provokes Sigurd into killing Fafnir. The dying dragon warns Sigurd that Regin will be a traitor to him. Regin cuts out Fafnir's heart, drinks his blood, and asks Sigurd to roast the dragon's heart. Then he goes to sleep. The titmice also warn Sigurd of

Regin and Sigurd consequently cuts off his head. Then he eats Fafnir's heart and drinks Regin's and Fafnir's blood. This makes him cunning and wise. Later Sigurd is in possession of costly goods and precious objects (see also the *Volsunga saga*).

In the *Þiðreks saga* Regin occupies the role of Fafnir and Mime has taken on the role of Regin. In the Eddic lays the brothers Regin and Fafnir are enemies; here Mime and Regin are friends (cf. "Young Sigurd").

[GW]

RERIR, son of Sigi in the *Volsunga saga*. He avenges his father's death by killing all of his maternal uncles, who, despite being the most trusted of Sigi's allies, had conspired to murder him. It is through the assistance of his grandfather, Odin (and the urging of the goddess Frigga), that Rerir's wife is eventually able to conceive a child when the couple is brought an apple of fertility by Hljod, one of Odin's wish maidens, and the daughter of the giant Hrimnir.

[WM]

RHINE. In the minds of many, the river and the *Nibelungenlied* are closely connected with one another. For instance, Heinrich Böll remembers that as a boy, he once believed that the Rhine consisted of dragon's blood that flowed down from the Odenwald. In the *Nibelungenlied* the Rhine constitutes the western axis of the scene of action. The Burgundian kings have their residence *ze Wormez bî dem Rîne* (at Worms on the Rhine; 6,1); Siegfried comes from Xanten *nidene bî dem Rîne* (down on the Rhine; 20,4); Gunther and Siegfried travel along the Rhine in order to win Brünhild (377,3); and Hagen finally sinks the treasure in the Rhine (1137), where it is allegedly still to be found today. However, the exact locations remain rather vague in the *Nibelungenlied* because the poet knew the Bavarian and Austrian regions far better.

Since the Romantic period at the beginning of the nineteenth century, the Rhine and the *Nibelungenlied* have been stylized both as elements of a national German mythology. Celebrated by romantic poets and painted by the artists of the Düsseldorf School of painting and the Rhine painters of Koblenz as well as English artists such as Turner and Webb, the Rhine eventually was declared to be "Teutschlands Strom" (Germany's river). Like no other river, the Rhine has been associated with historical events and political developments. Thus the river seemed to be particularly suited for preserving memories of a supposedly magnificent past and for ensuring their survival: "Memories of what the Germans once were and could be in the future are evoked nowhere so clearly as on the Rhine," wrote Friedrich Schlegel in 1803. About fifty years later the Rhine became, like the *Nibelungenlied* itself, a solid component of a national-political vocabulary that served the attempt to establish a new national order by regarding the past nostalgically.

[MH]

Bibliography
Brunner, Karl. "Ein 'Land' den 'Nibelungen'." In *Helden und Heldensage. Otto Gschwantler zum 60. Geburtstag,* edited by Hermann Reichert and Günter Zimmermann. Philologica Germanica 11. Vienna: Fassbaender, 1990, 45–56.
Gassen, Richard W., and Bernhard Holeczek, eds. *Mythos Rhein. Ein Fluß: Bild und Bedeutung.* Wilhelm-Hack-Museum Ludwigshafen am Rhein, 12. Juni bis 16. August 1992.
Hansen, Walther. *Wo Siegfried starb und Kriemhild liebte: Die Schauplätze des Nibelungenliedes.* Vienna: Ueberreuter, 1997.
van der Lee, Anthony. "Geographie, Toponymie und Chronologie im ersten Teil des Nibelungenliedes." *Neophilologus* 67 (1983): 228–241.
Volmari, Beate. "Am Rhein, am Rhein, am Deutschen Rhein." In *Die Nibelungen: Bilder von Liebe, Verrat, und Untergang,* edited by Wolfgang Storch. Munich: Prestel, 1987, pp. 162–165.

RHONE (ROTEN). In stanzas 1243 and 1244 of the *Nibelungenlied,* Kriemhild's brother, Giselher, is trying to persuade his sister to marry Etzel, saying that if she does marry Etzel, he will banish her sorrows and recompense her for her loss of Siegfried. He praises Etzel by saying "vome Roten zuo dem Rine, von der Elbe unz an daz mer,/so ist kunec deheiner so gewaltec niht" (From the Rhone to the Rhine, from the Elbe to the sea, there is no king so powerful 1244,2a–1244,3b). The form *Roten* is from Latin *Rhodanus,* the Rhone River in modern France.

[SMJ]

RISPA is Heime's horse, according to the *Þiðreks saga.* Heime's father, Studas, the administrator of Brynhild's stud, has tamed it for his son. Falka, Skemming, and Grani are Rispa's brothers. Rispa is a grey stallion and extremely beautiful and strong. When Heime and Widga have to cross the river Weser, Rispa and Skemming fly over the water like arrows.

[GW]

Bibliography

Tuppa, Gerlinde. "Die Bedeutung der Tiere und der Tiermotive in der germanischen Heldensage." Diss., Vienna, 1965, pp. 268f.

RITSCHART, mentioned briefly in the *Nibelungenlied* (2281,1) as one of Dietrich's men who is involved in the fighting in the Great Hall of Etzel.

[WM]

RIUZE (Russian). Russians are among the many nationalities at the court of Etzel in the *Nibelungenlied* (1339,1).

[WM]

ROGNIR is a proper name of Odin, perhaps cited in the *Sigrdrífumál.* In the *Atlakviða* the word simply means powerful prince or lord, and refers either to Atli or to Gunnar.

[GW]

Bibliography

Dronke, Ursula, ed. and trans. *The Poetic Edda.* Vol. 1 of *Heroic Poems.* Oxford: Clarendon Press, 1969, p. 68.

de Vries, Jan. *Altgermanische Religionsgeschichte.* Vol. 2. 2nd ed. Grundriss der germanischen Philologie 12/II. Berlin: de Gruyter, 1957, p. 84f.

ROTHINGEIR, lord of Bakalar and Attila's man in the *Þiðreks saga.* Attila sends him to Osantrix to request Erka's hand and, if refused, to threaten war. Osantrix rejects Attila's suit but sends Rothingeir back to Attila with gifts. Later, when Thidrek is forced out of Bern by Erminrek, he rides to Bakalar. Rothingeir accompanies Thidrek to Susa, where he fights valiantly for Atli and Thidrek. He rescues Hildibrand in the battle against Valdimar and leads one of Thidrek's armies in the latter's abortive at-

tempt to retake Bern. Rothingeir informs Atli and Erka of the deaths of their sons, Erp and Ortvin, and acts as an intermediary for the penitent Thidrek. When Atli marries Grimhild, Gunnar gives Rothingeir Sigurd's sword, Gram. The Niflungs stop at Bakalar on their journey to Húnaland, and Rothingeir receives them with great courtesy and generosity. He marries his daughter to Gislher and presents the groom the sword, Gram. He then gives Gunnar a helmet and Gernoz a new shield. Hogni is given Naudung's shield. Afterward Rothingeir accompanies the Niflungs to Susa. In the battle between the Niflungs and the Huns, Rothingeir remains neutral until he learns that Gernoz has killed Blothlin. He then attacks, killing many Niflungs. Gislher slays Rothingeir with Gram. Thidrek laments Rothingeir as "minn bezti vin" (my best friend) The role of the figure clearly parallels that of Rüdiger in the *Nibelungenlied.*

[FH]

RÜDIGER. In the *Nibelungenlied* and the *Klage,* one of the most sympathetic and well-liked characters whose tragic fate is particularly mourned by survivors of the cataclysmic confrontation at the court of Etzel. He has been regarded as *the* Christian warrior in the *Nibelungenlied,* although the epithet is not necessarily the most appropriate one. Rüdiger is margrave of Bechelaren (Pöchlarn) and a vassal in the service of Etzel. It is Rüdiger who brings the marriage suit from Etzel to Kriemhild and who makes the fateful promise in strophe 1256 to avenge any wrong done Kriemhild. While he is undoubtedly thinking of the future, Kriemhild's thoughts remain trained on the past.

Rüdiger's home at Bechelaren (with spouse Gotelind and daughter Dietlinde, who is, however, named only in the *Klage*) is portrayed as the epitome of a hospitable court, whether used as a stopover by Kriemhild in the twenty-first *âventiure* on her way to the land of the Huns to wed Etzel, or by the doomed Burgundians later in the twenty-seventh during their trip to the court of the Hunnish king. It is during their sojourn here that Rüdiger's daughter becomes betrothed to Giselher, thus helping to cement the close, friendly relationship between Rüdiger and his Burgundian guests, but also adding yet a further dimension to the tragic predicament in which he will find himself once fighting has broken out in Etzelnburg.

The dilemma faced by Rüdiger, one that is presented within a highly charged and complex dichotomy between *triuwe* and *untriuwe* (loyalty and disloyalty), is the matter of primary allegiance. He must choose between his liege lord Etzel and Kriemhild, by whom he is reminded of his earlier oath, and the Burgundians, as whose host and guide he has served since their arrival in the land of the Huns. The thirty-seventh *âventiure* is devoted entirely to the tragic situation in which Rüdiger finds himself, culminating in the fatal combat between himself and Gernot (who uses the very sword earlier given to him as a gift by Rüdiger to slay his opponent).

Although Rüdiger had believed that his very soul was in peril (note 2150), it is abundantly clear that the Burgundians fully recognize the dignity and integrity of Rüdiger and that his reputation among them, in any event, is in no way compromised by the decision he has taken. Until the end, he is loved and respected by friend and enemy alike, and the lamentation over his death, particularly as depicted in the *Klage,* reaches an incredible pitch that virtually defies description.

[WM]

Bibliography

Jones, George Fenwick. "Rüdigers Dilemma." *Studies in Philology* 57 (1960): 7–21.

Nagel, Bert. "Heidnisches und Christliches im Nibelungenlied." *Ruperto-Carola* 10 (24): 61–81 (1958).

Naumann, Hans. "Rüedegers Tod." *DVjs* 10 (1932): 387–403.

Splett, Jochen. *Rüdiger von Bechelaren: Studien zum zweiten Teil des Nibelungenliedes.* Heidelberg: Winter, 1968.

Wapnewski, Peter. "Rüdigers Schild: Zur 37. Aventiure des Nibelungenliedes." *Euphorion* 54 (1960): 380–410.

RUMOLD, master of the kitchen in the *Nibelungenlied* and protector of Burgundy during the absence of the Burgundian kings. Following the arrival of the Hunnish envoys Swemmel and Wärbel, and the announcement of Etzel's invitation to the Burgundians, Rumold concurs with Hagen's skepticism regarding the prudence of accepting the offer to come to the land of the Huns. He emphasizes the advantages to be had by remaining in Worms and the potential danger that awaits them at Etzelnburg, but his advice is immediately rejected by Gernot, who believes that Kriemhild no longer bears them a grudge and is well-disposed towards them. Just prior to the departure of the Burgundians, Rumold once again expresses his doubts over the wisdom of the journey and his regret that no one has been able to dissuade Gunther and the others from traveling to Etzel's court. Burgundian lands and the Burgundian women are entrusted by Gunther to his care. Rumold's attitude towards Hagen appears to be much more favorable in the *Nibelungenlied* than in the *Klage,* as he attributes there the loss of his lords to Hagen's arrogance and reflects that it was treacherous of Hagen to have killed Siegfried, who had never done anything to hurt him.

[WM]

SÆGARD (sea farm) is the name of Brynhild's castle in the *Þiðreks saga,* which is situated in Swabia. Brynhild lives here together with her foster father, Heime. Sægard is mentioned twice; the first time when the story of Studas is told and the second time when Sigurd tells Gunnar, his brother-in-law, that he should woo Brynhild. Later (perhaps after Brynhild's death) Sægard obviously belongs to Erminrich. In *Helreið-Brynhildar,* Brynhild and Heimir's place of residence is called Hlymdalir ("valleys of noise/din"). According to the *Ragnars saga loðbrókar,* Brynhild and Sigurd's daughter, Aslaug, grow up in Hlymdalir under Heimir's protection.

[GW]

SAXI, according to the *Guðrúnarkviða in Þriðja,* is a southern Germanic prince who is capable of consecrating the boiling kettle for a trial by ordeal. Gudrun asks for this ordeal in order to prove that she is innocent of adultery.

[GW]

SAXONS (MHG *Sahsen*), Germanic tribe, ruled by King Liudeger, according to the *Nibelungenlied,* a brother of the Danish King Liudegast. Both kings declare war on the Burgundians but are decisively defeated by an army commanded by Siegfried, and the two are taken prisoner. With two exceptions, the Saxons are mentioned in the *Nibelungenlied* only in the fourth *âven-*

tiure. Recollections of Charlemagne's campaigns against the Saxons between 772 and 804 as well as legal actions against Henry the Lion in 1180 have been suggested as a source for the image of the Saxons in the fourth *âventiure.* Saxons sometimes appear in other heroic poems (e.g., *Rabenschlacht* and *Biterolf und Dietleib*), but most of the information provided there is obviously taken from the *Nibelungenlied.*

[NV]

SAXONY (MHG *Sahsen lant*), territory in northern Germany between the Ems, Weser, and the lower Elbe rivers, bounded in the north by Denmark. It is named after the Germanic tribe of the Saxons who expanded their territory in this area starting in the second century a.d. Between 772 and 804 Saxony was conquered and converted by Charlemagne. In 852 the duchy of Saxony was founded by Louis the German; it became one of the five great tribal duchies of Germany. In 1180 Duke Henry the Lion was outlawed by Emperor Frederick Barbarossa. In the fourth *âventiure* of the *Nibelungenlied,* a campaign against Saxony is depicted in which the Burgundian army crosses the Rhine and marches through Hesse to Saxony (176).

[NV]

SCHILBUNG, brother of Nibelung (with whom he shares the kingship of Nibelungenland) in the *Nibelungenlied,* and son of Nibelung I, founder of the Nibelung dynasty. He is killed by Siegfried following a dispute over the Nibelungen treasure, resulting in Siegfried's acquisition of these riches.

[KM]

SCHRUTAN, in the *Nibelungenlied* one of Etzel's vassals. He is present at the festivities the Huns arrange in honor of their Burgundian guests. These festivities swiftly disintegrate into open hostility leading to the calamitous loss of life, which closes the epic. In the *Rosengarten* he is portrayed as a giant figure who loses his life fighting on the side of King Gibeche against Dietrich and his men.

[KM/WM]

SEYFRID (SEYFRIED, SEWFRID), Seifrid, Seyfrid and Seyfried are all normal Early New

High German reflexes of Middle High German Sîvrit, Sîfrit. The variant Sewfrid (also Süwfrid) occurs in a number of the sixteenth- and seventeenth-century editions of the *Lied vom Hürnen Seyfrid,* including the very earliest (cf. also Hans Sachs's play *Der hürnen Seufrid*), and whereas Max Herrmann and Wolfgang Golther regarded the dichotomy Seyfrid/Sewfrid as a significant criterion for grouping the editions, K. C. King clearly demonstrated that this view was untenable. The form Siegfried, more usual today, is not attested regularly until the seventeenth century.

[JLF]

Bibliography

Herrmann, Max. "Die Überlieferung des Liedes vom Hürnen Seyfrid." *ZfdA* 46 (1902): 61–89.

Golther, Wolfgang. *Das Lied vom Hürnen Seyfrid.* 2nd ed. Halle: Niemeyer, 1911.

King, K. C. *Das Lied vom hürnen Seyfrid.* Manchester: Manchester University Press, 1958, pp. 11f.

SIEGFRIED (see SEYFRID, SIGURD), in the *Nibelungenlied,* son of King Siegmund of Xanten and his wife Sieglinde; husband of Kriemhild. The narrative of his youth and upbringing as related in the second *âventiure* is presented as a parallel to the description of the young Kriemhild in the first. He is depicted as the favored scion of the royal family, brave, handsome, and, above all, just. It is a far cry from the descriptions of young Sigurd in the Scandinavian tales. Siegfried is an uneasy hybrid of the modern courtier and the archaic Germanic hero. On the one hand, when he is old enough, the poet reports, he "rides to court," where the ladies and maidens were happy to see him. He is also dubbed a knight during a magnificently lavish accolade that may have awakened memories of the emperor Friedrich Barbarossa's famous festival in Mainz for his sons in 1184, thus establishing a very modern context. Further, he is smitten by tales of the beautiful Kriemhild and determines to ride off and woo her, something that causes his parents great distress since they fear that their son will be slain by Gunther and his men. The fact that their son is the very same Siegfried who slew the Nibelungen kings and took possession of the Nibelungen treasure and later killed a dragon and bathed in its blood, which had the magical property of making him invulnerable (except for one spot) seems not to be present in their minds. What are they worried about, one might legitimately ask. Indeed, when Siegfried and his companions arrive at Worms, Hagen sets the scene by recounting the entire heroic prehistory of Siegfried, without mention of a possible connection with Brünhild (strophes 86–101). To compound matters, Siegfried temporarily forgets his original intention and challenges Gunther for his kingdom. The Burgundians refuse to be provoked with the exception of Ortwin, who is quickly put in his place by a very status-conscious Siegfried:

> Daz zurnde harte sêre   der helt von Niderlant.
> er sprach: "sich sol vermezzen   niht wider mich dîn hant.
> ich bin ein künec rîche,   sô bistu küneges man.
> jane dörften mich dîn zwelve   mit strîte nimmer bestân."

> [Then the hero of the Netherlands became enraged.
> He said: "Indeed, not against me shall your hand be gauged!
> I am a mighty king, and you but a retainer!
> Twelve of your sort could not prevail against me in anger."] (118)

The situation then gets tense as Ortwin calls for weapons, and Hagen murmurs darkly about the injustice of it all. But Gernot steps in and comes up with the solution before a battle is joined. He simply forbids his men to speak. The poet, thus, regains control of the scene and does not allow his characters to cross the line. Siegfried, he relates, then "remembered the glorious maiden" (123,4).

At this point the true tale of the *Nibelungenlied* Siegfried begins, and a complex one it is. True to the archaic Nibelungen tradition, Siegfried must marry Kriemhild, must come into contact with Brünhild, and must be killed by a member of Kriemhild's family. Further, the ostensible cause must be an apparent breach of faith between Siegfried and Gunther regarding Brünhild. Making full use of the epic form of narrative, the poet relates the slow development of a relationship of trust between Siegfried and the Burgundian kings, beginning with the "Saxon War" episode (fourth *âventiure*), when Hagen suggests that Gunther enlist Siegfried's

aid in the coming battle with Liudeger and Liudegast (151). Siegfried then leads a modest force of Burgundians against a numerically vastly superior army of Saxons and Danes. The poet depicts Siegfried in a series of battles, always in the thick of things. It is quite possible that he does so because this is the only opportunity in the *Nibelungenlied* for Siegfried to demonstrate his superb fighting prowess, in other words, his archaic, heroic side. Subsequent opportunities, as is well known, are limited to subterfuge: helping Gunther defeat Brünhild in Island and in the bedroom or in making his last stand after Hagen has cast his hunting spear into his back (scarcely the stuff of which legends are made). But a perhaps much more important purpose is served by this episode in that the beginnings of the ties that bind the Burgundians and Siegfried irrevocably together begin here. These ties are further intensified and at the same time made more opaque when Siegfried agrees to aid Gunther in his quest for Brünhild by posing as Gunther's vassal in return for the latter's consenting to the marriage of Siegfried and Kriemhild. Much has been written about this expedition, especially about the implications of Siegfried's pretense that he is Gunther's vassal. Whatever the symbolic impression such a masquerade might have made (i.e., whether the listeners really believed that Siegfried became Gunther's vassal) cannot be ascertained, and it is probably idle to continue speculating about it. Nonetheless, the fact does remain that in the work itself, Brünhild believes it (strophes 419–423), and becomes within the context of the narrative the motor driving Nibelungen society toward its inevitable tragic outcome. For as a status-conscious woman (strophes 423, 620, 622), she is dismayed to witness the betrothal of the princess, Kriemhild, to an apparent vassal which, if true, would be socially déclassé for her. Failing to receive a satisfactory explanation from Gunther, she employs her superhuman strength and hangs him on a nail until the first dawn of their marriage. Humiliated, Gunther confesses his unpleasant experience to Siegfried who promises to help him. Once again, Gunther readily accepts his aid under the condition that Siegfried not have intercourse with her. Wearing his cloak of invisibility, Siegfried subdues Brünhild, and she loses her great strength. Then, for some unfathomable reason, mysterious also to the poet, Siegfried takes with him her ring and belt and presents them to his wife, Kriemhild. Years later, at the culmination of the dispute about whose husband is of higher status, Kriemhild publicly flaunts these items in front of Brünhild before the cathedral, while declaring that it was Siegfried who took Brünhild's virginity and not Gunther:

> "Wen hâstu hie verkebset?"   sprach dô des küniges wîp.
> "daz tuon ich dich", sprach Kriemhilt.   "den dînen schoenen lîp
> den minnet' êrste Sîfrit,   der mîn vil lieber man.
> jane was ez niht mîn bruoder,   der dir den magetuom an gewan."

> [Cried the queen: "Whom are you calling whore?!"
> "You!" shouted Kriemhild, "and what's more he who pleasured you first was Siegfried, my sweet lover.
> He, not my brother, took your maidenhood's cover!"] (840)

Clearly, this is a terrible insult, made all the more malicious since Brünhild was claiming that Siegfried was Gunther's vassal. Kriemhild is not only accusing the Burgundian queen of having had sex with a man not her husband, but worse, with a man not her equal in status. Brünhild is discovered weeping by Hagen, who vows revenge. Hagen then presents the situation to Gunther, who eventually accedes to the former's demands and allows Siegfried to be treacherously slain.

The Nibelungen poet adheres closely to the necessary details of the Siegfried story while at the same time occasionally putting his own definite imprint on the events, and yet he is not always in complete control of them. His uncertainty is quite apparent with regard to Siegfried's relationship with Brünhild, for example. Did Siegfried already know Brünhild or not? Her greeting to him on Island makes that unclear. On the other hand, her immediate acceptance of his claim to be Gunther's vassal indicates that they had not enjoyed a previous relationship. But this shadowy "memory" remains, and the poet knows that the root cause for Siegfried's death has to do with a lie about the degree of his intimacy with Brünhild. Siegfried, however, has no opportunity for intimate contact on Island, and during the wrestling match with Brünhild in Worms, Gunther is present. The poet chooses to remain unclear on that point. He is clear, however, in his opinion of the murder. It is wrong. He casts the deed and his judgment of it in moral terms of loyalty, and the Burgundians are found severely wanting in this respect. Thus while the "story" of Siegfried remains, the justification for his death is not deemed acceptable by the poet. This moral judgment is unique to the *Nibelungenlied*.

[FGG]

Bibliography

Andersson, Theodore M. "Why Does Siegfried Die?" In *Germanic Studies in Honor of Otto Springer.* Pittsburgh: K & S Enterprises, 1978, pp. 28–39.

Ehrismann, Otfrid. *Nibelungenlied: Epoche, Werk, Wirkung.* Munich: Beck, 1987.

———. "Siegfried: Ein deutscher Mythos?" In *Mittelalter—Mythen 1,* edited by Ulrich Müller and Werner Wunderlich. St. Gallen: UVK, 1996, pp. 367–387.

Haymes, Edward. R. "Chevalerie und alte maeren: Zum Gattungshorizont des Nibelungenliedes." *Germanisch-romanische Monatsschrift* 65 (1984): 369–384.

Heinzle, Joachim. "Gnade für Hagen? Die epische Struktur des *Nibelungenliedes* und das Dilemma der Interpreten." In *Nibelungenlied und Klage: Sage und Geschichte, Struktur und Gattung. Passauer Nibelungengespräche 1985,* edited by Fritz Peter Knapp. Heidelberg: Winter, 1987, pp. 257–276.

Hoffmann, Werner. *Das Siegfriedbild in der Forschung.* Darmstadt: Wissenschaftliche Buchgesellschaft, 1979.

Ihlenburg, Karl-Heinz. *Das Nibelungenlied: Problem und Gehalt.* Berlin: Akademie Verlag, 1969.

Mackensen, Lutz. *Die Nibelungen: Sage, Geschichte, ihr Lied und sein Dichter.* Stuttgart: Hauswedell, 1984.

Müller, Gernot. "Zur sinnbildlichen Repräsentation der Siegfriedgestalt im Nibelungenlied." *Studia Neophilologica* 47 (1975): 88–119.

Müller, Jan-Dirk. "Sivrit: künec, man, eigenholt. Zur sozialen Problematik des Nibelungenliedes." *ABäG* 7 (1974): 85–124.

SIEGFRIED JR. In 718,4 of the *Nibelungenlied,* we learn that Gunther and Brünhild have one son and that they name him Siegfried, "out of love for the hero." Although he is not heard of again in the epic, the author of the *Klage*

(4006ff.) places emphasis on the knighting and crowning of the child proposed by the surviving Burgundians in Worms so that they will not be left without a leader.

[WM]

SIEGHARDUS, the father of the hero in the *Wunderschöne Historie vom gehörnten Siegfried.* In other Nibelungen texts he is commonly called Sigmund or Sigemunt. This prose version of the late medieval Seyfrid material has a tendency to change the traditional nomenclature in accordance with the prevailing taste of the time. Often, as in this case, names were chosen which were thought to be traditionally German. In the above text the names are commonly embellished with Latin endings to simulate a learned style.

[RB]

Bibliography
Jantz, Harold. "The Last Branch of the Nibelungen Tree." *MLN* 80 (1965): 433–440.
Schröder E. "Das Volksbuch vom gehörnten Siegfried." *DVjs* 5 (1892): 480–489.

SIEGMUND (Sigemunt), Siegfried's father in the *Nibelungenlied.* He has his court at Xanten, brings up his son with the help of his wife Sieglinde and, again with her, organizes a great festival in honor of his investiture (27–42). He tries to persuade Siegfried not to venture on the journey to Worms but then provides him with the appropriate fine equipment (66). When Siegfried and Kriemhild return to Xanten, Siegmund abdicates in favor of his son (713–714). He accompanies the party to Worms, but after the death of Siegfried and having failed in his attempts to persuade Kriemhild to return with him for the sake of her son, he goes back to Xanten and is not mentioned again. The idea that he might take revenge for the death of his son (a spontaneous response to the terrible deed and seemingly an obvious course of action) is dismissed by Kriemhild, who implies that she already has other plans (1033).

In Wagner's *Ring* cycle Siegmund is Wotan's son. He and his twin sister Sieglinde are the incestual parents of Siegfried (see SIGELIND I, SIGNY, SINFJOTLI)

[MEG]

SIFJAN, a king in the *Þiðreks saga* who is mentioned only once and who is called the father of King Sigmund of Tarlungaland.

[FH]

SIFKA, Ermenrich's treasurer and counselor in the *Þiðreks saga.* Ermenrich sends Sifka to Sarkasteinn and during his absence violates Sifka's wife, Odilia. Sifka secretly vows revenge. Under pretense of loyally advising Ermenrich, Sifka convinces him to send his son, Fridrek, to demand tribute of Osantrix. Sifka surreptitiously alerts his kinsman in Osantrix's realm and has Fridrek murdered. Then, complaining that Ermenrich has never received tribute from England, Sifka persuades Ermenrich to dispatch his son, Reginbald, to collect it. Sifka chooses the least seaworthy vessel for Reginbald, and Reginbald dies at sea. Later Sifka accuses Ermenrich's youngest son, Samson, of abducting Sifka's daughter. Ermenrich rides at Samson, grabs him by the hair so that the young man falls off his horse and is trampled by Ermenrich's mount. After Ermenrich has hanged his nephews, Egarth and Aki (who have been slandered by Odilia), Sifka warns him that Thidrek is disloyal. Ermenrich forces Thidrek from Bern. Years later, as Thidrek is returning to recapture Bern, he learns that Sifka has caused Ermenrich's death by offering fatal medical advice (i.e., "curing" Ermenrich's abdominal wound by drawing his entrails out). In the pivotal confrontation for control of the late Ermenrich's empire, Alibrand slays Sifka.

[FH]

SIGAR (1), a person named by Gudrun in the *Volsunga saga* as having taken one sister of Haki and Hagbard, the sons of Hamund, and having burned a second sister in her house.

[JHS]

SIGAR (2), one of two figures (the other is Siggeir) in the *Volsunga saga* whom Gudrun and Thora weave into a tapestry representing their battle at Fjon, a Danish island.

[JHS]

SIGEHER OF WALLACHIA, a nobleman in the *Klage* (347), but not mentioned in the *Nibe-*

lungenlied. Along with Herman of Poland, he is killed with all of his men at the court of Etzel while fighting to avenge Kriemhild's sorrow. The designation *Wallachia* (related to Old High German "Walah" = "foreigner," "of Romanic or Celtic extraction") would seem to indicate that Sigeher could have been identified with either Italy or France, but the name *Sigeher* tends to point closer to home. Perhaps he was viewed as Sigeher, conqueror of territory known as Wallachia. Although Sigeher does not appear in the *Nibelungenlied,* Walache is mentioned in 1339,2 as an ethnic group, and Ramung is named as one of their dukes in 1343,1. The editors of manuscript **B** of the *Nibelungenlied,* Bartsch/de Boor, believe that "Walache" is a reference to a southeastern Slavic people, although the latter cannot be more specifically defined.

[WM]

SIGELIND I (SIGELINT), wife of King Siegmund and mother of Siegfried, Sigelind, plays a small part in the *Nibelungenlied.* She is anxious when her son decides to go on his hazardous journey to Worms, but, unlike Siegmund, she does not try to dissuade him, though she cannot disguise her tears. When she realizes that he is determined, she helps him by preparing fine garments (63). She rejoices when he returns with his bride and rewards the messenger with *botenbrôt.* The last we hear of her is that she dies shortly after the birth of the child Gunther, thus ceding the place of first royal lady to Siegfried's wife Kriemhild (717). There seems to be no significance in the fact that one of the two water sprites (*mêrwîp*) bears the same name (1539,1).

In Wagner's *Ring* cycle, Sieglinde is Wotan's daughter. She and her twin brother Siegmund are Siegfried's incestual parents (see SIEGMUND, SIGNY, SINFJOTLY)

[MEG]

SIGELIND II, daughter of King Nitger in the *Klage.* He is a knight in the service of Dietrich who is killed by Giselher in the battle at Etzel's court.

[WM]

SIGELIND III is one of two water sprites in the *Nibelungenlied* whom Hagen encounters in the twenty-fifth *âventiure* of the *Nibelungenlied.* In

contrast to her companion, Hadeburg, she elects to tell Hagen the truth regarding the fate that awaits the Burgundians in the land of the Huns (1539ff.).

[WM]

SIGESTAB, nephew of Dietrich von Bern in the *Nibelungenlied.* He greatly laments the death of Rüdiger (2258,2–4), who has become a benefactor and a good friend to all those who have been exiled from their homelands. He is accorded high praise for his valor against the Burgundians in the fight in Etzel's Great Hall (2283), but is ultimately killed by Volker (2285) and his death is avenged by Hildebrand (2287). Sigestab is also mentioned in the *Klage.*

[WM]

SIGGEIR, a king in the *Volsunga saga* who rules over Gautland. He successfully woos Signy, the daughter of King Volsung, but is insulted by Sigmund, her brother, during the wedding festivities. In a treacherous act of revenge Siggeir attacks and kills the king. Sigmund is the only son who survives his father and eventually, with the compliance of his sister, he kills the two sons King Siggeir has by Signy. Siggeir perishes with all of his men and Signy, who voluntarily remains with him, when his Great Hall is set afire by Sigmund and Sinfjotli, Sigmund's son from an incestuous relationship with his sister.

[WM]

SIGI, in the *Volsunga saga,* Sigi is named as the son of Odin. Characteristic of numerous figures associated with the Volsung clan is the *Sig-* element in his name, the meaning of which is *victory.* He kills the thrall, Bredi, out of jealousy over the latter's greater success as a hunter. When the murder is discovered, Sigi is assisted by Odin in his escape. He subsequently establishes himself as ruler of Húnaland but is eventually killed by his wife's brothers.

[WM]

SIGIBERT, king of the Austrasian Franks (ruling at Metz, Rheims) from 561–575, married to Brunhild and murdered on the orders of Fredegund in 575. There are parallels with Siegfried in his name and in the manner of his death.

Sigibert also defeated the Danes and Saxons in 565 and aided his brother Gunthram, king of Burgundy, against the Saxons in 572.

[BOM]

SIGMUND, in the *Volsunga saga,* the son of Volsung and twin of sister Signy. He succeeds in removing a sword from a tree trunk into which it had been sunk during festivities celebrating the wedding of Siggeir and an unwilling Signy by a tall, aged, one-eyed stranger (Odin). Sigmund subsequently insults Siggeir (who, like others, was ostensibly also unsuccessful in his bid to remove the sword) and this leads to a battle between the Siggeir and King Volsung. Later Sigmund and Sinfjotli, a son he has conceived by his sister, Signy, are taken prisoner by Siggeir when they make an abortive attempt to kill him and avenge Volsung. They escape with Signy's assistance and set fire to Siggeir's Great Hall; however, they must bear witness not only to the death of Siggeir and his men, but also to that of their sister, who chooses to die alongside her husband. Sigmund subsequently reclaims the land of his father, marries Borghild, exiles her when she poisons Sinfjotli, remarries Hjordis, daughter of King Eylimi, but dies in battle (along with his father-in-law) against a rival suitor, Lyngvi. Hjordis later gives birth to his son, the hero Sigurd, in the land of the Vikings.

[WM]

SIGNY, the sister and twin of Sigmund in the *Volsunga saga.* She reluctantly marries King Siggeir of Gautland on the advice of her father, King Volsung. Siggeir later kills Volsung in battle after being insulted by Sigmund. With Signy's knowledge and connivance, Sigmund kills his sister's first two sons by Siggeir. He then produces a son, Sinfjotli, with Signy and later causes the death of Siggeir and all his men. Signy elects to die with Siggeir, stating that she is "not fit" to go on living, after having had no other purpose in life than to avenge their father. With respect to this trait, she bears a certain resemblance to Kriemhild in the *Nibelungenlied* and to Gudrun of the Old Norse tradition. Signy's role roughly corresponds with that of Sieglinde in Wagner's *Ring* cycle.

[WM]

SIGRDRIFA (BRYNHILDR) occurs only in the *Poetic Edda,* in the so-called *Fáfnismál* and *Sigrdrífumál* sections of the Sigurd tale, one time in each case. After having slain Fafnir, Sigurd receives the prophecy of birds, according to which he should take the hoard and buy a wife, Gjuki's daughter. The birds also tell him that he could awaken Sigrdrifa, whom Odin caused to fall into a deep sleep on Hindarfjall. Riding up Hindarfjall towards Franconia, he sees a light similar to burning fire. When he approaches, it turns into a fence of shields. He awakens the sleeper by cutting her armor. A prose section relates how she told Sigurd her name, Sigrdrifa, and introduced him to the mysteries of runic lore. The lay is fragmentary, caused by a lacuna in part of the codex.

The first occurrence of the word *sigrdrífa* in the lay could be an appellative ("driver to victory" = "valkyrja") or her name; the second time, in the prose version, it is her name. Possibly the author of the later *Prose Edda* misunderstood an appellative in the older lay as a name. The *Snorri Edda* tells this part of the story in a manner very similar to what one can find in the *Poetic Edda,* but the word *sigrdrífa* does not occur. According to the *Snorri Edda,* the valkyrie "named herself Hild, and also is called Brynhild." This is the same Brynhild that Sigurd woos for Gunnar.

The *Volsunga saga* and *Ragnars saga loðbrókar* extend this first meeting of Sigurd and Brynhild by telling how she conceived a daughter, Aslaug. In the German tradition Brünhild was a figure in a resuscitation myth, reflected in the name *lectulus Brunichilde* for the peak of the Feldberg near Frankfurt am Main. Other explanations of the name of the bed-shaped rock (such as those suggested by Friedrich Panzer) are not convincing.

In the *Þiðreks saga* Brynhild has several different functions. She is, for example, a sovereign who rules from her castle Saegard in Swabia where she has a stud farm from which the most famous stallions of German heroic poetry originate, including Sigurd's stallion Grani, which he obtains on the advice of the smith Mime. Although Sigurd enters Brynhild's castle by force and slays several guards in the process, she recognizes Sigurd, welcomes him, and tells him the names of his parents. Later, after his marriage to Grimhild, Sigurd tells Gunnar that

Brynhild is the most beautiful woman in the world and suggests that he might woo her. The courtship takes place without any fanciful scenery such as the wall of fire in the *Snorri Edda* and the *Volsunga saga*. In addition to Sigurd, Thidrek and Hogni also join Gunnar on the bridal quest. At Saegard, Brynhild is angry with Sigurd for having broken his oath not to have any other woman save her, although in the *Volsunga saga* no engagement was mentioned. Nonetheless, she agrees to the marriage plans. Elsewhere in the *Þiðreks saga,* Brynhild always appears as the wife of Gunnar in contrast to other versions of the tale.

The different perceptions of Brynhild can be attributed to contradictory sources. For the first occurrence even a homonymous figure was suggested, but this is impossible, as the *Volsunga saga* provides a link between the stud farm and Sigurd. The name of her castle, Saegard, and its iron door provide a link to Brünhild's castle in the *Nibelungenlied,* Isenstein (MHG *îsen* = "iron") in Island.

[HR]

Bibliography

Panzer, Friedrich. "Nibelungische Ketzereien." *PBB* 72 (1950): 463–499; 73 (1951): 95–123; 75 (1953): 248–272.

Reichert, Hermann. "Die Brynhildlieder der Edda im europäischen Kontext." In *Poetry in the Scandinavian Middle Ages.* Spoleto: Presso la sede del Centro studi, 1990, pp. 571–596.

———. "Zum Sigrdrífa-Brünhild-Problem." In *Antiquitates Indogermanicae: Studien zur indogermanischen Altertumskunde und zur Sprach- und Kulturgeschichte der indogermanischen Völker. Gedenkschrift für Hermann Güntert zur 25. Wiederkehr seines Todestages am 23. April 1973,* edited by Manfred Mayrhofer et al. Innsbrucker Beiträge zur Sprachwissenschaft 12. Innsbruck: Institut für Vergleichende Sprachwissenschaft der Universität Innsbruck, 1974, pp. 251–265.

SIGRUN, the daughter of King Hogni in the *Volsunga saga.* Her father promises her in marriage to King Hodbrodd. Sigrun tells Helgi, son of Sigmund and Borghild, that she does not wish to marry Hodbrodd and convinces him to prevent the marriage through battle. When Hodbrodd is killed by Helgi, Sigrun and Helgi are married. Sigrun is described by the anonymous poet as a

"shield maiden," possibly a euphemism for a valkyrie.

[WM]

SIGURD is the central figure of the Nibelung legend. His name appears in different versions: the Scandinavian authors write Sigurd (the corresponding German form would be Sigwart), the German writers use Siegfried, Sifrit, or Seyfrid. His story is told mainly in the lays of the *Poetic Edda, Snorra Edda, Volsunga saga, Nornagests þáttr, Þiðreks saga, Nibelungenlied,* and in *Das Lied vom Hürnen Seyfried.*

The author of the *Þiðreks saga* finishes his tale of Sigurd with the words "everyone said that no man now living or ever after would be born who would be equal to him in strength, courage, and in all sorts of courtesy, as well as in boldness and generosity that he had above all other men, and that his name would never perish in the German tongue, and the same was true with the Norsemen."

The most detailed account of his life is told in the *Poetic Edda* and in the *Volsunga saga.* Sigurd belongs to the family of the Volsungs or a South German family. His father is King Sigmund of Frakkland (Franconia), and his mother is Hjordis (or Sisibe in the *Þiðreks saga*). According to the two lays of Helgi Hundingsbani, Sigurd has two half brothers, Sinfjotli, son of Sigmund and his twin sister Signy (compare *Volsunga saga,* chapter 7), and Helgi, son of King Sigmund and Borghild.

There are different versions of Sigurd's youth. He grows up at the court of Alf, King Hjalprek's son, whom his mother married after Sigmund's death, or he is brought up by Regin (Mime in the *Þiðreks saga*), who forges Sigurd's sword, Gram. Regin provokes him into a fight against the dragon Fafnir (Regin in the *Þiðreks saga*), which watches over an immense hoard of gold. Sigurd takes revenge on Hunding's sons for his father's death. After the killing of the dragon on the Gnitaheath he decides to take the treasure with him, although the dying Fafnir warns him that the gold is cursed. In accordance with Regin's advice, he roasts Fafnir's heart. When he burns his finger, he puts it into his mouth and from that moment on he is able to understand the singing of the titmice, who warn him about Regin. Fearing that Regin may be treacherous and dangerous, Sigurd kills him. The birds then advise him to take his famous horse Grani and the gold. He should ride to Gjuki's court and woo Gjuki's daughter, Gudrun. The titmice also tell him about the valkyrie Sigrdrifa (according to the *Volsunga saga* she is Brynhild) on Hindarfjall. Sigurd awakens the valkyrie and falls in love with her. Brynhild and Sigurd then swear to be true and faithful to each other. Sigurd leaves her and arrives at Gjuki's court. There Grimhild, Gudrun's mother, brews an "ale of forgetfulness" for him, and so Sigurd forgets his betrothal and is willing to marry Gudrun. Sigurd swears oaths to Gjuki's sons, Hogni and Gunnar, and becomes their blood brother. He agrees to help Gunnar win Brynhild (who is here called daughter of Budli and sister of Atli. Her foster father is Heimir). Sigurd and Gunnar exchange shapes, because Gunnar is unable to pass through the wall of flame around Brynhild's hall. Disguised as Gunnar, he sleeps three (or eight) nights with Brynhild with a drawn sword between them. Sigurd and Gudrun and Gunnar and Brynhild marry on the same day. Sigurd has a happy married life with Gudrun, whereas Brynhild is unhappy and envies her sister-in-law. She even slanders Sigurd, claiming that he has broken the oaths. Gunnar and Hogni decide that their younger brother Guthorm should murder Sigurd, because Guthorm is not under oath. According to the *Volsunga saga,* Gudrun and Brynhild quarrel about their husbands, and while bathing in the river Gudrun shows Brynhild the ring Sigurd took from her while disguised as Gunnar.

There are also different versions of Sigurd's death. Some Eddic lays tell us that Sigurd, lying in bed beside Gudrun, was stabbed to death by Guthorm. Nevertheless, the dying Sigurd is still capable of killing Guthorm in revenge with his sword Gram. In other lays Hogni is obviously the murderer. Gudrun is paralyzed with grief and can only weep when Gullrond, her sister, uncovers Sigurd's dead body. Gudrun foretells that Sigurd's gold will bring the downfall of the Gjukungs. Another version says that Guthorm kills Sigurd outside in the open. According to a third version, Sigurd is killed returning from a "Thing" meeting. Gudrun looks for him in the woods and brings home Sigurd's dead body. Sigurd's and Gudrun's little son Sigmund is also murdered. Brynhild tells Gunnar that she lied

about Sigurd's betrayal and kills herself. She is laid with Sigurd on his funeral pyre.

Sigurd and Gudrun have a daughter (perhaps born after Sigurd's death) called Svanhild, who is murdered by Jormunrek. After Svanhild's death, Gudrun calls upon Sigurd to come back from Hel (the underworld) and take her with him to the beyond. According to the *Ragnars saga loðbrókar,* Sigurd and Brynhild have a daughter called Aslaug, who marries Ragnar, from whom the kings of Norway are descended.

Sigurd is certainly the most important figure of the Nibelungen legend for whom no historical model seems to exist, although attempts were made to compare Sigurd/Siegfried to various members of the Merovingian royal house or to the first-century Germanic leader Arminius. In all sources but the *Nibelungenlied,* where Siegfried is given a proper courtly upbringing at Sigmund's and Sieglind's court in Xanten, he is raised in the wild, in some versions not even knowing his name or his family. Only the German sources (including the *Þiðreks saga*) relate Sigurd's bath in the dragon's blood, which makes him invulnerable except at one spot where a leaf of a limetree has fallen (in the Swedish version of the *Þiðreks saga:* the leaf of a maple).

[GW]

Bibliography

Andersson, Theodore M. "Why Does Siegfried Die?" In *Germanic Studies in Honor of Otto Springer,* edited by Stephen J. Kaplowitt. Pittsburgh: K & S, 1979, pp. 29–39.

Beck, Heinrich. "Zu Otto Höflers Siegfried Arminius Untersuchungen." *PBB* (West) 107 (1985): 92–107.

Beyschlag, Siegfried. "Das Motiv der Macht bei Siegfrieds Tod." In *Zur germanisch-deutschen Heldensage,* edited by Karl Hauck. Darmstadt: Wissenschaftliche Buchgesellschaft, 1965, pp. 195–213.

de Boor, Helmut. "Hat Siegfried gelebt?" In *Zur germanisch-deutschen Heldensage,* edited by Karl Hauck. Darmstadt: Wissenschaftliche Buchgesellschaft, 1965, pp. 31–51.

Eifler, Günter. "Siegfried zwischen Xanten und Worms." In *Sprache, Literatur, Kultur: Studien zu ihrer Geschichte im deutschen Süden und Westen: Wolfgang Kleiber zu seinem 60. Geburtstag gewidmet,* edited by Albrecht Greule and Uwe Ruberg. Stuttgart: Steiner, 1989, 277–290.

Fechter, Werner. *Siegfrieds Schuld und das Weltbild des Nibelungenliedes.* Hamburg: Toth, 1948.

Fleet, Mary. "Siegfried as Gunther's Vassal." *Oxford German Studies* 14 (1983): 1–7.

Haimerl, Edgar. "Sigurd, ein Held des Mittelalters: Eine textimmanente Interpretation der Jung-sigurddichtung." *Alvísmál* 2 (1993): 81–104.

Haustein, Jens. "Siegfrieds Schuld." *ZfdA* 122 (1993): 373–387.

Haymes, Edward R., and Susann T. Samples. *Heroic Legends of the North: An Introduction to the Nibelung and Dietrich Cycles.* New York: Garland, 1996, 154–156.

Hoffmann, Werner. *Das Siegfriedbild in der Forschung.* Darmstadt: Wissenschaftliche Buchgesellschaft, 1979.

Höfler, Otto. *Siegfried, Arminius, und der Nibelungenhort.* Österr. Akad. d. Wiss. Phil.-Hist. Kl. 332. Vienna: Österreichische Akademie der Wissenschaften, 1978.

———. *Siegfried, Arminius und die Symbolik.* Heidelberg: Winter, 1961.

Kralik, Dietrich von. *Die Sigfridtrilogie im Nibelungenlied und in der Thidrekssaga I.* Halle: Niemeyer, 1941.

Peeters, Joachim. "Siegfried von Niderlant und die Wikinger am Niederrhein." *ZfdA* 115 (1986): 1–21.

Ploss, Emil. *Siegfried—Sigurd: Der Drachenkämpfer.* Cologne: Böhlau, 1966.

Quak, Arend. "Siegfried und die niederländischen Wikinger." *ZfdA* 116 (1987): 280–283.

Wenskus, Reinhard. "Der 'hunnische' Siegfried. Fragen eines Historikers an den Germanisten." In *Studien zum Altgermanischen: Festschrift für Heinrich Beck,* edited by Heiko Uecker. Reallexikon der germanischen Altertumskunde: Ergänzungsband 11. Berlin: de Gruyter, 1994, pp. 686–721.

SIGURD SNAKE-EYE, in the *Ragnars saga loðbrókar,* the youngest son of Ragnar and Aslaug and the grandson of Sigurd the dragon slayer. His name derives from a birthmark that resembles a snake winding about his eye. Aslaug foretells his birth and so proves to Ragnar that she is indeed the daughter of the famed Sigurd and thus worthy of marriage. Sigurd Snake-Eye gains great fame in battle and is said to be the father of Ragnhild, mother of Harald Fairhair of Norway. Sigurd (as Siward) also appears in Book IX of Saxo Grammaticus's *Gesta Danorum,*

where his nickname receives a different explanation.

[JKW]

SINDOLT, Gunther's cup bearer in the *Nibelungenlied.* He kills many of the enemy in the battle against the Saxons and the Danes, and prepares the courtly feasts in Worms. In the *Klage* Sindolt advises Brünhild to temper her grieving over Gunther's death and to crown young Siegfried soon in order to overcome her sorrow.

[BS]

SINFJOTLI, the son resulting from an incestuous relationship between the twins Sigmund and Signy (who has assumed the shape of a sorceress) in the *Volsunga saga.* Sinfjotli spends time with Sigmund who believes the boy to be the son of Signy's husband, Siggeir. Together with Sigmund, and wearing magical wolfskins, he experiences many adventures in Siggeir's kingdom. When he and Sigmund travel to Siggeir's home to kill him (to avenge the death of Volsung, Sigmund's father), Sinfjotli does not hesitate to slaughter, at Signy's instigation, her two sons, who have discovered the hiding place of the two men. Although captured by Siggeir's men, Sinfjotli and Sigmund escape and set fire to the Great Hall of Siggeir, killing him and his men. Together with Sigmund's son, Helgi, he helps defeat King Hodbrodd but subsequently kills the brother of Helgi's wife, Borghild, in a contest for the hand of a woman. He dies after drinking poison offered to him by Borghild at the funeral of her brother and is transported by Odin into the land of the dead.

[WM]

SINTRAM, the name of a nobleman in the *Klage* who resides in the Hungarian March. He has no equivalent in the *Nibelungenlied.*

[WM]

SISIBE, in the *Þiðreks saga,* daughter of King Nidung of Spain, mother to Sigurd. Sigmund of Tarlungaland sends messengers to Nidung requesting her hand in marriage. After Sigmund himself has traveled to Spain, Nidung marries Sisibe to Sigmund. Sigmund returns to Tarlungaland with his bride. When Sigmund is away at war, he leaves Artvin and Herman to guard his kingdom. Artvin attempts to seduce Sisibe, who rejects his proposition and threatens to tell Sigmund if Artvin repeats his advances. When Artvin sends Herman to speak to Sisibe on his behalf, Sisibe angrily rebuffs his request. Artvin continues to bring up the matter, but Sisibe remains resolute. When Sigmund returns, Artvin and Herman intercept him and accuse Sisibe of lying with a slave and of conceiving a child with him. Sigmund wishes to punish her and accepts Artvin's advice that she be banished to Svavaskog (lit., Forest of Swabia). Artvin and Herman lure Sisibe into the forest. Artvin is about to kill her by cutting out her tongue (to be taken to Sigmund) when Herman intervenes, protesting that Sisibe is innocent. He tells Artvin to cut out a dog's tongue instead. Artvin refuses, and they fight. At this moment, Sisibe goes into labor and bears a son. She places him in a small glass pot. Artvin kicks the container into a river just as Herman cuts off his head. Sisibe faints and dies.

[FH]

SISTRAM (SINTRAM), according to the *Þiðreks saga,* grandson of Boltram, Duke of Venice, and one of Thidrek's best men. He is a relative of Hildibrand. As a young man, Sistram rides out in order to meet Thidrek. During this journey he falls asleep and a dragon catches him and swallows him up to his shoulders. By chance Thidrek and Fasold find the dragon and free Sistram, who now joins Thidrek's knights. Later he is one of the opponents of the eleven sons of Isung. In the German heroic epics the story is told in the *Virginal,* an epic of the Dietrich cycle. Here the hero is called Rentwin, and Dietrich and Hildebrand save him. The fight against the dragon takes place in Arona near the Lago Maggiore. This may be an old feature of the story because the coat of arms of the family Visconte, the owners of the castle of Arona, shows the dragon carrying a naked baby/man in its mouth. A knight called Sintram is also mentioned in the *Klage, Biterolf und Dietleib, Dietrichs Flucht,* and *Rabenschlacht.* It is interesting that local legends of Switzerland tell a story about two brothers, Sintram and Beltram. Here it is Beltram whom the dragon almost swallows, and Sintram frees his younger brother. A sculpture on the

Cathedral of Berne shows the same event: a knight with the lion in his coat of arms (Dietrich von Bern) frees a man out of the dragon's mouth. Similar sculptures are to be seen in St. Peter in Straubing, in the church of Andlau in Alsace, and on the cathedral of Freising.

[GW]

Bibliography

Grimm, Wilhelm. *Die deutsche Heldensage.* 4th ed. Darmstadt: Wissenschaftliche Buchgesellschaft, 1957, p. 126.

Schneider, Hermann. *Germanische Heldensage.* Vol. 1, 2nd ed. Grundriss der germanischen Philologie 10/1. Berlin: de Gruyter, 1962, pp. 272f.

Tuppa, Gerlinde. "Die Bedeutung der Tiere und der Tiermotive in der germanischen Heldensage." Diss., Vienna, 1965, pp. 445f.

SIVARD (SNARENSVEND), "Young Sigurd the Rapid," is the hero of some Danish Nibelung ballads (*Folkevise*). The ballad *Sivard Snarensvend* relates us an episode of Sigurd's youth, the winning of his horse Grani. In *Sivard og Brynhild* the story of Sigurd's death is told: Sivard, a Danish prince, wins Brynhild on the glass mountain. When Signild (she represents Gudrun/Kriemhild) shows Brynhild a ring that Sivard gave her as a love token, the women start to quarrel. Hogni/Hagen (here called Haffue or Nielus), Sivard's companion, kills his friend with Sivard's own sword, Adelring, because otherwise Sivard would be invulnerable. Finally Hogni kills Brynhild and then turns the sword against himself. In *Kong Diderik og hans Kæmper Sivard,* Isse's or Isak's son (Isung), fights against Humlung (Amelung). Humlung loses the fight, but he finds out that he is Sivard's relative, and Sivard regards him as a friend. The ballads *Regnfred (Ragnar) og Kragelil* and *Karl* (a ballad name for Sigurd) *og Kragelil* retell elements of the story about Sigurd's daughter Aslaug (Svanelild or Adelrun).

[GW]

Bibliography

Holzapfel, Otto. *Die dänischen Nibelungenballaden: Texte und Kommentare.* GAG 122. Göppingen: Kümmerle, 1974, pp. 153ff.

SKADI, a powerful man who is mentioned at the beginning of the *Volsunga saga.* He is the owner of the thrall, Bredi, who is subsequently killed by Sigi, son of Odin.

[WM]

SKEMMING, Velent's horse in the *Þiðreks saga.* The excellent horse was raised on the stud farm of Brynhild, together with Falka, Grani, and Rispa. It can run as fast as a bird can fly. Velent gives the horse to his son, Vithga, who is very proud of Skemming, because the two of them can fly across the Weser, a broad river, like arrows. Only on one occasion does Vithga lend the horse to one of Thidrek's knights. The stallion is killed by Thidrek's brother, Thether. Vithga is so furious about the loss of Skemming that he kills Thether. In various German heroic epics of the Dietrich cycle, Schemming is (at least for some time) Dietrich's horse, and Witege obtains the horse from him.

[GW]

Bibliography
Tuppa, Gerlinde. "Die Bedeutung der Tiere und der Tiermotive in der germanischen Heldensage." Diss., Vienna, 1965, pp. 266ff.

SLEIPNIR, a horse belonging to Odin. In the *Volsunga saga* Brynhild refers to the runes that were etched on his reins.

[WM]

SNAEVAR, in the *Volsunga saga* one of the two sons of Hogni (the other being Solar), who travel with their father, Gunnar, and Orkning to the court of King Atli.

[WM]

SORLI, one of three sons (the others being Hamdir and Erp) born to Gudrun in her marriage to King Jonakr in the *Volsunga saga.* Together with Hamdir, he kills his brother Erp, and then the two proceed to the court of King Jormunrek, who has had their half sister, Svanhild, killed. While Hamdir cuts off the king's hands, Sorli cuts off his feet. He and his brother are then stoned to death by Jormunrek's men.

[WM]

SOEST, a city in northern Germany, in Westphalia, claimed by some to be the residence of King Attala in the Old Norse *Þiðreks saga,* where it appears as *Susat.* It is there, at Attala's court, that the Niflungen are all killed. The Old Norse saga may represent an earlier German stage in the development of the *Nibelungenlied,* and supporters of this theory usually fault the South German poet of the *Nibelungenlied* for not having understood the topography of the earlier material from which the *Nibelungenlied* poet crafted his material.

[SMJ]

Bibliography
Ritter-Schaumberg, Heinz. *Die Nibelungen zogen nordwärts.* 4th ed. Munich: Herbig, 1983. Paperback. St. Goar: Otto Reichl Verlag, 1987.
Böckmann, Walter. *Der Nibelungen Tod in Soest: Neue Erkenntnisse zur historischen Wahrheit.* 3rd ed. Düsseldorf: Econ Verlag, 1987.

SOLAR, in the *Volsunga saga,* one of the two sons of Hogni (the other being Snaevar), who travel with their father, Gunnar, and Orkning to the court of King Atli.

[WM]

SPANJE (Spain) is mentioned three times in the *Nibelungenlied* (1756,3; 1797,1; and 2344,3) as the homeland of a knight named Walther. This is the Walther of the Latin poem *Waltharius* (1456 hexameter lines from the ninth-tenth centuries), the fragmentary Anglo-Saxon poem *Waldere* (sixty-nine alliterative verses from about the year 1000), and the later Middle High German fragments usually called *Walther und Hildegund* (thirty-nine four-line stanzas from the 1220s-1230s). The story of Walther may be from a Germanic heroic lay or at least contain elements of that type of poetry. (Note also *Walthari* and *Walther of Spain.*) In the first passage in the *Nibelungenlied* Etzel mentions that Hagen and Walther had grown up at his court, that he had sent Hagen home, and that Walther and Hildegund had escaped. The second reference is made by one of Kriemhild's knights, who had known both Hagen and Walther previously and who does not want to fight against Hagen. In the third passage Hildebrand mocks Hagen for not having fought against Walter at the Wasgenstein, a locale in the Vosges mountains.

[SMJ]

Bibliography
Kratz, Dennis M., ed. and trans. *Waltharius and Ruodlieb.* GLML 13. New York: Garland, 1984.

SPESSART, the range of wooded hills to the east of Frankfurt, between the Vogelsberg and the Odenwald. The name can be translated as *woodpecker wood.* In the *Nibelungenlied* (967,3) Hagen explains the absence of wine on the hunting expedition that precedes the slaying of Siegfried by maintaining that he had misunderstood where the hunt was to take place and had arranged for the wine to be sent zem Spehtsharte (to the Spessart), probably a considerable distance from the actual location. Hagen's explanation is implausible, to say the least, and Siegfried is infuriated on two scores.

[MEG]

SPEYER, cathedral city and an ancient bishopric on the Rhine to the south of Worms in the German state of Rhineland-Palatinate. The Romanesque cathedral, one of the foremost cathdrals of the Middle Ages, was founded in the eleventh century and contains the remains of eight German emperors and kings. In the *Nibelungenlied* mention is made of an elderly (or sage) bishop of Speyer (". . . von Spîre, ein alter bischof," 1508,2) who makes a somewhat enigmatic comment to Ute on the preparations for the departure of the Burgundians in response to Etzel's invitation: "got müez' ir êre dâ bewarn" (1508,4b). The cleric's presence in Worms may be due to his relations to the royal family, to whom he is possibly related. Interestingly, the Bishop of Worms, who would have been the ecclesiastic that one would expect to be present to bless the Burgundians and see them off, does not appear here or anywhere else in the *Nibelungenlied.* Depending upon the understanding of the adjective "alt," scholars explain the significance of the episode differently. Two representative opinions are (1) *alt* in the sense of *sage;* for which the incident reflects the meeting in spring 1200 between the bishop of Speyer, Konrad III von Scharfenberg (then thirty years old), and Bishop Wolfger von Passau at the royal court in Nuremberg; and (2) *alt* in the sense of *elderly;* which means that the meeting was not between Wolfger and Konrad, but rather with the predecessor of Konrad, Otto von Henneberg.

The absence of a bishop of Worms may well reflect the fate of Bishop Lupold von Schönfeld (1196–1217). Lupold had been a follower of Philipp of Swabia and later seized the archbishopric of Mainz from the favored papal candidate, Siegfried von Eppstein. Lupold's excommunication in 1202, following this incident, may be the reason why he does not appear in the *Nibelungenlied.*

[MEG/OE]

Bibliography
Berendes, Hans Ulrich. "Die Bischöfe von Worms und ihr Hochstift im 12. Jahrhundert." Diss. Cologne, 1984.
Bienemann, Friedrich. *Conrad von Scharfenberg, Bischof von Speier und Metz und kaiserlicher Hofkanzler, 1200–1224.* Strassburg: Heitz, 1886.
Delbrück, Hans. "Das Werden des Nibelungenliedes." *Historische Zeitschrift* 131 (1925): 409–420.
Heusler, Andreas. *Nibelungensage und Nibelungenlied.* 6th ed. Dortmund: Ruhfus, 1965.

STUDAS, in the *Þiðreks saga,* ruler of a farmstead in a forest in Svavaland (lit., Swabia Land) belonging to Brynhild. Studas is wise and accomplished in many things but is preeminent as a horseman. His son is also named Studas but is known as Heimir. From Studas's stud come Thidrek's horse Falka, Heimir's mount Rispa, Velent's and Vithga's horse Skemming, and Sigurd's steed Grani.

[FH]

SUSA (also written **SUSAT** and **SUSAKK**), Atli's principal residence in the *Þiðreks saga,* possibly identical to the town of Soest in the Westphalian region of modern Germany. Much of the action of the *þiðreks saga* is centered around Susa.

[FH]

SVANHILD is Sigurd and Gudrun's daughter (perhaps born after Sigurd's death). She is very beautiful and has piercing eyes, and her mother loves her dearly. Svanhild grows up at Jonakr's court and marries the Gothic king Jormunrek. Bikki, Jormunrek's evil counselor, slanders her, maintaining that she is having an affair with Randver, Jormunrek's son. The king's pride is so deeply hurt that he sentences Randver to death by hanging, and Svanhild is trampled to death under the hooves of horses. Her stepbrothers, Hamdir and Sorli, are provoked by Gudrun to avenge their sister. But in the course of exacting revenge on Jormunrek, both are killed.

This story is told in the *Hamðismál*. Parallel versions are provided in the *Guðrúnarhvot* and in Snorri's *Skáldskaparmál* (*Prose Edda*). In the *Volsunga saga* Randver and Bikki bring Svanhild on a ship from Gudrun to Jormunrek's court. During their voyage Randver and Svanhild fall in love. When the horses are made to charge at her, she opens her shining eyes and the horses dare not trample her; a bag has to be put over her head.

The Svanhild legend is very old. The oldest poetic version is related in the skaldic poem *Ragnars drápa* (Ragnar's Poem of Praise) by Bragi Boddason, the first Norwegian skald (ninth century). Jordanes, the Gothic historian (mid-sixth century), relates the tale. Here Gudrun's daughter is called Sunilda, and her brothers are Ammius and Sarus. Sunilda is torn to death by wild horses. Whether the two different forms of Svanhild's execution were common or convenient methods of punishment cannot be proven with any certainty. Another version can be found in the *Gesta Danorum* written soon after 1200 by Saxo Grammaticus (died 1216). He is also familiar with the motif of Svanhild's piercing eyes. Svanilda can only be killed by the horses if she is placed face down.

[GW]

Bibliography

de Boor, Helmut. "Die nordische Swanhilddichtung." In *Erbe der Vergangenheit. Festgabe für Karl Helm zum 80. Geburtstage, 19. Mai 1951.* Tübingen: Niemeyer, 1951, pp. 47–62.

de Vries, Jan. *Altnordische Literaturgeschichte.* Vol. 1. 2nd ed. Grundriss der germanischen Philologie 15. Berlin: de Gruyter, 1964, pp. 73ff.

Dronke, Ursula, ed. and trans. *The Poetic Edda.* Vol. 1 of *Heroic Poems.* Oxford: Clarendon Press, 1969, pp. 168ff.

Gering, Hugo, and B. Sijmons. *Kommentar zu den Liedern der Edda.* 2. Hälfte: *Heldenlieder.* Germanistische Handbibliothek VII 3,2. Halle (Saale): Buchhandlung des Waisenhauses (Francke), 1931, pp. 270, 414, 425ff.

Schneider, Hermann. *Germanische Heldensage.* Vol. 1. 2nd ed. Grundriss der germanischen Philologie 10/I. Berlin: de Gruyter, 1962, pp. 243ff.

Tuppa, Gerlinde. "Die Bedeutung der Tiere und der Tiermotive in der Germanischen Heldensage." Diss., Vienna 1965, pp. 398ff.

SVEGGJUD, in the *Volsunga saga* a horse belonging to King Hodbrodd.

[WM]

SVEIPUD, the horse belonging to Granmar in the *Volsunga saga.*

[WM]

SWABIA (MHG *Swâben*), territory in southwest Germany, west of Bavaria, south of Franconia. Known first as Alemannia, it has been called Swabia since the eleventh century. In the Middle Ages, Swabia was one of the five great duchies of the empire. It is mentioned in the *Nibelungenlied* (1493,3) as the first stage of the return journey of Etzel's messengers, Wärbel and Swemmel, from Worms to the land of the Huns. The *Klage* (3494) and *Biterolf und Dietleib* also tell of journeys from Hungary to Worms through Swabia. In *Biterolf und Dietleib* and *Dietrichs Flucht,* Swabians are mentioned as allies of the Franks or Goths.

[NV]

SWALEVELT, a district mentioned once in the *Nibelungenlied* (1525,1) through which the Burgundians travel from East Franconia to the Danube. It is situated between Würzburg and Donauwörth and probably named after the Schwalb River, a tributary of the Wörnitz that runs into the Danube at Donauwörth. The name *Sualafeld* occurs in charters of the ninth through the eleventh centuries. The manuscripts have *Swanvelde* (**C, D, k,** and **b**), *Swanevelde* (**A**), *Salvelde* (**B**), and even *Swaben* (**d**).

[NV]

SWEMMEL, a minstrel in the service of Etzel who also plays the role of envoy in both the *Nibelungenlied* and the *Klage.* Together with Wärbel, he carries Etzel's invitation to the Burgundians to journey to Worms. In the *Klage* he brings the news of the slaughter at Etzel's court back to Worms.

[WM]

THEODERIC "THE GREAT" (ca. 454–526), king of the Ostrogoths who, encouraged by the

Byzantine emperor Zeno, led an invasion of Italy in 488. After defeating and murdering his rival Odoacer (of the Germanic Heruli tribe) in 493, Theoderic assumed the title king of Italy. He devoted resources to the repair of neglected Rome and attempted to bring about a cultural amalgamation of Germanic and Roman traditions, insisting that the Ostrogoths and the Romans live and work together. Confessional differences between the Arian Goths and the Catholic Romans prevented the envisioned amalgamation, and near the end of Theoderic's rule Rome sought an alliance with the recently converted Catholic Franks. During this time (523) Theoderic ordered the execution of the Roman statesman Boethius on the charge of treason (while awaiting execution, Boethius composed *De consolatione philosophiae*). The Ostrogothic kingdom of Italy did not long survive Theoderic, succumbing to the Byzantine emperor Justinian (552–555). However uneasy, the cultural alliance between a Germanic people and Rome brought about by Theoderic was the most significant previous to the empire of Charlemagne. Dietrich von Bern (i.e., Verona, Theoderic's capital), a literary figure who is mentioned in numerous medieval works besides the *Nibelungenlied* and who is the hero of an independent cycle of epics, is loosely based on the historical Theoderic.

[WRH]

THETLEIF (THETTLEIF) THE DANE, son of Biturulf, according to the *Þiðreks saga*. In his youth he is a dull, impassive young man, a layabout lying in ashes. During a robbery in the woods he turns out to be very strong and keen on weapons. His father gives him a suit of armor and sends him out to join Thidrek's knights. First he meets Sigurd the Greek and defeats him in single combat. Sigurd's man-mad daughter causes him some trouble. Finally he reaches Ermenrich's court and gives an expensive banquet which costs so much that he has to pawn the valuable weapons and horses of the nobles, including those of Thidrek and his knights. Waltari af Waskasteini scolds Thetleif for his behavior. Thetleif challenges Waltari to a contest and overcomes his opponent. In the end he proves himself worthy of joining Thidrek's court and is accepted as his liege man. Later he is one of the fighters

against the eleven sons of Isung and is killed in the battle between Hertnit and Isung. Perhaps Russian motifs of the *bylinies* (records of the folk) are the source of the story. The German heroic epic *Biterolf und Dietleib* tells a somewhat different story about Dietleib von Stîre (Styria/Austria). Dietleib is also mentioned in the *Rosengarten,* the *Rabenschlacht,* and *Dietrichs Flucht.*

[GW]

Bibliography
Haupt, Waldemar. *Zur niederdeutschen Dietrichsage. Untersuchungen.* Palaestra 129. New York: Johnson, 1970, pp. 1–82.
Haymes Edward R., and Susann T. Samples. *Heroic Legends of the North: An Introduction to the Nibelung and Dietrich Cycles.* New York: Garland, 1996, p. 147.
Schneider, Hermann. *Germanische Heldensage.* Vol. 1. 2nd ed. Grundriss der germanischen Philologie 10/I. Berlin: de Gruyter, 1962, pp. 326–328.

THIDREK (ÞIÐREK), in the *Þiðreks saga,* son of Thettmar and Odilia, knighted by his father at the age of twelve. He is Hildibrand's foster son. While hunting, young Thidrek captures the dwarf Alfrek from whom he gets the sword Naglhring as well as a promise of treasures which are in the possession of the berserk Grimr and his wife Hildr. Thidrek kills these two creatures and obtains their treasure plus the helmet Hildigrim. After his defeat by Vithga, an unaccompanied Thidrek leaves Bern to redeem his honor. He does this by slaying Ekka, king and guardian of Drekanfils, subduing Fasold, Ekka's brother, killing an "elefans" (elephant), and also a dragon from whose jaws he rescues Sistram.

When Thettmar dies, Thidrek becomes king of Bern. He helps Atli in his war against Osantrix and subsequently assists Ermenrich against Rimstein. At Aldrian's death Thidrek invites Gunnar and Hogni to a feast in Bern. He boasts that no one would dare challenge such a gathering. Herbrand chides Thidrek, telling him that Isung of Bertangaland, his eleven sons, and Sigurd are a match for Thidrek and his men. Thidrek immediately sets off for Bertangaland with his champions. He challenges Isung and his sons to single combat. All of Thidrek's men are defeated and bound except Omlung, Thettleif, and Vithga. In the final combat Thidrek over-comes Sigurd after a three-day battle, but only by deceiving Sigurd and using Mimung, the only sword that can cut Sigurd's otherwise invulner-able skin. Thidrek accepts Sigurd's services. Thidrek then rides to Niflungaland, is present when Sigurd marries Grimhild, and accompanies Gunnar, Hogni, and Sigurd to get Brynhild as Gunnar's wife. After Gunnar has married Brynhild, Thidrek returns to Bern. After he hears about Hild, daughter of Artus of Bertangaland, Thidrek sends his nephew Herburt to woo her by proxy. Herburt marries Hild instead. Thidrek, Fasold, and Thettleif then ride to Drekanfils where Thidrek requests and receives the late Drusian's eldest daughter, Guthilinda, as his wife.

Thidrek's troubles with Ermenrich result from Sifka's treachery. Confronted by Er-menrich's numerically superior forces, Thidrek withdraws, first to Rothingeir at Bakalar, then to Susa. Thidrek remains in exile with Atli for more than thirty years. He supports Atli against Osan-trix, then Valdamar, whose son (also called Thidrek) Thidrek captures as Atli retreats. Val-damar's army corners Thidrek's forces in a cas-tle, where Thidrek and his men are reduced to devouring their horses. Alerted by Ulfrath, Ro-thingeir arrives to liberate Thidrek. Thidrek pre-sents his namesake to Atli who casts him into a dungeon; both Thidreks are badly wounded. Erka, daughter of King Osantrix of Vilkinaland, nurses her kinsman, Valdamar's son, back to health, and he escapes. Despite his festering wounds, Thidrek of Bern sets out after him, catching up to him in Borgarskog (between Poland and Húnaland). Thidrek Valdimarsson refuses to accept silver or gold or offers of friendship to induce him return to Susa to save Erka's life. In the ensuing combat, Thidrek of Bern decapitates his namesake. He returns to Húnaland and flings Thidrek Valdimarsson's head at Erka's feet. Atli meanwhile has been routed by Valdimar. A recovered Thidrek urges an attack on Valdimar; the combined forces of Atli and Thidrek lay siege to Palteskja. Thidrek leaves the siege and invades Ruziland, besieging Smaland, and killing Valdimar. Once back in Húnaland, Thidrek requests Erka's support to regain his kingdom. Atli and Erka give Thidrek an army that includes their two sons Erp and

Ortvin. In the campaign Vithga kills Erp, Ortvin, and Thether, Thidrek's brother. Thidrek con-fronts Vithga who flees and disappears into the sea just as Thidrek has thrown his spear after him. Because of the deaths of Erp and Ortvin, Thidrek advances no further with Atli's army and returns to Susa. Atli and Erka forgive Thidrek for the loss of their sons.

After Erka's death, Thidrek accompanies Atli on his journey to Niflungaland to marry Grimhild. Gunnar gives Thidrek Sigurd's horse, Grani. Seven winters later, when the Niflungs arrive at Susa, Atli sends Thidrek out to greet his guests. Thidrek and Hogni are particularly fond of each other; Thidrek warns Hogni to be on guard as Grimhild weeps daily for Sigurd. Thidrek refuses to aid Grimhild but neither can he fight on the side of the Niflungs against the men of Atli, his lord. When Rothingeir falls, however, Thidrek attacks the remaining Niflungs. After a fierce battle Thidrek takes Hogni captive. Calling Grimhild a devil, Atli orders Thidrek to kill her. Thidrek cuts her in half with his sword. Soon thereafter Thidrek, Hil-dibrand, and Herath set out to regain Omlunga-land. Ermenrich has meanwhile died, and the men of Omlungaland choose Thidrek as their king over Sifka. After Alibrand slays Sifka and the men of Rome surrender, Hildibrand crowns Thidrek king with Ermenrich's crown. After Hil-dibrand's death Thidrek spends much of his time hunting. On one expedition he is abducted by the same dragon that has killed King Hernit. Thidrek slays the dragon and its brood, proceeds to Her-nit's castle, frees it from its besiegers, and mar-ries Isold, Hernith's widow. After Atli's death Thidrek becomes king of Húnaland.

Later Thidrek sends Heimir to collect tribute from the latter's former monastery. Thidrek joins Heimir in plundering the monastery. He then sends Heimir to take the treasure from an old giant. When the giant slays Heimir, Thidrek con-fronts him and kills him. As a very old man Thidrek hunts a great stag. In its pursuit he mounts a black horse that carries him off, never to be seen again (see DIETRICH VON BERN).

[FH]

THORA, daughter of Hakon in the *Volsunga saga.* After the death of Sigurd, Gudrun disap-pears into a forest. She eventually travels to Denmark where, for three-and-a-half years, she is accorded great hospitality by Thora.

[WM]

THURINGIA, a region in northeast Germany (modern German Thüringen). About 1130 King Lothar III bestowed the status of landgraves on the Ludowingers, one of the foremost dynasties in the region. The Wartburg, their great castle near Eisenach, became an important center of literature, particularly under Landgrave Hermann I (d. 1217). In the *Nibelungenlied* Thuringia is outside the action of the plot, like Denmark and Saxony. Irnfried is landgrave of Thuringia, living in exile at Etzel's court. His name is invariably coupled with that of Hawart of Denmark, likewise now in Gran.

[MEG]

TRAISEN, a right tributary to the Danube in Lower Austria. In the *Nibelungenlied* (1331ff.) it appears to form the border between territories under the influence of the Huns and Passau.

[HR]

TRAISMAUER, a town on the river Traisen. In the *Nibelungenlied* 1332,3 and 1336,1 it is the first castle belonging to Etzel on Kriemhild's journey to the Huns, and former residence of Helche. Kriemhild stays there for three days. The place name is given correctly by the manuscripts **C, R, a,** and **b.** Of the other manuscripts, **B** and **A** have the incorrect *Zeizenmûre* (Zeiselmauer), which is situated about thirty kilometers further east, between Tulln and Vienna. Manuscript **D** agrees with **C, R, a,** and **b** in the first instance, giving the correct place name; however in the second instance, it follows the incorrect usage found in **B** and **A.** In this second instance the term is used to localize the home of the poet or of the redactors of manuscripts **B** or **C.** Around 1200 Traismauer belonged to the archbishopric of Salzburg, Zeiselmauer to the bishopric of Passau. We do not know if this mistake should be attributed to the author or to the redactor of **B.** In the first instance the redactor of **C** corrected a mistake of the original based on his better knowledge; in the second instance of the term **B** made a wrong emendation and **C** just adhered to this model. If the mistake is attributed to the author, one must assume that his knowledge of the route

was not perfect, but fairly good (today people living within a few miles are not sure about the location of the two towns). He especially remembered names of properties of the Passau bishopric. Thus the author should be regarded as a person connected with the seat of Passau (200 kilometers northwest of Traismauer). The redactor of **C** in this case had better local knowledge, and the other manuscripts that follow this reading either depend on **C** or correct independently (as perhaps in the case of **d,** which belongs to the **B** tradition). If **B** is blamed for the mistake, it must have been original not only for **B** and **A,** but also for **D.** The **B** scribe must have known, then, the towns east of the Traisen only by a list of places belonging to the seat of Passau, so that he misinterpreted Traismauer as a reading for Zeizenmure. If so, then **B** probably was written down by a scribe at the seat of Passau. Nellmann's theory, that the mistake should be ascribed to an Alemannic redactor, is possible, but not supported by the evidence.

[HR]

Bibliography

Nellmann, Eberhard. "Zeizenmure im Nibelungenlied und in der Neidhart-Tradition." In *Festschrift für Siegfried Grosse zum 60. Geburtstag,* edited by Werner Besch et al. Göppingen: Kümmerle, 1984, pp. 401–425.

TRONEGE (Troneck) is the name of Hagen's birthplace in the *Nibelungenlied.* It is not to be fixed geographically (Troy?), which is in keeping with Hagen's relatively obscure origins and connection to the realm of lower mythology.

[WM]

TRÛNE (Traun), southern tributary of the Danube, mentioned in the *Nibelungenlied* (1304,1), and crossed by Kriemhild and her retinue before they arrive at Enns. It flows into the Danube near Linz, which is, strangely enough, not mentioned in the *Nibelungenlied.*

[NV]

TULNE (Tulln), town in Austria on the right bank of the Danube, about thirty kilometers east of Traismauer and about thirty-five kilometers west of Vienna. It is mentioned twice in the *Nibelungenlied* (1341,2 and 1361,2). Etzel comes to Tulne to meet Kriemhild. A tournament is held to celebrate her arrival. After a day of festivities, the party leaves for Vienna the next morning.

[NV]

UNGERLANT (Hungary). The term is part of an ambiguous topography in the *Nibelungenlied* which results from the attempt to situate the peoples of the heroic age at least partly within the historical conditions of the twelfth century. First of all, the term refers to the land of the Hungarians, whose king is Bloedelîn (1373,2), the brother of Etzel. This means that Ungerlant is also the *Hiunen lant* (land of the Huns; 1346,3–6), especially since Etzel's castle is situated there near Gran (Esztergom). During the twelfth century Gran was indeed a residence of the Hungarian kings which, under Bela III (died 1196), maintained diplomatic relations with the bishop of Passau.

[MH]

Bibliography

Gillespie, George T. "Das Mythische and das Reale in der Zeit- und Ortsauffassung des Nibelungenliedes." In *Nibelungenlied und Klage. Sage und Geschichte, Struktur und Gattung. Passauer Nibelungengespräche 1985,* ed. Fritz Peter Knapp. Heidelberg: Winter, 1987, pp. 43–60.

Hansen, Walter. *Die Spur des Sängers. Das Nibelungenlied und sein Dichter.* Bergisch Gladbach: Lübbe, 1987.

_____. *Wo Siegfried starb und Kriemhild lebte. Die Schauplätze des Nibelungenliedes.* Vienna: Ueberreuter, 1 997.

UTE, in the *Nibelungenlied* and the *Klage,* wife of Dancrat (deceased by the time the action of the *Nibelungenlied* takes place), and mother of Kriemhild, Gunther, Gernot, and Giselher. She is also the sister of Bishop Pilgrim of Passau. Her "interpretation" of Kriemhild's falcon dream is one of the early premonitions of the disaster to follow and causes her daughter to withdraw as a potential bride for ambitious suitors, at least until Siegfried arrives at Worms. Her role in the *Nibelungenlied* is not particularly prominent, although she is the epitome of courtly refinement. While she does not initially oppose the acceptance of an invitation to her sons to travel to Etzel's court, Ute does urge them to remain in Worms just prior to their departure, claiming that she has had a dream in which all of the birds of the land were dead. Hagen maintains that no stock should be put in dreams, although his later behavior after having met the water sprites would seem to indicate that he is less inclined to dismiss such "warnings" as might seem to be the case. Ute's innate sense that this will not turn out well finds reflection in a similar attitude of those women who gather on the riverbank to see their men off (1521). In the *Klage* Ute dies when she is later told of the slaughter of the Burgundians at the court of Etzel.

[WM]

VALDAMAR OF DENMARK (VALDAMARR AF DANMÖRK), one of the "men of great reputation" who accompany Grimhild and her sons to Denmark in order to compensate Gudrun for the murder of Sigurd in the *Volsunga saga.*

[JHS]

VELENT (VOLUND), in the *Þiðreks saga,* he is the son of Vathi and grandson of Vilkinus. When Velent is nine, his father sends him to apprentice with Mimir in Húnaland. Young Sigurd is with Mimir at this time. Velent remains with Mimir for three years. Vathi then takes Velent to apprentice with two dwarfs who live in a mountain. They instruct Velent for twelve months. At the end of this time, they do not want to release him and keep him for a second year. Velent becomes as skillful a smith as the dwarfs. When Vathi is crushed by a landslide, Velent finds the sword that his father has left for him, kills the dwarfs, and then sets out for Denmark. Unable to cross the Visara (Weser), he fashions a watertight container for himself and his implements from a tree trunk and floats ashore in Nidung's kingdom. Velent serves Nidung well. Velent and Amilias, Nidung's smith, wager their heads about who is the more accomplished artisan. When Velent tries to retrieve his own tools, he finds that they have been stolen. He identifies the thief by making a lifelike statue of him. Velent then forges the sword Mimung with which he cleaves Amilias's helmet and splits Amilias down to the belt. Nidung wants Mimung, but under pretense of fetching a scabbard, Velent brings Nidung a copy and keeps the original for himself. Velent accompanies Nidung on his campaign against a large enemy army. At

Nidung's request Velent rides back to Nidung's castle to retrieve the king's victory stone, for which Nidung has promised his daughter and half his realm. Intercepted by Nidung's steward who wishes to deliver the stone to the king, Velent kills the steward. Nidung banishes Velent, who later returns in disguise and tries to poison the king and his daughter. He is discovered, captured, hamstrung, and forced to work as Nidung's smith. Velent tricks Nidung's two young sons into walking backwards on newly fallen snow to his smithy, where he beheads them. He fashions goblets out of their skulls and other utensils from their bones. When Nidung's daughter breaks her ring and asks Velent to repair it, Velent locks the door to the smithy and violates the princess.

Egill, Velent's brother and a master archer, helps Velent make wings with which Velent escapes. Hovering above the rooftops, Velent tells Nidung the truth. Nidung orders Egill to shoot Velent. Egill's arrow strikes a bladder filled with blood under Velent's left arm. Unharmed, Velent flies to Sjoland.

Nidung dies, and his son Otvin becomes king. When Vithga has been born, Velent returns to Jutland, reconciles himself with Otvin, marries Nidung's daughter, and returns home with her and Vithga. Velent sends the twelve-year old Vithga out into the world armed with Mimung.

[FH]

Bibliography
Þiðreks Saga af Bern. Ed. Henrik Bertelsen. Samfund til udgivelse af gammel nordisk litteratur. 2 vols. Copenhagen: S. L. Mollers bogtrykkeri, 1905–1911.

VIENNA is mentioned several times in the *Nibelungenlied*. It is located seven days from Etzel's camp in Hungary (Gran) and is used by Rüdiger as a place to spend the night on his way back to Pöchlarn (1162,3; 1164,2a). It also serves as the location of Kriemhild's marriage to Etzel and the site of a magnificent seventeen-day celebration at Whitsuntide (1361,2, 1365,3a, and 1375,1).

Around 1200 Vienna was the capital of "Osterriche" under Leopold VII, and a commercial center of considerable importance. Leopold and his predecessors were responsible for the drama-

tic rise in the fortunes of the city. The Babenbergs maintained a policy of support for the Staufers; Margrave Heinrich II, called Jasomirgott (1112–1177) had by 1156 succeeded in obtaining control over Austria, and he and his successors were instrumental in garnering aid from the bishop of Passau and the Regensburg merchants for church— and mercantile— related activities in Vienna. Leopold VI and son Leopold VII enjoyed support from regional and local sources; both cultivated relationships with seigneurial lords and townspeople, and the result was an expanding center of commerce, finance, and political power.

[GCS]

VINBJORG, a place name in the *Volsunga saga*. The area is to be given to Gudrun (along with Valbjorg) by Grimhild and the sons of Gjuki to compensate her for the murder of her husband and son.

[JHS]

VINDLAND, an area between Germany and Poland, between the Schlei and the Vistula rivers, the region to the south of the Baltic Sea. Jarl Hornbogi rules here, according to the *Þiðreks saga*. Strangely enough, Sigurd tells us that he is a *frændi* (blood relative, blood friend) of Hornbogi (chapter 202).

[GW]

VINGI. His story is told in the *Atlamál* and in the *Volsunga saga*. He is the messenger sent by Atli to invite Gunnar and Hogni to the Hunnish court. In the *Atlakviða* the messenger is called Knefrod (also in the prose part *Dráp Niflungar*). The runes Gudrun carved in order to warn her brothers are altered by Vingi. Yet Glaumvor, Gunnar's wife, and Kostbera, Hogni's wife, guess the truth. So Vingi is forced to swear that he does not mean the Gjukungs any harm. When they arrive at Atli's court, Vingi confesses that he has deceived them and that they will soon be killed. Vingi is instantly beaten to death by Gunnar and Hogni with the back of their axes.

[GW]

Bibliography
Gering, Hugo, and B. Sijmons. *Kommentar zu den Liedern der Edda.* 2. Hälfte: *Heldenlieder.* Germanistische Handbibliothek VII 3,2. Halle

(Saale): Buchhandlung des Waisenhauses (Francke), 1931, pp. 288, 365.

VITHGA, son of Velent and of Nidung's unnamed daughter in the *Þiðreks saga*. At twelve Vithga declines Velent's offer to teach him his craft, preferring to become a knight. He sets out to test his mettle with the twelve-year-old Thidrek. Velent arms him with his sword Mimung. On his way Vithga encounters Hildibrand, Heimir, and Hornbogi. Discovering who he is and what he intends, Hildibrand and his companions conceal their identity and offer Vithga mutual aid. Confronted by twelve highwaymen, Vithga rejects their demands that he surrender his weapons. They attack, and Vithga kills seven of them. So that all may travel in peace, Vithga sets fire to their stronghold. Fearing for Thidrek's safety, Hildibrand steals Mimung. He then reveals his identity. The five surviving highwaymen are later slain by Vithga and Hornbogi. Thidrek welcomes Hildibrand, Hornbogi, and Heimir to Bern but will not speak to Vithga who challenges him to combat. When Thidrek threatens to hang Vithga, Hildibrand's remonstrations compel him to accept the challenge. After a long struggle Vithga's sword shatters. As Thidrek is about to slay him, Hildibrand pleads for Vithga's life. Thidrek remains intransigent, and Hildibrand returns Mimung to Vithga, who deals Thidrek five wounds. Thetmar intervenes and in vain offers Vithga a castle, an earldom, and a good marriage if he will spare Thidrek. When Vithga slices away half of Hildigrim and some of Thidrek's hair, Hildibrand separates them and effects a reconciliation. In the battle between Osantrix and the combined forces of Atli and Thidrek, Vitholf knocks Vithga unconscious. Heimir snatches up Mimung but leaves Vithga to be captured. Osantrix claps Vithga into a dungeon from which he is rescued by Vildifer. Vithga later slays Rimstein of Gerimsheim, receiving Thidrek's thanks. As Thidrek and his champions approach Isung's realm, Vithga enters the forest to fight the giant, Ethgeir (a kinsman). The victorious Vithga cuts out Ethgeir's tongue, bloodies himself and his horse, ties the tongue to his horse's tail, and rides back to Thidrek yelling that Ethgeir has dealt him a mortal wound. Only Thidrek stands his ground.

In the contest of Isung's and Thidrek's champions, Vithga defeats Isung's eleventh son and releases his captive companions. He then lends Thidrek Mimung so that Thidrek can defeat Sigurd. After Aki Omlungatrausti has been slain, Thidrek proposes to Ermenrich that Vithga marry Aki's widow, Bolfriana. Vithga does so and becomes Ermenrich's man. He later attempts to defend Thidrek against Sifka's treachery but is forced to fight on Ermenrich's side against Thidrek. He does not want to harm Thidrek or Thether. In the ensuing battle Vithga kills Nauthung, Ortvin, Erp, and Thether. Thidrek vows revenge and pursues Vithga, who retreats to the sea where he disappears beneath the surface as Thidrek flings his spear after him.

[FH]

VOLSUNG, in the *Volsunga saga,* son of Rerir, who experiences a remarkable birth so often associated with heroes. Etymologically, he is has been associated with a Scandinavian fertility god named Volsi. He remains in his mother's womb for six years, and later marries Hljod, daughter of the giant Hrimnir. She bears him ten sons and a daughter. King Volsung enjoys a considerable reputation as a ruler and warrior. He later falls into battle against his son-in-law, King Siggeir, who has been insulted by Sigmund, Volsung's son, during the marriage festivities.

[WM]

Bibliography
Byock, Jesse L., trans. *The Saga of the Volsungs: The Norse Epic of Sigurd the Dragon Slayer.* Berkeley: University of California Press, 1990. Also, New York: Penguin, 1999.

VOLKER VON ALZEY, a warrior knight who belongs to the highest echelon of the court at Worms and to the aristocracy that invariably surrounds the throne. Consequently he is mentioned very early in the *Nibelungenlied* (9,4a) and he is among the last to disappear in the work (2287); only Dancwart, Giselher, Gunther, and Hagen meet their death after him. Nevertheless Volker's presence in the text is uneven. He is a much stronger individual in the second part than in the first. His forefathers and family relations are not referenced, in contrast to those of the other protagonists.

Initially, Volker remains in the background. He does not play any role at decisive moments, such as the courtship of Brünhild, the strife between the queens, or the murder of Siegfried. Only once during the battles against the Saxons and the Danes does Volker come forward, but he does not take on any special role. In one instance in the first part of the epic, he is called a *spileman* (fiddler; 196,2b), but without any consequence to the plot. The absence of a singular perspective, a symptom of waning moral certainty in the *Nibelungenlied*, is reflected in Volker's case by his appearance on three different occasions.

Only during his second introduction, at the start of the Burgundians' journey into death, are Volker's musical capabilities underscored (1477), and they are not demonstrated until he is abroad (1705). His music is heard solely in connection with catastrophe and pain, moreover, not with his life in the court of Worms. Generally in the rest of the plot the function and understanding of music comports with the standards and realities of the era: Volker's music is designed to accompany lyrics and is more highly esteemed than sheer instrumental music. He does not belong to the musical practitioners whose works lack a basis in theory. Consistent with the medieval understanding of the string instruments' liberating and harmonizing powers, Volker's fiddling lulls the exhausted and troubled listeners to sleep. Rhythmic instruments, on the other hand, were thought to be a source of excitement, so mimicking those types of beat instruments Volker uses his bow in combat (1966; 1976; 2002). Unlike all the other heroes, only Volker's campaigns are often described in musical metaphors and only when he fights against the Huns, not the Saxons or the Danes. The semantic transgression, through which terms like *leich* (song) and *dôn* (melody) describe combat episodes, reflects a dynamic within the language that is uniquely Volker's. Volker repeatedly takes the liberty of breaking common rules and he actively explores new territory.

The third occurrence of Volker in the *Nibelungenlied* is as Hagen's friend (1584). From the commencement of their journey to the land of the Huns, Volker and Hagen discover their friendship as much as their new surroundings. Their connection is primarily intellectual. Their thoughts meet unintentionally and give birth to something new. Their camaraderie exists at first to avoid conflict, but in hostile situations it becomes provocative on the one hand and defensive on the other, like the image of fighter and thinker side by side, a fashionable theme of nineteenth-century painters and monument sculptors. The first interpretation of Volker stems incidentally from a time of boundless admiration of the union between power and art.

The *Klage* does not change Volker's image. Modern Nibelungen writers can take greater liberties: Hebbel sees Volker as a character with great knowledge and sensitivity. Thea von Harbou emphasizes the artist and neglects the warrior. In J. Fernau's interpretation Volker is the most detestable character in the text; whereas Volker Braun represents him from a multidimensional perspective as a critical intellectual.

[WL]

Bibliography
Eigner, Leopold. "Ueber den Spielmann im Nibelungenliede." In *Dritter Jahresbericht des niederösterreichischen Landes-Lehrer-Seminars in St. Pölten. Am Schlusse des Schuljahres 1878.* St. Pölten: Gutmannsthal und Völkl, 1878.
Hammerstein, Reinhold. *Diabolus in musica: Studien zur Ikonographie der Musik im Mittelalter.* Neue Heidelberger Studien zur Musikwissenschaft 6. Berne: Francke, 1974, pp. 50ff.
Storch, Wolfgang, ed. *Die Nibelungen. Bilder von Liebe, Verrat und Untergang.* Munich: Prestel, 1987.

VOSGES (MHG *Waskenwalt*), mountain chain west of the Rhine, opposite the Black Forest, the boundary between German-speaking Alsace and the rest of France. In the *Nibelungenlied* Vosges is mentioned as the scene of the hunt during which Siegfried was killed (911,3). The adapter of the **C** version replaced it with the Odenwald because, according to the poem, the hunt took place on the opposite bank of the river, whereas Worms and the Vosges are both situated on the left bank. The Waskenstein, to which reference is made in connection with Walther of Spain (2344,2), must not be confused with the Waskenwalt; it is a hill in the Palatine Forest north of the Vosges.

[NV]

WACHAU (also called **NIBELUNGENGAU**), term used to describe the area along the Danube in Austria between Melk and Krems. The Nibelungs/Burgundians travel through this territory on their way to Etzel's court.

[SSch]

WADE (also called **VAÐI**, **VATHI**, and **WATE**), a Germanic hero widely known throughout the Middle Ages in a variety of geographical localities (including England, Scandinavia, and Germany). He is the son of Wilcinus in the *Þiðreks saga* and the father of Velent (Welent) and grandfather of Vithga. He plays no role in the Nibelungen story per se, although certain parallels may be drawn between his character in *Kudrun* (ca. 1230–1240), whose author was undoubtedly familiar with the *Nibelungenlied*, and the figure of Hagen in the latter epic.

[WM]

Bibliography
McConnell, Winder. *The Wate Figure in Medieval Tradition.* Stanford German Studies 13. Berne: Lang, 1978.

WÄLSUNG, modern German equivalent of Old Norse "volsungr," as used by Wagner in his *Ring* cycle. Wagner's Wotan, wandering through the world, calls himself "Wälse." His human descendants, the twins Siegmund and Sieglinde, and their son Siegfried, are named "Wälsung" (plural "Wälsungen"). In the Norse *Volsunga saga,* King Volsungr is the father of Sigmundr and Signy, and grandfather of Sinfjotli and Sigurd. The relationship of Volsungr to a forefather (whose name must have been Volsi) remains unclear.

[UM]

WAERBEL, Etzel's minstrel in the *Nibelungenlied.* Together with Swemmel he serves as a messenger to the Burgundians, carrying Etzel's invitation to the Burgundians to journey to Gran, a message he imparts in good faith. He later loses a hand to Hagen's rage following the slaying of Ortlieb by the latter.

[KM]

WALBER, a noble freeman in the *Klage* who has led twelve hundred of his men from Turkey through Greece to the court of Etzel. He is mentioned in the same context as Herman of Poland and Sigeher of Wallachia and, like them, suffers, along with all of his men, the same fate. Walber is not mentioned in the *Nibelungenlied.*

[WM]

WALBERTUS (WALDBERTUS in some early editions), one of the sons of Gibaldus in the *Historia von dem gehörnten Siegfried.* He corresponds to Gernot in the *Nibelungenlied* and Gyrnot in the *Lied vom Hürnen Seyfrid.* His role in the *Historia* is minimal. The final chapter of the *Historia* tells how, after the death of his brother Hagenwald (Hagen), he and his other brother, Ehrenbertus, are hounded into exile. Walbertus is encountered by Siegfried's son Löwhardus in a forest on the way to Sicily.

[JLF]

WALBJORG is, according to the *Guðrúnarkviða onnur* and the *Volsunga saga,* a region which Grimhild offers Gudrun together with the district of Winbjörg, if her daughter will marry Atli. Gudrun finally agrees to her mother's plans. Both districts are accorded place names that are purely poetical.

[GW]

Bibliography
Gering, Hugo, and B. Sijmons. *Kommentar zu den Liedern der Edda.* 2. Hälfte: *Heldenlieder.* Germanistische Handbibliothek VII 3,2. Halle (Saale): Buchhandlung des Waisenhauses (Francke), 1931, p. 309.

WALDAR, king of the Danes, is mentioned in the *Guðrúnarkviða onnur;* the *Volsunga saga* refers to him as Waldamar. He is also among those knights whom Gunnar and Hogni ask to come to King Half's hall. Perhaps Waldar, along with Jarizkár, is Atli's vassal. The *Hervarar saga ok Heiðreks konungs* also mentions a Waldar, king of Denmark.

[GW]

Bibliography
Gering, Hugo, and B. Sijmons. *Kommentar zu den Liedern der Edda.* 2. Hälfte: *Heldenlieder.* Germanistische Handbibliothek VII 3,2. Halle (Saale): Buchhandlung des Waisenhauses (Francke), 1931, p. 301.

WALLACHIA. See SIGEHER OF WALLACHIA and RAMUNG.

WALTARI. According to the story of Waltari and Hildigund in the *Þiðreks saga*, Waltari is a hostage at Atli's court who escapes with his beloved Hildigund. They take treasures with them and therefore Waltari is engaged in battles with Hogni (according to other versions also with Gunnar) in the Vosges forest (Waskenstein). According to the Latin version of the legend, he loses one hand in his fight. He is called Waltari af Waskastein, son of Ermenrich's sister, in the saga. Other versions call him either Walter of Spain, of Aquitania, of Kerlingen, of Toledo, or of Langres. Sometimes his father is called Alphere and his mother is said to be a sister of Biterolf of Toledo. The *Nibelungenlied* tells us about his stay at Etzel's court together with Hagen and Rüdiger, who are his best friends. Here it is Hagen who flees from Etzel's court earlier than Walter and Hildegund. Later Hagen only fights against Walter in the Vosges forest because he is a liege man to Gunther. According to a later text (*Chronicle of Novalesa*), Walter grows very old and travels throughout the world. Finally he arrives in Novalesa. He becomes a gardener in the monastery and dies there.

[GW]

Bibliography

Raszmann, August. *Die Sagen von den Wölsungen und Niflungen, den Wilcen und König Thidrek von Bern in der Thidrekssaga.* 2nd ed. Hanover: Rümpler, 1863, pp. 289–297.

Schneider, Hermann. *Germanische Heldensage.* Vol. 1. 2nd ed. Grundriss der germanischen Philologie 10/I. Berlin: de Gruyter, 1962, pp. 331–344.

WALTHER OF SPAIN (WALTHER VON SPÂNJE), referred to in strophe 2344 of the *Nibelungenlied* by Hildebrand, who accuses Hagen of having refused to fight him at the Waskenstein. In *Waltharius* the hero Walthari defends a mountain pass against a series of warriors, including the reluctant Hagen, who had been his friend while they were hostages at the court of Attila. References to the tale are frequent. Walther's historical antecedent is probably the Visgothic king Walja (415–418).

[BOM]

WASKENSTEIN, a locale in the Vosges mountains in northeast France parallel to the Rhine. Before the final battle in the *Nibelungenlied* between Gunther and Hagen on the one side and Dietrich and Hildebrand on the other, Hildebrand exclaims in response to a taunt by Hagen:

Des antwurte Hildebrant: "zwiu verwîzet ir mir daz?
nu wer was, der ûf einem schilde   vor dem Waskensteine saz,
dô im von Spânje Walther   sô vil der friunde sluoc?
ouch habt ir noch ze zeigen   an iu selben genuoc." (2344)

[Hildebrandt replied: "Why do you rebuke me with that?
Who was it, I wonder, who sat on his shield at the Waskenstein,
while Walther of Spain slew his companions right and left?
Indeed, you are far from being above reproach."]

Hildebrand's comment refers to an episode in the Latin epic *Waltharius,* the date of composition of which lies between the latter half of the ninth century and the first half of the tenth (ca. 850–ca. 918). The epic, doubtless written by a monk of St. Gall (Switzerland), relates in 1456 hexameters the tale of three young people: Walther of Aquitaine, Hildigund of Francia, and Hagen of Burgundy, who grew up together as hostages at Attila's court. In due time, the three people became beloved by Attila and his wife and were accorded great honor and responsibilities. Walther and Hildigund became betrothed, and Hagen and Walther swore everlasting friendship. Eventually Hagen escapes back to Burgundy and to the service of the young Gunther, who has become king. Not long thereafter, Walther and Hildigund also escape with a great deal of Attila's treasure. Gunther, who is not a strong or even admirable king in the *Waltharius,* leads a group of men over Hagen's objections to steal the treasure from Walther. After a protracted series of individual battles near the Waskenstein, Walther has killed all the Franks except Gunther and Hagen. Through it all, Hagen has refused to fight his friend Walther. Even the murder of Hagen's nephew (son of his sister) is not sufficient to make Hagen break his vow of friendship.

Only when there is no one left to defend Gunther, the king, does Hagen agree to fight. He makes his reason clear to the king: "Know, my lord," [Hagen says], "not even for the sake of my beloved nephew [whom Walther killed] . . . Would I be willing to break my pledged friendship [to Walther] . . . . I go into certain danger for you alone, oh my king" (1112–1114).

When he enters the battle, however, this is not the explanation Hagen gives Walther. In response to Walther's question of why Hagen is breaking his pledge to him, Hagen replies that it is in retaliation for the death of his nephew at Walther's hands. Apparently the poet believed that this reason, avenging a family member's killing, would make sense to the hero, Walther, more so than Hagen adhering to his loyalty as a vassal to an unjust king. Walther accepts this argument and they engage in the final battle. Since the poem was most likely the work of a monk, there is a more or less happy ending. Gunther, Hagen, and Walther survive, each with rather serious wounds, about which Hagen and Walther make grotesque jokes while sitting around the campfire.

The statement by Hildebrand is interesting in the *Nibelungenlied* because it demonstrates that the audience was familiar with the *Waltharius* or at least with the episodes recounted in it; namely, Hagen fighting with his friend Walther. It is also fascinating because in essence Hagen refused to break his oath of loyalty to his friend and fight willy-nilly for his king, even though his own nephew was killed. Only when no one was left, did Hagen agree to fight, and even then he was unable to give the real reason to his friend. Was not Rüdiger in a similar situation in the thirty-seventh *âventiure* in which he had to make a decision between his feudal and his personal loyalties? Did not Hagen, this time, make the "right" choice in that same *âventiure* when he refused to raise a hand against Rüdiger, "ob ir si alle slüeget, die von Burgonden lant" (even if you slay all of them who have come from Burgundy; 2201,4)? Whatever the **B** poet intended can only be conjectured. It is clear, however, that the poet(s?) of the **C** version and the *Klage* did not agree with their colleague in this regard, since that would involve portraying Hagen in a positive light. Nonetheless it is entirely probable that the **B** poet wished to impart something specific to his audience by having the Waskenstein episode recalled to memory.

[FGG]

Bibliography

Gentry, Francis G. *Triuwe and Vriunt in the Nibelungenlied.* Amsterdamer Publikationen zur Sprache und Literatur 19. Amsterdam: Rodopi, 1975.

Waltharius. In *Waltharius, Ruodlieb, Märchenepen,* edited by Karl Langosch. Darmstadt: Wissenschaftliche Buchgesellschaft, 1967.

WASKENWALT, see VOSGES.

WELLGUNDE, see RHINE MAIDENS.

WICHART, in the *Nibelungenlied,* one of Dietrich's men whose death at Etzel's court, although not described, is greatly lamented (note 2281,1; 2323,2) by the leader of the Goths.

[WM]

WIDOLF. According to the *Þiðreks saga,* the giant Vidolfr mittumstangi (Widolf with the staff) is a brother of Etgeir, Aspilian, and Aventrod. The brothers are also mentioned in *Skíða ríma* (Skidi's poem), a humorous parody of heroic legends and myths, written about 1400. Here they sit together with Isung's sons, many other heroes, and Odin in Walhall. In the *Mágus saga jarls* (ca. 1350) the brothers, together with such other heroes as Sigurd, Gunnar, Hogni, Atli, and Thidrek, are brought back to life by the magic powers of the saga's main protagonist, Jarl Mágus, and have to engage in heavy fighting. Widolf's father is King Nordian of Sjaelland. Widolf is the strongest and tallest of all the giants and very cruel to human beings and animals. His weapon is a heavy and long iron staff. Not even twelve men can lift it. When Aspilian becomes king, he orders Widolf to be kept in chains because he fears his brother's strength. The brothers have to pay tribute to King Osantrix and during that time Widolf is killed by Wildifer, one of Thidrek's liege men. The figure is called Widolt in the German poem *Rother* (written after the middle of the twelfth century) and in the German epic *Reinfried von Braunschweig* (about 1300).

[GW]

Bibliography

Raszmann, August. *Die Sagen von den Wölsungen und Niflungen, den Wilcen und König Thidrek von*

Bern in der Thidrekssaga. 2nd ed. Hanover: Rümpler, 1863, p. 164.

Homan, Theo. *Skíðaríma: An Inquiry into the Written and Printed Texts, References, and Commentaries*. Amsterdam: Rodopi N.V., 1975.

Glauser, Jürg. *Isländische Märchensagas: Studien zur Prosaliteratur im spätmittelalterlichen Island*. Beiträge zur nordischen Philologie 12. Basel: Helbing & Lichtenhahn, 1983.

Simek, Rudolf, and Hermann Pálsson. *Lexikon der altnordischen Literatur*. Stuttgart: Kröner, 1987, pp. 239f., 320f.

WIESELBURG, town in Hungary (Hungarian, *Mosonmagyaróvár*), on a southern branch of the Danube (known as the Lesser Danube). In the Middle Ages Wieselburg was an important river port situated about 20 kilometers from the Austrian border. In the *Nibelungenlied* it is mentioned once as Misenburg (1377,1). Here Etzel and Kriemhild embark to travel the rest of the way by boat to Etzelnburg (= Esztergom) in the land of the Huns.

[NV]

WIGNANT. In the *Klage* Wignant appears as a warrior in the service of Dietrich and is killed by Gunther during the final battle at Etzel's court.

[WM]

WILCINUS, according to the *Þiðreks saga,* King Wilcinus, the eponymous hero of Wilcinaland and the Wilzen people. His people are known to the Marner. King Wilcinus is in conflict with King Hertnit of Russia and wins many battles against him. He has two sons, Nordian and the giant Wade of Sjaelland, whose mother is a mermaid. Wade is the father of Velent and the grandfather of Vithga.

[GW]

Bibliography

Grimm, Wilhelm. *Die deutsche Heldensage*. 4th ed. Darmstadt: Wissenschaftliche Buchgesellschaft, 1957, pp. 179f. 231.

Schneider, Hermann. *Germanische Heldensage*. Vol. 1. 2nd ed. Grundriss der germanischen Philologie 10/I. Berlin: de Gruyter, 1962, pp. 368f.

WILDIFER/WILD-EWER, one of Thidrek's liege men in the *Þiðreks saga*. His name is written Vildiver or Willifer in the *Þiðreks saga*. He is very tall and strong, and is strangely dressed and wears a heavy golden armlet. Initially he comes from Aumlungaland and wants to join Thidrek's court. Later Wildifer and Vithga become close friends, and he is one of Thidrek's fighters against the eleven sons of Isung. Wildifer is among Atli's knights during a hunt in the Lyrawoods. There he kills a huge bear and keeps its hide. When Vithga is kept in prison by King Osantrix, Wildifer tries to free him with the help of a minstrel called Isung. Isung takes the bear's hide and sews Wildifer into it so that he looks like a dancing bear, and Isung calls him Vizleo (white lion). Wildifer dances for Osantrix while Isung plays the harp. When Osantrix sets his sixty big dogs on the dancing bear and even tries to kill him, Wildifer gets so furious that he kills the king and two of his giants, Aventrod and Widolf. Vithga hears the noise and frees himself. The friends rush through the town and kill many brave men. Then Wildifer takes off the bear's hide and flees together with Vithga and Isung, and they return to Húnaland and to King Atli. Later Wildifer is killed by Waltari af Waskasteini in the battle of Thidrek and the Huns against Ermenrich at Gronsport. The scribe obviously interpreted the name Vildiver as wild boar, yet the story itself and the Low German fragment of the epic *Van bere Wisselaue* indicates that it primarily meant *wildi bero'* ("wild bear"), for Wisselaue is a popular etymological reinterpretation of Vaclov (Wenzel), the typical name for the Bohemian dancing bear. The name could also be interpreted as Víldivèr (wild man) with reference to the golden armlet, which is typical of a wild man.

[GW]

Bibliography

Bernheimer, R. *Wild Men in the Middle Ages*. Cambridge: Harvard University Press, 1952.

Schneider, Hermann. *Germanische Heldensage*. Vol. 1. 2nd ed. Grundriss der germanischen Philologie 10/I. Berlin: de Gruyter, 1962, pp. 329ff.

Tuppa, Gerlinde. "Die Bedeutung der Tiere und der Tiermotive in der germanischen Heldensage." Diss., Vienna, 1965, pp. 302ff, 358f.

WINGSKORNIR is Brynhild's horse. It is only mentioned in *Fáfnismál* and in the *hesta heiti* (names of horses) of the *Prose Edda*.

[GW]

Bibliography
Tuppa, Gerlinde. "Die Bedeutung der Tiere und der Tiermotive in der germanischen Heldensage." Diss., Vienna 1965, p. 272.

WITEGE is mentioned briefly in the *Nibelungenlied* as the warrior who killed Nuodung (1699,4), whose shield Gotelind presents to Hagen in the twenty-seventh *âventiure,* and whose land and bride are offered in the thirty-first by Kriemhild to Bloedelin as an incentive for supporting her cause. Note also VITHGA.

[WM]

WOGLINDE. See RHINE MAIDENS.

WOLFBRAND, one of Dietrich's men in the *Nibelungenlied.* Together with Helpfrich, Helmnot, and many other Amelungs, he laments the death of Margrave Rüdiger (2261). He is described as fighting magnificently during the battle in Etzel's Hall (2281,4), and Dietrich later regrets having lost him along with the rest of his men. Wolfbrand's actual death is not described in the *Nibelungenlied,* but the *Klage* poet intimates that he is killed by Dancwart.

[WM]

WOLFGER VON ERLA (d. 1218), confirmed as patriarch of Aquilea in northeastern Italy by Pope Innocent III in 1204, Wolfger (also known as Wolfger of Ellenbrechtskirchen) was bishop of Passau (named 1191) at the time of composition of the *Nibelungenlied.* Because of the prominence of a fictional counterpart (Bishop Pilgrim of Passau) within the epic, Wolfger is thought by some to have been the patron for the *Nibelungenlied,* though firm proof of this is lacking. In any event Wolfger was a patron of literature, as the poet Walther von der Vogelweide was evidently in his service. (See also ZEISELMAUER.)

[MR]

Bibliography
Boshof, Egon, and Fritz Peter Knapp, eds. *Wolfger von Erla: Bischof von Passau (1191–1204) und Patriarch von Aquileja (1204–1218) als Kirchenfürst und Literaturmäzen.* Germanistische Bibliothek, 3rd. ser., n.s., 20. Heidelberg: Winter, 1994.

WOLFHART, a warrior associated with Dietrich (note *Alpharts Tod,* 74,4, 89f.) who also appears in the *Nibelungenlied* and the *Klage.* In the Nibelungen tradition he is known as Hildebrand's nephew and in general he has the reputation of being something of a hothead. He and Giselher kill each other in the *Nibelungenlied.*

[WM]

WOLFWIN, in the *Nibelungenlied,* one of Dietrich's men, first mentioned in 2259,1 who, together with Sigestab, laments the death of Rüdiger, claiming that he could not be more affected if his own father had died. In the fighting in Etzel's Great Hall, he parts Wolfhart and Volker, but is subsequently killed, although no details of his demise are provided. (According to the *Klage* poet, he is killed by Giselher.) Dietrich laments him in 2322, along with Wolfhart, Sigestab, and Wolfprant, as key warriors on whom he would have depended to have formed a new realm in "der Amelunge lant" (2322,4).

[WM]

WORMS, the fictional capital of the Burgundian empire and the setting for much of the first half of the *Nibelungenlied,* Worms traces its roots back to the Roman fortress Borbetomagus, which was captured by the Burgundians in 413 a.d. There is no historical proof, however, that it ever became the Burgundian capital. Modern-day Worms identifies strongly with the prominent position it occupies in the *Nibelungenlied,* as numerous local place names allude to the epic. The north portal of the cathedral (begun 1171) may actually have provided the poet with his setting for the altercation between Brünhild and Kriemhild; in addition, a statue (erected 1905) on the west bank of the Rhine depicts Hagen sinking the Nibelungen treasure in the river.

[MR]

WOTAN, Wagner's variation on the name Odin. In the *Ring of the Nibelung* he is the chief god, the father of Brunnhilde and the other valkyries, and the ancestor of Siegfried. He also appears as "the wanderer," a one-eyed figure with magic powers. He is forced by Fricka to let Siegmund be killed by Hunding, and must punish Brunnhilde for trying to save Siegmund. He puts her into a deep sleep behind a wall of fire, where she must remain until a hero unafraid of the fire awakens her. This hero, of course, is Siegfried.

[JVM]

WULFFGRAMBÄHR, the name of the giant in *Wunderschöne Historie vom gehörnten Siegfried,* against whom the hero first has to fight in order to save the princess Florigunda, who has been captured by the dragon. In *Hürnen Siegfried* and in Hans Sach's drama, he is commonly called Kuperan, Kuperon, or Ruperan. This new name was obviously choosen to mark him as a dangerous, animal-like man.

[RB]

Bibliography

Jantz, Harold. "The Last Branch of the Nibelungen Tree." *MLN,* 80 (1965), 433–440.

Schröder, E. "Das Volksbuch von gehörten Siegfried." *DVjs* (1892), 480–489.

XANTEN, in the *Nibelungenlied,* a city on the Lower Rhine, the home of King Siegmund and his spouse, Sieglinde, parents of Siegfried. Although now situated in Germany, the epic sites Xanten in the "Niederlanden" (20). Siegfried returns here with Kriemhild after their marriage. He eventually returns to Worms (where he meets his death) following an invitation from Gunther that originally came from Brünhild.

[WM]

YOUNG SIGURD (Sigurðr svein) is the son of King Sigmund of Tarlungaland and his wife Sisibe, according to the *Þiðreks saga.* Sigurd is often referred to with the epithet "svein" throughout the whole *Niflunga saga* section. Here Sigurd's youth is of interest. King Sigmund is convinced by his advisors Hartwig and Hermann that his wife, Sisibe, is guilty of adultery and so he sends her away to Svavaskogr (Swabian woods, perhaps the Black Forest). There she gives birth to her son and puts the baby into a glass container, which rolls into a river. Sisibe dies soon afterwards. The container reaches the sea and on low tide is left behind on shore. The boy, having already grown a great deal, shatters the glass and begins to weep. A hind finds him and suckles him for one year, but at that time he

is as strong and tall as a four-year-old boy. He is found by Mime, a blacksmith in Húnaland. Sigurd is so strong that he hits Mime's twelve apprentices, even the strongest ones, Eckihard and Welent. When Mime wants Sigurd to forge an iron bar, the boy hammers the anvil into the ground. Mime begins to fear him and sends him to his brother Regin, who has changed into a dragon by magic, in the hope that Regin would kill him. Mime pretends that Sigurd should burn wood to make charcoal. When Regin approaches Sigurd, the young hero kills the dragon with a burning piece of wood. Because he is hungry, Sigurd boils the dragon. He burns his finger and puts it into his mouth to cool it. Now he can understand the birds, which warn him that Mime wants to avenge his brother's death. Sigurd bathes in the dragon's blood and gets a horny skin all over his body except for a spot between his shoulders. In the Swedish version of the saga a leaf of a maple falls between his shoulders. Then Sigurd returns home to Mime, bearing the dragon's head in his hands. Mime is so fearful that he tries to be reconciled by promising Sigurd the horse Grani, from Brynhild's stud, and by giving him a splendid suit of armor and weapons, in particular, the sword Gram. Sigurd kills Mime with this sword and leaves the woods. He reaches Brynhild's castle and kills seven serfs. Brynhild tells Sigurd about his royal heritage. Twelve men cannot catch Grani, and the horse runs to Sigurd voluntarily. Sigurd leaves the castle and reaches Bertangaland. There he becomes advisor to King Isung. In chapter 185 of the *Þiðreks saga* we are provided with an extensive description of young Sigurd and his heroic deeds. Here we are informed that the Wæringar (the Norsemen) call the dragon, which Sigurd killed, Faðmiþ; that is, Fafnir.

The story of Sigurd growing up without parents is also told in *Das Lied vom Hürnen Seyfried* and in the *Edda, Fáfnismál* 2–8. For a reference to Sigurd's first meeting with Brynhild, see also *Oddrúnargrátr* 17–18. Wilhelm Grimm also noticed the similarity between Sigurd's birth and the legend of Saint Genoveva of Brabant. The treatment of young Sigurd in the *Þiðreks saga* combines elements that we know from the northern and from the southern traditions preceding the *Nibelungenlied.* Yet the story of Sigmund and Sisibe and the birth of Sigurd is different from any other source.

[GW]

Bibliography

Boklund-Schlagbauer, Ragnhild. *Vergleichende Studien zu Erzählstrukturen im Nibelungenlied und in nordischen Fassungen des Nibelungenstoffes.* GAG 626. Göppingen: Kümmerle, 1996.

de Vries, Jan. *Altnordische Literaturgeschichte.* 2 vols. Grundriss der germanischen Philologie 15/16. Berlin: de Gruyter, 1964–1967.

Grimm, Wilhelm. *Die deutsche Heldensage.* 4th ed. Darmstadt: Wissenschaftliche Buchgesellschaft, 1957, pp. 81f.

Haymes, Edward R., and Susann T. Samples. *Heroic Legends of the North: An Introduction to the Nibelung and Dietrich Cycles.* New York: Garland, 1996, pp. 113ff.

Höfler, Otto. *Siegfried, Arminius, und die Symbolik: Mit einem historischen Anhang über die Varusschlacht.* Heidelberg: Winter, 1961, pp. 57f.

Schneider, Hermann. *Germanische Heldensage.* Vol. 1. 2nd ed. Grundriss der germanischen Philologie 10/I. Berlin: de Gruyter, 1962.

ZAZAMANC, a city situated in the Orient that is renowned for its silk. The name occurs in the *Nibelungenlied* (362,2) along with several other "silk capitals," the textiles of which are used by Kriemhild and her ladies to prepare fine clothes for the participants on her brother's wooing mission to Island. (See also AZAGOUC.)

[WM]

ZEISELMAUER, a small town on the Danube just above Vienna. According to the household accounts of Bishop Wolfger of Passau, it was here, on November 12, 1201, that he presented the money for a fur coat to the singer Walther von der Vogelweide. *Zeizenmûre* appears in manuscripts **A, B, H, J, d, g,** although manuscripts attributed to a later date instead mention *Traisenmûre.* Traismauer is on the River Traise (1332,1), and it has a great fortress (1332) where Kriemhild may appropriately have spent four days on the way to her meeting with Etzel. (See WOLFGER VON ERLA)

[MEG]

Bibliography

Herger, Hedwig. *Das Lebenszeugnis Walthers von der Volgelweide.* Vienna: Schendl, 1970.

ZIVELLES, a soldier made responsible for killing Hagenwald in the battle that Sieghardus unleashes to avenge Siegfried's death. Hounded by his enemies, Hagenwald imagines the cowardly Zivelles is more likely to show him mercy than is a more courageous soldier, but Zivelles takes advantage of Hagenwald's weariness and stabs him in his sleep. Later in the war Zivelles, too, is slain. For the fight between Jorcus and Zivelles in the *Historia von dem gehörnten Siegfried,* see JORCUS.

[JLF]

PART III

Themes, Motifs, Objects, and Key Words

ADELVRÎ (noble and free), is the term used to designate the free, dynastic aristocracy (Geburtsadel) in contrast to the originally unfree (and more numerous) "ministeriales" (Dienstadel), who functioned as adminstrators of feudal estates for members of the free aristocracy. Although the matter of whether a noble was originally of free or unfree status was erected as an ultimate and telling barrier between the two groups, the nobility of free origin was rapidly becoming little more than a memory in the eleventh century. Wars, vendettas, the growing shallowness of the gene pool, and impoverishment greatly reduced its numbers and influence by the late eleventh century. Thus since around the time of the *Nibelungenlied,* when a majority of the most powerful and wealthiest nobles in the German empire had their origins in the ministerial class, this distinction was no longer of real importance for many in the German empire. Consequently the term is found only once in the *Nibelungenlied* (828,1) when Kriemhild replies to Brünhild's charge that Siegfried is an "eigenman" (unfree vassal), and Kriemhild, as his wife, is an "eigendiu" (wife of an unfree vassal) and thus herself unfree: "You will see [yet] today that I am noble and free." Nonetheless (and surprisingly so) it is a key element in the acrimonious exchange between the two queens regarding the merits of their respective husbands. Clearly, as the literary sources of the *Nibelungenlied* indicate, the real reason for Siegfried's death ought to lie in Brünhild's frustrated love for Siegfried and her jealousy of Kriemhild (and on one level probably does). This subjective pretext is rejected by the *Nibelungenlied* poet, however, and he takes great care to craft the debate over status objectively. Troubling to Kriemhild is the accusation that Brünhild considers Siegfried unfree, not so much because it reflects unfavorably on her husband, but because of the implications for her own standing in the courtly world. For even if she is noble and free, if she married beneath her station, she would legally have to assume the status of her husband. Its sole occurrence in the *Nibelungenlied,* therefore, is telling in that it can be viewed as fulfilling the expectations of the unknown patron as well as, apparently, those of the poet's audience.

[FGG]

Bibliography

Bosl, Karl. *Die Grundlagen der modernen Gesellschaft im Mittelalter: Eine deutsche Gesellschaftsgeschichte des Mittelalters.* 2 vols. Stuttgart: Hiersemann, 1972.

Leyser, Karl J. *Medieval Germany and its Neighbours: 900–1250.* London: Hambledon Press, 1982.

AMBETLIUTE (servants) is derived from a Celtic word meaning *servant* or *member of a retinue.* By the time of the *Nibelungenlied* the word was used to denote a wide variety of usually ecclesiastic or royal administrators, from the lowest, unfree ministerial to an enfeoffed judge. The exact status of the ambetliute, who are mentioned only once in the *Nibelungenlied* (1505,1), is uncertain. They are the officials at Etzel's court who are ordered to prepare the royal hall with benches for the arrival of the Burgundians, an assignment carried out at Worms by the high court officials Hunold, the chamberlain, and Sindold, the cupbearer (563 and 776).

[RGS]

ANDVARANAUT (Andvari's gift), in both the *Reginsmál* and *Volsunga saga,* a ring that is part of an underwater treasure guarded by the dwarf Andvari at a waterfall. Upon losing the treasure to Loki, Andvari curses Andvaranaut, so that it and all the treasure will be the death of anyone who owns them. The ring's next owner, Heimdir, is killed by his son Fafnir. In the *Volsunga saga* Sigurd becomes owner of the ring after slaying Fafnir and gives it to Brynhild on their first encounter, later taking it back upon winning her to become Gunnar's bride. Sigurd then gives Andvaranaut to his wife, Gudrun, who shows it to Brynhild during their infamous dispute, which leads to Sigurd's murder and Brynhild's suicide. Apart from Gudrun, all the ring's owners, including the Niflungar (Burgundians), meet their deaths. According to the *Drap Niflungar* (Fall of the Niflungs), Gudrun sends Andvaranaut to Hogni in a vain attempt to warn her brothers away from accepting Atli's invitation to "Hunland." In Wagner's *Ring* cycle, Alberich is Andvari's counterpart.

[JKW]

AREBEIT (trials and tribulations, travail), is a common term in the courtly literature of the German Middle Ages. It hardly ever, however, signifies physical labor in these works, but rather is employed when poets wish to speak of great, and generally, wearisome effort, including the exertion expended in battle. Thus it is not surprising that the word is found in the *Nibelungenlied.* Its first appearance is in the second line of the first stanza:

Uns ist in alten mæren   wunders vil geseit
von helden lobebæren,   von grôzer arebeit, . . .

[In tales of old, true marvels are treasured, of heroes bold, of travails unmeasured . . .].

[FGG]

Bibliography
Gentry, Francis G. "Arbeit in der mittelalterlichen Gesellschaft: Die Entwicklung einer mittelalterlichen Theorie der Arbeit vom 11. bis zum 14. Jahrhundert." In *Arbeit als Thema in der deutschen Literatur vom Mittelalter bis zur Gegenwart,* edited by Reinhold Grimm and Jost Hermand. Königstein/Ts.: Athenäum, 1979, pp. 3–28.

ARM (powerless, non-noble). In the Middle Ages the term *arm* signified the state of being powerless rather than without means. Its Latin form, *pauper,* for example, consistently appears in documents as the antithesis of *potens* (powerful). It is, therefore, in this sense that *arm* is used in medieval writings. Near the end of the *Nibelungenlied* Dietrich von Bern learns from Hildebrand that all of his men have been lost at the hands of the Burgundians. Overwhelmed, he laments: ". . . ich armer Dietrîch./ich was ein künec hêre, vil gewaltec unde rîch" (". . . Alas, I poor Dietrich!/Once was I a king, great in power and in nobility rich" (2319,3–4). Here Dietrich is not bemoaning lost material wealth, but rather his men who were the outward symbol of his power and standing. Without them he may still be rich in a conventional sense, but is powerless as far as his status in the world is concerned.

[FGG]

Bibliography
Bosl, Karl. "Armut, Arbeit, Emanzipation: Zu den Hintergründen der geistigen und literarischen Bewegung vom 11. bis zum 13. Jahrhundert." In *Beiträge zur Wirtschafts- und Sozialgeschichte des Mittelalters: Festschrift für Robert Helbig zum 65. Geburtstag.* Cologne: Böhlau, 1976, pp. 128–146.
———. *Armut Christi: Ideale der Mönche und Ketzer, Ideologie der aufsteigenden Gesellschaftsschichten vom 11. bis zum 13. Jahrhundert.* Sitzungsberichte, Bayerische Akademie der Wissenschaften, Philosophisch-Historische Klasse, Heft I/81. Munich: Beck, 1981. 2 vols. Stuttgart: Hiersemann, 1972.

——. *Die Grundlagen der modernen Gesellschaft im Mittelalter: Eine deutsche Gesellschaftsgeschichte des Mittelalters.* 2 vols. Stuttgart: Hiersemann, 1972.

ÂVENTIURE (quest), a French loan word which came into use in Germany along with the influx of courtly elements from France during the twelfth century. *Âventiure* refers primarily to that which a knight encounters during his quests (Latin *advenire* "to come to"; cf. English "adventure"). *Âventiure* is employed in Middle High German with a rather broad range of meaning, denoting variously combat, fortune (whether good or bad), a chance happening, adventure, as well as the adventure story itself (and frequently even the literary source of such a tale). In the *Nibelungenlied* the noun *âventiure* is also used to designate each of the thirty-nine chapters of the epic.

[MR]

BALMUNG, the name of Siegfried's sword in the *Nibelungenlied* (note 95,1). Hagen acquires it after having murdered Siegfried, and Kriemhild uses it at the end of the epic to decapitate him. In Wagner's *Ring* cycle, Sigfried's sword, that had been forged by Wotan, is called Notung.

[WM]

BATTLE takes a wide range of forms in the *Nibelungenlied,* yet armed conflict between larger forces fighting in the open occurs only twice: a battle between one thousand Burgundians led by Siegfried and forty thousand Danes and Saxons commanded by Liudegast and Liudeger (139–220), and a rear-guard action between a Burgundian contingent consisting of sixty men led by Hagen and Dancwart and a party of seven hundred Bavarians following Gelpfrat (1602–1617). The most destructive combat occurs within Etzel's reception hall (1921–2379). The description focuses upon the principal warriors while the action of others is indicated indirectly by means of such details as the quantity of blood flowing on the ground or the body counts.

[VU]

BETROTHAL, a legally binding betrothal consisted of two parts (1) the pledge to give the bride to a suitor (e.g., Gunther's oath to Siegfried in *Nibelungenlied,* 334,1–4); (2) the actual giving of the bride (*Nibelungenlied,* 612,1–4). The *Nibelungenlied* contains four major betrothal promises, three of which are fulfilled. Brünhild's betrothal to Gunther follows his successful completion of the trials in Island in the seventh *âventiure.* Significantly Brünhild bestows her own hand on her suitor (*Nibelungenlied,* 466–469). Only then can Siegfried officially celebrate his betrothal to Kriemhild, his reward for helping Gunther win Brünhild. In the second part of the poem Kriemhild's betrothal to Etzel signals the beginning of the Burgundians' downfall. The fourth example, in which the betrothal has no hope of actual fulfillment, is that of young Giselher to Rüdiger's daughter Gotelind (*Nibelungenlied,* 1686). The betrothal is properly witnessed by the assembled company of the Burgundian army on their journey to Etzel's court. Interestingly the betrothal is perceived as a consummated marriage (*Nibelungenlied,* 2172). Furthermore the promise binds Rüdiger to the enemies of his queen, adding to his conflict of loyalty in the thirty-seventh *âventiure.*

[ASH]

Bibliography

Bornstein, Diane. "Betrothal." In vol. 2 of *Dictionary of the Middle Ages,* edited by Joseph R. Strayer. New York: Scribner, 1983, pp. 207–208.

Brundage, James. *Law, Sex, and Christian Society in Medieval Europe.* Chicago: University of Chicago Press, 1987.

Wemple, Suzanne. *Women in Frankish Society: Marriage and the Cloister, 500–900.* Philadelphia: University of Pennsylvania Press, 1981.

BIRDS. There is an ominous symbolism attached to birds in the *Nibelungenlied* (note also EAGLE and FALCON). In the twenty-fifth *âventiure,* prior to the departure of the Burgundians for Etzel's court, Ute dreams that all of the birds of the land are dead (1509; a similar dream is experienced by Oda, wife of King Irung of Niflungaland, in the *Þiðreks saga*). The warrior Ramung, duke of the Wallachians, journeys to the Hunnish court and supports Etzel in the struggle against the Burgundians. He brings along 700 men who are described as "flying birds" (1343) and who share the fate of others in the final conflagration at Etzel's court.

[WM]

BLOOD REVENGE, as the unalterable consequence of a vendetta or feud, is an entrenched component of Germanic heroic ethos and is as a result frequently encountered in Germanic heroic epic and song. It is a primary motif in the tales of the Nibelungen. The *Atlakviða* of the *Edda* provides one of the more spectacular examples from Old Norse literature. To avenge the slaying of her brothers Gunnar and Hogni, Gudrun kills her two sons, Erp and Eitell, and serves their hearts covered with honey to Atli. Even though Gunnar and Hogni were conspirators in the death of Sigurd, her first husband, Gudrun considers her ties to her blood relations to be more binding than those to either of her husbands or her children. In the *Nibelungenlied* the situation is reversed. Although Kriemhild is still responsible for the death of Ortlieb, her son by Etzel, her primary objective is to avenge the murder of Siegfried, her first husband, by being the prime force behind the fatal confrontation between the Burgundians and the Huns. Unlike Gudrun, however, Kriemhild earns no praise for her actions, but rather the opprobrium of the poet, demonstrating that, by the time of the *Nibelungenlied,* the Heroic Age was over.

[FGG]

Bibliography
Gentry, Francis G. *Triuwe and vriunt in the Nibelungenlied.* Amsterdam: Rodopi, 1975.
Zacharias, Rainer. "Die Blutrache im deutschen Mittelalter." *ZfdA* 91 (1962): 167–201.

BOTENBRÔT/BOTENMIETE (messenger's reward), are terms which appear to be interchangeable in denoting the reward that a messenger might expect for bringing good tidings. The messenger who gives Kriemhild a favorable account of Siegfried's performance in the war against the Saxons receives gold and splendid clothing (242–243). Sieglint rewards the messenger who brings the news of the approach of her son and his bride with silver and gold (705,1–2). The man who goes ahead of Rudiger believes that he will receive *botenbrôt* from Kriemhild for bringing the good news of Etzel's proposal (1216,3). One protracted little scene (556–558) makes it clear that the bestowal of such reward was enshrouded in ceremony: Siegfried has reason to hope for reward from Kriemhild when he rides ahead with the news that Gunther is safe and on his way home with his bride (553,1). Kriemhild, however, expresses her hesitation in giving him material reward, bearing in mind his status, though she declares that she will always be favorably disposed toward him. Siegfried in turn expresses his devotion to her, irrespective of his status, by saying that he would gladly receive such reward. When she gives it to him in the form of precious rings and bangles, he passes it on to some of her attendants, thus demonstrating that what mattered to him was not the gift itself but the gesture behind it. Added to the ceremonial aspects of this scene is the obvious factor of the growing affection between the two.

[MEG]

BREACH OF FAITH is a recurring motif in the *Nibelungenlied.* The betrayals enacted in the work are both political and personal. Siegfried's murder at the spring functions is the central betrayal that ultimately leads to the destruction of the Burgundian empire. Describing Gunther and Hagen's plot to kill Siegfried, the poet uses the word *untriuwe,* (faithlessness) seven times (876,2; 887,3; 911,4; 915,4; 916,2; 971,4; 988,4). Other pivotal scenes in which breach of faith occurs are when Siegfried professes his vassalage to Brünhild (420); when Kriemhild reveals Siegfried's vulnerable spot to Hagen (902); when Dancwart discloses to Hagen the extent of Kriemhild's enmity (1635); and when Hagen divulges to Kriemhild her brothers' agreement to hide the hoard and not reveal its location as long as one of them lives (2368). Episodes recounting such breaches of faith occur during critical junctures of the tale and serve to unify the text. In the Scandinavian tradition this motif is found in the *Volsunga saga,* in which Sigurd breaks his pledge to Brynhild and marries Gudrun. In both the *Brot af Sigurþarkviðu* and the *Volsunga saga,* Sigurd is falsely accused of having broken his oath not to violate Brynhild.

[LDT]

BUHURT (tourney), a knightly equestrian contest in which two opposing groups of knights face off and dash at one another with lances. Because the *buhurt* was conducted for sport, the knights' lances were customarily blunted. The noun (together with its related Middle High German verb *buhurdieren*) was borrowed directly from the Old French *bouhourt / behort,* which in turn was based upon a noun of Germanic origin; *hurt(e)* (thrust, impact). A typically courtly sport, the *buhurt* is practiced in the *Nibelungenlied* in the first half of the epic (e.g., at Siegfried's knighting and during Brunhild's welcome to Worms), but also in the second part, when the Burgundians ride against Etzel's knights.

[MR]

CLAN (MHG *sippe*), the Germanic notion of the clan is powerfully present in the background of the *Nibelungenlied,* although the word *sippe* is used on only three occasions, considerably less frequently than, for example, in the narrative works of Wolfram von Eschenbach. The power of blood relationships is, however, effectively reversed in the *Nibelungenlied,* in which Kriemhild is betrayed by her kinsmen, and she presides over the massacre of, among others, her own flesh and blood. Yet even as she prepares to torch the Great Hall, she recalls that she and the three kings are the children of one mother, and she offers to spare them if they will sacrifice Hagen (2104). Siegfried, in his death throes, prophesies that future generations will bear the guilt of this act (990), yet even then he commends Kriemhild to the care of her brothers (996–997). Kriemhild believes that when Hagen inquires about Siegfried's vulnerable spot, he is sincere in wishing to protect him because they are kinsmen (*mâc*) (898).

[MEG]

CONFLICT. The *Nibelungenlied* narrative steadily places conflict in the foreground of its story. Among the many conflicts presented are those of personal rivalry, marital strife, ethical dilemmas posed by contradictory loyalties, the competition for political power, assertions of social superiority through the conspicuous display of wealth, contests of physical might, tests of battlefield valor, and attacks by one nation on another's sovereignty. Taking the poem as a purveyor of Germanic lore, earlier scholarly opinion, especially in Germany, saw in the *Nibelungenlied*'s conflicts the forging of a people's moral, political, and military identity. In World War II German troops carried an official issue of the epic with them into battle. With postwar

scholarship far more diffident about any romanticization of the past, understanding of the poem's focus on conflict at every level has diverged in several directions: either toward the recognition of such universals in the human condition as tragedy (McConnell); toward the contextualization of the poem within the political milieu of the Hohenstaufen period (Haymes and Frakes); toward political, social, and cultural codes (Bekker, Gentry, and Udwin); and toward matters of text transmission and oral tradition (Andersson). All such studies pay tacit homage to the fact that every reader, no matter how modern and regardless of gender, national origin, or personal convictions, must confront the challenge to come to terms with the conflicts in which this story's characters are so complexly enmeshed. In observing and attempting to adjudicate these conflicts, the poem's audience is called upon to question its own gendered, political, social, and cultural attitudes, assumptions, and convictions in question. Thus the streams of textual criticism, having diverged in relation to the many facets of conflict presented by the poem, reconverge.

[VU]

Bibliography

Andersson, Theodore. *A Preface to the Nibelungenlied.* Stanford: Stanford University Press, 1987.

Bekker, Hugo. *The Nibelungenlied: A Literary Analysis.* Toronto: University of Toronto Press, 1971.

Frakes, Jerold. *Brides and Doom: Gender, Property, and Power in Medieval German Women's Epic.* Philadelphia: University of Pennsylvania Press, 1994.

Gentry, Francis G. *Triuwe and vriunt in the Nibelungenlied.* Amsterdam: Rodopi, 1975.

Haymes, Edward. *The Nibelungenlied: History and Interpretation.* Urbana: University of Illinois Press, 1986.

McConnell, Winder. *The Nibelungenlied.* Boston: Twayne Publishers, 1984.

Udwin, Victor. *Between Two Armies: The Place of the Duel in Epic Culture.* Leiden: Brill, 1999.

CONSUMMATION OF MARRIAGE. Several betrothals and marriages take place over the course of the *Nibelungenlied.* The consummation of two particular marriages has important ramifications for the entire plot, namely the marriages between Gunther and Brünhild and between Siegfried and Kriemhild. The contrasting experiences of these two couples on their wedding nights serve a twofold function in the design of the *Nibelungenlied.* The struggle for dominance between Gunther and Brünhild on their first night together, in which she hangs him on the wall of their bedchamber, provides comic relief (at least for the modern audience). Deeply embarrassed by his weakness, Gunther solicits Siegfried's aid in subduing his new wife.

There remains some question as to the exact nature of Siegfried's aid, namely whether Siegfried or Gunther actually consummates the relationship with Brünhild. The uncertainty is underscored by Siegfried's taking of Brünhild's belt and ring as victory tokens. The consummation of the marriage between Gunther and Brünhild thus lays the groundwork for the queens' argument in the fourteenth *âventiure.* Siegfried's oath heightens the ambiguity, for he swears only that he did not tell Kriemhild about any sexual involvement with Brünhild (*Nibelungenlied,* 857–860). The increased ambiguity threatens the security of Gunther's crown and Brünhild's position as queen. Brünhild's subsequent appeal to Hagen for help leads directly to Siegfried's murder.

[ASH]

DEGEN (hero, warrior) is a key word in the vocabulary of the heroic epic. Those designated as *degen* are considered to be brave, loyal, and valiant warriors. Other, similar terms from the heroic epic, all meaning warrior or hero, are *helt, wigant,* and *recke.* As is to be expected, all occur with great frequency in the *Nibelungenlied,* whereas in the courtly romances, *ritter* (knight) is most frequent, followed by *helt* (hero). In the *Nibelungenlied,* for example, the term *degen* is found twice as often as the word *ritter* (362/170), while in *Parzival* the word *ritter* occurs five times more frequently than *degen* (372/65). Likewise in Hartmann's *Iwein,* there are eighty-three occurrences of *ritter* and only four of *degen.* The term does not appear at all in Gottfried's *Tristan.*

[FGG]

Bibliography

Bumke, Joachim. *Studien zum Ritterbegriff im 12. und 13. Jahrhundert.* Heidelberg: Winter, 1964.

DESTRUCTION. The destruction that comes at the end of the *Nibelungenlied* consumes the entire Burgundian force consisting of nine thousand pages, one thousand knights, Hagen's personal cadre of sixty men, Hagen himself, Volker, Dancwart, and the three Burgundian kings. Of the Huns and their allies, seven thousand dead must be cleared from the hall at one point in the fighting. The twenty thousand then remaining are committed to battle and should be presumed killed. With the exception only of Etzel, Dietrich, and Hildebrand, all of the leading warriors die together with their cadres of elite fighters. The destruction thus engulfs warrior elites from Hunenland (east of Vienna) to the Danube and Rhine valleys, effectively underscoring the image of Armageddon and lack of continuity that prevails at the conclusion of the *Nibelungenlied.*

[VU]

DIENEST (service) is a cornerstone of the feudal system and as a result plays a great role in the literature of the courtly period, including the *Nibelungenlied.* In the feudal contract a vassal pledges his loyalty and service to a lord by promising his aid and counsel. By accepting this service the lord obligates himself to reward and protect the vassal. But this mutual obligation can also exist between individuals of equal status. While there are numerous occurrences in the *Nibelungenlied* that illustrate the former pattern, most notably during the preparations for the Saxon War, when Gunther actively seeks the counsel of his "friends" (allies, vassals, or family) with the intention of further requesting their aid in the war (strophes 147–162), it is the model of service that is of paramount importance for an insight into meaning of the *Nibelungenlied.* The relationship between Gunther and Siegfried, for example, can be characterized as one informed by "service." It is Siegfried who decisively aids Gunther in the Saxon War and in the wooing of Brünhild. Gunther's disregard not only of Siegfried's friendship, but also of his own obligations to Siegfried, earn him the censure of the poet, specifically for his disloyalty (*untriuwe*), that results from him taking part in the murder of Siegfried.

[FGG]

DRAGON'S BLOOD. In the *Nibelungenlied* Hagen refers in strophe 100 to Siegfried's bathing in the blood of the dragon he has slain which makes his skin *hurnîn* (hard as horn, callous, tough; here the sense of invulnerability). While some scholars are of the opinion that Siegfried's adventures in the otherworld, including his fight against the dragon, are downplayed by the poet of the *Nibelungenlied,* his sojourn in that world not only explains his near invulnerability, but also, at least to some degree, his tendency to act spontaneously and unpredicatably in his association with the Burgundians. Siegfried has assimilated some of the symbolic characteristics of the dragon, which manifest themselves when he returns to the world of knights and heroes. One of these most striking characteristics is his capacity to create chaos. In *Kudrun,* a heroic epic that is assumed to have been written down between thirty and forty years after the *Nibelungenlied,* the slaying of a *gabilûn,* a chameleonlike creature that had intended to devour the young prince Hagen, has been suggested by Bartsch as having taken Siegfried's battle against the dragon as a model (see *Kudrun,* edited Karl Bartsch, rev. 5th ed. by Karl Stackmann [Wiesbaden: Brockhaus, 1965], commentary to 101,2).

[WM]

DREAM. The purpose of a dream in the *Nibelungenlied* is to foreshadow an inexorable fate. In the first *âventiure,* Kriemhild's dream of a falcon and its death by two eagles (strophes 13–14) foretells the death of Siegfried, her future husband, through the treachery of Hagen and the faithless Gunther. The twenty-fifth adventure relates the foreboding dream of Ute, the queen mother (strophe 1509), in which " . . . all the birds of the land were dead." This admonition underscores the objection of Hagen and Rumold, the master of the kitchen, to Etzel's invitation: they fear the prospect of a vengeful Kriemhild and an ill-fated sojourn at the Hunnish court in Gran. Initially, however, Hagen refuses to accord Ute's dream any significance.

[EH]

DUEL. The duel occurs in several forms in the *Nibelungenlied,* but never with all of its elements, which include challenge, specification of terms, single combat, and resolution. Upon his arrival at Worms, Siegfried challenges Gunther to duel for control of land and people, but Hagen advises against combat and Siegfried is persuaded to enter the court as a guest. Brünhild's nuptial contest includes the specification of terms and an indirect combat, but the procedure is subverted by Siegfried's use of a magic cape. Siegfried's single combats with a Nibelung giant and Alberich are likewise reminiscent of dueling practice, as is the wrestling match in Gunther's wedding bed, explicitly characterized as a *strît* (combat) that nearly costs Siegfried his life. The hall battle that destroys the Burgundians and Huns is punctuated by two duels (without specification of terms): Iring's unsuccessful challenge of Hagen, and Hagen's defeat by Dietrich.

[VU]

DWARF/ELF, races of lower mythological beings in Germanic lore. Dwarves (the race of Dvalin) are connected in the Nibelung material with buried treasure. Though the demythologized *Nibelungenlied* leaves little room for such beings, Hagen knows that Alberich the dwarf keeps the Nibelungen hoard by Siegfried's leave. Perhaps the Nibelung warriors that Siegfried leads to Brynhild's land are dwarves as well. In the *Volsunga saga* Andvari, a dwarf who has taken the form of a pike, lives in the water where he keeps the treasure hoard, which ultimately becomes Sigurd's. In the *Lied vom Hürnen Seyfrid,* a dwarf named Nibling has hidden the treasure that Seyfrid later finds. Another dwarf, Eugel, helps Seyfrid rescue Krimhild from the dragon and later saves him with a *Nebelkappe,* which makes him invisible. (In *Von dem gehörnten Siegfried,* the dwarves' names are Egwardus and Egwaldus respectively, and the princess is Florigunda.)

Elves are connected with magic and often have a malevolent side. In the *Þiðreks saga* Oda is impregnated by an elf and bears Hogni; he is thus a half brother of Gunnar, Gislher, and Gernoz. His ancestry is said to account for his appearance: white, fierce, and troll-like. In the *Volsunga saga* the dying Fafnir tells Sigurd that some of the Norns are daughters of Dvalin, while others are the daughters of elves. Brynhild tells Sigurd that some secret runes are in the possession of the elves. There are several dwarfs in Wagner's *Ring* cycle: Alberich, his bother Mime, and the miners who work under the earth, whom Wagner calls Nibelungs.

[JKW]

EAGLE. The term *ar* (eagle) occurs once in the *Nibelungenlied* (13,3) in the plural form, *arn*, to describe the two birds of prey that descend upon and destroy Kriemhild's falcon in her dream. It is intriguing that in her interpretation of the dream Kriemhild's mother, Ute, identifies the falcon as a noble knight ("ein edel man;" 14,3), but offers no suggestion as to what the *arn* might represent.

[WM]

ECKE, ECKESAHS. Although Dietrich von Bern's sword (*Nibelungenlied* 2360,3) does not bear a specific name, from other sources we learn that it was called *Eckesahs* (cf. Heinrich von Veldeke, *Eneit* 5693; *Biterolf* 9269; *Þiðreks saga* [see Erichsen, p. 162]). The name doubtless means *sword with a (sharp) edge*, but heroic poetry relates how Dietrich won it from the warrior giant Ecke (i.e., "the sword of Ecke"), whose exploits are related in the *Eckenlied* and *Þiðreks saga*.

[JLF]

Bibliography

Bertselsen, H., ed. *Þidreks saga af Bern*. Copenhagen: Møller, 1905–1911.

Brévart, Francis B., ed. *Das Eckenlied. Mittelhochdeutsch/neuhochdeutsch*. Reclam UB 8339. Stuttgart: Reclam, 1986.

Erichsen, F., trans. *Die Geschichte Thidreks von Bern*. Thule 22. Reprint, Darmstadt: Wissenschaftliche Buchgesellschaft, 1967.

Jónsson, G., ed. *Þiðreks saga af Bern*. Reykjavik: Islendingasagnautgafan, 1951.

EIGENDIU (female bondservant) is encountered in the *Nibelungenlied* and is the term Brünhild uses to describe Kriemhild's status since Kriemhild is Siegfried's wife, and Siegfried is, in Brünhild's opinion, a bonded liege man. This status represents a significant escalation in their argument concerning the worth of their respective husbands.

[FGG]

EIGENHOLT (unfree, bonded), used by Brünhild to refer to Siegfried's and Kriemhild's betrothal. Asked the reason for her tears, Brünhild replies that she feels very sorry for Kriemhild who is betrothed to someone she considers an unfree vassal: "die [Kriemhild] sihe ich sitzen nâhen dem eigenholden dîn./daz muoz ich immer weinen, sol si alsô verderbet sîn" (I see her sitting close to the unfree and bonded one. I will always weep, if she is to be thus defiled; 620,3–4). Brünhild has cause for worry not only because such a union would be declassé for Kriemhild, but also would reflect poorly on Brünhild, who is marrying into the family.

[FGG]

EIGENMAN (male bondservant) occurs in the *Nibelungenlied* as a recurring structural motif in Brünhild's view of the relationship of Siegfried to Gunther. The Nibelungen poet chose to depict the tale of Siegfried, Brünhild, Kriemhild, and the Burgundians objectively, that is, in terms of status, and not subjectively, or in terms of personal emotions of love or jealousy. Thus Brünhild is led to believe this fabrication from her first meeting with Gunther on Island when she observes Siegfried holding the bridle of Gunther's horse while the king mounted it, a clear signal to Brünhild that Siegfried might well be of lower station than Gunther. This erroneous impression is reinforced a while later when Brünhild goes to greet the arrivals and speaks to Siegfried first (419), at which time Siegfried makes the fateful and false statement that Gunther is his lord ("herre," 420). Brünhild draws the logical conclusion that if Gunther is the lord, Siegfried must be his vassal (423). Viewed in this light, Brünhild's actions and assumptions within the text are completely logical. No matter how wealthy and powerful Siegfried may be, she reminds Gunther much later, the former still owes his liege lord service. *Eigenman*, together with *eigen*, *eigendiu*, and *adelvrî*, are key words within the free/unfree complex constructed by the poet to explain (though not justify) the murder of Siegfried.

[FGG]

ELLENDE. A key term in German heroic poetry which can be either a neuter noun meaning *a foreign country* or an adjective that means *exiled,* *away from one's homeland,* and with the implication of lacking the protection that being in one's homeland affords. In the *Nibelungenlied* it occurs as a noun when Rüdiger, in his effort to be released from an oath compelling him to fight against the Burgundians, declares to Etzel that he will leave and go by foot "in daz ellende" (2157,4), a powerful statement that indicates the intensity of Rüdiger's desperation. As an adjective, *ellende* occurs when Kriemhild refers to her friends who would be willing to live "far from home" for her sake (1282,2), to describe Kriemhild's status while at Bechelaren (1312,4), when Kriemhild refers to the pejorative manner in which she appears to be viewed by the Huns, namely, as the stranger from another land (1403,4), and to describe the followers of Rüdiger (2164,4), who had fled with him (from their homeland) to seek asylum with Etzel and for whom, along with his family, Rüdiger feels great concern prior to advancing into combat against the Burgundians.

[WM]

ERBARMEN (to be moved to pity, feel compassion). The capacity to feel compassion for another is one of the chief virtues of the knight in a courtly romance, but it is not necessarily considered a strength in heroic literature. Thus its appearance in the *Nibelungenlied* is noteworthy not only because it is unexpected, but also because it emanates from a highly unlikely source, namely, Hagen. The term occurs in the highly dramatic thirty-seventh *âventiure* after Rüdiger, feeling compelled to fulfill his feudal obligations to Etzel and Kriemhild, renounces his ties of loyalty to the Burgundians. Most of the Burgundians are unforgiving when they determine that Rüdiger will fight them. Only Hagen, who has known Rüdiger since he was held hostage (i.e., as a form of security that the Burgundians would pay annual tribute to the Huns) at Etzel's court (*Waltharius*) feels compassion. Hagen laments the loss of his shield, and Rüdiger presents him with his own shield together with the wish that Hagen might reach home again. Confronted with this last noble gesture of the brave Rüdiger, Hagen, too, makes an equally generous, indeed unheard-of offer: The poet describes the scene as follows:

Swie grimme Hagen wære   und swie herte gemuot,
ja erbarmte im diu gâbe,   die der helt guot
bî sînen lesten zîten   sô nâhen het getân.
    (2198,1–3)

[However grim and determined Hagen might be, however resolute, nonetheless the gift that the doughty hero [Rüdiger] gave so near to the end of his life moved him [Hagen] to compassion.]

"Nu lôn' ich iu der gâbe,   vil edel Rüedegêr,
swie halt gein in gebâren   dise recken hêr,
daz nimmer iuch gerüeret   in strîte hie mîn hant,
ob ir si alle slüeget   die von Burgonden lant."
    (2201)

["Now I intend to repay you for your gift, most noble Rüdiger, regardless of how these other warriors may act toward you, in that I will not strike you in battle here, even if you kill all who came from Burgundy."]

What is remarkable about the effects of his compassion is that Hagen has ultimately renounced his loyalty to his kings by refusing to protect them if they are attacked by Rüdiger. It is also striking that Hagen is joined by none other than Volker, the minstrel and fierce fighter, in offering his peace to Rüdiger. But perhaps most extraordinary of all is the fact that no other character in the scene, including the kings themselves, objects to Hagen's offer. One must be also forced to assume that Hagen's actions would conform to the expectations of the poet's audience.

[FGG]

Bibliography
Wapnewski, Peter. "Rüdigers Schild: Zur 37. Aventiure des Nibelungenliedes." *Euphorion* 54 (1960): 380–410.

ÊRE (honor) is a central concept in the heroic and courtly catalogue of virtues. It is, however, primarily an external value, in that the honor of a person or setting is visible to others. Wealth, generosity, and power are the marks of the honorable individual. The honorable king is the "treasure giver," the "giver of rings." Indeed a major reason for the first *âventiure* of the *Nibelungenlied* is not merely to provide a description of Kriemhild's home, but also to emphasize the honor of the Burgundian kings by pointing out their high-born heritage, boldness, and bravery, and the number of well-known and fierce warriors who served them.

[FGG]

FAIRY TALES, or rather motifs from folk tales, are to be found throughout the *Nibelungenlied,* especially in the stories about Siegfried's youth, a fact appreciated by the authors of the most influential collection of fairy tales ever assembled, Jacob and Wilhelm Grimm. Obvious examples include portentous dreams, bridal quests and contests, fearless dragon slayers, giants, dwarfs, nixies, and golden treasure. Some parallels are strikingly detailed. One example is Siegfried's acquisition of the Nibelungs' treasure and its parallels with the Grimms' tale, "The King of the Golden Mountain," in which the hero is asked by three giants to divide their father's possessions, including a sword and a cloak of invisibility. For Wilhelm Grimm, fairy tales and heroic epic drew on the same source of ancient Indo-Germanic religious myths. The fairy tales preserved by the common folk unwittingly transmitted elements of myth, while epics made myths historical by making the divine human. In the *Nibelungenlied* this process is incomplete, according to Grimm, hence the mythic motifs "in the background." Contemporary scholars of folklore are more uncertain about the relation of fairy tales and other forms of oral culture such as myth, legends, and heroic tales. It is often difficult and even impossible to trace the origin of common motifs and how their occurrence in one genre might bear upon their appearance in another.

[RGS]

Bibliography
Brüder Grimm. *Kinder- und Hausmärchen.* Vol. 3: *Anmerkungen.* Göttingen, 1856. Reprint edited by Heinz Rölleke. Stuttgart: Reclam, 1983, esp. 417ff.

FALCON, a symbol of the male beloved in medieval lyric and in the *Nibelungenlied.* Kriemhild's dream of a falcon that was attacked and killed by two eagles is correctly interpreted by her mother, Ute, as representative of a hero whom Kriemhild will lose unless God protects him. Even though Kriemhild rejects all possible thoughts of men and love in her life, the poet writes that she will become the wife of a bold warrior and that he is indeed the falcon about which she had dreamed (strophe 19).

[FGG]

FERRYMAN, on the twelfth day of their journey from Worms to Hunland in the *Nibelungenlied,* the Burgundians reach the Danube, which is in flood stage and unfordable. Hagen is sent to find a way across. He first encounters some water sprites, one of whom predicts that none of the travelers except the king's chaplain will survive the trip. He is also told how to find a ferryman. By pretending to be a missing Bavarian noble and by offering a gold bracelet as payment, he persuades the ferryman to cross the river to pick him up. But before landing, the ferryman, who happens to be the brother of the man Hagen is claiming to be, changes his mind and attacks Hagen with an oar. Hagen thereupon kills the ferryman and takes his boat to where the travelers are waiting. He tells Gunther that he had found the boat abandoned. Hagen then ferries the others across in a Charon-like fashion to what will become for the Burgundians the land of the dead. He throws the chaplain overboard, and when the clergyman reaches the shore safely, Hagen knows that the prediction of the water sprites will come true.

[JVM]

FOUNDLING. The motif of a person's unknown origin is widespread throughout the literature of the world. It gives the hero the opportunity to use his abilities without referring to his noble ancestors. He has to start his life in inadequate surroundings but will push forward his own claims over those of his opponents and gain self-confidence. In this manner he will prove his birthright. In parts of the German and Northern tradition, Siegfried/Sigurd's origin seems to be unknown. Only the *Nibelungenlied* tells us that he is a prince of noble birth, his parents are King Sigmund of the Netherlands and Queen Sigelind and he is given a proper courtly upbringing. In all other sources he is raised by a smith in the wild. According to *Das Lied vom Hürnen Seyfried,* he knew neither his father's nor his mother's name.

This motif also occurs in the *Þiðreks saga:* When Sigurd comes to Brynhild for the first time he does not know his parents or his family. *Fáfnismál* (2–8) and *Oddrúnargrátr* (17–18) also allude to the story of Sigurd growing up without parents. Sigurd seems to be an outstanding hero with a mysterious youth, a foundling whose story resembles that of Moses or Romulus and Remus, according to the *Þiðreks saga.* Sisibe, Sigurd's mother, is accused of unfaithfulness, and Sigmund banishes her. Her child is born in the wild and placed in a glass container, in which it floats to an island, a story we can compare with the birth of Moses (*Exodus* 2), a typical element of "hero birth." When young Sigurd is cast away by his dying mother, he is found by a hind who suckles him, as Romulus and Remus were suckled by a she-wolf. This motif may insinuate that Sigurd is similar in nature to a deer. Some events in Sigurd's life correspond to this idea (cf. Hindarfjall, Hjordis). Otto Höfler even associates Sigurd with the first-century Germanic leader Arminius, leader of the Cherusci, a tribal name meaning *deer people.* The motif of the hero's unknown origin is more appropriate for heroic epics than for courtly cycles. Yet it appears in Wolfram von Eschenbach's *Parzival,* in Ulrich von Türheim's *Rennewart* and in the anonymous tale *Wigamur.* In some heroic poems of the thirteenth century, stories similar to that of Sigurd's unknown origin are told in *Ortnit* and in *Wolfdietrich.* The function of the motif may also be to show the hero his predestined duties. This is typical for the early myths, often combined with the motif of the search or the revenge for the hero's father. This combination often takes on genealogical significance, as in the case, for instance, of Oedipus's birth. Many Anglo-Saxon and Old Norse genealogies of kings begin with Odin, a feature connected with Sigurd only in the *Volsunga saga.* Here King Volsung, Sigurd's grandfather, is an offspring of Odin. In the *Ragnars saga loðbrókar,* Ragnar, from whom the kings of Norway are descended, marries Aslaug, the daughter of Sigurd and Brynhild. The story of Sigurd's divine origin includes his duty to kill all those involved in the battle against his father Sigmund. The German legends about Siegfried do not contain the story that Sigurd avenged the murder of his father. Here Sigmund is simply a name.

[GW]

Bibliography

Frenzel, Elisabeth. *Motive der Weltliteratur: Ein Lexikon dichtungsgeschichtlicher Längsschnitte.* Stuttgart: Kröner, 1976, pp. 342–360.

Haymes, Edward R., and Susann T. Samples. *Heroic Legends of the North: An Introduction to the Nibelung and Dietrich Cycles.* New York: Garland, 1996.

Höfler, Otto. *Siegfried, Arminius und die Symbolik. Mit einem historischen Anhang über die Varusschlacht.* Heidelberg: Winter, 1961.

FOUR MAJOR COURT OFFICES. Since the crowning of Otto I in 936, the four major court offices included the *kamerære* (chamberlain), the *truchsæze* (seneschal), the *marschalch* (marshal), and the *schenke* (master of the cellars). The areas of responsibilities of these offices, all of which were held by high nobles, were the administration of the royal treasury (chamberlain), the administration of the royal household (seneschal), the leader of the army and the watch—originally master of the stables—(marshal), and the royal cupbearer (master of the cellars). Since the Burgundian kings are depicted as being of ancient heritage, that is, high-born, very powerful, and thus rich in honor, the poet of the *Nibelungenlied* provides their court with the full assortment of offices. In the work Hunold is the chamberlain, Ortwin the seneschal, Dancwart the marshal, and Sindolt the master of the cellars. An interesting addition to the four offices and one that was contemporary with the epic is the office of *kuchenmeister* (master of the kitchens), held by Rumold. The existence of this office is first attested in 1194 under Emperor Henry VI in Italy. In Germany, Heinrich von Rothenburg held the office of master of the kitchens from 1201 until at least 1217. These data could be used to establish an approximate date of composition of the *Nibelungenlied.*

[FGG]

FRIENDSHIP. Both in its betrayal and in its observance, friendship leads to disaster. The basic Nibelungen concept of friendship is that it always turns out badly. The first part of the work recounts the flawed friendship between Gunther and Siegfried and its fatal consequences. Faced with the Saxon threat to Worms and with little time to assemble his troops in the fourth *âventiure,* Gunther needs "true friends" (155). Upon

Hagen's advice Gunther confides his plight to Siegfried, who responds (156): "If you are looking for friends, let me be one. That I can promise, with honor, till my days are done." In the sixth through the ninth *âventiure* the poet tells of the ever-growing personal bonds between the two kings. Again it is Hagen who urges Gunther to seek the help of Siegfried, who agrees to take part in the deception of Brünhild under the condition that Kriemhild is to become his bride. Siegfried's trust in Gunther's friendship and that of the Burgundians proves to be ill-founded. *Âventiuren* twelve through sixteen tell of Siegfried's betrayal and murder at Hagen's behest to avenge Krimhild's public insult to Brünhild. Although he tries to save Siegfried by having him swear an exonerating oath, Gunther does not persevere and finally becomes a party to Siegfried's death. By betraying his obligations of friendship to Siegfried, Gunther embarks on a path that ultimately culminates in Kriemhild's revenge, his own destruction, and that of his family and followers.

The theme of friendship also contributes to the catastrophes of the second part of the work. The poet calls attention to the friendship between Hagen and Rüdiger of Bechelaren, who is bound to his lord Etzel and by oath to Kriemhild, yet bonded by kinship to the Burgundians through the betrothal of his daughter to Giselher. When Rüdiger can no longer avoid combat (*âventiure* thirty-seven), Hagen offers him a way out of his dilemma with honor. By announcing that he is without a shield, Hagen permits Rüdiger the opportunity to offer his own shield to him out of friendship. Accepting the gift, Hagen pledges not to lift a hand against him (2201): "even though you kill the whole of Burgundy." Friendship proves no deterrent to the impending doom. Though Hagen and Dietrich of Bern are also friends, Dietrich remains bound to Etzel and Kriemhild. Nevertheless the friendship of Hagen and Volker remains unencumbered by conflicting loyalties and the friends remain united, albeit by death, in a common cause.

[EH]

Bibliography

Gentry, Francis G., and James K. Walter, eds. *German Epic Poetry*. New York: Continuum, 1995, pp. 279, 284–285.

GEBRIEVEN (formally record, set down in writing), occurs just once in the *Nibelungenlied* (2233,2b), on the occasion of the death of Rüdiger. The use of a word that implies some kind of legal statement for posterity emphasizes the significance of this crucial event. It is linked here with the verb *gesagen* ("to say," "tell out loud"), and together the words attain a formulaic quality: no method of communication can express the enormity of what is happening (cf. *schrîber*).

[MEG]

GELEITE (escort), refers both to the group of people who escort another person or another group of people from one place to another in a strange land, and to the company thus afforded. Usually there is the additional suggestion of protection and safe passage. Gunther offers *geleite* to the messengers of Liudeger (164,4a); Etzel himself escorts his guests away after the killing of the Hun by Volker (1897,2a); Siegmund and his company decline *geleite* on their journey back to Xanten, relying on their own strength in the event of their being attacked (1095). The implication of *geleite* is extended when Rüdiger adds to his hospitality and gifts by escorting the Burgundians on their way to Etzel's court, a factor that he recalls poignantly when faced with his dilemma: "jâ was ich ir geleite in mînes herren lant" ("but I was their escort into the land of my lord;" 2144,3).

[MEG]

GIANTS mentioned in the *Nibelungenlied* are all to be found among the Nibelungs. In an account given by Hagen we learn that the princes Schilbung and Nibelung have a guard of twelve giants (94,1–2a), whom Siegfried defeats single-handed. When Siegfried later returns to the Nibelung stronghold to fetch a thousand warriors to serve as a guard for Brunhild's passage from Iceland to Worms, he finds the gate defended by a giant with whom he does combat as a demonstration of his own superiority (486–493). For the giants in Wagner's *Ring*, see FAFNER and FASOLT.

[VU]

GIFTS in the *Nibelungenlied* provide concrete evidence within the plot of the relationship between characters. Gunther gives his word that Siegfried will receive Kriemhild as a reciprocal gift for the hero's assistance in the wooing of Brünhild. Tragic relationships are also symbolized through gifts. For example, Rüdiger provides the Nibelungs with lavish gifts during their sojourn in Bechelaren and gives Gernot the sword with which the latter will later kill him. The feudal gift establishes the mutual relationship of loyalty and allegiance. As a vassal Rüdiger is forced by Etzel and Kriemhild to join in the battle against the Nibelungs, toward whom, however, he is obligated through the gifts of friendship and the escort he has already provided for them. Rüdiger cannot simply return Etzel's *beneficia* and annul the feudal contract. The inexorable nature of this legal concept is exemplified by the so-called gift of the shield. Hagen asks Rüdiger to give him his shield so that he will not have to fight against him. In the process he transgresses against his allegiance to the clan for the sake of friendship, an ideal that is symbolized by the gift of the shield.

[WW]

Bibliography
Wapnewski, Peter. "Rüdigers Schild: Zur 37. Aventiure des *Nibelungenlieds.*" *Euphorion* 54 (1960): 112–120.

GOLD, a central motif in the *Nibelungenlied,* is embodied most clearly in the Nibelungen hoard, which is said to consist of one hundred wagon loads of precious gems, and even more red gold (92). This golden treasure appears at key junctures of the tale and informs the narrative. We are told by Hagen that earlier, when Siegfried encountered Schilbung and Nibelung and was given the sword Balmung, he subsequently wrested the hoard from them and the *Tarnkappe* from Alberich (87–99). Later Siegfried presents the hoard to Kriemhild as his bridal gift; Kriemhild uses it to win the loyalty of heroes whom she hopes will avenge Siegfried's murder. Hagen, on the other hand, plots to steal and conceal the treasure from Kriemhild. In the final strophes of the epic the treasure becomes the focal point of the tale as Hagen, fettered before his nemesis, Kriemhild, boldly states that he will never reveal the location of the treasure as long as one of his kings lives (2368). Hagen's refusal

ensures the death of Gunther (2369) and leads to his own beheading (2373). In view of these tragedies it is no surprise that gold is a negative force throughout the epic. The red gold that Kriemhild offers the Huns lures them into battle and death. The desire for gold also makes warriors willing to betray their overlords. In Part II Hagen uses promises of golden rings to entice the ferryman to betray his loyalty to Gelpfrat and cross the Danube (1550–1554) and to win the loyalty of Eckewart, Kriemhild's retainer (1634–1635). Kriemhild lures Bloedel, who betrays his brother Etzel's authority (1903–1908), and Iring, the Hun who dares to battle Hagen (2025; 2068), into life-threatening combat with promises of red gold. The lust for gold and the negative consequences of this obsession constitute a major motif in all of the works in the Nibelungen tradition. In the *Sigurþarkviða hin skamma,* for example, golden rings and sunken treasure are used as an incentive to betray Sigurd. Likewise in the *Þiðreks saga* Brynhild promises Hogni as much gold, silver, and treasure as he desires if he will murder Sigurd. In the *Atlakviða* and the *Volsunga saga* Atli invites Gunnar and Hogni to his court promising them gifts of gold but in reality plans to seize Sigurd's treasure. In the *Þiðreks saga* it is Grimhild who convinces Atli to invite her brothers to court so that they might recover Sigurd's gold.

[LDT]

Bibliography
Gentry, Francis. *Triuwe and vriunt in the Nibelungenlied.* Amsterdam: Rodopi, 1975.

GRAM, in the *Þiðreks saga,* the name of the sword (known as "the best of all swords") given to Sigurd by the smith Mime, who is then killed by Sigurd with a blow from it. After Sigurd's death King Gunnar passes it on to Margrave Rodinger (Rüdiger in the *Nibelungenlied*) who subsequently makes a gift of it to Gislher. Rodinger is killed by Gislher (using Gram) in Atli's camp. Its last owner is Hildibrand, who "inherits" Gram after having killed Gislher. Gram is also mentioned in the *Volsunga saga.* It is a sword forged by Regin (who is ultimately beheaded by Sigurd) from the fragments of Sigmund's smashed sword. Sigurd also uses it to kill Lyngvi. Sigurd carries Gram in his hand when he exchanges shapes with Gunnar to ride through the circle of fire surrounding Brynhild's hall. He later places it unsheathed between himself and Brynhild on the three nights that they sleep together in the same bed. (Compare a variation of this motif with Tristan and Isolde in the lover's cave in Gottfried's romance.) It is also alluded to in the second strophe of the *Hyndluljóð* (The Lay of Hyndla), although not by name, as the sword passed on by Odin to Sigmund.

[WM]

GRIM (fierce), although used in many contexts in the *Nibelungenlied, grim* is employed time and again to illustrate Hagen's character and actions. The concept is, however, ethically neutral and is not intended to provide insight into the moral makeup of the individual. Thus it does not convey the negative implication that the term often does in modern English.

[FGG]

HAWK. In the twenty-sixth chapter of the *Volsunga saga* Gudrun tells her maidens that she has had foreboding dreams. In the one she saw a hawk with golden-colored feathers on her hand. One of her ladies-in-waiting suggests that the hawk represents a lover, but Gudrun, greatly disturbed over the matter, goes to Brynhild to ask her to interpret the dream. In the subsequent conversation with Brynhild, Gudrun relates another dream (chapter twenty-seven). This concerns a stag with golden fur, which Brynhild has chased away from her lap. Both dream narratives have prophetic character. Two opposing theories exist as to how the dreams came to be included in the saga: (1) that the author of the text interpolated the dream sequences into the material (Franz Rolf Schröder) or (2) that the dreams are part of an original, Eddic dream lay (Heusler, Eis). Literary dreams involving birds of prey and the symbolism of the bird of prey as the lover are an international phenomenon (Ploss, Schröder). There is also a similarity in the motif of the hawk dream in the *Volsunga saga* and Kriemhild's falcon dream in the *Nibelungenlied*. There is no definitive proof, however, of a direct connection between the two narratives (Panzer).

[BH]

Bibliography

Eis, Gerhard. "Das eddische 'Traumlied.'" *Arkvi för Nordisk Filologi* 71 (1956): 177–186.

Heusler, Andreas. "Die Lieder der Lücke im Codex Regius der Edda." In *Germanistische Abhandlungen. Hermann Paul zum 17. März 1902 dargebracht*, edited by Andreas Heusler et al. Straßburg: Trübner, 1902, pp. 1–98.

Panzer, Friedrich. "Nibelungische Ketzereien." *PBB* (Halle) 75 (1953): 248–272.

Ploss, Emil. "Byzantinische Traumsymbolik und Kriemhilds Falkentraum." *GRM* (Neue Folge) 8 (1958): 218—226.

Schröder, Franz Rolf. "Kriemhilds Falkentraum." *PBB* (Tübingen) 78 (1956): 319–348.

HELT (hero), as a concept, has its origin in Germanic heroic tradition. It is, thus, no surprise that the term is encountered more frequently in the *Nibelungenlied* than in the contemporary Arthurian epics where the term *ritter* (knight) is more common. Nonetheless both refer essentially to different facets of the same persona, an armed retainer. In the heroic epic, as would perhaps be expected, the aspect emphasized is that of the fighter, the one skilled in battle. The battles are most often scenes of mass confrontation (and destruction). However, the most important combats are presented as individual confrontations, because such scenes are more suitable for imparting the important lessons to be learned by the community of listeners (i.e., how one should act in a battle, how one should uphold one's own honor or the honor of one's lord, one's clan or family, etc.). While the knight in the Arthurian epics is likewise skilled in battle, and his battles, too, are individual encounters, the objective of a chivalric battle scene is infinitely more self-centered than in a heroic epic, which, whether it be the *Iliad* or the *Nibelungenlied,* is more concerned with the progress and fate of an entire people. In contrast, the romance focuses on the development and destiny of the individual knight.

[FGG]

HERRE is the standard Middle High German polite form of address for members of the nobility, the clergy, vassals, and husbands. A shortened form *hêr* corresponds to English *Sir* as in Sir Gawain.

[FGG]

HÊRSCHAFT (dominion) was defined in the Middle Ages by an alliterative formula characteristic of medieval vernacular law as lordship over people and lands (*liute unde lant*). The struggle for possession of *hêrschaft,* with its attendant determination of one's social and, to a certain extent, legal standing, is a major source of conflict in the *Nibelungenlied.* Siegfried boasts to his father and then later to Gunther himself that he will easily wrest people and land from the Burgundians (55; 109). Hagen obtains Gunther's approval of his plot to murder Siegfried in part by the allure of Siegfried's lands (870). As Siegfried lies dying at the spring, Hagen dismisses the Burgundians' laments and exults in his having finally put an end to Siegfried's *hêrschaft* (993).

[RGS]

HOARD. In the *Nibelungenlied,* Nibelung and Schilbung, the late King Nibelung's sons, ask Siegfried to divide up the hoard, consisting of more than one hundred wagons of jewelry and still more of gold, that had been hidden inside a mountain. His reward is Nibelung's sword. They are not content with his division and an argument ensues. Siegfried then slays them and defeats the dwarf, Alberich, taking his *tarnkappe* (cloak of invisibility). He later tells Kriemhild that she needs no dowry, as he can provide her with much gold from the hoard and territory in Nibelungenland. The nineteenth *âventiure* relates how, after the death of Siegfried, the Nibelungen treasure comes to Worms and what becomes of it. After Kriemhild has mourned for the death of Siegfried for three-and-a-half years, Hagen and Gunther plot to deprive her of the treasure, her rightful dowry. As a part of this plot, Hagen advises his king that such wealth would only grant Kriemhild the power to win favor among the people, especially among foreign knights, and in so doing, become "a mortal danger" (1128) for Burgundy. Once Kriemhild promises to reconcile herself with Gunther and does so with a kiss, her brothers retrieve the gold and jewels from Nibelungenland and bring them to Worms. Hagen soon sinks the treasure in the Rhine by stealth, perhaps in the hope of using it himself one day in the service of Worms (although the text is notably silent on this point) and her brothers swear oaths of secrecy (1137–

1140), thus becoming complicit in the act. Kriemhild's pain at the loss of her murdered husband is now heightened by the theft of her dowry. Her hatred of Hagen continues to grow and becomes a prelude to revenge. It culminates in her murder of him when he refuses to disclose the location of the stolen treasure (2367–2369). For some scholars the hoard is symbolic of Siegfried himself.

In the *Þiðreks saga* the hoard is not mentioned until Sigurd's death, when Grimhild's brothers deprive her of all the gold that Sigurd had. (In this version, the treasure is not submerged.) Grimhild persuades her second husband, Atli, to invite her brothers to his camp so that he might rob them of the hoard they had stolen from her. After the fall of the Niflungs the mortally wounded Hogni begets a son, Aldrian, with a woman, leaving her the key to Sigurd's cellar, where the hoard is hidden. His son, Aldrian, avenges his father by locking Atli in the cellar, so that the Atli starves to death in the midst of the treasure. Aldrian dies without revealing the hiding place to anyone.

The *Poetic Edda* accords the hoard a mythical prehistory: Odin, Honir, and Loki wandered through the world and Loki killed an otter (Otr) for food. Hreidmar, the father of the otter, demanded that he be compensated with gold for the loss of his son. Loki robs the dwarf Andvari of his hoard and a ring, but Andvari puts a curse on the hoard, stating that it will bring death to its owner. The curse is realized when Hreidmar's sons, Fafnir and Regin, kill their father. Fafnir then absconds with the hoard, turns himself into a dragon, and Regin incites Sigurd to slay his brother, although he himself is later killed by the hero. The dying Fafnir warns Sigurd that the hoard will bring death to him as well. Sigurd takes it nonetheless, advised by prophesying birds to use it later to procure Gudrun as his wife. The role likely played by the hoard in the lacunae of the manuscript can be surmised from the surviving lays: the first lay of Gudrun reveals that Gunnar had ordered the murder of Sigurd in order to acquire the hoard, but that he himself would die as a consequence. In the *Shorter Lay of Sigurd,* Brynhild declares that she would have preferred to marry Sigurd instead of Gunnar for the sake of Fafnir's hoard. In the *Slaughter of the Niflungs,* Gunnar and Hogni confiscate all of

Fafnir's gold after Sigurd's death. Later lays add different features: part of the hoard is used in the second lay of Gudrun to persuade her to marry Atli. In the *Lament of Oddrun,* Atli refuses to take the hoard Gunnar offers him as a penalty for the death of Brynhild, Atli's sister. In the much older Atli lays the avaricious Atli treacherously invites Gunnar and Hogni to his land in order to rob them of the hoard, but they prefer to die rather than reveal where they have hidden the gold in the Rhine. *Snorra Edda* and *Volsunga saga* correspond to the Sigurd and Atli lays of the *Poetic Edda.* In the *Volsunga saga* the hoard plays an important role: Grimhild, mother of Gudrun, Gunnar, and Hogni, arranges the marriage between Sigurd and Gudrun in order to procure the hoard.

[EH/HR]

Bibliography

Beyschlag, Siegfried. "Das Motiv der Macht bei Siegfrieds Tod." In *Zur germanisch-deutschen Heldensage,* edited by Karl Hauck. Wege der Forschung 14. Darmstadt: Wissenschaftliche Buchgesellschaft, 1965. First appeared in *GRM* 34 (1953): 95ff.

Haymes, Edward R., and Susann T. Samples. *Heroic Legends of the North: An Introduction to the Nibelung and Dietrich Cycles.* New York: Garland, 1996, p. 115.

HOCHGEMUOT (noble, proud, joyful), the spirit that should imbue every individual associated with a court. Festivals are especially viewed as occasions of *hôchgemuot.*

[FGG]

HOF (court), as well as a physical space, which in the *Nibelungenlied* usually designates the courtyard outside a palace (e.g., 1760), the gathering of the ruler and his or her followers and guests, regardless of where they are assembled. Almost every facet of royal life is encompassed by the court: deliberation and administration, justice, diplomacy, male-female relations, ceremony, and entertainment. By the twelfth century the members of the court had become bound by a highly refined code of behavior, the rule of courtesy ("hövescheit"), based in part on classical and Christian ideals, episcopal pedagogy, and on pragmatic stratagems for survival in an extraordinarily confined atmosphere of competition and intrigue. Essential to the interpretation of the *Nibelungenlied,* yet fiercely debated among scholars, is the evaluation of this courtly code that has been grafted onto precourtly figures and events, in particular as it is practiced by the members of the court of Worms.

[RGS]

Bibliography

Jaeger, C. Stephen. *The Origins of Courtliness: Civilizing Trends and the Formation of Courtly Ideals, 939–1210.* Philadelphia: University of Pennsylvania, 1985.

HÔHER MUOT (noble attitude, joy), a fundamental and frequently occurring phrase in both courtly and heroic literature. *Hôher muot* indicates the elation, the cheerfulness, the "elevation of spirits" which are characteristic of knights (and, to a lesser extent, of ladies) in the literature of the High Middle Ages. In the *Nibelungenlied* there are two basic situations that lead courtiers to experience *hôher muot:* love, as when Kriemhild and Siegfried first meet; and the relating or performing of knightly deeds, as when Siegfried readies himself for combat. In contrast to the phrase *hôher muot,* the Middle High German compound *hochmuot* signifies arrogance or pride (though on rare occasions *hôher muot* and *hochmuot* are interchanged in the literature). The modern German descendant *Hochmut* retains only the negative sense of haughtiness.

[MR]

HÔH(GE)ZÎT (festival), both the culmination and the most conspicuous external manifestation of the joy inherent in courtly life, the *hôhgezît* presented an occasion for both social and athletic interaction among medieval courtiers, real and fictional. In Middle High German the noun denotes not only the high festival itself (whether of secular or of religious character), but also the joy and the splendor attendant upon such celebrations. Not until the late Middle Ages did *hôhgezît* come to take on the narrower meaning which is still preserved in its modern-day cognate *Hochzeit* (wedding). In the *Nibelungenlied* many of the classical courtly conventions surrounding the *hôhgezît* are observed: the festivals are typically set in springtime (often at Whitsuntide), they provide an arena for the tournament, and they frequently witness a flowering of love between knights and ladies. Yet, in stark contrast to courtly tradition, the *Nibelungenlied* ultimately shows the joy of the festival to be fleeting. Indeed, it is expressly in the context of the *hôhgezît* that sorrow (in the form of open hostilities leading to bloodshed and death) asserts itself as the predominant, even primordial spirit of the heroic epic. This connection between joy and sorrow, between festival and death, is established in the very first strophe of the *Nibelungenlied*. The only truly joyful festival is the one that deals with Siegfried's knighting. This festival was possibly intended to recall the Mainzer Hoffest (Court Festival at Mainz; 1184) where the emperor Barbarossa had his two sons knighted amid great pomp and ceremony.

[MR]

HÔHVART (pride), together with its much more common synonym *übermuot,* (in the **B** version of the Nibelungenlied there are two examples of *hôhvart* and three of its adjectival forms compared with thirty-four instances of *übermuot*), is, in Christian moral theology, the first of the seven deadly sins, "the beginning of all sin," according to the Vulgate version of Ecclesiasticus 10.15. *Hôhvart,* unlike *übermuot,* appears to have no known cognate or related form in any other Germanic language. It is a learned and therefore ecclesiastical invention, first instantiated in the monastic teacher and translator Notker's works (ca. 950–1022). Despite its clear Christian heritage, however, the meaning of *hôhvart,* like that of *übermuot,* is somewhat ambivalent in the *Nibelungenlied.* Used negatively of Hagen (54,2) and, with a clear biblical echo, of Brünhild (474,3), it is also a positive military attribute of the Burgundians at Etzel's court (1882,4 and 1891,4).

[RGS]

Bibliography
Hempel, Wolfgang. *Übermuot diu alte . . . : Der Superbia-Gedanke und seine Rolle in der deutschen Literatur des Mittelalters.* Bonn: Bouvier, 1970.

HOLT (affectionate, favorably inclined) occurs frequently in the *Nibelungenlied* as a completely positive expression of an affectionate bond between individuals of the same as well as opposite sexes and between vassals and lords.

[FGG]

HÖVESCH/HÖVESCHEIT, rooted in *hof* (court) with the morpheme *-isch* (having the quality of . . .); the equivalent of Latin *curialitas* meaning *noble and well-bred behavior.* With the emphasis on ethical and social behavior, the concept is clearly and unmistakably linked with the nobility and the court. From the outset, the concept proved controversial. Negative comments about the court were uttered primarily by the clergy and moral-didactic poets, while, on the other hand, "courtly" became the rallying cry against peasant, bourgeois, and clerical social forms. Thus the term became a catchphrase for "civilization." As a result it developed a prescriptive connotation, and the court became the didactic locus where proper courtly/noble behavior was learned. The one instance highlighting this aspect in the *Nibelungenlied* is found in strophes 1916 and 1917 as Etzel asks the Burgundians to take his and Kriemhild's son, Ortlieb, back to Worms and raise him in a courtly fashion. Such glimpses are rare, however, for the *Nibelungenlied* poet is more interested in presenting courtly life in a social and ethical tension with the heroic, Germanic world. Indeed it is the inability of this opposition to realize a dialectic that contributes significantly to the tragedy of the epic.

[OE]

Bibliography
Bumke, Joachim. *Courtly Culture: Literature and Society in the High Middle Ages.* Translated by Thomas Dunlap. Berkeley: University of California Press, 1991.
———. "Höfische Kultur: Versuch einer kritischen Bestandsaufnahme." *PBB* 114 (1992): 414–492.
Elias, Norbert. *The Civilizing Process.* Translated by Edmund Jephcott. Oxford/Cambridge (Mass.): Blackwell, 1994.
———. *The Courtly Society.* Translated by Edmund Jephcott. New York: Pantheon, 1983.
Fleckenstein, Josef, ed. *Curialitas: Studien zu Grundfragen der höfisch-ritterlichen Kultur.* Veröffentlichungen des Max-Planck-Instituts für Geschichte 100. Göttingen: Vandenhoeck & Ruprecht, 1990.

Jaeger, C. Stephen. *The Origins of Courtliness: Civilizing Trends and the Formation of Courtly Ideals, 939–1210*. Philadelphia: University of Pennsylvania Press, 1985.

HORNY SKIN. In his account of the hero's previous exploits (*Nibelungenlied*, 86–101), Hagen relates how Siegfried had slain a dragon and bathed in its blood, from which his skin had grown so horny that no weapon could cut through it. In the *Lied vom Hürnen Seyfrid* (10–11) Seyfrid smears his body not with the dragon's blood but with molten horn. In the *Historia von dem gehörnten Siegfried* it is the dragon's fat that melts and, on cooling, turns into horn. (In woodcuts in some editions of the *Historia*, Siegfried is shown with horns, rather than as horny-skinned.) In itself the horny skin as such is of no real relevance in any version of the story: it is not the horn that protects him, but rather the unprotected spot between the hero's shoulder blades where the linden leaf fell that leaves him vulnerable. The horny-skin motif serves only to heighten the drama of his murder. By contrast, in the *Rosengarten* poems Dietrich von Bern overcomes Siegfried by melting his horn with his fiery breath.

Emil Ploss offers a wide-ranging discussion of references to dragon's blood and horn as armor in Scandinavian sources, the Old English *Beowulf*, and in such German sources as Lamprecht's *Alexanderlied*, *Orendel*, the *Kaiserchronik*, the *Jüngerer Titurel*, various poems about Dietrich von Bern, Wirnt von Gravenberg's *Wigalois*, and Heinrich von Neustadt's *Apollonius von Tyrlant*, as well as non-literary sources.

[JLF]

Bibliography

Ploss, Emil Ernst. *Siegfried-Sigurd, der Drachenkämpfer. Untersuchungen zur germanischdeutschen Heldensage*. Beihefte der Bonner Jahrbücher 17. Cologne: Böhlau, 1966, pp. 6–12; also pp. 21–28 on the motif of invulnerability, and pp. 35–42 on dragon's blood.

HROTTI, the name of a sword to be found among Fafnir's treasure in the *Volsunga saga*.

[WM]

INVITATION. Of the various invitations encountered in the *Nibelungenlied* (including Gunther's invitations to Siegfried, Liudiger and Liudegast to stay in Worms, and Kriemhild's invitation to Etzel's hymeneal envoy to her quarters), two emerge as central to the advancement of the plot and its tragic outcome. Both are used as vehicles to redress grave insults or injustices suffered, and both precede tragedies. In the twelfth *âventiure* Gunther requests the visit of Siegmund, Siegfried, and Kriemhild to Worms to an early summer festivity. Its consequence is the death of the hero: Hagen kills Siegfried. The second invitation occurs twenty-six years later, when Kriemhild asks her kinsmen to the solstice festival in Etzelnburg (twenty-third *âventiure* and *Klage*, verses 159–170). The outcome is the annihilation of all the Burgundians and most Huns and their vassals. Both invitations are triggered by the queens, Brünhild and Kriemhild, who cunningly manipulate their unsuspecting husbands to do their bidding. Their motivation, disguised as longing or friendship, is suspicion (and implied jealousy) in the case of Brünhild, and revenge in the case of Kriemhild. Greed only appears in the *Þiðreks saga*, where Atli, "the most avaricious of men," incited by Kriemhild, covets the Niflung treasure. There is an initial hesitation or uneasiness to comply with the invitation followed by the fateful assent. The narrative structure used to describe issuance and acceptance is very similar. Both commence with the dispatch of properly instructed and attired messengers, followed on arrival by cordial welcome ceremonies. The acceptance of the invitation and the return of the messengers trigger jubilant expectations (with varying motivations) and intense preparations for host and guest alike.

[OP]

JOUST, a favorite medieval pastime, jousting (combat between two mounted knights) is forever present in the *Nibelungenlied*. It appears to erupt spontaneously whenever knights meet, but it is also described as an integral part of planned tournaments. There is daily jousting after the war with the Saxons, at Brünhild's arrival in Worms, during Kriemhild's and Siegfried's doomed visit, on the plain before Enns, at Kriemhild's Vienna wedding, and also during the visit of the Burgundians to Etzelnburg. Jousting is depicted as a

boisterous equestrian sport, with shields re-
sounding under blows, lances splintering on impact, and magnificent horses kicking up clouds
of red dust, as if setting the land on fire. The word
tjoste (joust) is only mentioned three times
(596,2; 1609,2; 1878,3). Nonetheless allusions
to the sounds and pageantry of jousting are encountered throughout the poem. For example,
there are such sound inferences as: "one could
hear a loud noise" (*vil groezlîchen scal;* 306,1)
and "much clamor" (*vil lûte wart geschallet;*
1344,3); or "a great noise was heard before an
early Mass" (*dô huop sich aber schal/vor einer
vruomesse;* 807,2–3). Allusions to jousts are
also encountered wherever games and weapons
are mentioned, including references to "knightly
games" (*si pflâgen ritterschefte;* 1306,3); to "a
great tournament that began in the land" (*Dô
huop sich in dem lande vil harte hôhe ein spil;*
809,1); to the "many fine battles fought" (*vil
manegen puneiz rîchen;* 1353,3); or to the many
"broken lances" (*die schefte liezen vliegen;*
1354,2). Jousting was governed by strict rules of
combat and had to be performed with blunted
weapons. However, during the visit of the Burgundians to Etzelnburg, what begins in harmless
noise (*niwan schal;* 1881,1) turns to the killing of
the garish Hun by Volker (1889,3)—a prelude to
the mass combat to follow—as time honored
rules of conduct are no longer respected.

[OP]

Bibliography
Bernreuther, Marie Luise. *Motivationsstruktur und
Erzählstrategie im "Nibelungenlied" und in der
"Klage."* Wodan 41. Greifswald: Reineke, 1994.
Czerwinski, Peter. "Die Schlacht und Turnier-
darstellungen in den deutschen höfischen Romanen des 12. und 13. Jahrhunderts: Zur literarischen Verarbeitung militärischer Formen des
adligen Gewaltmonopols." Diss., Freie Universität Berlin, 1975.

KEBSE/KEBSEN (concubine, fornication),
powerful terms of insult and accusation occurring in the *Nibelungenlied* during the culmination of the queens' quarrel. Although they are
strong words in themselves, they must also be
understood within the context of the argument.
Neither Brünhild nor Kriemhild are primarily
concerned with whether Gunther or Siegfried is
the better husband, lover, or fighter, but rather

which of the two has more status. Believing that
Siegfried is a vassal of Gunther, albeit a powerful
one, Brünhild calls Kriemhild an *eigendiu,* the
woman of an unfree vassal, which is a calculated
insult. Kriemhild strikes back with the accusation that, if that is the case, Brünhild is the whore
of an unfree vassal since it was Siegfried,
Kriemhild avers, who took Brünhild's virginity.
This statement is, of course, not only humiliating
for Brünhild, but also diminishes her status as a
queen because it was delivered publicly. Here
again the poet is treading the fine line between
the subjective issue of commenting on the sexual
relationship of Siegfried and Brünhild), which is
part of the Nibelungen tradition, but which he
chooses not to emphasize, and the objective
question of status and power, a question that
must have been of significance to his audience.

[FGG]

KNEHT (squire), in addition to denoting a person of servile status (serf), Middle High German
kneht also means *lad or youth,* particularly a
noble youth training to become a knight (i.e., a
page or squire) as well as a person who has
already achieved chivalric status (i.e., a knight—
a noun which is itself cognate to *kneht*). All three
of these meanings occur in the *Nibelungenlied,*
but it is the sense of "squire" which predominates by far. Modern German *Knecht* retains only
the notion of servility.

[MR]

LÊHEN and its verb form *lîhen* refer to the most
tangible component of the feudal system, the fief
or benefice (verb: *to enfeoff*), generally a landed
estate or, in the case of a clerical benefice, a
church office. The fief is bestowed upon a vassal
by a lord as a reward for service but with the
express legal obligation on the part of the vassal
to advise and aid his lord (*consilium et auxilium*).
For his part the lord obligates himself to protect
the vassal. The glue that holds the bond together
is fidelity. If the vassal neglects his duties, the
fief is forfeit or if the lord himself misuses his
protection, the vassal has the right to renounce
his obligation of fidelity to the lord. The actual
conferring of a fief is encountered only once in
the *Nibelungenlied* (39,1) after Siegfried has
been knighted. The newly knighted Siegfried
grants estates and fortified manors to his fellows.

However, it is clear that the societal structure in the *Nibelungenlied* mirrors the feudal society of its listeners, clearly demonstrated by the centrality of the concept of *triuwe* (fidelity) in the work.

[OE]

Bibliography

Bloch, Marc. *Feudal Society.* Translated by L. A. Manyon. 2 vols. Chicago: University of Chicago Press, 1970.

Ganshof, François Louis. *Feudalism.* Translated by Philip Grierson. New York: Harper & Row, 1964.

Lehmann, K. "Lehnswesen." In vol. 3 of *Reallexikon der Germanischen Altertumskunde,* edited by Johannes Hoops. Straßburg: Trübner, 1915/1916, pp. 137–145.

Mitteis, Heinrich. *Lehnrecht und Staatsgewalt: Untersuchungen zur mittelalterlichen Verfassungsgeschichte.* Darmstadt: Wissenschaftliche Buchgesellschaft, 1974.

———. *Der Staat des hohen Mittelalters: Grundlinien einer vergleichenden Verfassungsgeschichte des Lehnzeitalters.* Darmstadt: Wissenschaftliche Buchgesellschaft, 1974.

LEIT/LEIDE (sorrow, pain, heartbreak, insult, with all adjectival, adverbial, and verbal forms and meanings), comprises half of the conceptual pair *liebe/leit* (love/sorrow) which forms a major leitmotif of the *Nibelungenlied*. Although *leit* is democratic in its operation and ultimately affects all in the work, it is in connection with Kriemhild that it achieves its greatest significance. It is first encountered at the beginning of the epic in the scene between Kriemhild and her mother Ute, as the latter interprets Kriemhild's disturbing dream about a falcon attacked and killed by two eagles. Ute prophesies that her daughter will marry a noble man whom misfortune will befall. Kriemhild rejects this prediction and indicates her resolve to remain unmarried. She replies to her mother: "ez ist an manegen wîben vil dicke worden scîn,/wie liebe mit leide ze jungest lônen kan" (It has been clearly shown in the case of many women how, at the end, love begets sorrow; 17,2–3). Subsequent events bear out the unfortunate truth of this assertion to an extent doubtless inconceivable to Kriemhild here at the beginning. The *leit* suffered by her because of the killing of Siegfried, the treachery of her relatives, and last not least, by the theft of her trea-

sure, is inexpressible and identified by the poet with Kriemhild's great loyalty (*triuwe*) toward Siegfried. But precisely in connection with Siegfried, *leit* undergoes a subtle change in emphasis and, in addition to meaning pain and sorrow it also comes to mean *insult*. This connotation is as structurally and semantically significant as *sorrow*, and Kriemhild's relentless plans for revenge are much more comprehensible when her *leit* is viewed under this rubric. But whether sorrow or insult, the end is all the same—tragic. And, in the penultimate strophe, the poet returns to the theme introduced in strophe 17, paraphrasing Kriemhild's words most closely:

Diu vil michel êre   was dâ gelegen tôt.
die liute heten alle   jâmer unde nôt.
mit leide was verendet   des küniges hôhgezît,
als ie diu liebe leide   z'aller jungeste gît. (2378)

[There lay the great armies humbled and dead.
The people were beset with torment and dread.
The king's festival ended in sorrow,
As, at the end, joy [always] turns to woe.]

[FGG]

Bibliography

Ehrismann, Otfrid. *Ehre und Mut, Aventiure und Minne: Höfische Wortgeschichten aus dem Mittelalter.* Munich: Beck, 1995.

Maurer, Friedrich. *Leid: Studien zur Bedeutungs- und Problemgeschichte, besonders in den großen Epen der staufischen Zeit.* 3rd ed. Berne: Francke, 1964, pp. 13–38.

LIME TREE (or linden), in the *Nibelungenlied*, connected with Siegfrid's death in that a lime tree leaf covers the hero's back and prevents the dragon's blood from rendering that spot invulnerable (902), and that Siegfrid is killed at a spring underneath a lime tree after leaning his spear against one of its branches (972, 977). This connection between the tree and Siegfrid's death and the dragon he kills may be reinforced by false etymology (Middle High German *linde*, lime tree, and *lintwurm/lint-drache*, dragon). In *Der Hürnen Seyfrid* and *Von dem gehörnten Siegfried*, the first dragon encountered by the hero actually lives by a lime tree.

[JKW]

LINTWURM, Middle High German for *dragon* or *large snake.* In the *Nibelungenlied* Hagen refers in strophe 100 to the dragon killed by Siegfried as a *lintrache* (<lint-drache). *Lint* itself originally meant dragon or snake; as this meaning became obscure, later words such as *wurm* or *drache* were added as clarifications. Though in Christian literature the dragon is identified with the devil, the *lintwurm* is connected in original Germanic lore with the hoarding of treasure (cf. the *wyrm* which Beowulf kills and by which he is killed [ll. 2200ff]). Beowulf also reminds his listeners of Sigmund (not Sigurd/Sigfrid) who killed a dragon/*wyrm* that guarded gold (875–897). The *lintwurm*/dragon is also a source of carefully guarded knowledge (see the *Fáfnismál).*

[JKW]

LIST. While the New High German word *List* conveys a sense of *cunning, guile, slyness, trickery,* its Middle High German predecessor could be endowed with more positive implications, like *cleverness* and *wisdom,* although a term such as *arger list* clearly meant *insincerity* or *disingenuousness.* It is used in the plural in the *Nibelungenlied* in 286,3 (von guotes meisters listen) to describe the manner that Siegfried appears in Worms as though he had been captured on parchment "through the art/the talents of a grand master." Its application in 337,4: "er warp mit grôzen listen daz vil hêrlîche wîp" to refer to Siegfried's "courting" of Brünhild tends, as indicated in the annotation to the verse in the Bartsch/de Boor edition of the epic, to come closer to the New High German meaning of the word. Whether *arger list* in 841,1, referring to Siegfried's "seducing" of Brünhild, is meant to convey the deception of Brünhild by Siegfried or, as the Bartsch/de Boor note to the verse suggests, alludes to Brünhild's full participation in the act of seduction, remains unclear. The *list* in which Hagen engages for tactical reasons in 1479,4 by preventing the Hunnish envoys from returning to Etzel until a week before the Burgundians themselves can journey to Hungary is the type of quality that would have been expected in someone of his position and would most certainly have been praised by his peers. It might be suggested that *list* is the most appropriate term to describe Kriemhild's method

of achieving vengeance, but as Walter Haug has demonstrated, we are dealing in this instance with a phenomenon that extends far beyond the often laudable and acceptable mode of behavior that *list* implies in medieval German literature.

[WM]

Bibliography

Haug, Walter. "Montage und Individualität im *Nibelungenlied.*" In *Nibelungenlied und Klage. Sage und Geschichte, Struktur und Gattung. Passauer Nibelungengespräche 1985,* edited by Fritz Peter Knapp. Heidelberg: Winter, 1987, pp. 277–293, esp. 281.

LOVE in the *Nibelungenlied* is expressed by two interrelated terms. *Liebe* exhibits its complete semantic range from *pleasure, joy,* and *delight* to *affection, love,* and *fondness,* both with and without erotic overtones. In addition *liebe* is frequently encountered in the prepositional form, *durch/ze liebe* (for the love of . . . ; for the sake of . . . ; because of . . . .). Of great importance for the understanding of the *Nibelungenlied* is the conceptual pair that informs the work, *liebe—leit* (love—sorrow), which contrasts *liebe* in the sense of the *joy* and *harmony* that should exist, with the *leit* (sorrow/discord) that has taken its place in the world.

Minne in the *Nibelungenlied* evinces the basic meanings commonly encountered in contemporary poetry of the late twelfth and early thirteenth centuries, connoting a state of love, peace, amity, and possibly affection between individuals. Reflecting the Germanic custom of cementing a legal relationship by exchanging gifts, for example, the phrase *ze minne(n)* is often used with verbs having the meaning *to give,* thereby intensifying the action and imparting the tone of good will or favor (e.g., Bishop Pilgrim "gap . . .den boten ze minne" [. . . gladly gave the messengers . . .,]; 1428,1). Or Hagen gives Eckewart six golden bracelets *ze minnen* (1634,3) in order to confirm their friendship. *Minne* is also employed to describe sexual intercourse. A case in point would be Gunther's and Brünhild's wedding night, when Brünhild refuses her new husband the *minne* (637,3) he so desperately desires. Of course the focus on the events of the wedding night casts *minne* in an ironic light, something that is made explicitly clear by designating sexually fulfilling marital intercourse as *edele minne* (629,3). Irrespective of the context, however, *minne* is supposed to be representative of a time of harmony, and the fact that *minne,* like *liebe,* so often leads to *leid* is but one of the great paradoxes and ironies that the poet puts at the core of the *Nibelungenlied.*

[OE]

Bibliography

Grönbech, Wilhelm. *Kultur und Religion der Germanen.* Vol. 2. Darmstadt: Wissenschaftliche Buchgesellschaft, 1991, pp. 55–77.

Schnell, Rüdiger. *Causa Amoris. Liebeskonzeption und Liebesdarstellung in der mittelalterlichen Literatur.* Berne: Francke, 1985.

——. "Die höfische Liebe als höfischer Diskurs über Liebe." In *Curialitas: Studien zu Grundfragen der ritterlich-höfischen Kultur,* edited by Josef Fleckenstein. Göttingen: Vandenhoeck & Ruprecht, 1990. pp. 231–301.

Wiercinski, Dorothea. *Minne: Herkunft und Anwendungsschichten eines Wortes.* Cologne: Böhlau, 1964.

MÂC, Middle High German for *blood relative.* The belief that ties of blood are primary and inviolate is ancient and universal. Conflict between kin is thus considered "tragic," the workings of a malign fate. Not surprisingly, then, are such strife and its consequences major themes in the Nibelungen tradition. In the Old Norse *Atlakviða,* for example, Gudrun slays Atli and her children to avenge the murder of her brothers Gunnar and Hogni, even though they were responsible for the death of her first husband, Sigurd. Events are changed in the *Nibelungenlied,* and Kriemhild is ultimately responsible not only for the death of her child, Ortlieb, but also for the demise of her brothers, all in order to avenge the murder of Siegfried.

It is clear that confidence in the integrity of kinship had greatly weakened the more kinship ties were being augmented and finally supplanted by feudal bonds. The most famous example of misplaced trust in one's kin in the *Nibelungenlied* is found in the scene between Kriemhild and Hagen, when the former reveals Siegfried's one vulnerable spot to her husband's future killer. She does so because she has faith in the power of the kinship she and Hagen share:

. . . "du bist mîn mâc,   sô bin ich der dîn.
ich bevilhe dir mit triuwen   den holden wine
    mîn,
daz du mir wol behüetest   den mînen lieben
    man." (898,1–3)

[. . . "we are of the same blood, we two.
Upon your oath I entrust my sweet darling to
    you,
so that you may well protect my beloved consort
    for me."]

[FGG]

Bibliography

Harms, Wolfgang. *Der Kampf mit dem Freund oder Verwandten in der deutschen Literatur bis um 1300.* Munich: Eidos, 1963.

MAGIC CAP, the *Tarnhelm* of Richard Wagner's *Ring* cycle. Siegfried recovers the helmet from the dead Fafner's hoard; it later allows him to appear in the guise of Günther and win Brünnhilde as bride. In the *Volsunga saga,* Fafnir's hoard includes the *aegishjalmr* (often translated as *helm of terror*), which Sigurd takes away with him. There is no further mention of the helmet in the *Volsunga saga,* but both the *Lay of Regin* and the *Lay of Fafnir* explain that this helmet strikes fear into the hearts of its wearer's enemies. None of the Scandinavian works explicitly connects this helmet with shape-shifting.

[JKW]

MAGIC CLOAK, Middle High German *tarnkappe* (*tarnhut* in *Nibelungenlied* 338,1), a garment obtained by Siegfried from the dwarf Alberich as part of the Nibelung treasure (97). The cloak enables Siegfried to become invisible (338) and gives him the strength of twelve men (337). Thus equipped, he is able to defeat Brünhild and win her hand in marriage for Gunther (seventh *âventiure*). In *Der Hürnen Seyfrid* and *Von dem gehörnten Siegfried* the hero is saved when the dwarf Eugel/Egwald renders him invisible with a magic *Nebelkappe.* In the *Volsunga saga* Sigurd takes a golden coat of chain mail from the dying Fafnir's treasure, but no magical qualities are attached to it in the saga.

[JKW]

MAGIC DRINK, an "ale of forgetfulness" given in the *Volsunga saga* to Sigurd by Grimhild, Gudrun's sorceress mother, so that he will forget his oaths to Brynhild and marry Gudrun instead. In the *Nibelungenlied* such a potion is unnecessary since Siegfried has (apparently) never met Brunhild. Later (also told in the *Second Lay of Gudrun*) Grimhild gives Gudrun a magic drink, described in some detail, which causes her to forget her grief over Sigurd and be free to marry Atli.

[JKW]

MAN (vassal), following the definition given by Marc Bloch, in the system of feudal law the term signifies *personal dependency as a principle.* In the *Nibelungenlied* the question of Siegfried's status, which is epitomized in his "stirrup service," functions as a vehicle for the development of the catastrophe, while it is unknown in the Nordic tradition. During his first encounter with the Burgundians, Siegfried is outraged at Ortwin's offer to accept his challenge and points to the difference in their status: "er sprach: 'sich sol vermezzen niht wider mich dîn hant./ich bin ein künec rîche, sô bistu küneges man'" (Do not think of lifting your hand against me. I am a powerful king while you are only a king's vassal; 118,3–4). In view of this reaction it seems rather surprising that Siegfried poses at Isenstein as Gunther's vassal (386,3, 420,4). This deceit concerning his status constantly perplexes Brünhild, who wonders why Siegfried does not fulfill his feudal duties, and leads finally to the quarrel between the two queens.

[MH]

Bibliography

Bloch, Marc. *Die Feudalgesellschaft.* Frankfurt a. M.: Ullstein, 1982.
Müller, Jan-Dirk. "Sivrit: künec—man—eigenholt. Zur sozialen Problematik des Nibelungenliedes." *ABäG* 7 (1974): 85–124.

MARCGRÂVE (margrave), the title given to one who is appointed to administer and protect the border lands (*marke,* cf. English *march*). There are a number of characters so described in the *Nibelungenlied.* It is the title of Gere (750,1) and Eckewart (1227,3), who is discovered by

Hagen sleeping at his post *ûf der marke* (on the march; 1631,3); as well as Gelpfrât (1612,2) and Iring (2028,1). Most frequently the title is used for Rüdiger, whose role as the custodian of Etzel's border territories contributes to his special commitment to Etzel, to whom he owes his wealth and his estate at Pöchlarn. From the twenty-seventh *âventiure* on it is he who is referred to when the word is used without further identification. His wife is the *marcgrâvinne* often with the adjective *edel* (noble), and their daughter has the same title, often with the adjective *junc.*

[MEG]

MEINRAETE/MEINRÂT, literally *false advice* (*meiner* [= evil] *rât*), the noun *meinrât* (906,3a) and the adjective *meinræte* (881,1) are used within a few strophes of one another to describe the behavior of those who are plotting to kill Siegfried. On the first occasion the word is used as an adjectival noun: these people are "the treacherous ones." The second occasion refers specifically to Hagen, who has just left Kriemhild, having exacted from her the information about Siegfried's vulnerable spot: "ich wæne immer recke deheiner mêr getuot/sô grôzer meinræte, sô dâ von im ergie" (I do not think that ever any warrior committed such treachery as he did). There are no other occurrences of the word in the *Nibelungenlied,* but this is a narrator who rarely makes explicit comments on the behavior of his characters. That he does so here is significant, leaving no doubt about his condemnation of this betrayal.

[MEG]

MILTE (generosity), one of the chief virtues that a noble can possess. Being generous adds to one's honor. Most examples of generosity encountered in the *Nibelungenlied* exist primarily to enhance the reputation of the generous one. Gunther did not agree to Siegfried's request to care for the Saxon and Danish prisoners and provide handsomely for their journey home out of a sense of Christian charity, nor was that the motive for Siegfried's making the request. By treating his prisoners well, Gunther is clearly demonstrating that he is more powerful than they and thus a man of great honor. But it should also be noted that, in spite of the aspect of self-interest, generosity was a social necessity during the medieval period. For by being generous those in power saw to it that the poor and powerless were provided for. Not only the sick and destitute who depended on alms were the objects of generosity, but also the traveling entertainers who appeared at every festival (e.g., strophe 41). But here, too, generosity expects reciprocity. For by aiding these less advantaged groups, nobles were remembered in prayers or celebrated in song and tale.

[FGG]

MIMUNG, in the *Þiðreks saga,* the name of Velent's sword, which Velent forged while serving Nithung. He later gives it to his son Vithga when the latter sets out to become a knight. Vithga joins up with Heimir, Hornbogi, and Hildibrand who are on their way to their master Thidrek in Bern. Recognizing the power of the sword and fearing for his master's life, Hildibrand steals Mimung from Vithga and replaces it with an ordinary sword. Once in Bern Vithga indeed challenges Thidrek, who agrees to the combat. During the fight Vithga's sword shatters in two on Hildigrim, Thidrek's helmet. Thidrek is about to slay him when Hildibrand intervenes and returns Mimung to its rightful owner. Newly empowered, Vithga proves a formidable and superior opponent for Thidrek and is not persuaded by Detmar, Thidrek's father, from breaking off the combat. Vithga proceeds to slice Hildigrim in half and to inflict serious wounds on his opponent. Hildibrand intervenes, disengaging the two combatants and forcing a reconciliation. Later in the story Vithga loses Mimung to Heimir, who snatches the sword away during the battle between the forces of Thidrek and Atli and those of Osantrix. Heimir is later forced to return the sword, however, when Vithga returns from captivity. Mimung changes hands once again when Vithga lends it to Thidrek, who uses it to defeat Sigurd. Ultimately both Vithga and Mimung disappear in a conflagration of traded allegiances and revenge. Vithga eventually transfers allegiance to Ermenrich, and is compelled to battle Thidrek and his forces. Trying to avert direct armed conflict with his previous master, Vithga avoids him and instead engages and kills Naudung, Ortvin, Erp, and Theter. Pained by the loss of his men, Thidrek vows revenge and pursues Vithga, who flees into the sea and vanishes with the sword.

[KQ]

MORT had two meanings in the Middle Ages. The most obvious is *murder,* indicating a premeditated crime that is carried out on someone. The other is *manslaughter.* It is clear which type is meant in the *Nibelungenlied.* Yet the word *mort,* referring to the slaying of Siegfried by Hagen, does not appear in the **B** redaction of the epic, only in the **C** version. The **B** poet is straightforward in his condemnation of the deed, but for him it remains on the ethical/moral level of a reprehensible breach of *triuwe,* while the **C** poet views the killing as murder with all its legal implications. In essence the **C** poet is attempting to construct a scenario that would make it permissible for Kriemhild to avenge Siegfried's murder on Hagen, who is repeatedly referred to as a "murderer" by the **C** poet.

[FGG]

Bibliography

Gentry, Francis G. "Mort oder Untriuwe? *Nibelungenliet* und *Nibelungennôt.*" In *Ergebnisse und Aufgaben der Germanistik am Ende des 20. Jahrhunderts: Festschrift für Ludwig Erich Schmitt zum 80. Geburtstag,* edited by Elisabeth Feldbusch. Hildesheim: Olms-Weidmann, 1989, pp. 302–316.

NORNS, Norse goddesses of destiny, originally having the name *Urd* (fate, destiny, cf. Old English *wyrd*), thus embodying the concept of fate. *Urd* was later taken to mean *past;* by the twelfth century other names, *Verdandi* (Present) and *Skuld* (Future), had been coined. The Norns guarded the Well of Urd, at the roots of *Yggdrasil,* the World Tree, and shaped the lives of all beings, human and divine. In literature the Norns frequently receive blame for unfavorable circumstances: in the *Volsunga saga* and *Lay of Regin,* Andvari claims that a Norn decreed he must live in water; in the *Short Lay of Sigurd* Brynhild blames the Norns that Sigurd is not hers; in *Gudrun's Plaint,* Gudrun accuses the Norns of causing her sad lot.

[JKW]

NÔT in addition to meaning *sorrow* or *hardship,* the Middle High German noun *nôt* has a broad range of other meanings, from *distress* [often in battle], *suffering, danger, fate,* all the way to *force, coercion,* or *necessity.* The noun is central to an understanding of the *Nibelungenlied,* not only because of the high frequency with which it occurs in diverse phrases, but also because of the so-called *nôt*-manuscripts, the most reliable of which are manuscripts **A** and **B,** in which *nôt* is the very final word in the epic: *daz ist der Nibelunge nôt.* By contrast, manuscripts of the *liet*-group, from which the title of the work was derived, end with *daz ist der Nibelunge liet.* The precise meaning of *nôt* in the closing verse of the epic has been the focus of considerable scholarly attention. In general it appears that the poet is speaking here not merely of the "military defeat" or "death" that the Nibelungs (i.e., Burgundians) suffer in Etzel's land, but rather, in a larger sense, of the ineluctable, fate-driven sorrow which inevitably must displace the joys of human existence.

[MR]

NUMBERS in the *Nibelungenlied* quantify fighting forces, from the single warrior (Siegfried and Hagen) to a guard of twelve *recken* (i.e., warriors; Siegfried and Rüdiger) or giants (Schilbung and Nibelung), to twenty-four princes (Etzel), to even companies that number in the hundreds (e.g., 500 for Rüdeger; 600 with Dietrich; 700 with Ramung, Gelpfrat, and Kriemhild; 1,000 for Hornbogen, Rüdiger, and the Burgundian kings; 2,000 for Brünhild; and 3,000 for Bloedelin). Numbers also quantify forces in other ways. For example, 1,200 warriors eat at Siegfried's table. The Burgundian expedition includes 9,000 pages, 1,000 knights, 60 of Hagen's men. The Hunnish forces number 20,000. Danes and Saxons together make 40,000. Also counted in the epic are the slain, maidens, messengers, packs of hunting dogs, transportation wagons, money, and days, which is a measure of distance in travel time. In the *Klage,* the narrator refers to 40,000 dead before Hagen met his death (236–237).

[VU]

ORDAL (ordeal; Latin *ordalium*) was a popular legal procedure during the early and High Middle Ages, particularly in cases when evidence was lacking and people believed that only God seemed able to determine the defendant's innocence or guilt. Charlemagne regulated the application of the *ordal* in his law books, and it was in widespread use up into the early thirteenth century when the Church, during the Fourth Lateran council in 1215, began to reject it and called it blasphemous. The *ordal* required the defendant, for example, to remove a ring from boiling water, or to hold a red-hot iron in the bare palm. If the skin did not begin to fester after three days, his innocence became manifest. If accused of murder, the defendant sometimes had to pass by the body of the victim. If the latter's wound(s) began to bleed again, the guilt of the defendant was established. After Siegfried's murder in the *Nibelungenlied,* Hagen also has to go through the test of the *ordal.* Although Siegfried's wounds bleed as before, King Gunther insists that robbers were the culprits (1045,4), but Kriemhild is not deceived and declares that she knows full well the identity of these "robbers" (1046,1).

[AC]

Bibliography

Bartlett, R. *Trial by Fire and Water, Ordeal.* Oxford: Clarendon, 1986.

Gibson, W. S. *On Some Ancient Modes of Trial.* London: J. B. Nichols & Son, 1848. Reprint, 1947, n.p.

Neilson, George. *Trial by Combat.* Glasgow: Hodge, 1979

PEASANTRY, in the *Klage* the *lant liute* ordered by the king to dig graves and bury the many dead. The *bûr* or peasantry's only role is to do the heavy, dirty, and distasteful work of burial after slaughter. In every other context in both the *Nibelungenlied* and the *Klage* the terms *volch* (*volc, volk*), *liut* (*liute*), *lant volch* or *gebûre* can be understood as terms that mean town dwellers, armies, the train and followers of the nobility, or the people as a whole. With the development of courtly/knightly literature the concept of courtliness became central. Things pertaining to life outside the towns and courts took on negative value as portraying the stupid, rude, or rough. The *Nibelungenlied* is superficially courtly, but its roots lie in the earlier time of epic heroes. Its recurrent themes of loyalty, honor, bravery, conquest, betrayal, revenge, and destruction are portrayed by figures larger than life in settings that exclude the limited, rough world of the peasantry.

[BC]

PREDICTIONS, in general, are an integral component of the narrative structure of an epic, in which future events are alluded to in advance. Predictions are as common to heroic epic as they are to the epic of the Bible, for example. In the *Nibelungenlied,* however, the intensity with which predictions occur is unlike any other epic. They are a striking characteristic of the style of the work and simultaneously one of the most important elements of form. Through the medium of the prediction the *Nibelungenlied* poet succeeds in linking the story of Siegfried with the demise of the Burgundians. Kriemhild's falcon dream and its interpretation in the first *âventiure* play a key role in the process. In accordance with the compactness of the epic framework, the predictions in the work are concentrated around the major events: the romantic meeting of Siegfried and Kriemhild, the quarrel of the queens, Siegfried's death, and the battle and the subsequent tragedy that transpire at the court of the Huns. By far the largest percentage of predictions is devoted to two catastrophes: Siegfried's death and the demise of the Burgundians. A formal characteristic of the predictions is the use of the adverb *sît* (later on, since then), but the forms that predictions assume are manifold and include dreams, warnings, fearful anticipation (particularly in departure scenes), and prophecies. Frequently the prediction is expanded to encompass an entire scene. The network of predictions that can be traced throughout the *Nibelungenlied* does not, however, compromise the inner tension of the epic, which is based on a riveting narrative and the complex motivations of its characters.

[BH]

Bibliography

Beyschlag, Siegfried. "Die Funktion der epischen Vorausdeutung im Aufbau des Nibelungenliedes." *PBB* (Halle) 76 (1955): 38–55.

Bonjour, Adrien. "Anticipations et prophéties dans le Nibelungenlied." *Etudes Germaniques* 7 (1952): 241–251.

Burger, Harald. "Vorausdeutung und Erzählstruktur in mittelalterlichen Texten." In *Typologia Litterarum. Festschrift für Max Wehrli,* edited by Stefan Sonderegger, Alois M. Haas, and Harald Burger. Zurich: Atlantis, 1969, pp. 125–153.

Gerz, Alfred. *Rolle und Funktion der epischen Vorausdeutung im mhd. Epos.* Germanische Studien 97. Berlin: Ebering, 1930.

Lämmert, Eberhard. *Bauformen des Erzählens.* Stuttgart: Metzler, 1955, pp. 139–194.

Wachinger, Burkhard. *Studien zum Nibelungenlied: Vorausdeutungen, Aufbau, Motivierung.* Tübingen: Niemeyer, 1960.

PROPHECY. In return for the clothing stolen from them by Hagen, the mermaids promise to make a prophecy concerning the trip to the Hunnish court and what it will bring. Hagen learns that the Burgundians have been invited there to die and that none will return alive to Burgundy save the king's chaplain (1540, 1542). Hagen puts the dreadful prophecy to the test by casting the chaplain, who cannot swim, into the Danube and trying to drown him. When the cleric succeeds in reaching the shore, Hagen knows the prophecy is true and his fears are well-founded: "All these men must die" (1580). See also Dream.

[EH]

RACE TO THE STREAM, a scene in the *Nibelungenlied.* Determined to kill Siegfried, Gunther and Hagen pretend that foreign invaders are about to attack. Siegfried offers to fight for the Burgundians, and Hagen tricks Kriemhild into telling him where Siegfried's one vulnerable place is. She sews a cross on the back of his shirt to mark the spot. The war is then called off and a hunting party is organized instead. Hagen has food delivered to where the hunters will be in the evening, but he sends the wine elsewhere. He then tricks Siegfried into suggesting a race to a nearby stream, where they can drink good water. They strip to their shirts for the race, though Siegfried carries all his weapons and equipment as a handicap. The hero of Xanten wins the race, lays down his equipment, waits for Gunther to drink first, and then bends to drink himself. Hagen moves Siegfried's sword and bow out of reach, then thrusts his spear into his back at the place marked by Kriemhild. Mortally wounded and unable to reach his sword, Siegfried hits Hagen with his shield before he dies. It is in this scene in the *Nibelungenlied* that Kriemhild's three dreams, beginning with the falcon dream, are fullfilled.

[JVM]

RECKE (warrior, adventurer). The term belongs, like *degen, helt, wigant,* and *ritter,* to a group of appellations for heroes in the *Nibelungenlied.* It designates fighting knights who are courageous and steadfast. Scholars have debated as to whether the original meaning of the term (warrior moving around on his own, cf. OHG *wrecheo, recko* = exiled person) is still active in the *Nibelungenlied.* While some argue that *in recken wîse* (341,1) must be interpreted to mean that Siegfried, Gunther, Hagen, and Dancwart set out for Iceland in order to win Brünhild in the manner of ancient heroes (i.e., without many companions), others claim that the expression refers primarily to the adventurous, non-belligerent character of the trip. During the Middle Ages the word *recke* vanished from the German language, and it was not until the beginning of the nineteenth century, against the backdrop of increasing interest in the Middle Ages, that it re-emerged as a way of describing Germanic heroes.

[MH]

Bibliography
Ehrismann, Otfrid. *Nibelungenlied: Epoche, Werk, Wirkung.* Munich: Beck, 1987, p. 123.
Hennig, Ursula. "Heldenbezeichnungen im Nibelungenlied." *PBB* (Tübingen) 97 (1975): 4–58.
Weber, Gottfried. *Das Nibelungenlied: Problem und Idee.* Stuttgart: Metzler, 1963, p. 159.

REVENGE. The *Nibelungenlied* illustrates the dreadful consequences of revenge for those who seek it, and who in turn bring it upon themselves. The poet's rebuke of Gunther and Hagen for avenging Kriemhild's insult to the queen by conspiring to kill Siegfried, and thus remove him as a threat to Gunther, is matched in full by the condemnation of Kriemhild when she plans revenge for Siegfried's murder and the wrongs she has suffered. The poet even attributes her obsession with revenge to her having heeded the counsels of the devil (1394). As Etzel's wife, Kriemhild once again possesses the wealth and power to pursue her revenge on Hagen (1396 and 1397). The consequence to which the poet alluded earlier, 'jâ muosen sîn engelten vil guote wîgande sint" (Many warriors paid the price in later years; 1002), comes to pass with the doom of Hagen, Gunther, their men, Etzel's son, innumerable warriors, and Kriemhild herself.

[EH]

Bibliography
Frakes, Jerold C. *Brides and Doom: Gender, Property, and Power in Medieval German Women's Epic.* Philadelphia: University of Pennsylvania Press, 1994, pp. 172–176.
Gentry, Francis G., and James K. Walter, eds. *German Epic Poetry.* New York: Continuum, 1995.

RHEINGOLD (RHINE GOLD). There are several versions in Old Norse tradition of how gold came into the possession of the dragon Fafnir (see, for example, OTR). Eventually Siegfried slew Fafnir and became lord of the treasure. On his death it should have gone to his wife, but Hagen threw it into the Rhine to prevent Kriemhild from using it for revenge. Wagner in his *Ring des Nibelungen* reduces the treasure to the symbolic ring, which is finally returned to the Rhine maidens. *Das Rheingold* is also the title of the first part of Wagner's opera. It tells how Alberich took the Rhine gold from the Rhine maidens to whom it had originally belonged, and how Alberich made the magic ring and had Mime make the *Tarnhelm* (magic cap). This part of the opera also describes how Loge persuaded the giants to accept the Rhine gold instead of Freia as their payment for building Valhall, how Loge then obtained the gold from Alberich by trickery, and how Alberich finally cursed the ring and its future owners.

[JVM]

RHINE MAIDENS, the three daughters of the Rhine river in Wagner's *Der Ring des Nibelungen* (The Ring of Nibelung), appearing in sections called *Das Rheingold* (The Rhinegold) and *Götterdämmerung* (Twilight of the Gods). They are the custodians of the Rhinegold that is stolen from them by Alberich. The three Rhine maidens, for whom Wagner invented the names Flosshilde, Wellgunde, and Woglinde, have no medieval counterparts, but the composer was certainly inspired by several mythical aquatic women, among others the two *merwîp,* the Danube water sprites, whom Hagen meets in the *Nibelungenlied* in the twenty-fifth *âventiure.*

[UM]

RÎCHE, one of the most frequently used terms in precourtly narrative and heroic literature. Its range of application extends from the description of characters and objects to the delineation of rank. It has the primary connotation of *power, authority,* and *sovereignty* (Latin *potens*) and only secondarily that of its modern cognate (*reich = wealthy*). In manuscripts **A** and **B** of the *Nibelungenlied* this meaning predominates. Manuscript **C,** on the other hand, employs *rîch(e)* more selectively and tends to use terms drawn more from courtly vocabulary. For example in manuscript **C,** Queen Mother Ute is called *frou Uote diu guote* (the honorable, noble Lady Ute; 1308) whereas in manuscripts **A** and **B,** she is identified as *Ute diu vil rîche* (the most noble, august Ute; **A:** 1225; **B:** 1285).

[OE]

Bibliography
Bosl, Karl. "Potens und Pauper: Begriffsgeschichtliche Studien zur gesellschaftlichen Differenzierung im frühen Mittelalter." In *Frühformen der Gesellschaft im frühen Mittelalter: Ausgewählte Beiträge zu einer Strukturanalyse der mittelalterlichen Welt.* Munich: Oldenbourg, 1964, pp. 106–134.
———. "Armut, Arbeit, Emanzipation: Zu den Hintergründen der geistigen und literarischen Bewegung vom 11. bis zum 13. Jahrhundert." In *Beiträge zur Wirtschafts- und Sozialgeschichte des Mittelalters. Festschrift Herbert Helbig,* edited by Knut Schulz. Cologne: Böhlau, 1976, pp. 128–146.
Ris, Roland. *Das Adjektiv reich im mittelalterlichen Deutsch: Geschichte, semantische Struktur, Stilistik.* Quellen und Forschungen zur Sprach- und Kulturgeschichte der germanischen Völker, NF 40. Berlin: de Gruyter, 1971.

RIDE THROUGH THE FLAMES. In the *Poetic Edda,* Sigurd, riding for the first time up Hindarfjall, sees a light similar to flames shooting up into the sky, just as some birds had earlier prophesied. The flames are interpreted as an obstacle intended to guard the sleeping Sigrdrífa against any but the most fearless suitor (in a later lay, *Brynhild's Ride to Hel,* the sleeping maid is called Brynhild). When he reaches the top, he finds in its place a *scialdborg* (fence of shields) with a flag. The sleeping maiden lies inside the fence. After the lacuna the manuscript continues in a Sigurd lay with a reference to a dangerous ride (obviously through the fire), which Sigurd undertook to woo Brynhild for Gunnar. This ride must have been described in a lay of the lacuna. In *Snorra Edda,* no light or flames are mentioned when Sigurd rides up Hindarfjall and awakens Brynhild, who corresponds to the Sigrdrífa of the *Poetic Edda.* Later he marries Gudrun and helps his brother-in-law Gunnar to woo Brynhild, who sits on Hindarfjall and has sworn to marry only a man brave enough to ride through her wall of flames, *vafrlogi.* Gunnar's horse will not go through fire, consequently Sigurd exchanges shapes with Gunnar, rides through the flames on his horse, Grani, and deceives Brynhild by calling himself Gunnar. The horse motif frees Gunnar from the accusation of cowardliness. When Brynhild and Gudrun quarrel as to who has the bravest husband, Brynhild claims that Gunnar is braver, for he rode through the flames and Sigurd dared not attempt it. Gudrun then reveals the fraud. In the *Volsunga saga* the flames that appear in the first Hindarfjall scene appear and vanish in the Sigurd section of the *Poetic Edda,* the awakened maiden is Brynhild as in the *Snorra Edda.* At their second meeting in her tower near the castle of her foster father Heimir, there are no supernatural obstacles. When Gunnar seeks Brynhild's hand, Heimir tells them that she will marry only that man who rides through the fire burning around her castle. As in the *Snorra Edda* only Sigurd's horse is able to ride through the flames, which burn fiercely. The earth shakes as he rides through the fire as though he were riding through the dark. Once he has passed through them, the flames are extinguished. The saga, however, includes two stanzas of a lost lay which, in contrast to the prose version, indicate that the fire extinguished itself before Sigurd and no one else. The report provided by the prose version corresponds to what is found in the *Snorra Edda,* but then mentions that on the return trip Sigurd once again had to pass the wall of flames. In her argument with Gudrun, Brynhild laments that Gunnar had shown himself to be less courageous than Sigurd, for he had not dared to pass through the fire, either on horseback or on foot. Here again the saga cites a stanza of a lost lay. In *Hürnen Seyfrid,* the story is told differently: Kriemhilt is the maiden sleeping on a mountain, guarded by dragons, and awakened by Seyfrid, who is almost killed by the flames and the intense heat on the peak; but here the flames originate from the breath of the dragons. Nevertheless the *Lied vom Hürnen Seyfrid* provides evidence that some kind of wall of fire existed in German tradition as well. In tales like "Sleeping Beauty," the sleeping maiden is protected by an obstacle of some sort which either vanishes at a certain point in time or at the approach of the hero, or else it has to be overcome by the hero. A psychological interpretation of all three variations could be that they are symbols for girls who are not interested in boys before a certain point in time or who are just waiting for the right one to come along, or who want, in fact, to be ravished.

[HR]

Bibliography
Bolte, Johannes, and Georg Polivka. *Anmerkungen zu den Kinder- und Hausmärchen der Brüder Grimm.* Vol. 1. Leipzig: Weicher 1913, pp. 434ff.
Heusler, Andreas. "Die Lieder der Lücke im Codex Regius der Edda." In *Germanistische Abhandlungen. Hermann Paul zum 17. März 1902.* Straßburg: Trübner, 1902.
Lehmgrübner, Wilhelm. *Die Erweckung der Walküre.* Halle: R. Mayr, 1935.
Panzer, Friedrich. "Nibelungische Ketzereien." *PBB* 72 (1950): 468–500; 73 (1951): 95–123; 75 (1953): 248–272.
Reichert, Hermann. "Zum Sigrdrífa-Brünhild-Problem." In *Antiquitates Indogermanicae: Studien zur indogermanischen Altertumskunde und zur Sprach- und Kulturgeschichte der indogermanischen Völker. Gedenkschrift für Hermann Güntert,* edited by Manfred Mayrhofer. Innsbrucker Beiträge zur Sprachwissenschaft 12. Innsbruck: Institut für Sprachwissenschaft der Universität Innsbruck, 1974, pp. 251–265.

RIDILL, in the *Volsunga saga,* the name of the sword used by Sigurd to cut out the dragon Fafnir's heart after he has killed him with the sword Gram.

[WM]

RIHTEN (to sit in judgment) is inseparable in the Middle Ages from rulership. The judge is either a ruler or his representative. In the *Nibelungenlied* therefore, *rihten* refers as much to ruling as it does to judging, as demonstrated by the humorous description of Rumold's "rihten" over his "subjects," namely his pots and pans (777). It has been argued that Hagen's provocative sitting with Siegfried's sword laid across his knees in Kriemhild's presence is, if not derived from, at least parallel to the symbolic posture of a judge sitting in judgment (1783). The evidence for this being a well-known gesture, however, is not compelling. While in medieval iconography the judge is indeed always seated, the sword, symbol of his authority, is typically held upright by one of his officials, and not by the judge himself.

[RGS]

Bibliography
Wynn, Marianne. "Hagen's Defiance of Kriemhilt." In *Medieval German Studies.* Presented to Frederick Norman. London: The Institute of German Studies, 1965.

RINC, formation into a ring was the traditional prelude to a legal judgment or undertaking. Thus the Burgundians form a circle as Siegfried prepares to declare his innocence on oath (859,4–860,1). On two occasions, the same formation is the setting for a formal betrothal between Kriemhild and Siegfried (614,3) and between Giselher and Rüdiger's daughter (1683,1). On the latter occasion, the narrator adds that this is in accordance with custom (*nâch gewonheite*), emphasizing the observation of correct procedure.

[MEG]

RING. When Loki steals the hoard of the dwarf Andvari in the *Poetic Edda, Snorra Edda,* and *Volsunga saga,* Andvari tries to withhold a ring. The reason for this is explained only in the *Snorra Edda.* The ring has the magical power to replenish the hoard. Andvari curses the ring Andvaranaut, which means *fellow (gift) of Andvari,* so that both it and the gold will bring death to their owner. When the gods hand over enough of the hoard to Hreidmar to cover the husk of Otr (otter), his son, killed by the god Loki, one whisker remains uncovered and Odin has to give up the ring to cover it. In the *Poetic Edda* the ring Andvaranaut is mentioned again only in the prose section dealing with the slaughter of the Niflungs. In this instance it is the ring sent by Gudrun to her brothers to warn them of Atli's treachery. In the Atli lays the ring is not named. In *Snorra Edda* the story of Andvaranaut continues after Sigurd has slain Fafnir. According to the story, Sigurd removes it from the hoard and later gives it to Brynhild when, disguised as Gunnar, he woos her and takes one of her rings in exchange. He gives this ring to Gudrun, who produces it in her quarrel with Brynhild to prove that Gunnar was not the one who rode through the wall of flames. After Sigurd's death Gunnar acquires Andvaranaut, but the ring is not mentioned when the hoard is submerged in the Rhine. The *Volsunga saga* initially follows *Snorra Edda,* but subsequently alters some of the details. In the *Edda,* Sigurd gives a ring (also Andvaranaut) to Brynhild when they renew their engagement at Heimir. Later, disguised as Gunnar, he takes Andvaranaut from her and gives her another ring from the hoard that he had taken from Fafnir (in contrast to *Snorra Edda*). Andvaranaut is thus the ring that Gudrun uses as proof in her quarrel with Brynhild. In the deliberations regarding the murder of Sigurd, the hoard is mentioned but not the ring, indeed it is not ever mentioned again. There is no indication in the *Volsunga saga* that the ring Gudrun used to warn her brothers against Atli's treachery was Andvaranaut. In the *Þiðreks saga* and the *Nibelungenlied,* the mythological antecedents of the ring are missing. Siegfried/Sigurd forcibly takes a ring from Brünhild when he overpowers her in the *Þiðreks saga,* and both a ring and a belt in the *Nibelungenlied.* Rings as bearers of magical powers occur in such Norse sources as the Wieland story (*Volundarqviða* of the *Poetic Edda*) and in the story of Odin's ring, Draupnir (*Snorra Edda*) (see WAGNER).

[HR]

RITTER (knight), first appeared in manuscripts of the eleventh century. Corresponding to Latin *miles,* its general meaning denotes a man serving on horseback in combat. Thus when encountered in earlier documents, the term primarily connoted heavily armed and select troops of horsemen. But by the end of the twelfth century, retainers from the originally unfree group of ministerials as well as soldiers of fortune were also called *ritter.* Gradually during this period,

however, *ritter* began to indicate social rank and "birthright," leading eventually to an understanding of knighthood as an order. In addition the ceremony of dubbing, which accompanied the induction to knighthood and was strictly secular in origin, assumed a more religious aspect, while still maintaining its secular significance. Of the two early thirteenth-century literary descriptions of the ceremony of dubbing, one is found in the *Nibelungenlied* when Siegfried and his companions are raised to knighthood (strophes 27–42) and the other is in Gottfried's *Tristan* (lines 4589–5068). During the latter half of the twelfth century *ritter* was a key concept in courtly life, and it became the repository of such male virtues as honor, fidelity, breeding, and generosity, thus establishing a new cultural identity quite distinct from that associated with the older terms for warrior, like *helt, degen, recke,* or *wîgant.*

[OE]

Bibliography

Arnold, Benjamin. *German Knighthood, 1050–1300.* Oxford: Oxford University Press, 1985.

Borst, Arno, ed. *Das Rittertum im Mittelalter.* Darmstadt: Wissenschaftliche Buchgesellschaft, 1989.

Bumke, Joachim. *Studien zum Ritterbegriff im 12. und 13. Jahrhundert,* Heidelberg: Winter, 1977.

———. "Höfische Kultur: Versuch einer kritischen Bestandsaufnahme." *PBB* 114 (1992): 414–492, here 460–470.

Hennig, Ursula. "Die Heldenbezeichnungen im Nibelungenlied." *PBB* 97 (Tübingen, 1975): 4–58.

Keen, Maurice. *Chivalry.* New Haven & London: Yale University Press, 1984.

Reuter, Hans Georg. *Die Lehre vom Ritterstand: Zum Ritterbegriff in Historiographie und Dichtung vom 11. bis zum 13. Jahrhundert.* Cologne: Böhlau, 1975.

Scaglione, Aldo. *Knights at Court: Courtliness, Chivalry, & Courtesy from Ottonian Germany to the Italian Renaissance.* Berkeley: University of California Press, 1991.

Weber, Gottfried. *Das Nibelungenlied: Problem und Idee.* Stuttgart: Metzler, 1963.

SCHILDWACHT, refers to the sentry duty performed by Hagen and Volker, the fiddler, in the *Nibelungenlied,* subsequent to the arrival of the Burgundians/Nibelungs in Etzelnburg. After a banquet hosted by Kriemhild and Etzel,

Kriemhild's brother Giselher agrees with Hagen that his sister is planning something treacherous against them. Hagen offers to protect the Nibelungs and stand watch while they are sleeping. Volker volunteers to stand watch alongside him, for which Hagen is duly grateful. The two men spend the night guarding the door of the Burgundian/Nibelung lodgings. In order to comfort the warriors inside, Volker sits down on a rock and begins to play the fiddle, eventually lulling the men to sleep. He then exchanges the fiddle for his shield and continues the watch. In the meantime Kriemhild sends a contingent of Huns to the Nibelungs' quarters to slay Hagen. As they approach, they see Hagen and Volker standing guard and, realizing the futility of a frontal attack, decide to retreat. Initially Volker wants to follow and engage them in battle, but Hagen counsels against it since this would leave the other Nibelung warriors unprotected. Persuaded to remain, Volker still manages to insult the retreating Huns by condemning their conspiracy to murder sleeping warriors as outright cowardice.

[KQ]

SCHRÎBER, elsewhere in medieval German also *schrîbære*. A scribe was a person, often a cleric of humble standing and sometimes attached to a *scriptorium*, who was charged with the task of committing material such as legal documents, genealogies, or sometimes works of literature to parchment or to wax tablets. The word occurs just once in the *Nibelungenlied* (2233,2a), when the poet is lamenting the enormity of the death of Rüdiger, stressing that it would surpass even the skill of a scribe to express the impact of his death in words.

[MEG]

SHE-WOLF, in the *Volsunga saga*, Siggeir and his men kill King Volsung and abduct Volsung's ten sons. Signy, Siggeir's wife and daughter of Volsung, wants to rescue her brothers and convinces her husband to keep them alive, fettered in stocks, rather than slaying them immediately. In the subsequent nine nights a she-wolf comes to the stocks at midnight, devouring one brother each night, until Sigmund alone is left. Before the tenth night Signy sends a servant to her brother who smears honey on Sigmund's face and in his mouth. When the she-wolf licks the honey out of Sigmund's mouth, he bites off her tongue and thus kills her. The narrator reports that the she-wolf might have been Siggeir's mother, a witch and shape shifter. Wolves are closely associated with the Volsungs, whose name is related to the word *ynglings* (wolflings). In the *Volsunga saga*, Sigmund and Sinfjotli, while living as outlaws, find wolf skins. When they wear them, they lose both their human shape and nature, turning into wolves and fighting and killing for five days. The wolf is also associated with Odin and the berserks, a group of warriors consecrated to Odin who are able to immerse themselves completely in the frenzy of the battle. According to Snorri, berserks fight "without mail coats, [. . .] frantic as dogs or wolves" (*Heimskringla,* "Ynglinga Saga," 6).

[BS]

SMITH/SMITHY. In the *Nibelungenlied* we are not offered many details on Siegfried's youth. There is only a very brief reference to his fight with the dragon and his winning of a treasure. Beyond the *Nibelungenlied* the dragon fight is associated with Siegfried's life in the woods, where he was raised by a smith. In the latest German version of the Nibelungen legend, the *Lied vom Hürnen Seyfrid* (The Song of Horn-skinned Seyfrid), Seyfrid is a prince, the son of Sigmund, who behaves so badly that his parents send him away to a smith who burns charcoal at the edge of the woods. Seyfrid enters service with the man but soon he gets into trouble and wreaks so much havoc in the smithy that the smith tries to get rid of him. He sends Seyfrid off to the forest, hoping that a dragon will kill him. In fact Seyfrid kills more than one dragon and sets fire to the beasts. When their horny skin melts in the fire, he covers himself with this substance, hoping that it will protect him from all weapons. Only one spot between his shoulders remains uncovered. According to *Rosengarten A,* Siegfried possesses a breastplate which Eckerich, a master smith, has forged. Siegfried was brought up in Eckerich's smithy. A lost late manuscript of the *Nibelungenlied* seems to have incorporated these adventures of Siegfried's youth in detail, at least its table of contents (the *Darmstädter Aventiurenverzeichnis*) refers to them, but it does not mention the smithy.

The story of Siegfried/Sigurd's growing up without parents is also told in the *Þiðreks saga* (see MIME, YOUNG SIGURD) and in *Reginsmál* and *Fáfnismál* (see REGIN). Since it is unlikely that the Norse stories of Sigurd's travelled south into Germany, it is more likely that they were already current in some form in Germany during the thirteenth century. At least in the Norse tradition, smiths are not ordinary humans; they always evince supernatural features. Often smiths are (like Regin) cunning dwarfs, giants, or elves and" magicians capable of forging extraordinary jewelry and weapons, among them the time-honored swords for the great heroes in German poetry (see MIMUNG). Siegfried's youth in a smithy belongs to folk legend rather than heroic poetry.

[GW]

Bibliography

Flood, John L. "Siegfried's Dragon-Fight in German Literary Tradition." In *A Companion to the Nibelungenlied,* edited by Winder McConnell. Studies in German Literature, Linguistics, and Culture. Columbia, SC: Camden House, 1998, pp. 42–65.

Haymes, Edward R., and Susann T. Samples. *Heroic Legends of the North: An Introduction to the Nibelung and Dietrich Cycles.* New York: Garland, 1996, pp. 129–131.

Schneider, Hermann. *Germanische Heldensage.* Vol. 1. 2nd ed. Grundriss der germanischen Philologie 10/I. Berlin: de Gruyter 1962, pp. 115–120.

SPILMAN (minstrel). In the *Nibelungenlied* the most famous *küene spileman* (brave minstrel) and *videlære* (fiddler) is Volker von Alzeye, a high vassal and intrepid warrior of the Burgundian court. Explicitly characterized as *edel* (noble), he has nothing in common with an ordinary traveling minstrel, instead his musical abilities allude to his courtly education. Less clear, on the other hand, is the social status of Etzel's minstrels, Wärbel and Swemmel, who are sent as messengers to Worms in order to invite the Burgundians to the Hunnish court. As professional minstrels who are not, like Volker, primarily warriors, they do not seem, in spite of their splendid equipment, entirely suited to represent the power of Etzel, particularly if one considers the fact that all the other messengers in the *Nibelungenlied* are of higher position. However, in the *Þiðreks saga,* minstrels are used as messengers as well, so it is possible that the motif lies in the precourtly tradition.

[MH]

Bibliography

Wailes, Stephen L. "Wärbel und Swemmel. Zur verräterischen Botschaft im Nibelungenlied." *Archiv für das Studium der neueren Sprachen und Literatur* 219 (1982): 261–276.

STÆTE (constancy, steadfastness), is closely connected with the other important virtues like *triuwe* and *êre*. Indeed after *triuwe/getriuwe* it is the most important attibute an individual can possess in medieval literature. While a necessary quality in kings, of course, in the works stress is laid on the necessity of this virtue in abundant measure in vassals whom kings must be able to trust implicitly. Thus in every context in which it appears, even in environments not connected with the relationship between lord and vassal, the term denotes absolute reliability and unwavering firmness. The "constant" individual is someone who can be trusted in all circumstances to keep his word. It is in this regard, for example, that Kriemhild admonishes Rüdiger to keep his promise to her:

Si sprach: "gedenke, Rüedegêr,   der grôzen triuwe dîn,
der stæte und ouch der eide,   daz du den schaden mîn
immer woldest rechen   und elliu mîniu leit."
  (2151,1–3)

[She spoke, "Remember Rüdiger your great loyalty, remember your constancy and also your oath that you would ever be ready to avenge all my afflictions.]

Rüdiger knows that without constancy, there can be no true fidelity, and without true loyalty, there can be no honor, and he believes that he has no choice but to fight against the Burgundians. But paradoxically he also knows that it is wrong and he stands to lose precisely those good character traits that impel him to do battle in an unjust cause.

[FGG]

SUONE (reconciliation), is the opposite of re-venge (2229,3) and acquires its meaning in the context of *strît* (argument, battle), *schulde* (guilt), and *vride* (peace). Generally *suone* describes a process of reconciliation after or during an argument or dispute, in order to prevent a subsequent fight or act of revenge. In the *Nibelungenlied* the defeated Danes refer to their losing many warriors at the hands of the Burgundians and therefore insist on the necessity of arranging durable peace settlements (*stæte suone,* 311,3) before their departure. Gernot's reaction to Siegfried's challenge to do battle is equally directed at the avoidance of a fight and is therefore criticized by Ortwin as being inadequate: "disiu suone diu ist mir harte leit" ("I do not care at all for this reconciliation" 116,3). Kriemhild's doubly futile attempt at *suone* is of central relevance for the development of the plot. During her meeting with Hagen before the campaign (892–894) she shows her willingness to attempt a reconciliation, admits her guilt in the quarrel between the queens, and refers to her repentance in order to win Hagen as a protector of Siegfried. Hagen's remark, "ir wert versüenet wol nâch disen tagen" ("You [and Brünhild] will soon be reconciled" 895,1), can be interpreted, given Siegfried's fate, not only as a possible reconciliation of the two queens, but may also ironically mean "you'll get what is coming to you. " Nor does Kriemhild's second reconciliation with her brothers after the murder of her husband, from which Hagen is explicitly excluded (1115), prove viable, Kriemhild loses the hoard as well. In the second part of the *Nibelungenlied* the aspect of atonement is prevalent in the use of the term *suone.* After the fighting at Etzel's court has begun, it is the Burgundians who offer first *buoze unde suone* (atonement and reconciliation 1991,3) and then *vride unde suone* (peace and reconciliation 1997,2) respectively, which are, however, rejected by Etzel saying, "vride unde suone sol iu gar versaget sîn" (You shall be denied peace and reconciliation 2090,4). Kriemhild is only willing to talk with her brothers about *suone* if she can have Hagen as a hostage (2104), and later Dietrich and Hildebrand demand that Gunther and Hagen be taken hostage as *suone* for the death of Rüdiger (2336f., 2432).

[MH]

Bibliography

Bender, Ellen. *Nibelungenlied und Kudrun: Eine vergleichende Studie zur Zeitdarstellung und Geschichtsdeutung.* Europäische Hochschulschriften. Reihe 1: Deutsche Sprache und Literatur 994. Frankfurt a. M.: Lang, 1987, esp. pp. 168f.

SWERTDEGEN (squire)/**SWERTGENÔZ** (brother-in-arms). *Swertdegen* are squires, the young men who attend knights and who are themselves candidates for knighthood. *Swertgenôz* refers to those squires who are knighted together at the same ceremony. Thus, although essentially two different groups, in the *Nibelungenlied* they basically refer to the same people, namely those four hundred young men who are to be knighted together with Siegfried (strophes 30 and 39).

[FGG]

TOURNAMENTS. The word *tournament* (*turnier, turnîr, turner,* or *türnier*) is never mentioned in the *Nibelungenlied.* Most festivities, however, depict simulated battles (*spil* or *puneiz*), prowess of arms, pageants, or sports competitions, all characteristic for this most spectacular social ritual of feudal courts. Seven such festivals with tournaments are described in the epic: during Siegfried's knighthood festivities in Xanten, during Siegfried's first stay in Worms, after the peace "treaty" with Liudeger and Luidegast, at Gunther's wedding, during Siegfried and Kriemhild's visit to Worms, during Kriemhild's wedding ceremonies, and during the Burgundians' visit to Etzelnburg. (The latter is also mentioned without further details in verse 351 of the *Klage.*) The tournaments include the bohort, an equestrian group battle with shields, capped lances and blunted swords (*bûhurt* or *bûhurdieren* appears fifteen times); the joust, a battle between a pair of contestants on horseback (*tjoste* is mentioned only three times but alluded to on many more occasions); and stone (*stein*) or javelin (*scaft*) throwing. Celebrations surrounding tournaments display similar descriptive details: there are tents, pavilions, and seats built for the noble spectators, sumptuous banquets, elegant fabrics and garments, magnificent gifts of clothing and gold. The court attends Mass before or after the events. The boisterous tournaments serve as backdrop to the ever shifting, progressively deteriorating mood of the epic. It changes from serene happiness and chivalric gentility during the Xanten and Worms games, to suspicion and brooding during Gunther's wedding celebrations. It further permutes to anger and confrontation during the festival celebrating Kriemhild's visit to Worms. In Etzelnburg both spectators and participants sense a murderous tension rise: Dietrich and Rüdiger, aware of the hostility of the Burgundians, forbid their men to bohort or joust. Watching the games from her window, Kriemhild plots revenge. Finally the mood of the tournament turns deadly during the last bohort in "native style," when Volker kills a garish, young Hun. This last tournament signals the beginning of the carnage.

[OP]

Bibliography

Jackson, William Henry. "Das Turnier in der deutschen Dichtung des Mittelalters." In *Das ritterliche Turnier im Mittelalter,* edited by Josef Fleckenstein. Göttingen: Vandenhoeck & Ruprecht, 1986, pp. 257–295.

TRIUWE (loyalty, fidelity, love, allegiance)/**GETRIUWE** (loyal). *Triuwe* is arguably the most important concept in medieval German literature of the classical period. It is in Wolfram's *Parzival* that *triuwe* finds its most sublime expression, namely, not only connoting the spirit of loyalty and constancy that should lie at the base of all human relationships, but also the concept of divine love (*Parzival,* 448, 7–12).

While the use of *triuwe* in the *Nibelungenlied* remains on a more mundane level, the term itself together with all that it implies has long been recognized as the basic structural component of the Nibelungen narrative. If the noun *triuwe* embodies the ethical foundation of the characters, its adjectival form *getriuwe* (loyal) provides the defining attribute of a relationship or character. It is the most enduring and noble trait that one can have. It is the essential quality of character that nourishes all other virtues, such as steadfastness, honor, good breeding, and noble attitude, without which they would wither. In short *triuwe/getriuwe* informs and defines every human association in the *Nibelungenlied,*

whether within the feudal social structure or that of personal relationships.

Within feudal society, *triuwe* is the cement that holds the feudal bond together, the tenor of which is marked by the conceptual pair, *vel auxilium vel consilium* (both aid and advice). It is the vassal's responsibility to offer his lord protective aid and advice whenever the latter requires the one or the other. The lord, for his part, is expected to treat his vassal justly, to reward him for his services, and to protect him. If both parties perform their duties correctly, they are praised as being *getriuwe.* Both aspects of the feudal tie are frequently observed in the *Nibelungenlied.* For example, regarding the matter of advice, when Gunther is first apprised of the imminent attack of the Saxons and the Danes by a messenger of his enemies, he refuses to make any decision until he has discussed the matter with loyal advisors:

"Nu bîtet eine wîle,"   sprach der künec guot,
"unz ich mich baz versinne.   ich künd' iu mînen
   muot.
hân ich *getriuwer* iemen,   dîne sol ich niht
   verdagen
disiu starken mære   sol ich mînen friwenden
   klagen."
(147, emphasis mine)

["Now wait a bit," said the good king, "until I
   consider
[the matter] better. I'll let you know my decision.
   If I
have any loyal [followers], from them I will not
   hide these
grave tidings; I will lament [my plight] to my
   friends."]

In this instance Gunther is doing precisely what would be expected of a wise ruler in the feudal age, seeking the counsel of his "friends" (i.e., advisors, vassals, relatives). Regarding aid, engaging in battle on the side of one's lord, dramatically illustrates the concept of *triuwe* in this way. Yet the actual use of the term in the text is found not in descriptions of combat, but rather primarily in important scenes that precede the fighting itself. The best-known illustration of this aspect of *triuwe* is found in the scene between Rüdiger and Kriemhild after Rüdiger has delivered Etzel's offer of marriage. Kriemhild rejects Etzel's proposal until Rüdiger swears to serve and protect her in the land of the Huns:

Mit allen sînen mannen   swuor ir dô Rüedegêr
mit *triuwen* immer dienen,   unt daz die recken hêr
ir nimmer niht versageten   ûz Etzelen lant,
des si êre haben solde,   des sichert' ir Rüedegêres hant.
(1258, emphasis mine)

[Then [together] with all his men, Rüdiger swore to her to serve [her] ever faithfully. [Further, he pledged] that the noble warriors would never deny her anything that would honor her in Etzel's land. Rüdiger gave her his surety on that.]

Of course, it is this offer of service and protection that brings Rüdiger to grief later at the ill-fated festival at Etzel's court. It is clear that he did not understand his pledge to include plans for avenging Siegfried's death, but Kriemhild did, as she makes obvious in the following strophe when she muses: "waz ob noch wirt errochen des mînen lieben mannes lîp" (Might it yet well be that my dear husband's death will be avenged? 1259,4).

The reciprocal nature of the bond between lords and vassals is also highlighted during the final battle at Etzel's court. When it is clear that the Burgundians will not be victorious, Kriemhild offers to let all surviving Burgundians go in exchange for the surrender of Hagen. In reply to her offer of amnesty, Giselher unequivocally voices the lord's obligation to his vassal:

"Wir müesen doch ersterben,"   sprach dô Gîselher.
uns enscheidet niemen   von ritterlîcher wer.
swer gerne mit uns vehte,   wir sîn et aber hie,
wande ich deheinen mînen friunt   an *den triuwen* nie verlie."
(2106, emphasis on *triuwe* mine)

[Then Gislher said: "we will certainly have to die. No one will prevent us from [mounting a] chivalric defense. Whoever would like to do battle with us—[well] here we are! For I have never failed to fulfill my oath to a friend."]

And just a few stanzas later after the Burgundians have scorned Kriemhild's demand to surrender Hagen and the bloodshed in the hall begins, the poet underscores, once more, the importance of this bond between lord and vassal:

Die noch hie ûze stuonden,   die tribens' in den sal
mit slegen und mit schüzzen,   des wart vil grôz der schal.
doch wolden nie gescheiden   die fürsten und ir man.
sine konden von ir *triuwen*   niht ein ander verlân.
(2110, emphasis mine)

[They [the Huns] drove those who were still standing outside [the Burgundians] back into the hall with swords and arrows. For that reason the din [of battle] was very great. Nonetheless, the princes [Burgundian kings] and their vassal [Hagen] did not wish to be separated. They were incapable of abandoning their pledge of loyalty, one to the other.]

Triuwe is also used to define the character of personal relationships which, in some instances in the *Nibelungenlied,* have more importance than the relationships defined by the feudal bond. Three groups comprise the spectrum of personal relationships within the epic: blood relatives, spouses, and friends. The obligations of *triuwe* imposed on the members of these groups were qualitatively the same as those of the feudal structure, and, indeed, it is often difficult to draw the line between the two groups, as far as the concept is concerned, since individuals could be members of both groups. Hagen, for example, exists in a feudal relationship with the Burgundian kings, but is also a blood relative (something that is mentioned by Kriemhild in strophe 898,2 and by Giselher in 1133,3), as well as being a friend of Rüdiger. Although in the realm of friendship the concept of *triuwe* is more often implied than expressed, it is nonetheless the complex bond of friendship that plays the most important role in the *Nibelungenlied,* as for example in the relationship of Rüdiger to the Burgundians. The ties binding Rüdiger to the Burgundians are several: (1) He gives his daughter in marriage to Giselher, the youngest Burgundian king (1682); (2) The Burgundians are his guests, and he provides them with an escort to Etzel's palace; and (3) He also enjoys a long-standing friendship with Hagen. An important part of the tragedy in the second half of the *Nibelungenlied* is that these obligations of friendship come into dramatic conflict with those incurred by his pledge of personal loyalty to Kriemhild, something of which she reminds him (2151). In addition Etzel recalls Rüdiger's vassal loyalty and demands that the latter render the service that he owes the king. Caught between the seemingly diametrically opposed obligations of his loyalty to his lord and to his friends, Rüdiger eventually accedes to the pleas of the royal couple and fulfills his vassal loyalty. He believes, however, that by doing so he is jeopardizing his immortal soul (strophes 2150; 2166). This dilemma lends dramatic emphasis to the central theme of the *Nibelungenlied:* the paradox of *triuwe* becoming *untriuwe* (disloyalty, faithlessness).

In general, *untriuwe* does not merely mean no *triuwe,* but rather an absence of *triuwe* where one would expect to find it. In addition to the scene depicting Rüdiger's quandary, Siegfried's death provides another good illustration of this point. For the hero's death and the events surrounding it mark the first attempt on the part of the poet to indicate clearly the terrible consequences that *untriuwe* could have. On seven occasions, the poet personally intrudes into his text in order to express his outrage at the act. He repeatedly describes Siegfried's killing as one of unparalleled faithlessness (876,1–2; 887,3; 911,4; 915,4; 916,1–2; 971,4; 988,3–4). On one further occasion (1074,1–2), he has Sigmund, Siegfried's father, refer to his son's death as a faithless action. It is obvious that the poet is outraged at Hagen's deed. But it is equally as obvious that Hagen has cause to seek Siegfried's death since his lady, Brünhild, has been publicly humiliated by Kriemhild, Siegfried's wife.

In both scenes the poet has put his characters into situations in which conflicting obligations of feudal and personal *triuwe* are highlighted. In both instances the issue also revolves around the taking of apparently justified revenge for an injury or insult done to the king and queen. Further, both times the protagonists, Hagen and Rüdiger, respectively act with apparent justification, the one case involving an action to restore the honor and thus the ruling viability of Gunther, and the other to avenge the severe losses incurred by Etzel and Kriemhild, including the slaughter of their young son Ortlieb. Yet neither reason meets with the approbation of the poet. Clearly he is asking his characters to distinguish among conflicting obligations and not always choose to

honor those that appear to be legitimized by custom (vendetta), but rather to look closely at the relationships humanized by the bond of friendship, something Gunther was unable to do with regard to Siegfried and Rüdiger with regard to the Burgundians. The answers that the Nibelungen poet offers his audience with regard to the obligations of *triuwe* are definitely not comfortable. He is asking them to make distinctions, to come to decisions that may fly in the face of accepted tradition. The tragedy of the *Nibelungenlied* is that the strict adherence to *triuwe,* the bond of society, actually sunders Nibelungen society and ultimately destroys it.

[FGG]

Bibliography

Ehrismann, Otfrid. *Ehre und Mut, Aventiure und Minne: Höfische Wortgeschichten aus dem Mittelalter.* Munich: Beck, 1995.

Emmel, Hildegard. *Das Verhältnis von êre und triuwe im Nibelungenlied und bei Hartmann und Wolfram.* Frankfurt: Diesterweg, 1936.

Gentry, Francis G. *Triuwe and Vriunt in the Nibelungenlied.* Amsterdam: Rodopi, 1975.

McConnell, Winder. *The Nibelungenlied.* Boston: Twayne, 1984.

TUGENT (virtue) is one of the most complex terms in the courtly literature of the Middle Ages. It can refer either to single virtues or to a totality of good qualities that reflects a more or less clearly defined ideal of courtly perfection. In the *Nibelungenlied, tugent* is specified, on the one hand, as emanating from noble predisposition combined with courtly education, and is therefore closely connected to the concept of *zuht* (discipline). On the other hand the original meaning of *tugent* (physical and mental prowess, especially with respect to an individual's fighting skills; cf. the verb *tugan* = to be suitable, to be of use) is still evident in the work. The term is used for both males and females. However, specific differences can be noted with regard to the kind and range of the qualities attributed to various figures. At the top of the scale one can find Rüdiger, the "vater aller tugende" (father of all virtues; 2202,4; cf. also 1637,4), and Siegfried. He is characterized as "an allen tugenden ein riter küen' unde guot" (possessing all merits of a brave and excellent knight; 230,4). He demonstrates this when he spares defeated adversaries or when he allows Gunther to be the first to go to the spring. The behavior of the Burgundian kings, as well as that of their ancestors, is guided by notions of *tugent* and *êre* (honor and reputation; 1148,3). The term is not applied at all to describe Etzel, and the author uses it only once to describe Hagen and remarkably in a context that stresses primarily his practical abilities. During their journey to Etzel's court Gunther tells Hagen to stop expressing doubts about their venture "durch iuwer selbes tugende" (because of your own virtue), and to find a place to ford the Danube (1529). *Tugent* attributed to female protagonists (especially Kriemhild and Helche, Etzel's first wife) is synonymous with *milte* (generosity) and *triuwe* (faithfulness, steadfastness, loyalty). Although Brünhild's virtue is not often referred to, it is her *tugende* that eventually prompts her to release Gunther from the nail on the wall during their wedding night.

[MH]

Bibliography

Eifler, Günter, ed. *Ritterliches Tugendsystem*. Wege der Forschung 56. Darmstadt: Wissenschaftliche Buchgesellschaft, 1970.

Rupp, Heinz. "Tugend." *Saeculum* 2 (1951): 465–472.

ÜBERMUOT (arrogance, pride), a characteristic attitude of most of the major figures of the *Nibelungenlied*, particularly of Siegfried and Hagen. Siegfried's *übermuot* is most notable during his initial confrontation with the Burgundian kings upon his arrival in Worms (strophe 117) and in the struggle between Siegfried and Brünhild in Gunther's bed (Bartsch notes that the *hôhen muot* referred to in strophe 680 can be understood as *übermuot*). The subsequent murder of Siegfried can be traced back to his theft of Brünhild's ring and belt and to the arrogance/pride that instigated this theft. Hagen manifests his *übermuot* during the Burgundians' fateful visit to Etzel's court when he lays the sword of the murdered Siegfried across his leg in the presence of Kriemhild and her armed host (strophe 1783). *Übermuot* has a positive or a negative value according to the perspective from which it is considered. From a theological standpoint *übermuot* is related to *hochvart* (*superbia*), one of the seven deadly sins, and is thus reprehensible. Conversely *übermuot* may once have been the central feature of a Germanic warrior ethos that may be visible in the *Hildebrandslied* and in the *Poetic Edda*. It is also consistent with the qualities of vigor, boldness, brutality, and greed that the historian Robert Bartlett puts forward as the defining characteristics of the conqueror.

[WRH]

Bibliography

Bartlett, Robert. *The Making of Europe: Conquest, Colonization, and Cultural Change, 950–1350*. Princeton: Princeton University Press, 1993.

UNDERTÂN (subject), in most cases the term corresponds to a conception of rule in which the ruler's legitimacy is based on his personal strength. In the *Nibelungenlied* the first and most important representative of this idea is Siegfried, who gains new *undertânen* by means of physical power and fighting force (95,4). His bold challenge at the court in Worms demonstrates his confidence in his physical superiority: "ich wil an iu ertwingen swaz ir muget hân:/lánt únde bürge, daz sol mir werden undertân" ("I intend to take whatever you have; your lands and your castles will become subject to me" 110,3–4). The number of subjects also indicates the scale of a ruler's power and authority (8,2; 1215,3; 1477,2), in which his wife participates even after his death (1385,1; 1075,3; 1236,2; 619,3), although she is, in principle, subject to her husband (46,4; 1157,2). After the victory over Brünhild, Gunther also acquires her followers as *undertânen* (466,4), while Brünhild tells Kriemhild of her conviction that Siegfried, as Gunther's *undertân*, is obliged to serve her as well (823, cf. also 816, 821). A double meaning of the term, this time referring to another form of legitimation of rule (*von rehte;* 115,4), is evident in Gunther's reaction to Siegfried's provocative announcement: "allez daz wir hân,/geruochet irs nâch eren, daz sî iu undertân" (All that we have is at your disposal, if you will accept it within the bounds of honor" 127,1–2). He is offered merely admission to court, which implies no power; here

Gunther does not submit himself to Siegfried's authority.

[MH]

Bibliography

Müller, Jan-Dirk. "Sivrit: künec—man—eigenholt. Zur sozialen Problematik des Nibelungenliedes." *ABäG* 7 (1974): 85–124.

URLIUGE (war). The terms for *war* (*urliuge*), *military campaign* (*hervart*), and *combat* (*strît*) are used so loosely and interchangeably in the *Nibelungenlied* as to make it seem unlikely that the composers of the various manuscripts distinguish clearly among them. *Urliuge* can mean *fighting*, as when daylight allows for a resumption of combat during the battle in Etzel's Great Hall (2128,2), but it can also mean the general preparations to repel a *hervart*, an invasion, or war (note 171,2). In the description of Gelpfrat's men as those who had proven destructive *in starken urliugen* (1597,3), *urliugen* may be a reference to combat of any scope. The emphasis here, however, would appear to be on starken, i.e., the intensity of the violence, hence, "in hard fights."

[VU]

VÂLANDINNE (she-devil). Following the arrival of the Burgundians at Etzel's court in the twenty-eighth *âventiure* of the *Nibelungenlied*, Dietrich von Bern warns them that Kriemhild has not relented in her lamenting of Siegfried's death (1724,4), and that no good will come of it as long as Kriemhild is alive (1726,2). When Kriemhild realizes that the Burgundians have been forewarned because they will not give up their shields, she threatens the person who has alerted them with death (1747). An angry Dietrich responds that he is the one who has informed the Burgundians of the true state of affairs and concludes with a challenge to Kriemhild: "nu zuo, vâlandinne, du solt michs niht geniezen lân" (Well then, come on, you she-devil, don't let me get away with it; 1748,4). This has been considered premature by most scholars, a stylistic lapse on the part of a later compiler of the epic, as Kriemhild's "degeneration" has not yet manifested itself to an extent that would in any way justify such an appellative. It rings truer when uttered by Hagen in 2371,4, following the

slaughter of tens of thousands, as he asserts that Kriemhild will never get a hold of the Nibelungen hoard: "der sol dich, vâlandinne, immer wol verholn sîn" (it will always remain hidden from you, you she-devil). The term also appears in its masculine form in the twenty-third *âventiure*: "Ich wæne der übel vâlant Kriemhilde daz geriet,/daz sie sich mit friuntschefte von *Gunthere* schiet" (I believe the foul devil prompted Kriemhild to take her leave of Gunther in friendship 1394,1–2), the sense being that, already at this point, Kriemhild demonstrated an association with the demonic through a feigned reconciliation with her brother(s) as part of her overall plan to exact revenge, even if at some undetermined point in the future. Contemporary reaction to this derogatory depiction of Kriemhild was undoubtedly split between those, such as the scribe of manuscript **B**, who would likely have sided with Etzel and Hildebrand's condemnation of her following the death of Hagen, and others, such as the scribe of manuscript **C** and the anonymous author of the *Klage,* who would have praised her for the unswerving devotion and loyalty she displayed towards Siegfried until the bitter end.

[WM]

VALKYRIES, in Norse myth, warrior maidens who flew over battlefields and conducted fallen heroes to Odin's Valhalla. They are most often found in groups of nine, though thirteen names of valkyries are given in the *Lay of Grimnir.* In the *Poetic Edda,* Sigrun, wife of Hunding, is a valkyrie; her appearance in the *Volsunga saga* with a band of "shield maidens" must reflect her original identity. The most important valkyrie figure in the *Volsunga saga,* also not identified as such, is Brynhild. Brynhild of the *Edda* is already connected to the valkyrie Sigrdrifa in that major events in the lives of the two women as told in the *Lay of Sigrdrifa* and *Brynhild's Ride to Hel* overlap to a large extent. From Brynhild's explanation to Sigurd in the *Volsunga saga* of how she came to be asleep behind a wall of flame, it is obvious that the author of the *Volsunga saga* chose to identify Sigrdrifa the valkyrie with Brynhild. Typically this author avoided any unnecessary inclusion of Norse mythology, and thus the word *valkyrie* is not found. In the *Nibelungenlied* Brünhild's physical prowess and aversion to marriage can best be understood if her original character had been a valkyrie. Her relationship to Odin/Wotan (valkyries were the god's servants), hinted at in the *Lay of Sigrdrifa*, is elaborated considerably by Richard Wagner in his *Die Walküre*.

[JKW]

VOG(E)T (ruler). Always implying the idea of protection, the term is used in the *Nibelungenlied* in three different ways. In most cases *voget* refers to a king or a patron (e.g., Gunther, Etzel, Ortlieb, Rüdiger, Dietrich, Wolfwin, and Liudeger, ruler of the Saxons). However, there is no unambiguous reference here to the organization of feudal relations connected with its usage. Rüdiger, "voget von Bechelâren," is also a vassal of Etzel. Secondly *voget* can describe the governor or acting representative of a ruler: Brünhild chooses her mother's brother as *voget* to whom her castles and her land are entrusted until Gunther assumes the reign (522,8–523,8). Finally *voget* is used in the meaning of guardian, as when, for example, Kriemhild asks her brother Giselher during the treasure argument to become her *voget* and care for "beidiu lîbes unde guotes" (both life and property; 1135,2f.).

[MH]

WASKE, the name of the sword belonging to Iring the Dane in the *Nibelungenlied,* with which he wounds Hagen, just before being slain by the latter (note 2064ff.).

[WM]

WATER SPRITES are encountered in the twenty-fifth *âventiure* of the *Nibelungenlied*. During the Burgundians' trip to Etzel's court in Hungary, Hagen comes across them while they are bathing in the Danube. He steals their clothes and Hadeburg, one of the sprites, offers to tell him how they would fare on their trip. Because they float on the water, Hagen believes they are gifted with second sight. Hadeburg informs him that the Burgundians can ride with confidence to Etzel's and win glory, a proclamation that pleases Hagen, who then returns their clothes. However, Sieglind, Hadeburg's companion (aunt?), informs him that Hadeburg has lied, that he should turn back, otherwise he and all the others will die, except for the king's chaplain,

advice that Hagen did not heed nor impart immediately to the others. Inquiring how he and his companions might cross the river, he is told by Sieglind that his travels on the other side, where the margrave Else and his brother, the warrior Gelpfrat, cause much trouble, will be precarious. She also indicates that the ferryman, who owes homage to Gelpfrat, is ferocious and must be paid his due. If he does not come promptly, Hagen should say that his name is Amelrich and he will appear. Hagen bows in thanks, and departs. The prophetic words of Sieglind are later realized.

[SJM]

WEDDINGS. Middle High German *hochzît/hochgezît* can refer to any secular or religious festivals but also specifically to the lengthy celebrations that constitute medieval weddings. The promises of three betrothals in the *Nibelungenlied* culminate in a public wedding celebration after a period of courtship. Siegfried goes as a youth to Worms with the intent of winning Kriemhild, a plan that includes a certain term of service on the part of the young suitor. Siegfried must fight in Gunther's service for approximately two years before he may ask for Gunther's promise that he may receive Kriemhild's hand in marriage. As a condition of Gunther's oath, Siegfried must further help Gunther win Brünhild before the anticipated wedding may take place. With Siegfried's superhuman aid, Gunther must in turn compete with Brünhild in wrestling, spear throwing, and stone throwing and win before she will accept him as her husband. Etzel, the king of the Huns, does not have to woo Kriemhild in such a way. However, he is an extremely powerful king in his own right. Although her brothers consult with one another before they permit Rüdiger to plead Etzel's case to Kriemhild personally, the decision is then hers to make in response to Rüdiger's request. Furthermore Gunther and Hagen are all too eager to see her married and "safely" under the control of a husband once more. As Siegfried's widow, she caused her brothers considerable political embarrassment through her gift giving (1128–1130), an act that could also have led to civil war in Burgundy.

The weddings are characteristically celebrated following the consummation of the relationship (see 644,1–4). The unions are formalized with the celebration of a Mass, in keeping with the traditions of medieval nobility before the fourth Lateran Council, though this receives only brief mention in the *Nibelungenlied.* Fourteen days of feasting and jousting in Worms follow the double marriage of Gunther with Brünhild and Siegfried with Kriemhild (see 686ff.) As such, weddings are court functions, designed to make public the marriage consummated the night before. Wedding celebrations solidify, then, not only the personal relationships between the couples involved but perhaps more importantly the political alliances thus formed. For this reason Gunther's first wedding day is actually bittersweet, since he is incapable of consummating his marriage with Brünhild until after his public celebration has gotten underway. His wedding is virtually a sham, since he and his wife are not "really" married at the time the public celebration occurs.

[ASH]

Bibliography

Brooke, Christopher. *The Medieval Idea of Marriage.* Oxford: Oxford University Press, 1989.

Brundage, James A. *Law, Sex, and Christian Society in Medieval Europe.* Chicago: University of Chicago Press, 1987.

Gies, Frances and Joseph. *Marriage and the Family in the Middle Ages.* New York: Harper and Row, 1987.

WOLF'S HAIR. In the *Volsunga saga* Gudrun, suspecting Atli's treachery towards her brothers, tries to warn them by sending along a message for them with Vingi: a gold ring with a wolf's hair tied onto it. Looking at the ring, Hogni suspects that Gudrun wants to warn them that Atli regards them in the way a wolf would view its prey. In *Atlakviða* the ring is wrapped in an entire piece of wolf's skin and delivered by a messenger called Knefrodr, but interpreted in the same way by Hogni.

[BS]

PART IV

Manuscript Collections and Literary/Historical Analogues

AMBRASER HELDENBUCH, a sumptuous parchment manuscript (cod. Vind. Ser. nov. 2663) now housed at the Austrian national library (Österreichische Nationalbibliothek) in Vienna. It was previously stored in the castle Ambras near Innsbruck from the late sixteenth century until 1806. In its table of contents the manuscript refers to itself as a *Heldenpuch* (book of heroes), and it is designated as such by several documents that were produced during the time of its composition. The *Ambraser Heldenbuch* was composed by Hans Ried, who is mentioned in documents of the imperial chancery of Maximilian I beginning in 1496. After Maximilian commissioned the manuscript in 1504, Ried worked on it, probably copying from what is now a lost manuscript (the *helldenpuch an der Etsch*) and other sources until his death in 1516. During this time Ried also worked in the imperial chancery (1512–1514) and as tax collector in the towns of Bozen (1500–1508) and Eisack (1514–1516). The illustrator of the border decorations in the *Ambraser Heldenbuch* is made known only by the initials *VF* on folio 215. Because fifteen of the twenty-five different narratives in the *Ambraser Heldenbuch* are unique, this manuscript is of great importance for the study of medieval German literature, even if it is often difficult to establish how faithful the *Ambraser*

Heldenbuch remained to the original narratives, which were composed some three centuries earlier in the latter part of the twelfth and thirteenth centuries. An antiquarian interest seems to underlie the three-part structure of the *Ambraser Heldenbuch*, which is divided into an initial section containing courtly narratives (1. Der Stricker, *Frauenehre,* 2. *Moriz von Craun,* 3. and 4. Hartmann von Aue, *Iwein* and *Die Klage,* 5. *Das [zweite] Büchlein,* 6. Heinrich von dem Türlin, *Der Mantel,* and 7. Hartmann von Aue, *Erec*), a middle section containing heroic epics (8. and 9. *Dietrichs Flucht* and *Rabenschlacht,* 10. and 11. *Das Nibelungenlied* and *Die Klage,* 12. *Kudrun,* 13. *Biterolf,* 14. *Ortnit,* and 15. *Wolfdietrich*), and a final section consisting of various shorter epic works (16. *Die böse Frau,* 17., 18., 19., and 20. Herrand von Wildonie, *Die treue Gattin, Der betrogene Gatte, Der nackte Kaiser,* and *Die Katze,* 21. Ulrich von Lichtenstein, *Frauenbuch,* 22. Werner der Gärtner, *Der Meier Helmbrecht,* 23. Der Stricker, *Pfaffe Amis,* 24. Wolfram von Eschenbach, *Titurel,* and 25. *Priesterkönig Johannes*). Although it is the most recent complete version, the copy of the *Nibelungenlied* in the *Ambraser Heldenbuch* (manuscript **d**), which contains rhymes corresponding closely to those found only in manuscript **B** and in the *Þiðreks saga,* has been regarded by

Helmut de Boor as significant for the reconstruction of the original work.

[WRH]

Bibliography

Ambraser Heldenbuch [Facsimile]. Edited by Franz Unterkircher. Graz: ADEVA, 1973.

Janota, Johannes. "Ambraser Heldenbuch." In vol. 1/2 of *Verfasserlexikon.* 2nd ed., edited by Kurt Ruh et al. Berlin: de Gruyter, 1977.

BRANWEN, DAUGHTER OF LLYR, one of the four *Mabinogi,* medieval Welsh prose tales from the tenth century (fourteenth-century manuscripts). *Branwen* forms the second "branch" of the *Mabinogi.*

Found here is a tale, somewhat parallel to the Nibelung material, of a bride taken to a foreign land by her new husband, whose brothers later visit but are attacked and die in battle. Besides the broader outline of the plot, *Branwen* may share some minor elements with the best known Nibelung works. Branwen is the sister of Bran, King of the Isle of the Mighty (Britain). She has two brothers, Manawydan and Nisien, and a half brother, Efnisien. Matholwch, King of Ireland, comes to Britain to ask for Branwen's hand in marriage and Bran consents. Efnisien destroys Matholwch's horses in an act for which Bran must pay compensation to keep peace. Matholwch accepts payment and takes Branwen back to Ireland.

Though Branwen bears Matholwch a son, he is pressured by kinsmen who are angry over Efnisien's affront and begins to mistreat Branwen. She writes her brothers a letter of complaint, which a bird brings to Bran. Bran gathers an army and sails to Ireland. When Matholwch seeks to make peace by abdicating his throne in favor of Gwern, his son by Branwen, Bran accepts. The Irish prepare a feast in a special hall where they hide two hundred armed men in flour bags. Entering the hall, Efnisien squeezes the bags, crushing the heads of the men inside. During the feast Efnisien seizes Gwern and casts him into the fire, and a battle ensues. The Irish possess a magic cauldron which allows the revivification of dead warriors placed inside; pretending to be a dead Irishman, Efnisien is placed in the cauldron, where he stretches out,

destroying the cauldron and killing himself. The battle ends with seven British warriors and Branwen still living. Bran is struck by a poisoned spear. Dying, he orders his head to be cut off and taken back to Britain. The seven return home with Branwen, where she laments her role in the destruction of two islands and dies of grief.

For Kurt Wais, *Branwen* held a major place in his reconstruction of the development of the Nibelung legend. Because of the appearance of certain motifs in the Welsh story he placed the tale on a "middle layer" in the evolution of his hypothetical "Krimhild Legend," which deals with the marriage of a young woman into a foreign family, and the strife that arises out of this arrangement. Important elements for Wais were Efnisien's destruction of the Irish horses, retained in Hagen's reference to the inadequacy of the Huns' horses in the *Nibelungenlied* (1273,3). Wais also compared Efnisien with Hagen in that both men kill their host's son. Other similarities between *Branwen* and various Nibelung works are the flour bag incident (Sigmund and the sons of Signy in the *Volsunga saga*), the return of a remnant of the visitors to their home (*Finnsburg Lay*), and Efnisien as half brother to the royal brothers and their sister (Hogni in the *Þiðreks saga*).

[JKW]

Bibliography

Ford, Patrick, trans. and ed. *The Mabinogi and Other Medieval Welsh Tales.* Berkeley: University of California Press, 1977.

Wais, Kurt. *Frühe Epik Westeuropas und die Vorgeschichte des Nibelungenliedes.* Tübingen: Niemeyer, 1953.

Williams, Ifor, ed. *Pedeir Keinc y Mabinogi.* Cardiff: Gwasg Prifysgol Cymru, 1951.

CANTAR DE LOS INFANTES DE LARA (The Young Noblemen of Lara), a lost medieval Spanish epic poem, closely reflecting the military and political circumstances of the late tenth-century Castilian frontier. It is known in two different redactions that were transcribed in thirteenth- and fourteenth-century Spanish and Portuguese chronicles. According to the story an escalating series of insults and violent confrontations deepen the enmity between the Castilian nobleman Ruy Velázquez and his seven impetuous nephews from Lara. The quarrel is exacerbated by Velázquez's manipulative, tempestuous wife, Doña Lambra (Latin *flamula*). Eager for vengeance, Ruy Velázquez lures the seven brothers into a battle with the Muslims and then abandons them to certain death. Their heads are taken as trophies to Córdoba and are presented to Almanzor (i.e., Mohammed ibu abi-Amir al-Mansur, chief minister of the Omayyed Caliphate; died 1002). The caliph asks Gonzalo Gustioz, father of the young men, who has come to Córdoba as a Christian emissary, to identify the heads. Overwhelmed with grief, he seizes a sword and kills a Muslim courtier. Almanzor, taking pity on him, has him imprisoned. Gustioz is visited by a Muslim noblewoman, who later bears him a son, Mudarra (Arabic for 'son of an Arab and a non-Arab'). The caliph eventually frees his prisoner, who returns to Castile, to live in abject poverty. His son, Mudarra, is brought up as a Muslim at Almanzor's court. Learning of his father's identity, Mudarra takes an army of Muslim followers to Castile, converts to Christianity, hunts down the treacherous Ruy Velázquez, and delivers him, gravely wounded, to Doña Sancha, mother of his seven half brothers. She decrees his punishment: he will be tied to a scaffold and spears will be thrown at him. Later the fiery-tempered Doña Lambra is burned at the stake.

The presence of two strong-willed women-bent on vengeance, Lambra and Sancha, whose actions in various ways inform the narrative, is strongly reminiscent of the *Nibelungenlied*. The story of the legendary Mudarra, whose sole raison d'être is to take vengeance in the name of his aged father and his murdered half brothers, also finds echoes in Germanic heroic narrative. Such features would perhaps seem to reinforce R. Menéndez Pidal's arguments in favor of the Spanish epic's ultimately Germanic origins in Visigothic heroic poetry. K. Wais has pointed out further parallels between the Spanish poem and the *Nibelungenlied,* but his suggestions are not conclusive and have not been accepted by Spanish critics. Menéndez Pidal concludes: "I cannot agree with Wais's abundant parallels . . ., in passages having distant and inexact resemblances, [which] are insufficient for establishing . . . genetic relationships . . ., but rather point to a simi-

lar atmosphere shared by the two legends: women's hatred, offenses, vengeance, the faithful tutor, etc." (Menéndez Pidal 1992:484, n. 69).

[SGA]

Bibliography

Menéndez Pidal, Ramón. *La leyenda de los infantes de Lara.* 3rd ed. Madrid: Espasa-Calpe, 1971.

———. *La épica medieval española.* Vol. 1, edited by Diego Catalán and María del Mar Bustos. Madrid: Espasa-Calpe, 1992.

Wais, Kurt. *Frühe Epik Westeuropas und die Vorgeschichte des Nibelungenliedes.* Vol. 1. Tübingen: Niemeyer, 1953.

CANTAR DEL CERCO DE ZAMORA (The Siege of Zamora), a lost medieval Spanish epic poem, ultimately reflecting historical events of the late eleventh century, known principally through thirteenth- and fourteenth-century prosifications. The story is as follows: On his deathbed Ferdinand I of Castile and León (1016?–1065) divides his kingdom between his three sons, Sancho, Alfonso, and García, and wills the city of Zamora to his daughter, Urraca. Sancho, who becomes king of Castile, refuses to honor his father's testament, seizes his brothers' lands, and lays siege to Zamora. A Zamoran traitor, Vellido Dolfos, pretends to flee from the town, ingratiates himself with the Castilian king, and feigning that he can show him a secret gate giving access to the city, lures Sancho into the no-man's-land between the Castilian lines and the city wall, and stabs him through the back with a spear. Pointing out various similarities between the circumstances of Sancho's death and the murder of Siegfried in the *Nibelungenlied,* E. von Richthofen suggests the possibility of some genetic relationship between the two poems: "Previous warning, blind confidence, departure on horseback, rest by a river, murder with a spear, which the traitor thrusts through the back of his unsuspecting victim" (von Richthofen 1944:81; 1954:131). Even in combination, such commonplace details offer an insufficient basis upon which to relate two otherwise completely different narratives. Von Richthofen's suggestion has not been received favorably by Hispanomedievalists.

[SGA]

Bibliography

Reig, Carola. *El Cantar de Sancho II y cerco de Zamora.* Madrid: Consejo Superior de Investigaciones Científicas, 1947.

Richthofen, Erich von. *Studien zur romanischen Heldensagen des Mittelalters.* Halle: Niemeyer, 1944.

_____. *Estudios épicos medievales.* Madrid: Gredos, 1954.

CHRONICA HUNGARORUM, a history of the Hungarian people by Johannes de Thurocz, (Janos Thuroczy), printed in 1488. Johannes, a clerk and judge in Buda, who compiled his work from a number of earlier chronicles, marks the end and culmination of medieval Hungarian historiography. In the first part of the chronicles he gave final and authoritative form to the false identification of Scyths, Huns, and Magyars as being one and the same people that has dominated Hungarian historiography up to modern times. As the progenitors of the Hungarians, the Huns appear in a very favorable light. Attila in particular is a very positive figure, a view that prevails in Hungary to this day. The material in the *Chronica Hungarorum* that relates to the *Nibelungenlied* differs in detail from the western tradition. In the chronicles Attila/Ethele dies at his wedding to a Bactrian princess named Mycolth. One of his other wives is Kremheylch, a Bavarian princess whose son is Aladarius. After Attila's death the disloyal Germanic princes at the Hunnish court, spurred on by Detricus de Verona, a former foe but later counselor of Attila's, rally round Aladarius in the fight for the succession. (The "ch" in the name Kremheylch may suggest cognation with the name (H)ildico in Jordanes's history of the Goths as well as with Helche in the *Nibelungenlied.*)

[WLH]

Bibliography

Johannes de Thurocz. *Chronica Hungarorum,* edited by Elisabeth Galanti and Julius Kristo. Vol 1 of *Textus.* Budapest: Akademiai Kiado, 1985.

DARMSTÄDTER AVENTIURENVERZEICHNIS (Darmstadt Index of *Âventiuren*), manuscript 3249, a single vellum leaf, located in the Hessen State and University Library in Darmstadt (Hessische Landes- und Hochschulbibliothek). Staub and Sänger correct a previous dating and site it in the middle or second half of the fourteenth century. This *Nibelungenlied* manuscript, categorized as manuscript **m,** disappeared prior to 1540. The leaf contains a list of the first twenty-eight *âventiure* headings and is from a version of the *Nibelungenlied* that remains otherwise unattested. This version followed the known plot of the epic with a few deviations. In the first *âventiure* the tale of Siegfried's battle against the dragon and his acquisition of the hoard occurs before Siegfried's departure for Worms. In the seventh to the ninth *âventiure* Gunther's bridal quest is interrupted by the tale of Kriemhild's abduction by a dragon and rescue by Siegfried. This material is also found in the *Lied vom Hürnen Seyfrid.* Strangely the name Kriemhild is used three times where one would expect Brünhild's name to appear. Parallel occurrences of this transfer of names are found in manuscripts **a** and **n.** Possible connections between the manuscripts **m, a, b,** and **n** remain in need of examination.

The importance of this version does not lie solely in the history of the material, but rather in the issue of how the structure and narrative style of a text change when a new element is incorporated into an organic whole. From the standpoint of the high medieval epic, the tales of the young Siegfried with which we are acquainted through the *Lied vom Hürnen Seyfrid* constitute new and foreign elements. The version found in **m** is a result of a symbiosis of two separate narrative traditions: on the one hand, the epic, and on the other, the continued oral poem.

[PG]

Bibliography

Bartsch, Karl. *Der Nibelunge Not.* Vol. 1. 1870. Reprint, Hildesheim: Olms, 1966, pp. XXV–XXVIII.

Batts, Michael S. *Das Nibelungenlied: Paralleldruck der Handschriften A, B und C nebst Lesarten der übrigen Handschriften.* Tübingen: Niemeyer, 1971, pp. 799–800.

de Boor, Helmut. "Die Bearbeitung m des Nibelungenliedes." *PBB* (Tübingen) 81 (1959): 176–178.

Göhler, Peter. "Bemerkungen zur Überlieferung des Nibelungenliedes." In *3. Pöchlarner Heldenliedgespräch. Die Rezeption des Nibelungenliedes,* edited by Klaus Zatloukal. Philologica Germanica 16. Vienna: Fassbaender, 1995, pp. 67–69.

Hennig, Ursula. "Zu den Handschriftenverhältnissen in der *liet*-Fassung des Nibelungenliedes." *PBB* (Tübingen) 94 (1972): 117–120.

Staub, Hans, and Thomas Sänger, eds. *Deutsche und niederländische Handschriften: Mit Ausnahme der Gebethandschriften.* Handschriften der Hessischen Landes- und Hochschulbibliothek Darmstadt 6. Wiesbaden: Harrassowitz, 1991.

Weigand, Friedrich Ludwig Karl. "Zu den Nibelungen: Bruchstück des Verzeichnisses der Aventiuren aus einer Handschrift der Nibelunge." *ZfdA* 10 (1856): 142–146.

DAUREL ET BETON and BEUVE DE HANTONE,

two epic poems. *Daurel,* in Old Provençal, and *Beuve,* in Norman and Continental French, embody the wild boar hunt motif leading up to a protagonist's murder by a treacherous enemy, thus suggesting a possible relationship to Siegfried's death at the hands of Hagen. In *Daurel* it is the protagonist's lord, Bove, who dies, while in *Beuve,* it is the young hero's aged father, Count Guy. *Daurel* and *Beuve* are certainly genetically related, though at numerous points the narratives differ radically. The definite chronology of the works also remains in question. *Daurel* may date from as early as 1130, while the earliest preserved Old French forms of *Beuve,* which later spread all over Europe, seem to date from after 1200. Building on earlier work by Andreas Heusler, Bumke and Schröder study the *Eberjagd* (boar hunt) scenes rigorously and in meticulous detail. Bumke brings in an additional parallel from Apuleus's *Golden Ass* and identifies seven narrative stages in the various accounts that would suggest a common origin. Schröder proposes a complex stemma. But we may ask, are *Daurel* and *Beuve* somehow related to the *Nibelungenlied?* Andersson (pp. 209–212) has reviewed previous scholarship and remains unconvinced of any relationship. In traditional and at least partially oral literature problems of chronology and of the exact relationship of whatever texts may have been preserved put us on notably treacherous ground. An alternate possibility also suggests itself. Wild boar and stag were the most popular of medieval game animals and hunting them was a commonplace activity. Bowman (pp. 55–58) has shown that the motif of the protagonist's murder during a boar (or stag) hunt can be found in no fewer than six *chansons de geste* (including *Daurel* and *Beuve*).

From the perspective of the Parry-Lord theory of formulaic composition, the *Eberjagd* scenes emerge as examples of a migratory formulaic theme (Lord, p. 68), thus obviating the need to relate the romance poems directly to the *Nibelungenlied,* beyond the three epics' sharing in the common poetic rhetoric of medieval minstrelsy.

[SGA]

Bibliography

Andersson, Theodore M. *The Legend of Brynhild.* Ithaca: Cornell University Press, 1980.

Bowman, Russell K. *The Connections of the "Geste des Loherains" with other Other French Epics and Medieval Genres.* New York: Bowman, 1940.

Bumke, Joachim. "Die Eberjagd im *Daurel* und in der Nibelungendichtung." *GRM* 41 (1960): 105–111.

Kimmel, Arthur S., ed. *Daurel et Beton.* Chapel Hill: University of North Carolina Press, 1971.

Lord, Albert B. *The Singer of Tales.* Cambridge: Harvard University Press, 1964.

Schröder, Franz Rolf. "Sigfrids Tod." *GRM* 41 (1960): 111–122.

Stimming, Albert, ed. *Der anglonormanische Boeve de Haumtone.* Halle: Niemeyer, 1899.

———. *Der festländische Bueve de Hantone.* 5 vols. Dresden: Niemeyer, 1911–1920.

FINNSBURG LAY, the tale of a battle between Danes and Frisians at Finn's hall. It exists in two parts. The first is a fragment of a manuscript from the collection of Sir Robert Bruce Cotton, which was lost in the disastrous fire of 1731 in London that destroyed the building in which the collection was housed and damaged a number of Anglo-Saxon manuscripts, including that of *Beowulf.* The current text is based on the eighteenth-century transcription by George Hickes, the dependability of which is somewhat questionable. The original manuscript, like the Old English *Beowulf* manuscript, probably dated to the late tenth century; composition is usually assigned to the eighth century. The second part of the lay is found as a digression within the text of *Beowulf* (lines 1063–1159).

In the fragment, Hnaef and his fellow Danes are apparently guests of Finn, an East Frisian king who has married Hnaef's sister Hildeburh. For unknown reasons Finn has attacked the Danes by night, and there the fragment picks up with a five-day battle in which many warriors on both sides are killed.

When the *Beowulf* digression begins, Hnaef has already been killed. The remaining Danes, led by Hengest, are forced to swear oaths of peace with Finn. The son of Finn and Hildeburh (unnamed), also killed in the fight, is burned on the same funeral pyre as his uncle Hnaef. After spending the winter with Finn, Hengest's duty to avenge his fallen comrades outweighs any oaths he has sworn to Finn; he therefore leads the Danes in an attack in which Finn is killed. The Danes then depart and take Hildeburh back to Denmark. Due to the fragmentary nature of the lay, a number of questions cannot be answered: Why were the Danes invited to Finnsburg? What, precisely, is the role of Hildeburh in her kinsmen's deaths? (She mourns the fallen and goes home with Hengest, and therefore seems to be on good terms with her family.) Was the hall set on fire? How did the son of Finn and Hildeburh die? On whose side did he fight?

The *Finnsburg Lay* parallels the story of the fall of the Nibelungs and related stories of a foreign wife whose relatives are invited to her new home and then attacked and killed. One more particular similarity is seen at the fragment's opening, where Hnaef and another man, while standing guard, see the glint of enemy helmets and arms in the moonlight (thirtieth *âventiure* of the *Nibelungenlied*, particularly 1837, where Hagen and Volker spot the enemy's approach). Other shared elements include Hnaef's having sixty men (six hundred survive the burning of the hall in the *Nibelungenlied*), a remnant that survive the fight (seven Britons survive in *Branwen Daughter of Llyr*); and the now-widowed sister who returns home with survivors (also in *Branwen*). The *Finnsburg Lay* also mentions a certain Frisian named Gudere (Gunther/Gunnar) and a warrior Sigeferd (Siegfrid/Sigurd), here a member of a Danish tribe.

Kurt Wais counted the *Finnsburg Lay* among those tales making up a "middle layer" in his reconstruction of the growth of the Nibelung legend. In this "layer" are found certain elements which relate to a hypothetical "Krimhild Legend" about a young woman who is married into a foreign family, an arrangement which leads to

strife. He cited as important the fact that Finn is killed in revenge for Hnaef's death, just as Atli is killed by Hogni's son in the *Volsunga saga*. He also compared the desire of Garulf the Frisian to fight the Danes (Hnaef and companion) who stand guard by night with Iring's desire to go against Hagen in the *Nibelungenlied,* despite the efforts of others to dissuade them (Gudere plays that role in the *Lay*). Wais postulated as well that Sigeferd was the son of Finn and Hildeburh, who fought alongside his uncle against his father.

Despite its incomplete state, a good case can be made that the events described in the *Finnsburg Lay* at the very least reflect a transposition of the story of the fall of the Burgundians onto a Frisian or Danish tale of a wife's kinsmen betrayed by her in-laws.

[JKW]

Bibliography

Klaeber, Friedrich, ed. *Beowulf and the Fight at Finns-burg.* Lexington, MA: Heath, 1950.

Wais, Kurt. *Frühe Epik Westeuropas und die Vorge-schichte des Nibelungenliedes.* Tübingen: Niemeyer, 1953.

HELDENBUCH-PROSA. *Heldenbücher* (literally *books of heroes*) is the term used to designate collections of Middle High German heroic epics in manuscript or printed form. Usually they contain tales of Dietrich (Theoderich) and the double epic *Ortnit/Wolfdietrich*. The *Nibelungenlied* is only found in Lienhart Scheubel's *Heldenbuch* of the late fifteenth century (manuscript **k**). However, the transmission complex of the so-called *Straßburger Heldenbuch,* to which two Straßburg manuscripts (from 1476 and ca. 1480) and six printed versions (from 1479 to 1590) belong, contains a text that is considered one of the most important attestations of the Nibelungen tale: the so-called *Heldenbuch-Prosa.* Two versions are extant, the manuscript version in the *Heldenbuch des Diebolt von Hanowe* (ca. 1480) and the printed version in the six printed editions of the *Heldenbuch* as well as in excerpts contained in two sixteenth-century printed editions of the Dietrich epics. The manuscript version is conceived as a preface, the printed version as an appendix (which is why in older research the text is either called "preface" or "appendix to the Heldenbuch"). The text provides a brief survey in prose form of the most important figures and events of German medieval heroic poetry. They are presented in interlocking cycles as a quasi-historical depiction of a former heroic age, which starts with the creation of the heroes and ends with their downfall. The Nibelungen story is built into the tale of Dietrich von Bern. It is reported that Siegfried was slain by Dietrich during the fighting in the rose garden at Worms. (In earlier Dietrich epics "Rosengarten" is the geographical name of an Alpine massif in South Tyrol.) This act brought Kriemhild's hatred upon Dietrich and his followers, and she marries Etzel in order to avail herself of the possibility of destroying them. For this purpose she invites all the heroes to Etzel's court with treacherous intent and asks Hagen to sow discord among the guests. Hagen declares this inconsistent with his honor but that he would do his best if another started the fighting. Then Kriemhild asks her ten-year-old son to strike Hagen in the face. The boy obeys and Hagen warns him that if the boy were to do it again he would not tolerate it. Kriemhild is happy about this and lets the boy strike Hagen another time, to which Hagen says: "You did not do this of your own volition" ("von dir selber") and chops the child's head off. An uproar arises and the heroes massacre each other. Old Hildebrand escapes with a serious injury and informs Dietrich von Bern, who is in another building. Dietrich rushes to the place of action, happens upon two of Kriemhild's brothers, wrestles them to the ground, and leaves them there fettered. Kriemhild finds them and chops their heads off. Dietrich, having witnessed Kriemhild's brutality, cuts her in half. Then he rides off with Hildebrand. Outside Dietrich's city, Bern, new fights arise, in the course of which Kriemhild's brother Gunther kills old Hildebrand (only in the printed version) and finally all remaining heroes meet their deaths. Only Dietrich remains and is led out of this world by a dwarf.

Clearly the depiction offers a mixture of old story material and ad hoc invention. The provocation of Hagen by Etzel's son (urged on by his mother) is certainly old, as is the killing of her two brothers and also Dietrich's graphic dispensing of Kriemhild. All these features are also found in the *Þiðreks saga,* which the author of the *Heldenbuch-Prosa* can not possibly have known. Of special interest is the provocation scene, which matches the one in the *Þiðreks saga* even down to the words in Hagen's speech ("you have not done this of your own volition") in the *Heldenbuch-Prosa.* It can be determined that the scene was contained in an earlier version of the *Nibelungenlied* and was known to its author. It is this version from which the *Nibelungenlied* strophe 1912 (Bartsch/de Boor edition) must derive, where the text says that Kriemhild sent for her son because the battle she desired could not have been brought about in any other way. In the context of the *Nibelungenlied* the statement makes no sense because there the fighting has already begun. This leads to a general assumption that the features shared by the *Þiðreks saga* and the *Heldenbuch-Prosa,* as opposed to the *Nibelungenlied,* belong to an older version of the downfall of the Burgundians, one that was handed down in Germany into the late Middle Ages alongside that in the *Nibelungenlied.* That can only have happened orally, and thus the *Heldenbuch-Prosa* is an important piece of evidence for the existence of an oral tradition that took place after and during the time of the transcription of the *Nibelungenlied.*

[JH]

Bibliography

Heinzle, Joachim, ed. *Heldenbuch: Nach dem ältesten Druck in Abbildung.* Vol. 1: *Abbildungsband;* Vol. 2: *Kommentarband.* Litterae 75/I,II. Göppingen: Kümmerle, 1981; 1987.

Kofler, Walter. *Das Strassburger Heldenbuch. Rekonstruktion der Textfassung des Diebolt van Hanowe.* 2 vols. Göppingen: Kümmerle, 1999.

JAUFRE, a 10,956-verse Arthurian romance. *Jaufre* was composed in Spain (Aragon) in Old Provençal (circa 1169–1170) by two consecutive authors. According to the romance, the youthful nobleman Jaufre, seeking knighthood, arrives at Arthur's court at the moment when a tyrannical knight, Taulat de Rogimon, rides fully armed into the hall, kills a courtier, and insults Arthur and his queen. Jaufre begs royal permission to pursue Taulat and avenge the insult. Arthur knights Jaufre, who then departs on his quest, experiencing diverse adventures and eventually defeating and capturing Taulat. During his wanderings Jaufre arrives at the impregnable castle of Monbrun, ruled by the autocratic, strong-minded, willful, young noblewoman, Brunesen, whom, after many more adventures, Jaufre eventually marries, to the detriment of his knightly calling. Fleischman identifies a parodic subtext in the seemingly heroic narrative. Kurt Wais, in his extensive article that touches on many other problems, seeks to compare and relate Brünhild and Brunesen. Wais's Germanic etymology, through a hypothetical intermediate *Brunissent,* is convincing and is suggestive, too, of the imperious girl's iron will: compare Gothic *brunjo* with OHG *brunja* (coat of mail), which became the German *Brünne* and the English *byrnie;* and Gothic *swinths* with MHG *swint* (strong), which became the German *gesund* and the English *sound.* Förstemann even lists this exact combination in the term *Prunswid* (also Piel and Kremer 50, 360). There are significant similarities between Brunesen and Brünhild. Both are strong-willed and implacable, both live in fortified strongholds, and both command numerous warlike retainers. But there are also radical differences. Unlike Brünhild, Brunesen is not carried off under false pretenses to live in frustrated obscurity. On the contrary, her destiny is quite the opposite: through her marriage to Jaufre, the young warrior is tamed, abandons his heroic path, and settles into a domestic situation dominated by the strong-willed girl. Wais's work is eminently learned and the juxtaposition of Brünhild and Brunesen is certainly suggestive, but aside from the Provençal name's Germanic origin, other parallels could well be coincidental.

[SGA]

Bibliography

Fleischman, Suzanne. "*Jaufre* or Chivalry Askew." *Viator* 12 (1981): 101–129.

Förstemann, Ernst. *Altdeutsches Namenbuch.* Vol. 1. 2nd ed. Bonn: Hanstein, 1900.

Gómez Redondo, Fernando, trans. *Jaufré.* Madrid: Gredos, 1996.

Lavaud, René, and René Nelli, eds. and trans. *Les troubadours.* 2 vols. Bruges: Desclée de Brouwer, 1960/1966.

Piel, Joseph M., and Dieter Kramer. *Hispano-gotisches Namenbuch.* Heidelberg: Winter, 1976.

Wais, Kurt. "Brunissen im *Jaufre* und die Tradition Brünhild/Brunehout." In *Studia Occitania,* 2 vols., edited by Hans-Erich Keller et al. Kalamazoo, MI: Medieval Institute, 1986, pp. 211–232.

LEX (LEGES) BURGUNDIONUM, the codification of Burgundian laws made around 516 by King Gundobad (474–516), son of Gundioch I, a relative of the Gothic king Athanaric, and brother of Gundomar, Godigisel and Chilperic. The introduction refers to several royal ancestors including Gibica, Gundomar, Gislahari, and Gundahari, three of these providing names for the *Nibelungenlied.*

[BOM]

Bibliography

Beyerle, Franz, ed. *Leges Burgundionum.* In *Germanenrechte.* Texte und Übersetzungen 10. Weimar: Böhlau, 1936.

RODRIGO DÍAZ DE VIVAR (EL CID ca. 1043–1099). Renowned Castilian knight, a vassal of King Alphonse VI, whom he served loyally in the conquest of Toledo (1085) and later of Moslem Valencia (1094–1102). In his monographic study of Rüdiger von Bechelaren, Jochen Splett weighs the problem of a putative connection between the Spanish national hero (and central character of the epic *Cantar de Mio Cid,* died ca. 1140) and the *Nibelungenlied*'s Rüdiger, on the basis of various similarities first pointed out by B. Q. Morgan. Splett decides affirmatively. He is convinced it may be possible that Rodrigo Díaz could have served as a model or a prototype for Rüdiger. Their names are similar, both heroes are exiles, both fight in the service of a foreign king, both are scrupulously loyal vassals. There are also other apparent similarities, though any and all of these parallels hardly seem sufficiently distinctive to preclude the alternate possibility that they may be polygenetic and purely coincidental. That the Cid fought in Muslim Spain, for instance, just as Rüdiger had fought in Arabia (according to *Biterolf*), can hardly be considered conclusive evidence, nor is the presence of Spanish and Arabian elements and reminiscences any great novelty in medieval Germano-Latin or German literature (e.g., *Ruodlieb, Kudrun, Parzival,* and *Willehalm*). On the Romanist side, Menéndez Pidal did not look unfavorably on the possibility of a Rodrigo-Rüdiger correlation, perhaps through the mediation of German-speaking minstrels visiting the tomb of St. James in Galicia (II, 618, n. 2). Leo Spitzer, by contrast, preferred to attribute the heroes' convergence to aesthetic or poetic motivations: "The Nibelung poet had to contrast the plotters of treachery and reprisal with a uniquely worthy personage, a noble exile, a paragon of chivalric virtues—a type widely known in medieval Europe" (657). In sum, though the similarities between Rodrigo and Rüdiger are highly suggestive, their direct relationship has not been definitively demonstrated and alternative theories concerning Rüdiger's enigmatic origins abound in critical literature.

[SGA]

Bibliography

Ehrismann, Otfrid. *Nibelungenlied: Epoche, Werk, Wirkung.* Munich: Beck, 1987.

Hamilton, Rita, and Janet Perry, trans. *The Poem of the Cid.* New York: Penguin, 1984.

Menéndez Pidal, Ramón. *La España del Cid.* 4th ed. 2 vols. Madrid: Espasa-Calpe, 1947.

Montaner, Alberto. *Cantar de Mio Cid.* Barcelona: "Crítica," 1993.

Morgan, B. Q. "Rüdiger." *PBB* 37 (1912): 325–336.

Spitzer, Leo. *Romanische Literaturstudien.* Tübingen: Niemeyer, 1959.

Splett, Jochen. *Rüdiger von Bechelaren.* Heidelberg: Winter, 1968.

Wunderlich, Werner, and Ulrich Müller, eds. "*Waz sider da geschach.*": *American-German Studies on the Nibelungenlied.* Göppingen: Kümmerle, 1992.

THOUSAND AND ONE NIGHTS. This vast, multisecular compilation of medieval and postmedieval Arabic narratives, *Alf laila wa-laila,* first documented in a later ninth-century fragment, continued to expand its variegated contents well into the nineteenth century. In the introduction to his 1997 translation, the Spanish Arabist Juan Vernet briefly compares the complex story of Jawdar ben Umar to the legend of the Nibelungen hoard. The Arabic story, of Egyptian origin, involves a problematic search for the fabulous treasure of King Samardal, which is guarded by multiple enchantments and hidden behind seven doors in a golden-doored chamber at the bottom of a river. The key to overcoming these intricate obstacles is a magic, but cursed ring, destined to bring about the death of all who seek the treasure, including Jawar himself and his envious brothers, Sālim and Salīm, who quarrel over who will possess the riches and the power they bestow. After the murderous brothers poison the generous, forgiving Jawdar, Sālim has Salīm killed and then insists on marrying Āsīya, Jawdar's heroic widow, who apparently accedes to Sālim's wishes, but then manages to poison him and to break the enchanted ring, thus ending its fatal spell. Similarities between the Jawdar story and the Nibelung legend are so distant and so topical and the narratives' cultural contexts are so radically different and so widely separated in time and space that our initial reaction is to discount any relationship out of hand. All the same, José Pedrosa's bold comparative research on all legends (in a multilingual and multicultural perspective comprising peoples of all six inhabited continents) suggests the possibility of a significant correlation at an archetypal level. Both stories embody Aarne-Thompson tale-type 763, The Fatal Treasure, of which Pedrosa has now uncovered and analyzed a repertoire of over 150 narratives, both traditional and learned, including Chaucer's *Pardoner's Tale,* B. Traven's *Treasure of the Sierra Madre,* and Faulkner's *The Hamlet.*

[SGA]

Bibliography

Aarne, Antti. *Verzeichnis der Märchentypen.* English. *The types of the folktale: a classification and bibliography: Antti Aarne's Verzeichnis der Märchentypen. (F F Communications 3).* Translated and enlarged by Stith Thompson. 2nd revised edition. Helsinki: Suomalainen Tiedeakatemia, Academia Scientarum Fennica, 1981.

Abbott, Nabia. "A Ninth-Century Fragment of the 'Thousand Nights.'" *Journal of Near Eastern Studies,* 8 (1949), 129–164.

Littmann, Enno. *Tausendundeine Nacht in der arabischen Literatur.* Tübingen: Mohr, 1923.

Payne, John, trans. *The Book of the Thousand Nights and One Night.* 9 vols. London: [privately printed], 1884.

Pedrosa, José Manuel. "¿Existe el hipercuento?: Chaucer, una leyenda andaluza y la historia de *El tesoro fatal* (AT 763)." *Revista de Poética Medieval,* 2 (1998), 195–223.

Schröder, Werner. *Nibelungenlied-Studien.* Stuttgart: Metzler, 1968, pp. 157–184.

Vernet, Juan, trans. *Las mil y una noches.* 2 vols. Barcelona: Planeta, 1997.

PART V

Scholarship

"ÄLTERE NIBELUNGENÔT" (Elder Nibelungenôt) is the designation given by Andreas Heusler to a source, the existence of which he inferred, for the second part of the *Nibelungenlied.* Heusler proposed that the "Elder Nibelungenôt" was a written version of the history of the downfall of the Burgundians that was authored by a learned minstrel at the behest of Duke Heinrich II Jasomirgott of Austria (1141–1177) sometime in the 1160s. If this source truly existed, this minstrel author would have been a pioneer in two respects. First, he would have been the first to have put the oral tradition (in Heusler's terms, lay tradition) of the Nibelungen matter into writing and in epic form. Second, for this epic he would have used the long-line strophe that had just recently been introduced by the twelfth-century lyric poet, Der von Kürenberg. With that he would not only have discovered the authentic form for the epic composition of the Nibelungen matter, but also would have established the tradition of the strophic epic in Middle High German literature. Heusler assumed that the "Elder Nibelungenôt" was also used in the Norwegian *Þiðreks saga* from the middle of the thirteenth century, by means of a Low German mediation, as well as in a Norwegian ballad that was lost but could be inferred from later texts, especially the Danish ballad "Kremold's Rache." Through a comparative analysis of these texts as well as the *Heldenbuchprosa* and the Eddic tradition, Heusler reconstructed the hypothetical work in detail and impressively described the artistic achievement of the poet. Apart from the introduction of the new strophic form, he also saw this achievement as the first example of a new narrative technique, one that transformed the taut, episodic style of the supposed lay source into an embellished description of events, changing "balladic conciseness" into "epic breadth." According to Heusler, this had been effected not only by textual expansion and more detailed description, but also by means of the creation of new characters and scenes, especially the new heroic roles of Volker, Iring, and Rüdiger, all associated with spectacular scenes. Significant, too, were the portrayals of Gernot, Giselher, and Hildebrand. The new heroic roles, according to Heusler, were not original ideas from the epic poet, but were also influenced by other narrative traditions, including Rüdiger, from what then was an as-yet-to-be discovered contemporary tale of Dietrich von Bern (Theoderich the Great); and Iring, from the tribal history of the Thuringians. In the figure of Rüdiger, according to Heusler, the epic writer had, like the author of the hypothetical Dietrich epic, commemorated his patron, the Austrian duke.

The poet of the *Nibelungenlied,* according to Heusler, then combined the "Elder Nibelungenôt" with the story of Siegfried's death, which he retold in the strophic form of the "Elder Nibelungenôt." In particular this poet had (a) matched the two epic narrative traditions as well as possible in content and length; (b) modernized the sense of courtly culture in the narrative of the "Elder Nibelungenôt;" (c) refined the language and smoothed out the meter of the texts, while at the same time preserving some archaic elements in order not to totally extinguish the "handwriting" of the revered master of the "Elder Nibelungenôt"; and (d) lengthened the story through the introduction of new characters and scenes and through in-depth psychological portrayals of the characters. Heusler's hypothesis was accepted almost unanimously by scholars of his day. The "Elder Nibelungenôt" has long been treated as a truly historical text, and scholars differed in their opinions solely about details like the length of the work, which Heusler postulated at 400 strophes, and the absence or presence of certain elements of the action in the text or its source. Today this kind of optimism in questions of reconstruction is shared by very few, mainly by the Nordist scholar Theodore M. Andersson, who in a series of important studies has tried to reestablish Heusler's position). To be sure, now as before one is aware of the possibility that the *Nibelungenlied,* in addition to oral sources, the existence of which is undisputed, had at least one, if not several, preliminary textual epic versions. However, there is no longer much speculation about their exact content. What scholars now consider important and firmly established is that the use of the Nibelungen strophe, and along with it the development of the specific style of the *Nibelungenlied,* can be attributed to lost Nibelungen epics of the second half of the twelfth century and that the author of the *Nibelungenlied* utilized individual strophes from these epics, and probably even whole sequences of strophes, in a more or less unchanged form. Scholars exercise more caution when dealing with the question of the sources of the *Þiðreks saga.* It is assumed that its author, through whatever mediation, also had access to the *Ältere Nibelungenôt,* but he is further presumed to have used the *Nibelungenlied* itself. As a result the possibilities of reconstructing textual forerunners of the *Nibelungenlied* are significantly hampered.

[JH]

Bibliography

Andersson, Theodore M. *A Preface to the Nibelungenlied.* Stanford: Stanford University Press, 1987, pp. 118ff, 210ff.

Heinzle, Joachim. *Das Nibelungenlied: Eine Einführung.* 2nd ed. Fischertaschenbuch 11843. Frankfurt a. M.: Fischer, 1996, pp. 31ff.

Heusler, Andreas. *Nibelungensage und Nibelungenlied: Die Stoffgeschichte des deutschen Heldenepos.* 1921. Reprint, 6th edition. Dortmund: Ruhfus, 1965, pp. 37ff.

Hoffmann, Werner. *Das Nibelungenlied.* 6th ed. Sammlung Metzler 7. Stuttgart: Metzler, 1992, pp. 63–64.

ANONYMITY. Neither the extant manuscripts of the *Nibelungenlied* nor contemporary poets quoting it mention the name of an author, in contradistinction to poets of courtly romances who mention their names or refer to each other in their works regularly. In the beginning of the nineteenth century, the anonymity of the *Nibelungenlied* was explained to be a result of the fact that the oldest extant text was not created as a whole by an individual poet, but rather that it was a collection of originally separate poems emanating from the anonymous *Volksgeist* (the collective mind of the nation) and put together by a redactor in the early thirteenth century. In the beginning of the twentieth century this hypothesis was replaced by another, which advances the theory that the poet was a member of the lowest class among the nobility, a minstrel, who did not dare reveal his name. Half a century later, a new hypothesis was suggested, according to which poets who relate the history of a nation do not consider themselves to be the creators of the stories they tell but merely the transmitters. This would explain why they never mention their names. Another possible explanation of the poet's anonymity is the assumption that the *Nibelungenlied* was transmitted orally and that the one who wrote it down for the first time was not considered to be the poet but just a scribe.

[NV]

Bibliography

Fromm, Hans. "Der oder die Dichter des Nibelungenliedes?" In *Colloquio italo-germanico sul tema: I Nibelunghi.* Rome: Accademia Nazionale dei Lincei (Atti dei Convegni Lincei 1), 1974, pp. 63–74.

Höfler, Otto. "Die Anonymität des Nibelungenliedes." *DVjs* 29 (1955): 167–213.

AUDIENCE INVOLVEMENT.

Although scholars may debate the authorship of the *Nibelungenlied,* there remains little doubt that the poet targeted a courtly audience in his work. In the verses that frame the poem (particularly in manuscript **C**), the poet addresses this audience directly (1,4 and 2379,1). He also includes himself in this audience, using the inclusive "uns" (1,1) and "wir" (1655,1). These narrative devices assume involvement on the part of the audience, although the *Nibelungenlied* poet maintains a much more discreet distance from his audience than his contemporaries Hartmann and Wolfram. For example, the poet tantalizes the audience's imagination by posing the question about a possible touching of hands between Siegfried and Kriemhild and then refusing to answer (294,1–2) whether or not it occurred. Later he speaks to the audience by insisting on the truth of his description of the Burgundians' arrival in Bechelaren on their fatal journey to Etzel's court (1654,4).

Performed in a social setting, like most courtly literature, the *Nibelungenlied* not only supplied entertainment but also functioned as a vehicle for the dissemination of certain cultural values to its courtly audience. The poet's asides, however infrequent, compel his audience to interact with the text and to follow and complete his thoughts. This form of interaction between recipient and text illustrates how the poem directed the dissemination of values. Above all the idealized portrayals of character-types in the stylized setting of courtly epic provide an opportunity for the poet to communicate a certain code of behavior for the audience, offering noblemen and noblewomen desirable role models to emulate. The negative portrayals of Kriemhild and Brünhild, for instance, show the audience that both have ultimately behaved in ways unbecoming to a woman.

[ASH]

Bibliography

Frakes, Jerold C. *Brides and Doom: Gender, Property, and Power in Medieval German Women's Epic.* Philadelphia: University of Pennsylvania Press, 1994.

Jaeger, C. Stephen. "The Nibelungen Poet and the Clerical Rebellion against Courtesy." In *Spectrum Medii Aevi: Essays in Early German Literature in Honor of George Fenwick Jones,* edited by William C. McDonald. Göppingen: Kümmerle, 1983, pp. 177–207.

Liebertz-Grün, Ursula. "On the Socialization of German Noblewomen 1150–1450." *Monatshefte* 82 (1990): 17–37.

AUTHORSHIP.

The extant manuscripts of the *Nibelungenlied* do not contain the name of any author. To some degree, that is in keeping with the genre. Virtually the entire corpus of heroic poetry written in the vernacular remained anonymous into the thirteenth century. In the introductory strophe of the *Nibelungenlied,* as contained within manuscripts **A** and **C,** the narrator informs us that his source is an old story. To base a source on hearsay is a formulaic device that attests to the oral transmission and thus the basic truth of the story that is being told. In the narrator role in the introductory strophe, the Nibelungen author portrays himself as the transmitter of a narrative tradition. With this as his main task his individuality occupies a secondary role. Just as Virgil in his *Aeneid,* the Nibelungen poet is only a transmitter, an advocate, and a witness for what has been handed down, which he once again brings up for discussion. He is not the originator or its creator. Thus, both the aesthetic conception and literary elements of form allow us to assume that the *Nibelungenlied,* in the epic form in which it has been passed down to us, worked from the tradition of oral narrative and used it as a poetic idiom. This was most likely achieved by an individual person, probably in the service of a patron, when one considers the enormous costs involved in producing a medieval epic and writing it out by hand. Even when narrative tradition was written down, there did not arise any sort of authorial claim to a text as "the one and only" that was to be identified solely with a particular person. The various strains of the tradition demonstrate how diversely scribes wrote down the narrative work, which obviously was not seen as an untouchable work of art.

The epic is aimed at a public: "muget ir nu wunder hoeren sagen" (You will now hear wonderous stories told). In this manner the author introduces indirectly the role of the minstrel. It is also an indication that the epic exists in a more or less variable form of text that is occasioned by oral recitation, regardless of whether it is composed from memory or based on an available text. This variable form is likely because given different singers and different performance situations, we can assume that both improvisation and variation must have occurred within a narrative framework that remained constant. In this respect each of the singers who gave a performance in some way participated in authoring the story of the Nibelungen.

If there is any conclusion to be drawn from the controversial discussion that has raged for decades regarding the oral and written origins of the *Nibelungenlied* as well as its original text, the following point can be made with all probability vis-à-vis the matter of authorship. An individual poet undoubtedly combined elements from oral narrative tradition and one or more written transmissions to create the epic, which subsequently underwent several editing processes. Further, it is in the nature of the genre that the poet does not name himself. In manuscripts **A** and **B** we have the so-called "Nôt"-version, in manuscript **C** the so-called "Liet"-version, named after the last word in the two variations of an original text. Apart from the written tradition, certain influences were exerted on the entire complex of the Nibelungen tradition and its transformation process throughout the entire Middle Ages down to the time of Emperor Maximilian's *Heldenbuch,* influences which were based on the oral form of presentation and an oral narrative tradition that still exists.

There are indirect leads regarding the period of time when the author was at work on the epic. In Wolfram von Eschenbach's *Parzival* (VIII 420,26), Liddamus quotes the Burgundian kitchen master Rumold, who advises against the trip to the Huns and who remains in Worms as the Imperial Regent. Scholars have assumed that Wolfram composed this passage about 1204/1205 and at a time when he must have been familiar with the *Nibelungenlied* in its epic form, even if it is not possible to determine which one of the versions was available to him. The year 1213 has recently been assumed as the *terminus post quem,* because parallels are presumed between the downfall of the House of Andechs in the years 1208 to 1213 and the plot of the *Nibelungenlied.* Judging by the language of the *Nibelungenlied,* its author likely hailed from southeast Germany. The few traces of dialect that can be detected in the author's rhymes do not permit a more specific localization than the Bavarian-Austrian area. There are also strikingly accurate and detailed place references to this region, which can be found in the second part of the epic. The accuracy even exceeds the precision of topographic and geographic allusions in the first part of the work. Several smaller and clearly identifiable towns situated along the Danube, particularly between Donauwörth and Vienna, are cited by name. Above all, the site of Passau at the confluence of the Danube, Inn, and Ilz Rivers is described with notable accuracy.

Another connection with Passau occurs with the figure of Bishop Pilgrim. The *Klage* refers to him as the patron who commissioned the recording of the Nibelungs' fate. The historic Bishop Pilgrim (971–991) was a member of the Bavarian nobility, the Sigharding clan, among whom numerous Nibelungen names can be detected. Consequently, there is a theory that Pilgrim could have brought the Nibelungen saga along with him to Passau and had its Latin version composed by an unknown author among his followers either in the form of poetry or as a chronicle, and then later written down by a cleric called Konrad in order to associate his name with a narrative tradition. At the time that the composition of the Middle High German epic was assumed to have taken place, Wolfger von Erla was residing in Passau (1191–1204). He later served as Patriarch of Aquileia until his death in the year 1218. Wolfger was a promoter and patron of authors such as Walther von der Vogelweide and Thomasin von Zirklaere. It is thus quite possible that he might also have engaged someone from his circle at the bishopric court in Passau with the composition of the *Nibelungenlied.*

The unknown author was not content with simply regurgitating the old *maeren* (stories) and preserving what had been handed down. In the overall narrative composition of the epic, his own aesthetic achievement is to be found in the courtly and poetic medium of rhyming couplets and long verses. His literary creativity lies in the accentuation of substantive elements, such as the dramatic dialogues, the way in which he conveys mood and atmosphere in the various scenes, climaxes and changes that essentially make viewers out of listeners, the monologues, the delineation of specific characters in the plot, and the portrayal of contemporary chivalric and courtly forms of life. His own intellectual achievement is to be found in the manner in which he gives a contemporary meaning to the *mæren* that have been passed down by waxing critical about the idea of the heroic, the virtues and ideals of which, such as loyalty and honor, lost their validity against the backdrop of a contemporary crisis under the deteriorating Hohenstaufen leadership. Narrative incongruities and inconsistencies are not to be attributed to incompetency on the part of the author, but are instead relics of oral transmission and should be considered simply contradictions in epic narrating. They do not hold any significance for the inexorability and inevitable nature in which the plot unfolds.

The unknown author's knowledge of literary tradition is attested. Not only did he know the saga cycle that dealt with the story of Siegfried and Kriemhild, with Brünhild, and the demise of the Burgundians, and present all of this in an epic as a panoramic tour de force, he was also familiar with Hagen's youthful adventures as they are imparted in the Latin *Waltharilied,* a work that continues in the epic tradition of Virgil, as well as with feudal conflicts of loyalty as they are related with respect to Charlemagne's nephew Roland in the French chanson de geste *Renaut de Montauban.* It can only be speculated whether or not the anonymous poet had an archive or a library in Passau at his disposal.

It cannot be determined from the *Nibelungenlied* alone whether we are justified in attributing a marked Hohenstaufen prejudice to the author of the epic, or whether we can detect in him a poet with a decidedly critical awareness of the time in which he lived; someone who, during the reign of Philip of Swabia would caution that leadership that is not based on strength must, by necessity, falter. However, the *Nibelungenlied* author counters the overly idealistic image of the chivalrous world as it is found in both Arthurian romance or *Minnesang* with a set of norms and values that are highly problematic; namely the inexorable nature of an ideal of loyalty and heroic absoluteness that has its basis in abject sorrow.

There are also no compelling facts or arguments that will allow us to determine the class to which the author of the epic may have belonged. Previously, scholars had a romanticized idea of the author as a troubador, a minstrel, who even identified himself with Volker in the *Nibelungenlied.* They considered the possibility that he might have been a wandering poet, a knight, or even a town citizen. The predominant view held today is that he was a "cleric." This does not mean that he was necessarily a member of the clergy, but rather someone who was educated within the church, a person who had attended a monastery or a church school. He would have been an individual who could both read and write, a person who would have been introduced to the basic elements of the Latin tradition of education. If we search for the author at the court of Passau, then he could, in fact, have been employed in Wolfger's court chancellery as a notary, scribe, diplomat, or administrator.

Since the rediscovery of the *Nibelungenlied* in 1755, the nebulous situation with regard to the source of the work has repeatedly raised the question of who the enigmatic poet of this anonymously transcribed epic might have been. Der von Kürenberg, Bishop Pilgrim of Passau, Friedrich von Hausen, Der Marner, Heinrich von Traunstein, Bligger von Steinach, Rudolf von Ems, Heinrich von Ofterdingen, Sighard von Lorsch, Wirnt von Grafenberg, Wolfram von Eschenbach, Walther von der Vogelweide, Konrad von der Vogelweide, Konrad von Würzburg, Konrad von Fussesbrunnen, Konrad von Göttweig, Konrad von Russbach, and a Niedernburg nun have all been suggested as possible authors. But no historical person has, to date, been unequivocally identified as the author of the *Nibelungenlied.*

The final verses of the *Nibelungen Klage* contain the only lead to be found in the sources as to a possible identification of the author. The *Klage* provides a "truth certificate" for the demise of the Nibelungen, which is characteristic for heroic saga and heroic epic, namely, the claim that it is based on the report of an eyewitness. According to the information at the end of the *Klage,* Bishop Pilgrim gave his scribe, Master Konrad, the task of writing down in Latin the history of the Nibelungen in accordance with the eyewitness report of the Hunnish messenger, Swämmel. That the Latin version attributed to him is supposed to have been actually undertaken gives the later vernacular dissemination an aura of serious historiography. If one does not consider these references to be fictitious, then the Master Konrad to which the *Klage* refers was just the scribe and by no means the author of the *Nibelungenlied*.

[WW]

Bibliography

Curschmann, Michael. "'Nibelungenlied' und 'Klage.'" In vol. 6 of *Die deutsche Literatur: Verfasserlexikon*. 2nd ed., edited by Kurt Ruh et al. Berlin: de Gruyter, 1987, cols. 926–929.

Heinzle, Joachim. *Das Nibelungenlied: Eine Einführung*. Fischer Taschenbuch 11843. Frankfurt a. M. Fischer Taschenbuch Verlag, 1994, pp. 47ff., 77ff.

Hoffmann, Werner. *Das Nibelungenlied*. 6th ed. Sammlung Metzler 7. Stuttgart: Metzler, 1992, pp. 91–104.

Höfler, Otto. "Die Anonymität des Nibelungenliedes." *DVjs* 9 (1955): 167–213.

Mackensen, Lutz. *Die Nibelungen: Sage, Geschichte, ihr Lied und sein Dichter*. Stuttgart: Hauswedell, 1984, pp. 79–192.

Meves, Uwe. "Bischof Wolfger von Passau, sîn schriber, meister Kuonrât und die Nibelungenüberlieferung." *Montfort* 32 (3/4): 246–243.

Reichert, Hermann. "Autor und Erzähler im Nibelungenlied: Seine Mündlichkeit, Schriftlichkeit, Bildung, Trinkgewohnheiten, und sonstigen Charakteristika." In *Helden und Heldensage: Otto Gschwantler zum 60. Geburtstag*, edited by Hermann Reichert und Günter Zimmermann. Philologica Germanica 11. Vienna: Fassbaender, 1990, pp. 287–327.

Salvina-Plawen, Luitfried. "Zur Datierung des Nibelungenliedes: Bezüge zum Haus Andechs-Meranien." *Mitteilungen des Instituts für Österreichische Geschichtsforschung* 103 (1/2): 26–43.

Wunderlich, Werner. "The Authorship of the Nibelungenlied." In *Companion to the Nibelungenlied*, edited by Winder McConnell. Columbia, SC: Camden House, 1998, pp. 251–277.

BLIGGER VON STEINACH (BLIGGER II, ca. 1165–ca. 1210).

In his *Alexander* fragment Rudolf von Ems praises Bligger von Steinach as a poet who has experienced great adventures. Gottfried von Strassburg compares Bligger favorably with Hartmann von Aue and Heinrich von Veldeke in his *Tristan,* because of the poet's wonderful "umbehanc," the metaphorical term for a poem that weaves a story like a medieval tapestry. This work remains unknown to this day and is presumed lost. The Manesse Codex contains a miniature and only three courtly love songs by Bligger II, lord of the castle of Steinach on the Neckar. Recent historical and literary studies by the Breuers (see bibliography) have revealed close connections between Bligger II and Wolfger von Erla, who was bishop of Passau in the years 1191 to 1204 and the patriarch of Aquileia from 1204 to 1218. There is some circumstantial evidence that Wolfger, a patron of considerable repute, might also have been Bligger's patron. Moreover, the Breuers have found evidence of a genealogical connection between Bligger II and names and places in the *Nibelungenlied*. Bligger's brother Konrad was provost of Speyer and could be the writer Cuonrat, who is mentioned at the conclusion of the *Klage*. The Breuers are convinced that the bishop of Worms had the *Nibelungenlied* composed as a private commission in his name (Hausdichtung), a work that was to mirror the glory of the empire from the time of Charlemagne. They interpret the decline of the empire to the war between the Hohenstaufen and the Welfs for the German throne. According to scholar Peter Honegger, it is not Bligger II, but rather Bligger III (d. 1228) who, although there is no definitive evidence to prove this, is most likely the author of manuscript **A** of the *Nibelungenlied* and of the complementary version of manuscript **B** (see RUDOLF VON EMS).

[WW]

Bibliography

Breuer, Dieter, and Jürgen Breuer. *Mit spaeher rede: Politische Geschichte im Nibelungenlied*. Munich: Fink, 1995.

Hoffmann, Werner. "Bligger von Steinach als Dichter des Nibelungeliedes? Zu Peter Honeggers neuer These." *ZfdPh* 112 (3): 434–441 (1993).

Honegger, Peter. "Bligger von Steinach als Verfasser und Rudolf von Montfort als Bearbeiter des Nibelungenliedes." In: *"Waz sider da geschach." American-German Studies on the Nibelungenlied*, edited by Werner Wunderlich and Ulrich Müller. GAG 564. Göppingen: Kümmerle, 1992, 9–54.

CHANSONS DE GESTE is the term given to Old French heroic epics, which are akin to such heroic poems in German as the *Nibelungenlied.* The extant Old French poems, dating from around 1100, precede the Middle High German ones of roughly 1200. However, the extant versions of both the French and German poems apparently derive from earlier oral poetry now lost. They all have features of what we know to be common in oral poetry: the strophic form, which indicates that they were originally sung; the repetition of set epithetic phrases and line fillers; lengthy dialogues and monologues; and descriptions of prodigious feats of arms in battle scenes. The term *chanson de geste* means *song of heroic deeds* with *geste* coming from Latin *gesta* (things done or deeds, i.e., heroic deeds). The Old French songs are grouped into cycles with one main cycle of poems centering around Charlemagne and his paladins and the other chief cycle dealing with Guillaume d'Orange and various members of his family. Quite possibly the oldest chanson is the well-known *Chanson de Roland.* The chansons are composed in stanzas called *tirades* or *laisses* of a varying number of ten-syllable (five stresses), assonantal lines. The lines frequently have a caesura after the fourth syllable, and some chansons later adopt the alexandrine line of twelve syllables, with caesuras after the sixth syllable. Each laisse is a more or less self-contained unit, frequently connected to the preceding and the subsequent stanza by a line or so at the end that recapitulates the content of the laisse and is then paraphrased at the beginning of the next stanza. In contrast, the *Nibelungenlied* has a regular stanzaic structure. The origins and the development of the chansons are still controversial.

[SMJ]

CODEX SANGALLENSIS 857 (MS. B), a manuscript bought in 1768, along with 114 other manuscripts, from the estate of the Catholic humanist Aegidius Tschudi (1505–1572) of Glarus by Abbot Beda Angehrn for the Abbey Library in St. Gall. The motivating factor for the purchase was, however, not the Nibelung manuscript, but rather the presence of works of the Helvetic Church and monastery documents that were found among the manuscripts. The first editor of the *Nibelungenlied* (manuscript), the

Zurich scholar Johann Jacob Bodmer, had expressed an interest in Tschudi's Nibelung manuscript, but the city officials could not afford the collection.

Cod. Sang. 857 consists of 318 parchment leaves. At least six or seven scribes were involved in constructing the manuscript in a scriptorium probably located in South Tyrol. Prior to 1250 they wrote the works down in two columns in the following order: pages 5–288 contain Wolfram von Eschenbach's *Parzival* (MS. **D**) pages 291–416 the *Nibelungenlied* (MS. **B**), pages 416–451 the *Klage* ("Lament," MS. **B**), pages 452–588 Stricker's *Karl der Große* ("Charles the Great," MS. **C**), pages 561–691 Wolfram von Eschenbach's *Willehalm* (MS. **G**, formerly MS. **K**). In the third quarter of the thirteenth century, an unknown hand wrote down the last page of the Codex (693) five stanzas of the gnomic poetry of Friedrich von Sonnenburg. Originally the Codex contained two other poems, the first five leaves (pages 694–703) of which form an incomplete "quarternion," and are to be found today in the Staatsbibliothek Preussischer Kulturbesitz in Berlin (Ms. germ. fol. 102). These leaves contain more than the first third of the religious poem *Die Kindheit Jesu* (The Childhood of Jesus, MS. **L**, vv. 1–114) by Konrad von Fussesbrunnen, a nobleman from Lower Austria. The fifth scribe, who wrote down the largest section of the *Nibelungenlied* and the complete *Klage,* was also responsible for transcribing the Berlin fragments. According to another fragment on a later page that was published in 1919 and that is no longer extant, the Codex originally concluded with a second religious work, the Mariologic poem "Unser vrouwen hinvart" (The Ascension of our Lady, MS. **E**) by Konrad von Heimesfurt. The Berlin fragment was part of the estate of the scholar Friedrich Heinrich von der Hagen, who, in August 1816, spent six days in St. Gall working in the abbey library. In the course of his sojourn in St. Gall, von der Hagen must have acquired the six leaves in question under circumstances which even today remain a mystery. The return of the missing texts from the Cod. Sang. 857 will undoubtedly give rise to new investigations into the nature of the repertoire of the original, complete manuscript.

[WW]

Bibliography

Ochsenbein, Peter. "Tatsachen und Mutmassungen über den Verlust zweier geistlicher Dichtungen in der St. Galler Nibelungenhandschrift." In *"Waz sider da geschach." American-German Studies on the Nibelungenlied,* edited by Werner Wunderlich and Ulrich Müller. GAG 564. Göppingen: Kümmerle, 1992, pp. 55–70.

EPIC SINGING. The singing of tales and epics has been a worldwide phenomenon, and the old tradition of epic singing can still be found in some regions, for example, in the Germanic Faroese Islands, in some Slavic and Arab countries, and in Africa, India, Central Asia, and China. The singer usually accompanies himself by playing a string instrument. The performances of epic singing which were recorded in Yugoslavia in 1934 and 1935 by Milman Parry, and which are now housed at the Harvard University Library, had a decisive influence on Classical and Medieval Studies, as well as on research into oral poetry. Most scholars agree today that there was also epic singing *(Sangvers-Epic)* in the German Middle Ages. Scholars also agree that all MHG strophic epics (i.e., German heroic poetry, including the *Nibelungenlied*) were sung or at least could have been sung. Nevertheless, the musical quality of the MHG heroic epics is neglected or even ignored by most philologists. Fifteen forms of stanzas of MHG epics have been handed down to us but only eight melodies: *Hildebrandston, Titurel-Weise, Winsbecke-Ton, Schwarzer Ton, Bernerton, Herzog-Ernst-Ton, Heunenweise,* and the *Angstweise* of Michel Beheim. The melody of the *Nibelungenstrophe* presumably can be reconstructed. A few musicologists even emphasize that courtly epics such as Wolfram's *Parzival* were also sung. Two contemporary musicians are particularly renowned for their performance of Middle High German epics: Eberhard Kummer (Vienna) and Reinhold Wiedenmann (Habelsee/Germany). (see HILDEBRANDSTON, NIBELUNGEN PROSODY, SANGVERSEPIK, ORAL POETRY, KUMMER.)

[UM]

Bibliography

Finnegan, Ruth H. *Oral Poetry: Its Nature, Significance, and Social Context.* Cambridge and New York: Cambridge University Press, 1977.

Foley, John Miles. *The Theory of Oral Composition: History and Methodology.* Bloomington: Indiana University Press, 1988.

Lord, Albert Bates. *Epic Singers and Oral Tradition.* Ithaca: Cornell University Press, 1991.

———. *The Singer of Tales.* Cambridge: Harvard University Press, 1960.

———. *The Singer of Tales in Performance.* Bloomington: Indiana University Press, 1995.

Popovic, Tatyana. *Prince Marko: The Hero of South Slavic Epics.* Syracuse: Syracuse University Press, 1988.

FEMINIST AND GENDER STUDIES ON THE *NIBELUNGENLIED*. Feminist literary discourse on the *Nibelungenlied,* which has increased since the 1980s and has been advanced more by women than by men, mirrors the scholarly change in emphasis from Women's Studies (beginning with the women's movement in the 1960s) to Gender Studies, i.e., the move from locating and elucidating unknown sources that could provide information regarding the life, history, and achievements of women, to the discussion of different ways of thinking, as well as systems of signs and symbols that are gender specific. To be sure, already in the '60s and '70s there were attempts to view the *Nibelungenlied* as a "woman's biography" (for example, in the work of Hugo Kuhn [1969/1973], but also Günther Schweikle [1981]). Berta Lösel-Wieland-Engelmann tried in 1980 and 1983 to demonstrate that the *Nibelungenlied* had been authored by a woman and theorized that manuscript **C** was the original manuscript of the *Nibelungenlied* and that **A** and **B** were "reactions of protest by males to the assigning of guilt to Hagen." Heide Göttner-Abendroth (1980) und Albrecht Classen (1991; 1992) searched for traces of a matriarchy in the text of the *Nibelungenlied,* although with different premises. According to Göttner-Abendroth's claims, proof of a matriarchy can only be demonstrated in the oldest phases of the Siegfried sagas, where Brünhild appears as a goddess of love and fertility. Brünhild's belt in the *Nibelungenlied* is seen as an example of a series of transformations of matriarchal mythology, which the author also believes can be detected in the Lancelot cycle as well as in the tales of Parzival and Tristan. Göttner-Abendroth defines and analyzes the term *matriarchy* in her articles in a historically much more accurate way than Albrecht Classen, who has been criticized for the vagueness of his terminology (matriarchy seen as the reverse side of patriarchy; compare Bennewitz 1995). Walter Seitter approaches the text of the *Nibelungenlied* more from a sociopolitical perspective and directs his main focus to the female protagonists and their political careers in aristocratic feudal society. He designates, for example, Kriemhild's ascension to Queen of the Huns as the "Brunhild-ization of Kriemhild" (1987). Jerold C. Frakes (1994) also concentrates on the fate of women in the *Nibelungenlied*. Although the author does not always clearly differentiate with respect to gender and gender relations between literary product and historical "reality," his textual analyses of the term *heimlîche* demonstrate that the parameters of intimacy and sexuality with regard to the possibilities for communication between men and women in the *Nibelungenlied* are of considerable weight. Frakes concurs with Ingrid Bennewitz (1995) that women in the *Nibelungenlied* are basically isolated from one another while their male counterparts always act together as a group. Frakes and Bennewitz independently assert that women do not have direct access to political activities and processes. In this regard Bennewitz (1995) is more specific when she addresses the matter of "objectivization" of women in the *Nibelungenlied* who identify themselves through their spouses, who see their own destiny determined by that of their husbands, and who, if they wish to see something changed in the existing *ordo*, must attempt to do so via representatives of the reigning feudal aristocratic class. In an article dating from 1996 Bennewitz concentrates on the conversations of women in the *Nibelungenlied* and the way they are staged. Monika Schausten's reading of the *Nibelungenlied* (1999) emphasizes the "function of bodies" in the work. The author inquires as to the function of, and relationship between, "body" and "gender."

[AKN]

Bibliography

Bennewitz, Ingrid. "Das Nibelungenlied: Ein 'Puech von Chrimhilt'? Ein geschlechtergeschichtlicher Versuch zum *Nibelungenlied* und seiner Rezeption." In *Philologica Germanica* 16, edited by Klaus Zatloukal. Vienna: Fassbaender, 1995, pp. 33–52.

———. "'Frauen'-Gespräche: Zur Inszenierung des Frauendialogs in der mittelhochdeutschen Literatur." In *Das Mittelalter: Frauen-Beziehungsgeflechte im Mittelalter,* vol. 1, no. 2, edited by Hedwig Röckelein and Hans-Werner Goetz. Berlin: Akademischer Verlag, 1996, pp. 11–26.

Classen, Albrecht, ed. *Women as Protagonists and Poets in the German Middle Ages: An Anthology of Feminist Approaches to Middle High German Literature.* Göppingen: Kümmerle, 1991.

———. 'The Defeat of the Matriarch Brünhild in the Nibelungenlied, with Some Thoughts on Matriarchy as Evidenced in Literary Texts." In *"Waz sider da geschach." American-German Studies on the Nibelungenlied,* edited by Werner Wunderlich and Ulrich Müller. Göppingen: Kümmerle, 1992, pp. 89–110.

Frakes, Jerold C. *Brides and Doom: Gender, Property, and Power in the Medieval German Women's Epic.* Philadelphia: University of Pennsylvania Press, 1994.

Göttner-Abendroth, Heide. *Die Göttin und ihr Heros: Die matriarchalen Religionen in Mythos, Märchen, und Dichtung.* Munich: Verlag Frauenoffensive, 1980.

Göttner-Abendroth, Heide. *Das Matriarchat II, erste Stammesgesellschaften in Ostasien, Ozeanien, Amerika.* Stuttgart: Kohlhammer, 1991.

Kuhn, Hugo. "Kudrun." In *Kleine Schriften II: Text und Theorie.* Stuttgart: Metzler, 1969; reprinted in *Nibelungenlied und Kudrun,* edited by Heinz Rupp. Wege der Forschung 54. Darmstadt: Wissenschaftliche Buchgesellschaft, 1976, pp. 502–514.

———. "Tristan, Nibelungenlied, Artusstruktur." In *Liebe und Gesellschaft* (Kleine Schriften 3). Stuttgart: Metzler, 1980, pp. 12–35.

Lösel-Wieland-Engelmann, Berta. "Verdanken wir das Nibelungenlied einer Niedernburger Nonne?" *Monatshefte* 72 (1980): 5–25.

———. "Die wichtigsten Verdachtsmomente für eine weibliche Verfasserschaft des Nibelungenliedes." In *Feminismus: Inspektion der Herrenkultur. Ein Handbuch,* edited by Luise Pusch. Frankfurt a. M.: Suhrkamp, 1983, pp. 149–170.

Schausten, Monika. "Der Körper des Helden und das 'Leben' der Königin. Geschlechter- und Machtkonstellationen im Nibelungenlied." *ZfdPh* 118 (1999): 27–49.

Schweikle, Günther. "Das Nibelungenlied: Ein heroisch-tragischer Liebesroman?" In *De poeticis medii aevi quaestiones. Käte Hamburger zum*

85. Geburtstag, edited by J. Kühnel et al. Göppingen: Kümmerle, 1981, pp. 59–84.

Seitter, Walter. *Das politische Wissen im Nibelungenlied. Vorlesungen.* Merve-Titel 141. Berlin: Merve, 1987.

———. *Versprechen, versagen: Frauenmacht und Frauenästhetik in der Kriemhild Diskussion des 13. Jahrhunderts.* Merve-Titel 154. Berlin: Merve, 1990.

FORMULAIC CONSTRUCTIONS. Recurrent, syntactic metrical/rhythmical patterns that cover a whole verse or hemistich. In formulaic constructions all elements are interchangeable with other elements of the same word class and structure (number of syllables, accentuation, etc.). Whether tense, number, case, and so on have to be the same is a matter of definition, in contradistinction to the oral formula, which expresses, according to the founders of the theory of oral-formulaic composition, Milman Parry and Albert B. Lord, the same essential idea whenever it occurs and which is consequently unchangeable. The nature of formulaic constructions, however, resides in the recurrent, syntactic metrical/rhythmical pattern and is independent of the semantic content. In the *Nibelungenlied* a hemistich such as "Dô sprach diu küneginne" ("Then the queen said. . . " 416,1") occurs eighteen times and is considered to be a formula, but as such it is part of a system that also includes lines such as "Dô sprach der videlaere" ("Then the minstrel said" 1412,1) "Dô kom diu küneginne" ("Then the queen came" 2066,), and so on. If a hemistich such as "Dô sprach zer küneginne" ("Then x said to the queen" 1283,1) is considered to be part of the same system, it will be obvious that it is rather difficult to define the notion of "formulaic construction" adequately. In his concordance to the *Nibelungenlied,* Franz H. Bäuml presents all key words within the context of the hemistichs that are classified according to their syntactical structure, but avoids the term *formula* or *formulaic construction* and speaks instead of *patterns.*

[NV]

Bibliography

Bäuml, Franz H. and Eva-Maria Fallone. *A Concordance to the Nibelungenlied.* Leeds: W. S. Maney & Son Ltd. 1976.

FORNYRÐISLAG, a meter for old sagas/poems consisting of a four-syllable, two-foot alliterating line, with about eight lines forming one stanza.

[GW]

GERMAN HEROIC POETRY (DEUTSCHE HELDENDICTUNG) is, like heroic poetry in general, the poetic expression of Germanic heroic myth, first in oral then in written form. The first part (Helden-) of the German word "Heldendictung" relates, as is obvious, to special warriors or warrior-bands of a tribe or nation in times of conquest and/or the foundation of an empire. These warriors are retained in the collective memory, and by means of creative memory they are glorified and typified along the lines of mythical models that are taken as historical fact. Many texts focusing on heroic individuals or the events and groups with which they are involved are organized in larger cycles, e.g., the Dietrich von Bern cycle or the Nibelungen cycle.

German heroic poetry reflects the age of a great migration of peoples in Europe and the subsequent formation of Germanic kingdoms and empires (the so-called *Völkerwanderung*) from the fourth to the sixth century. This formative era is focused on the aristocracy, which defines itself through such overriding—and mandatory—ethical concepts as honor and fidelity among family, followers, and friends, all of which the aristocracy viewed as being confirmed by their history. Further, the poetry is anonymous and presents an epic as opposed to a reflective narrative. Happy endings are rare, and the heroic death generally follows close on the performance of a great deed.

Heroic song (comprising from 50–500 verses) is generally accepted as the older form of heroic poetry in contrast to the epic. The singer focuses his lay on peaks of action and tension, alternating between short epic narrative and dramatic dialogue and employing a whole range of fixed epic formulas, motifs, and patterns of storytelling. The Germanic heroic lay, as far as one can trace it back to the period of migrations, exhibits even in its earlier stages an advanced and relatively structured type of lay with individual nuances, e.g., the Old High German *Hildebrandslied* from the beginning of the ninth century, the Old English *Battle of Finnsburgh,* known to the *Beowulf* poet but only surviving in a copy made in 1705, and the Old Norse Eddic lays.

Heroic epic was viewed by scholar W. P. Ker and later Andreas Heusler as an amplification of the lay itself and not the simple addition of epic lays. It is distinguished from the lay mainly because of its greater length, owing to style and content. Even after the transition from oral to written form, the oral narrative techniques continue to be clearly visible in the heroic epic, however difficult they may be to recognize (e.g., formulaic constructions, variation, parallelization, and foreshadowing). The transformation of the Germanic heroic song to a written epic in Germany began with the *Nibelungenlied* about 1200, doubtless due to the close contact with and reception of the Arthurian romances. Germanic heroic epic in Germany is represented by the *Nibelungenlied, Kudrun,* and the extensive cycle around Dietrich von Bern (*Dietrichs Flucht, Rabenschlacht, Alpharts Tod, Goldemar, Eckenlied, Sigenot, Virginal, Laurin, Rosengarten zu Worms, Biterolf und Dietleip, Ortnit, Wolfdietrich,* and *Walther und Hildegund*).

[OE]

Bibliography

Beck, Heinrich, ed. *Heldensage und Heldendichtung im Germanischen.* Berlin: de Gruyter, 1988.

Betz, Werner. "Die deutsche Heldensage." In vol. 3 of *Deutsche Philologie im Aufriß.* 2nd ed. Berlin: Schmidt, 1962, cols. 1871–1970.

Bowra, C. M. *Heroic Poetry.* London: Macmillan, 1952.

Chadwick, H. M. *The Heroic Age.* Cambridge: Cambridge University Press, 1912.

———, and N. K. Chadwick. *The Growth of Literature.* 3 vols. Cambridge: Cambridge University Press, 1932–1940.

Heusler, Andreas. *Lied und Epos in germanischer Sagendichtung.* Dortmund: Ruhfus, 1905. 3rd ed., Darmstadt: Wissenschaftliche Buchgesellschaft, 1960.

Hoffmann, Werner. *Mittelhochdeutsche Heldendichtung.* Berlin: Schmidt, 1974.

Ker, W. P. *Epic and Romance.* New York: Dover, 1957. Reprint of 1908 edition.

Kuhn, Hans. "Heldensage vor und außerhalb der Dichtung." In *Zur germanisch-deutschen Heldensage,* edited by Karl Hauck. Wege der Forschung 14. Darmstadt: Wissenschaftliche Buchgesellschaft, 1965, pp. 173–194.

Schneider Hermann, and Wolfgang Mohr. "Heldendichtung." In vol. 1 of *Reallexikon der deutschen Literaturgeschichte,* edited by Werner Kohlschmidt and Wolfgang Mohr. 2nd ed. Berlin: de Gruyter, 1958, cols. 630–646.

Tiefenbach, Heinrich, Hermann Reichert, and Heinrich Beck. "Held, Heldendichtung und Heldensage." In *Reallexikon der germanischen Altertumskunde,* edited by Johannes Hoops. Vol. 14, edited by Heinrich Beck, Dieter Geuenich, and Heiko Steuer. 2nd rev. ed. Berlin: de Gruyter: 1999, pp. 260–282.

Uecker, Heiko. *Germanische Heldensage.* Sammlung Metzler 106. Stuttgart: Metzler, 1972.

HEINRICH VON OFTERDINGEN, the name of Heinrich von Ofterdingen is mentioned for the first time in the so-called "Fürstenlob" (Panegyric to Princes) in the medieval gnomic poem *Der Wartburgkrieg* ("The Wartburg Contest," 1240–1260). In the poem the poets assembled at the Wartburg compete in their praise of the best sovereign. Heinrich, who favors the Babenberg Duke Leopold VI, is defeated by Walther von der Vogelweide, who supports Landgrave Hermann I of Thuringia. The late Middle Ages clearly assumed that Heinrich was a real poet. Herman Damen lists him among the dead poets and minstrels. The Jena and Kolmar collections of songs name Heinrich as the inventor of melodies, and the *Heldenbuch* version of *Laurin* names him at the end as its author or source. It is uncertain whether Heinrich's fictitious role in the *Wartburgkrieg* is a reflection of an unknown author or perhaps even of the actual author of this poem. It may well be that later adapters of heroic epic used the popular name as a kind of pseudonym. We have no historical evidence that would allow us to identify Heinrich with persons having similar names that occur in legal documents. In 1802 Friedrich von Hardenberg (Novalis) modeled the major protagonist of his popular, fragmentary romance, *Heinrich von Ofterdingen,* on the medieval precursor. Although the basis for their arguments was shaky at best, a number of authors, poets, historians, and philologists, including August Wilhelm and Friedrich Schlegel, Friedrich Heinrich von der Hagen, Anton Ritter von Spaun, Christian Dietrich Grabbe, Friedrich Rückert, Joseph Victor von Scheffel, and Adalbert Stifter (but not Jacob Grimm or Johann August Zeune) assumed that Heinrich von Ofterdingen was the author of the anonymous *Nibelungenlied.*

[WW]

Bibliography

Ehrismann, Otfrid. *Nibelungenlied 1755–1920: Regesten und Kommentare zu Forschung und Rezeption.* Beiträge zur deutschen Philologie 62. Gießen: Schmitz, 1986, pp. 17f., 30, 76, 166f.

HEROIC AGE. Hesiod introduced the notion of "a godlike race of human heroes who are called semidivine." These were the warriors who fought before the walls of Thebes and Troy. The notion of a Germanic heroic age similarly suggests a mythical past inhabited by men and women larger and more powerful than those living in the narrator's present. To some late-nineteenth and early-twentieth century Germanists, the parallels between the *Nibelungenlied* and the Greek epic tradition suggested an attractive symmetry between German and classical Greek culture, a view that reached the height of its political popularity during the period of German National Socialism. Following the disaster of World War II, Germanists eschewed any further interest in a German heroic age. Instead, efforts have been made to anchor the *Nibelungenlied* in a particular historic period; whether that of the late twelfth century, in which it was composed and recorded in its present form, or else that of a "migration age," the period in which Germanic tribes grew in strength, expanded, sought new territories, and established themselves widely throughout Northern Europe and Britain. While the historicity of the *Nibelungenlied* and other Germanic narratives remains quite problematic, their reference to a common set of characters and exploits continues to promote the concept of an age, albeit mythical, in which warriors possessed of superhuman size, strength, and magical properties met each other, did battle, and, most frequently, died a violent death.

[VU]

HEUNENWEISE, a form of a Middle High German epic strophe, called by the late medieval Mastersingers the "Hönweise Wolframs (von Eschenbach)." The *Heunenweise* is a late medieval adaptation of the *Hildebrandston,* with the rhymes of the latter expanded. The *Heunenweise* was used in several late medieval heroic epics.

[UM]

HILDEBRANDSTON (see Fig. 1, p. 217), a form of a Middle High German epic strophe, used as melody for the *Jüngere Hildebrandslied* and the *Lied vom Hürnen Seyfried.* The melody is transmitted in Georg Rhau's (Rhaw's) *Bicinia,* a collection of songs published in 1545 (vol. 1, no. 94). The form is metrically very similar to the *Nibelungenstrophe:* the last *Kurzzeile* (short line) of the *Hildebrandston* has three stressed syllables, just like the other *Kurzzeilen,* whereas the last *Kurzzeile* of the *Nibelungenstrophe* usually, although not always, has four. The *Hildebrandston* was used for a late medieval adaptation of the *Nibelungenlied,* contained within Lienhart Scheubel's *Heldenbuch* (Vienna, *Piaristen-Handschrift: Nibelungenlied* version **k**). There are compelling reasons to believe that not only the metrical form, but also the melody of the *Hildebrandston,* is very similar to the lost melody of the *Nibelungenlied.* The *Hildebrandston* currently offers the most reliable basis for any attempt to reconstruct the Nibelungen melody, and it was probably used for several more late Middle High German epics (see NIBELUNGEN PROSODY; EPIC SINGING).

[UM]

KONRAD VON FUSSESBRUNNEN (ca. 1165–ca. 1220), author of the religious poem "Die Kindheit Jesu" (The Childhood of Jesus), written between 1195 and 1200 and preserved at the end of the St. Gall Codex 857, which also includes manuscript **B** of the *Nibelungenlied.* Purely speculative is the assumption that he might also have been the long-sought author of the *Nibelungenlied.* It has been suggested that Bishop Wolfger of Passau gave Konrad, who hailed from Fussesbrunnen, belonging to the bishopric of Passau, the task of composing the *Nibelungenlied* after the short epic about the marriage of Maria and Joseph and the miracles of the child Jesus had been completed. The evidence for this is seen in Konrad's declaration in his religious work that he regretted having earlier authored secular poetry. To be sure, this statement is no more proof of his authorship of the *Nibelungenlied* than the reference to the town of

Traismauer on the Trais River, where in manuscript **C** Kriemhild is said to have spent four days before moving on to Etzel's court. Feuersbrunn, the old Fussesbrunnen and Konrad's home, lies within the vicinity of Traismauer. In order to bring his homeland to some degree into the work, the rather far-fetched claim is made that Konrad used the gimmick of transforming Traismauer into Zeiselmauer, a town that lay further to the east and a place name that also appears in manuscripts **A** and **B**.

[WW]

Bibliography
Hansen, Walter. *Die Spur des Sängers: Das Nibelungenlied und sein Dichter.* Bergisch Gladbach: Lübbe, 1987.

KONRAD VON GÖTTWEIG, eleventh-century cleric, canon in Passau, and prior of the monastery of Göttweig, was suggested as the poet of the *Nibelungenlied* by Wilhelm Gärtner, a professor of German Language and Literature in Pest in the nineteenth century.

[OE]

Bibliography
Gärtner, Wilhelm. *Chuonrad, Prälat von Göttweig und das Nibelungenlied: Eine Beantwortung der Nibelungenfrage.* Pest, Vienna, Leipzig: Hartelben, 1857.
———. *Beleuchtungen: Nachwort zu meiner Nibelungenschrift, und eine Antwort auf die Kritik des Herrn Joseph Diemer.* Pest: G. Kilian, 1857.
Ehrismann, Otfrid. "Das goldne Haar im Weichselzopf: Zum Briefwechsel zwischen Friedrich Hebbel und Wilhelm Gärtner über dessen Nibelungenbuch." *Brüder-Grimm-Gedenken* 11 (1995): 144–157.

KONRAD VON RUSSBACH, thirteenth-century Austrian chaplain who had received the parish of Russbach as a benefice. There is evidence to demonstrate that between 1207 and 1232 Konrad von Russbach served as a cleric and notary in the bishopric chancellery of Passau and the ducal chancellery of Vienna. He has thus been considered by some as the author of the *Nibelungenlied,* which was written down about 1204. This theory is based on the concluding verses of the *Klage,* according to which Bishop Pilgrim of Passau had his clerk, Konrad, write down in Latin the events that transpire in the epic.

[WW]

Bibliography
Kralik, Dieter. *Wer war der Dichter des Nibelungenliedes?* Vienna: Österreichischer Bundesverlag für Unterricht, Wissenschaft und Kunst, 1954.

DER KÜRENBERGER, Lower Austrian lyric poet who has been suggested as the author of the *Nibelungenlied,* although there is no proof to substantiate this hypothesis. He was the first (about 1150–1160) to use in his rhythmic style two long-line rhyming couplets with three measures in the second half-lines of the first three verses and four measures with a slight crescendo at the conclusion of the strophe. Scholars' use of the designation *Nibelungenstrophe* to describe the form of his stanza was clearly suggestive enough to have them searching time and time again for further geographic and genealogical evidence to prove that Kürenberg was the author of the *Nibelungenlied* (see NIBELUNGEN PROSODY).

[WW]

Bibliography
Krogmann, Willy. *Der Dichter des Nibelungenliedes.* Philologische Studien und Quellen 11. Berlin: Schmid, 1962.
Pfeiffer, Franz. "Der Dichter des Nibelungenliedes." In F. P., *Freie Forschung: Kleine Schriften zur Geschichte der deutschen Litteratur und Sprache.* Vienna: Tendler, 1867, pp. 1–52.

LITERACY/ILLITERACY, in the early Middle Ages, had to do with knowledge of Latin, or lack thereof. Originally, the terms *litteratus* and *illitteratus* indicated the ability or inability (respectively) to read and write in Latin. Without exception everyone fell into one category or the other. These terms also generally divided the clergy (as *litterati*) and the lay population (as *illitterati*) until the thirteenth century when lay nobles began to develop the ability to read and write in the vernacular (Grundmann). Such distinction between *litteratus* and *illitteratus* can be misleading, however. Since the transmission and reception of knowledge was socially conditioned, one must consider degrees of (il)literacy in the Middle Ages (Bäuml). Bäuml describes three categories, each depending upon the functions required of the individual in the realm of literacy: (1) the fully literate; (2) the individual who must rely on the literacy of another for access to written transmission; and (3) the illiterate without means or need of such reliance. To describe the second group, Bäuml advocates the use of the term "quasiliterate," since "those *illitterati* who must and do have access to literacy are, in respect to their dependence on the written word for the exercise of their sociopolitical function, to be classified with the *litterati*" (Bäuml, 246). More recently, in this context, D. H. Green discusses an intermediate form of medieval literary reception that combined the skills of *hoeren unde lesen* (listening and reading). Such evidence suggests the likelihood that the audience of the Middle High German *Nibelungenlied* would have practiced these intermediary forms of reading and listening.

The text of the *Nibelungenlied* could appeal to both the literate and illiterate people of the time. Clearly the *Nibelungenlied* shows evidence of oral transmission in its traditional material as well as in its oral formulaic constructions. In the manuscript form of the thirteenth century, however, the poem offers a written message designed to reach an audience through a reading or reciting intermediary. Indeed, the poet involves his audience of listeners at times in the poem. In the prologue, for instance, the poet promises: "nu muget ir wunder hoeren sagen" ("now you will hear told wonderous stories" 1,4). Shortly before Siegfried's murder, the poet recognizes his obligation to continue his story to the end, though he may not wish to: "Sît daz ich iu diu mære gar bescheiden sol" ("Since I am to tell you the whole story" 956,1; see also 2379,1a).

The *Nibelungenlied* stands at the crossroads of oral and written culture around 1200, and its message reflects the influence of the developing literate culture: "As experience became richer, deeper, and more complex, it also demanded a different shape. Interpretive models evolved from texts, whether disseminated by verbal or written means, were increasingly called upon to provide explanations for behavioral patterns" (Stock, 455). As the *Nibelungenlied* offers commentary on the behavior of its actors, the poem crosses "the line from illiteracy to literacy"

(Bäuml and Spielmann, 256) and constructs (or reconstructs) heroic models for its courtly audience to emulate (Jaeger).

[ASH]

Bibliography
Bäuml, Franz. "Varieties and Consequences of Medieval Literacy and Illiteracy." *Speculum* 55 (1980): 237–265.

———, and Edda Spielmann. "From Illiteracy to Literacy: Prolegomena to a Study of the *Nibelungenlied*.' *Forum for Modern Language Studies* 10 (1974): 248–259.

Green, Dennis H. *Medieval Listening and Reading: The Primary Reception of German Literature 800–1300.* Cambridge: Cambridge University Press, 1994.

Grundmann, Herbert. "*Litteratus-illiteratus:* Der Wandel einer Bildungsnorm vom Altertum zum Mittelalter." *Archiv für Kulturgeschichte* 40 (1958): 1–65.

Jaeger, C. Stephen. "The Nibelungen Poet and the Clerical Rebellion against Courtesy." In *Spectrum Medii Aevi: Essays in Early German Literature in Honor of George Fenwick Jones,* edited by William C. McDonald. Göppingen: Kümmerle, 1983, pp. 177–207.

Stock, Brian. *The Implications of Literacy: Written Language and Models of Interpretation in the Eleventh and Twelfth Centuries.* Princeton: Princeton University Press, 1983.

LITERARY PATRONAGE OF THE *NIBELUNGENLIED.*

There is no documentary evidence for sponsorship of the *Nibelungenlied.* In the absence of acrostics or direct allusions by the anonymous Nibelungen poet, research on the patronage of the work must therefore rest on deductive reasoning. Factors in singling out the sponsor are the dating of the *Nibelungenlied,* the provenance of manuscripts, the financial resources for producing a poem of this scope, clues in the epic itself, and a literary patron of sufficient reputation to make reasonable the promotion of the *Nibelungenlied.* Scholarly consensus identifies this person as the Austrian Wolfger of Erla, who was bishop of Passau from 1191 until 1204, the generally accepted dates for composition of the *Nibelungenlied,* and Patriarch of Aquileia from 1204 until his death in 1218.

Wolfger of Erla was a crusader, a masterly Church diplomat and a generous, if somewhat indiscriminating, Maecenas. The important Passau court of this *homo nobilis* persuasively fulfills the conditions for bringing forth the poem. Wolfger is a documented patron of the arts, having granted Walther von der Vogelweide money *pro pellicio* ("for a fur coat") on St. Martin's Day in 1203. (It has been speculated that Walther, and even Wolfger himself, were the authors of the *Nibelungenlied*.) Other poets linked to Wolfger's name, however tenuously, are Bligger von Steinach, Albrecht von Johansdorf and Thomas of Circlaria or Zerclaere. Wolfger of Erla opened his gates to scores of entertainers of every stripe, from noble minnesinger to low-bred and low-brow mimic actors and comedians. It is impossible to state with certainty, but the anonymous author of the *Nibelungenlied* was probably a cleric in the chancellery of the episcopal court in Passau. This would make him possessor of a religious education, thus able to read and write. The bishop surely had the necessary resources to provide literary source texts, parchment, and scribes for the composition and recording of the poem. And in Passau, in Wolfger's entourage, the Nibelungen poet certainly could have come to know the courtly culture.

Passau and its surrounding area command the attention and affiliation of the *Nibelungenlied* poet. The city figures importantly in the text, and the Danube region between Passau and Vienna is clearly the geographical realm best known to him. Note that the *Klage,* a poem in verse couplets attached as a kind of epilogue and appendix to most manuscripts of the *Nibelungenlied,* also features Passau prominently. Its opening lines tell how Bishop Pilgrim of Passau had a certain "meister Kuonrat" (Master Conrad) record a tale in Latin concerning the subject matter of the *Nibelungenlied.* This passage, identified in research as an attestation of the authenticity of the *Nibelungenlied* in respect to historical truth ("Echtheitszertifikat," per Heinzle), is also a testimonial to the episcopal sponsorship of the work.

A Bishop Pilgrim of Passau, "Pilgerin," also appears in the *Nibelungenlied:* "In der stat ze Pazzouwe saz ein bischof" (In the town of Passau resided a bishop, 1296,1). Pilgrim, maternal uncle of Kriemhild and the Burgundian kings, hosts his niece on her bridal journey to the land

of the Huns. This Bishop Pilgrim, mentioned in stanzas 1296, 1428, 1495, and 1628, seems to be a twofold monument in verse to the Passau episcopate, as well as to the presumed episcopal sponsor of the poem, Wolfger von Erla. First, the Nibelungen poet had not far to seek for a model for the poetic Pilgrim, the historical Bishop Pilgrim of Passau (971–991), whose tomb in the city was opened in 1181 to attendant miracles and emphatic veneration. Second, the favorable treatment of a bishop of Passau in the *Nibelungenlied* would allow the current holder of the seat to bask in reflected glory. Said veneration would thus be an intentionally anachronistic tribute. Observe that Wolfger was consecrated as bishop in 1191, exactly 200 years after Bishop Pilgrim's death in 991; and that Wolfger, as a participant in the crusade of 1197–1198, had himself earned the title of "pilgrim." Looking beyond the memorialization of the sponsor and the Passau episcopate, one is tempted to explain the writing of the *Nibelungenlied* as a reaction to the regnant Arthurian romances. Since the *Nibelungenlied* diverges so sharply from these, one surmises that the sponsor, having little use for knights of the Round Table, the reconciliation of all the plot strands and the wonted happy endings of Arthurian tales, promoted a deliberately "antimodern" poem that maintains its distance from contemporary aesthetics and literary fashion.

[WCM]

Bibliography

Andersson, Theodore. *A Preface to the Nibelungenlied.* Stanford: Stanford University Press, 1987.

Heger, Hedwig. *Das Lebenszeugnis Walthers von der Vogelweide: Die Reiserechnungen des Passauer Bischofs Wolfger von Erla.* Vienna: Schendl, 1970.

Heinzle, Joachim. *Das Nibelungelied.* Munich and Zurich: Artemis, 1987.

Hempel, Heinrich. "Pilgerin und die Altersschichten des Nibelungenliedes," *ZfdA* 69 (1932): 1–16.

Heuwieser, Max. "Passau und das Nibelungenlied," *Zeitschrift für bayerische Landesgeschichte* 14 (1943): 5–62.

Muenz, Walter. "Zu den Passauer Strophen und der Verfasserfrage des Nibelungenliedes," *Euphorion* 65 (1971): 345–367.

Voorwinden, Norbert. "Pilgerin und das Bistum Passau im Nibelungenlied." In *Pöchlarner Helden-*

liedgespräch: Das Nibelungenlied und der mittlere Donauraum, edited by Klaus Zatloukal. Vienna: Fassbaender, 1989, pp. 139–156.

LJÓÐÁHÁTTR, tune/melody of songs, an alliterating stanza consisting of two four-syllable lines with two feet, forming one long line, and a single line with three feet without a caesura (= full line).

[GW]

MAJOR TRENDS IN *NIBELUNGENLIED* SCHOLARSHIP. Although critical opinion about the *Nibelungenlied* has been ongoing since the writing down of the *Klage* in the thirteenth century, the genesis of Nibelungen scholarship is inextricably bound up with the ever-nascent tendencies of German patriotism and chauvinism as well as with the beginnings of the discipline of German philology in the nineteenth century and of German literary research in the twentieth. The individuals mentioned in this article represent only pars pro toto of the great and near-great scholars of German studies and Nibelungen research. This is especially true of scholars from the modern period, with its ongoing redefining of existing methodologies and development of new ones. More detailed information on many items and individuals mentioned in the course of this article can be found throughout the encyclopedia, especially in those entries on RECEPTION, MANUSCRIPTS, and ÄLTERE NIBELUNGENNÔT.

The Establishment of a Discipline.—The field of Germanic philology as well as the inception of *Nibelungenlied* scholarship can fairly be said to have originated with the treatise *Über die ursprüngliche Gestalt des Gedichts von der Nibelungen Noth,* written in 1816 by the classical philologist Karl Lachmann (1793–1851). Together with Jacob Grimm, Lachmann fashioned the new discipline. While a student in Göttingen, he attended lectures on older German literature delivered by Georg Friedrich Benecke, professor of English and older German. This experience left a lasting mark on Lachmann, and he dedicated the rest of his life to both classical and German philology. In addition to his pioneering work in the new discipline, he also continued to be active in the area of classical philology, among other things editing the works of Propertius and Lucretius. As a German philologist

Lachmann's greatest achievement is without doubt the grand edition of the works of Wolfram von Eschenbach.

His work on the *Nibelungenlied* was no less impressive in its effect on scholarly discourse, especially in the nineteenth century. Lachmann concerned himself primarily with two issues: (1) the identification of the primary manuscript, which in his opinion would be the least complete version—something that would speak for its greater age; and (2) the determination of the structure of the epic. With regard to the first, he determined that manuscript **A,** because of its lack of polish and apparent lacunae, was the earliest and therefore the primary manuscript, an assumption that would later be shown to be false. Further, Lachmann applied Friedrich August Wolf's theory on the origin of the Homeric epics to the *Nibelungenlied* in a theory he called "Liedertheorie" (song/lay theory). Wolf had postulated that the *Iliad* and the *Odyssey* were not the work of one poet but rather of a series of poets or singers who composed short pieces which were then later ordered, edited, and combined into the epics known by subsequent ages as being composed by Homer. By 1836, in his *Anmerkungen zu den Nibelungen und zur Klage,* Lachmann had refined his "Liedertheorie" to the extent that he had determined that there were twenty individual *Lieder,* or rhapsodies, that comprised manuscript **A.**

From the beginning, Lachmann's views were questioned, most notably by Friedrich Heinrich von der Hagen (1780–1856), the first academic to hold the professorship for German Language and Literature in Berlin. Von der Hagen had published an edition of the *Nibelungenlied* himself in 1807. Unfortunately, this edition was not characterized by scholarly or any other kind of rigor and it received little positive notice from the scholarly community. Then in 1809 Wilhelm Grimm wrote about it: "It [the edition] is a modernization, which is worse than the original, and yet not at all modern." As a result, von der Hagen's protests failed to gain any significant support.

The "Nibelungenstreit" and Its Aftermath.—After Lachmann's death, a scholarly struggle over his theories that concerned both the primary manuscript and the genesis of the epic ensued. The dispute, the so-called "Nibelungenstreit," was characterized by unusual vituperation and ad hominem attacks. It centered around followers of Lachmann, like Karl Müllenhoff (1818–1884), who not only advocated the primacy of manuscript **A,** but also applied Lachmann's "Liedertheorie" to the epic *Kudrun;* and the "dissidents," like the Heidelberg professor Adolf Holtzmann (1810–1870) and Friedrich Zarncke (1825–1891), professor at Leipzig, who claimed primacy for manuscript **C.** Holtzmann's *Untersuchungen über das Nibelungenlied* (1854) not only advocated manuscript **C** but also rejected Lachmann's "Liedertheorie" out of hand. He was joined in the same year by Zarncke, who later modified his support after Karl Bartsch (1832–1888) became the first to espouse manuscript **B** (1865). Today Bartsch is credited with putting together the most widely-used critical edition of the *Nibelungenlied,* which is based on **B.** The decision in favor of **B** was put forth by Wilhelm Braune (1850–1926) in his study *Die Handschriftenverhältnisse des Nibelungenliedes* (1900), in which he posited a stemma of the *Nibelungenlied,* on the basis of which he demonstrated that the three main manuscripts form two branches **AB* and **C,* and all derive from one original **x.* In 1963, in his *Beiträge zur Handschriftenkritik des Nibelungenliedes,* Helmut Brackert subjected Braune's theory to a rigorous examination. Brackert concluded that the presupposition upon which Braune constructed his stemma, namely that there was an original (**x*), was simply not verifiable. Brackert's equally controversial position theorizes that there never was one single work that could be considered the original *Nibelungenlied.* The common text appearing to lie behind the transmitted texts is actually just one of several versions. As could be expected, Brackert's theories were likewise felt to be in need of some revision, for while most agree that in light of Brackert's work Braune's stemma can no longer be considered viable, to draw the conclusion that there can be no original work to which the transmitted texts can trace their roots is tantamount to throwing out the baby with the bathwater. Joachim Heinzle's comments may be taken as exemplary in this regard. Heinzle agrees with Brackert regarding Braune's stemma, but, he cautions: "We can infer an original in the sense that the *Nibelungenlied* tradition goes back

to an original or basic text, in whose author we may see the poet of the *Nibelungenlied.* **AB* and **C* are revisions of this basic text, which is fairly well preserved in **AB* whereas **C* represents a systematic reworking, which in turn, however, influenced the total **AB* tradition secondarily. In general, one has to take into consideration also the repeated impact of oral epic tradition on the written, but it is not the rule as Brackert thought. We have to see the written tradition as essentially closed. In spite of these facts, it is just as impossible to reconstruct the basic text."

The other Lachmann hypothesis, the "Liedertheorie," was also rejected in the new century. In his classic work, *Lied und Epos in germanischer Sagendichtung* (1905), Andreas Heusler (1865–1940) convincingly demonstrated the untenability of Lachmann's position. Heusler differentiated between "lay" and "epic" as follows: "A lay does not relate [just] an episode, but rather a cohesive narrative. The epic narrative and the lay content are the same." More concretely put: "According to [Lachmann's] theory, the epic stands in the same relationship to a lay as a group of trees to an individual tree . . . . In reality, however, the epic stands in relationship to a lay as a grown person to an embryo." Heusler's work provided the final nail in the "Liedertheorie" coffin. While Heusler's differentiation between lay and epic is generally regarded as valid, scholars like Franz Rolf Schröder (1960) objected to the rigidity of the Heuslerian hypothesis. Schröder states: "In his confrontation with the 'Liedertheorie,' Heusler fell into the other extreme. We must reckon with songs of two types, those that narrate a lengthy series of events . . . and those that relate [just] one episode from the life of a hero." With the Lachmannian ghosts finally laid to rest, Nibelungen research in the twentieth century was ready to strike out in new directions in addition to adhering to previously trodden paths. Source studies, either reaffirming Heusler's proposals (e.g., the many writings of Theodore M. Andersson) or seeking sources in myth (e.g., the assumptions of scholars like de Vries, Franz Rolf Schröder, and Höfler) continued to be written. Friedrich Panzer sought the origin of the epic in fairy tales, specifically in a Russian fairy tale about a wooing expedition. The theories proposing the genesis of the *Nibelungenlied* in either myth or fairy tale met with great resistance and were by and large not influential in determining the course of scholarship in the twentieth century. One new area of speculation that started off promisingly was the consideration of the work in terms of Milman Parry and Albert B. Lord's oral-formulaic theories. Scholars like Franz Bäuml strongly endorsed the hypothesis that the origins of the *Nibelungenlied* are to be sought in the oral tradition. Edward Haymes endorses Bäuml's assertion with some reservations regarding the apparent restriction of the formulaic to the oral sphere, arguing that written poetry is likewise formulaic. Ultimately, oral-formulaic considerations evolved into the ongoing significant research of Michael Curschmann, Dennis H. Green, and Alois Wolf. But by and large the concentration of scholars in the twentieth century was fixed on the *Nibelungenlied* as a work of great literature.

Research Trends in the Twentieth Century. —While the wars of liberation in the nineteenth century as well as the periods of World War I, the Weimar Republic, and World War II in the twentieth provided ample opportunity for the use of the *Nibelungenlied* as a nationalistic artifact, the twentieth century also witnessed a new era in viewing the epic as a work of literary art. To be sure, there had been some scholars who voiced this literary viewpoint in a few isolated writings, including Josef Körner in 1921, Ernest Tonnelat in 1926, and Julius Schwietering in 1940, but the literary genie really came out of the bottle only after World War II. In 1949 Friedrich Maurer declared his intention to examine the epic as a unified work and to consider the poet as a creative genius, not merely as one redactor in a long line of such. Since Maurer's time numerous studies of the *Nibelungenlied* as a literary phenomenon have appeared, each attempting a general interpretation of the work: (a) the *Nibelungenlied* vis-à-vis the courtly romance (Dürrenmatt, Mergell, Schulze); (b) the characters as representations and the psychology of the characters (W. J. Schröder, Bekker, G. Weber, W. Schröder, McConnell); (c) the *Nibelungenlied* as tragedy (Nagel); (d) the *Nibelungenlied* within its socio-historical epoch (Beyschlag, Ihlenburg, Gentry); and (e) the reception of the *Nibelungenlied* (O. Ehrismann, U. Müller, Wunderlich); (f) music (Brunner, U. Müler).

This brief review demonstrates that as perspicacious as he may have been in other cases, Frederick the Great was very much off the mark with his 1784 comment about the *Nibelungenlied* and other medieval literary works: "In my opinion, such 'poems' are not worth a rap and do not deserve to be lifted from the dust of obscurity. At any rate, I would not tolerate such miserable stuff in my library but would toss it out!"

[FGG]

Bibliography

Andersson, Theodore M. *A Preface to the 'Nibelungenlied.'* Stanford: Stanford University Press, 1987.

―――. *The Legend of Brynhild.* Islandica 63. Ithaca: Cornell University Press, 1980.

Bartsch, Karl. *Untersuchungen über das Nibelungenlied.* Vienna: Braumüller, 1865.

Bäuml, Franz H., and Donald J. Ward. "Zur mündlichen Überlieferung des Nibelungenliedes." *DVjs* 41 (1967): 351–390.

―――, and Edda Spielmann. "From Illiteracy to Literacy: Prolegomena to a Study of the Nibelungenlied." *Forum for Modern Language Studies* 10 (1974): 248–259.

Bekker, Hugo. *The Nibelungenlied: A Literary Analysis.* Toronto: Toronto University Press, 1971.

Beyschlag, Siegfried. "Das Motiv der Macht bei Siegfrieds Tod." *GRM* 33 (1951/1952): 95–108.

―――. "Das Nibelungenlied als aktuelle Dichtung seiner Zeit." *GRM* 43 (1967): 225–231.

Brackert, Helmut. *Beiträge zur Handschriftenkritik des Nibelungenliedes.* Quellen und Forschungen zur Sprach- und Kulturgeschichte der germanischen Völker. N.F. 11. Berlin: Schmidt, 1963.

Braune, Wilhelm. "Die Handschriften-Verhältnisse des Nibelungenliedes." *PBB* 25 (1900): 1–222.

Curschmann, Michael. "'Nibelungenlied' und 'Nibelungenklage': Über Mündlichkeit und Schriftlichkeit im Prozeß der Episierung." In *Deutsche Literatur im Mittelalter: Kontakte und Perspektiven,* edited by Christoph Cormeau. Stuttgart: Metzler, 1979, pp. 85–119.

Dürrenmatt, Nelly. *Das Nibelungenlied im Kreis der höfischen Dichtung.* Berne: Lang, 1945.

Ehrismann, Otfrid. *Das Nibelungenlied in Deutschland: Studien zur Rezeption des Nibelungenliedes von der Mitte des 18. Jahrhunderts bis zum ersten Weltkrieg.* Münchner Germanistische Beiträge 14. Munich: Fink, 1975.

Fohrmann, Jürgen, and Wilhelm Voßkamp, eds. *Wissenschaft und Nation: Zur Entstehungs-*

geschichte der deutschen Literaturwissenschaft. Munich: Fink, 1991.

———, eds. *Wissenschaftsgeschichte der Germanistik im 19. Jahrhundert.* Stuttgart: Metzler, 1994.

Gentry, Francis G. *Triuwe and vriunt in the Nibelungenlied.* Amsterdamer Publikationen zur Sprache und Literatur 19. Amsterdam: Rodopi, 1975.

Heinzle, Joachim. "The Manuscripts of the Nibelungenlied." In *A Companion to the Nibelungenlied,* edited by Winder McConnell. Studies in German Literature, Linguistics, and Culture. Columbia: Camden House, 1998, pp. 105–126.

Heusler, Andreas. *Lied und Epos in germanischer Sagendichtung.* 1905. Reprints, Darmstadt: Gentner, 1956; Darmstadt: Wissenschaftliche Buchgesellschaft, 1960.

Höfler, Otto. *Siegfried, Arminius, und der Nibelungenhort.* Sitzungsberichte der Österreichischen Akademie der Wissenschaften. Philosophisch-Historische Klasse 332. Vienna: Verlag der Österreichischen Akademie der Wissenschaften, 1978.

Holtzmann, Adolf. *Untersuchungen über das Nibelungenlied.* Stuttgart: Krabbe, 1854.

Ihlenburg, Karl Heinz. *Das Nibelungenlied: Problem und Gehalt.* Berlin: Akademie Verlag, 1969.

Kolk, Rainer. *Berlin oder Leipzig? Eine Studie zur sozialen Organisation der Germanistik im "Nibelungenstreit."* Studien und Texte zur Sozialgeschichte der Literatur 30. Tübingen: Niemeyer, 1990.

Körner, Josef. *Das Nibelungenlied.* Aus Natur und Geisteswelt 591. Leipzig: Teubner, 1921.

Kralik, Dietrich. *Die Sigfridtrilogie im Nibelungenlied und in der Thidrekssaga.* Halle: Niemeyer, 1941.

Lord, Albert Bates. *The Singer of Tales.* Harvard Studies in Comparative Literature 24. Cambridge: Harvard University Press, 1981.

Maurer, Friedrich. "Das Leid im Nibelungenlied." In W. M., *Leid: Studien zur Bedeutungs- und Problemgeschichte besonders in den großen Epen der staufischen Zeit.* Bibliotheca Germanica 1. Berne: Francke, 1951, pp. 13–38.

McConnell, Winder. *The Nibelungenlied.* Twayne's World Authors Series 712. Boston: Twayne Publishers, 1984.

Mergell, Bodo. "Nibelungenlied und höfischer Roman." *Euphorion* 45 (1950): 305–336.

Müller, Jörg Jochen. *Germanistik und deutsche Nation 1806–1848: Zur Konstitution bürgerlichen Bewußtseins.* Literaturwissenschaft und Sozialwissenschaften 2. Stuttgart: Metzler, 1974.

Nagel, Bert. *Das Nibelungenlied: Stoff, Form, Ethos.* 2nd ed. Frankfurt: Hirschgraben, 1970.

Neumann, Friedrich. *Studien zur Geschichte der deutschen Philologie: Aus der Sicht eines alten Germanisten.* Berlin: Schmidt, 1971.

———. *Studien zum Nibelungenlied.* Frankfurt: Diesterweg, 1945.

Panzer, Friedrich. *Das Nibelungenlied: Entstehung und Gestalt.* Stuttgart: Kohlhammer, 1955.

Parry, Milman. *Serbocroation Herioc Songs.* Collected by Millman Parry, edited and translated by Albert Bates Lord. Cambridge: Harvard University Press; Belgrade: Serbian Academy of Sciences, 1953– [vol. 1, 1954]

Schröder, Franz Rolf. "Siegfrieds Tod." *GRM* 41 (1960): 111–122.

Schröder, Werner. *Nibelungenlied-Studien.* Stuttgart: Hirzel, 1968.

Schulze, Ursula. Das Nibelungenlied. Stuttgart: Reclam, 1997.

Schwietering, Julius. Die deutsche Dichtung des Mittelalters. 1940; reprint. Darmstadt: Gentner, 1957.

Tonnelat, Ernest. *La Chanson des Niberungen. Étude sur la Composition et la Formation du Poème Épique.* Publication de la Faculté des lettres de l'Université de Strasbourg fasc.30. Paris: Paris, Société d'édition: Les Belles lettres, 1926.

Weber, Gottfried. *Das Nibelungenlied. Problem und Idee.* Stuttgart: Metzler, 1963.

Wolf, Alois. *Heldensage und Epos: Zur Konstituierung einer mittelalterlichen volkssprachigen Gattung im Spannungsfeld von Mündlichkeit und Schriftlichkeit.* Tübingen: Narr, 1995.

Wunderlich, Werner. *Der Schatz des Drachentödters: Materialien zur Wirkungsgeschichte des Nibelungenlieds.* Literaturwissenschaft, Gesellschaftswissenschaft 30. Stuttgart: Klett-Cotta, 1977.

MALAHÁTTR ("quotation tone"), a stanza consisting of eight (short) lines, each of which contains two metric feet, a meter very similar to the fornyrðislag (meter for old sagas/poems).

[GW]

MANUSCRIPTS OF THE *NIBELUNGENLIED* are thirty-five in number: eleven complete (or nearly complete), one version based only on a few remaining traces (**c**), and twenty-three fragments, the most recent of which (**W**) was discovered in 1997/1998 at the monastery of Melk in Austria. The oldest attested texts (**C** and **S**) date from the second quarter of the thirteenth century; the most recent (**d**) was written at the beginning of the sixteenth century. In addition there is a fragment of a Dutch adaptation (**T**) from the second half of the thirteenth century.

The manuscripts deviate from one other, sometimes considerably, in content and in form. Generally they can be assigned to two groups representing two versions: the *AB or *Nôt*-version and the *C or *Lied*-version, named in each case according to the most important manuscripts: **A**, **B**, and **C**, or according to the wording of the last verse: "daz ist der Nibelunge nôt" (that is the downfall of the Nibelungs) or "daz ist der Nibelunge liet" (that is the lay/song of the Nibelungs).

The 'signatures' **A**, **B**, and **C** were assigned by the scholar Karl Lachmann, who laid the foundation for the manuscript criticism of the epic. The distribution reflects his assessment of the value of the manuscripts with respect to textual criticism. In his opinion the transmitted text of **A** came closest to the surmised original, and **B** represented a first systematic reworking of the text, which was in turn subjected to a more recent, thorough revision, as represented by the text in **C**. Therefore, he based his edition of 1826, which aimed at the textual reconstruction of the original, on **A**. Lachmann's evaluation of the manuscripts is also tied to his understanding of the genesis of the *Nibelungenlied*. He was convinced that it was not a homogeneous poetic work, conceived as one piece, but ultimately the product of a redactor who had joined together several episodic songs or lays (Lachmann's "Liedertheorie" or "Song/Lay Theory") without being able to dissolve the heterogeneous quality of the materials. With this supposition, Lachmann applied the theory of the genesis of the Homeric epics, which his teacher Friedrich August Wolf had developed, to the *Nibelungenlied*. Since the text of **A** is the most unwieldy of all in style, metre, and narrative coherence, Lachmann believed that, fashioned after Wolf's genesis theory, in its unpolished state it must most nearly approximate the idea of the original text. Not long after Lachmann's death, a fierce dispute arose about his theories. During the conflict the two theoretically possible alternatives were defended one after the other: First the relative primacy of **C** (version *C); then the relative primacy of **B** (version *B). Adolf Holtzmann and Friedrich Zarncke (1854) accorded priority to *C, while Karl Bartsch was the first to claim it for *B (1865). The overall decision in favor of *B was brought about by Wilhelm Braune's study on *Die Handschriftenverhältnisse des Nibelungenliedes* (1900). Together with Heusler's work, *Lied und Epos in germanischer Sagendichtung* (1905), which demonstrated the untenable position of Lachmann's song theory, Braune's treatise ended the *Nibelungenlied* dispute. Objections that were raised here and there against his combinations went unnoticed until Helmut Brackert took them up in his 1963 work, *Beiträge zur Handschriftenkritik des Nibelungenliedes,* in which he subjected Braune's construct to an extensive examination. The result of his criticism, which was aimed at the methodological presuppositions of the construction of the stemma, was devastating. Braune's model, according to Brackert, was untenable, and incapable of being proved in its decisive points. Basically Brackert's position amounts to the assumption that an original of the *Nibelungenlied* in the sense of a single poetic work never existed and that the common text discernible behind the transmitted body of texts represents only one of several versions. The discussion of Brackert's theses yielded the consensus that while Braune's stemma indeed is not viable, Brackert's criticism is exaggerated with respect to its further conclusions. We can infer an original in the sense that the *Nibelungenlied* tradition goes back to an original or basic text, in whose author we may see the poet of the *Nibelungenlied*. *AB and *C are revisions of this basic text, which is fairly well preserved in *AB. *C represents a systematic reworking, which in turn, however, influenced the total *AB tradition secondarily. In general one must take into consideration the repeated impact of oral epic tradition on the written, but it is not the rule, as Brackert thought. We have to see the written tradition as essentially closed. In spite of these facts it is just as impossible to reconstruct the basic text, which probably originated in Passau around 1200, as it is to reconstruct the *AB-version. It must also remain undecided which is closer to the basic text, *B or *A. Both the *AB-version as well as the *C-version must have originated very early, directly following the writing of the basic text and in the same area. There is a connection between the new version *C and the *Klage*, an appendix in rhyming couplets. Both share a similar line of interpretation and thus shaped the impression that medieval people came to have of the terrible events recounted by the *Nibelungenlied*. With two exceptions (**k** and **n**), the *Klage* is to be found as a kind of reader's guide or initial commentary on the great epic in all complete manuscripts of the *Nibelungenlied.*

The question of priority, whether the *Klage* is based on the *C-version of the *Nibelungenlied* or the *C-version is based on the *Klage,* is controversial. Joachim Bumke has argued for priority of the *C-version for good reasons. It is safe to say that around the year 1200 there existed a kind of Nibelungen workshop,that produced in rapid sequence, perhaps even simultaneously, the basic text, both the *AB- and *C-versions and the *Klage*. The typical content, style, and form of the *C-version have been described repeatedly. Although the redactor's ultimate aim has not been sufficiently understood because of this-version's special status between the oral and written tradition, the *C-version represents the attempt to adapt the customary oral tradition to written literary conventions, while at the same time going beyond the achievements of the basic text or those of the *Nôt*-version. This means that the basic text/*Nôt*-version and the *Lied*-version show us two phases or text stages in process of transforming the matter of the Nibelungen into the written *Nibelungenlied*. The advanced book status of *C first becomes evident in the redactor's work of systematically abolishing or reducing all inconsistencies and deficits in motivation. This concerns the microstructure of the text, individual phrases or strophes, which he touched up by textual reformulating, erasing, or adding. But most of all, it concerns the macrostructure which, dictated by the subject itself, is contradictory. In the first part Hagen appears as a faithless murderer and Kriemhild as a victim. The second part, however, depicts Hagen as the great hero and selfless protector of the Burgundians, while Kriemhild is portrayed as a brutal murderer. The *C-redactor (like the poet of the *Klage*) retained a consistency of interpretation between the first and second parts of the epic. In the latter, he presented Hagen as the villainous author of all evil, Kriemhild, however, as the suffering and loving woman, whose acts, no matter how terrible their consequences, are guided by the Christian virtue of loyalty, the unswerving love for Siegfried. This satisfies the prescribed concern for a logical course of action as well as the ethical Christian assessment of the events by the categories of guilt/sin and innocence/virtue. At the same time this evaluation means that the redactor must at times detach himself from tradition, and this occurs whenever the redactor points out problems in the historicity of the narrative, to which, however, he adheres—like his predecessors.

The *Lied*-version dominated the Nibelungen tradition from the very beginning as the most advanced textual stage of the *Nibelungenlied* in book form. The earliest literary echo of the text we know is a passage in Wolfram von Eschenbach's *Parzival* (1204/1205). And probably the oldest textual evidence of the *Nibelungenlied* itself is manuscript **C**, which, as mentioned, was written in the second quarter of the thirteenth century. In the second half of the thirteenth century this version is attested to by no fewer than six manuscript fragments (**E, F, G, R, X, Z**), in the fourteenth century by an additional fragment (**U**), and in the fifteenth century by the important manuscript **a**. A *C-text was also said to be contained in the inferred manuscript ****Db**. However the *Lied*-text had been available only for a short time so that one had to resort to a *Nôt*-text as a model for the greater part of the work (the division runs in the area of strophes *C 270/271). This mixed version was first attested in the second quarter of the thirteenth century through the fragment complex **S**, after that in the fourteenth century through manuscript **D** as well as fragments **N**, **P**, and **V**, and in the fifteenth century through manuscript **b**, the only one with detailed illustrations. Manuscript **k** is the only other illustrated manuscript and it contains only one illustration. The importance of the *Lied*-version is further underscored by the mixed versions *J and *d, in which a series of characteristic *C-strophes is built into the *Nôt*-text. It is conceivable that the initial manuscript was a *Nôt*-manuscript of the *J or *d type, which was modernized by adding the *C-strophes in the margins and that from this manuscript then a manuscript of the other type was augmented. It is unlikely that the mixture found in *J and *d match just by chance. Thus, through the interpolation the position of the *C-redactor in the context of the *Nôt*-version is brought into focus. This mixed complex has been attested since the late thirteenth century. Listed under group *J are the manuscripts **J** (around 1300) and **h** (fifteenth century) as well as the fragments **K** (around 1300) and **Q**, **Y**, and **l** (fourteenth century); under group *__d__ are listed the fragments **O** (end of the thirteenth century) and **H** (fourteenth century) as well as manuscript **d**, which was perhaps directly copied from **O**, the famous *Ambraser Heldenbuch* written for Emperor Maximilian I at the beginning of the sixteenth century. Evidence of the *Nôt*-variations outside of these mixed versions is sparse. Of *__A__ there are, besides manuscript **A** (fourth quarter of the thirteenth century), only the fragments **L**, **M** (both fourteenth century) and **g** (fifteenth century, copy of **L**). *__B__ is attested with certainty only in manuscript **B** (around 1260) so that here only the *__d__ group of the mixed complex *__Jd__ is available as a means of examining the manuscript tradition (sometimes the small remnants and traces of manuscripts **i** and **c** are included under *__B__, although this classification is extremely tenuous).

Three manuscripts that have not yet been discussed do not fit into the above-mentioned manuscript tradition of the *Nibelungenlied*. They present radical adaptations of the text, falling back upon the oral tradition that was alive at the time of their writing. The Darmstadt manuscript **m** (middle or second half of the fourteenth century) is a fragment that contains a listing of the *âventiuren* (*Darmstädter Aventiurenverzeichnis*). We can gather that the tale of the abduction of Kriemhild by a dragon and her liberation by Siegfried was incorporated into this text. The story was known by way of the *Lay of the Hürnen Seifried*. The second Darmstadt manuscript, **n** (1449 or around 1470/1480), has a text that offers only the downfall of the Burgundians in a relatively free reworking of the story. Finally there is manuscript **k** (end of the fifteenth century), a *Heldenbuch*, a collection of heroic epic texts, in which the *Nibelungenlied* appears in a stylistically and metrically radical transformation adapted to the literary conventions of the time.

There is a noticeably strong geographical concentration in the transmission of the *Nibelungenlied*. The large majority of manuscripts (all of them until ca. 1300) originated in the Bavarian-Austrian region, southeast of the German-speaking area. A second center emerges in the Rhine-Franconian area with **L**, **g**, **m**, and **n** in the fourteenth and fifteenth centuries. It is

perhaps not by accident that these two centers correspond to the geographical areas of the story: in the southeast the area of the Danube and the Alpine realm of the Dietrich epics; and in the west, the Rhenish kingdom of the Burgundians at Worms. In both areas the *Nibelungenlied* could be viewed as local tradition.

[JH]

Bibliography
Facsimile editions listed on pp. 327–328.

Brackert, Helmut. *Beiträge zur Handschriftenkritik des Nibelungenliedes*. Quellen und Forschungen zur Sprach- und Kulturgeschichte der germanischen Völker, N.F. 11. Berlin: de Gruyter, 1963. Reviewed by Joachim Bumke in *Euphorion* 58 (1964): 428–438.

Bumke, Joachim. *Die vier Fassungen der Nibelungenklage*. Quellen und Forschungen zur Literatur- und Kulturgeschichte 8. Berlin: de Gruyter, 1996.

Glaßner, Christine. "Ein Fragment einer neuen Handschrift des Nibelungenliedes in Melk." *PBB* 120 (1998): 376–394.

Göhler, Peter. "Bemerkungen zur Überlieferung des Nibelungenliedes." In *3. Pöchlarner Heldenliedgespräch. Die Rezeption des Nibelungenliedes*, edited by Klaus Zatloukal. Philologica Germanica 16. Vienna: Fassbaender, 1995, pp. 67–79.

Heinzle, Joachim, and Klaus Klein. "Zu den Melker Fragmenten des Nibelungenlieds." *ZfdA* 127 (1998): 373–380.

Hoffmann, Werner. "Die Fassung *C des Nibelungenliedes und die Klage." In *Festschrift Gottfried Weber*, edited by Heinz Otto Burger and Klaus von See. Bad Homburg: Gehlen, 1967, pp. 109–143.

Springeth, Margarete. "Beobachtungen zur Nibelungenrezeption in der Wiener Piaristenhandschrift (k)." In *3. Pöchlarner Heldenliedgespräch. Die Rezeption des Nibelungenliedes*, edited by Klaus Zatloukal. Philologica Germanica 16. Vienna: Fassbaender, 1995, pp. 173–185.

MYTH can be understood as "statements about the relations between the world and the proper existence of man" or "statements about religious facts impossible to prove rationally," or simply "stories in which gods or other supernatural beings appear as acting figures." Therefore, the question as to what is mythological in the Nibelungen tradition can be answered in different ways. Gods appear as actors in the *Poetic Edda*,

Snorra Edda, and above all in the *Volsunga saga.* In these sources the Volsungs descend from Odin, who intervenes in their destinies, beginning with their ancestor Sigi and continuing through to the last descendants, Hamdir and Sorli.

Odin's part is dominant in the passages concerning Sigmund and his sons, up to the point when Sigurd awakens a valkyrie (Brynhild or Sigrdrífa). He helps, for example, by providing Sigmund with a magic sword, but finally causes his death when Sigmund's magic sword breaks against his magic spear.

Mythological aspects are most striking in the first part of the Sigurd traditions (starting with the prehistory of the hoard and especially parts concerning the cursed golden ring), in which gods walk on earth, kill an animal for food, and have to pay *wergeld,* and in which supernatural beings transform themselves into animals. The symbolic value inherent to the struggle for gold, power, and revenge, already apparent in the mythical prehistory of the world is considerable. Sigurd's deeds, for example, are more a reflection of initiation rites than acts of bravery: the dragon, Fafnir, is not killed in a fight, but from below, with a sword thrust from a ditch. When Sigurd, counseled by prophesying nuthatches, ascends a mountain surrounded by fire to awaken a valkyrie, he does not have to brave the flames, as they vanish before he arrives. The ride through flames has to be performed only when the disguised Sigurd woos Gunnar. Obstacles like this are interpreted as symbols of a transition to an otherworld. The dialogue scenes were regarded by scholar Bertha Phillpotts as texts of a ritual drama. Her thesis is now generally rejected, and theories that suggest comparisons to initiation rites must be viewed critically as well. Individual motifs do occur both in rites and in literature, but a rite consisting of several steps—getting a horse and a sword, then killing a cosmic monster and finally being introduced into magic lore and sexuality, as in the longest versions of the Sigurd story—is most unlikely. Similar combinations of motifs, including the hero's later marriage to a woman in conflict with the otherworld bride, can be found in several literary traditions, including the story of the Greek Jason, Tristan in the Celtic tradition, and in fairy tales.

The *Nibelungenlied* has fabulous motifs rather than mythical ones. In the Brünhild subplot supernatural elements prevail. It is thus incorrect to theorize that the poet has Hagen relate Siegfried's adventures (hoard, dragon) instead of the narrator to keep his distance from incredible elements of the tale. A better explanation is the assumption that he concentrated on Kriemhild and Hagen in the epic and not on Siegfried.

In the *Þiðreks saga* there are few supernatural elements to be noted with respect to Gunnar's wooing of Brynhild. But this work includes more mythological material pertaining to the birth of Sigurd. He is set adrift in a bottle on a river, comparable to Moses, who is placed in a crib of bulrushes on the Nile, then fostered by a hind, analogous to Romulus and Remus, who are suckled by a she-wolf. The *Þiðreks saga* follows German traditions with respect to name-giving by using the name Sigfrodr, from German Siegfried, instead of Sigurdr.

[HR]

Bibliography

Beck, Heinrich. See his articles on "Helreið," "Brynhildar," "Reginsmál," "Fáfnismál," "Sigrdrífomál." In *Kindlers Literatur Lexikon: Werke.* 7 vols. Zurich: Kindler, 1965–1971.

de Vries, Jan. *Altgermanische Religionsgeschichte.* 2 vols. 3rd ed. Berlin: de Gruyter, 1970.

Eliade, Mircea. *Traité d'Histoire des Religions.* Paris: Payot, 1949.

Kuhn, Hugo, and Kurt Schier, eds. *Märchen, Mythos, Dichtung. Festschrift zum 90. Geburtstag Friedrich von der Leyens.* Munich: Beck, 1963.

Motz, Lotte. *The Beauty and the Hag: Female Figures of Germanic Faith and Myth.* Philologica Germanica 15. Vienna: Fassbaender, 1993.

Phillpotts, Berta S. *The Elder Edda and Ancient Scandinavian Drama.* Cambridge: Cambridge University Press, 1920.

Polomé, Edgar C., ed. *Old Norse Literature and Mythology: A Symposium.* Austin: University of Texas Press, 1969.

Reichert Hermann. *Nibelungensage und Nibelungenlied.* Böhlau Studien Bücher. Vienna: Böhlau, 1985.

Schier, Kurt. "Edda." In vol. 3 of *Enzyklopädie des Märchens: Handwörterbuch zur historischen und vergleichenden Erzählforschung,* edited by Kurt Ranke and Hermann Bausinger. Berlin: de Gruyter, 1981, pp. 979ff.

Steblin-Kamenskij, Michail Ivanoviè. *Myth: The Icelandic Sagas and Eddas.* Ann Arbor: Karoma, 1982.

——. "Valkyries and Heroes." *ANF* 97 (1982): 81–93.

Weber, Gerd W. "Irreligiosität und Heldenzeitalter: Zum Mythencharakter der altisländischen Literatur." In *Speculum norronum. Norse Studies in memory of Gabriel Turville-Petre,* edited by Ursula Dronke et al. Odense: Odense University Press, 1981, pp. 474–505.

NIBELUNGEN PROSODY. The *Nibelungenstrophe*—designed for oral, sung delivery—is the narrative building-block for the Nibelungen epic, which is comprised of 2,376 strophes in manuscript **B,** the manuscript on which the most popular print editions are based. Each strophe has four *Langverse* (longlines) arranged as rhyme pairs: aabb; and each longline is broken by a *Zäsur* (caesura) into an *Anvers* (ascending halfline) and an *Abvers* (descending halfline). Manuscript **B** clearly marks the strophic divisions, either by an initial majuscule or by an initial letter in the manuscript margin or both. The longlines are also clearly indicated by rhyme dots and tend to coincide with a major syntactic juncture. Evidence for the halfline unit is not immediately apparent in the manuscript. Only seventy-two of 9,504 longlines have a rhyme dot in the medial position, and only thirteen of these rhyme dots actually mark a *Zäsurreim* (caesural rhyme), a phenomenon that is rare in the Nibelungen verse. The most convincing evidence for the existence of the halfline unit is the strong tendency for minor syntactic juncture (i.e., clausal and phrasal juncture) to occur in the medial position of longlines.

Terminological confusion has long been a part of the Nibelungen prosodic tradition. Although the strophic model established by Andreas Heusler in his *Deutsche Versgeschichte* (1925–1929) has long been predominant, the earlier model by Karl Lachmann is the base for seminal studies of the nineteenth century and much of the early twentieth century. Since Heusler accepts several of Lachmann's terms into his system and applies each according to a set of fundamentally different assumptions, it is not at all surprising that contemporary readers of prosodic studies are often confused. In describing a strophic model for the Nibelungen verse,

Lachmann and Heusler share a focus on the halfline-final cadences; that is, on the final cadence of the four ascending halflines in the caesural position and on the final cadence of the four descending halflines in the rhyme position. The strophe below contains the predominant halfline cadence-types in the verse and demonstrates by direct comparison the scansion and terminology of the Lachmannian and Heuslerian approaches:

Heusler:

∧ | Nách den | hérge- | sél- | lèn ∧|| ∧ | wárt ein | bóte ge- | sánt | ∧ ∧||

∧ | ób si | wólden | scóu- | wèn ∧|| ∧ | níuwez | ír ge- | wánt | ∧ ∧||

ob | éz den | hélden | wáe- | rè ∧|| ze | kúrz und | óuch ze | lánc | ∧ ∧||

ez | wás in | réhter | má- | zè ∧|| des | ságten | sí den | fróuwen | dánc||

1. 4 Hebungen, 2-silbig klingend|| 4 Hebungen, 1-silbig stumpf||
2. 4 Hebungen, 2-silbig klingend|| 4 Hebungen, 1-silbig stumpf||
3. 4 Hebungen, 2-silbig klingend|| 4 Hebungen, 1-silbig stumpf||
4. 4 Hebungen, 2-silbig klingend|| 4 Hebungen, 1-silbig voll||

(*Hebung*—metrical stress; *klingend*—feminine cadence; *stumpf*—masculine cadence; *1-silbig*—monosyllabic; *2-silbig*—disyllabic; *voll*—a full four measures actualized in the language material, i.e., Heusler's *Viertakter* without paused unstresses or paused stresses or paused measures.)

Lachmann:

Nách den hérgeséllen wárt ein bóte gesánt
ób si wólden scóuwen níuwez ír gewánt
ob éz den hélden wáere ze kúrz und óuch ze lánc
ez wás in réhter máze des ságten sí den fróuwen dánc

1. 3 Hebungen, klingend 3 Hebungen, stumpf
2. 3 Hebungen, klingend 3 Hebungen, stumpf
3. 3 Hebungen, klingend 3 Hebungen, stumpf
4. 3 Hebungen, klingend 4 Hebungen, stumpf

A closer look at the Heuslerian model reveals two fundamentally different assumptions in his prosodic system as compared with his predecessor Lachmann. First, he has established the *Viertakter* (four-measure line) as the line unit for the entire Germanic verse tradition from Otfried to Opitz. He does not allow for longer or shorter actualization of the halfline units, as does Lachmann, and this necessitates paused stress or unstress ("?") or paused measures ("? ?") in his system, as well as the additional meaning he attributes to the phrase *klingend* (paused final unstress) and to the phrase *stumpf* (paused final measure). A second assumption in Heusler's system is that of isochronism: he compares the performance of the verse line to the playing of a violin with a metronome. He envisions the passage of an equal amount of time from stress to stress, and thus his notational system includes the division of halflines into measures (the "|") and the marking of *Viertakter* boundaries (the "||"). Lachmann's approach is not anchored either in the *Viertakter* or isochronism. He simply notes the final cadence as *klingend* (feminine) for the ascending halflines and as *stumpf* (masculine) for the descending halflines and allows for longer and shorter actualization of the halfline units.

Both Heusler and Lachmann agree that the final halfline of the *Nibelungenstrophe*, the fourth descending halfline or the *Strophenschluß*, is to be seen as a prosodic environment different from the other seven halflines in the strophe. Whether measured by the number of stresses or by the relative fullness with respect to the *Viertakter* or by the average number of syllables, this concluding halfline is consistently longer than the other halflines in the strophe. There is also a distinctive sequence of stresses and unstresses in this halfline which appears to be part of the underlying metrical pattern of the verse. The halfline-type below illustrates this pattern:

vor állen júncfróuwen jách.

The pattern involves stresses two and three realized as contiguous stress positions, and Lachmann described this configuration just that way: as the omission of *Senkung* (unstress) between two *Hebungen* (stresses). Only later did this pattern come to be known as the *beschwerte Hebung* (heavy stress) cadence. The *beschwerte*

Hebung may occur in other halflines of the strophe, but it is only in the *Strophenschluß* where its frequency affects the underlying pattern of the verse, which is overwhelmingly alternating (stress-unstress-stress-etc.) in the other seven strophic halflines. Recent analysis of the *Strophenschluß* indicates an underlying dipodic pattern in the halfline: secondary stress-primary stress, followed by secondary stress-primary stress, and so on.

In addition to the dominant halfline-types, the *Nibelungenstrophe* also has infrequent occurrences of *Kadenzentausch* (cadence exchange), as evinced by the appearance of masculine cadences in ascending halflines and feminine cadences in descending halflines. The following examples illustrate *Kadenzentausch*: Ascending Halfline:

flúhe méister Híldebránt

Descending Halfline:

mit mínem schílde

These halfline-types provide a particular challenge for Heusler's *Viertakter*, since they appear to establish strong evidence for long and short actualization in the verse. Heusler, to account for this length variation, is required to label the first example *voll*, thereby suggesting a radical wandering of the *Strophenschluß*, and to create a new term for the second, *überstumpf* (extra-masculine). The term *überstumpf* is especially counterintuitive for those accustomed to the predominant pattern of labeling disyllabic cadences of the type *schilde* as *klingend* (feminine). The frequency of cadence exchanges is extremely low, comprising less than 5 percent of the halflines in the manuscript B corpus.

As in all strophic epics, the form of the stanza provides a flexible frame for the poet and singer. The melody of the *Nibelungenstrophe* has not survived, but there have been several attempts to reconstruct it. Since the 1950s the so-called "Trier–Alsfeld melody" (passed down in two religious plays from Trier and Alsfeld) was thought to be identical with the lost Nibelungen melody (Bertau/Stephan). It is more likely, however, that the lost melody can be reconstructed by adhering to the *Hildebrandston* (Beyschlag,

Müller) because it is nearly identical to the *Nibelungenstrophe* and it is closely related to the Nibelungen poetry of the later Middle Ages. Notably, the Austrian musician Eberhard Kummer has employed the *Hildebrandston* to great effect in his performances of the *Nibelungenlied* since the 1980s.

Altogether fifteen forms, but only eight melodies, of Middle High German epic strophes have survived. It is by no means certain that all of them have Germanic roots. Some scholars have suggested that the *Nibelungenstrophe* originated from the Latin *Vagantenstrophe* (especially Kabell). The *Vagantenstrophe* also has four rhyming longlines and was very popular in the Middle Ages. It is unlikely that the *Nibelungenstrophe* can be traced to French roots, and recent attempts by the ensemble Sequentia (Ben Bagby) to use a medieval French melody to perform the *Nibelungenlied* have been unconvincing. The lyrical *Kürenbergerstrophe,* used by the first Middle High German love poet, the Kürenberger, is metrically identical with the epic *Nibelungenstrophe.* Yet it cannot be ascertained whether or not the two forms of strophes were sung using the same melody. The chronological relationship between them is also unclear. (see HILDEBRANDSTON, EPIC SINGING, SANGVERSEPIK; for recordings see COMPACT DISCS, GERMANY)

[RW/UM]

Bibliography

Bertau, Karl H., and Rudolf Stephan. "Zum sanglichen Vortrag mhd. strophischer Epen." *ZfdA* 87 (1956/57): 253–270.

Beyschlag, Siegfried. "Langzeilen-Melodien." *ZfdA* 93 (1964): 157–176.

Bischoff, Karl, ed. *Das Nibelungenlied und die Klage. Handschrift B.* Cologne: Böhlau, 1962.

Brunner, Horst. "Epenmelodien." In *Formen mittelalterlicher Literatur,* edited by Otmar Werner and Bernd Naumann. Göppingen: Kümmerle, 1970, pp. 149–178.

———. "Strukturprobleme der Epenmelodien." In *Deutsche Heldenepik in Südtirol,* edited by Egon Kühebacher. Bozen: Athesia, 1979, pp. 300–328.

de Boor, Helmut. "Die schweren Kadenzen im *Nibelungenlied.*" *BGDSL* 94 (1972): 81–112.

———. "Zur Rhythmik des Strophenschlusses im *Nibelungenlied.*" In *Festgabe für Ulrich Pretzel.* Berlin: Schmidt, 1963.

Heusler, Andreas. *Deutsche Versgeschichte.* 3 vols. Berlin: de Gruyter, 1925/29.

———. *Nibelungensage und Nibelungenlied.* 6th ed. Dortmund: Ruhfus, 1965.

Hoffmann, Werner. *Das Nibelungenlied.* 6th ed. of *Nibelungenlied* by Gottfried Weber and Werner Hoffmann. Sammlung Metzler 7. Stuttgart: Metzler, 1992. "Die metrische Form des Nibelungenliedes," pp. 114–125.

Kabell, Aage. *Metrische Studien II. Antiker Form sich nähernd.* Uppsala: Lundequistika Bokhandeln, 1960.

Kulsdom, Gerard Jan Hendrik. *Die Strophenschlüsse im Nibelungenlied: Ein Versuch.* Dortmund: Ruhfus, 1979.

Lachmann, Karl. *Anmerkungen zu den Nibelungen und zur Klage.* Berlin: Riemer, 1836.

Müller, Ulrich. "Aufführungsversuche zur mittelhochdeutschen Sangversepik: Zur allmählichen Entstehung eines altgermanistischen Forschungsschwerpunktes am Institut für Germanistik." *Jahrbuch der Universität Salzburg 1985–1987.* Salzburg: Universität, 1989, pp. 191–197.

———. "Das Nibelungenlied: Ein Sangvers-Epos." In *"Waz sider da geschach." American-German Studies on the Nibelungenlied,* edited by Werner Wunderlich and Ulrich Müller, with the assistance of Detlef Scholz. Göppingen: Kümmerle, 1992, pp. 249–265. With Bibliography 1980–1990/91.

———. "Eberhard Kummer und die mittelhochdeutsche Sangversepik." *Österreichische Musikzeitschrift,* 1989, 234–238.

———. "Überlegungen und Versuche zur Melodie des 'Nibelungenliedes,' zur Kürenberger-Strophe und zur sog. 'Elegie' Walthers von der Vogelweide." *Zur gesellschaftlichen Funktionalität mittelalterlicher deutscher Literatur.* Greifswald: Universität, 1984, pp.27–42, 136.

Rompelmann, T. A. "Zur Strophik des Nibelungenliedes." In *Altgermanische Beiträge,* edited by Friedrich Maurer and Cola Minis. Amsterdam: Rodopi, 1977.

Wakefield, Ray M. *Nibelungen Prosody.* The Hague: Mouton, 1976.

Zarncke, Friedrich. "Einleitung Metrisches." In *Das Nibelungenlied,* edited by Friedrich Zarncke. 5th ed. Leipzig: Wigand, 1875. Most concise and complete compendium of Lachmann's prosodic system.

NONNE VON NIEDERNBURG (Nun of Niedernburg), an anonymous nun of the Benedictine convent at Niedernburg who has been

NL Der was der sel - be val - ke den si'n ir troume sach
K Ich zoch mir ein - nen val - ken me - re dan'ein jar
W O - we war sint ver-swun - den al- liu miniu jar

NL den ir be-schiet ir muo - ter wie se- re si daz rach
K do ich in ge- zame - te als ich in wol-te han
W ist mir min leben ge-trou - met o- der ist ez war

NL an ir næh-sten ma - gen die in sluo-gen sint
K und ich im sin ge- vide - re mit gol-de wol be- want
W daz ich ie wand'ez wae - re waz daz al- lez iht

Ey - ia

NL durch sin ei - nes ster- ben starp vil maneger muo - ter kint.
K er huob sich uf vil ho - he und floug in an - de - riu lant
W dar - nach han ich ge- sla - fen und en - weiz ez · niht
ie- mer mer ou -we

U. M.

Figure 1

suggested as the author of manuscript **C** of the *Nibelungenlied.* It has been asserted that since this version is more sympathetic to women, it is the earlier one. Manuscript **B,** on the other hand, is regarded as an example of male chauvinism, revised according to sexist criteria. Apart from the lack of any proof of the historical circumstances, the more favorable depiction of women detected in manuscript **C** is hardly sufficient evidence to draw the conclusion that the author was a woman.

[WW]

Bibliography

Bennewitz, Ingrid. "Das Nibelungenlied ein *Puech von Chrimhild?* Ein geschlechtergeschichtlicher Versuch zum Nibelungenlied und seiner Rezeption." In *3. Pöchlarner Heldenliedgespräch: Die Rezeption des Nibelungenliedes,* edited by Klaus Zatloukal. Vienna: Fassbänder, 1995, pp. 33–52.

Lösl-Wieland-Engelmann, Berta. "Verdanken wir das Nibelungenlied einer Niedernburger Nonne?" *Monatshefte* 72 (1980): 5–25.

_____. "Die wichtigsten Verdachtsmomente für eine weibliche Verfasserschaft des Nibelungenliedes." In *Feminismus: Inspektion der Her-*

renkultur. Ein Handbuch, edited by Luise F. Pusch. Edition Suhrkamp 1192 (n.s. 192). Frankfurt a. M.: Suhrkamp, 1993.

ORAL-DICTATED TEXT. An orally composed text that has been dictated to a scribe. The founders of the theory of oral-formulaic composition, Milman Parry and Albert B. Lord, proceeded from the principle that oral and written literature are mutually exclusive: a text is either composed orally or in writing. Orally composed medieval literature, however, has necessarily come down to us in writing. To explain the transition from oral to written, it has been suggested that a singer who had learned to write could have dictated the text to himself, or that a singer could have dictated the text to a scribe for the use by those colleagues who were able to read in order to refresh their memories, or that a text was dictated to a scribe at the request of a rich patron following a performance, as has been suggested in the case of the *Nibelungenlied.* None of these three possibilities are likely, however, because contemporary singers find it extremely difficult either to recite slowly enough for someone to follow them in longhand or to write their songs down themselves.

[NV]

Bibliography

Borghart, K. H. R. *Das Nibelungenlied: Die Spuren mündlichen Ursprungs in schriftlicher Überlieferung.* Amsterdam: Rodopi, 1977.

Curschmann, Michael. "Oral Poetry in Mediaeval English, French, and German Literature: Some Notes on Recent Research." *Speculum* 42 (1967): 36–52.

Lord, Albert, B. "Homer's Originality: Oral-Dictated Texts." In *Transactions and Proceedings of the American Philological Association* 84 (1953): 124–134.

ORAL POETRY serves in preliterate societies as an important medium for the preservation and dissemination of culturally sensitive information and values, whether across the generations within a society or across political or ethnic boundaries between neighbors, trade partners, or rivals. Etzel's choice of minstrels as his emissaries to Worms may still carry a trace of oral poetry's earlier role in communication between polities. A single poem may be either conservative or innovative, depending on whether it is used to inculcate traditional values in a new generation or to introduce strangers to the experiences and values of an alien cultural system. The mechanics of accurately preserving very long poems has been ascertained through observation of oral performances in Yugoslavia, Indonesia, and Africa. Through such studies we have come to understand poetic recitation as an act of composition derived from formulaic language, stereotyped scenes and motifs, and traditional narrative materials. Familiarity with these conventions also informs oral poetry's reception as audiences apply well-developed sets of expectations to the type scenes and stock characters encountered during a performance. Although in its present form influenced by the process of written composition, the *Nibelungenlied* can be presumed to derive at least in part from a preliterate society, and thus still to carry some of the information and values that would have been a concern to the Germanic peoples during the migration age (third to fifth centuries A.D.) or even earlier. Parallels are to be found in poems, folktales, and legends, both in other Germanic contexts (Old High German, Anglo-Saxon, Danish, and Norse), as well as in less clearly connected sources (Greek, Persian, and Hebrew). The wide distribution of traditional scenes testifies to oral poetry's remarkable portability and durability, and above all, to its utility.

[VU]

PIARISTENHANDSCHRIFT (Piarist Manuscript). A (paper) manuscript dating from the fifteenth century containing diverse works from the Middle Ages. It is to be found in the Österreichische Nationalbibliothek in Vienna, cod. 15478. The manuscript was discovered in the nineteenth century in the Piarist Monastery of St. Thekla an der Wieden (Vienna), from which it derives its name. The codex is also called "Lienhart Scheubels Heldenbuch" after the name of the person presumed to be its first owner, the Nuremberg citizen Lienhart Scheubel.

Though it is primarily known as the manuscript containing *Nibelungenlied* **k**, it consists of seven narratives or parts of narratives, some of which, including the Nibelungenlied, had been circulated singly before being bound together. 1. *Virginal,* a "Dietrich epic"; 2. *König Anteloy,* also called Antelan, an Arthurian narrative named for its hero, a dwarf king. Then a series of heroic epics: 3. *Ortnit;* 4. *Wolfdietrich;* 5 *Nibelungenlied I* (1152 strophes); 6 *Nibelungenlied II* (1290 strophes). Finally, 7. *Lorengel,* a version of the Arthurian Lohengrin story.

There seems to be a plan in the selection and sequencing of the narratives. All depict the testing of young warriors; all except *Anteloy* are concerned with *Brautwerbung* ("winning a bride"). *Virginal, Anteloy,* and *Ortnit* are connected through the depiction of dwarfs in important roles. The *Nibelungenlied* and *Lorengel* might be connected through a mention of Etzel at the beginning of *Lorengel.* Moreover, like the *Heldenbuch-Prosa* "prose supplement to the anthology," the heroic epics span the entire "heroic age," incorporating the biography of Dietrich von Bern.

Nibelungenlied **k** is clearly a product of the fifteenth century. It is composed in *Hildebrandston,* a late adaptation of the *Nibelungenstrophe* that lacks the extended last line. The text, based on the C version, has been extensively adapted to the tastes of a fifteenth century, primarily middle-class audience. This kind of adaptation is seen in increased emphasis upon courtly etiquette and protocol; in hyperbolic descriptions of battle, clothing, and weapons; and in the emotional intensity with which the love between Kriemhild and Siegfried is depicted.

[RHF/MS]

Bibliography
Becker, Peter Jörg. *Handschriften und Frühdrücke mittelhochdeutscher Epen.* Wiesbaden: Reichert, 1977, pp. 156–158.
Ertzdorff, Xenja von. "Lienhart Scheubels Heldenbuch." In *Festschrift für Siegfried Gutenbrunner,* edited by Oskar Bandle et. al. Heidelberg: Winter, 1972.
Heinzle, Joachim. "Heldenbücher." In *Die deutsche Literatur des Mittelalters: Verfasserlexikon,* edited by Kurt Ruh, vol. 3. Berlin: de Gruyter, 1981, cols. 947–956, here 951–952.
Hoffman, Werner. "Die spätmittelalterliche Bearbeitung des Nibelungenliedes in Lienhart Scheubels Heldenbuch." GRM, 60 (1979) 129–145.
Keller, Adalbert von, ed. *Das Nibelungenlied nach der Piaristenhandschrift.* Stuttgart: Verlag des Litterarischen Vereins, 1879.
Kornrumpf, Gisela. "Strophik im Zeitalter der Prosa: Deutsche Heldendichtung im ausgehenden Mittelalter." In *Literatur und Laienbildung im Spätmittelalter und in der Reformationszeit,* edited by Ludger Grenzmann et al. Stuttgart: Metzler, 1981, pp. 316–340.
Menhardt, Hermann. *Verzeichnis der altdeutschen literarischen Handschriften der österreichischen Nationalbibliothek.* Vol. III. Deutsche Akademie der Wissenschaften zu Berlin. Berlin: Akademie-Verlag, 1961.
Springeth, Margarete. "Beobachtungen zur Nibelungen Rezeption in der Wiener Piaristenhandschrift (k)." In *3. Pöchlarner Heldenliedgespräch: Die Rezeption des Nibelungenliedes,* edited by Klaus Zatloukal. Vienna: Fassbaender, 1995, pp. 173–185.
————. "Die Dekonstruktion des Heroischen: Überlieferungsgeschichtliche und rezeptionsästhetische Untersuchungen zum Nibelungenlied in der Wiener Piaristenhandschrift (Fassung k)." Diss., Salzburg, 1997.

PSEUDO-ORAL FORMULA. A traditional, recurrent, metrically or rhythmically organized, lexically variable but semantically stable group of words that in a written text does not necessarily imply that we are dealing with oral composition but refers to the oral tradition. Its link to the oral tradition has a sociohistorical implication; that is, that oral poetry addresses an illiterate social subgroup, whereas written literature applies to an educated stratum of society. The *Nibelungenlied* is considered to be a pseudo-oral-formulaic composition which means that it can be regarded as a commentary on the oral Nibelungen tradition.

[NV]

Bibliography
Bäuml, Franz, H. "Medieval Texts and the Two Theories of Oral-Formulaic Composition: A Proposal for a Third Theory." *New Literary History: A Journal of Theory and Interpretation* 16 (1984/85): 31–49.

RECEPTION OF THE *NIBELUNGENLIED* IN GERMANY has its roots in the scholarly and artistic interests of the educated bourgeoisie and lesser nobility in the mid- to late eighteenth century. As is the case with much of the later reception of the epic, its beginnings must also be viewed against the larger historical and cultural background of the age. Johann Jakob Bodmer (1698–1783), a major opponent of Johann Christoph Gottsched (1700–1766, Professor of Literature at Leipzig, leading Enlightenment theoretician, dramatist, translator, and editor) and his brand of Prussian rationalism, together with his friend Johann Jakob Breitinger, published in 1757 the last third of the *Nibelungenlied* and the *Klage* under the title *Chriemhilden Rache, und die Klage; Zwey Heldengedichte aus dem schwäbischen Zeitpuncte.* The excerpts were taken from a manuscript found by Jakob Hermann Obereit, a physician with antiquarian interests, in the library of the Count of Hohenems on June 28, 1755. This manuscript was later designated manuscript **C.** In 1782 Christoph Heinrich Müller (or Myller) published the complete text of the *Nibelungenlied* utilizing the newly discovered manuscript **A** (1779) for the first half and **C** for the second. He dedicated his edition to the Prussian king, Frederick the Great, who dismissed the epic and, indeed, medieval literature in general by declaring that the work was "not worth powder and shot [i.e., was worthless] and did not merit being raised up from the dust of obscurity." In spite of his daunting judgment, once the *Nibelungenlied* genie was out of the bottle it was impossible to put it back in. Toward the end of the eighteenth century, a time that was influenced by Herder's concept of the nation ("Volk") and his call for a national myth, the reception of the Middle Ages in general and the *Nibelungenlied* in particular developed its own dynamic and was able to assert itself against the ideals of the Enlightenment and classicism. Not until the nineteenth century, however, would the seeds of interest in the *Nibelungenlied* bear fruit.

Novalis's *Die Christenheit oder Europa* (1799) begins with the lines: "Those were times of beauty and splendor when Europe was one Christian land," a statement that effectively raises the curtain on the Eurocentric myth of the Middle Ages. Romanticism delved deep into Christian myth, and romantic writers, like Friedrich Schlegel, Friedrich Schelling, Georg Wilhelm Friedrich Hegel, Friedrich Hölderlin, expanded that myth with their desire for a "new mythology," one with roots in the antiquity. This "new mythology" would not replicate or merely reflect classical mythology, but rather, as Friedrich Schlegel wrote in his *Rede über die Mythologie,* would become a "new accommodation and receptacle for the ancient and eternal font of poesy and even of the unending poem itself which cloaks the seeds of all other poems." In a lecture devoted exclusively to the *Nibelungenlied,* one in a series delivered in Berlin dealing with the "history of romantic literature" (1803/1804), August Wilhelm Schlegel concluded with the clarion call: "After we [the Germans] have been roaming all around the world long enough, we should finally begin to take advantage of our own national literature." Using the *Iliad* as a model, the "neue Mythologie" took on a national focus for which Schlegel retrieved the *Nibelungenlied.* Anchored within the romantic theory of universal poesy, he extolled it as a "marvel of nature" and a "grand work of art." His brother, Friedrich, hoped that it would become the "foundation and cornerstone of our poesy." According to Schelling, the "new mythology" would be the agent that would guide philosophy (or science), actualized in the dawn of poesy, back to poesy, which itself is "not the invention of the individual poet . . . ." Echoing this sentiment, August Wilhelm Schlegel said of the *Nibelungenlied:* "Such a work is too grand for one individual; it is the product of the total energy of an age." Ludwig Tieck, who promoted German medievalism with a revival of the old chapbooks, also concurred in his preface to *Die altdeutschen Minnelieder* (1803). He published the songs in an archaic, literary language, believing that their ancient essence manifested itself most purely in the old tongue. In this sense he also attempted, albeit unsuccessfully, to reconstruct the Nibelungen myth, joining the *Nibelungenlied* together with Nordic sagas. Tieck, the brothers Schlegel, and even Schelling, combined the song/lay theory developed by F. A. Wolf with Herder's ideas on the so-called "Volks-, National- or Naturpoesie," and their own theories regarding the "new mythology" and universal poetry. For them the *Nibelungenlied* itself was a collective creation that reflected the "German national character" (A. W. Schlegel), whereby they followed the practice of the patriotic eighteenth century and identified "German" with "Germanic."

The conflict with philology was inevitable. Friedrich Heinrich von der Hagen, who had attended lectures by A. W. Schlegel in Berlin and had been a friend of Tieck, came completely over to their side after his translation of the *Nibelungenlied* in 1807. He wished to strengthen the patriotic features of romantic medievalism, which was becoming more and more nationalistically focused as a result of Napoleon's military successes and the fall of the Holy Roman Empire in 1806. In the face of the desolate state of the empire, von der Hagen hoped for a "return of German glory" on a new foundation of the Nibelungen values. His topical view made a strong impression on the educated middle class that was searching for a national myth. It also favorably influenced the creative reception of the work in art and poetry. His approach afforded a contrast to the philology of manuscript criticism or the naive, even if mythologically saturated, position of Jakob Grimm, who vehemently rejected any attempts at providing the work with contemporary appeal. In von der Hagen's opinion, the epic would "certainly find acceptance by the people [*Volk*] and probably more on its own merits than through teaching in a school." A. W. Schlegel, on the other hand, demanded ten years after his lecture on the *Nibelungenlied* that along with the Bible the epic should become "once again a major text [used] in the education of youth."

Art, too, participated in the medieval revival. A group of early nineteenth-century German artists known as the Nazarenes (earlier called the Lukasbrüder) offered a new kind of art constructed around the works of Albrecht Dürer and Raphael. The secularization of Christian painting carried out by Peter Cornelius, Karl Gangloff, Karl Philipp Fohr, Ludwig Sigismund Ruhl, and others was also applied to scenes from the *Nibelungenlied*.

Throughout the course of the nineteenth century romantic medievalism gradually lost its visionary intensity directed toward the future of humanity and suffered a general decline, becoming a nostalgic imitation of the Middle Ages. An excellent example of this development can be seen in the impressive frescoes by Schnorr von Carolsfeld in the Wittelsbach palace in Munich. Although still influenced by the Christian aspirations of the Nazarenes, he was able to harmonize the Nibelungen of the epic with Bavarian feudalism. By encroaching upon the historic, art disarmed myth. The theme "Middle Ages" found a secure spot in all genres, with dramas, including those dealing with the *Nibelungenlied*, being the most popular. A new and specifically German stimulus for medievalism came from opera, especially the medieval works by Richard Wagner. Wagner replaced the idyll with the myth of splendor and grandioseness as well as heroism for their own sakes. In the shadow of the archaic *Ring*, the Nibelungen myth flourished again, thus benefiting the *Nibelungenlied*, whose importance had been relentlessly promoted by eager philologists and teachers. Slowly the literature of the Middle Ages seeped into the school curricula, mainly Walther von der Vogelweide and the *Nibelungenlied*. Editions and translations were made for schools, teaching materials on the work were revised, and soon children's books appeared.

By the beginning of the twentieth century, the romantic "popular epic" had become the "heroic epic." The development of the Nibelungen myth reacted to political movements, but it cannot be convincingly demonstrated that the myth itself developed its own momentum in unifying the nation. Gradually, then, the idealistic romantic vision of such unifying power that was connected to the myth faded away.

Nonetheless, the *Nibelungenlied* provided the German-speaking lands with powerful stereotypes that would be used through World War II. In his 1814 edition of the *Nibelungenlied*, Johann August Zeune celebrated the liberation of the German territories from Napoleon's rule with the exultant words: "Yes! The mighty dragon slayer [Siegfried] has risen and rid our sacred German soil of foreign vermin!" In addition to the image of Siegfried the dragon slayer, a number of other motifs and images have been taken from the Nibelungen myth. The fable of the "stab in the back" (the "Dolchstoßlegende") as the explanation for the defeat of the German army in World War I is one such motif. Both Hitler and Hindenburg helped to establish this fiction as truth and claimed that Germany lay in ashes because of the enemy within. Other motifs and images from the epic have included: youth in all its positive aspects (strength, beauty); the (blond) German in general; invincibility; Hagen (the sinister killer, but also the man of state); the determined and death-defying warrior; the Nibelungen treasure (used in many ways as a positive symbol for something with undefined proportions); Kriemhild (the merciless avenger and the typical blond German maiden); Brünhild (the barbaric maiden); Kriemhild vs. Brünhild (the quarreling woman, and civilization/culture vs. nature); Rüdiger (nobleness and fidelity); and *Nibelungentreue* (Nibelungen loyalty—a key political concept used by the chancellor of the empire, Fürst von Bülow, to describe the relationship between Germany and Austria). The inspiration for these stereotypes, however, was scarcely to be sought in the medieval epic, but rather in the chapbook about Siegfried as well as in Wagner's operas.

A stubborn refusal to accept the humiliating defeat in World War I, as well as a widespread cultural pessimism among the middle classes, made Germans more susceptible to the Nibelungen stereotypes being employed with great success by radical and antidemocratic movements. In the politically unstable climate of the years between the world wars, these groups, most notably National Socialism, advanced the theory of the strong leader (Führer), proclaimed "germanicized medievalism" as its political and social program, and looked more toward the Nibelungen myth than the *Nibelungenlied*. The *Edda,* for example, describes a new country rising from the flood with an eagle soaring high, the eagle being the heraldic bird of the nation. Germany became "Nibelungenland." Images, derived from the Nibelungen story and directed especially toward youth, and a Germanism that was cultivated in part within broad academic circles, became widespread. For example, in his speech on January 30, 1943, the tenth anniversary of the National Socialists' coming to power, Hermann Göring elevated the hopeless battle of Stalingrad into the realm of myth by comparing it to the burning of the great hall at Etzel's court. Hans Naumann, a professor of German Studies, proposed molding the life of Hitler into something resembling the tales of the hero Dietrich von Bern. But it should not be forgotten that there was also a secret and "nonvulgar" reception of the work in these years, especially in art, as for example in the charcoal drawings by Ernst Barlach or in the paintings by Josef Hegenbarth and Max Slevogt.

The fascist perversion of the Nibelungen myth had such a widespread influence abroad that in 1945 the work was completely banned for a short time after World War II by the British Occupation authorities in Hamburg. Later, in the early years of the Federal Republic of Germany, the *Nibelungenlied* took its place in the more or less favored educational canon of the secondary schools, without, however, any national encumbrance. The tales from the chapbooks and myth found their place in children's books, as was also the case in the German Democratic Republic. The former national stereotypes were stripped bare of all political associations and lived on as pure superman fiction. With few exceptions literary reception of the *Nibelungenlied* was muted. The reception of the Middle Ages, on the other hand, flourished in both the Federal Republic of Germany and the German Democratic Republic, especially during the 1960s and 1970s. Several relatively successful novels and dramas with medieval subject matter as well as biographies of medieval poets continue to be published. This German phenomenon coalesced with the American medievalism that has been thriving since the 1960s and to some degree has been associated with the presidency of John F. Kennedy. In the 1980s, then, a positive image of the Middle Ages became established among broad segments of the population. It is now linked to tourism, castles, and exhibitions, medieval fairs, and the architectural renaissance of city centers and villages into idyllic, preindustrial, half-timbered buildings. This situation may provide an opportunity for the *Nibelungenlied* to be stripped of unacceptable mythological baggage so that it can be presented to all in its grandeur and dignity. Outside Germany and Scandinavia the reception of the Nibelungen theme has, for the most part, occurred via the medium of Richard Wagner's *Ring* tetralogy, although the *Nibelungenlied* has been translated into many languages. (see section on translations below.)

[OE]

Bibliography

Arendt, Dieter. "Barbarossa im Kyffhäuser oder der literarische Traum vom 'geheimen Deutschland.'" *Damals, Zeitschrift für geschichtliches Wissen* 14 (1982): 554–573, 646–667.

Brackert, Helmut. "Nibelungenlied und Nationalgedanke: Zur Geschichte einer deutschen Ideologie." In *Mediaevalia litteraria. Festschrift Helmut de Boor zum 80. Geburtstag.* Munich: Beck, 1971, pp. 343–364.

Ehrismann, Otfrid. *Das Nibelungenlied in Deutschland: Studien zur Rezeption des Nibelungenliedes von der Mitte des 18. Jahrhunderts bis zum ersten Weltkrieg.* Munich: Fink, 1975.

———. *Nibelungenlied: Epoche, Werk, Wirkung.* Munich: Beck, 1987.

———. *Nibelungenlied 1755–1920: Regesten und Kommentare zu Forschung und Rezeption.* Gießen: Schmitz, 1986.

———. "Siegfried: Ein deutscher Mythos?" In *Herrscher, Helden, Heilige,* edited by Ulrich Müller and Werner Wunderlich. St. Gall: UVK, 1996, pp. 367–387.

Frühwald, Wolfgang. "Wandlungen eines Nationalmythos: Der Weg der Nibelungen ins 19. Jahrhundert." In *Wege des Mythos in der Moderne: Richard Wagner, Der Ring des Nibelungen,* edited by Dieter Borchmeyer. Munich: Deutscher Taschenbuch Verlag, 1987, pp. 17–40.

Gentry, Francis G. "Die Rezeption des Nibelungenliedes in der Weimarer Republik." In *Das Weiterleben des Mittelalters in der deutschen Literatur,* edited by James F. Poag and Gerhild Scholz Williams. Königstein/Ts.: Athenäum, 1983, pp. 141–156.

Grunewald, Eckhard. *Friedrich Heinrich von der Hagen, 1780–1856: Ein Beitrag zur Frühgeschichte der Germanistik.* Berlin: de Gruyter, 1988.

Hermand, Jost, and Francis G. Gentry. "Neue Romantik? West-Östliches zum Thema 'Mittelalter.' " In vol. 9 of *Basis: Jahrbuch für deutsche Gegenwartsliteratur,* edited by Reinhold Grimm and Jost Hermand. Frankfurt am M.: Suhrkamp, 1979, pp. 122–148, 264–266.

Hoffmann, Werner. "Nibelungenromane." In *Helden und Heldensage: Otto Gschwantler zum 60. Geburtstag,* edited by Hermann Reichert and Gunter Zimmermann. Vienna: Fassbaender, 1990, pp. 113–142.

Kimpel, Harald, and Johanna Werckmeister. "Leidmotive: Möglichkeiten der künstlerischen Nibelungen-Rezeption seit 1945." In *Die Nibelungen: Ein deutscher Wahn, ein deutscher Alptraum. Studien und Dokumente zur Rezeption des Nibelungenstoffs im 19. und 20. Jahrhundert,* edited by Joachim Heinzle and Anneliese Waldschmidt. Frankfurt a. M.: Suhrkamp, 1991, pp. 284–306.

Koebner, Thomas. "Minne Macht: Zu Richard Wagners Bühnenwerk *Der Ring des Nibelungen.*" In *Die Nibelungen: Ein deutscher Wahn, ein deutscher Alptraum. Studien und Dokumente zur Rezeption des Nibelungenstoffs im 19. und 20.*

Jahrhundert, edited by Joachim Heinzle and Anneliese Waldschmidt. Frankfurt a. M.: Suhrkamp, 1991, pp. 309–332.

Körner, Josef. *Nibelungenforschungen der deutschen Romantik.* 1911. Reprint, Darmstadt: Wissenschaftliche Buchgesellschaft, 1968.

Krüger, Peter. "Etzels Halle und Stalingrad: Die Rede Görings vom 30.1.1943." In *Die Nibelungen: Ein deutscher Wahn, ein deutscher Alptraum. Studien und Dokumente zur Rezeption des Nibelungenstoffs im 19. und 20. Jahrhundert,* edited by Joachim Heinzle and Anneliese Waldschmidt. Frankfurt a. M.: Suhrkamp, 1991, pp. 151–190.

Lankheit, Klaus. "Nibelungen-Illustrationen der Romantik: Zur Säkularisierung christlicher Bildformen im 19. Jahrhundert." In *Die Nibelungen: Ein deutscher Wahn, ein deutscher Alptraum. Studien und Dokumente zur Rezeption des Nibelungenstoffs im 19. und 20. Jahrhundert,* edited by Joachim Heinzle and Anneliese Waldschmidt. Frankfurt a. M.: Suhrkamp, 1991, pp. 193–218.

Martin, Bernhard R. *Nibelungenmetamorphosen: Die Geschichte eines Mythos.* Munich: Iudicium, 1992.

Mertens, Volker. "Richard Wagner und das Mittelalter." In *Richard-Wagner-Handbuch,* edited by Ulrich Müller and Peter Wapnewski. Stuttgart: Kröner, 1986, pp. 19–59. Engl. ed.: *Wagner Handbook,* edited by Ulrich Müller and Peter Wapnewski, translated and edited by John Deathridge. Cambridge: Harvard University Press, 1992.

Müller, Ulrich. "Das Nachleben mittelalterlicher Stoffe." In *Epische Stoffe des Mittelalters,* edited by Volker Mertens and Ulrich Müller. Stuttgart: Kröner, 1984, pp. 424–448.

Müler, Ulrich. "Die Auferstehung der Nibelungen: Beobachtungen zur Rezeption des Nibelungen-Mythos in den Achtziger Jahren." In *Soziokulturelle Kontexte der Sprach- und Literaturentwicklung: Festschrift für Rudolf Grosse zum 65. Geburtstag,* edited by Sabine Heimann, et al. Stuttgart: Heinz, 1989, pp. 495–506.

Schmidt, Siegrid. "Die Nibelungen in der Jugend- und Unterhaltungsliteratur zwischen 1945 und 1980." In *Mittelalter-Rezeption,* edited by Peter Wapnewski. Stuttgart: Metzler, 1986, pp. 327–345.

Schröder, Werner. "Das Nibelungenlied in unserer Zeit." In *Hohenemser Studien zum Nibelungenlied,* edited by Achim Masser. Dornbirn: Vorlarlberger Verlagsanstalt, 1981, pp. 9–18.

Schulte-Wülwer, Ulrich. *Das Nibelungenlied in der deutschen Kunst des 19. und 20. Jahrhunderts.* Gießen: Anabas-Verlag Kampf, 1980.

———. "Das Nibelungenlied: Ein Nationalepos?" In

Die Nibelungen, edited by Joachim Heinzle and Anneliese Waldschmidt. Frankfurt a. M.: Suhrkamp, 1991, pp. 43–110.

Storch, Wolfgang, ed. *Die Nibelungen: Bilder von Liebe, Verrat, und Untergang.* Munich: Haus der Kunst, 1987.

Wappenschmidt, Heinz-Toni. "Nibelungenlied und Historienmalerei im 19. Jahrhundert: Wege der Identitätsfindung." In *Die Nibelungen: Ein deutscher Wahn, ein deutscher Alptraum. Studien und Dokumente zur Rezeption des Nibelungenstoffs im 19. und 20. Jahrhundert,* edited by Joachim Heinzle and Anneliese Waldschmidt. Frankfurt a. M.: Suhrkamp, 1991, pp. 219–250.

Wunderlich, Werner. "'Ein Hauptbuch bey der Erziehung der deutschen Jugend . . . .' Zur pädagogischen Indienstnahme des Nibelungenlieds für Schule und Unterricht im 19. und 20. Jahrhundert." In *Die Nibelungen: Ein deutscher Wahn, ein deutscher Alptraum. Studien und Dokumente zur Rezeption des Nibelungenstoffs im 19. und 20. Jahrhundert,* edited by Joachim Heinzle and Anneliese Waldschmidt. Frankfurt a. M.: Suhrkamp, 1991, pp. 119–150.

——. *Der Schatz des Drachentödters: Materialien zur Wirkungsgeschichte des Nibelungenliedes.* Stuttgart: Klett/Cotta, 1977.

——. "Total krasse Helden." In *Sammlung, Deutung, Wertung: Ergebnisse, Probleme, Tendenzen und Perspektiven philologischer Arbeit; mélanges de littérature médiévale et de linguistique allemande; offerts à Wolfgang Spiewok à l'occasion de son soixantième anniversaire,* edited by Danielle Buschinger. Amiens: Université de Picardie. Centre d'Etudes Médiévales, 1988, pp. 369–383.

ROMANCE. Intended for a secular and noble audience, the class of literature known as the romance celebrated the feudal court and its way of life. In addition to entertainment the romance showed its audience "wie man zer werlte sollte leben" ("how one should live in the world" Walther von der Vogelweide). It also dealt with issues of immediate concern for the nobility, such as ideals of rulership, courtliness (*hôher muot*), loyalty (*triuwe*), honor (*êre*), and love (*minne*). Characteristic of the romance is a distinct *Doppelwegstruktur,* in which the male hero's quest leads him on two sets of adventures; the second guides him to his appropriate role in courtly society. This structure allowed the poet to explore various cultural spaces, as well as the margins of those areas. In fact, the relationship between the peripheral and the central remains a defining characteristic of the romance. The process of *âventiure* structures this movement between the center and the margins, providing some experiences that courtly society cannot accommodate. Indeed, according to Erich Auerbach, adventure signals a "chosen" condition. Southern also interprets the quest as a fundamentally spiritual experience. The quest offered a solitary knight (like the individual soul) the opportunity to undertake a secular journey toward self-knowledge. For Vinaver, the narrative strategy of the romance invites the reader to share in the quest for meaning. Finally, the romance is concerned not with human realities but with problems and how they may be elaborated and solved. In other words the romance offers an experiment that we could perhaps classify as "fiction" (Haug). According to Green, the German romance poets perfected the art of representing fictional truth. This does not, of course, discount the possibility of a higher truth in the fiction; it merely underscores the importance of the written form as a legitimation of this truth. Thus Green circumvents Auerbach's argument that the romance represents a detour into the world of the fairy tale, unlike the more "factual" *chanson de geste.*

The *Nibelungenlied,* while drawing primarily on sources anchored in the tradition of the heroic epic, also incorporates elements typical of thirteenth-century romance. The elements are most evident in Kriemhild's dream of the falcon (13,1–4) and the depiction of the relationship between Siegfried and Kriemhild as an example of *hôhe minne.* In addition, the courtly episodes in the *Nibelungenlied* serve to heighten the tension between the courtly and the feudal systems and between epic and romance traditions.

[ASH]

Bibliography

Auerbach, Erich. *Mimesis: Dargestellte Wirklichkeit in der abendländischen Literatur.* Berne: Francke, 1946.

Green, Dennis H. *Medieval Listening and Reading: The Primary Reception of German Literature 800–1300.* Cambridge: Cambridge University Press, 1994.

Haug, Walter. *Literaturtheorie im deutschen Mittelalter von den Anfängen bis zum Ende des 13. Jahrhunderts: Eine Einführung.* Darmstadt: Wissenschaftliche Buchgesellschaft, 1985.

————. "Wandlungen des Fiktionalitätsbewußtseins vom hohen zum späten Mittelalter." In *Entzauberung der Welt: Deutsche Literatur 1200–1500,* edited by James F. Poag and Thomas C. Fox. Tübingen: Francke, 1989, pp. 1–18.

Southern, R. W. *The Making of the Middle Ages.* New Haven: Yale University Press, 1953.

Vinaver, Eugene. *The Rise of Romance.* Oxford: Oxford University Press, 1971.

RUDOLF VON EMS (ca. 1200–ca. 1254), a "Ministeriale" in the service of the Landgrave of Montfort in the Austrian territory of Vorarlberg, who had his residence at Hohenems. Rudolf had close connections to the Hohenstaufen dynasty and the courts of Frederick II and Konrad IV. He was the author of several epics, including *Der guote Gêrhart, Barlaam und Josaphat, Willehalm von Orlens,* and *Alexander,* and he wrote a world chronicle dedicated to the Hohenstaufen emperor Konrad IV. It has been suggested that Rudolf might be the poet who revised and wrote down the *Nibelungenlied* in the version passed down to us in manuscript **C**, which was found in 1755 in the castle library of Hohenems, the ancestral seat of the Montfort dynasty. In Albert Ritter's novel, *Das Nibelungenjahr* (The Nibelungen Year, 1912), Rudolf is portrayed as the author, scribe, and performer (singer) of this manuscript. Peter Honegger has theorized that Bligger III of Steinach was the author of manuscripts **A** and **B** and that one of his Swiss kinsmen from the village of Steinach on Lake Constance inspired Rudolf to write down the version found in manuscript **C**. In Honegger's opinion the miniature of "Rudolf the Scribe" that appears in the Manesse Codex could refer to Rudolf von Ems. There is, however, no concrete evidence for all of these hypotheses.

[WW]

Bibliography

Brackert, Helmut. *Rudolf von Ems: Dichtung und Geschichte.* Heidelberg: Winter, 1968.

Ertzdorff, Xenia von. *Rudolf von Ems: Untersuchungen zum höfischen Roman im 13. Jahrhundert.* Munich: Fink, 1967.

Hoffmann, Werner. "Bligger von Steinach als Dichter des Nibelungenliedes? Zu Peter Honeggers neuer These." *ZfdA* 112 (1993): 434–441.

Honegger, Peter. "Bligger von Steinach als Verfasser und Rudolf von Montfort als Bearbeiter des Nibelungenliedes." In *"Waz sider da geschach." American-German Studies on the Nibelungenlied,* edited by Werner Wunderlich and Ulrich Müller. GAG 564. Göppingen: Kümmerle, 1992, pp. 9–54.

SANGVERSEPIK, the singing of epics and tales. The word was introduced by Ulrich Müller, inspired by Karl Bertau's "Sangverslyrik," to stress the decisive role of music and singing in performing epic poetry. (see NIBELUNGEN PROSODY, HILDEBRANDSTON, EPIC SINGING.)

[UM]

SCHNEIDERSTROPHE (Tailor's stanza). The poet of the *Nibelungenlied* was apparently very much concerned with the splendors of courtly life, especially in its physical aspects. Evidence of this is his manifest interest in costly articles of clothing. Whole strophes of the poem deal with the wearing apparel of the leading figures and have come to be known as *Schneiderstrophen.* See, for example, stanza 362: "Die arâbîschen sîden wîz alsô der snê/unt von Zazamanc der guoten grüen' alsam der klê/dar in si leiten steine; des wurden guotiu kleit./selbe sneit si Kriemhilt, diu vil hêrlîche meit" (Arabian silks as white as snow and the ones from Zazamanc, green as clover,—into them they stitched precious stones, thus making fine clothes. Kriemhild, that very noble maiden, tailored them herself). The four strophes that follow continue the description of the clothing and how it was made, thereby making five *Schneiderstrophen* in a row.

[SMJ]

SIGEHART VON LORSCH, an abbot considered the possible author of manuscript **C.** The search for the author of the *Nibelungenlied* has been particularly intense with regard to manuscript **C,** the so-called "liet"-version of the epic. The striking idiosyncrasies of **C** suggest that a scribe took it upon himself to modernize the language of an already extant text, expand the content, and provide a moral interpretation of the plot. Sigehart was a grandson of Uta von Calw, who lived at a court situated close to Lorsch. Because one can read in **C** that Ute resided at a court near Lorsch Monastery, it was suggested that this provides a justification for associating the *Nibelungenlied* with Sigehart, who is presumed, about 1150, to have combined the Lay of Brünhild and the story of the Nibelungs' demise into a Rhenish-Franconian poem. This poem formed the basis for the composition of the *Nibelungenlied* that was undertaken some five decades later. It was also claimed that the considerable familiarity with Middle Rhenish localities also supports the theory that Sigehart was the author of manuscript **C**.

[WW]

Bibliography

Dietrich, Julius R. *Der Dichter des Nibelungenliedes: Ein Versuch.* Darmstadt: [E. Bekker], 1923.

Selzer, Wolfgang. "Lorsch und das Nibelungenlied." In *Laurissa jubilans: Festschrift zur 1200-Jahrfeier von Lorsch.* Mainz: Gemeinde Lorsch, 1964, pp. 106–114.

Voorwinden, Norbert. "Lorsch im Nibelungenlied: Die Hs. C als Bearbeitung einer schriftlich fixierten mündlichen Dichtung." In *Stauferzeit: Geschichte, Literatur, Kunst,* edited by Rüdiger Krohn et al. Stuttgart: Klett-Cotta, 1978, pp. 279–284.

SIMROCK, KARL JOSEPH (1802–1876), German philologist and poet. Simrock became well-known for his many translations of Middle High German epics and lyric poetry, among them the poems of Walther von der Vogelweide and the *Nibelungenlied.* His translation of the *Nibelungenlied* became probably the most influential modern German translation of the epic. In 1843, 1846, and 1849 he published the *Amelungenlied,* a collection of epics in modern German telling the story of the "Amelung" Dietrich von Bern and his clan. The *Amelungenlied* consists of eight parts: (1) Wieland der Schmied (Wieland the Smith), (2) Wittich Wielands Sohn (Wittich, Son of Wieland), (3) Ecken Ausfahrt (Ecke's Departure), (4) Dietleib, (5) Sibichs Verrat (Sibich's Treachery), (6) Die beiden Dietriche (The Two Dietrichs), (7) Die Rabenschlacht (The Battle at Ravenna), and (8) Die Heimkehr (The Homecoming). Parts three and seven are translations of late MHG epics, the other parts are accounts composed by Simrock in which he used the metrical pattern of the Nibelungen stanza. The *Amelungenlied* was highly praised at its time, but is nearly forgotten today. Simrock also wrote two poems entitled "Der versenkte Hort" (The Sunken Treasure) and "Der Nibelungenhort" (The Nibelungen Treasure) in which he reveals that the mythical "Hort" of the Nibelungs is not gold but the golden Rhine wine.

[UM]

Bibliography

Heinzle, Joachim. "'. . . diese reinen kräftigen Töne.' Zu Karl Simrocks Übersetzung des 'Nibelungenliedes.'" In *Die Nibelungen: Ein deutscher Wahn, ein deutscher Alptraum. Studien und Dokumente zur Rezeption des Nibelungenstoffs im 19. und 20. Jahrhundert,* edited by Joachim Heinzle and Anneliese Waldschmidt. Frankfurt a. M.: Suhrkamp, 1991, pp. 111–118.

Mertens, Volker. "Amelungenlied und Nibelungenlied. Richard Wagner und Karl Simrock." In *La chanson des Nibelungen hier et aujourd'hui: Actes du Colloque Amiens 12 et 13 janvier 1991.* Greifswald: Reineke, 1991, pp. 113–128.

Moser, Hugo. *Karl Simrock: Universitätslehrer und Poet, Germanist und Erneuer von "Volkspoesie" und älterer "Nationalliteratur." Ein Stück Literatur-, Bildungs- und Wissenschaftsgeschichte des 19. Jahrhunderts.* Berlin: Schmidt, 1976.

Müller, Ulrich. "Heldenlieder aus Minnesangs zweitem Frühling: Karl Simrock's 'Amelungenlied' (1843–1849)." In *4. Pöchlarner Heldenliedgespräch. Heldendichtung in Österreich, österreichische Heldendichtung,* edited by Klaus Zatloukal. Vienna: Fassbaender, 1997, pp. 171–188.

Simrock, Karl. *Ausgewählte Werke in zwölf Bänden,* edited by Gotthold Klee. 12 vols. Leipzig: Hesse, 1907.

STEREOTYPICAL SCENES. Traditional elements of a story, recurring within the same poem but also being used in other poems. There are longer stereotypical scenes, like "The Sending of Messengers" or "The Summoning of the Council," which can consist of a considerable number of lines, and smaller ones, like "The Hero on the Beach" or "The Beasts of Battle," which consist of only a few lines. All stereotypical scenes have a stable semantic structure. They are considered to be a feature of oral composition ("composition by theme") but they also occur in written texts.

Several such stereotypical scenes can be found in the *Nibelungenlied.*

[NV]

Bibliography

Renoir, Alain. "Oral-Formulaic Theme Survival: A Possible Instance in the 'Nibelungenlied.'" *Neuphilologische Mitteilungen* 65 (1964): 70–75.

TRADITIONAL NARRATIVE MATERIAL.
Narrative materials of which the *Nibelungenlied* is composed are not unique to this poem. They also appear in German and Norse analogues, which themselves show signs of derivation from earlier stories transmitted orally or in writing but are in any case lost to us. Such materials reflect a tradition of reuse and recycling of narrative elements over time, and also a crossing of geographic and even linguistic boundaries. The traditional materials are of three distinct kinds: themes, type scenes, and stories. Themes include generic plot elements such as the wooing expedition. Type scenes refer to generic situations, such as the hero on the beach and the formal duel. Stories refer to the combination of character name and deed, such as Hildebrand's service to Dietrich or Siegfried's killing of a dragon and bathing in its blood. Even when a very high percentage of a poem's materials appear to stem from narrative traditions, as is certainly the case for the *Nibelungenlied,* each retelling of the tale represents a fresh act of composition, for new combinations of themes, type scenes, and stories create new contexts that lend a narrative its own distinct character. The Nibelungen poet's use of themes and type scenes that also appear in Homer and other pre-Germanic stories may suggest the longevity of some traditional narrative materials.

[VU]

Bibliography

Andersson, Theodore M. *A Preface to the Nibelungenlied.* Stanford: Stanford University Press, 1987.
Renoir, Alain. *A Key to Old Poems.* University Park: The Pennsylvania State University Press, 1988.
Udwin, Victor. *Between Two Armies: The Place of the Duel in Epic Culture.* Davis Medieval Texts and Studies. Leyden: Brill, 1999.

TRANSITION FROM ORAL TO WRITTEN. Prior to the introduction of writing, Germanic heroic poetry was composed and transmitted orally. The poems in the extant manuscripts exhibit some features of oral literature, which raises the question as to whether these texts were first composed orally and written down later or composed in a "transitional period," when both types of composition were used by the same poet. According to the founders of the theory of oral-formulaic composition, oral and written literature are mutually exclusive and the existence of "transitional texts" or of a "transitional period" is rejected. If the notion of transition is not limited to the technique of verse-making but applied to the stance of the narrator towards the story he tells, the process of transition from oral to written can be illuminated in the case of the *Nibelungenlied.* Heroic poetry claims to relate historical truth and idealizes the heroes of a nation. In the *Nibelungenlied,* however, the narrator assumes an ironical stance towards the heroes, which means that this poem must have shifted shortly after 1200 from its oral existence among an illiterate social subgroup into a literate stratum of society.

[NV]

Bibliography

Bäuml, Franz H. "The Unmaking of the Hero: Some Critical Implications of the Transition from Oral to Written Epic." In *The Epic in Medieval Society,* edited by Harald Scholler. Tübingen: Niemeyer, 1977, pp. 86–99.
———. "Medieval Texts and the Two Theories of Oral-Formulaic Composition: A Proposal for a Third Theory." *New Literary History: A Journal of Theory and Interpretation* 16 (1984–1985): 31–49.

VAGANTENSTROPHE, the most popular Middle Latin form of lyric strophe, consisting of four rhyming long verses. It is unlikely, however, that the *Nibelungenstrophe* originated from this Latin form.

[UM]

WALTHER VON DER VOGELWEIDE (1170/75–ca. 1230) is widely recognized as the greatest lyric poet of the German Middle Ages. He is also thought by some scholars (e.g., Friedrich Heinrich von der Hagen) possibly to have been the poet of the *Nibelungenlied,* although the evidence for this hypothesis is both circumstantial and conjectural. For one thing Walther is known to have received in the year 1203 a sum of money for a fur coat from Wolfger of Erla, who was not only Bishop of Passau during the time of composition of the *Nibelungenlied,* but who has also been tentatively identified as a possible patron of the anonymous *Nibelungenlied* poet. Whether or not that poet was also Walther remains uncertain, but it does appear quite likely that Walther was in the service of Wolfger and that he was commissioned to compose some type of work for him. Additionally in a well-known passage Walther claims Austria as the geographic region in which he had learned *singen unde sagen* (to sing [songs] and to tell [stories]); it has been suggested that the latter activity, the telling of stories, might possibly refer to Walther's role as poet of the *Nibelungenlied.* In fact, Werner Falk sees in the person of Volker a self-portait of Walther. At any rate, Walther's enduring fame rests not upon his hypothetical authorship of the *Nibelungenlied,* but rather upon his richly transmitted corpus of lyrics, which include political poetry, love songs of varying types, and religious poems.

[MR]

Bibliography
Delbrück, Hans. "Das Werden des Nibelungenliedes." *Historische Zeitschrift* 131 (1925): 409–420.
Falk, Werner. *Das Nibelungenlied in seiner Epoche: Zur Revision eines romantischen Mythos.* Heidelberg: Winter, 1974.
Hagen, Friedrich Heinrich von der. *Minnesänger: Deutsche Liederdichter des 12., 13., und 14.*

Jahrhunderts. Vol. 4. Leipzig: Barth, 1838, pp. 186–187 (repr. Aalen: O. Zeller, 1963).
Jones, George Fenwick. "Ze oesterrich lernt ich singen unde sagen (Walther 32, 14)." *Leuvense Bijdragen* 58 (1969): 69–77.

WOLFRAM VON ESCHENBACH (fl. 1200), Middle High German author. An important piece of chronological data relevant to the *Nibelungenlied* can be derived from his romance *Parzival.* It involves the advice given to the Burgundian kings by Rumold, Master of the Kitchen, namely, that rather than make the trip to Etzel's court, they ought to remain at home and enjoy the courtly life (*Nibelungenlied,* 1467,3–1469,4). When Duke Liddamus wants to make it clear that he considers it senseless to fight against Gawein, he cites Rumold's advice (*Parzival* 420,26–30). Quite clearly, then, Wolfram had access to a version of the *Nibelungenlied* around the year 1205. This chronology is derived from the dating of the preceding seventh book of *Parzival,* in which there is a reference to the still visible devastation of the Erfurt vineyards (379,18ff.), which actually occurred in 1203 during the war between King Philip of Swabia and Count Hermann von Thuringia.

[WW]

Bibliography
Parzival: A Romance of the Middle Ages. Translated by Melen M. Mustard and Charles E. Passage. New York: Vintage, 1961.
Wolfram von Eschenbach. Edited by Karl Lachmann. 7th edition by Eduward Hartl. Berlin: de Gruyter, 1952.

PART VI

The Literary Reception of the Nibelungen Theme in Germany, Austria, and Switzerland

ALBRECHT, PAUL (1863–?). See PART II, ARMINIUS.

ANTZ, AUGUST (1881–1959), German author, one of a number of writers who, during the Weimar Republic, published adaptations of the Nibelungen material but otherwise remained largely unknown. His version of *Das Nibelungenlied* (1926), written in an archaic style, was published as a "Klassenlektüre als Ergänzung des Lesebuches" (special supplementary reading materials for the classroom). In the introduction the *Nibelungenlied* is characterized as the "erste große deutsche Dichtung" (the first great German poem) and as a "gewaltiges nationales Heldenepos" (powerful national heroic epic) that represents at the same time "das Hohelied der deutschen Treue" (the Song of Songs of German loyalty). The piece was primarily addressed to the typical German boy, who was expected to read the story of the strong and noble Siegfried "mit heißen Wangen" (his cheeks aglow). The author anticipated that such a tale of heroism would fire the heart of a boy and raise his courage with "der überweltlichen Größe der Sagengestalten" (greater-than-life stature of the epic heroes).

[MH]

Bibliography

Antz, August. *Das Nibelungenlied: Erzählt.* Klassen-lektüre als Ergänzung des Lesebuches. Saarlouis: Hausen Verlagsgesellschaft, 1926.

ARND, FRIEDRICH (1839–1911), pseudonym for Friedrich Arnd-Kürenberg, director of the Geographical Institute in Weimar and from 1886 on an official of the Ottoman Ministry of Education. His tragedy *Kriemhild* (1875) glorifies faith and obedience as quintessential German values that are absolute and that must be maintained until death.

[WW]

Bibliography

Arnd, Friedrich. *Kriemhild: Trauerspiel.* Leipzig: Wagner, 1875.

AYREN, ARMIN (b. 1934), a contemporary German narrator, teacher, critic, and author of several novels and short stories. In 1987 he published the novel *Meister Konrads Nibelungenroman* (Master Conrad's Nibelungen Novel), a modern retelling of the *Nibelungenlied* in the first person from an anonymous Konrad's point of view. According to the story, Konrad, a descendant of the *Minnesänger* known as Der von Kürenberg, is the chaplain who was thrown by Hagen into the Danube River to drown during a trip to the Huns. Hagen threw him into the river in order to verify the mermaid's prophecy that only the chaplain would survive the trip. The chaplain, who can't swim, manages to get out of the river, thus proving the mermaid's words to be true. Master Konrad, a clerk in the service of the bishop of Passau, reminisces and reflects on these events at the end of his life. In his role as both a medieval chronicler and a modern psychologist, he records the history and destiny of the Nibelungs.

[WW]

Bibliography

Meister Konrads Nibelungenroman. Baden-Baden: Elster Verlag, 1987. The pocketbook edition contains the author's name: Ayren, Armin. *Meister Konrads Nibelungenroman.* dtv 11432. Munich: Deutscher Taschenbuch Verlag, 1991.

BARTELS, ADOLF (1862–1945), a German nationalist poet, editor, and cultural historian with antisemitic tendencies who, in later life, had close connections to the National Socialists. His poem, "Nibelungenland" (1896), is written in the first person and praises the Nordic homeland as the genuine world of the strong and superior race.

[WW]

Bibliography

Sergel, Albert, ed. *Saat und Ernte: Die deutsche Lyrik unserer Tage.* Berlin: Bong, 1925, p. 38.

Fuller, Steven Nyole. *The Nazis' Literary Grandfather: Adolf Bartels and Cultural Extremism.* New York: Lang, 1996.

BARTSCH, KURT (b. 1937), a contemporary German poet whose "Nibelungenlied" (1985) is based on a nursery rhyme and parodies the heroic rallying cries of the National Socialists at the end of World War II. The Nibelungs represent Hitler and his paladins in the Führerbunker in Berlin, where a grotesque showdown takes place.

[WW]

Bibliography

Bartsch, Kurt. *Weihnacht ist und Wotan reitet.* Berlin: Rotbuch, 1985, p. 77.

BAUMANN, HANS (1914–1988), the author of historical plays and literature for young readers. His drama *Rüdiger von Bechelaren* (1939) holds up war as proof of heroism and a

means by which the true sense of one's being can be fulfilled.

[WW]

Bibliography

Baumann, Hans. *Rüdiger von Bechelaren: Das Passauer Nibelungenspiel.* Jena: Diederichs, 1939.

BECK, FRIEDRICH (1806–1888), teacher and editor of the *Münchener Politische Zeitung.* His poem "Die Heldenschlacht" (The Battle of the Heroes) addresses the controversial issue of whether humanistic or Teutonic educational ideals and subjects should be advocated for young German males in general and the secondary schools in particular. The poem depicts, in a rather simplistic way, how Siegfried, Hagen, Gunther, and other Nibelungs, as Christian warriors, defeat the Greek pagans Achilles, Ajax, and Ulysses.

[WW]

Bibliography

Hub, Ignaz, ed. *Deutschlands Balladen- und Romanzen-Dichter.* Vol. 3. Karlsruhe: Creuzbauer, 1870, pp. 24f.

BEHEIM-SCHWARZBACH,   MARTIN (1900–1985), a translator and novelist with a mystical bent to his writings. His novel *Der Stern von Burgund* is a retelling of the *Nibelungenlied* from both a realistic and a fantastic perspective, with the emphasis on Brünhild's fate. She is depicted as a pagan who is deceived by the court of Worms. At the conclusion of the work she throws herself onto Siegfried's funeral pyre. Brünhild's fate is tied to the destiny of Burgundy whose star has waned as a consequence of human failings.

[WW]

Bibliography

Beheim-Schwarzbach, Martin. *Der Stern von Burgund: Roman der Nibelungen.* Munich: Bertelsmann, 1961.

BEHREND, OTTO (1857–?), author of the poem "Sigfrid" (1892), whose great dramatic tension is propelled and enhanced by a forceful, urgent rhythm. The central theme is the inexorable tragic nature of the heroic fate to which both Sigfrid and Hagen are bound.

[WW]

Bibliography
Behrend, Otto. *Sigfrid.* Leipzig: Renger, 1892.

BENZER, RICHARD (1888–1967), a popular writer from Hohenems in Vorarlberg (western Austria), author of the tragedy *Kriemhild* (1951), in which Rudolf von Ems appears as a poet, scribe, and performer (singer) of the *Nibelungenlied,* the plot of which is presented in ten dramatic scenes. The play belongs to that segment of postwar German literature which, against the backdrop of a terrible war and the catastrophic conditions that prevailed immediately following it, tends to repress questions of guilt. The Nibelung plot serves, in a somewhat tasteless and unctuous way, to make apocalyptic forces and enigmatic twists of fate responsible for the lot of man and thus pronounce the individual free of guilt.

[WW]

Bibliography
Benzer, Richard. *Kriemhild: Romantisches Trauerspiel (nach dem Nibelungenliede) in zehn Bildern mit einem Vor- und Nachspiel. Hohenemser Heimatspiel.* Hohenems: Eigenverlag der Marktgemeinde, 1951.

BLEIBTREU, KARL (1859–1928), German literary critic, dramatist, and Naturalist author. His novel, *Der Nibelunge Not* (1884), deals with the fictitious character Konrad von Bechelaren, an eyewitness to the traumatic events described in the *Nibelungenlied.* Konrad's epic, which is also titled "Der Nibelunge Not," is based on its author's reminiscences.

[WW]

Bibliography
Bleibtreu, Karl. *Der Nibelunge Not.* Berlin: Auerbach, 1884.

BLEY, WULF (1890–1961), alludes in his poem "Die Gibichunge" (1934) to the Nordic tradition of the Nibelungs and presents the characters as Aryan beings, proud of their superior physical and mental qualities. Like other literary renditions of the Nibelung theme during the Third Reich (Bley was a member of the SS), "Die Gibichunge" mirrors and attempts to legitimate Nazi racial ideology.

[WW]

Bibliography
Bley, Wulf. *Die Gibichunge.* Berlin: Hobbing, 1934.

BLUNCK, HANS FRIEDRICH (1888–1961), a North German dramatist and author of novels and stories dealing with Nordic and Hanseatic topics. He adapted the *Nibelungenlied* from the Middle High German and depicted the figure of Siegfried as the ideal Nordic man.

[WW]

Bibliography
Blunck, Hans Friedrich. *Das Nibelungenlied. Mit Bildern aus der Hundshagenschen Handschrift.* Leipzig: Bibliographisches Institut, 1934.

BRAUN, MAX (1874–1967). His novel *Nibelungenland* (1931) is set against the backdrop of the disastrous economic situation prevailing in Germany during the Weimar Republic. The work underscores the strong desire of the Right to overcome the political and social inertia of Germany and the Germans. Contemporary politics are historicized through reference to the myth of Siegfried. The plot revolves around the story of the reborn Siegfried who appears in the industrial Rhineland which has been occupied by the French Army subsequent to the Versailles Treaty. Utilizing pathos and a grandiose style, Siegfried is portrayed as a symbol of hope, strength, the power of work, and as the harbinger and progenitor of a new generation.

[WW]

Bibliography
Braun, Max. *Nibelungenland: Roman der deutschen Westmark in zwei Büchern.* Ludwigshafen: Walkirch, 1931.

BRAUN, VOLKER (b. 1939), East German author, playwright, and poet. His *Siegfried Frauenprotokolle Deutscher Furor* (1983–1984, performed 1986) shows how German myths (e.g., Grimmelshausen's *Simplicissimus* or Schiller's *Demetrius*) may be reshaped. Each of the three acts treats the subject differently: as mythology, as family tragedy, and as historical narrative, presenting the entire myth from the story of Siegfried to that of Etzel's court. Worth noting are Braun's use of chronology and logic and his infusion of modern material. Siegfried is slain twice and in different ways. The figures of both the historically attested Aetius and the literary-based Etzel appear; characteristic German war widows begin and end the play. The highly ambiguous language alludes to the *Nibelungenlied*, Hebbel's *Nibelungen*, and other texts and historical epochs, from biblical times to the present day. Braun's notes consider women's struggle for emancipation and the establishment of missile bases during the 1980s, which opened up the prospect of nuclear warfare on German soil.

[RK]

Bibliography
Braun, Volker. *Siegfried Frauenprotokolle Deutscher Furor.* In vol. 8 of V. B., *Texte in zeitlicher Folge.* Halle: Mitteldeutscher Verlag, 1992, pp. 172–248.

BRECHT, BERTOLT (1898–1956), German playwright, poet, theater director, and literary theorist. His poem, "Siegfried hatte ein rotes Haar" (1922), possibly a twenty-line fragment, which was published in Brecht's *Gesammelte Werke* in 1982, uses cross-rhymed quatrains to tell the balladlike story of four men's erotic attraction to one another. Siegfried, who is loved by Hagen, is more attracted to Giselher. Consequently Hagen kills him, and, in turn, contemplates a relationship with either Giselher or Gunter. No hints are given as to the time, place, age, or social status of the characters. The homosexual implications are clear, though never stated explicitly, and the whole poem is marked by a gentle sense of irony.

[RK]

Bibliography
Brecht, Bertolt. "Siegfried hatte ein rotes Haar." In *Werke: Grosse kommentierte Berliner und Frankfurter Ausgabe,* edited by Werner Hecht, Jan Knopf, Werner Mittenzwei, Klaus-Detlef Müller. Vol. 13: *Gedichte 3. Gedichte und Gedichtfragmente, 1913–1927,* edited by Jan Knopf and Brigitte Bergheim. Berlin: Aufbau; Frankfurt a. M.: Suhrkamp, 1993, 255f., 492.

BÜSCHING, GUSTAV GOTTLIEB (1783–1829), a professor of ancient history in Breslau whose writings aimed mainly at nourishing a national consciousness by popularizing medieval German culture and literature. His verse translation of the *Nibelungenlied* (1815) was introduced by dedicatory poems to two of his close friends and fellow campaigners. In both poems Büsching (who calls himself "The Charcoal Burner"), combines the classical sonnet form with the romantic-mystic style typical for the early propagators of things medieval. The first poem is addressed to Friedrich de la Motte Fouqué, whom he calls "Volker" and whom he credits for first introducing him to the story. The second is directed to the scholar Friedrich Heinrich von der Hagen, whom he calls "Hagen" and whom he lauds for long-time cooperation and his work on the *Nibelungenlied.*

[WLH]

Bibliography
Büsching, J. G. G. *Das Lied der Nibelungen.* Leipzig: Brockhaus, 1815. Metrisch übersetzt.

BUHL, HERBERT ERICH (1905–1948), head of the *Reichsschrifttumskammer* (Reich Literature Board) in the Third Reich. His novel, *Krone der Frauen* (1939), deals with the love of Siegfried and Brunhild which is based on a mixture of racial affinity, eroticism, and Nordic heroism. The couple is regarded as a model for the coming generation, for which a heroic race is to be established through the hegemony of National Socialism in Germany and eventually throughout all of Europe.

[WW]

Bibliography
Buhl, Herbert Erich. *Krone der Frauen: Roman der Königin Brunhild.* Berlin: Reichel, 1939.

BURLESQUE. Some literary and nonliterary works of the twentieth century are designed to ridicule attitudes, style, or subject matter by treating the *Nibelungenlied* in a trivial manner or with comic mimicry through satirical imitation. Robert Neumann's parody, *Das Buch Treue* (1962) attacks Werner Jansen's Nibelung novel of the same title (1916), which glorified "Nibelungian" virtues such as military prowess against the backdrop of the First World War. Herbert

Schneider's book, *Die Nibelungen in Bayern* (1974), provides an anachronistic and comical new version of the Nibelungs as settlers in modern Bavaria. Its illustrations make light of the stubbornness of the Bavarians as well as the heroism of the Nibelungs. The anonymous Austrian or Bavarian satirical songs ("Schnadahuepfeln") in the book *s'Nibelungen-Ringerl* ("The Little Nibelungen Ring," 1976) refer to Richard Wagner's opera cycle as well as to the *Nibelungenlied*. Angerer's *Nibelungenlied* (1984) juxtaposes selected stanzas translated into modern German with witty descriptions in slang and caricatures of the epic milieu. Leopold Swossil's *Nibelungen-Travestie* (1984) is a parody which deals with the *Nibelungenlied* in a flippant way. While making use of the Nibelung stanza, it situates the story within the Viennese milieu of rogues and scoundrels. The unusual application of the old heroic and epic style, as well as the epic form of narration to what would today be considered a humorous detective story, is burlesque. Uta Claus wrote the text and Rolf Kutschera drew the cartoons of *Total krasse Helden* (1986). This comic book is based on the story of the Nibelungs and has transformed it into slapstick humor aimed at appealing to contemporary youth. The predominantly slang language is that of the disco or the student milieu. Burlesque renditions of the *Nibelungenlied* parody the tendency in the nineteenth and twentieth centuries to portray the epic as the conveyor of national, racial, or ethical ideals. *Mord und Totschlach: Datt Nibelungenlied (Für Jürgen Lodemann)* (Murder and Manslaughter: The Nibelungenlied [For Jürgen Lodemann]) by the journalist and writer, Elke Heidenreich, is a witty piece of gossip told from the naive point of view of a simpleminded housewife living in the Ruhr district.

[WW]

Bibliography

[Angerer, Rudolf]. *Angerers Nibelungenlied.* Munich: Universitas Verlag, 1984.

Claus, Uta, and Rolf Kutschera. *Total krasse Helden: Die bockstarke Story von den Nibelungen.* Frankfurt a. M.: Eichborn, 1986.

Heidenreich, Elke. *Mord und Totschlach: Datt Nibelungenlied (Für Jürgen Lodemann).* In *Mit oder ohne Knochen: Das Letzte von Else Stratmann.* rororo 5829 Reinbek: Rowohlt, 1986, pp. 105–123.

Neumann, Robert. *Das Buch Treue: Ein Domelanen-Roman.* In R. N., *Die Parodien.* Munich: Desch, 1962, pp. 80ff.

Schneider, Herbert. *Die Nibelungen in Bayern.* Pfaffenhofen: Ludwig, 1974. Mit Zeichnungen von Horst Haitzinger.

Nibelungen-Ringerl von v. Miris: Respektlose Schnadahüpfeln zu einem grandiosen Thema. Passau: Passavia Verlag, 1976.

Swossil, Leopold. *Nibelungen-Travestie.* Wiener Neustadt: Weilburg, 1984.

CHILDREN'S LITERATURE. There are three major ways in which the *Nibelungenlied* has been adapted for children (1) into books containing legends (*Sagenbücher,* about sixty titles), including several cycles of myths; (2) into books that deal only with the *Nibelungensage* (about thirty titles), or even one aspect of it, such as *Siegfried's Death* or *Kriemhild's Revenge;* and (3) those books that tell a story that simply integrates some persons, themes, or motifs lifted from the *Nibelungenlied*. The legends have been published under titles such as *Deutsche Heldensagen, Deutsche Rittersagen, Germanische Sagen, Götter und Helden, Sagenbuch,* and *Heldensagen.* The basic source for the story is the medieval *Nibelungenlied,* in some cases augmented by material garnered from Scandinavian tradition. These books have their roots in the nineteenth century and were written primarily for adults. In the early twentieth century, partly owing to the efforts of various educational movements, these stories were then adapted for children aged ten to fourteen. It is intriguing to note that some of these books, published over a hundred years ago, are still being reprinted in contemporary editions, for instance, the volumes by Gustav Schalk and Wilhelm Wägner. Modern renditions, however, have not altered the basic story line, in contrast to other adaptations of the *Nibelungenlied* which appeared after World War II. Many of the latter are given to parody and irony. The writers of the *Sagenbücher,* however, used an antiquated language. The normative standards presented by the stories are somewhat old-fashioned with respect to gender delineation and the significance attributed to authority. Certain nationalistic tendencies are in evidence as well as some antipathy towards foreigners, underscoring the relatively conservative bent of the genre as a whole. Martin Beheim-Schwarzbach represents a notable exception with his *Helden-sagen, Rittersagen* and, in particular, *Der Stern von Burgund*, a novel about the Nibelungs aimed at adults. He attempts to offer a detached and differentiated point of view. In contrast to other children's books that deal with the Nibelungen legend, his include complementary illustrations in the first edition. Those books that recount only the tale of the *Nibelungenlied*, from the beginning of this literature in the 1950s to the latest adaptation by Willi Fährmann, have the same literary roots and, in general, the same normative tendencies as described above. One Austrian author, Auguste Lechner, deserves particular mention, as her work has been influential in forming the impression of generations of teenagers with regard to their impressions of medieval literature, in general, and the *Nibelungenlied*, in particular. Wolfgang Hohlbein, who is also Austrian, has published a great number of fantasy novels and in his description of the events of the *Nibelungenlied*, has adopted Hagen's point of view. The main difference from the other versions is that Hagen loves Kriemhild and this love constitutes the reason for Hagen's course of action. Hohlbein's story ends with Siegfried's and Brünhild's death, mirroring Scandinavian tradition. The story ends here, however, as Kriemhild does not seek revenge. Her last words to Hagen are: "Oh no, Hagen, sword and spear or dagger, these are your weapons . . . . I don't want you to die. You shall live, Hagen, for a long time. I shall take away everything you ever owned, or that you loved . . . . That is my weapon, Hagen . . ." (p. 442).

Other stories can be discerned that deal solely with individual sections of the *Nibelungenlied*. They may recount contemporary events, such as children learning in school about the Nibelungs and beginning to look for the treasure or the magic hood, or parts of the old story that are included in another fictional medieval story.

[SSch]

I. General Collections

Aick, Gerhard. *Deutsche Heldensagen I.* Illustrated by Willi Widmann. Vienna: Ueberreuter, 1950. Subsequent editions in 1961 and 1965. [*Gudrun, Walther and Hildegunde, The Nibelungen, Dietrich of Bern and His Companions*, and *The Saga of Roland*]

Beheim-Schwarzbach, Martin. *Deutsche Helden-sagen*. Illustrated by Walter Grieder. Vienna: Ueberreuter, 1980. Subsequent edition in 1982. [*A War Because of Gudrun, Stories about Dietrich of Bern, The Saga of Siegfried the Dragon Killer, Nibelung's Treasure and Kriemhild's Revenge*, and *The Adventures of Wolfdietrich*]

Hecht, Gretel and Wolfgang. *Deutsche Heldensagen*. Leipzig: Kiepenheuer, 1969. Subsequent edition in 1981. [*Dietrich of Bern, The Nibelungen, Wieland the Blacksmith, Walther and Hildegunde, Ortnit and Wolfdietrich*, and *Hilde and Kudrun*]

Schalk, Gustav. *Deutsche Heldensagen*. Braunschweig: Klinhardt & Biermann, 1964. First edition in 1891. [*Wieland the Blacksmith, Siegfried and the Nibelungs*, and *Beowulf Frithjof*]

Wägner, Wilhelm. *Deutsche Heldensagen*. Hanover: Neue Jugendschriften, 1867. New edition: Erlangen, 1984. [*The Amelungen, The Nibelungen, The Hegelingen, Beowulf, Sagas of Karl*, and *King Arthur and the Holy Grail*]

II. Novels for Children and Adolescents

Fährmann, Willi. *Siegfried von Xanten. Eine alte Sage neu erzählt*. Illustrated by Werner Bläbst. Stuttgart: Thienemann, 1987.

_____. *Kriemhilds Rache. Eine alte Sage neu erzählt*. Illustrated by Werner Bläbst. Stuttgart: Thienemann, 1988.

Hohlbein, Wolfgang. *Hagen von Tronje. Ein Nibelungen-Roman*. Vienna: Ueberreuter, 1986.

Lechner, Auguste. *Die Nibelungen. Nacherzählt für die Jugend*. Innsbruck: Tyrolia, 1981 (first edition 1956).

III. Records for Children

Die Nibelungen. Radio play by Peter Folken, narrated by Will Quadflieg. Music by Wolfram Burg. Hamburg, n.d.

Nibelungen. Siegfried der Drachentöter. Siegfried und Brunhilde. Schallplattenhörspiel. Tyrolis n.p., n.d.

Nibelungen. Siegfrieds Tod. Kriemhilds Rache. Schallplattenhörspiel. Tyrolis n.p. n.d.

IV. Novels Dealing with Specific Themes or Figures

Beyerlein, Gabriele. *Wie ein Falke im Wind*. Hamburg: Dressler, 1993.

Mader, Eva. *Die Nibelungen sind an allem schuld*. Hamburg: Oetinger, 1966.

Sieg, Wolfgang. *Siegfrieds Tarnkappe*. Hanover: Fackkelträger, 1974.

V. Satire and Parody

Claus, Uta, and Rolf Kutschera. *Total krasse Helden: Die bockstarke Story von den Nibelungen.* Frankfurt a. M.: Eichborn, 1986.

Hoop, Hein. *Lisa, Gudrun, Freya, alle hin, auweia . . . Satirische Bretterlieder.* Hamburg: Struck, [1978].

Kiefer, Sepp. *Die Isar-Nibelungen: Eine zünftig-tragische Geschichte aus blau-weißer Perspektive.* Composed and illustrated by Sepp Kiefer. Mainburg: Pinsker, [1963].

Kreye, Walter. *De Nibelungen: Fidele Weltgeschichte op Platt*(deutsch) *1. Murd un dootslag bi den nibelungen. Gudrun—oder: von de waschbütt op'n Königsthorn.* Leer: Schuster, 1970/78.

Schneider, Herbert. *Die Nibelungen in Bayern.* With illustrations by Horst Haitzinger. Pfaffenhofen/Ilm: Ilmgau, 1974.

VI. Secondary Literature

Schmidt, Siegrid. "Die Nibelungen in der Jugend- und Unterhaltungsliteratur zwischen 1945 und 1980." In *Mittelalter-Rezeption: Ein Symposion,* edited by Peter Wapnewski. Stuttgart: Metzler, 1986, pp. 327–345.

————. *Mittelhochdeutsche Epenstoffe in der deutschsprachigen Literatur nach 1945: Beobachtungen zur Aufarbeitung des Artus- und Parzival-Stoffes in erzählender Literatur für Jugendliche und Erwachsene mit einer Bibliographie der Adaptationen der Stoffkreise Artus, Parzival, Tristan, Gudrun und Nibelungen 1945–1981.* GAG 495 I/II. Göppingen: Kümmerle, 1989, pp. 234–278; 338.

Schreier-Hornung, Antonie. "Mittelalter für die Jugend: Auguste Lechners Nacherzählungen von *Nibelungenlied, Rolandslied, Parzival* und *Kudrun.*" In *Mittelalter-Rezeption III: Mittelalter, Massenmedien, Neue Mythen.* GAG 479. Göppingen: Kümmerle, 1988, pp. 32–49.

COMICS. About the middle of the 1950s, popular literature began to take an interest in the heroes of the Nibelungen myth which were already known to a young public from the numerous publications on "German Heroic Sagas" by various authors. The name of the hero of the comic series "Sigurd" is taken from the Siegfried myth. Although this comic figure has the Nordic name of the Nibelungen hero, the individual issues and episodes have, however, nothing to do with the Nibelungen theme. Sigurd demonstrates characteristics that can be identified with Tarzan and Superman, and his being is reduced to mere physical strength and courage. As an unconquerable, blond muscle man, he functions in a fantastic world of adventure in which the era of the Germanic tribes and that of the Middle Ages no longer represent anything more than background sets. Tailored to correspond to the need of a youthful public to assert its independence, Sigurd is the ultimate hero, a man who speaks for all readers when he uses his fists to solve his problems.

The name of Curt Linda might also be mentioned here. He was the author of the German TV cartoon, "Die Nibelungen oder Was Richard Wagner nicht wußte" (The Nibelungs or: What Richard Wagner did not know), a series in twenty-four parts produced by ZDF (Second German Television) in 1976.

[WW/UM]

Bibliography

Kimpel, Harald, and Johanna Werckmeister. "Leidmotive: Möglichkeiten der künstlerischen Nibelungen-Rezeption seit 1945." In *Ein deutscher Wahn, ein deutscher Alptraum: Studien und Dokumente zur Rezeption des Nibelungenstoffs im 19. und 20. Jahrhundert,* edited by Joachim Heinzle and Anneliese Waldschmidt. Frankfurt a. M.: Suhrkamp, 1991, pp. 288, 290.

CONSENTIUS, RUDOLF OTTO (1813–1887), a former artillery officer from Berlin and an actor in Dresden who wrote historical dramas and was influenced by Ludwig Tieck. *Königin Brunhild* (1842) dramatizes the bloody conflict between the Merovingian brothers, King Sigibert of Austrasia and King Chilperich of Neustria. This contest of arms from the sixth century is assumed to be a part of the historical background of the *Nibelungenlied.* A confused plot and dozens of characters are intended to demonstrate that quarrels and feuds never lead to the establishment of a powerful and peaceful empire.

[WW]

Bibliography

Consentius, Rudolph Otto. *Königin Brunhild: Historisches Trauerspiel in fünf Akten.* Karlsruhe: Macklot, 1842.

DAHN, FELIX (1834–1912), a professor of German legal history at the University of Munich and a representative of literary historicism. His national and ethnic poems, ballads, plays, and novels deal on both a scholarly and popular level with events of Germanic and medieval history and literature. Political poems such as "Der Bundestag" (The Federal Parliament, 1856), "An Napoleon III" (To Napoleon III, 1859), "Deutsche Lieder" (German Songs, 1859), "Die Rheinmädchen und das Rheingold" (The Rhine Maidens and the Rhine Gold, 1868), "An die Deutschen in Böhmen" (To the Germans in Bohemia, 1870), and "An die Deutschen in Siebenbürgen" (To the Germans in Transylvania, 1870) make use of such motifs as the Nibelung treasure as a symbol for the real political "treasure," which was the German unity so intensely desired at the time. The play *Markgraf Rüdiger von Bechelaren* (Margrave Rüdiger of Bechelaren, 1875) and poems such as "Lied Siegfrieds" (The Song of Siegfried), "Siegfrieds Leichenfahrt" (Siegfried's Funeral Journey), "Hagens Sterbelied" (Hagen's Death Song), and "Krimhilde" (all written around 1870), take as their themes episodes from the *Nibelungenlied*. Dahn's works glorify loyalty as a German virtue and heroic death as a German ideal, which allowed them to be used in the cause of nationalistic and imperialistic aspirations.

[WW]

Bibliography
Felix Dahn's sämtliche Werke poetischen Inhalts. Vols. 16 and 18. Leipzig: Breitkopf & Haertel, 1898.
Wunderlich, Werner. *Der Schatz des Drachentödters: Materialien zur Wirkungsgeschichte des Nibelungenliedes.* Stuttgart: Klett–Cotta, 1977, pp. 37ff.

DRAMA. Since the "rediscovery" of the *Nibelungenlied* there have been attempts to use its theme for drama. Above all, tragedy has been able to adapt for its purposes the conflict of interests and the catastrophic conclusion, as well as the fate of individual protagonists. Plots have been developed using diverse aesthetic perspectives and underscoring different interpretations of the work. In particular, dramas were produced after the Second World War that took critical issue with the tradition of the Ni-

belungen theme from an ideological point of view. See the various articles included in this section.

[WW]

ECK, MIRIAM (1861–1915), pseudonym of Käte Sebaldt, German lyricist who, in her later years, also turned to writing religious drama. With the onset of the First World War, the poem "Unseren Brüdern" (To Our Brothers, 1914) invokes the "höchste Gemeinschaft" (supreme community) of women and men. Eck defines women's wish to be "Sporn und Schild" (spur and shield) to their sons, lovers and brothers as their supreme desire and glorifies death mythologically by drawing on material from the story of the Nibelungen: "Die Starken von uns, sie tragen Euch aus den Schlachten/Zum Gott aller Helden, wie den Siegmund einst trug Brunhild" (The strong ones among us, they will carry you out of the battles/To the God of all heroes, like Brunhild once carried Siegmund).

[MH]

Bibliography
Eck, Miriam. "Unseren Brüdern." In *Das Volk in Eisen: Kriegsgedichte der "Täglichen Rundschau."* Berlin: Verlag der Täglichen Rundschau, 1914, p. 32.

EICHHORN, CARL FRIEDRICH (1804–1836), professor of mechanical engineering in Hanover. His tragedy, *Chriemhildens Rache* (1824), draws on romantic medieval myths and the nostalgia for national unification, and projects these onto the character of Siegfried. Like Arminius, Siegfried is seen as the personification of liberation and unification, who is killed by the envious and malicious enemies of a strong Germania.

[WW]

Bibliography
Eichhorn, Carl Friedrich. *Chriemhildens Rache: Ein Trauerspiel, nach dem Nibelungenliede bearbeitet.* Göttingen: Rosenbusch, 1824.

EISENSTEIN, KARL VON (1889–?), pseudonym of Eisner von und zu Eisenstein, German lyricist, narrative writer, and translator. In 1926 he published the tragedy *Siegfrieds Tod* (Siegfried's Death), which he addresses especially to "die lieben jungen Freunde" (dear young friends). He suggests that the play be performed "im Papierpuppen-Theater im Kreise der Familie" (with a paper-doll theater in a family setting). As with many other adaptations of the *Nibelungenlied* in the Weimar Republic, Hagen is portrayed in a positive light. He honors his pledge of loyalty while the king proves to be helpless: "Wüsst König Gunther Königs Last zu tragen, man säng das Lied von Hagen, dem Getreuen" (If King Gunther knew how to bear a king's burden, one would sing the song of faithful Hagen).

[MH]

Bibliography

Eisenstein, Karl von. *Siegfrieds Tod: Ein Spiel für die deutsche Jugend.* Die Schatzgräber-Bühne 41. Munich: Callwey, 1928.

Gentry, Francis G. "Die Rezeption des Nibelungenliedes in der Weimarer Republik." In *Das Weiterleben des Mittelalters in der deutschen Literatur,* edited by James F. Poag and Gerhild Scholz-Williams. Königstein/Ts.: Athenäum, 1983, pp. 142–156.

ERNST, (KARL FRIEDRICH) PAUL (1866–1933), German author of narrative, dramatic, and theoretical writings. Ernst disassociated himself from the artistic ideas of neoromanticism and naturalism and turned to neoclassical attitudes. He believed that the quality of poetry was first of all determined by strictness of form, a criterion he appreciated especially in the *Nibelungenlied.* Furthermore a work of art should present us with values "die uns das Herz brennen machen." This artistic conception found concrete realization in many dramas that emphasized moral and heroic values, which are mainly expressed in the relationship between a leader and his followers. The tragedy *Brunhild* (1909) shows Siegfried and Brunhild as great and good heroes who are meant for each other and who finally die together. Opposed to them are Gunther and Kriemhild, who appear as small and bad characters, and Hagen, who in spite of his goodness is forced to serve the small and bad. By developing the myth of the superior man who, in a world ruled by baseness, can find fulfillment only in tragic decline, Ernst helped prepare the way for the later blood-and-soil mysticism. In *Chriemhild* (1919), a tragedy about the end of the

Nibelungs at Etzel's court, written under the impression of the lost World War, Ernst presents a critique of the nation. He calls the Nibelungs "Germans" and criticizes an understanding of loyalty and duty that is bereft of content and leads both to blind obedience and blind rage. Ernst creates a contrast in Gudrun, Rüdiger's daughter, who yearns for the security of a primordial state in mythological timelessness. In his lifetime Ernst was respected rather than appreciated, and only under National Socialism was he held in high esteem because his conservative views were, in an appropriately simplified form, eminently suited for the underpinning of nationalistic ideology.

[MH]

Bibliography

Ernst, Paul. *Brunhild: Trauerspiel in drei Aufzügen.* In *Gesammelte Werke,* Sec. 2, Vol. 2: *Dramen.* Munich: Albert Langen, Georg Müller, 1933, pp. 67–125.

_____. *Chriemhild: Trauerspiel in drei Aufzügen.* In *Gesammelte Werke,* Sec. 2, Vol. 2: *Dramen.* Munich: Albert Langen, Georg Müller, 1933, pp. 127–167.

ETTMÜLLER, ERNST MORITZ LUDWIG (1802–1877), author of the play *Sigufried* (1870), which presents the title character as a young, victorious hero who, as the epitome of valor and loyalty, represents a model for the "young" German Empire founded in 1871 at the conclusion of the Franco-Prussian War.

[WW]

Bibliography

Ettmüller, Ernst Moritz Ludwig. *Sigufried: Schauspiel in fünf Handlungen.* Zurich: Bürkli, 1870.

FÄHRMANN, WILLI (born. 1929), author of several German heroic tales for young readers. *Siegfried von Xanten* (1987) is an abbreviated rendering of the first part of the *Nibelungenlied.* Fährmann's version omits the more brutal scenes traditionally associated with the epic and avoids any glorification of heroic actions. Furthermore he does not deal with the concept of ominous fate which, usually endowed with magical and ritualistic overtones, constitutes a bond between the main characters in similar works intended for younger readers. *Siegfried von Xanten* was followed in 1988 by *Kriemhilds Rache: Eine alte Sage neu erzählt* (Kriemhild's Revenge, An Old Story told Anew), and in 1989 Fährmann published a work on the most popular hero of the period, Dietrich von Bern. Werner Bläbst provided illustrations for the first two aforementioned books.

[WW]

Bibliography

Fährmann, Willi. *Siegfried von Xanten: Eine alte Sage neu erzählt.* Stuttgart: Thienemann, 1987.

———. *Kriemhilds Rache: Eine alte Sage neu erzählt.* Stuttgart: Thienemann, 1988.

———. *Dietrich von Bern: Eine alte Sage neu erzählt.* Stuttgart: Thienemann, 1989.

———. *Deutsche Heldensagen.* Stuttgart: Thienemann, 1993.

FANTASY. It is well known that modern fantasy and science fiction, in books, comics, TV, movies, and even computer games, are based on motifs and topics of medieval courtly and heroic literature, and that they use them frequently. Many modern adventure stories are, consciously or unconsciously, based on the pattern of the medieval quest, especially the grail quest. This pattern is part of the worldwide myth of "the hero with a thousand faces," called the "monomyth" by Joseph Campbell. It is also quite probable that the Germanic myth of Sigurd/Siegfried, the strongest man of his time and one of the most famous dragon slayers, might have influenced modern heroic fantasy. Examples of such influence may be found in the books about Conan by Robert E. Howard and his associates (since 1933), about fantasy heroes fighting with dragons and monsters, or Ann McCaffrey's novels about the Dragonriders of Perth that have been published since 1968. German translations of various works were often more successful than the English originals. For example, Stephan Grundy's *Rheingold* novel first appeared in a German translation and was on *Der Spiegel*'s bestseller list for weeks. In contrast, however, the multi-authored novels of the cycle *Die Nibelungen,* based on an idea by the writer Kai Meyer (b. 1969) and which appeared in 1997 in Econ Taschenbuch Verlag (Düsseldorf), did not enjoy any particular success.

[UM]

Bibliography

Campbell, Joseph. *The Hero with a Thousand Faces.* Princeton: Princeton University Press, 1949.

Müller, Ulrich. "Schwerter, Motorräder und Raumschiffe: Versuch über eine Gruppe von epischen Universalien." In *Mittelalter-Rezeption III: Gesammelte Vorträge des 3. Salzburger Symposions: "Mittelalter, Massenmedien, Neue Mythen"* Göppingen: Kümmerle, 1968, pp. 697–712.

FEDDERSEN, FRIEDRICH AUGUST (1838–1908), author of the *Nibelungenkranz* (1876), a cycle of different types of poems, tells the story of *Siegfrieds Tod* and *Chriemhilds Rache.* Each part consists of twelve poems which are, in terms of both style and metrics, of poor quality and imbued with unintended humor. In accordance with the "spirit of the time," the heroic characters in Feddersen's work are portrayed in an exaggerated way in order to provide an impressive demonstration of "German" virtues such as obedience and courage.

[WW]

Bibliography

Feddersen, F[riedrich] A[ugust]. *Nibelungenkranz: Balladen und Dichtungen.* Hamburg: Richter, 1876.

FERNAU, JOACHIM (1909–1988), German journalist and author. He published various popular treatments of historical themes, all of which were very successful: *Rosen für Apoll: Die Geschichte der Griechen* (Roses for Apollo: History of the Greeks, 1961), *Caesar läßt grüßen: Die Geschichte der Römer* (Caesar sends his regards: History of the Romans, 1971), *Disteln für Hagen:. Bestandsaufnahme der deutschen Seele* (Thistles for Hagen: An Inventory of the German soul, 1966). The latter work offers a modern retelling of the *Nibelungenlied* and ostensibly takes a critical stance on ideology. Fernau has been justifiably reproached, however, for remaining stalwartly within the old folk tradition of Nibelungen interpretation. It was even suggested, particularly by Peter Wapnewski, that his book contains uncritical vestiges of National Socialist ideology.

[UM]

Bibliography

Fernau, Joachim. *Disteln für Hagen: Bestandsaufnahme der deutschen Seele.* Munich: Herbig, 1966.

Bachorski, Hans-Jürgen. "Alte Deutungen in neuem Gewande: J. Fernaus 'Disteln für Hagen' und H. Reinls 'Nibelungen-Filme.'" In *Mittelalter-Rezeption III,* edited by Jürgen Kühnel et al. Göppingen: Kümmerle, 1988, pp. 339–358.

FOUQUÉ, FRIEDRICH DE LA MOTTE

(1777–1843), remembered probably above all for his fairy tale *Undine* (1811), Fouqué used also the material of the Scandinavian sagas for his trilogy *Der Held des Nordens* (The Hero of the North, 1810), which was comprised of *Sigurd der Schlangentödter* (Sigurd the Dragon Slayer, first appeared 1808), *Sigurds Rache* (Sigurd's Revenge), and *Aslauga.* The first part, a dramatic poem in six sections ("Abenteuer"), is the most important, with its dedication to the German patriot and philosopher, Johann Gottlieb Fichte (1762–1814) which provides early testimony to the impact of the *Nibelungenlied* in the nineteenth century and anticipates the dramatizations of Hebbel and Wagner. An interesting addition to the study of this work that was largely disregarded after its first appearance is a review dated 1808 by Wilhelm Grimm in collaboration with Achim von Arnim. This review offers a telling indication of the reaction of near–contemporaries and also refers to the projected sequels to the first part. In his pungent essay *Die Romantische Schule in Deutschland* (1836), Heinrich Heine dismisses Fouqué's hero as having "as much courage as a hundred lions and as much sense as two donkeys."

[MEG]

Bibliography

Fouqué, Friedrich Baron de la Motte. *Sigurd, der Schlangentödter.* Berlin: Hitzig, 1808.

Hinrichs, Gustav, ed. *Kleinere Schriften von Wilhelm Grimm.* Vol. 1. Berlin: Dümmler, 1881, pp. 237–244.

FRIEDRICH, ALOIS

(1840–1919), teacher and author of school plays. His *Jung Siegfried* (1911) is a play for boys, designed to demonstrate to them the meaning of German character and the nature of the German: courageous, strong, proud, and endowed with an awareness of national identity.

[WW]

Bibliography

Friedrich, Alois. *Jung Siegfried: Dramatische Dichtung in einem Aufzug. Für die männliche Jugend verfaßt.* Munich: Höfling, 1911.

FÜHMANN, FRANZ

(1922–1984), journalist and author in the former German Democratic Republic. His retelling of the *Nibelungenlied* (1971) adheres closely to the epic and is written in modern prose. Fühmann avoids false pathos and any tendency to glorify events or characters. His poem, "Der Nibelunge Not" (The Demise of the Nibelungs, 1956) does not deal with the medieval epic per se, but is rather concerned with coming to terms with the Third Reich and the purposes to which it used the epic. In a style reminiscent of expressionist poetry, nine stanzas condemn the horrors of war as well as the misery of social exploitation. The same tendency and intention characterizes Fühmann's rough draft for the screenplay *Der Nibelunge Not* (1971/1972). The catastrophe was not something brought on by fate, but was rather the result of men's actions. The story begins with Etzel's wooing of Kriemhild and ends with the bloody massacre. The film was intended as a warning against the abuse of power, but it was never completed.

[WW]

Bibliography

Fühmann, Franz. "Der Nibelunge Not." In *Das Gedicht: Jahrbuch für zeitgenössische Lyrik* 3 (1956): 71–73.

———. *Das Nibelungenlied.* Neu erzählt von Franz Fühmann. Berlin: Neues Leben, 1971.

———. *Der Nibelunge Not: Szenarium für einen Spielfilm,* edited by Peter Göhler. Berlin: Aufbau Taschenbuch Verlag, 1993.

Venne, Ingmar ten. "Der Nibelunge Not: Franz Fühmanns Interpretation des Nibelungenliedes in einem Filmszenarium." In *La Chanson des Nibelungen hier et aujourd'hui: actes du colloque, Amiens, 12 et 13 janvier 1991,* edited by Danielle Buschinger and Wolfgang Spiewok. Wodan 7. Amiens: Université de Picardie, 1991, pp. 177–190.

GEIBEL, EMANUEL (1815–1884), from 1843 to his death in 1884, official poet to the Prussian king in Lübeck. He is known primarily as a lyric poet, but his interest in the Middle Ages found expression also in dramatic and epic writings. *König Sigurds Brautfahrt* (King Sigurd's Wooing Expedition) is an epic poem which in the manuscript bears the subtitle "eine nordische Sage" (a Nordic legend). It was composed in the mid-1840s and published in the collection of Geibel's poems called the "June songs." This poem is composed in four-line strophes which attempt to echo, often very clumsily, the form of the *Nibelungenlied.* In five sections, each with an explanatory heading, it tells the tragic tale of the obsessive love of old King Sigurd for Alfsonne, the lovely young daughter of Alf the Wise. In the tale Alf's daughter drinks poison rather than accept Sigurd as her husband. Her brothers also die in a clash with Sigurd's massive army, which had been brought to take Alf's daughter by force. Sigurd, learning of her death, abdicates in favor of his son Ragnar and himself seeks death in the flames of the otherworld as his ship bears her body away with him.

Brunhild appeared in book form in 1857 and was later performed briefly in Munich, Berlin, and Weimar, then in Geibel's native Lübeck in 1876. The material is derived from the first part of the *Nibelungenlied* and concentrates on the unrequited love of Brunhild for Siegfried (their earlier relationship is evoked in conversation between them) and the jealousy of Gunther. These two factors culminate in the murder of Siegfried, demanded by Gunther as a matter of honor and perpetrated offstage by Hagen. The action ends with the suicide of Brunhild after a passionate declaration of her love and her desire for eternal reunion with Siegfried. The later events of the *Nibelungenlied* are prophesied by the priestess Sigrun, one of the few figures introduced by Geibel, in a final speech which refers to the devastation of the land in which Kriemhild wanders with blood-stained sword, holding out a crowned head to the few survivors. The final word of the drama is one of resigned acceptance from Hagen. Motifs of the epic occur throughout, yet some central features, notably Siegfried's cloak of invisibility, are omitted or unexplained. Although the play has some impressive moments, it is a strange mixture, with its imitation of classical drama, its often clumsy language, and its wooden characters. Nonetheless it is an intriguing phenomenon and provides evidence of the fascination of the *Nibelungenlied* for the nineteenth century, a fascination that is echoed in later attempts to dramatize the material.

"Volkers Nachtgesang" (1870) is a lyric poem in six strophes, evoking through the song of Volker the scene in the thirtieth *âventiure* of the *Nibelungenlied.* Here, too, Volker is very much the minstrel warrior, whose instruments are both the fiddle and the sword. The poem is pervaded by the atmosphere of the night and the threat of impending conflict. The clash of swords betrays the enemy lurking outside or, as he puts it, death itself creeping about in the darkness. The present mood of foreboding is set against memories of youthful victories and of love, and the sharp contrasts of the poem culminate in the address to Death which, when day dawns in its bloody garment, will play its merry tune for them. An effective poem which, in the manner of its own age, succeeds in evoking the mood of the medieval epic.

"An Deutschland" bears the date January 1871 and thus marks the victory of Germany over France in the Franco-Prussian War and with that the foundation of the Prussian-dominated Second Reich. It is a poem full of the patriotic fervor which made Geibel so popular in his time. It urges Germany to abandon the widow's veil that she has worn for sixty-four years (since the abolition of the Holy Roman Empire) and assume her rightful place as victor, at the heart of Europe. It recalls the past conflict with the archenemy ("der Franze") and greets the present triumph as an hour sent by God, when the "marrow of the Nibelungs" again runs "like ore" through the limbs of Germany. The twelve stanzas of the poem throb with passion, with image heaped upon image, and the whole culminating in the declaration that the bridegroom is approaching, "the hero and the emperor" who will lead Germany home in glory.

[MEG]

Bibliography

Stammler, Wolfgang, ed. *Geibels Werke.* 3 vols. Leipzig: Bibliographisches Institut, 1920.

GEISSLER, HORST WOLFRAM (1893–1983), German author of popular novels in which the action is often set in the Biedermeier and Rococo period or in Greek antiquity. Until the Second World War, Geissler was a feature writer for several German papers. In 1966 he published a prose translation of the *Nibelungenlied*. His aim was to replace what he viewed as "entmutigende" (discouraging) prose adaptations of the nineteenth century with a modern version written in up-to-date language. However a deeper understanding of the original is occasionally hampered by Geissler's somewhat artificial style.

[MH]

Bibliography

Geissler, Horst Wolfram, trans. *Das Nibelungenlied.* With four illustrations by Ernst Barlach. Munich: Ehrenwirth, 1966.

GERLACH-BERNAU, KURT (1889–1976), author of *Der Nibelungen-Leich* (1933), an epic poem which is composed of lyric and narrative elements of the medieval lay. Irregular stanzas glorify the racist and aggressive behavior of pure-blooded Nibelungs as a parable for the historical legitimation of Nazi ideology and the politics of conquest for "Lebensraum" (living space), as well as the subjugation of "inferior" peoples.

[WW]

Bibliography

Gerlach-Bernau, Kurt. *Der Nibelungen-Leich.* Breslau: Hirt, 1933.

GÖRRES, GUIDO (1805–1852), son of Joseph Görres. He retells the story of the *Hürnen Seyfried,* i.e., the adventures of young Siegfried, who kills the dragon and frees the king's daughter. In keeping with the intentions of his father, the younger Görres wished to revitalize German heroic legends in order to provide some models of "truth" and "honor," and thus encourage the German people and the German fatherland to move forward into a glorious future.

[WW]

Bibliography

Görres, Guido. *Der hürnen Siegfried und sein Kampf mit dem Drachen: eine altdeutsche Sage.* Schafthauser: Hurter, 1843.

Wolzogen, Hans von. *Der Nibelungenmythos in Sage und Literatur.* Berlin: Weber, 1876, pp. 97f.

GÖRRES, JOHANN JOSEPH VON (1776–1848), the most influential German publicist of his time who opposed, especially as the editor of the important journal *Rheinischer Merkur,* both the Napoleonic empire and the following Restoration. In his later years he became a leading voice of Catholic liberalism. Görres also had some import as an editor (of *Lohengrin* and of poetry), critic, and promoter of medieval German literature. He was one of the first to describe the Norse versions of the Nibelungen tale, and he helped popularize the *Nibelungenlied* by praising it in his typically rhetorical, often mystic style, with its flood of romantic imagery.

[WLH]

Bibliography

Görres, Joseph. "Der gehörnte Siegfried und die Nibelungen." *Zeitschrift für Einsiedler.* April 15, 1808, pp. 36–40. Reprinted in vol. 3 of *Gesammelte Schriften,* edited by Günther Müller. Cologne: Gilde, 1926, pp. 304–308.

———. "Der gehörnte Siegfried." In *Die teutschen Volksbücher.* Heidelberg: Mohr/Zimmer, 1807, pp. 208ff.

———. "Heldenthum, Heldengesänge, Minne unter den christlich-germanischen Völkern des Mittelalters." *Eos* (99/104), June 1828. Reprinted in vol. 15 of *Gesammelte Schriften,* edited by Ernst Deuerlein. Cologne: Backen, 1951, pp. 56–66.

Schultz, Franz. *Joseph Görres als Herausgeber, Litteraturhistoriker, Kritiker im Zusammenhang mit der jungen Romantik dargestellt.* Berlin: Mayer, 1902.

GRILL, ERICH (1883–1949), German historian, director of the local museum in Worms (1921 to 1933). His poem "Abend am Rhein" (Evening by the Rhine, 1926) can be seen as representative of the political treatment of the *Nibelungenlied* during the twenties and thirties that directly or indirectly relates Siegfried's fate to the "Dolchstoßlegende" (stab-in-the-back myth) and the alleged fate of the Germans in the First World War. Grill presents Siegfried as "a glorious hero" who, after the conspiracy of Brünhild and Hagen, "vom feigen Mörderstahle durchbohrt (wird)" (is run through by the murderer's cowardly blade). In the poem the red light of the setting sun on the Rhine not only corresponds to Siegfried's hot blood, which colored the grasses crimson red, but in this context also evokes the memory of the battlefields of the war.

[MH]

Bibliography

Grill, Erich. "Abend am Rhein." *Volk und Scholle: Heimatblätter für beide Hessen, Nassau und Frankfurt a. M., Nibelungen-Nummer 4* (1926), 12–13.

Wunderlich, Werner. *Der Schatz des Drachentödters: Materialien zur Wirkungsgeschichte des Nibelungenliedes.* Stuttgart: Klett-Cotta 1977, pp. 71–73.

GRIMM, WILHELM (1786–1859), author of *Das Lied von der Frau Grimhild und ihren Brüdern* (The Song of Lady Grimhild and her brothers). Although his popular claim to fame rests with the collections of fairytales that he made with his brother Jacob, Wilhelm Grimm's scholarly contributions to the understanding of the German language and older literature are very significant. Of these his joint achievement with his brother in initiating the great German dictionary (1852) must count as the outstanding one, but his independent contribution on the German heroic legend (*Die deutsche Heldensage*, 1829) is important, together with his editions of older German texts. The volume which appeared in 1811 and which was dedicated to two of the central figures of the German romantic movement, the poets Achim von Arnim and Clemens Brentano, is remarkable for the insights that it offers into the perception of the nature of older literature, and for its revelation of Grimm's own poetic gifts. His appendix to his renderings of Old Danish heroic songs, ballads and fairytales casts important light on his own appreciation of the literature that he is offering to his German public at a time when so little was generally known about it and when scholars were only beginning to comprehend its scope. The ballad that bears the title *Das Lied von der Frau Grimhild und ihren Brüdern* is placed at the beginning of the section called "Heroic Songs," and Grimm explains that he opens his volume

with this account because it represents the most splendid point of the legend ("den glänzendsten Punct der Sage"). This is not a translation but a retelling of the story of Grimhild's revenge, with material derived from Nordic and Germanic sources, and not only from the *Nibelungenlied* ("bald der einen, bald der anderen," as he puts it). The result is a strange and often contradictory account of events, emanating, it emerges, from the murder of Siegfried, and culminating in the deaths of the brothers Hogen and Folqvard Spielemann. The three "songs" are composed in the rhythmic meter of the traditional ballad.

[MEG]

Bibliography

Grimm, W. C., trans. *Altdänische Heldenlieder, Balladen und Märchen.* Heidelberg: Mohr and Zimmer, 1811.

GROTE, HANS-HENNING VON (1896–1946), officer and author, whose poem, "Das Lied von Siegfried" (The Lay of Siegfried, 1934), displays characteristics typical of the literature produced during the Third Reich. In the poem Providence gives new life to the myth of Siegfried, the liberator of Germany, who, as a new hero and idol, brings renewed hope to the land through his killing of the dragon, an allegory of the evil powers that had suppressed the German people.

[WW]

Bibliography

Jelusich, Mirko, ed. *Deutsche Heldendichtung.* Leipzig: Verlag Das Neue Deutschland, 1934, pp. 55–57.

GRÜN, ANASTASIUS (pseudonym of Anton Alexander Graf von Auersperg; 1806–1876), Austrian author and politician. Since 1830 opposed to the Metternich system, in 1838 he published anonymously the *Spaziergänge eines Wiener Poeten* (Strolls of a Viennese Poet), a lyrical cycle that represents the earliest statement of the prerevolutionary *Vormärz* period in Austria. In 1838 Metternich gave him the alternative of either ceasing publication or leaving the country. Grün chose the first option but maintained his opposing position even when he assumed, through marriage, a representative function at court. Having been fiercely criticized for this behavior by German *Vormärz* poets, he answered with the humorous epic *Nibelungen im Frack* (Nibelungen in Tails, 1843). In his effort to reach the hearts of his critics, Grün makes deliberate use of the Nibelungen stanza, the use of which he characterizes as his "Kriegsgallione" (galleon of war) and "Sängerbarke" (singer's barque). He accuses these poets, sarcastically calling them "Sänger der Freiheit" (singers of freedom), of wanting to oppress their own mother (i.e., poetry), "ausschliesslich im Feldrock der Politik zu fechten" ([by having her] fight exclusively in the uniform of politics), i.e., by having her become a mere instrument of politics. He also insists that even "Fürstenlippen" (the lips of princes) should be allowed to speak freely.

[MH]

Bibliography

Grün, Anastasius. *Nibelungen im Frack.* In vol. 4 of *Gesammelte Werke in 5 Bänden,* edited by Ludwig August Frankl. Berlin: Grote, 1877, pp. 5–78.

HAGENDORFF, HUGO (1813–1860), retells the story of *Hürnen Seyfried* in a cycle of nineteen romances of poor literary quality. The language and the metric elements oscillate between pathos and unintended humor.

[WW]

Bibliography

Hagendorff, Hugo. *Die Mähr vom hürnen Siegfried: Balladenkranz nach dem Volksbuche.* Nebst einem Anhange. Zeitz: Julius Schieferdecker, 1837.

HAUSER, OTTO (1896–1946), translator and author, whose epic poem, *Das Nibelungenlied* (1923), glorifies in pseudoreligious fashion the newborn Siegfried as the sun's progeny and liberator of the defeated and humiliated German people following the Treaty of Versailles.

[WW]

Bibliography

Hauser, Otto. *Das Nibelungenlied: Nachdichtung.* Weimar: Duncker, 1923.

HEBBEL, FRIEDRICH (1813–1863), poet and one of the most significant German dramatists. Hebbel worked for one and a half years on his trilogy *Die Nibelungen* (*Der gehörnte Siegfried, Siegfrieds Tod,* and *Kriemhilts Rache*) and

finished it in March 1860. It was first performed in Weimar under Dingelstedt in 1861, and published in 1862. At this time plays with a medieval theme were in fashion (e.g., *Der Nibelungenhort* (1828) by Ernst Raupach and *Brunhild* (1857) by Emanuel Geibel), and Hebbel was eager to write a national drama with historical dimensions using the epic and not the myth as its foundation. He achieved this dimension with the help of Schelling's *Philosophie der Mythologie und der Offenbarung.* Hebbel attended Schelling's lectures in Munich and put the philosopher's thoughts and ideas into the play. He wrote in the *Vorwort zur Maria Magdalena* that the aim of dramatic art is not to topple contemporary historical processes or existing human political, religious, and moral institutions, but rather to provide an even more stable foundation. Art is understood as philosophy that has been translated into reality, a definition which affirms the words of Schelling that "art is the sole true and eternal guide and, at the same time, document of philosophy (*System des transcendentalen Idealismus,* p. 695). Hebbel's feigned modest words that he had merely been the interpreter of someone superior, does not exclude the endowment of the epic matter with a remarkable philosophical profusion.

In the work itself, for example, the chaplain, endowed by Hebbel with a greater importance than in the *Nibelungenlied,* clearly works within the parameters of Schelling's category of obedience when he begs Kriemhild to renounce revenge. But the play transcends the Christian principle of reconciliation, and its heroine pulls the trigger of final justice (5441). Here the historical dimensions are mercilessly followed through until the end of Christianity and beyond. At one level, Dietrich von Bern appears to epitomize the true Christian knight, and as in the epic he gives meaning to the incident. He frees himself from possessions and power. Yet, while he follows the principle of poverty at Etzel's court (3953–3962), he still remembers heathen mythology, which is for him the ideal era (4812). As we already know from the Old Norse *Voluspá,* he, too, listens to the riddle of the world at the well of the water nymphs, to the history of the great sun year with its eternal circling of the world, the destroying autumn, and the new spring (4823–4831). He wants to know about the forthcoming changes, but clumsily he frightens away the water nymphs.

In the character of Dietrich, history faces itself and he himself is at its end. The mythological process of the play has to be understood in connection with Schelling's philosophy of revelation, which states that following the stage of mythical timelessness, history moves on to posthistory. This concept is transferred to the characters of the drama, as follows: the time of Frigga, which represents prehistory, is followed by Brünhild and Siegfried. Then come the Burgundians, followed by Etzel and Dietrich. Brünhild, "the proud descendant of the Valkyries" (1341), is made manifest with her entrance into history (namely, the approach to the Burgundian court), and she is "historicized" through her loss of virginity. Siegfried's convergence on history happens through the devaluation of the mythical gold to a mere product, to a bridal gift. Siegfried, connected to the dragon by means of his armored skin, introduces (unknowingly) the satanic principle into history, and wins his bride through deceit. The mover of this painful process is the "spirit" that allies itself with culture, and opposes the predominance of nature by weakening and deflowering it. At the other end is Dietrich, who personifies the dream of eternal peace. Mediating between the principle of Siegfried and the principle of Dietrich is Etzel. Etzel did not turn away completely from life as a heathen. He admits that he came to conquer the world, an admission for which the author evokes an image of a horseman of the Apocalypse (4733–4739), but before the horseman can take over Rome, a frightening vision forces him to give up his plans (4752f.) and he yields to the authority of the Pope (4757f.). From now on, however, Etzel wants to become a peaceful ruler and avenge Kriemhild only according to law, without treachery and villainy (4796) and without violating hospitality. His apocalyptic horse is "still saddled" (4760), indeed "it is even half way out of the stable" (4761). But "out of pity and compassion" (4764) it hides its head into the clouds (4763), tries to be blind and indifferent. It is a code for Etzel himself, a symbol for the choice to preserve or to destroy. Because anti-Christ and Christ are ultimately one, according to Hebbel, pity always prevails. Like Christ, Etzel took up the task of supporting humankind, but could not keep it from sinning. Trying to reconcile between God and spirit, Etzel became the eternal mediator, divided and full of discord.

In the final analysis, it must be left open how deeply Hebbel wanted to embed the philosophy of revelation into his drama, but without it any understanding of his drama is empty and nonhistorical. This philosophy is by no means a chimera. It is substantially integrated into the work about the Nibelungen myth, which has been revived as a "German tragedy." It is the dramatized "German" myth concerning the then common belief that the Germans were the legitimate successors of Germanic society. Utilizing national myth, the process of world history is simulated in the work, and its course is not determined by humans but by history itself. People are subject to its rule, and it becomes very difficult to put the Nibelungen characters into a play which demands, according to Hegel's determination, critical reflection and a deep psychological examination. Because of this Hebbel first shied away from starting the work but later found the courage and put (like the poet of the *Nibelungenlied*) reflection and psychology into acting and myth and consciously molded his characters according to those elements.

[OE]

Bibliography

de Boor, Helmut, ed. *Friedrich Hebbel. Die Nibelungen. Vollständiger Text. Dokumentation.* Frankfurt a. M.: Ullstein, 1966.

Ehrismann, Otfrid. "Hebbels Nibelungen: Der Dichter als Dolmetscher." In vol. 1 of *Mittelalter-Rezeption.* Göppingen: Kümmerle, 1979, pp. 311–343.

———. "Dietrich oder die Produktivität der Tränen: Verhinderte Trauerarbeit am Nibelungenlied." *Diskussion Deutsch* 18 (1987): 306–320.

———. "Philosophie, Mythologie, und Poesie: Hebbels Schellingrezeption in den Nibelungen." In *Friedrich Hebbel: Neue Studien zu Werk und Wirkung,* edited by Hilmar Grundmann, Heide: Westholsteinische Verlagsanstalt Boyens, 1982, pp. 85–102.

———. "Siegfried: Studie über Heldentum, Liebe, und Tod. Mittelalterliche Nibelungen, Hebbel, Wagner." *Hebbel-Jahrbuch* 36 (1981): 11–48.

Glaser, Horst Albert. "Ein deutsches Trauerspiel: Friedrich Hebbels Nibelungen." In *Die Nibelungen: Ein deutscher Wahn, ein deutscher Alptraum. Studien und Dokumente zur Rezeption des*

Nibelungenstoffs im 19. und 20. Jahrhundert, edited by Joachim Heinzle and Anneliese Waldschmidt, Frankfurt a. M.: Suhrkamp, 1991, pp. 333–350.

Hermand, Jost. "Hebbels Nibelungen: Ein deutsches Trauerspiel." In *Hebbel in neuer Sicht,* edited by Helmut Kreuzer, Stuttgart: Kohlhammer, 1963, pp. 315–333.

Stockinger, Ludwig. "Anmerkungen zu Hebbels Position im Religionsdiskurs der Moderne." *Hebbel-Jahrbuch* 51 (1996): 129–149.

HEIDNER, MARTIN (pseudonym for Wolfgang Hohlbein, b. 1953), contemporary German author whose novel, *Der Drachentöter* (1989), relates the story of Siegfried's youth and his maturation from a youthful, reckless adventurer to a responsible adult. This popular juvenile tale of Siegfried has virtually nothing in common with the medieval epic, is poorly written, and tends to be full of standard, black-and-white clichés.

[WW]

Bibliography

Heidner, Martin. *Der Drachentöter: Ein Roman nach Motiven des Nibelungenlieds.* Bindlach: Löwe, 1989.

HEINE, HEINRICH (1797–1856), renowned German lyric poet and satirist for whom the Middle Ages and, occasionally, the tale of the Nibelungs, provided narrative fodder. In his *Romanzero* (1851), for example, he compares the Hungarian Revolution of 1849 to the Nibelungen tales. "It is the same fate of heroes [as in the tales of the Nibelungs]," Heine writes. "They are the same ancient tales, just the names have been changed. But yet these like those are valiant heroes." Heine also recognizes the ultimate similarity between the Hungarian revolution and the Nibelungs: they are doomed to failure and cannot succeed against Austria and Russia. "It is the same fate, too—no matter how proud and free the banners wave, the hero, due to custom old, must fall to brutishly bloody powers."

Siegfried, too, experiences an interesting transformation, from tragic hero to the naive child of the sun. In his poem "Deutschland ist noch ein kleines Kind" from 1840 Heine muses: "Germany is still a small child, but the sun is its nurse who nourishes it not with milk, but with fire!" He goes on to compare Germany to Siegfried, an unpredictable and clumsy "little giant" whose course of action is still undetermined. The ultimate meaning of this poem and its allusions is still uncertain, which is typical for Heine's poetry at this time. Nonetheless the national, indeed nationalistic, content is clearly recognizable. The "little giant," be it Siegfried or Germany, growing fast like a curiosity of nature, is still "clumsy." But when it is fully grown, the easygoing youngster will unfold his still dormant mighty powers. In which direction? In a barbaric way, wreaking havoc on the dominant cultures, on civilization itself? Well-meaning but nevertheless clumsy, and, therefore, not controllable?

This image of the "little giant" looks ahead to the nationalistic treatments of the *Nibelungenlied* in the late nineteenth and early twentieth century. But by that time it has become clear that Siegfried/Germany is no longer the "sun child," and its apologists know full well in which direction they want its powers to lead.

[OE/FGG]

Bibliography

Brummack, Jürgen, ed. *Heinrich Heine: Epoche, Werk, Wirkung.* Munich: Beck, 1980.

Clasen, Herbert. *Heinrich Heines Romantikkritik: Tradition, Produktion, Rezeption.* Hamburg: Hoffmann and Kampe, 1979.

Hinck, Walter. *Die Wunde Deutschland: Heinrich Heines Dichtung im Widerstreit von Nationalidee, Judentum und Antisemitismus.* Frankfurt a. M.: Insel, 1990.

Kanowsky, Walter. *Vernunft und Geschichte: Heinrich Heines Studium als Grundlegung seiner Welt- und Kunstanschauung.* Bonn: Bouvier, 1975.

Mucke, Georg. *Heinrich Heines Beziehungen zum deutschen Mittelalter.* 1908. Reprint, Hildesheim: Gerstenberg, 1978.

Pongs, Ulrich. *Heinrich Heine: Sein Bild der Aufklärung und dessen romantische Quellen.* Frankfurt a. M.: Lang, 1985.

Windfuhr, Manfred. *Heinrich Heine: Revolution und Reflexion.* Stuttgart: Metzler, 1969.

HEINRICH WITTENWILER'S *RING*. Horst Brunner has pointed out that the *Ring,* written about 1410, shows the same negativity as the *Nibelungenlied* and *Reinhart Fuchs,* as well as the *Trojanerkrieg.* In each instance the work concludes with the complete destruction of the epic world. The *Ring* contains several names from the *Nibelungenlied* and the *Nibelungensage*. However, the major source for the *Ring* from the fourteenth century, the *Bauernhochzeits-schwank*, which exists in two versions, *Meier Betz* and *Metzes Hochzeit*, already contains some of these names from the Nibelungen tradition. The *Bauernhochzeitschwank* also evinces several Nibelungen names that are found in the *Ring*. Ortlieb (der Hün), which was the name for Attila and Kriemhild's son in the *Nibelungen-lied*, appears only in *Metzes Hochzeit*. In both versions one finds Sifrit (*Metzes Hochzeit*) and Seifrid (*Meier Betz*), Nodung (*Meier Betz*) and Nuodung (*Metzes Hochzeit*), Elckenpolt (*Meier Betz*) and Erckenbolt (*Metzes Hochzeit*) and Dietrich der Übelfar (*Metzes Hochzeit* and *Meier Betz*).

None of the names from *Metzes Hochzeit* and *Meier Betz* that pertain to German heroic epic is repeated in Wittenwiler's *Ring* except for Dietrich, this time correctly named "von Bern." The title itself, denoting simultaneously a piece of jewelry, a treasure, and a wedding gift, might ironically refer to Andvari's ring. In fact at least one of the sources for Wittenwiler could have been the manuscript **m** of the *Nibelungenlied* (Darmstadt), dating from about 1400, in which the first part of the epic has been compiled with the deeds of the hero of the *Hürnen Seyfrid*. One of the major sources, in turn, for the *Hürnen Seyfrid* was the *Rosengarten*. The name Hagen is treated in a comical way, because it is given to the donkey, who has his own series of adventures during the fighting in the *Ring* (see RING, PART III).

[SJ]

Bibliography

Brunner, Horst. "Hürnen Seyfried." In vol. 4 of *Die deutsche Literatur des Mittelalters. Verfasser-lexikon*, 2nd ed., edited by Kurt Ruh. Berlin: de Gruyter, 1983, cols. 317–326.

Wießner, Edmund. *Kommentar zu Heinrich Witten-wilers 'Ring.'* Deutsche Literatur: Sammlung lit-erarischer Kunst- und Kulturdenkmäler in Ent-wicklungsreihen. Reihe Realistik des Spätmittelalters. Kommentar zu Band 3. Ergän-zungsband. 1936. Reprint, Darmstadt: Wissen-schaftliche Buchgesellschaft, 1964.

Wittenwiler, Heinrich. *Der Ring: Frühneuhoch-deutsch/Neuhochdeutsch*, after the text by Ed-mund Wießner, edited and translated by Horst Brunner. Stuttgart: Reclam, 1991.

HENNE, JOSEF ANTON (1798–1870), Swiss politician, journalist, and teacher of German and history in the canton of St. Gall. He was also director of the public record office and later li-brarian of the abbey library of St Gall. In 1825 he began republishing various works dealing with the Nibelung tradition: the *Edda, Volsunga saga, Amelung saga*, and the *Nibelungenlied*. Dur-ing the course of his lifetime, he planned to publish the complete cycle of German heroic tales, but it never appeared in print. In 1868 Henne published the romantic novella *Des hl. Gallus Zelle an der Steinach im Jahre 614* (The Cell of St. Gallus on the Steinach in the Year 614). The story takes place in the time of the Irish wanderer, Gallus, patron saint of the later monas-tery of St. Gall. Historical events as well as the legendary traditions surrounding the Lake Con-stance area of the seventh century provide motifs and episodes for the narrative, which is dedicated to a so-called Sunadar, a minstrel of the Walser, a German-speaking alpine people from Raetia. This Sunadur travels to the Merovingian court of Brunihild at Worms and performs the "Joy and Sorrow of the Nibelungs." He explains the mythological references and tells of the fabu-lous sources of the Nibelung tradition. After that he sings six songs in the *Nibelungenton* and the *Nibelungenstrophe* which recount for his lis-teners the course of the epic up to the death of Siegfried.

[WW]

Bibliography

Henne, Anton. *Des hl. Gallus Zelle an der Steinach im Jahre 614*. St. Gall: Altwegg-Weber, 1868.

Pfrunder, Peter. *Josef Anton Henne (1798–1870), Sagenerzähler und Sagensammler der Schweiz: Studien zur Produktion volkstümlicher Geschich-te und Geschichten vom 16. bis zum frühen 20. Jahrhundert*, edited by Rudolf Schenda and Hans ten Doornkaat. Berne: Haupt, 1988, pp. 331–350.

HERMANN, FRANZ RUDOLPH (1787–1823), author of a drama trilogy that presents the plot of the *Nibelungenlied* as a romantic and patriotic play aimed at revitalizing the Teutonic spirit and the poetic magic of the epic in order to promote the self-confidence and national identity of the German people following the war of liberation against Napoleon. This explains why Hermann historicizes the figure of Etzel, calling him Attila, to whom various knights, such as Rüdiger, are bound. Such alliances weaken the position of the Nibelungs, just as was the case with the German states, which did not join together in the fight against Napoleon. The drama is dedicated to von der Hagen, Büsching, Fouqué, and Tieck who, with their editions and literary studies, were responsible for the "rebirth of the Nibelungs."

[WW]

Bibliography

Hermann, Franz Rudolph. *Die Nibelungen in drei Theilen: 1. Der Nibelungen Hort, 2. Siegfried, 3. Chriemhildens Rache.* Leipzig: Brockhaus, 1819.

HERWEGH, GEORG (1817–1875), a fervent, political-revolutionary poet and member of the "Young Germany" movement, who emigrated from Prussia to France and Switzerland. His satirical and critical poem, "Den Siegestrunknen. Januar 1872" (To Those intoxicated by Victory. January 1872), admonishes the victor of the Franco-Prussian War, "Bismarck-Siegfried," who had slain the French dragon and won the Nibelungen hoard (i.e., German unification), not to fall prey to chauvinism.

[WW]

Bibliography

Werner, Hans-Georg, ed. *Herweghs Werke in einem Band.* Berlin: Aufbau, 1975, pp. 273f.

HERZOG, RUDOLF (1869–1943), German author who retells the story of the Nibelungs, stressing battle scenes and other heroic actions. The first part deals with Siegfried, the young hero who meets his death as a result of rivalry between Kriemhilde and Brunhild. The second part is concerned with the battle between the Nibelungs and the Huns. The catastrophe is interpreted as an act of cruel revenge for the murder of a "sun hero." The demise of the Nibelungs may be seen as an allegory of the sacrifice required of all mankind for the death of Siegfried.

[WW]

Bibliography

Herzog, Rudolf. *Die Nibelungen: Des Heldenliedes beide Teile. Neu erzählt.* Die Koehler Reihe. Berlin: Ullstein, 1913.

HOFFMEISTER, HERMANN (1839–1916), his poem, "Der eiserne Siegfried" (Iron Siegfried, 1885) is dedicated to the German chancellor, Bismarck, who was referred to in the press as "the Iron Chancellor." The elder statesman is compared in an obsequious and ridiculous way with a young Siegfried who is the embodiment of strength. Bismarck is seen as protecting the German people from such evils as social democracy, which is considered as vicious as the dragon Fafnir.

[WW]

Bibliography

Hoffmeister, Hermann. *Der eiserne Siegfried:Eine neuzeitliche Nibelungenmär.* Berlin: Ebhardt, 1885.

HOHLBEIN, WOLFGANG (b. 1953; see also HEIDNER, MARTIN) German author of adolescent and fantasy literature. His novel *Hagen von Tronje* is set against the historical backdrop of the great migrations in the fifth century and contains a mixture of history and fantasy. The plot and the motifs of the *Nibelungenlied* serve simply as the decorative basis for a suspenseful, pseudohistorical, but trivial tale. The narrator provides, for instance, details regarding Brünhild's deflowering as well as vivid descriptions of bloody battles. The protagonists lack any psychological depth, with the result that the main character, Hagen, does not transcend the image of a vassal and sinister warrior.

[WW]

Bibliography

Hohlbein, Wolfgang. *Hagen von Tronje: Ein Nibelungen-Roman.* Vienna: Ueberreuter, 1986.

Martin, Bernhard R. *Nibelungen-Metamorphosen: Die Geschichte eines Mythos.* Munich: Iudicium, 1992, pp. 200–210.

HOOP, HEIN (b. 1927) Danish-born author of poems and songs, satirist. In the first poem of his collection he deals with the problems of violence and killing, and the last verses constitute the title of his book: "Lisa, Gudrun, Freya, alle hin, auweia!" (Lisa, Gudrun, Freya, alas, all gone!).

[SSch]

Bibliography
Hoop, Hein. *Lisa, Gudrun, Freya, alle hin, auweia! Satirische Bretterlieder.* Hamburg: n.p., [1978].

HOSÄUS, WILHELM ABSALOM (1827–1900), librarian and author of the tragedy, *Kriemhild* (1866), which is concerned with the dichotomy between Christianity and paganism. In her destructive drive for revenge Kriemhild rejects basic Christian virtues, such as forgiveness, and her triumphant quest for vengeance ultimately destroys both herself and all of the Nibelungs.

[WW]

Bibliography
Hosäus, Wilhelm Absalom. *Kriemhild: Trauerspiel in fünf Aufzügen.* Paderborn: Schöningh, 1866.

HÜTTIG, ERNST German teacher (Saxony) and author of amateur plays. During the Weimar Republic, Hüttig published several children's and Christmas plays, and in the 1930s he wrote a number of festival plays in celebration of National Socialism. In his play *Siegfried* (1934), he equates the guileless hero with Germany, which was also considered to be a victim of treachery. Myth and history are intended to demonstrate here how Germany will never again suffer such a fate. The hero, Siegfried, is the embodiment of German loyalty and the German's willingness to make sacrifices, evoking a future of "heroic Teutonism."

[MH/WW]

Bibliography
Hüttig, Ernst. *Siegfried: Festliches Spiel in drei dramatischen Szenen und zwei Bühnenbildern, mit Sprechchören oder Gesängen.* Turnerbühne: Eine Sammlung von Theaterstücken, besonders für Turnvereine geeignet 54. Leipzig: Jahn-Verlag, 1934.

JÄHNS, MAX (1837–1900), Prussian author of military works. After the victory over France in the Franco-Prussian War and the founding of the Second German Empire, Jähns composed in Versailles "Ein preussisches Festspiel" (A Prussian Festival Play). In it he portrayed the Nibelungen hoard as a metaphor for patriotic German unification while the personified Rhine was depicted as an allegorical protector of German unity.

[WW]

Bibliography
Jähns, Max. *Ein preussisches Festspiel.* 3rd ed. Berlin: Pactel, 1896.

JANSEN, FRITZ (1892–197?), German author of amateur plays and works aimed at the youth of Germany. During the Weimar Republic Jansen published two plays based on the Nibelungen material, *Siegfrieds Tod* (Siegfried's Death, 1924) and *Siegfried* (1927). Although the titles seem to suggest otherwise, the emphasis is actually on the figure of Hagen, whose role is central to the action and whose loyalty is paramount, an adaptation quite similar to the interpretation predominating in other Nibelungen works of that period. Hagen, "der Treu um Treue brach" (who was disloyal for the sake of loyalty) is depicted as bearing the entire burden of responsibility because his king proves inept.

[MH]

Bibliography
Jansen, Fritz. *Siegfrieds Tod: Ein ernstes Spiel von deutscher Treue in fünf Aufzügen.* Jugend- und Volksbühne 429. Leipzig: Strauch, 1924.
———. *Siegfried: Ein deutscher Heldengesang in fünf Aufzügen.* Volksbühne 115. Warendorf: Wulf, 1927.
Gentry, Francis G. "Die Rezeption des Nibelungenliedes in der Weimarer Republik." In *Das Weiterleben des Mittelalters in der deutschen Literatur,* edited by James F. Poag and Gerhild Scholz Williams. Königstein: Athenäum, 1983, pp. 142–156, esp. pp. 150–152.

JANSEN, WERNER (1890–1943), German author whose work *Das Buch Treue* (The Book of Loyalty, 1916), enjoyed considerable popularity during World War I. Jansen attempts to revive what he views as the key idea of the medieval epic. He suggests that the virtues of the old Nibelungs instilled courage in those Prussian soldiers sent to fight against Napoleon's army in 1815. Jansen aspires to renew that fighting spirit with his novel, the plot of which centers around a nationalistic recounting of the demise of the Nibelungs as they fought for their homeland in a foreign country. The main protagonist is Hagen, the "chancellor," a personification of absolute loyalty to king, people, and fatherland.

[WW]

Bibliography

Jansen, Werner. *Das Buch Treue: Nibelungenroman.* Braunschweig: Westermann, 1921.

Hoffmann, Werner. "Nibelungenromane." In *Helden und Heldensage,* edited by Hermann Reichert and Günter Zimmermann. Philologica Germanica 11. Vienna: Fassbaender, 1990, pp. 113–142.

JORDAN, WILHELM (1819–1904), German translator and author who combined elements of classical and Germanic poetry in his writings. His retelling of the *Nibelungenlied* is reminiscent of the epic style of Homer and characterized by alliterative meter. *Die Nibelunge* is divided into two parts, *Sigfridsage* (The Saga of Sigfrid, 1869) and *Hildebrands Heimkehr* (Hildebrand's Homecoming, 1874). The Volsung Sigfrid, a foundling, is the legal ruler of Burgundy. He falls victim to the Nibelung Hagen's conspiracy. After the catastrophe at the court of Etzel and after Kriemhild's suicide, Hildebrant, who is modeled on Ulysses, sets out and returns home safely after a number of adventures. His son, Hadubrant, and Sigfrid's daughter, Schwanhild, marry and produce a new generation of Wulfings (note use of this tribal name in *Beowulf*), who represent the hope and future of the German nation during the Middle Ages. Jordan projects his romantic dreams of the awakening of a strong, vital German people and a powerful German nation back into legendary prehistoric times. They are also linked to the *Nibelungenlied* and to the present. Sigfrid was born too early, because Germany still needs to undergo 1,000 years of strife, up to the dawn of the Middle Ages, in order to prove itself. Thereafter it still requires several more centuries in order to overcome a lack of unity, symbolized by the hoard and the ring of the Nibelungs. After the founding of the German Empire, the Second Reich, in 1871, the historical aim of German domination throughout the world (in line with the belief that "might makes right"), is to be attained through the Hohenzollern dynasty, who inherit the Wulfings' legacy. Jordan's ultimate objective was to re-create a heroic myth that would have national significance.

[WW]

Bibliography

Kühnel, Jürgen. "Der Hort, Held Sigfrid und die Hohenzollern: Zu Wilhelm Jordans Epos 'Die Nibelunge.'" In *3. Pöchlarner Heldengespräch: Die Rezeption des Nibelungenliedes,* edited by Klaus Zatloukal. Philologica Germanica 16. Vienna: Fassbaender, 1995, pp. 127–146.

Wilhelm Jordans Nibelunge. Erstes Lied: Sigfridsage. Frankfurt a. M.: Selbstverlag, 1869.

Wilhelm Jordans Nibelunge. Zweites Lied: Hildebrants Heimkehr. Frankfurt a. M.: Selbstverlag, 1874.

KEVERING, WOLFGANG, the author of "Das Nibelungenlied," a short poem consisting of fifteen rhyming couplets which relate in concentrated form the entire story of the Nibelungs by referring simply to characters, motifs, and actions. Kevering's laconic style transforms the originally somber epic into a humorous and rapid succession of references to jealousy, the breaking of oaths, murder, revenge, and slaughter.

[WW]

Bibliography

Kevering, Wolfgang. "Das Nibelungenlied." *Fantasia* 28/29 (1986): 37.

KIEFER, SEPP, German author of a Nibelungen story that claims that the plot unfolded not on the Rhine, but rather on the Isar River. The heroes in the work are Bavarians and Swabians, including Hagen. Bavarian dialect is used throughout. The Burgundians journey to visit Etzel and Kriemhild on the occasion of their son's baptism. The work does not conclude with a battle; instead Kriemhild puts a special powder into the Bavarians' beer that gives them terrible stomachaches. The moral of the story is that, had there been enough breweries in existence at the time, it would not have been necessary for Siegfried to drink water and Hagen would not have had an opportunity to kill him during the race to the stream.

[SSch]

Bibliography

Kiefer, Sepp. *Die Isar-Nibelungen: Eine zünftigtragische Geschichte aus blau-weißer Vorzeit.* Composed and illustrated by Sepp Kiefer. Mainburg: Pinsker, [1963].

KINDLEBEN, CHRISTIAN WILHELM (1748–1785), German writer, author of the prose work *Der gehörnte Siegfried* (1783).

[WW]

Bibliography
Kindleben, Christian Wilhelm. *Der gehörnte Siegfried: Ein Volksroman.* N.p., 1783.

KINKEL, JOHANN GOTTFRIED (1815–1882), professor of German in London and later . of art history in Bonn and Zurich. Persecuted as an adherent to the republican "Jungdeutsche" movement, he emigrated to England and later to Switzerland. He is an epigonic author of sentimental poems, stories, and verse dramas, whose romance *Brynhildis* (1843) relates the tragedy of the deceived valkyrie.

[WW]

Bibliography
Hub, Ignaz, ed. *Deutschlands Balladen- und Romanzen-Dichter.* Vol. 3. Karlsruhe: Creuzbauersche Buchhandlung, 1870, p. 226.

KIRST, HANS HELLMUT (1914–1989), German author of the novel *Die Nacht der Generäle* (The Night of the Generals) in which the major protagonist, General Wilhelm Tanz, is portrayed both as the insane murderer of prostitutes during and after World War II, as well as the commander of the elite German armored division "Nibelungen," assembled to carry out particularly "difficult" missions. *Night of the Generals* was also the title of a British-made film (1967) based on Kirst's novel, with Peter O'Toole in the role of the fictitious (Wehrmacht, and then, without explanation for the transformation, Waffen-SS) General Tanz, commander of what in this context is the equally fictitious Panzer Division "Nibelungen" in Poland, and subsequently SS Panzer Division "Nibelungen" in France. (see also NIBELUNGEN DIVISION)

[WM]

Bibliography
Kirst, Hans Hellmut. *Die Nacht der Generäle.* Munich: K. Desch, 1962.
———. *The Night of the Generals,* translated by J. Maxwell Brownjohn. New York: Harper & Row, 1963.

KÖHLMEIER, MICHAEL (b. 1949), Austrian author who grew up in Hohenems, the town in which two significant Nibelungen manuscripts were discovered (**A** and **C**). For most of his life Köhlmeier, who lives in the west Austrian province of Vorarlberg, has taken an interest in the story of the Nibelungs. His retelling of the *Nibelungenlied* appeared in 1999. His prose, characterized by its laconic style, recounts the events of the tale in a highly concentrated fashion and he makes rich use of dialog. Despite the many abridgements in his work, Köhlmeier has been successful in capturing the epic tone and in imparting the high drama associated with the events of the medieval poem.

[WW]

Bibliography
Köhlmeier, Michael. *Die Nibelungen neu erzählt.* Serie Piper 2882. Munich: Piper, 1999.

KOPISCH, AUGUST (1799–1853), a popular German artist and the author of folkloristic, romantic poems. In his drama *Chrimhild* (1846) the central character is Hagen, whose arrogance, obstinacy, and uncompromising harshness drive the action of the play to its final catastrophe. Kriemhild's revenge is considered absolutely legitimate because a man would have acted in exactly the same way.

[WW]

Bibliography
Behr, Hans-Joachim. "Die Faszination des Bösen: Das 'Nibelungenlied' als Dramenstoff im 19. Jahrhundert." In *3. Pöchlarner Heldenliedgespräch: Die Rezeption des Nibelungenliedes,* edited by Klaus Zatloukal. Philologica Germanica 16. Vienna: Fassbaender, 1995, pp. 17–32.
Kopisch, August. *Gesammelte Werke.* Vol. 4, edited by Carl Boetticher. Berlin: Weidmann, 1856.

KREYE, WALTER ARTHUR (b. 1911), German author who retells the story of the Nibelungs in Low German verse. The dialect and accompanying illustrations lend the volume a humorous touch.

[SSch]

Bibliography
Kreye, Walter Arthur. *De Nibelungen: Fidele Wortgeschichte op Platt. 1. Murd un dootslag bi de ni-*

belungen. Gudrun—oder: von de waschbütt op'n königsthron. Leer: Schuster, 1970.

KUBY, ERICH (b. 1910), German author whose short poem "Genug!" (Enough!) takes as its subject the Munich exhibition titled "Die Nibelungen: Bilder von Liebe, Verrat, und Untergang" (The Nibelungs: Images of Love, Betrayal, and Catastrophe," 1987/1988). The theme of the exhibition had been the occurrence of the Nibelungs in German art since the period of romanticism. Kuby's poem consists of a mere two stanzas that suggest that the *Nibelungenlied* be regarded as a distant myth or as a mirror reflecting the misery of German history. Its concluding sentiment is reflected in the title of the poem.

[WW]

Bibliography
Storch, Wolfgang, ed. *Die Nibelungen: Bilder von Liebe, Verrat, und Untergang.* Munich: Prestel, 1987, p. 113.

LERNET-HOLENIA, ALEXANDER (1897–1976), Austro-Hungarian author who in 1937 published the somewhat fanciful novel *Der Mann im Hut* (The Man in the Hat), which tells of the modern search for the grave of the Hunnish king Attila and his treasures, and which also tries to unearth traces of the demise of the Burgundians.

[MS]

Bibliography
Springeth, Margarete. "Attila (II). Der Attila-Mythos in der nordischen und in der deutschen Literatur." In *Herrscher, Helden, Heilige,* edited by Ulrich Müller and Werner Wunderlich. Mittelalter-Mythen 1. St. Gall: UVK-Verlag, 1996, pp. 29–46.

LERSCH, HEINRICH (1889–1936), a former boilermaker who became an enthusiastic supporter of the National Socialist movement. His poems and novels are characterized by an ecstatic glorification of race and the strength of the German worker. The novel *Siegfried,* which was published posthumously in 1941, relates the story of Siegfried, who is reborn from the Rhine. The hero is cast as an Aryan prototype who restores to the German people its strength as a nation of workers as well as its self-confidence following the devastating effects of the Versailles treaty.

[WW]

Bibliography
Lersch, Heinrich. *Siegfried und andere Romane aus dem Nibelungenlied,* edited by C. Jenssen. Hamburg: Hanseatische Verlagsanstalt, 1941.

LIBIGER, RICHARD (1882–1957), German lyricist. In 1922 he published a rhyming adaptation of the *Nibelungenlied,* in which Hagen appears, in contrast to Gunther, as a shining example of virtue through his loyalty and steadfastness until the final downfall of the Nibelungen. Hagen tells Gunther at the end that "aller Helden kühner Tod" (the bold death of all heroes) signifies "nur das Morgenrot zu neuen Ruhmestagen" (only the dawn of new days of glory). Libiger turns this notion into an appeal to the Germans to adopt this stance in the aftermath of the lost World War, because "es geht, auch in schwerster Stunde, kein treues Volk zugrunde" (even in times of utmost difficulty, a steadfast people cannot perish).

[MH]

Bibliography
Libiger, Richard. *Die Märe von Siegfried und den Nibelungen.* Dresden: Pierson, 1922.
Gentry, Francis G. "Die Rezeption des Nibelungenliedes in der Weimarer Republik." In *Das Weiterleben des Mittelalters in der deutschen Literatur,* edited by James F. Poag and Gerhild Scholz-Williams. Königstein: Athenäum, 1983, pp. 142–156, esp. pp. 151ff.

LIENHARD, FRIEDRICH (FRITZ) (1865–1929), German lyric poet, dramatist, and narrator of neoromantic, regional literature. His drama *Heinrich von Ofterdingen* (1903) depicts Bishop Pilgrim at the beginning of the thirteenth century as a collector and a translator of Latin Nibelung lays which Ludwig the Pious had earlier destroyed. However, because he considers his work to be imperfect, Pilgrim consigns it to the flames. Out of love for the girl Mechthild and at the instigation of Klingsor, Heinrich occupies himself with the national theme and molds it into the German *Nibelungenlied,* with which he emerges triumphant in the singing competition against Wolfram von Eschenbach's *Parzival* and the prevalent French literary fashions. Lienhard presents Heinrich's work as an alternative to modernism, which is felt to be decadent, and as a point of orientation from the turn of the century, which people experienced as a period of critical upheaval in both society and culture.

[WW]

Bibliography

Lienhard, Fritz. *Wartburg: Dramatische Dichtung in drei Teilen, I. Heinrich von Ofterdingen: Drama in fünf Aufzügen.* Stuttgart: Greiner & Pfeifer, 1903.

LODEMANN, JÜRGEN (b. 1936), contemporary German critic and novelist. His work *Siegfried* (1986) focuses on German history, the German mentality, and the reception of the Nibelungs with a critical lens. The novel is written from a contemporary perspective, and Siegfried is the embodiment of the "life-is-struggle" adage which served as a model for much of the German political scene in the nineteenth and the first half of the twentieth century. Siegfried's exploits are depicted as inconsiderate, simpleminded, and brutal. He brings about his own demise and this, in turn, constitutes the genesis of a disastrous legacy for Germany. The novel is intended as a parable on German history.

In *Der Mord* (The Murder, 1995), which contains images of significant figures and episodes of the *Nibelungenlied* by Erhard Göttlicher, Lodemann casts himself as the most recent translator of the late fifth-century manuscript of Gislahar, the youngest of the Burgundian kings. This manuscript claims to transmit the true story of Siegfried, who is portrayed as the hero of pagan polytheism and early Celtic Christianity. Siegfried represents a close relationship between the natural and supernatural worlds which is ultimately overcome by representatives of Roman Catholicism (e.g., the misogynistic bishop Ringwolf) and its cynical political allies (Hagen), who isolate and demonize the natural world in order to dominate it. Lodemann's narrative is multilayered, consisting of both the postulated translation and frequently elaborate parenthetical commentaries relating events surrounding the death of Siegfried to the later cultural history of the Germans.

[WW/WRH]

Bibliography

Lodemann, Jürgen. *Siegfried: Die deutsche Geschichte im eintausendfünfhundertsten Jahr der Ermordung ihres Helden nach den ältesten Dokumenten erzählt.* Stuttgart: Thienemann, 1986.

———. *Der Mord: Das wahre Volksbuch von den Deutschen.* Frankfurt a. M.: Büchergilde Gutenberg, 1995.

Martin, Bernhard R. *Nibelungen-Metamorphosen:: Die Geschichte eines Mythos.* Munich: Iudicium, 1992, pp. 187–200.

Wunderlich, Werner. "Total krasse Helden." In *Sammlung, Deutung, Wertung: Ergebnisse, Probleme, Tendenzen, und Perspektiven philologischer Arbeit; mélanges de littérature médiévale et de linguistique allemande; offerts à Wolfgang Spiewok à l'occasion de son soixantième anniversaire,* edited by Danielle Buschinger. Amiens: Université de Picardie. Centre d'Etudes Médiévales, 1988, pp. 369–383.

LUBLINSKI, SAMUEL (1868–1910), a representative of neoclassicism and author of historical dramas. His tragedy *Gunther und Brünhild* (1908) idealizes Siegfried and Brünhild as human beings who live according to a higher ethic and who are destined for each other. Gunther is portrayed as a tragically unhappy man, unable to accept his inferior position with regard to both Siegfried and Brünhild in terms of personality, character, and ethics. By not accepting his fate, but rather acting against it, he precipitates the ensuing catastrophe.

[WW]

Bibliography

Lublinski, Samuel. *Gunther und Brunhild: Tragödie.* Berlin: Bard, 1908.

LUSERKE, MARTIN (1880–1969), German author of stage plays. *Brunhilde auf Island* (Brunhild on Island, 1922) concentrates on the contest set by the queen and the deception that is associated with it. A sad and wretched Brunhilde is forced to leave her beloved Island and follow Gunther to the Burgundian court. In a somewhat naive fashion, the play contrasts the pseudoromantic and "natural" world of the valkyrie with the decadent world of the Burgundians.

[WW]

Bibliography
Luserke, M[artin]. *Brunhilde auf Island: Ein wahrhaft romantisches Sonnenwendspiel.* Wickersdorfer Bühnenspiele, series 2, vol. 2. Lauenburg: Saal, 1922.

LYRIC POETRY. In contrast to other genres, poems and ballads that take the story of the Nibelungs as their theme tend to be fewer in number. Especially in the nineteenth century and in the first half of the twentieth, there are quite a few sentimental and hymnic verses which celebrate individual figures such as Siegfried and Hagen, certain virtues such as loyalty, or a heroic demise determined by fate. The postwar period also produced poems which dealt in an ironic and satirical way with this particular strain of Nibelungen reception.

[WW]

MARZIK, TRUDE (pseudonym of Edeltrud Marczik, b. 1923), Austrian authoress. From 1946 until 1975 Markzik worked for an airline in Vienna, and since 1971 she has been publishing poetry and prose. The poem "Nibelungen-Kurzfassung" (Nibelungen—Abridged Version) presents, in fourteen stanzas, a burlesque summary of the *Nibelungenlied* in Viennese dialect.

[MH]

Bibliography
Marzik, Trude. "Nibelungen-Kurzfassung." In *A Jahr is bald um. Gedichte.* Vienna: Zsolnay, 1981, pp. 70f.

MELL, MAX (1882–1971), German author, whose two-part drama *Der Nibelungen Not* had its premiere in Vienna, the first part on January 23, 1944, and the second, almost seven years later, on January 8, 1951. Kriemhild tries in vain to save Siegfried; Brunhild goes on board a ship and sets it afire, hoping to join Siegfried in death. At the conclusion of the work, only Gunther and Hagen are still alive; Etzel realizes that Kriemhild has never really loved him and decides to banish her, but she is killed by Hildebrand. Etzel abandons Dietrich's Christian and humane perspective that he had earlier admired, and desires only "to leave the garden and return to the steppes." For his killing of Kriemhild, Hildebrand has to take his leave of Dietrich and the rest of his men and he disappears into the darkness, riding a black horse.

[SSch]

Bibliography
Mell, Max. *Der Nibelungen Not: Dramatische Dichtung in zwei Teilen.* Salzburg: Müller, 1951.

MEVERT, ERNST (1834–1910), his novel, *Die neuen Nibelungen* (The New Nibelungs, 1864), written in the first person, recounts the life and death of the young German Hermann, who is an enthusiastic supporter of the movement for national unification prevailing during the 1840s. The "New Nibelungs" are a group of brave patriots fighting in the Prussian campaign of 1848. Their aim is the liberation of the principalities Schleswig and Holstein from Danish rule and ultimately their unification. Prussia had sought to establish its rule over this territory between North and Baltic Sea and to increase its hegemony in the northern parts of Germany. The novel glorifies this war as a part of the German struggle for unity, which is to be seen as the true hoard of the Nibelungs. Hermann gives his life to this end. The connection of Mevert's novel to the *Nibelungenlied* itself consists of nothing more than vague allusions to some names and motifs.

[WW]

Bibliography
Mevert, Ernst. *Die neuen Nibelungen: Zeitroman.* 4 vols. Hamburg: Hoffmann und Campe, 1864.

MIEGEL, AGNES (1879–1964), German writer of stories, poetry, and ballads in the neoromantic tradition. Having grown up in East Prussia, she often integrates the landscapes, history, and legends of her home into her work. Her neoromantic inclination towards fairy tales, magic, and the demonic is evident in the ballad "Die Nibelungen" (1905). In the ballad Volker sings three songs, the last one being a chilling lay about the overwhelming greed for gold, blood, and revenge. Kriemhild, who is contemplating revenge for Siegfried's murder, listens with malicious pleasure while the heroes are disconcerted and gloomy. Their premonitions of their own deaths are prefigured not so much by Volker's song as by Kriemhild herself.

[AH]

Bibliography
Miegel, Agnes. *Gesammelte Balladen.* Vol. 6 in *Gesammelte Werke in 6 Bänden.* Düsseldorf: Diederichs, 1953, pp. 29–31.

MÜLLER, HEINER (1929–1995), East-German author, principally a dramatist. In the early 1970s, Müller became recognized as one of the most important German-speaking authors of the late twentieth century. Two major themes in his writings are the fatal continuity that is peculiar to German history and the question of betrayal. The Nibelungen motif is for him "der deutscheste aller deutschen Stoffe."

Germania Tod in Berlin (1971, premiere 1978), begun in 1956, gives a nonchronological, sometimes satirical survey of German history from the period of migrations through the building of the Berlin Wall in 1963. In a scene of grotesque parody, the Nibelungs Gunter, Hagen, Volker, Gernot, appear as the undead in the Battle of Stalingrad. The latter is depicted as mirroring the conflagration in Etzel's Great Hall, where the Burgundians fight imaginary Huns night after night. In a quarrel over who murdered Siegfried, whether he was a traitor, and whether or not the continual fighting is pointless, they finally kill each other. The scene ridicules their never-ending, senseless belligerence, their auto-eroticism, and autoaggressivness.

Germania 3 (published posthumously 1996, premiere 1996) is another but shorter survey from the Middle Ages through unification. Historically situated once again during the Battle of Stalingrad, Kriemhild and Hagen argue over who has been unloyal to whom. While Hagen reproaches her for having been unfaithful to her first husband, she justifies the abhorrent marriage to Etzel by declaring it necessary to seek revenge for Siegfried. Hagen is identified with the Wehrmacht, Kriemhild with an antifascist Germany, forced to ally itself with the Red Army. Most of the text is taken literally, if structurally re-arranged, from Hebbel's play *Die Nibelungen, Kriemhilds Rache* (1862; IV, 3, 4, 6).

Müller also refers to the Nibelungs occasionally in other texts, including his autobiography and in interviews. The work has been translated into a number of different languages, including English, French, Spanish, Italian, and Japanese.

[RK]

Bibliography
Müller, Heiner. *Germania Tod in Berlin.* Rotbuch 176. Berlin: Rotbuch, 1977, pp. 35–78.
_____. *Germania 3.* Cologne: Kiepenheuer & Witsch, 1996. [English translation by Carl Weber under the title: *Explosion of a Memory: Writings by Heiner Müller.* New York: PAJ Publications, 1989]
Schmitt-Sasse, Joachim. "Die Kunst aufzuhören: Der Nibelungen-Stoff in Heiner Müllers Germania Tod in Berlin." In *Die Nibelungen: Ein deutscher Wahn, ein deutscher Alptraum. Studien und Dokumente zur Rezeption des Nibelungenstoffs im 19. und 20. Jahrhunderte,* edited by Joachim Heinzle and Anneliese Waldschmidt. Suhrkamp Taschenbuch 2110. Frankfurt a. M.: Suhrkamp, 1991, pp. 370–396.

MÜLLER, JOHANN WILHELM (1794–1827), composer of very popular hiking songs and romantic poetic cycles, including *Die schöne Müllerin* (The Pretty Miller Woman) and *Die Winterreise* (Winter's Journey), which were set to music by Franz Schubert. He was named "Griechen-Müller" (Müller the Greek) for the enthusiasm with which he undertook studies of Greek classical literature. The tragedy *Chriemhilds Rache* (Chriemhild's Revenge, 1822), is to be included among a number of literary and intellectual post-romantic efforts to accord the Nibelung tradition the dignity and significance of ancient Greek poetry and ethics. Müller's play uses the choir as the harbinger of disaster and portrays Kriemhild as a masochistic heroine comparable to Heinrich von Kleist's Penthesilea. She is not personally responsible nor does she bear guilt for the catastrophe, which is brought about by the tragic dynamics of the events themselves. Kriemhild commits suicide with the same sword she had used to kill Hagen.

[WW]

Bibliography
Müller, Johann Wilhelm. *Chriemhilds Rache: Trauerspiel in drey Abteilungen, mit dem Chor.* Heidelberg: Groos, 1822.

MÜNCHHAUSEN, BÖRRIES FREIHERR VON (pseudonym for H. Albrecht, 1874–1945). German author who wrote a series of poems that deal with the Nibelungen theme. Some are based on the *Edda,* and they include "Wodans Ritt" (Wodan's Ride), "Weissagung der Wala" (Wala's Prophecy), "Thöks Trotz" (Thök's Defiance), "Wodans Lied vom Ymir-Kampf" (Wodan's Song of the Battle with Ymir). Others, derived from characters and events in the *Nibelungenlied,* include "Kind Hagen" (Hagen the Child), "Hagen und die Donaufrauen" (Hagen and the Danube Maidens), "Das Lied Volkers" (The Song of Volker), and "Hunnenzug" (The March of the Huns).

[SSch]

Bibliography
Münchhausen, Börries Freiherr von. *Das Balladenbuch.* Ausgabe letzter Hand. Stuttgart: Deutsche Verlags-Anstalt, [1951].

NAUMANN, FERDINAND (1819–1876), German lawyer and journalist. Until the age of 50, he was senior legal counsel and editor in Hameln. In 1869 he moved to Vienna where he became "Direktionsrat" of the municipal theater. The *Nibelungenlied in Romanzen* (1866) is a free rendering of the *Nibelungenlied* in the form of the romance, which Naumann regarded as a modern substitute for the older epic form. By omitting "die typischen Wiederholungen" (characteristic repetitions) as well as "unbedeutende Partien" (irrelevant parts), he sought to make the work more accessible to the public. Contemporary critics responded very positively to the adaptation. One article that appeared in the *Westfälische Zeitung* (1/13/1866) included the statement that there could not be "a more charming gift for educated young ladies" (ein reizenderes Geschenk für gebildete junge Damen).

[MH]

Bibliography
Naumann, Ferdinand. *Das Nibelungenlied in Romanzen.* 2nd ed. Vienna: Rosner, 1875.

NEUMANN, OTTO, German author whose *Sigurd und Brünhilde* (1929) is one of numerous plays that draw on the Norse Nibelungen traditions found in the *Edda.* Sigurd and Brünhild are accorded homage as cult figures representing a pseudoreligious racism.

[WW]

Bibliography
Neumann, Otto. *Sigurd und Brünhilde.* Leipzig: Payne, 1929.

NOVEL. The novel as a genre offers the possibility of depicting the fate of an unusual individual's life, or it can portray the totality of an event with all of its associations. From the second half of the nineteenth century on, the Nibelungen theme became the subject for a wide range of novels from new narratives of the entire plot or of the fate of individual figures, to completely new and independent accounts of the theme, parodies, and works which attempt to come to terms with the Nibelungen reception from an ideological perspective.

[WW]

OTTO, LOUISE i.e., **LUISE OTTO (-PETERS),** (1819–1895), an idealistic German poetess of the nineteenth-century, revolutionary "Vormärz" movement. Motivated by an essay of Friedrich Theodor Vischer, who had recommended the Nibelungen theme as the subject of an opera and who himself had prepared a detailed overview of the plot, Louise Otto immersed herself in the subject. She wrote the libretto *Die Nibelungen* and sent a copy of the published work (1854) to Robert Schumann, who had particular praise for the musicality of a scene involving Volker. In line with the emancipatory perspective of the author, the central figures are Brunhilde, "the free, courageous woman," and "the bloodthirsty she-wolf" Chriemhilde, whose fate is intended as a warning to Otto's own time. In 1847 the Danish composer Niels Gade set the scene to music in which Volker sings of Siegfried's fight against Schilbung and Nibelung.

[WW]

Bibliography
Otto, Louise. *Die Nibelungen: Text zu einer großen heroischen Oper in 5 Acten.* Gera: Verlag der Hofmeisterschen Zeitungs-Expedition, 1852.

PESCH, HELMUT W. (b. 1952). A specialist in fantasy literature, Helmut Pesch published a book for young readers in 1998 in which are to be found elements from the Nordic Nibelungen tradition. Three children, Hagen, who hails from Manchester, and the German brother and sister Gunhild and Siggi, enter a world of fantasy that is full of adventure. A merciless war is raging between the "dark elves" and the "light elves." The children must resist the slings of hatred and jealousy, avarice, and egocentricity and stand together in "Nibelungen loyalty." Thus they come to understand that war only causes misery and that solidarity is a societal obligation for the individual.

[WW]

Bibliography
Pesch, Helmut W. *Die Kinder der Nibelungen.* Märchenmond ed. Vienna: Ueberreuter, 1998.
Tirschner, Susanne. "Artus- und Nibelungenstoff in der Fantasy: Ein Lied von gestern?" In *Wormser Symposium zur Rezeptionsgeschichte des Nibelungenliedes,* edited by Gerold Bönnen and Volker Gallé. Der Wormsgau, Beiheft 35. Worms: Stadtarchiv, 1999, pp. 203–220.

PFARRIUS, GUSTAV (1800–1884), a Rhenish writer of poems, tales, and stories. He retells the second part of the *Nibelungenlied* in a comprehensive and modest prose work titled *Chriemhildens Rache* (Chriemhild's Revenge).

[WW]

Bibliography
Pfarrius, Gustav. *Chriemhildens Rache.* Cologne: Kohnen, 1844.

PICHLER, KAROLINE (1769–1843), ran one of the most important literary salons in Vienna. The salon became the meeting spot of romantics and literary figures of the revolutionary German *Vormärz* period of the 1830s, in which the bourgeoisie aspired to political power. Karoline Pichler, who was friends with Dorothea Schlegel, became known as a popular narrator of patriotic novels with themes lifted from Austrian history. She made Heinrich von Ofterdingen (as the poet of the *Nibelungenlied*) into a character in a historical novel. In *Friedrich der Streitbare* (Friedrich the Quarrelsome, 1831) Heinrich von

Ofterdingen is portrayed as a participant in the *Minnesänger* competition at the Wartburg, where he performs his *Nibelungenlied.* Heinrich is also an unhappy lover who is not allowed to marry the courtly noblewoman Jutta von Raueneck until he has completed many heroic acts of chivalry. Some of the characteristics of the figure are drawn from the lyric poetry of Walther von der Vogelweide. Just like the latter, Heinrich also receives his plot of land, presented to him by his lord, the Austrian Duke Friedrich II, for loyal and brave service.

[WW]

Bibliography
Pichler, Karoline. *Friedrich der Streitbare.* 4 pts. In vols. 46 to 49 of *Sämmtliche Werke.* Vienna: Anton Pichler, 1832.
Knapp, Fritz Peter. "Die altdeutsche Dichtung als Gegenstand literarhistorischer Forschung in Österreich von Jacob Grimms Wiener Aufenthalt (1814/15) bis zum Tode Franz Pfeiffers (1868)." In *Die österreichische Literatur: Ihr Profil im 19. Jahrhundert (1830–1880),* edited by Herbert Zeman. Graz: Akademische Druck- und Verlagsanstalt, 1982, pp. 160–171.

PLOGSTEDT, AXEL, author of the 1975 play, *Die Nibelungen,* a satire on heroic behavior and a warning against the escalating danger of blind revenge. Plogstedt intersperses his own text with the original Middle High German. Heroic clichés are parodied through the use of pop scenes and slapstick comedy during the stage performance.

[WW]

Bibliography
Plogstedt, Axel. *Die Nibelungen.* © 1975, Axel Plogstedt.
Schödel, Helmut. "Plogstedts Nibelungen in Landshut." *Theater heute* 11 (1975): 67.

QUALTINGER, HELMUT (1928–1986), author of the cabaret text *Siggy and Bess oder Der Swing der Nibelungen.* Siggy is an auto mechanic in New Orleans. His quest is to locate the treasure of the Mississippi, which is guarded by the monster Frankenstein. Siggy defeats him by asking him if he is a member of the Communist party. Bess is a modern Brünhild, the daughter of Wotan. She falls in love with Siggy because he offers her a role in a Hollywood film. Reality is somewhat different, however, and they find employment on a showboat, Siggy as a waiter-singer and Bess as a bar girl. The leader of the boat's band is called Edelhagen and he is also interested in Bess. He challenges Siggy to a baseball game, musicians against waiters, in the course of which he hits Siggy with his baseball bat and it appears he has killed him. Edelhagen then wishes to marry Bess, but at the last moment, Siggy reappears as a Tarzanlike figure and calling out like Popeye the Sailor. Edelhagen and his companions fight against Siggy, who is rescued by the cavalry. The text concludes with Siggy and Bess disappearing in a water ballet.

[SSch]

Bibliography

Qualtinger, Helmut. *"Brettl vor dem Kopf" und andere Texte fürs Kabarett.* Werkausgabe. Vol. 2. Vienna: n.p., 1996, pp. 91–106.

RAUPACH, ERNST (1784–1852), professor of history and literature in St. Petersburg, Russia. An imitator of Schiller, Raupach was the author of numerous historical plays and comedies. His 1834 drama, *Der Nibelungen-Hort* (The Nibelungen Hoard), is a romantic tragedy and among the few Nibelung plays ever performed. The adventures of young Siegfried are derived from both the *Edda* and *Hürnen Seyfried* (Horny-skinned Siegfried). The first part of the play portrays Siegfried and Kriemhild as an innocent couple, whose love and lives are destroyed by a rash political decision aimed at stabilizing Gunther's rule. Hagen's act is that of an unselfish man who is concerned about the welfare of his king. In the second part of the drama Kriemhild is transformed from a lamenting widow into an avenger because her brothers force her to marry Etzel. Subsequent to the destruction of the Nibelungs, she kills Etzel, a motif taken over from the Nordic tradition. The surviving Dietrich von Bern assumes power as a Christian ruler and restores order and peace to the empire.

[WW]

Bibliography

Raupach, Ernst. *Dramatische Werke ernsterer Gattung.* Vol. 14. Hamburg: Hoffmann und Campe, 1834.

REIMAR, REINALD (pseudonym of Adolf Glaser, 1829–1916), author of the five-act tragedy *Kriemhildens Rache* (Kriemhild's Revenge, 1853). The work is written in blank verse, and it follows the *Nibelungenlied* with regard to its basic plot. In a prelude, Gunther and Siegfried hatch the following scheme: Siegfried is secretly to defeat Brünhild in Gunther's place. As a reward, he is to receive Kriemhild as his wife. The conflict arises from the rivalry between Kriemhild and Brünhild, who both claim to be married to the most outstanding warrior. Hagen murders Siegfried, and Kriemhild realizes her revenge at Etzel's royal court in Vienna. With considerable pathos the tragedy celebrates obedience as the highest virtue and the duty to remain loyal as the highest ideal of human action. Hagen, Rüdiger, or Dietrich are models for such behavior, while Kriemhild, motivated by a female lust for revenge, breaks her promises. Defying the oath she had sworn to Dietrich, she kills both Gunther and Hagen. The play ends with Dietrich asserting the primacy of loyalty above everything else and depicting it as an eternal sign of hope for the future. Reimar's tragedy is a typical product of the type of Nibelungen reception that takes the medieval epic as a pretext for extolling loyalty and obedience as timeless virtues for which no sacrifice is too great.

[WW]

Bibliography

Reimar, Reinald. *Kriemhildens Rache: Trauerspiel.* Hamburg: Meißner & Schirges, 1853.

RITTER, ALBERT (pseudonym for Karl von Winterstetten, 1872–1931), author of the novel *Das Nibelungenjahr* (The Nibelungen Year, 1912), which relates a story derived from elements of the *Nibelungenlied* and the making of an illuminated manuscript. The fable refers to events, personalities, and circumstances in the year 1226. Among the followers of the Hohenstaufen emperor Friedrich II is the poet and minstrel of Montfort, Rudolf von Ems. He is the one who produced the so-called Hohenems manuscript of the *Nibelungenlied* (manuscript C), and who is the first to recite the epic in the presence of the royal couple and their retinue.

[WW]

Bibliography

Heinzle, J. "Albert Ritter. Leben und Werk." Diss., Vienna, 1935.

Ritter, Albert. *Das Nibelungenjahr: Kultur-Roman aus der Zeit der Hohenstaufen.* Leipzig: Dietrich, 1912.

RODENBERG, JULIUS (pseudonym for Julius Levy, 1831–1914), wrote one of the numerous patriotic festival plays dedicated to the German victory over France and the founding of the second German empire in 1871. The rhymed, two-act play *Vom Rhein zur Elbe* (From the Rhine to the Elbe) was performed in the royal court theater of Dresden, capital of Saxony, to celebrate the return of Saxon troops. Karl Krebs conducted the music for the work. The first act is an allegorical play. The personified rivers, the Rhine, Moselle, Saar, and Elbe, mirror German history and its goal of becoming a united nation, now achieved through the victorious war against France. In the central scene the Rhine tells the story of the treasure of the Nibelungs, the Rhinegold, which is symbolic of German unification. Out of the waves of the Rhine there emerges the new imperial crown, the new hoard of the Nibelungs.

[WW]

Bibliography

Rodenberg, Julius. *Vom Rhein zur Elbe: Festspiel in zwei Abtheilungen zum feierlichen Einzug der Sächsischen Truppen für das Dresdner Hoftheater gedichtet.* Musik von Karl Krebs. Dresden: n.p., [1871].

ROESS, GEORG RICHARD (1872–1945), German author who, in 1905, published nine poems under the title *Neun Bilder aus dem Nibelungenliede* (Nine Scenes from the *Nibelungenlied*), written in the style of the *Nibelungenstrophe*. They were used as the lyrical background of a festival play performed in Worms and depict, in concentrated form, the plot of the complete *Nibelungenlied,* accompanied by music from Richard Wagner's opera *Rienzi.*

[WW]

Bibliography

Roess, Georg Richard. *Neun Bilder aus dem Nibelungenliede: Dem zweiten Rosenfeste.* Worms, [1905].

SACHS, HANS (1494–1576), author of *Ein Tragedia mit 17 personen: Der huernen Sewfrid* (A Tragedy with 17 Characters: The Horny-Skinned Sewfrid, 1557). For the poetically prolific Nuremberg shoemaker, who drew for his sources upon everything from the Bible and the classics to contemporary literature and history, this was his only excursion into German heroic material. In his dramatization Sachs on the whole follows the course of *Das Lied vom Hürnen Seyfrid* (The Lay of Horny-skinned Seyfrid, Nuremberg, ca. 1530) with the understanding that for the combat between Dietrich von Bern and Siegfried the so-called *Grosse Rosengarten* (Large Rose Garden) was the main source. The notable exception is that he has Hagen slay Siegfried in his sleep with a dagger then recognized by Kriemhild as belonging to her brother. Goetze in the introduction to his edition follows Wilhelm Grimm's assumption of a third source.

[PS]

Bibliography

Grimm, Wilhelm. *Die deutsche Heldensage.* 4th ed. Darmstadt: Wissenschaftliche Buchgesellschaft, 1957, pp. 349–351.

Sachs, Hans. *Der huernen Sewfrid,* edited by Edmund Goetze. Tübingen: Niemeyer, 1967.

Das Lied vom Hürnen Seyfrid. Critical edition with introduction and notes by K. C. King. Manchester: Manchester University Press, 1958.

SAGERER, ALEXEIJ, contemporary German dramatist and director who in 1992 produced the *Nibelungenströme* in the Munich off-theater "proT." He portrays the German myth of the Nibelungen as a mania, the chief characteristics of which are horror and terror. Germany is depicted as a slaughterhouse in which the Nibelungs commit their outrageous acts.

[WW]

Bibliography

Sagerer, Alexeij. *Nibelungenströme.* © 1992 Alexeij Sagerer.

SCHÄFER, WILHELM HILDEBRAND (1868–1952), a popular narrator and dramatist, who dealt particularly with historical and heroic topics from the Germanic past. In his tragedies *Siegfried* and *Grimhild* (both 1914), he depicts in an epigonic manner the world as a stage, upon which Siegfried appears as a visionary representative of a superior form of man who, however, falls victim to the evil in the world.

[WW]

Bibliography

Schäfer, Wilhelm Hildebrand. *Siegfried.* Mannheim: Lämmel, 1948.

————. *Grimhild.* Mannheim: Lämmel, 1948.

SCHEFFEL, JOSEPH VIKTOR VON (1826–1886), during his lifetime and throughout the first half of the twentieth century, one of the most popular German writers of historical novels, epics, epigonic poems, as well as student songs. Scheffel theorized that "meister Cuonrât"—according to the *Klage,* the alleged poet of the *Nibelungenlied*—was also the author of the Latin *Nibelungias* in the tenth century, and that Heinrich von Ofterdingen had translated that epic into Middle High German for his performance during the "Sängerkrieg" (war of the minstrels) at the Wartburg. From 1857 on, Scheffel devoted much of his time to an attempt to verify his hypothesis regarding the authorship of the *Nibelungenlied.* He sketched the outline for a novel titled *Meister Konrad* (Master Konrad) which was to provide, through a blending of fact and fiction, the biography of the Latin author Konradus, an ancestor of Volker von Alzey. In addition it was to recount the history of the origins of the German epic. The novel was never written; only the outline has been passed down, as well as several poems written from the perspective of Konrad's lyrical "I," such as "Meister Konradus Donaulied" (Master Konrad's Danube Song, 1859), or the cycle "Des Meister Konrads Spur" (The Trail of Master Conrad, 1863).

[WW]

Bibliography

Wunderlich. Werner. "Wer war der Greis, den Worms solch Lied gelehrt? Der erfundene Dichter: Joseph Viktor von Scheffels Version vom Autor des *Nibelungenliedes* (mit einem Textanhang)." *Euphorion* 89 (1995): 239–270.

SCHENKENDORF, MAX VON (1783–1817), appealed to the mood of his generation, with the patriotic fervor of his poems and their vigorous exhortation to those who were fighting for freedom. The majority reflect the mood and events of his age, and they include "Freiheit" (Freedom); "Das Eiserne Kreuz" (The Iron Cross), "Die Preußen an der Kaiserlichen Grenze. August 1813" (The Prussians on the Imperial Border. August 1813), and "Te Deum nach der Schlacht bei Leipzig" (Te Deum after the Battle of Leipzig). Two poems, "Auf der Wanderung nach Worms" (On the Journey to Worms, 1814) and "Das Lied vom Rhein" (The Song of the Rhine, 1815), contain explicit references to the *Nibelungenlied,* relating the heroic deeds of the past to places significant in the present turmoil. The Rhine is the hero and the king; Worms is "heilig," made sacred by the past and awaiting the time when "a good German word" will resound again. Another, more personal, poem, is addressed to his "oldest friend," Karl, Graf von der Gröben, on the occasion of his marriage to Selma von Dörnberg (1816). This time the echo is not in the content, which is very much in the manner of an occasional poem, with eulogy and rejoicing, but in the metrical form, which mimics precisely that of the *Nibelungenlied.* Moreover the opening lines are a blatant near translation:

> Uns klingt aus alten Mähren
> Viel Wunders alter Zeit,
> Von Helden reich an Ehren
> Und arbeitvollem Streit.
>
> [From old tales we hear
> Of remarkable deeds from older times,
> Of heroes rich in honor
> And of fierce battles.]

[MEG]

Bibliography

Schenkendorf, Max von. *Gedichte.* Stuttgart: Cotta, 1815.

Max von Schenkendorf's sämmtliche Gedichte. Erste vollständige Ausgabe. Berlin: Eichler, 1837.

SCHERER, WILHELM (1873–1937), Catholic theologian and professor of German philology and dogma. The martial "war songs" contained in his *Nibelungentreue* (Nibelungen Loyalty, 1916) derive from the political slogan used by German Chancellor von Bülow to describe the relationship between the Reich and Austro-Hungary prior to the First World War. His lyrics relate a Siegfried raised from the dead who fights alongside all the other Nibelungs (including his murderer, Hagen) against Germany's enemies on both the Eastern and Western Front.

[WW]

Bibliography
Scherer, Wilhelm. *Nibelungentreue: Kriegsgesänge.* Regensburg: Pustet, 1916.

SCHLEGEL, FRIEDRICH (1772–1829), one of the leading lights of the early romantic movement in Germany, Friedrich Schlegel is not noted primarily as a poet. His poem "Am Rheine" (On the Rhine, 1802) evokes a heroic age imbued with the virtues of chivalry, when Franks and Germans and Burgundians strove for fame. In somewhat monotonous and contrived couplets the poem praises the Rhine as the custodian of a past now lost forever but recalled in the songs which blossom still and speak above all of loyalty. The tears of grief at the loss of cherished values give way to a mood of confidence in a future based on the past and expressed in the continuity of the great river.

[MEG]

Bibliography
Friedrich von Schlegel's Sämmtliche Werke. Vol. 10. 2nd (original) ed. Vienna: Klang, 1846, p. 93.

SCHMIDT, ARNO (1914–1979), post-World War II German author who experiments with narrative styles and plays on words and forms, often with parodistic and critical effect. In his novel, *KAFF auch mare crisium* (Godforsaken Hole in the Ground and Sea of Crisis, 1960), Schmidt presents a parody of the *Nibelungenlied* that undermines the ideological role of the model of heroism and national identity ascribed to the legend by National Socialist propaganda. The scene is an imagined colony on the moon, one of two narrative settings in the novel, established after the destruction of the earth by nuclear weapons. The legend of the Nibelungen, hailed as a great national epic, is broadcast over the moon radio. In this national epic the Germans appear only as beaters in the hunt, at the end of which Siegfried is killed by Hagen; the Nibelungen heroes are American soldiers in the headquarters of the occupation army in Heidelberg in 1948: General Grünther (King Gunther), Sergeant H. G. Trunnion (Hagen von Tronje), Alabama-Dillert (Siegfried), and Cream-hilled

(Kriemhild). The Nibelungen legend is retold within the framework of this postwar setting. The work ends with Kriemhild's revenge: the Nibelungen heroes are invited by Cream-hilled into the Soviet Zone in Berlin and are killed there by Russian soldiers (the Huns).

[AH]

Bibliography
Schmidt, Arno. *KAFF auch mare crisium.* Vol. 7 of *Das erzählerische Werk in 8 Bänden.* Zurich: Haffmans/Arno Schmidt Stiftung Bargfeld, 1985.

SCHNABEL, HEINRICH (1885–1917), German writer who was killed in action at the Somme. Only the first act of his tragedy *Kriemhild* was published in 1910 in the monthly journal *Die Tat.* Kriemhild is a calculating, vindictive woman who plays her part as Etzel's wife and mother of their son with only one purpose in mind: revenge. She pays Werbel to carry out the murder and promises him the hoard as blood money. The play is one of numerous sentimental literary documents which uses the Nibelungs as models for larger-than-life characters.

[WW]

Bibliography
Schnabel, Heinrich. *Kriemhild: Erster Akt.* In *Die Tat: Wege zu freiem Menschentum. Eine Monatsschrift,* edited by Ernst Horneffer, vol. 2, no. 4 (1910): 189–212.

SCHNEIDER, HERBERT (b. 1922), author of *Die Nibelungen in Bayern,* a novel which tells, in twenty chapters, the story of the story of the Burgundians in Bavaria. In the last chapter of the work the author is described as having received a letter from a disabled Burgundian who had remained in Worms after the battle that led to the downfall of the Burgundians. His intention was to depart from the more bloodthirsty aspects of the epic and allow the old heroes to end their days in peace. The work contains references to the Bavarian earls Franz Josef and Alfons, clearly an attempt to imbue the work with a contemporary aura with allusions to Franz Josef Strauß and Alfons Goppel.

[SSch]

Bibliography
Schneider, Herbert. *Die Nibelungen in Bayern.* With illustrations by Horst Hitzinger. Pfaffenhofen/Ilm: Ilmgau, 1974.

SCHNEIDER, REINHOLD (1903–1958), prolific German author whose novel *Die Tarnkappe* (The Magic Cap) concentrates on a short section of the Nibelungen theme, namely, from the quarrel between Kriemhild and Brünhild to Kriemhild's lament for her murdered husband. Magic has a significant symbolic function in the work. Paradoxically, Schneider, whose works were banned in 1941 by the National Socialists, focused after the war on the Nibelungen theme, a favorite subject of the regime he had opposed.

[SSch]

Bibliography
Schneider, Reinhold. *Die Tarnkappe.* Wiesbaden: Insel, 1951.

SCHNEIDER, ROLF (born 1932), German novelist whose *Tod des Nibelungen* tells the story of a sculptor who, during the era of National Socialism, comes to terms with its leaders and serves them with his art. His oscillation between diverse possibilities of art is represented by the figures in the Nibelungen myth, who are viewed as antipodes, and by the paintings of El Greco. He decides on a monumental glorification of the fascist image of the superman, and to this purpose uses, or misuses, the figures of the Nibelungen saga. His pact with those wielding power is interpreted as a variation on the motif of the man who makes a pact with the devil. This is underscored already in the title through through the obvious association with Thomas Mann's novel *Dr. Faustus*. Schneider's choice of literary composition is based on the questionnaire form, which had already been employed by Ernst von Salomon in *Der Fragebogen* ("The Questionnaire," 1951). The reception of motifs lifted from the Nibelungen saga is of secondary importance (even if the title of Schneider's work is clearly based on the Nibelungen tradition). Their use reflects the polemical stance of the author towards the appropriation of the *Nibelungenlied* and the Nibelungen saga by an aggressive, racist ideology in the twentieth century.

[PG]

Bibliography
Schneider, Rolf. *Der Tod des Nibelungen. Aufzeichnungen des deutschen Bildschöpfers Siegfried Amadeus Wruck, ediert von Freunden.* Rostock: Hinstorff, 1970.

SCHNELLEN, BERNHARD (1921–1990), German novelist whose *Nibelungenleid* (1986) is basically a modern-day soap opera. In the novel the physical education student Brünhilde Norden is in love with the tennis star Siegfried von Xanten, who marries Kriemhilde, the daughter of a wine dealer. What ensues is an absurd collage of trivial clichés adapted from such television series as *Dallas* and the plot of the medieval epic.

[WW]

Bibliography
Schnellen, Bernhard. *Nibelungenleid. Roman* (Haag ed.). Frankfurt a. M.: Haag & Herrchen, 1986.
Wunderlich, Werner. "Total krasse Helden." In *Sammlung, Deutung, Wertung: Ergebnisse, Probleme, Tendenzen, und Perspektiven philologischer Arbeit; mélanges de littérature médiévale et de linguistique allemande; offerts à Wolfgang Spiewok à l'occasion de son soixantième anniversaire,* edited by Danielle Buschinger. Amiens: Université de Picardie. Centre d'Etudes Médiévales, 1988, p. 376.

SCHREYVOGEL, FRIEDRICH (1899–1976), professor of literature in Vienna, chief dramatic adviser to the Burgtheater, and author of historical as well as religious plays and novels. *Die Nibelungen,* under the title *Heerfahrt nach Osten* (Campaign in the East), was first published in 1938, the year Austria joined the German Reich. Schreyvogel deals with the second part of the epic and depicts Hagen, his main character, as the protagonist of heroic destruction who cannot escape his destiny.

[WW]

Bibliography
Schreyvogel, Friedrich. *Die Nibelungen. Roman.* Berlin: Zeitgeschichte-Verlag, 1940.

SCHRÖTER, ADALBERT (1851–1905), librarian of the Royal Library in Berlin. In 1882 he composed a New High German translation of the *Nibelungenlied* into a verse form which he considered the only one appropriate for a contemporary rendering and revitalization of the epic. In line with Lord Byron's *Don Juan,* he chose the eight-line Italian stanza (*ottava rima*), which consists of eight iambic verses with five stressed syllables, in which two rhymes alternate three times with each other and then close with two consecutive rhymes (ab ab ab cc). The language and style of this translation are old-fashioned in terms of both vocabulary and style.

[WW]

Bibliography
Das Nibelungenlied. In der Oktave nachgedichtet von Dr. Adalbert Schroeter. 2nd ed. Berlin: Costenoble, 1902.

SIGISMUND, REINHOLD (1834–1900), German author whose tragedy *Brynhilde* (1874) is one of numerous plays that focus on the valkyrie and the Nordic tradition. In the story the sleeping Brynhilde is awakened by Sigurd. He swears an oath to become her husband, which he subsequently breaks, deceiving her in the contest in order to procure Gunnar's sister Gudrun as his wife. Sigurd is murdered because Gunnar cannot stand the fact that Sigurd preceded him as Brynhilde's lover. Brynhilde then elects to follow Sigurd to Hel.

[WW]

Bibliography
Sigismund, Reinhold. *Brynhilde: Tragödie in fünf Aufzügen.* Rudolfstadt: Stageskript, 1874.

SOMMER, EDUARD, uses Nordic sources as well as the *Nibelungenlied* in his account of the tragic love story of Siegfried and Brunhilde in the poem "Siegfried" (1890), consisting of fifteen epic songs. Although Siegfried is Brunhilde's equal, he rejects her, deceives her in the suitor's contest, and marries Kriemhild. Following Siegfried's murder, Brunhilde commits suicide as penance and predicts with her dying breath the catastrophe that is to befall the Nibelungs at King Etzel's court. The poem typifies some of the pathos to be found in the literary reception of the Nibelung theme in Germany at the end of the nineteenth century.

[WW]

Bibliography
Sommer, Eduard. *Siegfried.* Danzig: A.W. Kafemann, 1890.

SPAUN, ANTON RITTER VON (1790–1849), a Linz official and a philological dilettante, author of a biographical novel on Heinrich von Ofterdingen. Motivated by patriotism, von Spaun claims that the fictitious poet of the *Nibelungenlied* can be shown from the sources to have been a historical person and that he was the national poet of Austria during the Middle Ages.

[WW]

Bibliography
Spaun, Anton Ritter von. *Heinrich von Ofterdingen und das Nibelungenlied: Ein Versuch den Dichter und das Epos für Österreich zu vindiciren.* Linz: Haslinger, 1840.

STECHER, CHRISTIAN (1832–1885), Austrian Jesuit, editor of a series that presents works of German poetry in adapted or revised form for use in Christian instruction and edification in families and schools. With this in mind Stecher offers a modified version of the *Nibelungenlied* (1881) in thirty-four "adventures," using the *Nibelungenstrophe.* The first part takes place in the time of the Merovingians, the second in the time of the Carolingians. Stecher wishes to underscore the victory of the Christian spirit over the pagan world. To this end, he invents a son of Siegfried, Gunther, who personifies the Christian idea of knighthood as the shining hope against pagan-motivated revenge, which ultimately leads to catastrophe.

[WW]

Bibliography
Das Nibelungen-Lied: Ein Helden-Epos. Umgedichtet von Christian Stecher. Graz: Styria, 1881.

STIEGLITZ, HANS, a Bavarian educator, whose 1919 work, *Das Nibelungenlied,* retells in eighteen chapters the plot of the medieval epic in the authentic dialect of old Bavaria (the region between the Isar and the Inn Rivers and the Alps). Stieglitz uses the vigorous language and the somewhat rough vocabulary typical for this southern German idiom and its native speakers, to portray the energy, the obstinacy and the willpower of the main characters Siegfried, Kriemhild, and Hagen. The narrative is intended as a parable for the eternal struggle between power that is motivated by a noble cause (Siegfried) and power that is driven by bold-faced pragmatism (Hagen). Both form the basis for the blind hatred that characterizes the feminine force (Kriemhild), which ultimately prepares its own destruction. The book appeared in 1919 and purports to be a mirror of Germany's fate to have been defeated in World War I as a consequence of the "female" spirit of the political parties.

[WW]

Bibliography
Stieglitz, Hans. *Das Nibelungenlied: Altbayerisch erzählt.* Munich: Oldenbourg, 1919.

STIFTER, ADALBERT (1805–1868), the most significant Austrian writer of the nineteenth century, a product of the bourgeois *Biedermeier* world. He moved from early romantic beginnings to the classical ideal of humanity. In 1855 Stifter began work on the novel *Witiko* which ultimately appeared in three volumes between 1865 and 1867. This prose epic deals with the early period of the founding of the Czech state and recounts the story of Witiko, who fought for the unity and independence of Bohemia. At the end of the novel he is invited to the Whitsuntide Festival held in 1184 in Mainz. The poets and minstrels Heinrich von Ofterdingen and Kürenberg come into his tent in order to perform the *Nibelungenlied.* Stifter leaves the question open, however, as to whether or not they are also the authors of the epic.

[WW]

Bibliography
Enzinger, Moriz. "Stifter und die altdeutsche Literatur." In M. E., *Gesammelte Aufsätze zu Stifter.* Vienna: Österreichische Verlagsanstalt, 1967, pp. 328–364.
Stifter, Adalbert. *Witiko: Eine Erzählung.* In *Adalbert Stifter: Werke und Briefe. Historisch-kritische Gesamtausgabe,* edited by Alfred Doppler and Wolfgang Frühwald. Vol. 5, 3. Stuttgart: Metzler, 1986.

STROBL, KARL HANS (1877–1946), Austrian writer, who wrote a festival play commissioned by the *Nibelungenverein* (Nibelungen Society). The play, *Die Nibelungen an der Donau*

(The Nibelungs on the Danube), was to be performed by amateur actors in the Nibelungen city of Pöchlarn. The action takes place at the castles of Rüdiger (Pöchlarn) and Etzel (Hainburg). The characters speak in modern German, and the tragic conflicts are trivialized due to the modest plot, which primarily stresses the interaction of the heroes. Strobl introduces the Kürenberger as a kinsman of Rüdiger and a surviving eyewitness of the events that unfold following the arrival of the Burgundians at Pöchlarn.

[WW]

Bibliography
Strobl, Karl Hans. *Die Nibelungen an der Donau: Ein Festspiel in vier Abteilungen.* Berlin: Fontane & Co., 1907.

TIECK, LUDWIG (1773–1853), a major writer of German romanticism. Like Novalis, the Schlegel brothers, and other Romantics, Tieck studied and appreciated German medieval literature. His tale, *Der getreue Eckart und der Tannhäuser* (Loyal Eckart and Tannhäuser, 1799), introduces Eckart (Eckewart) who, in the *Nibelungenlied,* meets the Nibelungs on the border of Etzel's empire and urges Hagen von Tronje to beware of the Huns. In Tieck's tale, however, Eckart appears in the context of other, newly combined medieval legends. A poem, "Der getreue Eckart" (Loyal Eckart) first published as a part of this tale, deals with the role Eckart played in the Harlungen legend (as told in the Nordic *Þiðreks saga*).

After 1803, Tieck began (but never finished) a translation of the *Nibelungenlied.* In 1804 he wrote two romances on Siegfried's youth, *Siegfrieds Jugend* (Siegfried's Youth) and *Siegfried der Drachentöter* (Siegfried the Dragon Slayer) in which Siegfried is portrayed as a fierce, violent man of great strength and little kindness. Both romances tell about Siegfried's stay with Mimer the Smith, his fight with and slaying of the dragon, and his bathing in the dragon's blood, which made him semi-invulnerable. In the second romance a bird foretells Siegfried's acquisition of the Nibelung treasure; the poem also tells about the vulnerable spot between Siegfried's shoulders, thus foreshadowing his death. Tieck's primary source for the poems is not the *Nibelungenlied,* in which Siegfried's youth is mentioned only briefly in the third *âventiure,* but a later prose version of the epic: the chapbook *Das Lied vom Hürnen Seyfried* (The Lay of Horny-skinned Seyfried, sixteenth century). Tieck's romances are assumed to have influenced Wagner's *Ring des Nibelungen* (The Ring of Nibelung).

In 1805/1806, Tieck journeyed through Italy. Among the travel poems he wrote, the one on Verona (1805) mentions Dietrich von Bern and recalls the names of heroes of the *Nibelungenlied:* Hildebrand, Wolfart, and Dietlieb. During his travels Tieck studied manuscripts of the *Nibelungenlied* in Munich, Rome, and St. Gall.

[AH]

Bibliography

Brinkler-Gabler, Gisela. *Poetisch-wissenschaftliche Mittelalter-Rezeption: Ludwig Tiecks Erneuerung altdeutscher Literatur.* GAG 309. Göppingen: Kümmerle, 1980.

Tieck, Ludwig. *Phantasus.* Vol. 6 of *Schriften in zwölf Bänden,* edited by Manfred Frank. Frankfurt a. M.: Deutscher Klassiker Verlag, 1985, pp. 149–183.

_____. *Gedichte.* Vol. 7 of *Schriften in zwölf Bänden,* edited by Ruprecht Wimmer. Frankfurt a. M.: Deutscher Klassiker Verlag, 1995, pp. 171–172; 377–380; 380–388.

TRALOW, JOHANNES (1882–1968), German journalist, director, and author. His play *Die Mutter* (The Mother, 1914) depicts Siegfried and Brunhild as identical in character and in their roles as superior beings. The Expressionist pathos characterizing the play celebrates the hero and the valkyrie as protagonists of a higher race and Brunhild herself as the mother of a new mankind.

[WW]

Bibliography

Tralow, Johannes. *Die Mutter: Eine Bühnenhandlung in drei Abschnitten.* Munich: Müller, 1914.

UHLAND, (JOHANN) LUDWIG (1787–1862), German lyricist, dramatist, Germanist, and politician. While studying law, he developed, in close contact with the romanticist circle in Tübingen, a strong interest in the Middle High German epic. In 1807 Uhland published a "Bruchstück aus dem Nibelungen-Liede mit Beziehungen aufs Ganze" (Fragment from the *Nibelungenlied* with references to the entire work) in the *Sonntagsblatt für die gebildeten Stände* (Sunday paper for the educated classes). In the Schmidt/Hartmann edition of the *Nibelungenlied* (1898), the ferrying of the Burgundians across the Danube (twenty-fifth *âventiure*) was accorded the title "Hagen und die Meerweiber" (Hagen and the Water Sprites). Uhland characterizes the *Nibelungenlied* in his introduction as "ein wahres Epos" (a true epic poem), that shows unmistakably "einen Welt-Lauf" (a way of the world) because it represents "gewaltig wie nirgends . . . den Untergang einer ganzen Heldenwelt" (more powerfully than anywhere else . . . the demise of an entire world of heroes): "ein grosses Verhängnis waltet über der Handlung, bildet die Einheit derselben und wird uns beständig im Hintergrund gezeigt" (a great, dark destiny dominates the action, constitutes the latter's unity, and is constantly presented to us in the background). In 1812 he adapted the story of how Siegfried forged his own sword, as told in the *Þiðreks saga* and the *Lied vom Hürnen Seyfrid* (The Lay of Horny-skinned Seyfrid), for his ballad "Siegfrieds Schwert" (Siegfried's Sword). His attempt to dramatize the action of the *Nibelungenlied,* which he began in 1817 at the suggestion of Wilhelm Schlegel and Friedrich Heinrich von der Hagen, remained a fragment with only the following acts intact: I. Siegfrieds Tod (Siegfried's Death), and II. Chriemhildens Rache (Chriemhild's Revenge). Uhland regarded heroic sagas as less applicable to the dramatic genre because they were more orientated to "das äußerliche Leben und auf körperliche Kraft" (external life and physical power). Later, as a professor of German language and literature, his interest centered on the psychological motivation of the characters in the *Nibelungenlied.* His interpretation that the psychological development of Kriemhild from "der jedes Herz gewinnenden Jungfrau . . . zur furchtbaren Rachegöttin, zum blutdürstenden Ungeheuer" (the virgin who wins every heart . . . to a frightening goddess of revenge, a bloodthirsty monster) forms the unity of the poem has remained influential even for today's interpretations.

[MH]

Bibliography

Ehrismann, Otfrid. *Das Nibelungenlied in Deutschland: Studien zur Rezeption des Nibelungenlieds von der Mitte des 18. Jahrhunderts bis zum Ersten Weltkrieg.* Münchner Germanistische Beiträge 14. Munich: Fink, 1975, pp. 127–129, 248.

Uhland, Ludwig. "Bruchstück aus dem Nibelungen-Liede mit Beziehungen aufs Ganze." In *Werke,* edited by Hartmut Fröschle and Walter Scheffler. Vol. 2: *Sämtliche Dramen und Dramenfragmente, dichterische Prosa, ausgewählte Briefe.* Munich: Winkler, 1980, pp. 413–418.

———. "Siegfrieds Schwert." In *Werke,* edited by Hartmut Fröschle and Walter Scheffler. Vol. 1: *Gedichte.* Ausgabe letzter Hand. Munich: Winkler, 1980, pp. 210f.

———. "Die Nibelungen." In *Werke,* edited by Hartmut Fröschle and Walter Scheffler. Vol. 2 *Sämtliche Dramen und Dramenfragmente, dichterische Prosa, ausgewählte Briefe.* Munich: Winkler, 1980, pp. 335–350.

———. "Geschichte der altdeutschen Poesie: Vorlesungen an der Universität Tübingen gehalten in den Jahren 1830 und 1831." Pt. 1. Stuttgart, 1865 (= *Uhlands Schriften zur Geschichte der Dichtung und Sage.* Vol. 1)

WACHTER, FERDINAND (1794–1861), a

scholar of Nordic literature and philology whose tragedy, *Brunhild* (1821), written in blank verse, relates the story of the Austrasian king Siegbert and his wife Brunhild, daughter of the West Gothic king Athanagild. This historical play is based on Merovingian history and dramatizes the bloody conflicts between the ruling families of Austrasia and Neustria. These political events of the years between 566 and 584 could have provided part of the historical background of the *Nibelungenlied* and it is for this reason that Wachter alludes in his drama to the "Nibelungen tradition."

[WW]

Bibliography

Wachter, Ferdinand. *Brunhild: Ein Trauerspiel in fünf Aufzügen.* Jena: Bran, 1821.

WALDMÜLLER, ROBERT (pseudonym for

Edouard Duboc, 1822–1910), German translator and dramatist. His play *Brunhild* (1863) is based on both mythical Nordic tradition and the characters of the medieval epic. The tragedy concentrates on Brunhild, who is reminiscent of the Chinese princess Turandot and her deadly bridal contests. Brunhild's fate is linked to Siegfried; both protagonists enjoy equal status with respect to their strength and incredible willpower. Brunhild, however, is of divine descent, while Siegfried is mortal, a noble hero and king. No human love relationship is possible for them in this life, where they fail in the realm of social order and ideals. The murder of Siegfried is tragic, but nevertheless necessary. As he lies dying, Siegfried declares his love for Brunhild who is subsequently killed by thunder and lightning. Both are then united in the otherworld.

[WW]

Bibliography

Waldmüller, Robert. *Brunhild: Trauerspiel in fünf Aufzügen.* Deutsche Schaubühne 1. Leipzig, 1863. Also under Duboc, Edouard. *Brunhild. Trauerspiel in fünf Aufzügen.* Leipzig: Reclam, 1873.

WEINHEBER, JOSEF (1892–1945), Austrian

lyric poet whose work is characterized by both classical Roman/Greek and German tradition. His poem "Siegfried—Hagen" (1936) is a lament in four stanzas: a hero such as Siegfried inevitably evokes envy, which will eventually lead to his entrapment and death. Through this image Weinheber makes an oblique allusion to the political situation of the German Reich three years after the National Socialists had gained power.

[WW]

Bibliography

Josef Weinheber. Gedichte. Vol. 2 of *Sämtliche Werke,* edited by Josef Nadler and Hedwig Weinheber. Salzburg: Müller, 1954, p. 246.

WIEMER, RUDOLF OTTO (b. 1905), Ger-

man poet whose montage, "abstrakta konkreta," combines key words in the Nibelungen tradition that convey an abstract ideal, such as "mannentreue" (loyalty among men) with concepts that allude to real experiences and concrete aims, such as "mündige menschheit" (humanity come of age), with the purpose of decrying any attempt at ideological posturing.

[WW]

Bibliography

Wiemer, Rudolf Otto. *Beispiele zur deutschen Grammatik.* Berlin: Fietkau, 1972.

WILBRANDT, ADOLF (1857–1911), author of "Künstlerromane" (artist novels) and comedies. His tragedy *Kriemhild* (1877), written in iambic pentameter, is one of numerous historical plays that appeared after the founding of the second German Reich in 1871. It is characterized by a nationalist tenor, inflated heroism, and a tendency to employ "type" characters to glorify all things "German."

[WW]

Bibliography

Wilbrandt, Adolf. *Kriemhild: Trauerspiel in drei Aufzügen.* Vienna: Rosner, 1877.

ZAUNER, GEORG, contemporary German novelist whose 1985 work, *Die Erinnerungen des Helden Sigfrid* (Memoirs of the Hero Sigfrid), presents an original version of the myth of Siegfried employing C. G. Jung's theory of the eternal repetition of myth as destiny. Siegfried, black-haired and short in stature, is the embodiment of a brutal and vicious warrior, the catalyst of death and destruction. Poisoned because of his role in planning the coup d'état in Burgundy, Siegfried is reborn in the nineteenth century as a mass murderer who is condemned to death. The Jewish prison warden reveals Siegfried's true spirit in a series of hypnotic séances. The novel reflects the dichotomy between the pseudomythological rantings of German racism and the ill-fated relationship between Germans and Jews.

[WW]

Bibliography

Zauner, Georg. *Die Erinnerungen des Helden Sigfrid.* Zurich: Benziger, 1985.

PART VII

The Literary Reception of the Nibelungen Theme in Non-German-Speaking Countries

BALDWIN, JAMES (1841–1925), American writer whose 1882 work, *The Story of Siegfried,* is a children's classic. This prose adaptation combines elements from the *Poetic* and *Prose Edda* and the *Volsunga saga* with passages from the *Nibelungenlied.* Baldwin narrates the life of Siegfried in twenty "adventures," beginning with his apprenticeship in Mimer's smithy, where Balmung is crafted, and ending with his murder and the sinking of the hoard in the Rhine. In an effort to introduce young children to a broader spectrum of Nordic myths and legends, the author weaves into his story the legends of Ægir, Balder, Idun, and Thor. Copious notes at the end of the book offer further guidance and explanations. To the contemporary reader Baldwin's antiquated prose, replete with long-winded imaginary dialogue, may appear awkward and cumbersome. However, at the time, *The Story of Siegfried* enjoyed great popularity, as is evident from the two dozen reprints and editions published between 1882 and 1959. Baldwin was a teacher and superintendent of schools in Indiana, a prolific author of schoolbooks, and a creative adapter of world legends for the young. Scribner's attracted two of America's most prominent children's-book illustrators for the project: Howard Pyle, admired for his woodcut style drawings inspired by Dürer, and Peter Hurd, a student of N. C. Wyeth, the artist who became internationally acclaimed for his watercolors of Southwestern landscapes. Hurd began to produce his illustrations for the work with the 1925 edition. At the time of his contract with Scribner's, he considered his Siegfried pictures his best illustrative work. These enchanting color plates were reproduced from paintings in gouache on illustration board.

[OP]

Bibliography
Baldwin, James. *The Story of Siegfried.* New York: Scribner's, 1882.

BENSON, EDWARD FREDERIC (1867–1940), author of *The Valkyries: A Romance Founded on Wagner's Opera* (illustrated by T. Noyes Lewis). Benson, best known as the creator of the hilarious *Lucia* novels, and Lewis, primarily an illustrator of children's books, collaborated on this turn-of-the-century example of Wagner worship and, indirectly through Wagner, and representation of the *Nibelungenlied.* The book is, in Benson's words, "an attempt . . . to render as closely as possible into English narrative prose the libretto of Wagner's *Valkyries.*" As the subtitle suggests and the "rendering" of *Die Walküre* as a plural makes clear, Benson's work is not a translation, but a recasting of the drama as a romance novel. To this end he has added numerous descriptive passages and reduced dialogue (though what remains is surprisingly faithful to Wagner's text), and succeeds in changing the style from Wagner-heroic to art nouveau. Lewis's illustrations of plump valkyries with winged helmets enhance this impression.

[RHF]

Bibliography

Benson, Edward Frederic. *The Valkyries: A Romance Founded on Wagner's Opera.* Illustrated by T. Noyes Lewis. London: Dean & Son, 1903. American edition: Boston: L. C. Page and Company, 1905.

BRINK, ANDRÉ (b. 1935), South African writer, whose books have enjoyed worldwide success, including his Nibelungen novel, *States of Emergency* (1988). The work is based primarily on Wagner's version of the Nibelungen legend, intertwining the latter with the situation that prevailed in South Africa in the 1970s and 1980s. In Brink's own words, "[t]he tragic and gloomy situation in South Africa today . . . seems to re-enact many of the underlying tensions in the 'Ring.'"

[UM]

Bibliography

Brink, André. *States of Emergency.* London: Faber and Faber, 1988.

Müller, Ulrich. "Die Nibelungen und Richard Wagner in modernen englischsprachigen Romanen: David Gurr (1987), Tom Holt (1987/1988), André Brink (1988)." In *Fide et amore: A 'Festschrift' for Hugo Bekker,* edited by William C. McDonald and Winder McConnell. Göppingen: Kümmerle, 1990, pp. 273–288.

BUCK, KATHERINE M[ARGARET] (1874–ca. 1930), embarked upon, but did not complete, a massive retelling in English blank verse of the entire Wayland-Dietrich Saga, including the Nibelungen story. In particular she used elements from the *Þiðreks saga,* but she also integrated bits from the *Elder Edda,* Saxo Grammaticus, and others. Only Part I was published (in substantial volumes, 1924–1928), covering far more than just the Wayland story. The publisher, A. H. Mayhew, collaborated on an index volume and the line-illustration plates are by Elizabeth Goodman.

[BOM]

Bibliography

Buck, Katherine M. *The Wayland-Dietrich Saga: The Saga of Dietrich of Bern and His Companions, Preceded By That of Wayland Smith,* Pt. 1. *The Song of Wayland.* 9 vols. London: Mayhew, 1924–1928.

CIXOUS, HELENE (b. 1937). In 1994 contemporary French writer Helene Cixous, best known for her previous theatrical work with Ariane Mnouchkine's world-renowned Théâtre du Soleil, had her newest play, *L'histoire, qu'on ne connaîtra jamais* (The story we will never know), produced and directed by French theater director Daniel Mesguich. In Cixous's play we rediscover Sigfrid and his bride Kriemhilde, king and queen of the Netherlands, as well as Gunther and Brunhilde, the royalty of Iceland from the medieval Nibelungen story. Notice that the "Sigfrid" of Cixous's play is spelled without "e," in an effort to maintain a distance between this contemporary version of the legend and the original, which the author has long found a haunting tale.

As in the ancient text, *L'histoire* tells a tale of nuptials and alliances between diverse heroic figures, a story of forgetting and forgiving, a primitive, legendary story inhabited by the gods, whom Cixous calls the "Big High One" and the "Little High One." The play announces its intention to tell the truest story, the Nibelungen tale that has not been transmitted heretofore, the one we do not know but that could have been. The play is a political piece, but above all it is a reflection on the nature of memory and on the work that is mourning.

Cixous has stated in interviews that she chose to work with this myth because of its extraordinary richness, believing it to be on a par with *The Iliad* and *The Odyssey* in Western culture. Unlike the Greek texts, however, the Nordic myth, according to Cixous, speaks not only of war, but also of love. Furthermore Cixous was also interested in displacing what she calls the false image of the Nibelungen offered us by Wagner, whose tetralogy was exploited by the Nazis.

In Cixous's version we see a Sigfrid who, always the hero, maintains the many qualities with which we are familiar, but we also meet the character of Edda, who, rather than being the Edda of the legend, is portrayed as the oldest woman in the world. And the "author" of the Nibelungen story, Snorri Sturlusson (in real life a Scandinavian poet and historian, 1179–1241), also makes an appearance at the beginning of the play, when the gods ask him to write a new page in the book of Sigfrid's destiny, which in turn will be the unfolding of the play itself. The play asks us, "Why couldn't a poet change history?" and in Cixous's play Sturlusson is not only a poet, but also a historian. He is not passive, he is active, not just a poet, also a character in his own text, thus an agent with regard to the events that are in the process of happening. As for the two queens, Brunhilde and Kriemhilde, in L'histoire they refuse the wicked jealousies and grudges of the original, and reject the sterile idea of eternal revenge. Thanks to them, hope is reborn. "I brought an element of subversiveness to the story," Cixous asserts. "In the legend, all the characters die. I wanted to put the brakes on the horrible cycle of revenge. Nothing obliges current societies to cut each other's throats. We are witnessing attempts at reconciliation both in the Israeli-Palestinian conflict and in South Africa. Why shouldn't we cut the threads of hatred?" This is the question asked by Cixous's play, which tells the story told in Wagner's *Twilight of the Gods* of a meeting between the two couples, Sigfrid and Kriemhilde and Gunther and Brunhilde, years after the fateful act by which Sigfrid was made to forget his first love. "The play talks a lot about the mystery of forgetting," says Cixous. "I am struck by the power of forgetting. We construct barriers against forgetting, but do we succeed? Why is it so difficult to have been forgotten? Why is it so difficult to forget? In both cases, the wound is deep."

[CM]

Bibliography

Cixous, Helene. *L'histoire, qu'on ne connaîtra jamais.* Paris: Des Femmes, 1994.

EVSLIN, BERNARD, contemporary American writer of novels, books on mythology, and plays. His tale *Fafnir* (1989) is part of a series of works on monsters of mythology. It recounts the myth of the bloodthirsty ogre Fafnir, who can change himself into a number of ferocious creatures, of which a dragon is the most dangerous, and who is finally killed by the Germanic hero Siegfried.

[MH]

Bibliography

Evslin, Bernard. *Fafnir.* Monsters of Mythology. New York: Chelsea House, 1989.

GIBB, JOHN (1835–1915), Professor at the Presbyterian Theological College in London, he was the author of a number of scholarly works on theology and known principally for his translations of the writings of St. Augustine. His interest extended also to medieval literature, and he was apparently able to read both French and German, as well as Latin and Greek. His volume of 1881, *Gudrun and other Stories from the epics of the Middle Ages,* which was popular enough for a second edition in 1884, was doubtless intended as a presentation volume for children, with its gilt edges and attractive, if stylized, illustrations. It contains six stories: "Gudrun," "Hilda," "Wild Hagen," "Beowulf," "The Death of Roland," and "Walter and Hildegund." This selection is not surprising, bearing in mind his clear intention of providing edifying examples of courage and heroism, while entertaining "English boys and girls with the wild and terrible adventures" of which they tell. His obvious enthusiasm for *Kudrun,* which he describes as one of the most beautiful poems in German, led to his devoting half the volume to what he represented as the three self-contained stories ("Gudrun," "Hilda," "Wild Hagen"). Also, given the emphasis on the importance of Christian values in his prefatory note, it is hardly surprising that he omits the *Nibelungenlied,* while conceding that it actually surpasses *Kudrun.* These are not translations but fairly faithful renderings in language meant primarily for children. The tone is at times rather patronizing, not to mention sermonizing, but the volume probably achieved its aim.

[MEG]

Bibliography

Gibb, John. *Gudrun and Other Stories from the Epics of the Middle Ages.* With twenty illustrations. London: Marshall Japp and Company, 1881.

GJELLERUP, KARL ADOLPH (1857–1919), Danish author and dramatist, whose tragedy, *Brynhild,* deals with the fate of the Nordic valkyrie.

[WW]

Bibliography
Gjellerup, Karl Adolph. *Brynhild: En tragedie.* Kopenhagen: 1884.

GRUNDY, STEPHAN (b. 1967), American author who, while a student studying at Cambridge, used the songs of the *Edda* and the *Volsunga saga* as well as Richard Wagner's *Ring des Nibelungen* for his voluminous novel, *Rhinegold* (1992/1994). In three books the narrator relates the history of the Volsunga clan starting with the moment when the gods commit murder and abscond with the Rhinegold. As the story goes, the treasure is then cursed and this curse determines the fate of the Volsunga, the mortal descendants of Wotan. Sigland and Sigmund engage in an incestuous relationship and produce the mighty Sigfrid, who, however, falls victim to his own naive innocence. After marrying Kriemhild, an evil Attila lures the Burgundians to his residence where the battle over the treasure takes place. Sigfrid's widow, Gudrun, and Hagen are the only survivors of the battle, and they return the hoard to the bottom of the Rhine. Following Wagner, Grundy provides an interpretation of the world as a myth of gods and heroes in an effort to find answers to the timeless questions of love and death, war and violence, and man and nature.

In his second Nibelungen novel, *Wodan's Curse,* Grundy casts Hagen (spelled Hagan) as the central character in the plot, one who is dark and secretive. The material for the work is derived from historical Burgundian sources, the Nordic Nibelungen tradition, the *Nibelungenlied,* and the Latin poem *Waltharilied.* In the novel, Hagan, whose relationship to his own clan is ambiguous, is the second son of Grimhild, who is versed in magic, and the Burgundian king Gebica. He goes in the place of his brother Gundahari as a hostage to the court of Attila, who is portrayed as a tolerant ruler with respect to religions. Hagan, who fervently holds to his belief in the Germanic gods, strikes up a friendship with Waldhari, a Christian by conviction. Waldhari's flight with his beloved Hildegund, herself a hostage of Attila's court, is a painful experience for Hagan, who is torn between his duty as a vassal and his loyalty to his friend. During a visit to the bishop of Passau, Hagan clearly recognizes the influence and the power of Christianity as a new religion. Grundy points in his novel to the basic contradiction that exists between the Christian idea of brotherly love and the realities of power.

[WW]

Bibliography
Grundy, Stephan. *Attila's Treasure.* New York: Bantam, 1997.
———. *Wodans Fluch.* Translated from the English by Manfred Ohl and Hans Sartorius. Frankfurt a. M.: Krüger, 1999.
———. *Rhinegold.* New York: Bantam, 1994.
———. *Rheingold.* Translated from the English by Manfred Ohl and Hans Sartorius. Frankfurt a. M.: Krüger, 1992.

GURR, DAVID (b. 1936), Canadian novelist. In *The Ring Master* (1987), he uses many medieval myths, particularly Wagner's version of the Nibelung legend, to depict the modern reception of the *Nibelungenlied.* The work also portrays Wagner's exploitation by the National Socialists. It is the story of incestuous twins, born in England but fascinated by Bayreuth and Nazism. *The Ring Master* bears some resemblance to the novel *Der Feuerkreis* (The Circle of Fire) by the Austrian novelist Hans Lebert (1971).

[UM]

Bibliography
Gurr, David. *The Ring Master.* New York: Atheneum, 1987.
Müller, Ulrich. "Die Nibelungen und Richard Wagner in modernen englischsprachigen Romanen: David Gurr (1987), Tom Holt (1987/1988), André Brink (1988)." In *Fide et amore: A 'Festschrift' for Hugo Bekker,* edited by William C. McDonald and Winder McConnell. Göppingen: Kümmerle, 1990, pp. 273–288.

HOLT, TOM (b. 1961), British novelist. His work, *Expecting Someone Taller* (1987/1988), presents a "continuation" of Wagner's version of the Nibelung legend in modern times, emphasizing the utopian and optimistic potentials of Wagner's *Ring.*

[UM]

Bibliography

Holt, Tom. *Expecting Someone Taller.* London: St. Martin's Press 1987, and New York: McMillan, 1988.

Müller, Ulrich. "Die Nibelungen und Richard Wagner in modernen englischsprachigen Romanen: David Gurr (1987), Tom Holt (1987/1988), André Brink (1988)." In *Fide et amore: A 'Fest-schrift' for Hugo Bekker,* edited by William C. McDonald and Winder McConnell. Göppingen: Kümmerle, 1990, pp. 273–288.

JEFFERS, ROBINSON (1887–1962), highly talented and controversial California poet, who is the author of the verse drama *At the Birth of an Age* (1935). Its main character is Gudrun (Kriemhild of the *Nibelungenlied,* and Gudrun of the *Volsunga saga*) and the plot appears to be an intermeshing of elements from both the *Nibelungenlied* and the Old Norse *Volsunga saga,* to which Jeffers himself refers in the preface to his poem. The action begins subsequent to Sigurd's death and Gudrun's marriage to Attila with the arrival of Gunnar, Hoegni, and Carling (Gislher) at the court of the Hunnish leader. As in the *Nibelungenlied,* Gudrun has extended an invitation to her brothers to visit her in the camp of the Huns. In contrast to both the medieval epic and the *Volsunga saga,* however, Attila demonstrates virtually no interest in the Burgundians, engaged as he is in a siege of the city of Troyes. At no point in time do the "guests" constitute the center of his attention.

With respect to the Burgundians, the initiative is taken entirely by Gudrun. In contrast to the *Volsunga saga,* in which Gudrun attempts to warn her brothers that Atli's motive in inviting them to his camp is treacherous and that he intends solely to procure the treasure that had formerly belonged to Sigurd, the relationship of Gudrun to her brothers—specifically Gunnar and Hoegni, who are responsible for the death of her first husband, Sigurd—is thoroughly ambivalent in Jeffers's poem. She does, however, remain closely attached to Carling, a reflection of Kriemhild's relationship to Giselher in the *Nibelungenlied.* The antagonistic relationship between Hoegni and Gudrun is reminiscent of the antipathy that exists between Hagen and Kriemhild in the German epic, and in Jeffers's poem Hoegni even attempts to stab Gudrun in the presence of Attila and taunts her repeatedly

with his sarcastic remarks about her marriage to the "toad." Whereas the Gudrun of the *Volsunga saga* reaffirms her loyalty to the clan and joins with her brothers in the struggle against the Huns, her counterpart in "At the Birth of an Age" reflects much of the limbo status, the spiritual loneliness, and barrenness of Kriemhild in the *Nibelungenlied.* While Gudrun may also share with Kriemhild a fondness for power and its trappings, she is ultimately depicted in a terrible state of spiritual isolation, caught between hatred of what her brothers have done to Sigurd and a deep, sincere familial bonding, between the desire for revenge and the need for reconciliation.

Jeffers portrays Gudrun as standing on the threshold between Teutonic paganism and its ethos of revenge and the advent of (by no means unproblematic) Christianity with its new ethos of forgiveness. Gudrun's brothers are killed at the court of the Huns while trying to overpower their captors, and Gudrun commits suicide. Jeffers allows her, however, to "reappear" in the form of a reflecting shade who makes remarkable pronouncements on her motivations while she was still alive, among other things, that she had placed ambition above love and, furthermore, that she bore responsibility for the death of Gunnar and Hoegni and had even consented in the death of her first husband Sigurd. Unlike the *Nibelungenlied,* which offers no vision for the future in either this world or the next, Jeffers's poem concludes on a philosophically positive note, as the shade Gudrun acquires awareness of the inevitability of rejuvenation and resurrection within an ontological order based on the myth of the eternal return.

[WM]

Bibliography

Eliade, Mircea. *Cosmos and History. The Myth of the Eternal Return.* Translated from the French by Willard C. Trask. New York: Harper, 1959.

Jeffers, Robinson. *The Selected Poetry of Robinson Jeffers.* New York: Random House, 1959, pp. 505–561.

McConnell, Winder. "Robinson Jeffers and the *Nibelungenlied.* The 'Fourth' Source of His Poem: 'At the Birth of an Age.'" In *"Waz sider da geschach." American–German Studies on the Nibelungenlied Text and Reception,* edited by Werner Wunderlich and Ulrich Müller, with the assistance of Detlef Scholz. GAG 564. Göppingen: Kümmerle, 1992, pp. 217–229. With Bibliography 1980–1990/91.

———. "Why Does Gudrun Act This Way? On Robinson Jeffers's 'At the Birth of an Age.'" In *In hôhem Prîse: A Festschrift in Honor of Ernst S. Dick,* edited by Winder McConnell. GAG 480. Göppingen: Kümmerle Verlag, 1989, pp. 235–242.

LUDLAM, CHARLES (1943–1987), American dramatist and director of the "Ridiculous Theatrical Company" (Greenwich Village, New York; founded in 1967). He composed the satirical *The Ring Gott Farblonjet: A Masterwork,* based primarily on Wagner's version of the Nibelung legend. The drama was successfully staged at Ludlam's Greenwich theater in 1977 and posthumously in 1990.

[UM]

Bibliography

Müller, Ulrich Müller. "'Los, spreng die Welt in die Luft!' Von 'normalen' und alternativen Opern und von einer 'toten' Gattung." In *Theater für Bayreuth: 10 Jahre Studiobühne Bayreuth.* Bayreuth: Krauss, 1991, pp. 88–96. With illustrations.

MORRIS, WILLIAM (1834–1896), known primarily as a decorator and designer, and as a founding member of the group which became the Socialist League and propounded the early doctrines of Socialism, William Morris was also a prolific poet. His writings, like his art, had their roots in the past and particularly in the Middle Ages. An early work, *The Hollow Land* (1856), a visionary romance inspired by medieval themes, begins with the first strophe of the *Nibelungenlied,* quoted in the English translation of Thomas Carlyle in his essay of 1831.

The Earthly Paradise, which appeared in three volumes between 1868 and 1870, is a long and elaborate work explicitly inspired by Chaucer's *Canterbury Tales.* Beginning with a lengthy prologue, "The Wanderers," it is a collection of twenty-four stories, two assigned to each month of the year and taken from medieval, classical, Eastern, and Norse legends. The tellers of the tales are the wanderers who have fled from their plague-ridden city in search of the island where they will find the fabled land of lasting happiness, "the earthly paradise." The six strophes that open the work, the so-called "Apology," contain two of the most quoted self-assessments of Morris as "the idle singer of the empty day" and "dreamer of dreams, born out of my due time." The dominant theme of the tales is escape, freedom from the ugliness and oppression of the modern world, and ultimately even from death itself.

The longest single tale is *The Lovers of Gudrun,* assigned to November. This is a retelling of part of the *Laxdælsaga,* and it reflects Morris's early interest in Icelandic literature, but does not display the special insight he gained through his visits there that are reflected above all in *Sigurd the Volsung.* Essentially a heroic tale, *The Lovers of Gudrun* is tempered by romantic sentimentality, and it was well received in the England of the mid-nineteenth century. The Gudrun of the story is the daughter of Oswif of Bathstead and her inescapable fate, foretold in the prophecy with which the poem begins, takes its tragic course and culminates in the cry which she utters, old and blind: "I did the worst to some I loved the most." Popular though it was at the time, the poem is little admired by experts on Icelandic literature, who point to the betrayal of the material through the softening of events and motivation.

For *The Fostering of Aslaug* (December), Morris took his material from the version of the story of Aslaug, which he found in Volume I of Benjamin Thorpe's *Northern Mythology* (London 1851/1852). This, in turn, was based on the Aslaug material appended, possibly by a redactor, to the *Volsunga saga.* As the story goes, Aslaug, daughter of Sigurd and Brynhild, is brought up in poverty and obscurity, until Ragnar, son of Sigurd of Sweden, happens to meet her, is struck by her beauty, and eventually marries her. The version by Morris is again a sentimentalization of the original, as he tells of the joy of the lovers (untainted by the increasing hardening of Aslaug's character in the source) and the heroic death of Ragnar in battle. Purists again justifiably point to his distortion of the emphasis of the original.

Morris undoubtedly appreciated the true qualities of the literature which he was refashioning for his own age, and his view of the heroic evolved a great deal as he became more familiar with Icelandic literature. The most significant impetus to his lasting preoccupation with Iceland and things Icelandic came with his meeting in the autumn of 1868 with Eiríkr Magnússon, the scholar who was in England, engaged on work on a Norse New Testament and a Norse dictionary, and who undertook to teach Morris Icelandic. They collaborated on a number of translations, notably *The Story of the Volsungs and the Niblungs* (1870). By now Morris had come to see the *Volsunga saga* as the "grandest tale that ever was told," though initially he doubted his ability to retell it in English verse, fearing that he could produce only a "flatter and tamer version of a thing already existing." He likewise despised Wagner for his foolhardiness in rendering such sublime material as an opera, writing of the incongruity of the resultant "tweedle-deeing over the unspeakable woes of Sigurd." The poem that he eventually did produce, *Sigurd the Volsung* (1876), is generally believed to be his greatest poetic achievement and important to him both as a person and as an artist.

Sigurd the Volsung is divided into four books ("Sigmund," "Regin," "Brynhild," "Gudrun"), and Morris uses some important details from the *Nibelungenlied* to support the material that is essentially derived from the *Volsunga saga.* The heart of the poem is the life and death of the hero, as contained in the second and third books, but framing this is the account of the "earlier days of the Volsungs," the death of Sigmund before the birth of his son, and finally the fate of the the Niblungs ("their woeful need") and the fall of the house of Atli. Morris's early view of the poem as a tale of tragic love was augmented, but not contradicted, by his growing conception of Sigurd as the precursor of a better world, not in some earthly paradise, apart from the real world, but within that world. In that sense the work marks an important transition in Morris's development as a political figure. Artistically, it is a pivotal work and opens up the way to the fusion of his poetic and political concerns in the writings of his last years (*The House of the Wolfings,* 1888; *The Roots of the Mountains,* 1889; *News from Nowhere,* 1890; *Glittering Plain,* 1890; *The Wood beyond the World,* 1894; *The Well at the World's End,* 1896; and *The Sundering Flood,* 1898.)

[MEG]

Bibliography

Morris, William. *Sigurd the Volsung.* With a new introduction by Jane Ennis. Bristol: Thoemmes, 1994.

PAXSON, DIANA L. (b. 1943), a contemporary American writer of historical fiction/fantasy novels, author of *Wodan's Children,* a trilogy based on the legends surrounding Sigfrid, Brunahild (sic), the Burgundians, and the Huns. The series consists of *The Wolf and the Raven* (1993), which covers the childhoods of Sigfrid and Brunahild, and culminates in Sigfrid's rescue of Brunahild and their subsequent brief life together; *The Dragons of the Rhine* (1995), which treats the couple's marriages into the Burgundian royal family and the tensions leading to Sigfrid's murder; and *The Lord of the Horses* (1996), which takes up the events that give rise to the Burgundians' downfall. Paxson derives her material primarily from the *Volsunga saga* and the *Nibelungenlied* (though there is a good deal that is original), and places events in Central Europe of the fifth century. The discrepancies between her sources are generally resolved as are conflicts with actual events of the time period. The author tells her story from the viewpoints of several of the major characters, complementing it with material from other Germanic legends and with a wealth of information concerning the details of daily life, warfare, and religion in this period. Religion is her chief interest, and the god Wodan's interactions with the major characters provide a unified justification for their actions in the three novels. Paxson seeks to depict what she sees as the clash of three spiritual traditions: Wodan's warrior cult, the Christian faith and an old "earth-religion," In addition her work reflects a number of elements drawn from contemporary "New Age" spirituality. Other novels by the author include *The White Raven* (1988) and *The Serpent's Tooth* (1991).

[JKW]

Bibliography

Paxson, Diana L. *The Wolf and the Raven.* New York: William Morrow, 1993.

———. *Dragons of the Rhine.* New York: William Morrow, 1995.

———. *The Lord of the Horses.* New York: William Morrow, 1996.

RAGOZIN, ZENAÏDE ALEXEIEVNA

(1835–1924), Russian-born historian and author of children's works (naturalized in the USA in 1874). *Siegfried, the hero of the North, and Beowulf, the hero of the Anglo-Saxons* was the first volume in the series, "Tales of the Heroic Ages," fiction intended for children that was chosen for "moral purity and profound wisdom" and "high literary worth, besides historical value, as the source from which all the poetry, drama, romance of the world have flowed" (xii). The *Nibelungenlied* was chosen not only for its intrinsic values, but also to counteract the effect of the popularity of Wagner's operatic treatment of the themes and restore the epic itself to the public eye. The story is presented in a condensed format consisting of twenty-one books, remaining faithful to the original "poetical beauties, [and] picturesque traits" and using as much of the dialogue as possible. An appended "Note on the Nibelungenlied" presents information on the writing down of the tale, the manuscripts, and the relationship of events in the story to known historical facts. Four full-page illustrations are included.

[BC]

Bibliography

Ragozin, Zénaïde Alexeïevna. *Siegfried, the hero of the North, and Beowulf, the hero of the Anglo-Saxons.* London: Putnam, 1898; 2nd ed. New York: Knickerbocker, 1903.

SCHERMAN, KATHARINE, American writer whose work, *The Sword of Siegfried* (1959), was illustrated by Douglas Gorsline. This children's story, with its extensive cast of characters, tells the tale of Siegfried, who is directly descended from the chief Germanic deity, Odin. The god takes an active but silent role in Siegfried's life. He bestows upon him gifts such as the brilliant sword Branstock and the horse Greyfell, and with the help of these gifts Siegfried kills Fafner the dragon, who is really a dwarf and brother to Siegfried's teacher Regin. After tasting the dragon's blood, Siegfried understands the language of the birds who tell him to kill Regin, take all of the dragon's gold, and to then go to the mountain of fire, Hindarfall. Brynhild, a former valkyrie warrior of Odin turned mortal, lies sleeping there and Siegfried frees her, falls uncontrollably in love with her, gives her a gold ring from the dragon treasure, and leaves, promising to return. He then kills King Lygni of the Hundings, who killed Siegfried's father before he was born, and proceeds to the land of the Nibelungs to the court of King Giuki and Queen Grimhild, who is really a witch. She gives Siegfried a potion to make him forget Brynhild and to marry her daughter Gudrun. After Giuki dies, Gunnar becomes king and needs a wife. Siegfried, remembering nothing and disguised as Gunnar, fetches Brynhild as Gunnar's bride. Brynhild is angry, yet must go with him. At the wedding the spell is broken and Siegfried recognizes her. The court intends to kill Siegfried and he is stabbed in the back by Guttorm during a boar hunt. Siegfried then kills Guttorm, dies, and Greyfell follows him to Valhalla. In the end Brynhild stabs herself and is put on Siegfried's pyre with Branstock between them.

[SJM]

Bibliography

Scherman, Katharine. *The Sword of Siegfried.* With illustrations by Douglas Gorsline. New York: Random House, 1959.

SIMON, EDITH (b.1917) British authoress, who published, in 1955, the 365-page novel *The Twelve Pictures,* composed of twelve parts called pictures. The work draws not only on the *Nibelungenlied,* but on other similar epics and on various versions of the Siegfried myths. It begins with two weddings: Siegfried the Volsung, heir to the Lowlands and King of the Nebelland, to Kriemhild, princess of the Burgundians, and King Gunter of the Burgundians to Queen Brunhilde of Eisenland. A sordid, sad tale follows with the queens quarreling and Siegfried being murdered in the Odenwald Forest. Kriemhild woos and marries Attila of the Huns. She takes her revenge as had been prophesied and destroys the Burgundian court and herself. The final picture is that of the two remaining queens, Brunhilde and her mother-in-law, the queen mother Uta, who have become somewhat unbalanced. They sit in the ruins of their castle

and spend endless hours weaving their memories into twelve tapestries so that their tragic story will not die.

[SJM]

Bibliography
Simon, Edith. *The Twelve Pictures*. New York: Putnam, 1955.

THE HEROIC LIFE AND EXPLOITS OF SIEGFRIED THE DRAGON SLAYER: AN OLD GERMAN STORY (1848), with eight illustrations by Wilhelm Kaulbach.

This children's tale, consisting of fourteen adventures, is loosely based on the *Nibelungenlied,* although most of the story takes place before the *Nibelungenlied* actually begins. The focus is on the development of "Siegfried the Swift" into a hero after he leaves Konigsburg, the supportive court of his parents. From there he seeks out the dragon, whom he slays and in whose blood he bathes. His skin becomes horny and impenetrable, except for the one small spot on his back which is missed because a leaf landed there. Siegfried the Swift learns the art of the smith from Mimer, smithy to the giants, a race of cruel people who also inhabit the world. In his adventures he meets King Englein of the dwarves and King Kuperan the Faithless, king of the giants. Together with them on an adventure deep into the earth to Drachenstein, Siegfried battles for and wins the great sword Balmung. He uses this sword to fight the mighty dragon and succeeds, thus rescuing the imprisoned daughter of the Rhine King, Princess Kriemhilda of Worms. The two know their destiny is to be together and they marry immediately, after which the dwarf king sings about the tragic fate of their future together.

[SJM]

Bibliography
The Heroic Life and Exploits of Siegfried the Dragon Slayer: An Old German Story. With eight illustrations by Wilhelm Kaulbach. London: Cundall, 1848.

THE RECEPTION OF THE NIBELUNGEN THEME IN JAPAN.

The earliest reception of the Nibelungen theme in Japan began in the twentieth century during the third period (1908–1922) and the fourth period (1923–1945) of a genre referred to as "translation literature" in modern Japanese culture following the Meiji Restoration in 1868. The first attempt to translate the *Nibelungenlied* into Japanese, *Hokuou Shinwa* ("Nordic Mythology," Vol. 1: *Nibelungen Monogatari* [epic]), by Takeshi Takeda, was published in 1917. It is not a verbatim translation of the original, but rather an abridged rendering of the whole Nibelungen story. The primary authentic Nibelungen translation in Japan, by Toshio Yukiyama (1939 and 1942), is based on the edition of manuscript **B** by Karl Bartsch. Yukiyama translated the manuscript into colloquial Japanese and tried to reproduce an analogical structure of the Nibelungen strophe in his translation. Masaki Hattori also translated Bartsch's edition in 1944 (revised in 1977) in pseudoclassical style, using manuscript **B** with **C** as a variant. Following his initial Nibelungen translation of the Bartsch edition in 1952, Morio Sagara's second modern Japanese translation in 1955 replaced the Yukiyama version as the standard work in Iwanami paperbacks. Sagara published his third, revised translation in 1975 as an idiomatic translation and it enjoyed long-term success on the Japanese book market. The last three translators, who were also Germanists, consulted the commentary of Paul Piper's late nineteenth-century edition of *Der Nibelunge Not*. The latest translation of the *Nibelungenlied* by Tadahiro Okazaki, only the first part of which was published (1989), combines literalness with linguistic-philological accuracy. In the field of Germanic philology, research into the *Nibelungenlied* has also been heavily influenced by methodological changes which were determined by socio-political conditions in modern Japan. Yukiyama, the first authentic medievalist in Japanese *Germanistik,* composed his monumental work in 1934, *Nibelungen no Uta* (Lied): *Kiso no Kenkyu* (research of the basics), in which fundamental themes of Nibelungen studies are examined in detail. His work consists of three parts. In the introduction several important terms such as *Lied, Epos, Sage, Naturpoesie,* and *Kunstpoesie* are critically scrutinized and a description provided of previous philological research into the *Nibelungenlied.* In the second part the historical textual criticism and tradition are discussed in detail, and each major theory is summarized and evaluated. In the third the generative history of the subject matter, the primary and secondary traditions of the Nordic materials are sketched out, the prehistory of the production process of the *Nibelungenlied* in relation to the *Edda* and the *þiðreks saga* is explained, and the problems of authorship and the generative process of the work are debated. In contrast to Yukiyama's synthetic, objective description, stands Teiji Yoshimura's *Nibelungen Densetsu* (legend), published during World War II. It had immense influence on Japanese Germanists who were promoting nationalistic ideology. Yoshimura placed methodological emphasis on the *Nibelungenlied* as a literary object that was written in 1205, within the framework of German *Ideengeschichte*. This aesthetic-ideological stance was closely related to Japanese Shintoistic nationalism during the war. Yoshimura intended to provide a genealogy of the "folk" gods for German *Ideengeschichte* and to assign Siegfried an appropriate position within the history of ideas. After the war most of the traditional philological research in Japan was resumed, with no reflection on the responsibility for contributions made to the war effort. In *Doitsu Chusei Jojishi Kenkyu* (Research on German Medieval Epic, 1948), Sagara was alone in issuing a stern warning against the danger of a heroism that lacked humanity. Since the 1970s, there has been more of a tendency to concentrate on linguistic or textual-linguistic analyses of the *Nibelungenlied,* as is the case with Okazaki (1972) and Shitanda (1983). With respect to the Nordic variants of the Siegfried legends, the *Edda* and *Volsunga saga*

have been translated into Japanese prose by Yukio Taniguchi (1973/1979).

[SS]

Bibliography

Hattori, Masaki, trans. *Jojishi Nibelungen Zoku no Kinan.* Tokyo: Youtokusha, 1944.

———, trans. *Nibelungen no Uta.* Tokyo: Toyo shuppan, 1977.

Okazaki, Tadahiro. "Der Nibelunge Not ni okeru Hiteihyougen no Kenkyu." *Gaikokugo Gaikokubungaku* 2 (1972): 17–41.

———, trans. *Nibelungen no Uta.* Vol. 1. Hiroshima: Keisuis ha, 1989.

Sagara, Morio. *Doitsu Chusei Jojishi Kenkyu.* Tokyo: Fuji shuppan, 1948.

———, trans. *Nibelungen no Uta.* Sekaibungaku Zenshu 3. Tokyo: Kawade shobo, 1952.

———, trans. *Nibelungen no Uta.* 2 vols. Tokyo: Iwanami shoten, 1955; 1975.

Shitanda, So. "Kommunikative Funktionen der epischen Vorausdeutungen im Nibelungenlied." *Doitsu Bungaku Ronshu* 16. Kochi: Asahi shuppansha,1983, 68–85.

Takeda, Takashi. *Hokuou Shinwa: Nibelungen Monogatari.* Vol. 1. Tokyo: Kouryusha, 1917.

Taniguchi, Yukio, trans. *Edda: Kodai Hokuou Kayoushu.* Tokyo: Shinchosha, 1973.

———, trans. *Iceland Saga.* Tokyo: Shinchosha, 1979.

Yoshimura, Teiji. *Nibelungen Densetsu.* Kamakura: Kamakura shobo, 1943.

Yukiyama, Toshio. *Nibelungen no Uta. Kiso no Kenkyu.* Tokyo: Ouokayama shoten, 1934.

———, trans. *Nibelungen no Uta.* 2 vols. Tokyo: Iwanami shoten, 1939; vol. 2: 1942.

PART VIII

Music and Composers

BRAUN, CHARLES, English composer of the dramatic cantata *Sigurd* (libretto by E. Brook), which premiered in Liverpool in December 1890. It subsequently fell into obscurity.

[UM]

BRENDEL, KARL FRANZ (1811–1868), German musicologist, who, like Anton Wilhelm Florentin von Zuccalmaglio, Friedrich Theodor von Vischer, and Louise Otto-Peters, tackled the aesthetics of the Nibelungen theme and the possibilities it offered as a play and as a German opera. He called for a composer who could become the "man of the hour."

[WW]

Bibliography
Neue Zeitschrift für Musik 23 (1845): 120–146.

D'ALBERT, EUGEN (FRANCIS CHARLES) (1864–1932), German composer and pianist. Born in Glasgow of Italian ancestry, D'Albert composed many operas and musical comedies. *Tiefland* (1903) was a hit for several decades, the most successful opera of German verismo. By contrast, his Nibelungen opera, *Gernot,* was a failure (libretto by G. Kastropp; Mannheim, April 11, 1897).

[UM]

Bibliography
Heisig, H. "D'Alberts Opernschaffen." Diss., Leipzig, 1942.

DAS BARBECÜE. A NEW MUSICAL COMEDY, English-German title of an American Nibelungen musical conceived by Jim Luigs, who wrote the stage play and the lyrics, and Scott Warrender, who composed the music. The musical is primarily based on Wagner's version of the Nibelungen legend, but it transposes the story to Texas. It was commissioned by the Seattle Opera and played in several theaters across the United States. In 1997, under the subtitle *Nibelungen Go Texas,* it was performed with considerable success, even in the "Nibelungen city" of Linz (Austria). A CD recording of the work is available (Varese Sarabande VSD-5593, 1995).

[UM]

Bibliography
Eder, Annemarie, Ulrich Müller, Siegrid Schmidt, and Margarete Springeth. "Helden für das Dritte Jahrtausend? Siegfried, Faust und der Freischütz auf der Musical-Bühne." In *Ethische and ästhetische Komponenten des sprachlichen Kunstwerks: Festschrift für Rolf Bräuer zum 65. Geburtstag,* edited by Jürgen Erich Schmidt, Karin Cieslik, and Gisela Ros. GAG 672. Göppingen: Kümmerle, 1999, pp. 37–60.

DRAESEKE, FELIX (AUGUST BERN-HARD) (1835–1913), German composer. Four of Draeseke's five operas had medieval topics: *Sigurd* (1853–1857), *Herrat* (1877–1879), *Gudrun* (1884), *Bertran de Born* (1892–1894), and *Merlin* (1903–1905), and for these works the composer also wrote the librettos. Draeseke composed his first opera, *Sigurd,* after having heard Wagner's *Lohengrin* in Weimar (conducted by Franz Liszt). The opera was praised by Liszt, but only fragments of it were performed (Meiningen, 1867). It has nothing to do with the Nibelungs, but rather was based on Eduard Geibel's poem, "König Sigurds Brautfahrt" (1846) and tells of the ominous wooing of young Alfsonnes by old King Sigurd. *Herrat,* which deals with Dietrich von Bern, was performed in Dresden in 1892.

[UM]

Bibliography
Fischer, Jens Malte. "Singende Recken und blitzende Schwerter: Die Mittelalteroper neben und nach Wagner, ein Überblick." In *Mittelalter-Rezeption: Ein Symposion,* edited by Peter Wapnewski. Stuttgart: Metzler, 1986, pp. 517–519.
Roeder, Erich. *Felix Draeseke: Der Lebens- und Leidensweg eines deutschen Meisters.* 2 vols. Dresden: Limpert, 1932–1937.

GADE, NIELS WILHELM (1817–1890), Danish composer. In 1847 Gade set to music a scene from the libretto *Die Nibelungen* by Louise Otto. Volker, the fiddler, sings about Siegfried's victory over Schilbung and Nibelung and how he becomes the owner of the Nibelungen hoard. This fragment of a musical score with the title *Siegfried og Brünhilde* is preserved as a handwritten original in the Royal Library in Copenhagen.

[WW]

Bibliography
Jost, Christa. "Die Nibelungen auf dem Weg zur Oper." In *Nibelungenlied und Klage: Ursprung, Funktion, Bedeutung,* edited by Dietz-Rüdiger Moser and Marianne Sammer. Munich: Institut für Bayerische Literaturgeschichte, 1998, pp. 483–497.

GLÄSER, PAUL (b. 1871), German composer. He composed an oratorio entitled *Giselhers Brautfahrt* (Giselher's Wooing Mission, libretto by Hermann Römpler; Plauen ca. 1900), a work which is not well-known today

[UM]

GRIMM, HEINRICH, German composer. He composed the librettos and music of three operas, two of them with Nibelung topics. Both operas, *Krimhild* (Augsburg, April 10, 1891), and *Sigurd* (Metz, February 1894) were unsuccessful.

[UM]

HOPPE, UWE, German dramatist and director of the Studiobühne Bayreuth. He conceived and produced several satirical renditions of Wagnerian operas, among them Wagner's version of the Nibelung legend, *Der Ring des Liebesjungen* (The Ring of the Lover Boy, 1982) and *Der Ring des Nibelungen* (The Ring of the Nibelung, 1996). Hoppe and his company were invited to perform at the Deutsche Oper Berlin in 1984.

[UM]

Bibliography
Müller, Ulrich. "'Donna Giovanni' und 'Der Ring des Liebesjungen': Versuch über alternative Opern." In *Opern und Opernfiguren,* edited by Ursula and Ulrich Müller. Anif: Müller-Speiser, 1989, pp. 411–426.

KUMMER, EBERHARD (b. 1940), Austrian musician and singer, who specializes in the performance of historical music. Since 1982 he has enjoyed considerable success singing excerpts of the *Nibelungenlied* in the *Hildebrandston* throughout Europe and the United States. In 1988 and 1989 at the Danube Festival of Krems and at the Wiener Festwochen (Vienna Festival Weeks), he sang the whole epic poem over a period of five days and a total of thirty-three hours.

[UM]

KUNKEL, MAX (b. 1875), German composer of the libretto and music for the opera *Sigurds Ring* (Würzburg, March 3, 1911), which is, however, no longer performed.

[UM]

LASS' DAS, HAGEN!, (Stop that, Hagen!), a German radio musical about the Nibelungs. The libretto was conceived by Horst Pillau (b. 1932), with music by Siegfried Ulbrich (1922–1991). The musical was produced by the Berlin Broadcasting Service (RIAS) in 1967 and aired several times. It is a witty and ironic re-telling of the *Nibelungenlied,* probably inspired by Joachim Fernau's book *Disteln für Hagen* (1966).

[UM]

Bibliography

Eder, Annemarie, Ulrich Müller, Siegrid Schmidt, and Margarete Springeth. "Helden für das Dritte Jahrtausend? Siegfried, Faust und der Freischütz auf der Musical-Bühne" In *Ethische und ästhetische Komponenten des sprachlichen Kunstwerks: Festschrift für Rolf Bräuer zum 65. Geburtstag,* edited by Jürgen Erich Schmidt, Karin Cieslik, and Gisela Ros. GAG 672. Göppingen: Kümmerle, 1999, pp. 37–60.

Fernau, Joachim. *Disteln für Hagen. Bestandsaufnahme der deutsche Seele.* 2nd ed. Munich: Herbig, 1966.

Schmidt, Siegrid and Ulrich Müller. "'Lass' das, Hagen!' Ein Nibelungen-Musical von Horst Pillau und Siegfried Ulbrich (1967)." In *Verstehen durch Vernunft: Festschrift für Werner Hoffmann.* Vienna: Fassbaender, 1997, pp. 313–347. With libretto.

MENDELSSOHN BARTHOLDY, JAKOB LUDWIG FELIX (1809–1847), German composer, conductor, and pianist. In 1840 Fanny Hensel attempted to persuade her brother Felix to compose a Nibelungen opera. Mendelssohn was very enthusiastic about the idea and corresponded with his sister about it. Together they studied Ernst Raupach's drama *Der Nibelungen-Hort* (The Nibelungen Hoard, 1834). However, because of the dramaturgical difficulties encountered in the attempt to create an appropriate conclusion, as well as the contemporary demonstration of nationalism in connection with the Nibelungen theme, Mendelssohn eventually distanced himself from the project.

[WW]

Bibliography

Breig, Werner and Hartmut Fladt, eds. *Dokumente zur Entstehungsgeschichte des Bühnenfestspiels 'Der Ring des Nibelungen.'* (Richard Wagner, *Sämtliche Werke,* vol. 29,1) Mainz: Schott, 1976, p. 15.

Jost, Christa: "Die *Nibelungen* auf dem Weg zur Oper." In *Nibelungenlied und Klage: Ursprung,* *Funktion, Bedeutung,* edited by Dietz-Rüdiger Moser and Marianne Sammer. Beibände zur Zeitschrift *Literatur in Bayern* 2. Munich: Institut für Bayerische Literaturgeschichte, 1998, pp. 483–497.

OPERA. Both the Nordic and Middle High German Nibelungen traditions played an important role in the development of a national opera following the split from Italian models at the beginning of the nineteenth century. In the course of the disputes regarding the aesthetic concepts of the music drama (see FRIEDRICH THEODOR VISCHER), the possibilities of using the Nibelungen theme for the opera stage were discussed. Composers such as Felix Mendelssohn and Robert Schumann considered setting the plot to music; others, such as Niels Gade, Heinrich Dorn, and Felix Draeseke, produced Nibelungen operas. Another music drama comes in the form of a burlesque Nibelungen operetta by Oscar Straus. On the whole, however, apart from the music dramas of Richard Wagner, none of the Nibelungen operas of the nineteenth century has been able to maintain a place in the repertoire.

[WW]

POTTGIEFOR, KARL, German composer. His *Festspiel* entitled *Das Nibelungenlied (Siegfried von Xanten und Kriemhild)* was unsuccessful; the first and probably only performance was in Cologne in 1892.

[UM]

REINTHALER, KARL (MARTIN) (1822–1896), German composer. Reinthaler, who was a friend of Brahms, composed the opera *Edda,* which was successfully performed in Bremen (February 22, 1875) as well as in some other opera houses. It is no longer known today.

[UM]

RELLSTAB, LUDWIG (1799–1860), pseudonym for Freimund Zuschauer, a Berlin author, music critic, editor of the *Vossische Zeitung* and the music journal *Iris.* Rellstab wrote several libretti for opera. In 1847 he included with a letter to Giacomo Meyerbeer, a French composer of operas, two acts of a script for a Nibelungen opera. The opera was intended to illustrate the effect of the norns and valkyries on the fate of the

Nibelungs. As far as we know, Meyerbeer did not concern himself with the project and Rellstab did not complete the text. The scene alluded to in the letter has been lost.

[WW]

Bibliography

Meyerbeer, Giacomo. *Briefwechsel und Tagebücher,* edited by Heinz and Gudrun Becker, vol. 4: 1846–1849. Berlin: de Gruyter, 1985, pp. 276–277.

REYER, (LOUIS-ETIENNE) ERNEST (1823–1909), French composer and critic. The fifth of his six operas, *Sigurd* (libretto: C. du Locle, A.Blau), is based on the *Nibelungenlied.* It recounts Sigurd's wooing of Brünhild "au lieu de" Gunther. *Sigurd,* composed between 1870 and 1872, is a French Grand Opéra, but it was not until 1884 that it enjoyed a successful premiere at the Théâtre de la Monnaie in Brussels. Like Reyer's last opera, *Salammbo,* (Brussels, 1890), *Sigurd* survived in France and Brussels for several decades. In recent years a complete recording of the opera has been made.

[UM]

Bibliography

Fischer, Jens Malte. "Singende Recken und blitzende Schwerter: Die Mittelalteroper neben und nach Wagner, ein Überblick." In *Mittelalter-Rezeption: Ein Symposion,* edited by Peter Wapnewski. Stuttgart: Metzler, 1986, pp. 519–520.
Kühnel, Jürgen. " 'La tétralogie du pauvre': L'opéra de Ernest Reyer 'Sigurd.' L'épopée allemande comme grande opéra." In *La Lettre et la Figure: La littérature et les arts visuels à l'époque moderne,* edited by Wolfgang Drost and Géraldi Leroy. Heidelberg: Winter, 1989, pp. 89–103.

RUSSELL, ANNA (ANNA CLAUDIA RUSSELL-BROWN) (b. 1911), soprano and musical satirist. She quotes from her "analysis" of Wagner's *Ring,* generally taken as one of her most brilliant spoofs, in the prologue to her autobiography: "Anybody here remember Alberich? . . . And Wotan? . . . Mrs. Wotan? . . . Siegfried and Brünnhilde and my friend Erda? I've made a career doing my version of Wagner's *Ring.* Of course, I *tell* the story of the *Ring* and sing only bits of it, such as the Jo-ho-to-ho bit. While Wagner didn't exactly intend his opera cycle to

be a comedy, I have made a career out of doing just that—finding the comical in serious music."

[PS]

Bibliography

Russell, Anna. *I'm Not Making This Up, You Know: The Autobiography of the Queen of Musical Parody,* edited by Janet Vickers. New York: Continuum, 1985.
[Richard] Wagner–[Anna] Russell. "The Ring of the Nibelungs" On side 1 of *The Anna Russell Album?* Columbia Masterworks MG 31199.

SCHUMANN, ROBERT ALEXANDER (1810–1856), a renowned German composer of the romantic period. His "project journal" indicates that in 1840 Schumann was considering the *Nibelungenlied* as the basis for an opera, but it was an idea that he never realized. Within the context of his Rhine songs, he set Karl Immermann's poem about the Nibelungen hoard to music in 1842. The result was "Auf dem Rhein" in F major (Opus 51, No. 4). The treasure represents in this case a metaphor for those secrets that remain locked in one's heart and which never find overt expression.

[WW]

Bibliography

Jost, Christa. "Die Nibelungen auf dem Weg zur Oper." In *Nibelungenlied und Klage: Ursrung, Funktion, Bedeutung,* edited by Dietz-Rüdiger Moser and Marianne Sammer. Beibände zur Zeitschrift *Literatur in Bayern* 2. Munich: Institut für Bayerische Literaturgeschichte, 1998, pp. 483–497.

STRAUS, OSCAR (1870–1954), Austrian composer. Straus composed the successful operettas *Ein Walzertraum* (A Waltz Dream, 1907), *Der tapfere Soldat* (The Brave Soldier, after G. B. Shaw, 1908; which in the United States became known as "The Chocolate Soldier"), and the score for the film, *La ronde* (after Arthur Schnitzler, 1950). His first success was the "burlesque operetta" *Die lustigen Nibelungen* (The Merry Nibelungs, Vienna, November 12, 1904; libretto by Rideamus [F. Oliven]), a funny and entertaining parody à la Offenbach. The action revolves around Siegfried, Gunther, Kriemhild, and Brunhild, and the work concludes on a happy note. In recent years, the operetta has enjoyed several successful productions.

[UM]

Bibliography

Grun, Bernard. *Prince of Vienna: The Life, Times, and Melodies of Oscar Straus.* London: W. H. Allen, 1955.

Hellmuth, Leopold. "'Die lustigen Nibelungen' in Österreich: Eine Ergänzung zur Geschichte des Nibelungenstoffes." In *Österreich in Geschichte und Literatur* 31 (1987): pp. 275–300.

Klotz, Volker. "Ungebrochen durch vielerlei Brechungen: 'Die lustigen Nibelungen.' Hinweis auf Oscar Straus' Burleske Operette von 1904." In *Mittelalter-Rezeption II*, edited by Jürgen Kühnel et al. Göppingen: Kümmerle, 1982, pp. 661–673.

Straus, Oscar. *Die lustigen Nibelungen.* Kölner Rundfunkchor and Kölner Rundfunkorchester. Chorus led by Helmut Froschauer and Godfried Ritter, orchestra conducted by Siegfried Köhler. Westdeutscher Rundfunk Köln and Capriccio. Compact disk WDR 10 752. Burlesque operetta in three acts by Rideamus.

VATKE, ROLF. German author whose work, *Das Nibelungenlied,* is presented in spoonerisms combining material from both the medieval epic and Wagner's opera.

[SSch]

Bibliography

Vatke, Rolf. *Das Nibelungenlied.* Motive aus Wagners *Ring des Nibelungen,* a musical parody by Funtastex/Jürgen Franke. Narrator: Hanns-Dieter Hüsch. Baden-Baden, 1996. CD with text.

VERDI, GIUSEPPE (1813–1901), greatest musical dramatist of Italian opera. His opera *Attila* (libretto by Temistocle Solera and Francesco Maria Piave; Venice, March 17, 1846) has nothing to do with the Nibelungen legend, but is based on Zacharias Werner's historical play *Attila, König der Hunnen* ("Attila, King of the Huns"). There are at least fourteen more operas that deal with Attila, all of them are completely forgotten today. According to Franz Stieger, these fourteen operas were composed between 1672 and 1895.

[UM]

Bibliography

Stieger, Franz. *Opernlexikon. Teil I: Titelkatalog.* Vol. 5. Tutzing: Schneider, 1975, pp. 120–121.

VISCHER, FRIEDERICH THEODOR (1807–1887), German philosopher, literary critic, dramatist, and satirist. Although a liberal, his approach to the German Middle Ages was rather conservative. In his essay "Vorschlag zu einer Oper" (Proposal for an Opera, 1844), he argued that a heroic opera, not a drama, would be the best medium to use in recreating the *Nibelungenlied,* as it provided the most appropriate forum for expressing the emotions of the heroes. Vischer composed the framework for five acts. The plot begins with the arrival of Gunther and Brunhild in Worms and ends with the death of Kriemhild by the hand of Hildebrand. Vischer anticipated the ideas and concepts of Richard Wagner, including the performance of the work over the space of five evenings. In several articles he also praised the Nibelungen illustrations painted by Schnorr von Carolsfeld as well as other artists in Munich.

[UM/WW]

Bibliography

Vischer, Friederich Theodor. "Vorschlag zu einer Oper." In *Kritische Gesänge,* vol. 2. Tübingen: Fues, 1844, pp. 399–436.

Schulte-Wülwer, Ulrich. *Das Nibelungenlied in der deutschen Kunst des 19. und 20. Jahrhunderts.* Gießen: Anabas, 1979, pp. 108–111.

WAGNER, RICHARD (1813–1883), German poet-composer. Richard Wagner is certainly the most important figure associated with nineteenth-century German opera. He is also the most hotly debated, not only for his music and his poetry, but also for political and ideological reasons. His operas and especially his writings were used, as was the *Nibelungenlied,* for political propaganda, first by the right-wing national movement in Germany, by many Wagnerians of the so-called "Bayreuth Circle," and above all by the National Socialists. The Wagner family (especially Winifred Wagner, the English-born wife of Siegfried Wagner) entertained close connections to Hitler and the ideology he espoused. After the Second World War, Wagner's grandsons, Wieland and Wolfgang, were relatively successful, with the assistance of many scholars and progressive opera producers, in establishing a new and different image of Wagner.

Wagner and his operas have done far more to familiarize modern audiences with the tales surrounding Tannhäuser and Lohengrin, Siegfried and the Nibelungs, Tristan and Isolde, and Parzival than entire generations of philologists with their scholarly publications. Wagner's version of the Nibelungen myth, *Der Ring des Nibelungen* (the first complete performance was given at the Bayreuth Festival in 1876), has proven without a doubt to be the most influential re-creation of this legend in modern times. *The Ring*, or parts of it, are regularly produced at the great and even some ambitious middle-sized opera houses throughout the world. Video and audiocassettes have further helped to bring the work to a wider audience. Some scholars call the *Ring* not only a masterpiece of musical theater, but also one of the great dramatic works of modern literature.

The Ring of the Nibelung is a tetralogy, designated by Wagner as "Ein Bühnenfestspiel für drei Tage und einen Vorabend" (A Stage Festival for Three Days and a Preliminary Evening). Wagner wrote both the libretto and the music to the drama, as was his custom. The opera consisted of: *Das Rheingold, Die Walküre, Siegfried, Götterdämmerung* (Twilight of the Gods). He created a story which symbolizes the cosmic fate of the world and of mankind, beginning with the creation of the world and ending with an inferno of fire and water, but with the promise of a better future. *The Ring* is centered around the story of the god Wotan, his family and descendants (including the valkyrie Brünnhilde and the "Wälsungen" Siegmund, his twin sister, Sieglinde, and their son Siegfried). It relates the ongoing struggle between the gods at Valhalla and the "Nibelungs," a breed of dwarfs living and working deep under the earth, with Alberich as their master. Both sides are dominated by the irreconcilable dichotomy between eros and power politics, between the restless and destructive male principle and the conservative female principle. The symbol of their ambitious fighting to rule the world is a golden ring. Alberich, after having stolen the Rhinegold and renounced love, forges this ring in order to become master of the whole world. However, when he is deceived and robbed

by Wotan and the gods, he curses his lost ring (i.e., the "ring of the Nibelung") and all the future "lords of the ring." By the end of the work, the whole world—gods, Nibelungs, giants, and the human race, all of whom are fighting for power—are witness to a final catastrophe, the end of the Old World of power politics.

In terms of its dramatic construction, the *Ring* was written "retrogressively" (Peter Wapnewski). Wagner began in the autumn of 1848 by sketching and writing out "Siegfried's Tod" (Siegfried's Death). This was a time of violent political and prerevolutionary activity in Dresden, and the text contains clear references to contemporary events. In 1851 and 1852, during his period of exile in Zurich, Wagner expanded the action by adding three further dramas (*Der junge Siegfried, Die Walküre, Das Rheingold*). The complete text was now largely finished, and it was in this form that Wagner had it privately printed in Zurich in a limited edition of fifty copies. Various other changes were made to the text during the following two decades while, it, in part renamed, was being set to music in accordance with the chronological order of the story: *Rheingold*, 1853–1854; *Walküre*, 1854–1856; *Siegfried*, 1856–1857, 1864–1865, and 1869–1871; and *Götterdämmerung*, 1869–1874. *Rheingold* and *Walküre* had their first performances in Munich in 1869 and 1870, respectively. They were commissioned by King Ludwig II, Wagner's royal patron and sponsor. The complete *Ring* cycle had its première at the first Bayreuth Festival in 1876, which had been founded by Wagner to afford the *Ring* the most appropriate staging.

Wagner concentrated from the outset on the lives of Siegfried and Brünnhilde in his treatment of the Nibelung legend, omitting entirely all references to the cycle of legends surrounding Etzel/Attila and the vengeance wrought by Kriemhild/Gudrun. He began by singling out sections of the plot and individual motifs from the *Nibelungenlied* before moving on to the entire Germanic tradition, including the relevant secondary literature of his time. In the course of his research into the available material, it was the Norse tradition, and, in particular, the *Volsunga saga* and the *Edda*, that grew in importance for him. For the Siegfried story Wagner found the essential outline of the plot in the *Nibelungen-lied,* which also provided him with individual scenes such as Siegfried's arrogant arrival at the court in Worms and his challenge to Gunther, his defense of his role as Gunther's "substitute," and his murder while hunting. From the second part of the *Nibelungenlied* came such important ideas as the Danube water sprites and Hagen's nocturnal vigil at the court. Important characters in *Siegfried* and *Götterdämmerung* bear the same names as characters in the first part of the *Nibe-lungenlied,* but a great deal has been changed, most notably the figures of Gunther and Kriemhild (Gutrune in Wagner's *Ring*), and even more, Hagen and Brünnhilde. Much has been omitted, including Siegfried's royal ancestry, his campaign against the Saxons and Danes, his lengthy courtship of Kriemhild, the quarrel between the queens (which Wagner already had used in Lohengrin, Act II), Gunther's brothers and followers, Ute the queen mother, and the whole courtly ambience. In contrast, the story of Siegfried and Brünnhilde, the history and role of the ring, the magic potion that causes amnesia, the sensational scenes at the double wedding, and the whole prehistory and mythological superstructure (with the Rhine maidens, the gods, Nibelungs, giants, and Wotan and his descendants) have either been lifted from the various Norse versions or newly invented by Wagner. In this process a by no means negligible role was played by the myths and dramas of classical Greece, especially by the works of Aeschylus, the influence of which can be seen on Wotan and Fricka in particular. In general, Wagner has used a technique which can be described as "mythic reportage" (Volker Mertens, "Wagner's Middle Ages," *Wagner Handbook* p. 248). Inspired, it would seem, by contemporary philology (including that of Jacob and Wilhelm Grimm, Franz Joseph Mone, Karl Simrock, and Karl Ettmüller), he built up a uniform and coherent story by amending the whole existing Nibelungen tradition. The sources of the *Ring* have, therefore, been neither expanded nor reduced, but rather compiled and concocted from existing material.

Taken as a whole and on their own terms, these medieval sources did not have any clear and comparable message. The Norse cycle of legends is more amorphous in this respect, being dependent at best upon a single principle, which is that of an all-powerful fate and an overriding sense of tragedy. In this regard it is "senseless" in the truest meaning of the word. Much the same may be said of the *Nibelungenlied.* Writers on the subject have yet to agree on a basic interpretation of the work comparable to the relatively unambiguous messages of Wolfram von Eschenbach (*Parzival*) and Gottfried von Straßburg (*Tristan*). Wagner used the medieval sources of the Nibelungen legend to construct a mythical framework, within which he provided the varied and often contradictory elements and individual versions of the tradition with a real degree of coherency and significance, a process that involved incorporating ideas already implicit in these sources, if only in rudimentary form.

The Old Norse sources also inspired Wagner to use alliterative verse in an effort to arrive at a new relationship between language and music. Some verses have "aroused amusement and incomprehension at least from the time of the first public performance," but "by recreating that (Germanic-style) language, Wagner hoped to address a direct emotional appeal to the stultified hearts of his nineteenth-century listeners, and arouse in them a sense of the human emotions which he felt had been destroyed by the corrupting influence of modern civilisation" (Spencer p. 141; for the language of the *Ring,* see also Werner Breig and Peter Branscombe in *Wagner Handbook,* and Panagl 1988).

[UM]

Bibliography

Cord, William O. *The Teutonic Mythology of Richard Wagner's "The Ring of the Nibelung."* 3 vols. London: Mellen, 1989–1991.

Finch, R. G. "The Icelandic and German Sources of Wagner's 'Ring of the Nibelung.'" *Leeds Studies in English,* 1986, pp. 1–23.

Magee, Elizabeth. *Richard Wagner and the Nibelungs.* Oxford: Clarendon Press, 1990.

Millington, Barry, ed. *Wagner Compendium: A Guide to Wagner's Life and Music.* London: Thames and Hudson, 1992.

Müller, Ulrich. "The medieval sources of Wagner's 'Der Ring des Nibelungen.' 1: A documentary study" (in collaboration with Oswald Panagl); "2: A critical commentary with four propositions." *Bayreuther Festspiele 1988, Programmheft II/III*

(Das Rheingold, Die Walküre), pp. 123–151 and 147–168. Also in German and French.

———, and Peter *Wapnewski*, eds. *Wagner Handbook*, translated by John Deathridge. Cambridge: Harvard University Press, 1992.

———, and Ursula Müller, eds. *Richard Wagner und sein Mittelalter.* Anif/Salzburg: Müller-Speiser, 1989, pp. 157–170.

———, and Oswald Panagl et al. *Ring und Gral: Materialien und Beiträge zu Wagners späten Musikdramen.* Würzburg: Königshausen und Neumann, 2002.

Spencer, *Stewart.* "The Language and Sources of 'Der Ring des Nibelungen.'" In *Richard Wagner und sein Mittelalter 1989,* edited by Müller and Müller, pp. 141–155.

Wapnewski, Peter. *Der traurige Gott. Richard Wagner in seinen Helden.* Munich: Beck, 1978.

ZUCCALMAGLIO, ANTON WILHELM FLORENTIN VON (1803–1869) (a.k.a. Wilhelm Vonwaldbruehl, Gottschalk Wedel, Dorfküster Wedel, Schulmeister Wedel, Blum Keulenschwinger, Diamond).

Zuccalmaglio, whose forebears came from Upper Italy, was a talented musician, writer, and artist. He was acquainted with the representatives of Heidelberg romanticism, such as Robert Schumann, Carl Maria von Weber, and Felix Mendelssohn-Bartholdy. He composed many poems, wrote short stories, stage plays, and libretti which were based on medieval themes. In 1837 he wrote an essay entitled "Die deutsche Oper" (The German Opera) in which he made concrete proposals for a stage adaptation of the Nibelungen theme as well as for setting it to music. During a period as resident mentor of the Russian Count Gortschakoff in Warsaw, he authored four libretti for Mozart operas: *Die Entführung aus dem Serail, Idomeneo, Die Zauberflöte,* and *La clemenza di Tito.* The libretti have only survived in manuscript form. Zuccalmalgio wished to adapt Mozart's operas, in a romantic way, to the patriotic spirit that prevailed at the time. He thus composed new plots aimed at underscoring national history and Teutonic values such as duty and noble-mindedness. In 1834 he produced the new libretto to *Die Zauberflöte* under the title *Der Kederich.* It includes the theme of the Crusades, the Loreley saga, the chivalric romance, and also motifs from the Nibelungen tales. In *Der Kederich* one of the tests which the crusader Rudhelm (Tamino from the *Zauberflöte*) must pass in order to win Garlinde (Pamina in the *Zauberflöte*) deals with the Nibelungen treasure that has been sunk in the Rhine. Rudhelm can see the treasure from the top of the cliff, called Kederich, but must temper his greed and by passing this test provides the country with a national model. The protectors of the treasure sing: "Nicht irdischem Dienste frommt des Erbe Teil,/ Dem edlen deutschen Vaterlande nur zum Heil!" Rudhelm resists every temptation and in the end is united with Garlinde. Zuccalmaglio's libretto is one of the many documents testifying to the reception of so-called medieval opera in the nineteenth century, which also included several Nibelungen operas.

[WW]

Bibliography

Feller, Karl *Gustav.* "Mozarts Zauberflöte als Elfenoper." In *Symbolae Historiae Musicae. H. Federhofer zum 60. Geburtstag.* Mainz: Schott, 1971, pp. 229–240.

———. "A. W. *Zuccalmaglios* Bearbeitungen Mozartscher Opern." *Mozart-Jahrbuch* 1976/77 (1978): 21–58.

Fischer, Jens Malte. "Singende Recken und blitzende Schwerter: Die Mittelalteroper neben und nach Wagner, ein Überblick". In *Mittelalter-Rezeption: Ein Symposion,* edited by Peter Wapnewski. Germanistische Symposien Berichtsbände 6. Stuttgart: Metzler, 1986, pp. 511–530.

Jost, Christa. "Die Nibelungen auf dem *Weg* zur Oper." In *Nibelungenlied und Klage:. Ursprung, Funktion, Bedeutung,* edited by Dietz-Rüdiger Moser and Marianne Sammer. Beibände zur *Zeitschrift Literatur in Bayern* 2. Munich: Institut für Bayerische Landesgeschichte, 1988, pp. 483–497.

Zuccalmaglio, Anton Wilhelm Florentin von. *Der Kederich.* Manuscript in the Öffentliche Bibliothek Aachen, Sign. Zucc. I 11c.

PART IX

Art, Artists, Film, Filmmakers, Sculpture, and Sculptors

BALLENBERGER, KARL (1801–1860), German painter, member of the Gesellschaft für Deutsche Altertumskunde von den drei Schilden (see Schwanthaler) in Munich. Using the old Dutch painting style, he copied Nibelungen illustrations from Schnorr von Carolsfeld, Cornelius, and others.

[UM]

Bibliography
Schulte-Wülwer, Ulrich. *Das Nibelungenlied in der deutschen Kunst des 19. und 20. Jahrhunderts.* Gießen: Anabas, 1979, pp. 98–100.

BARLACH, ERNST (1870–1939), expressionist German sculptor and artist. Between 1908 and 1922 Barlach drew and sketched many scenes from the second part of the Nibelungen legend. They became known to a wider public only after being printed in the German Democratic Republic (East Germany) in 1982. Some of his other drawings and sculptures also seem to reflect images from the Nibelungenlied, although they have no explicit Nibelungen titles.

[UM]

Bibliography
Kramer, Günter, trans. *Das Nibelungenlied. Aus dem Mittelhochdeutschen übertragen.* Mit 33 Zeichnungen von Ernst Barlach. With an essay by Elmar Janssen titled "Zu Barlachs Zeichnungen." Berlin: Verlag der Nationen, 1982. Also published in the Federal Republic of Germany: Hanau: W. Dausien, 1983.
Schulte-Wülwer, Ulrich. *Das Nibelungenlied in der deutschen Kunst des 19. und 20. Jahrhunderts.* Gießen: Anabas, 1979, pp. 168, 172.
Storch, Wolfgang, ed. *Die* Nibelungen: *Bilder von Liebe, Verrat und Untergang.* Munich: Prestel, 1987, pp. 7, 89, 98, 226, 226–227, 231, 246–249, 308–309.

BEARDSLEY, AUBREY (1872–1898), probably the most famous illustrator of English art deco. In 1892 and 1893 he produced sketches illustrating Richard Wagner's *Ring des Nibelungen*. His illustrations of Wagner's *Rheingold* were printed in 1896.

[UM]

Bibliography
Storch, Wolfgang, ed. *Die* Nibelungen: *Bilder von Liebe, Verrat und Untergang.* Munich: Prestel, 1987, pp. 115, 128, 130, 182–183, 308.

BECKMANN, MAX (1884–1950), German expressionist painter. One of his paintings from 1933, depicting a naked couple with a sword between them, was originally called *Siegmund und Sieglinde,* characters from Wagner's *Walküre,* but was officially titled *Geschwister* (Brother and Sister). After having read Karl Simrock's translation of the *Nibelungenlied,* he created two drawings based on the epic, *Krimhild* and *Kampf der Königinnen* (The Fight between the Queens) (1949).

[UM]

Bibliography

Kimpel, Harald, and Johanna Werckmeister. "Leidmotive: Möglichkeiten der künstlerischen Nibelungen-Rezeption seit 1945." In *Die Nibelungen: Ein deutscher Wahn, ein deutscher Alptraum. Studien und Dokumente zur Rezeption des Nibelungenstoffs im 19. und 20. Jahrhundert,* edited by Joachim Heinzle and Anneliese Waldschmidt. Frankfurt a. M.: Suhrkamp, 1991, p. 288.

Storch, Wolfgang, ed. *Die Nibelungen: Bilder von Liebe, Verrat und Untergang.* Munich: Prestel, 1987, pp. 262–263, 274–275, 309.

BECKMANN, OTTO (1900–1997), Austrian artist and sculptor who was born in Vladivostok, Russia. He produced several artworks with the Nibelungen theme, a computer graphic that provides an interpretation of the beginning of the *Nibelungenlied* and an *objet trouvé* made out of bones with the title *Klagende Kriemhilde* (A Lamenting Kriemhild).

[UM]

Bibliography

Pausch, Oskar. "Altdeutsche Literatur und bildende Kunst heute: Beispiele zum Nibelungenlied." In *Mittelalter-Rezeption: Ein Symposion,* edited by Peter Wapnewski. Stuttgart: Metzler, 1986, pp. 357, 359.

BINDER-STASSFURTH, BERNHARD and **ELFRIEDE,** German illustrators. They provided the colorful illustrations for East German Franz Fühmann's retelling of the *Nibelungenlied* (1971).

[UM]

Bibliography

Fühmann, Franz. *Das Nibelungenlied, neu erzählt von Franz Fühmann.* Berlin: Neues Leben, 1971.

BOSSARD, JOHANN MICHAEL (1874–1950), German artist. In 1926 Bossard began to build a large *Kunsttempel* (see also FIDUS) in Lüllau near Jesteburg, situated close to Hamburg where he was a professor at the Kunstgewerbeschule (College of Arts and Crafts). The *Kunsttempel* had rooms full of woodcarvings, bronze sculptures, and paintings, among them an *Edda-Saal* (Edda Room) filled with Nibelungen motifs.

[UM]

Bibliography

Storch, Wolfgang, ed. *Die Nibelungen: Bilder von Liebe, Verrat und Untergang.* Munich: Prestel, 1987, pp. 260–262, 309.

BÜHLER, ADOLF (1877–1951), pupil of the German painter Hans Thoma. Between 1906 and 1908 he worked on two Nibelungen paintings. One of them, *Die Nibelungen* (1907/1908), depicts Siegfried, Kriemhild, and Brünhild as nudes in the heroic style.

[UM]

Bibliography

Kastner, Jörg. *Das Nibelungenlied in den Augen der Künstler vom Mittelalter bis zur Gegenwart.* Exhibition catalog. Passau: Passavia Universitätsverlag, 1986, p. 75.

Schulte-Wülwer, Ulrich. *Das Nibelungenlied in der deutschen Kunst des 19. und 20. Jahrhunderts.* Gießen: Anabas, 1979, pp. 176–177.

BÜRCK, PAUL, German artist. In 1942 he produced several Nibelungen frescoes with scenes from the first part of the *Nibelungenlied* for a metalwork business called the Dürener Metallwerke in Berlin. In these frescoes the Nibelungs are glorified as Aryan heroes.

[UM]

Bibliography

Kastner, Jörg. *Das Nibelungenlied in den Augen der Künstler vom Mittelalter bis zur Gegenwart.* Exhibition catalog. Passau: Passavia Universitätsverlag, 1986, p. 175.

Schulte-Wülwer, Ulrich. *Das Nibelungenlied in der deutschen Kunst des 19. und 20. Jahrhunderts.* Gießen: Anabas, 1979, p. 175.

BURKART, ALBERT (1898–1982), German artist. He produced many Christian pieces of art but also created a cyclic fresco now found in the Kriegsschule (War College) at Fürstenfeldbruck that depicts the Nibelungs as Arthurian knights rather than Germanic heroes.

[UM]

Bibliography

Kastner, Jörg. *Das Nibelungenlied in den Augen der Künstler vom Mittelalter bis zur Gegenwart.* Exhibition catalog. Passau: Passavia Universitätsverlag, 1986, pp. 83–84.

CORINTH, LOVIS (1858–1925), German impressionist painter.

Several of his works depict medieval settings and knights in armor. In 1912 he also designed scenery for Wagner's *Rheingold*.

[UM]

Bibliography

Storch, Wolfgang, ed. *Die Nibelungen. Bilder von Liebe, Verrat und Untergang.* Munich: Prestel, 1987, pp. 199, 222–223, 225, 236–237, 256–257, 309.

CORNELIUS, PETER VON (1783–1867), German painter.

After having illustrated Goethe's *Faust* (1808) during his visit to Rome, he produced six drawings on the *Nibelungenlied* (1812), of which engravings were published in 1817. Cornelius also created several Nibelungen sketches and paintings. His illustrations of 1812, which betray a patriotic-romantic style, later influenced many other Nibelungen pictures and were often reprinted. The painter hoped to be commissioned by the Bavarian king Ludwig I to paint the Nibelungen frescos at the royal residence in Munich, but the commission was instead awarded to Schnorr von Carolsfeld.

[UM]

Bibliography

Kastner, Jörg. *Das Nibelungenlied in den Augen der Künstler vom Mittelalter bis zur Gegenwart.* Exhibition catalog. Passau: Passavia Universitätsverlag, 1986, pp. 60–61.
Lankheit, Klaus. "Nibelungen-Illustrationen der Romantik." In *Die Nibelungen: Ein deutscher Wahn, ein deutscher Alptraum. Studien und Dokumente zur Rezeption des Nibelungenstoffs im 19. und 20. Jahrhundert,* edited by Joachim Heinzle and Anneliese Waldschmidt. Frankfurt a. M.: Suhrkamp, 1991, pp. 193–218. First published in 1953; also reprinted in *Die Nibelungen: Bilder von Liebe, Verrat und Untergang,* edited by Wolfgang Storch. Munich: Prestel, 1987, pp. 77–84).
Schulte-Wülwer, Ulrich. *Das Nibelungenlied in der deutschen Kunst des 19. und 20. Jahrhunderts.* Gießen: Anabas, 1979, pp. 30–45, 85–87, 90.

Storch, Wolfgang, ed. *Die Nibelungen: Bilder von Liebe, Verrat und Untergang.* Munich: Prestel, 1987, pp. 145–149.

CZESCHKA, CARL OTTO (1878–1960), commercial artist,

design teacher in Vienna (1902–1907) and Hamburg (1907–1943), a member beginning in 1905 of the *Wiener Werkstätte* (Vienna Workshop), and a first-rate, though somewhat neglected, representative of Art Nouveau. In 1907 Czeschka worked on a project for costumes and stage sets for the production of Hebbel's *Nibelungen* at the Vienna Raimund Theatre. He was able to use this experience and draw upon his earlier interest in depicting knights for the book design and eight double-paged illustrations of *Die Nibelungen* (1909), a work with text by Franz Keim that is part of a book series for youths called *Gerlachs Jugendbücherei*. The illustrations have a strong appeal to the modern eye. Influenced by the Bayeux Tapestry (c. 1077), Czeschka's book inspired costumes, interiors, architecture, and scenes in the Nibelung films by Fritz Lang (1923/1924).

[RK]

Bibliography

Keim, Franz. *Die Nibelungen: Dem deutschen Volke wiedererzählt.* Bilder und Ausstattung von C. O. Czeschka. Gerlachs Jugendbücherei 22. Vienna: Gerlach und Wiedling, [1909].
Die Nibelungen: In der Wiedergabe von Franz Keim. Mit Illustrationen von Carl Otto Czeschka. Vor- und Nachwort von Helmut Brackert. Im Anhang die Nacherzählung *Die Nibelungen* von Gretel und Wolfgang Hecht. Frankfurt: Insel, 1972.
Fanelli, Giovanni. *Carl Otto Czeschka: Dalla secessione viennese all'Art Deco.* Firenze: Cantini, 1989, pp. 18–20.
———. *Wiener Jugendstil: Die Druckgraphik.* Translated by Peter Hahlbrock. Berlin: Propyläen, 1992, pp. 65–66.
Schulte-Wülwer, Ulrich. *Das Nibelungenlied in der deutschen Kunst des 19. und 20. Jahrhunderts.* Gießen: Anabas, 1979, pp. 160–167.
Storch, Wolfgang, ed. *Die Nibelungen. Bilder von Liebe, Verrat und Untergang.* Munich: Prestel, 1987, pp. 4, 117, 212–213, 309.

DES COUDRES, LUDWIG (1820–1878),

German artist, a pupil of Schnorr von Carolsfeld. His series of Nibelungen illustrations done in pencil are now housed in the Kunsthalle Karlsruhe.

[UM]

Bibliography

Kastner, Jörg. *Das Nibelungenlied in den Augen der Künstler vom Mittelalter bis zur Gegenwart.* Exhibition catalog. Passau: Passavia Universitätsverlag, 1986, p. 70.

DOLL, FRANZ, German artist who in 1939 and 1940 created the Gobelin painting *Siegfrieds Tod* (Siegfried's Death), which glorified the death of a hero.

[UM]

Bibliography

Kastner, Jörg. *Das Nibelungenlied in den Augen der Künstler vom Mittelalter bis zur Gegenwart.* Exhibition catalog. Passau: Passavia Universitätsverlag, 1986, p. 82.
Schulte-Wülwer, Ulrich. *Das Nibelungenlied in der deutschen Kunst des 19. und 20. Jahrhunderts.* Gießen: Anabas, 1979, pp. 179.

DÜSSELDORFER MALERSCHULE (Düsseldorf School of Painters), a group of painters active during the 1830s and 1840s, supported by the liberal bourgeoisie in Düsseldorf. Some members, influenced by romanticism and by German painter Peter Cornelius, produced several Nibelungen pictures, especially for inclusion in an illustrated Nibelungen translation by Gotthard Oswald Marbach that was put out by the Leipzig publisher Wigand to celebrate the four hundredth anniversary of book printing (1840). The group included Eduard Bendemann, Alfred Rethel, Julius Hübner, Anton Stilke, Heinrich Mücke, and H. W. A. Dörnberg.

[UM]

Bibliography

Lankheit, Klaus. "Nibelungen-Illustrationen der Romantik." In *Die Nibelungen: Ein deutscher Wahn, ein deutscher Alptraum. Studien und Dokumente zur Rezeption des Nibelungenstoffs im 19. und 20. Jahrhundert,* edited by Joachim Heinzle and Anneliese Waldschmidt. Frankfurt a. M.: Suhrkamp, 1991, pp. 193–218. First published in 1953; also reprinted in *Die Nibelungen: Bilder von Liebe, Verrat und Untergang,* edited by Wolfgang Storch. Munich: Prestel, 1987, pp. 77–84.

Schulte-Wülwer, Ulrich. *Das Nibelungenlied in der deutschen Kunst des 19. und 20. Jahrhunderts.* Gießen: Anabas, 1979, pp. 64–67, 138–144.
Storch, Wolfgang, ed. *Die Nibelungen: Bilder von Liebe, Verrat und Untergang.* Munich: Prestel, 1987, p. 153, 313.

EGGER-LIENZ, ALBIN (1868–1926), Austrian painter who in 1909 and 1910 created the Jugendstil fresco *Der Einzug Etzels in Wien* (Attila's Entry into Vienna) for the city hall in Vienna.

[UM]

Bibliography

Kastner, Jörg. *Das Nibelungenlied in den Augen der Künstler vom Mittelalter bis zur Gegenwart.* Exhibition catalog. Passau: Passavia Universitätsverlag, 1986, pp. 76–77.
Schulte-Wülwer, Ulrich. *Das Nibelungenlied in der deutschen Kunst des 19. und 20. Jahrhunderts.* Gießen: Anabas, 1979, p. 176.
Storch, Wolfgang, ed. *Die Nibelungen. Bilder von Liebe, Verrat und Untergang.* Munich: Prestel, 1987, pp. 210–211, 236.

ENSOR, JAMES (1860–1949), Belgian artist. Two of his paintings depict the "Ride of the Valkyries" (ca. 1888 and 1938, respectively) in an expressionist-fantastic style.

[UM]

Bibliography

Storch, Wolfgang, ed. *Die Nibelungen: Bilder von Liebe, Verrat und Untergang.* Munich: Prestel, 1987, pp. 190, 294, 309.

ERNST, MAX (1891–1976), German surrealist painter. Out of all the artist's works, at least one linocut, titled *Siegfried der Drachentöter* (Siegfried the Dragon-Slayer) from 1912, has an explicitly Nibelungen theme.

[UM]

Bibliography

Storch, Wolfgang, ed. Die *Nibelungen: Bilder von Liebe, Verrat und Untergang.* Munich: Prestel, 1987, pp. 181, 192, 258–259, 266–267, 278, 310.

EWALD, ERNST, German painter. He decorated the new building of the Nationalgalerie in

Berlin with Nibelungen wall paintings that were strongly influenced by Schnorr von Carolsfeld.

[UM]

Bibliography

Schulte-Wülwer, Ulrich. *Das Nibelungenlied in der deutschen Kunst des 19. und 20. Jahrhunderts.* Gießen: Anabas, 1979, pp. 155–156.

FANTIN-LATOUR, HENRI (1836–1904), French painter, especially interested in music and an ardent Wagnerian. He provided many illustrations (lithographs as well as paintings) for Richard Wagner's operas, including the *Ring des Nibelungen* (1876–1888).

[UM]

Bibliography

Storch, Wolfgang, ed. *Die Nibelungen: Bilder von Liebe, Verrat und Untergang.* Munich: Prestel, 1987, pp. 166–170, 310 (there erroneously referred to as Jean Théodore Fantin-Latour, who was his father and also a painter.)

FELLNER, FERDINAND (1799–1859), German artist who produced more than fifty drawings based on the *Nibelungenlied.* He was particularly interested in the second part of the poem. Fellner was a specialist in the history of medieval costumes and arms, and was later used as a source by both Moritz von Schwind and Schnorr von Carolsfeld.

[UM]

Bibliography

Kastner, Jörg. *Das Nibelungenlied in den Augen der Künstler vom Mittelalter bis zur Gegenwart.* Exhibition catalog. Passau: Passavia Universitätsverlag, 1986, p. 64.
Schulte-Wülwer, Ulrich. *Das Nibelungenlied in der deutschen Kunst des 19. und 20. Jahrhunderts.* Gießen: Anabas, 1979, pp. 73–79.

FEUERBACH, ANSELM (1829–1880), one of the leading German painters of the nineteenth century. As a young man he drew two Nibelungen sketches that were both influenced by Peter Cornelius.

[UM]

Bibliography

Kastner, Jörg. *Das Nibelungenlied in den Augen der Künstler vom Mittelalter bis zur Gegenwart.* Ex-

hibition catalog. Passau: Passavia Universitätsverlag, 1986, pp. 70–71.
Storch, Wolfgang, ed. *Die Nibelungen: Bilder von Liebe, Verrat und Untergang.* Munich: Prestel, 1987, p. 151.

FIDUS [pseudonym of **HUGO HÖPPENER**], (1868–1948), German artist, known for his theosophical mysticism. In 1897 he created a sketch for a *Walhall-Panorama,* a round building with a circular canvas.

[UM]

Bibliography

Storch, Wolfgang, ed. *Die Nibelungen: Bilder von Liebe, Verrat und Untergang.* Munich: Prestel, 1987, pp. 88–90, 206–207, 310.
Y [!], Rainer. *Fidus, der Tempelkünstler: Interpretationen im kunsthistorischen Zusammenhang mit Katalog der utopischen Architekturentwürfe.* Göppingen: Kümmerle, 1985.

FOHR, CARL PHILIPP (1795–1818), German artist. While living in Heidelberg and then in Rome, Fohr painted several Nibelungen pictures in a romantic-patriotic style. Among them were sketches for a large, neogothic triptychon (1813–1814; Städtische Galerie Frankfurt a. M.). He had been inspired by the philologist Bernhard Joseph Docen to read the *Nibelungenlied,* as had his friends in Rome, Ludwig Sigismund Ruhl and Wilhelm von Harnier, who also produced several paintings based on Nibelungen themes.

[UM]

Bibliography

Kastner, Jörg. *Das Nibelungenlied in den Augen der Künstler vom Mittelalter bis zur Gegenwart.* Exhibition catalog. Passau: Passavia Universitätsverlag, 1986, pp. 62–63.
Lankheit, Klaus. "Nibelungen-Illustrationen der Romantik." In *Die Nibelungen: Ein deutscher Wahn, ein deutscher Alptraum. Studien und Dokumente zur Rezeption des Nibelungenstoffs im 19. und 20. Jahrhundert,* edited by Joachim Heinzle and Anneliese Waldschmidt. Frankfurt a. M.: Suhrkamp, 1991, pp. 193–218. First published in 1953; also reprinted in *Die Nibelungen: Bilder von Liebe, Verrat und Untergang,* edited

by Wolfgang Storch. Munich: Prestel, 1987, pp. 77–84).

Schulte-Wülwer, Ulrich. *Das Nibelungenlied in der deutschen Kunst des 19. und 20. Jahrhunderts.* Gießen: Anabas, 1979, pp. 52–60, 86.

Storch, Wolfgang, ed. Die *Nibelungen: Bilder von Liebe, Verrat und Untergang.* Munich: Prestel, 1987, p. 150.

FORTUNY Y MADRAZO, MARIANO (1871–1949), Spanish painter of the late nineteenth and early twentieth century. He was a Wagnerian and particularly fascinated with *Parsifal,* even designing Kundry's costume for the Bayreuth Festival in 1911. Two of his paintings completed after 1890 depict Wotan, and another, produced in 1893, takes Siegmund and Sieglinde as its theme.

[UM]

FÜSSLI, JOHANN HEINRICH (1741–1825), Swiss painter, who spent most of his life in England. He became famous for his illustrations for Shakespeare and Milton works and for paintings in a heroic-romantic style. Under the influence of Johann Jacob Bodmer and after having read the edition of the *Nibelungenlied* by Christoph Heinrich Myller (1782), Füssli became the first modern illustrator of the epic. Between 1798 and 1820 he conceived a series of drawings and eight paintings combining classical antiquity and post-Renaissance Mannerism (above all Michelangelo). He also wrote some poems about the Nibelungs; in one of them, "Der Dichter der 'Schwesterrache'" (The Poet of the "Revenge of the Sister," 1795), he praised Siegfried as a "revived, superior Achilles" (". . . in Sivrit ein bessrer Achill/Wieder vom Grabe erstand"). Among his Nibelungen pictures are: *Kriemhild zeigt Hagen das Haupt Gunthers* (Kriemhild shows Hagen the head of Gunther, drawing, 1805; Kunsthaus Zürich); *Brunhild betrachtet den von ihr gefesselt an der Decke aufgehängten Gunther* (Brunhild looks at Gunther whom she has bound and suspended from the ceiling, drawing, 1807; Nottingham Castle Museum), *Kriemhild sieht im Traum den toten Siegfried* (Kriemhild sees the dead Siegfried in her dream, painting, 1805–1810; Kunsthaus Zürich).

[UM]

Bibliography
Lankheit, Klaus. "Nibelungen-Illustrationen der Romantik." In *Die Nibelungen: Ein deutscher Wahn, ein deutscher Alptraum. Studien und Dokumente zur Rezeption des Nibelungenstoffs im 19. und 20. Jahrhundert,* edited by Joachim Heinzle and Anneliese Waldschmidt. Frankfurt a. M.: Suhrkamp, 1991, pp. 193–218. First publication 1953; also reprinted in *Die Nibelungen: Bilder von Liebe, Verrat und Untergang,* edited by Wolfgang Storch. Munich: Prestel, 1987, pp. 77–84.

Schulte-Wülwer, Ulrich. *Das Nibelungenlied in der deutschen Kunst des 19. und 20. Jahrhunderts.* Gießen: Anabas, 1979, pp. 12–16.

Storch, Wolfgang, ed. *Die Nibelungen: Bilder von Liebe, Verrat und Untergang.* Munich: Prestel, 1987, pp. 124–139. Includes all of Füssli's Nibelungen paintings.

GANGLOFF, KARL (1790–1814), German painter who was inspired by Ludwig Uhland to conceive a plan for a series of *Nibelungenlied* illustrations. However, his early death prevented him from completing the series, and he in fact only completed a single drawing in 1812. The drawing was published in 1821 together with a sonnet by Uhland titled "Auf Karl Gangloffs Tod" (On the Death of Karl Gangloff). A lithograph of the drawing was produced by Ernst Fries.

[UM]

Bibliography
Kastner, Jörg. *Das Nibelungenlied in den Augen der Künstler vom Mittelalter bis zur Gegenwart.* Exhibition catalog. Passau: Passavia Universitätsverlag, 1986, p. 61.

Schulte-Wülwer, Ulrich. *Das Nibelungenlied in der deutschen Kunst des 19. und 20. Jahrhunderts.* Gießen: Anabas, 1979, pp. 46–49.

GOJOWCZYK, HUBERTUS (b. 1943) Silesian-born artist. He created a "Buch-Objekt" (book object) in 1970 that consists of a *Nibelungenlied* edition, the middle section of which is cut away.

[UM]

Bibliography
Schulte-Wülwer, Ulrich. *Das Nibelungenlied in der deutschen Kunst des 19. und 20. Jahrhunderts.* Gießen: Anabas, 1979, pp. 8–9.

GROSS, HANS, German artist. He created a series of woodcuts with Nibelungen scenes about 1920. In 1939 he used them as the basis for fifteen large paintings that glorified heroism and "*deutsche Treue bis zum Untergang*" (German loyalty to the very end).

[UM]

Bibliography

Schulte-Wülwer, Ulrich. *Das Nibelungenlied in der deutschen Kunst des 19. und 20. Jahrhunderts.* Gießen: Anabas, 1979, pp. 179–182.

GROSZ, GEORGE (1893–1959), German-American expressionist and satirical painter. He designed a front page for the satirical magazine *Die Pleite* (November 1923), depicting Hitler as Siegfried.

[UM]

Bibliography

Storch, Wolfgang, ed. *Die Nibelungen: Bilder von Liebe, Verrat und Untergang.* Munich: Prestel, 1987, pp. 90, 254, 271, 311.

GRÜTZKE, JOHANNES (b. 1939), German artist who painted two Nibelungen pictures in 1984, *Siegfrieds Tod* (Siegfried's Death) and *Wie Hildebrandt und Kriemhilde* (Just like Hildebrand and Kriemhild), the latter of which depicts the beheading of a woman by a naked man.

[UM]

Bibliography

Storch, Wolfgang, ed. *Die Nibelungen: Bilder von Liebe, Verrat und Untergang.* Munich: Prestel, 1987, pp. 284–285, 311.

HAHN, HERMANN (1868–1942), German sculptor. He created a heroic sculpture of Siegfried for a Bismarck monument near Bingerbrück (Rhineland). The monument was never completed.

[UM]

Bibliography

Kastner, Jörg. *Das Nibelungenlied in den Augen der Künstler vom Mittelalter bis zur Gegenwart.* Exhibition catalog. Passau: Passavia Universitätsverlag, 1986, pp. 88–89.

Storch, Wolfgang, ed. *Die Nibelungen: Bilder von Liebe, Verrat und Untergang.* Munich: Prestel, 1987, pp. 94, 165, 225, 270, 311.

Wappenschmidt, Heinz-Toni. "Nibelungenlied und Historienmalerei im 19. Jahrhundert." In *Die Nibelungen: Ein deutscher Wahn, ein deutscher Alptraum. Studien und Dokumente zur Rezeption des Nibelungenstoffs im 19. und 20. Jahrhundert,* edited by Joachim Heinzle and Anneliese Waldschmidt. Frankfurt a. M.: Suhrkamp, 1991, pp. 219–250; 252.

HANSEN-BAHIA, KARL-HEINZ, German-Brazilian artist. In 1963 he produced a series of satirical woodcuts titled *Tittmoninger Nibelungenlied* (Tittmoning *Nibelungenlied*). Tittmoning is a small town in Bavaria.

[UM]

Bibliography

Kimpel, Harald, and Johanna Werckmeister. "Leidmotive: Möglichkeiten der künstlerischen Nibelungen-Rezeption seit 1945." In *Die Nibelungen: Ein deutscher Wahn, ein deutscher Alptraum. Studien und Dokumente zur Rezeption des Nibelungenstoffs im 19. und 20. Jahrhundert,* edited by Joachim Heinzle and Anneliese Waldschmidt. Frankfurt a. M.: Suhrkamp, 1991, p. 288.

HARBOU, THEA VON (1888–1954), German writer of light literature and film scripts. Her second marriage was to the Austrian-born writer and director Fritz Lang. Harbou wrote the scripts for the films that Lang made between 1920 and 1932, some of which were based on her own novels. The most significant and successful films on which they worked include *Dr. Mabuse* (1921/1922), *Metropolis* (1925/1926), as well as *Die Nibelungen* (1922/1924). When Fritz Lang emigrated to America in 1933, Harbou remained in Germany and became one of the film stars of the Third Reich. After the war she wrote a series of scripts for popular films, including *Dr. Holl.*

[WW]

Bibliography

Kleiner, Reinhold. *Thea von Harbou und der deutsche Film bis 1933.* 2nd ed. Studien zur Filmgeschichte, vol. 2. Hildesheim: Olms, 1991.

HARNIER, WILHELM VON, German artist. After his visit to Rome with his friends Carl Philipp Fohr and Ludwig Sigismund Ruhl, Harnier, while studying law at Göttingen, produced the drawing *Siegfried auf der Jagd* (Siegfried on a Hunt, 1818; Hessisches Landesmuseum Darmstadt). The romantic style evident in the work clearly displays the influence of Peter von Cornelius.

[UM]

Bibliography

Schulte-Wülwer, Ulrich. *Das Nibelungenlied in der deutschen Kunst des 19. und 20. Jahrhunderts.* Gießen: Anabas, 1979, pp. 61–64, 87.

HARRACH, GRAF FERDINAND VON (1832–1915), German painter. After returning from the Franco-Prussian War (1870/1871), he decorated his newly purchased residence, Tiefhartsmanndorf in Silesia, with Nibelungen frescoes.

[UM]

Bibliography

Schulte-Wülwer, Ulrich. *Das Nibelungenlied in der deutschen Kunst des 19. und 20. Jahrhunderts.* Gießen: Anabas, 1979, pp. 155, 222 (35).

HARTMETZ, RAINER (1925–1981), a German artist who created a series of thirty-two drawings depicting the reception of the Nibelungs in the nineteenth and twentieth centuries. His realistic images expose the ideological character of much of that reception, including the manner in which Nibelung themes and motifs were used for political purposes. Particularly poignant are those drawings that portray the consequences of glorifying battle and death during both world wars. In each instance he juxtaposes for ironic effect a stanza from the epic with a scene depicting the brutal reality of total annihilation.

[WW]

Bibliography

Hartmetz, Rainer. *Die Nibelungen: Eine neue Folge kritischer Zeichnungen.* An exhibition catalog. Hanover: Wilhelm-Busch-Museum, 1975.

Kimpel, Harald, and Johanna Werckmeister. "Leidmotive: Möglichkeiten der künstlerischen Nibelungen-Rezeption seit 1945." In *Die Nibelungen: Ein deutscher Wahn, ein deutscher Alptraum. Studien und Dokumente zur Rezeption des Nibelungenstoffs im 19. und 20. Jahrhundert,* edited by Joachim Heinzle and Anneliese Waldschmidt. Frankfurt a. M.: Suhrkamp, 1991, pp. 288–289.

Pausch, Oskar. "Altdeutsche Literatur und bildende Kunst heute: Beispiele zum Nibelungenlied." In *Mittelalter-Rezeption: Ein Symposion,* edited by Peter Wapnewski. Stuttgart: Metzler, 1986, pp. 356–358.

HEGENBARTH, JOSEF (1884–1962), German painter and illustrator. In 1922 he painted twenty-five watercolors illustrating the *Nibelungenlied* and the "most terrible events" portrayed therein. In the same year he also published twenty-three engravings of the *Nibelungenlied.*

[UM]

Bibliography

Hegenbarth, Josef. *23 Originalradierungen zum Nibelungenlied.* Mit einführenden Worten von Oskar Bie. Dresden: Ernst Arnold, 1922.

Kastner, Jörg. *Das Nibelungenlied in den Augen der Künstler vom Mittelalter bis zur Gegenwart.* Exhibition catalog. Passau: Passavia Universitätsverlag, 1986, pp. 78–79.

Storch, Wolfgang, ed. *Die Nibelungen: Bilder von Liebe, Verrat und Untergang.* Munich: Prestel, 1987, 244–245, 311.

HEINE, THOMAS THEODOR (1867–1948), German painter, illustrator, and caricaturist (especially for the weekly *Simplicissimus*). In 1920 he painted Siegfried as a small bulldog sitting on a chair.

[UM]

Bibliography

Storch, Wolfgang, ed. *Die Nibelungen: Bilder von Liebe, Verrat und Untergang.* Munich: Prestel, 1987, pp. 254, 311.

HIRT, JOHANNES (1859–1907), German sculptor. A wealthy businessman in Worms, Cornelius W. Freiherr Heyl zu Herrnsheim (see also Schmoll von Eisenwerth), commissioned a Nibelungen monument from Hirt in 1905. It depicts Hagen throwing the Nibelungen treasure into the Rhine. The monument is still standing today. Hirt was strongly influenced by Schnorr von Carolsfeld.

[UM]

Bibliography

Wappenschmidt, Heinz-Toni. "Nibelungenlied und Historienmalerei im 19. Jahrhundert." In *Die Ni-*

belungen: Ein deutscher Wahn, ein deutscher Alptraum. Studien und Dokumente zur Rezeption des Nibelungenstoffs im 19. und 20. Jahrhundert, edited by Joachim Heinzle and Anneliese Waldschmidt. Frankfurt a. M.: Suhrkamp, 1991, pp. 219–250; 252.

HÖFER, WERNER (b.1941), Austrian architect. Receiving his inspiration from medieval maps, Höfer designed the color print *Begegnung Kriemhilds mit Etzel* (Kriemhild meets Etzel) in 1981. The print was conceived as a prototype for a tapestry that his wife later made.

[UM]

Bibliography

Pausch, Oskar. "Altdeutsche Literatur und bildende Kunst heute: Beispiele zum Nibelungenlied." In *Mittelalter-Rezeption: Ein Symposon,* edited by Peter Wapnewski. Stuttgart: Metzler, 1986, pp. 359, 361.

HOLLEMANN, BERNHARD (b. 1935), Austrian artist who produced a series of thirty drawings in the early 1980s dealing with the Nibelungen theme. Twenty of them are variations on Siegfried's death, six depict the scene with Hagen and the mermaids, and four have as subject matter Gunther's struggle with Brünhild on his wedding night. Some of them are included in the booklet that accompanies Eberhard Kummer's 1983 recording of the *Nibelungenlied.*

[UM]

Bibliography

Pausch, Oskar. "Altdeutsche Literatur und bildende Kunst heute: Beispiele zum Nibelungenlied." In *Mittelalter-Rezeption: Ein Symposon,* edited by Peter Wapnewski. Stuttgart: Metzler, 1986, pp. 361–363.

———. "Bernhard Hollemann 'bezeichnet' mittelhochdeutsche Texte." In the booklet accompanying the record of the *Nibelungenlied* by Eberhard Kummer (1983).

HOLZBAUER, SIEGFRIED (b. 1955), Austrian artist. His work *daz nibelungenlied* is intended to illustrate significant sections of the text by using colored squares which, in an abstract manner, symbolize the interrelationships of the figures in the epic and certain plot structures. The project is to be completed by 2002 and can be

viewed on the Internet as a work in progress at www.nibelungen.com.

[MS]

HOVEN, ADRIAN. (1922–1981) Director of the pornographic film *Siegfried und das sagenhafte Liebesleben der Nibelungen* (Siegfried and the fabulous love life of the Nibelungs), made in West Germany in 1970. Hoven's film contains most elements of the first part of the *Nibelungenlied,* but he has introduced as many bed scenes as possible into the story and has populated the castles with dozens of scantily clad and naked women. Despite such liberties taken with the plot, the main problems of the story are dealt with in a convincing way, especially the quarrel of the two queens and its consequences. Some elements are taken from earlier films on the theme, including the dark-haired and one-eyed Hagen, the blond Siegfried and Kriemhild, and the dark-haired Brunhild. A new addition in this work is the happy ending, in which Kriemhild prevents Hagen in the last minute from killing Siegfried and she persuades Siegfried to refrain from revenge.

[NV]

HRDLICKA, ALFRED (b. 1928), Austrian painter and sculptor. Inspired by Johann Heinrich Füssli, Hrdlicka produced five Nibelungen prints as part of a series titled *Blake & Füssli* in 1983. One year later he portrayed Richard Wagner as Wotan in a piece called *Wotan Wagner, der Wanderer* (Wotan Wagner, the Wanderer). He also "merged" Wagner with the Austrian poet Adalbert Stifter (1805–1868) in another piece in 1985.

[UM]

Bibliography

Hrdlicka, Alfred. *Alfred Hrdlicka: Adalbert Stifter/ Richard Wagner, Richard Stifter/Adalbert Wagner. Reaktionär und Revolutionär,* edited by Ernst Hilger. Vienna: Edition E. Hilger, 1985.

Pausch, Oskar. "Altdeutsche Literatur und bildende Kunst heute: Beispiele zum Nibelungenlied." In *Mittelalter-Rezeption:Ein Symposon,* edited by Peter Wapnewski. Stuttgart: Metzler, 1986, pp. 362, 364.

Storch, Wolfgang, ed. *Die Nibelungen: Bilder von Liebe, Verrat und Untergang.* Munich: Prestel, 1987, pp. 280, 311.

JOSEPHSON, ERNST (1851–1906), Swedish artist. Two of his approximately two thousand drawings depict the Germanic god Odin (1890–1900).

[UM]

Bibliography

Storch, Wolfgang, ed. *Die Nibelungen: Bilder von Liebe, Verrat und Untergang.* Munich: Prestel, 1987, pp. 191, 312.

KIEFER, ANSELM (b. 1945), German painter. He produced large paintings of lofts and landscapes between 1973 and 1975 that were intended to focus on the connection between Germanic myths, Wagner and Wagnerianism, and modern German history.

[UM]

Bibliography

Kimpel, Harald, and Johanna Werckmeister. "Leidmotive: Möglichkeiten der künstlerischen Nibelungen-Rezeption seit 1945." In *Die Nibelungen: Ein deutscher Wahn, ein deutscher Alptraum. Studien und Dokumente zur Rezeption des Nibelungenstoffs im 19. und 20. Jahrhundert,* edited by Joachim Heinzle and Anneliese Waldschmidt. Frankfurt a. M.: Suhrkamp, 1991, pp. 295–300.

Storch, Wolfgang, ed. *Die Nibelungen: Bilder von Liebe, Verrat und Untergang.* Munich: Prestel, 1987, pp. 7, 298–303, 312.

KIENHOLZ, EDWARD (1927–1994), American sculptor. He created nineteen installations between 1976 and 1977 using music from Wagner, old radios of the Third Reich called *Volksempfänger* (People's Radios), and garbage. Some of the installations were given Nibelungen names, such as *Brünnhilde, Die Nornen* (The Fates), *Notung, Die Rheintöchter* (The Rhine Maidens) to present his belief that the Nibelungs, Wagner, and National Socialism are closely interrelated.

[UM]

Bibliography

Kimpel, Harald, and Werckmeister, Johanna. "Leidmotive: Möglichkeiten der künstlerischen Nibelungen-Rezeption seit 1945." In *Die Nibelungen: Ein deutscher Wahn, ein deutscher Alptraum. Studien und Dokumente zur Rezeption des Nibelungenstoffs im 19. und 20. Jahrhundert,* edited by Joachim Heinzle and Anneliese Waldschmidt.

Frankfurt a. M.: Suhrkamp, 1991, pp. 292–296.

Storch, Wolfgang, ed. *Die Nibelungen: Bilder von Liebe, Verrat und Untergang.* Munich: Prestel, 1987, pp. 282–283, 312.

KIRCHBACH, FRANK (1859–1912), German painter. Together with Ferdinand Wagner he decorated the "Nibelungenzimmer" at Schloß Drachenburg. The neogothic Drachenburg, situated on the Rhine near Königswinter, was commissioned by a wealthy businessman named Stephan Sarter (1833–1902); Kirchbach's frescoes, which betray the influence of Schnorr von Carolsfeld, became well known, but Sarter, forced by economic problems to go to France, never had the opportunity to live in his neoromantic castle.

[UM]

Bibliography

Kastner, Jörg. *Das Nibelungenlied in den Augen der Künstler vom Mittelalter bis zur Gegenwart.* Exhibition catalog. Passau: Passavia Universitätsverlag, 1986, pp. 72–73.

Schulte-Wülwer, Ulrich. *Das Nibelungenlied in der deutschen Kunst des 19. und 20. Jahrhunderts.* Gießen: Anabas, 1979, pp. 158–160.

Wappenschmidt, Heinz-Toni. "Nibelungenlied und Historienmalerei im 19. Jahrhundert." In *Die Nibelungen: Ein deutscher Wahn, ein deutscher Alptraum. Studien und Dokumente zur Rezeption des Nibelungenstoffs im 19. und 20. Jahrhundert,* edited by Joachim Heinzle and Anneliese Waldschmidt. Frankfurt a. M.: Suhrkamp, 1991, pp. 219–250; 227–238.

KLEE, PAUL (1879–1940), Swiss artist and painter. One of his last sketches, which dates from 1940, depicts a "Walküre," apparently inspired by Wagner.

[UM]

Bibliography

Storch, Wolfgang, ed. *Die Nibelungen: Bilder von Liebe, Verrat und Untergang.* Munich: Prestel, 1987, pp. 274, 294, 312.

KOLBE, CARL WILHELM, DER JÜNGERE (1781–1853), German painter. Kolbe, the most important *Historienmaler* in nineteenth-century Berlin, created Nibelungen paintings for chambers in the Marmorpalais, a palace built in Potsdam after 1845 for the Prussian king Friedrich Wilhelm IV. The pictures were completed by Ossowsky and Lampeck. Kolbe's conception was explicitly influenced by Schnorr von Carolsfeld's Nibelungen illustrations.

[UM]

Bibliography

Schulte-Wülwer, Ulrich. *Das Nibelungenlied in der deutschen Kunst des 19. und 20. Jahrhunderts.* Gießen: Anabas, 1979, pp. 111–122.

LANG, FRITZ (1890–1976), Austrian-born film director, active in both Germany and the United States. Lang was one of the leading film directors in Germany during the twenties and the early thirties. His most important movies from that period are *Dr. Mabuse, der Spieler* (1922), *Die Nibelungen* (1924), *Metropolis* (1927), *M— Eine Stadt sucht einen Mörder* (1931), and *Das Testament des Dr. Mabuse* (1933). After immigrating to the United States, Lang went to Hollywood where he directed many pictures, including *Fury* (1936), *The Return of Frank James,* (1940), *Manhunt,* (1941), *Hangmen also die,* (1943), and *Human Desire,* (1954). "It wasn't his fascination with the psychopathology of violence, but the fascinating visual means he chose to express it that made him one of the creative giants in the history of both German and American cinema" (Katz). *Die Nibelungen*—in two parts: "I. Siegfried" and "II. Kriemhilds Rache" (Kriemhild's Revenge)—is based primarily on the medieval *Nibelungenlied* but was also influenced by Wagner. The film is impressive owing to its imaginative scenery, as well as the highly stylized settings and costumes. Lang, who produced the film together with his wife, Thea von Harbou, stated that they intended to depict Germany's legendary past at a time of pressing political problems. Later there were several adaptations of Lang's *Nibelungen,* without the filmmaker's authorization, and soundtracks were added. In the 1980s the original version was restored under the direction of Enno Patalas at the Munich Filmmuseum, using the original orchestral music composed by Gottfried Huppertz. An unimpressive remake of Lang's classical film was directed by Harald Reinl (*Die Nibelungen: I. Siegfried von Xanten, II. Kriemhilds Rache*) in Germany in 1966. It transformed the legend and Lang's black-and-white original into a colorful and sometimes unintentionally ridiculous adventure movie.

[UM]

Bibliography

Armour, Robert A. *Fritz Lang.* Boston: Twayne, 1988.

Bogdanovich, Peter. *Fritz Lang in America.* London: Studio Vista, Praeger, 1967/1969.

Eisner, Lotte H. *Fritz Lang.* London: Secker and Warburg, 1976.

Harbou, Thea von. *Das Nibelungenbuch. Munich: Drei Masken Verlag, 1923.*

Heller, Heinz-B. " 'Man stellt Denkmäler nicht auf den flachen Asphalt.' Fritz Langs 'Nibelungen'- Film." In Die Nibelungen: Ein deutscher Wahn, ein deutscher Alptraum. Studien und Dokumente zur Rezeption des Nibelungenstoffs im 19. und 20. Jahrhundert, edited by Joachim Heinzle and Anneliese Waldschmidt. Frankfurt a. M.: Suhrkamp, 1991, pp. 351–369.

Humphries, Reynold. *Fritz Lang: Genre and Representation in His American Films.* Baltimore: Johns Hopkins University Press, 1982.

Jenkins, Stephen, ed. *Fritz Lang: The Image and the Look.* London: British Film Institute, 1981.

Kanzog, Klaus. "Der Weg der Nibelungen ins Kino: Fritz Langs Film-Alternative zu Hebbel und Wagner." In *Wege des Mythos in der Moderne: Richard Wagner "Der Ring des Nibelungen,"* edited by Dieter Borchmeyer. Munich: dtv, 1987, pp. 202–223.

Kaplan, Elizabeth Ann. *Fritz Lang: A Guide to Reference and Resources.* Boston: Hall, 1981.

Kracauer, Siegfried. *From Caligari to Hitler.* Princeton: Princeton University Press, 1947.

Müller, Ulrich. "'Das geistige Heiligtum einer Nation': Die 'grand opera cinematographique' über die Nibelungen von Fritz Lang und Thea von Harbou (1924)." In *Alban Bergs "Wozzeck" und die Zwanziger Jahre,* edited by Peter Csobadi et al. Anif/Salzburg: Müller-Speiser, 1999, pp. 645–657.

Ott, Frederick W. *The Films of Fritz Lang.* Secaucus: Citadel Press, 1979.

Storch, Wolfgang, ed. *Die Nibelungen: Bilder von Liebe, Verrat und Untergang.* Munich: Prestel, 1987.

LAUFFER, EMIL JOHANN (1837–1909), German artist who concentrated on historical themes. In 1879 he completed a monumental painting for the Rudolphinum (a neo-

Renaissance building erected in 1876 as a museum and parliament; since 1946 it is a concert hall) in Prague: *Kriemhilds Klage an der Bahre Siegfrieds* (Kriemhild's Lament at the Bier of Siegfried), in which a parallel was suggested between Siegfried and Christ.

[UM]

Bibliography

Kastner, Jörg. *Das Nibelungenlied in den Augen der Künstler vom Mittelalter bis zur Gegenwart.* Exhibition catalog. Passau: Passavia Universitätsverlag, 1986, p. 72.

Schulte-Wülwer, Ulrich. *Das Nibelungenlied in der deutschen Kunst des 19. und 20. Jahrhunderts.* Gießen: Anabas, 1979, pp. 153–154.

LEHMBRUCK, WILHELM (1881–1919), German sculptor. One of his earlier works is a heroic sculpture entitled *Siegfried* (1902).

[UM]

Bibliography

Storch, Wolfgang, ed. *Die Nibelungen: Bilder von Liebe, Verrat und Untergang.* Munich: Prestel, 1987, pp. 232–235, 238, 312.

LUCAS, AUGUST (1803–1863), German artist. Along with his friend Carl Sandhaas, he created several illustrations of the *Nibelungenlied* in Darmstadt around 1820.

[UM]

Bibliography

Schulte-Wülwer, Ulrich. *Das Nibelungenlied in der deutschen Kunst des 19. und 20. Jahrhunderts.* Gießen: Anabas, 1979, pp. 68, 72.

MAISON, RUDOLF (1854–1904), German sculptor. Working with images from Richard Wagner's opera *Rheingold,* he created a model of a "Rheingold" fountain for the city of Aachen around the year 1895 that glorified Emperor Wilhelm I as Siegfried. He did not, however, receive the commission to actually do the fountain. Instead, he used his prototype for two smaller Nibelungen sculptures that he completed in 1897.

[UM]

Bibliography

Schulte-Wülwer, Ulrich. *Das Nibelungenlied in der deutschen Kunst des 19. und 20. Jahrhunderts.* Gießen: Anabas, 1979, p. 154.

Storch, Wolfgang, ed. *Die Nibelungen: Bilder von Liebe, Verrat und Untergang.* Munich: Prestel, 1987, pp. 200–201, 234–235, 312.

MAKART, HANS (1840–1884), the most influential Austrian painter of the Viennese *belle époque.* In 1883 he created eight large paintings illustrating scenes from Wagner's *Ring des Nibelungen.* Makart used the same theme for a fresco ceiling in Vienna between 1870 and 1872.

[UM]

Bibliography

Storch, Wolfgang, ed. *Die Nibelungen: Bilder von Liebe, Verrat und Untergang.* Munich: Prestel, 1987, pp. 174–177, 312–313.

METZNER, FRANZ (1870–1919), German sculptor, and professor of art in Berlin. He conceived Nibelungen monuments and sculptures. His most famous piece is the Völkerschlachtdenkmal (monument for the battle of the nations) near Leipzig.

[UM]

Bibliography

Kastner, Jörg. *Das Nibelungenlied in den Augen der Künstler vom Mittelalter bis zur Gegenwart.* Exhibition catalog. Passau: Passavia Universitätsverlag, 1986, pp. 87–88.

Storch, Wolfgang, ed. *Die Nibelungen: Bilder von Liebe, Verrat und Untergang.* Munich: Prestel, 1987, pp. 31, 209, 218, 269, 313.

Wappenschmidt, Heinz-Toni. "Nibelungenlied und Historienmalerei im 19. Jahrhundert." In *Die Nibelungen: Ein deutscher Wahn, ein deutscher Alptraum. Studien und Dokumente zur Rezeption des Nibelungenstoffs im 19. und 20. Jahrhundert,* edited by Joachim Heinzle and Anneliese Waldschmidt. Frankfurt a. M.: Suhrkamp, 1991, pp. 219–250; 252.

MÜNCHEN (MUNICH) EXHIBITION. By far the largest exhibition dealing with the medieval and modern reception of the Nibelungen legend was conceived and organized by Wolfgang Storch for the Haus der Kunst (House of Art, formerly House of German Art) in Munich (December 5, 1987–February 14, 1988). The catalog from the exhibit contains the most comprehensive listing of Nibelungen paintings, graphics, and sculptures ever published. Much smaller Nibelungen exhibitions were organized at Hohenems in 1979, Passau in 1986, and Pöchlarn in 1996. For Munich's Nibelungen tradition of the nineteenth century, see BALLEN-BERGER, NEUSCHWANSTEIN, SCHNORR VON CAROLSFELD, and SCHWANTHALER.

[UM]

Bibliography

Ausstellung zur Erinnerung an die Auffindung der Handschrift A des Nibelungenlieds im Jahre 1779 im Palast zu Hohenems. Bregenz: Vorarlberger Landesmuseum, 1979.

Kastner, Jörg, ed. *Das Nibelungenlied in den Augen der Künstler vom Mittelalter bis zur Gegenwart.* Exhibition catalog. Passau, 1986.

Storch, Wolfgang, ed. *Die Nibelungen: Bilder von Liebe, Verrat und Untergang.* Munich: Prestel, 1987.

NETZER, HUBERT (1865–1939), German sculptor. He created a war memorial for the city of Duisburg depicting Siegfried as a "symbol of German heroism," a description Netzer himself gave in a letter to a well-known colleague, Wilhelm Lehmbruck, dated March 19, 1919.

[UM]

Bibliography

Storch, Wolfgang, ed. Die *Nibelungen: Bilder von Liebe, Verrat und Untergang.* Munich: Prestel, 1987, pp. 238, 313.

NEUBER, FRITZ (1857–1889), German artist. The Hamburg businessman Paul P. H. von Schiller commissioned Neuber in 1870 to create a wooden frieze in his Buckhagen mansion (Schleswig). The wooden Nibelungen reliefs inspired by Wilhelm Jordan's epic, *The Nibelunge,* depict various Nibelungs as members of the Schiller family.

[UM]

Bibliography

Schulte-Wülwer, Ulrich. *Das Nibelungenlied in der deutschen Kunst des 19. und 20. Jahrhunderts.* Gießen: Anabas, 1979, pp. 157, 159, 222–223 (42).

NEUSCHWANSTEIN, the neogothic "Grail Castle" of the Bavarian King Ludwig II (d. 1886) near Füssen. The castle was built between 1869 and 1890 and evinces influences of the Wart-burg which was restored and partly reconstructed in a Romantic way between 1838 and 1890. Its construction was overshadowed both by the king's health problems and by financial difficulties. The "Magic Castle," as it is now known, is today visited every year by thousands. It is full of frescoes with medieval themes. The design of the paintings in the castle was conceived by the philologist, historian, and writer Hyacinth Holland. Most of them have to do with Richard Wagner's operas, but there are also twenty-two Nibelungen frescoes painted by Wilhelm Hauschild, Joseph Munsch, Ferdinand von Piloty, and Karl Schultheiß between 1882 and 1884. They do not depict the Nibelungen legend according to the Middle High German *Nibelungenlied* or Wagner's *Ring des Nibelungen,* but rather follow the Nordic tradition of the Eddic ballads. Frescoes that illustrated scenes from Wagner's *Ring* were commissioned by Ludwig II for the *Nibelungengang* of the Residenz in Munich and were painted by Michael Echter (1864–1865) in close cooperation with Wagner.

[UM]

Bibliography

Mück, Hans Dieter. "Das historische Mittelalterbild Ludwigs II: Die Entwicklung Neuschwansteins von der Burg Lohengrins und Tannhäusers zum Gralstempel Parzivals." In *Mittelalter-Rezeption II,* edited by Jürgen Kühnel et al. Göppingen: Kümmerle, 1982, pp. 195–246.

Schulte-Wülwer, Ulrich. *Das Nibelungenlied in der deutschen Kunst des 19. und 20. Jahrhunderts.* Gießen: Anabas, 1979, pp. 146–147.

NIGHT OF THE GENERALS, THE (film). See KIRST, HANS HELLMUT IN PART VI.

RACKHAM, ARTHUR (1867–1939). Rackham, a successful English illustrator, produced illustrations for *Grimm's Fairy Tales, Peter Pan, Gulliver's Travels, A Midsummer Night's Dream,* and other books. His illustrations to accompany Wagner's *Ring des Nibelungen* (1911–1912, Heinemann, London) were well known and had an influence on the Nibelungen films of Austrian-born filmmaker Fritz Lang.

[UM]

Bibliography
Storch, Wolfgang, ed. *Die Nibelungen: Bilder von Liebe, Verrat und Untergang*. Munich: Prestel, 1987, pp. 197, 313.

RAHL, KARL (1812–1865), Austrian artist who, in 1835 and 1836, produced three colorful Nibelungen paintings in oil.

[UM]

Bibliography
Kastner, Jörg. *Das Nibelungenlied in den Augen der Künstler vom Mittelalter bis zur Gegenwart*. Exhibition catalog. Passau: Passavia Universitätsverlag, 1986, p. 68.

RAMBERG, JOHANN HEINRICH, German artist. When he was sixty years old (ca. 1820), he painted a caricature of students from Göttingen as the Nibelungs (*Niebelungs Naturen d'après nature*).

[UM]

Bibliography
Schulte-Wülwer, Ulrich. *Das Nibelungenlied in der deutschen Kunst des 19. und 20. Jahrhunderts*. Gießen: Anabas, 1979, pp. 66–67.

REDON, ODILON (pseudonym for Berbard-Jean Redon, 1840–1916), French avantgarde painter. Among his *peinture wagnériennes* are three pictures of Brünnhilde—two lithographic "portraits" of Brünnhilde from 1886 and 1894 respectively, and a pastel from about 1905 called *Brünnhilde Riding.*

[UM]

Bibliography
Storch, Wolfgang, ed. *Die Nibelungen: Bilder von Liebe, Verrat und Untergang*. Munich: Prestel, 1987, pp. 188–189, 313.

REINL, HARALD. See LANG, FRITZ.

RETHEL, ALFRED (1816–1859), German artist and draftsman. In addition to his woodcuts for a danse macabre and his frescoes for the Aachen town hall, he was well known for his illustrations in the modern German deluxe edition of the *Nibelungenlied,* published by Gotthard Oswald Marbach in the year 1840.

[WW]

Bibliography
Marbach, Gotthard Oswald, trans. *Das Nibelungenlied.* With woodcuts based on original sketches by Alfred Rethel et al. Leipzig: Wigand, 1840.

RICHTER, TRUDE, German illustrator, especially of children's books. In 1960, together with Felix Richter, she published *Das Nibelungenlied . . . Respektlos betrachtet* (The Song of the Nibelungs . . . viewed disrespectfully). It is a humorously written and illustrated rendition of the *Nibelungenlied* with legal comments on the story from the perspective of the German Criminal Code of the 1960s. The work sought to replace "Pathos durch Humor und nationalistische Begeisterung durch nüchterne Betrachtung"; (pathos with humor and nationalistic enthusiasm with sober examination).

[MH]

Bibliography
Richter, Trude and Felix. Das *Nibelungenlied . . . Respektlos betrachtet.* Munich: Münchner Buchverlag, 1960.

ROME, GERMAN PAINTERS IN. During the first three decades of the nineteenth century, several German and Austrian artists and painters were living and working in Rome, among them a group of artists called Nazarener (Nazarenes). Ludwig Tieck, who was studying in 1805 at the Vatican Library, inspired several painters to read the *Nibelungenlied.* Some of them produced paintings and drawings of the Nibelungen legend in a romantic-patriotic style, including Joseph Anton Koch, Carl Philipp Fohr, Ludwig Sigismund Ruhl, Wilhelm von Harnier, Karl Schuhmacher, and Peter Cornelius. Cornelius, who was the most influential of the group, was also one of the founders of the Lukasbrüder, an artistic group whose name was later changed to Die Nazarener. During the second decade of the nineteenth century, Friedrich Heinrich von der Hagen, Friedrich Rückert, and the historian J. F. Böhmer, all of them studying in libraries in Rome, also exercised some influence on these Nibelungen painters.

[UM]

Bibliography
Schulte-Wülwer, Ulrich. *Das Nibelungenlied in der deutschen Kunst des 19. und 20. Jahrhunderts.* Gießen: Anabas, 1979, pp. 83–89.

ROPS, FELICIEN (1833–1898), French painter. His watercolor *L'Attrapade* (The Quarrel) could very well represent Kriemhild and Brünhild in a modern setting.

[UM]

Bibliography
Storch, Wolfgang, ed. *Die Nibelungen: Bilder von Liebe, Verrat und Untergang.* Munich: Prestel, 1987, pp. 196, 313.

ROTHAUG, ALEXANDER (1870–1946), Austrian artist. His painting, "Der grimmige Hagen," dates from the second decade of the twentieth century.

[UM]

Bibliography
Storch, Wolfgang, ed. *Die Nibelungen: Bilder von Liebe, Verrat und Untergang.* Munich: Prestel, 1987, pp. 211, 313.

RUHL, LUDWIG SIGISMUND, German artist. In 1816 the young German painter created a series of nineteen drawings based on the Nordic *Wilkina-* and *Niflunga-Saga,* of which only four have survived (Museum der Bildenden Künste, Leipzig). Like his friends, Carl Philipp Fohr and Wilhelm von Harnier in Rome, Ruhl had been inspired by Bernhard Joseph Docen to read the *Nibelungenlied.*

[UM]

Bibliography
Schulte-Wülwer, Ulrich. *Das Nibelungenlied in der deutschen Kunst des 19. und 20. Jahrhunderts.* Gießen: Anabas, 1979, pp. 60–61, 86.

RYDER, ALBERT PINKHAM (1847–1917), American romantic and visionary painter. His painting *Siegfried and the Rhine Maidens,* created after a performance of Wagner's *Götterdämmerung* in New York in 1888 and 1889, was acquired by the National Gallery in Washington, D.C. To purchase the painting, the museum had to pay the highest price ever asked for an American painting at the time.

[UM]

Bibliography
Storch, Wolfgang, ed. *Die Nibelungen: Bilder von Liebe, Verrat und Untergang.* Munich: Prestel, 1987, pp. 171, 313.

SALOMÉ (b. 1954), German-born painter who moved to New York in 1982. Inspired by a performance of Wagner's *Götterdämmerung* at the Metropolitan Opera in New York, he created nine large pieces called "Wagner paintings." These works consisted of a series of approximately 150 drawings and several installations between 1984 and 1987 that tried to illustrate Wagner's version of the Nibelungen legend in a very personal way.

[UM]

Bibliography
Kastner, Jörg. *Das Nibelungenlied in den Augen der Künstler vom Mittelalter bis zur Gegenwart.* Exhibition catalog. Passau: Passavia Universitätsverlag, 1986, pp. 85–86.
Kimpel, Harald, and Johanna Werckmeister. "Leidmotive: Möglichkeiten der künstlerischen Nibelungen-Rezeption seit 1945." In *Die Nibelungen: Ein deutscher Wahn, ein deutscher Alptraum. Studien und Dokumente zur Rezeption des Nibelungenstoffs im 19. und 20. Jahrhundert,* edited by Joachim Heinzle and Anneliese Waldschmidt. Frankfurt a. M.: Suhrkamp, 1991, pp. 300–304.
Storch, Wolfgang, ed. *Die Nibelungen: Bilder von Liebe, Verrat und Untergang.* Munich: Prestel, 1987, pp. 286–287, 313.

SANDHAAS, CARL (1801–1859), German artist and friend of artist August Lucas. About 1824, together with Lucas he produced some illustrations in Darmstadt of the *Nibelungenlied.*

[UM]

Bibliography
Schulte-Wülwer, Ulrich. *Das Nibelungenlied in der deutschen Kunst des 19. und 20. Jahrhunderts.* Gießen: Anabas, 1979, pp. 68–70.

SATTLER, JOSEF (1867–1931), German artist. He created Jugendstil illustrations for a folio edition of the *Nibelungenlied* (manuscript **A**), published between 1898 and 1904 by the Reichsdruckerei (Imperial Printing Office) Berlin for the World Exhibition in Paris.

[UM]

Bibliography

Schulte-Wülwer, Ulrich. *Das Nibelungenlied in der deutschen Kunst des 19. und 20. Jahrhunderts.* Gießen: Anabas, 1979, pp. 160–163.

SCHLEEF, EINAR (b. 1944), German artist and director, asks the question "Was gehen uns die Nibelungen an?" (Of what concern are the Nibelungs to us?) in a modern painting produced for the Munich exhibition titled "Die Nibelungen" (1987). Schleef responds to his own question with a poem that alludes to the myth of nationality, chauvinistic aggression, and nationalist and racist ideology, all of which have led to catastrophe in German history. He provides a laconic answer: the heroes are finished.

[WW]

Bibliography

Storch, Wolfgang, ed. *Die Nibelungen: Bilder von Liebe, Verrat und Untergang.* Munich: Prestel, 1987, p. 113.

SCHMOLL VON EISENWERTH, KARL (1879–1948), Austrian painter. Cornelius W. Freiherr Heyl zu Herrnsheim, a wealthy businessman living in Worms who commissioned several Nibelungen works of art (see Hirt, Johannes) and played an important role in promoting the Nibelungen renaissance in the Rhineland, engaged the architect Theodor Fischer to construct a large building with a Festsaal (banquet- or ballroom) for the Worms Rathaus called the Cornelianum between 1905 and 1910. The building was decorated with sculptures by Georg Wrba of Munich (1872–1939), who had been a professor in Dresden since 1907. A Siegfried-Brunnen (Siegfried fountain) constituted part of the project. It was created in 1905 by Adolf von Hildebrand (also from Munich) but was not erected in front of the Cornelianum until 1921. Theodor Fischer asked painter and designer Schmoll von Eisenwerth, who had been Fischer's colleague at the Technische Hochschule Stuttgart since 1907, to decorate the Festsaal with monumental frescoes of the *Nibelungenlied.* Schmoll von Eisenwerth conceived the paintings in 1910

and completed them between 1912 and 1915. These Jugendstil frescoes depict heroic scenes but are also overshadowed by a feeling of impending catastrophe. The Festsaal and the frescoes were destroyed in World War II, but some of the original large drafts and multicolored photographs survived. During World War I Schmoll von Eisenwerth used his frescoes as the basis for gloomy, heroic illustrations of the *Nibelungenlied* that were printed in a soldiers' newspaper in October 1917.

[UM]

Bibliography

Kastner, Jörg. *Das Nibelungenlied in den Augen der Künstler vom Mittelalter bis zur Gegenwart.* Exhibition catalog. Passau: Passavia Universitätsverlag, 1986, pp. 97–99.

Schmoll, J. A. (called Eisenwerth). "Der Wormser Nibelungen-Wandbildzyklus von Karl Schmoll von Eisenwerth." In *Die Nibelungen: Ein deutscher Wahn, ein deutscher Alptraum. Studien und Dokumente zur Rezeption des Nibelungenstoffs im 19. und 20. Jahrhundert,* ed. Joachim Heinzle and Anneliese Waldschmidt. Frankfurt a. M.: Suhrkamp, 1991, pp. 251–283.

Storch, Wolfgang, ed. *Die Nibelungen: Bilder von Liebe, Verrat und Untergang.* Munich: Prestel, 1987, pp. 82, 125, 214–222, 314.

SCHNORR VON CAROLSFELD, JULIAN (1794–1872), one of the most important German painters of the nineteenth century. Between 1827 and 1867, together with many collaborators, he designed and created the Nibelungen frescoes for the Royal Residenz in Munich, a project that was intended to demonstrate royal power and historical tradition. Schnorr was living in Rome, a member of the artists' group called Die Nazarener, when he received this commission from the Bavarian king Ludwig I. For the five royal chambers he designed a theatrical Nibelungen theme, dominated by historical scenes of dubious accuracy. The Nibelungen frescoes became a nuisance for Schnorr, due to his commitments to other projects and to the problems encountered when he lost sight in his left eye. Although Schnorr's *Historienmalerei* (historical painting) was not appreciated by most experts, the frescoes did exert some influence on other Nibelungen paintings, including those by Carl Wilhelm Kolbe, and they were also used for illustrating popular editions of the *Nibelungenlied* from 1843 and 1852. Schnorr von Carolsfeld used many sketches in the preparation of the frescoes, as well as other Nibelungen drawings and paintings.

[UM]

Bibliography

Kastner, Jörg. *Das Nibelungenlied in den Augen der Künstler vom Mittelalter bis zur Gegenwart.* Exhibition catalog. Passau: Passavia Universitätsverlag, 1986, pp. 65–67.

Nowald, Inken. *Die Nibelungenfresken von Julius Schnorr von Carolsfeld im Königsbau der Münchener Residenz. 1827–1867.* Diss., Heidelberg, 1975, Kiel: Kunsthalle, 1978.

Schulte-Wülwer, Ulrich. *Das Nibelungenlied in der deutschen Kunst des 19. und 20. Jahrhunderts.* Gießen: Anabas, 1979, pp. 90–111.

Storch, Wolfgang, ed. *Die Nibelungen: Bilder von Liebe, Verrat und Untergang.* Munich: Prestel, 1987, pp. 154–159.

Wappenschmidt, Heinz-Toni. "Nibelungenlied und Historienmalerei im 19. Jahrhundert." In *Die Nibelungen: Ein deutscher Wahn, ein deutscher Alptraum. Studien und Dokumente zur Rezeption des Nibelungenstoffs im 19. und 20. Jahrhundert,* edited by Joachim Heinzle and Anneliese Waldschmidt. Frankfurt a. M.: Suhrkamp, 1991, pp. 219–250.

SCHUMACHER, CARL GEORG CHRISTIAN (1797–1869), German painter who produced several Nibelungen illustrations, among them the painting *Siegfrieds Abschied von Kriemhilde* (Siegfried's Departure from Kriemhild), completed in Rome about 1822 to 1823.

[UM]

Bibliography

Kastner, Jörg. *Das Nibelungenlied in den Augen der Künstler vom Mittelalter bis zur Gegenwart.* Exhibition catalog. Passau: Passavia Universitätsverlag, 1986, p. 63.

SCHWANTHALER, LUDWIG (1802–1848), German sculptor. In Munich, as a member of the Gesellschaft für Deutsche Altertumskunde von den drei Schilden (Society for German Classical Studies of the Three Shields, founded 1831), Schwanthaler developed a special interest in medieval chivalry. From 1842 to 1843 he produced a silver centerpiece for the wedding festivities of the Bavarian crown prince with scenes from the Nibelungen and Dietrich legends. The matching porcelain plates, made at the Royal Nymphenburger Manufaktur, also had scenes from the *Nibelungenlied* that were copied from Schnorr von Carolsfeld's frescoes.

[UM]

Bibliography

Schulte-Wülwer, Ulrich. *Das Nibelungenlied in der deutschen Kunst des 19. und 20. Jahrhunderts.* Gießen: Anabas, 1979, pp. 98–104.

SCHWEGERLE, HANS (1882–1950), German artist. In 1933 he produced a heroic sculpture of Wotan.

[UM]

Bibliography

Storch, Wolfgang, ed. *Die Nibelungen: Bilder von Liebe, Verrat und Untergang.* Munich: Prestel, 1987, pp. 105, 314.

SINDING, STEPHAN (1846–1922), Danish sculptor. He produced several sculptures of a riding Valkyrie (1902–1910) and of an embracing couple (*Sigmund and Sieglinde,* ca. 1910; *Siegfried and Brunhilde,* 1906–1914). Replicas cast in marble, terracotta, or bronze were manufactured in Berlin by his gallery, Keller and Reiner, and by the factory Aktiengesellschaft Vermals H. Gladenbeck und Söhn.

[UM]

Bibliography

Storch, Wolfgang, ed. *Die Nibelungen: Bilder von Liebe, Verrat und Untergang.* Munich: Prestel, 1987, pp. 194–195, 314–315.

SLEVOGT, MAX (1868–1932), German designer and impressionist painter. Popular and prolific illustrator of works by Rilke, Goethe, Grimm, Musäus, James Fenimore Cooper, and others. He was particularly renowned for his lithographs. Slevogt was extremely interested in operas, especially those by Mozart and Wagner. He produced several Nibelungen paintings, some illustrating the *Nibelungenlied* and some drawings, wood cuttings, and wall-paintings of Wagner's *Ring des Nibelungen* in his home at Neukastel.

[UM]

Bibliography
Blinn, Hans. *Max Slevogt und seine Wandmalereien.* Landau i. d. Pfalz: Verlag Pfälzer Kunst, Dr. Hans Blinn, [1983].
Guse, Ernst-Gerhard, Hans-Jürgen Imiela, Berthold Roland, eds. *Max Slevogt: Gemälde, Aquarelle, Zeichnungen.* Stuttgart: G. Hatje, [1992].
Schulte-Wülwer, Ulrich. *Das Nibelungenlied in der deutschen Kunst des 19. und 20. Jahrhunderts.* Gießen: Anabas, 1979, pp. 168, 171.
Slevogt, Max. *Die Nibelungen. 7 Holzschnitte für die Verbindung zur Förderung deutscher Kunst, vormals Verbindung für Historische Kunst.* Charlottenburg: Panphesse, [1925].
Storch, Wolfgang, ed. *Die Nibelungen. Bilder von Liebe, Verrat und Untergang.* Munich: Prestel, 1987 [Exhibition: Haus der Kunst, Munich, 1986–1987], pp. 7, 240–243, 315.

STAEGER, FERDINAND, German painter. During World War II he produced Nibelungen paintings that glorified heroic fighting and death.
[UM]

Bibliography
Schulte-Wülwer, Ulrich. *Das Nibelungenlied in der deutschen Kunst des 19. und 20. Jahrhunderts.* Gießen: Anabas, 1979, pp. 176–179.

STASSEN, FRANZ, German artist who painted a number of illustrations based on Wagner's operas and the Nibelungen legend. Hitler also engaged Stassen to design large tapestries with heroic-monumental scenes from the Edda for the New Reich Chancellery in Berlin.
[UM]

Bibliography
Kastner, Jörg. *Das Nibelungenlied in den Augen der Künstler vom Mittelalter bis zur Gegenwart.* Exhibition catalog. Passau: Passavia Universitätsverlag, 1986.
Schulte-Wülwer, Ulrich. *Das Nibelungenlied in der deutschen Kunst des 19. und 20. Jahrhunderts.* Gießen: Anabas, 1979, p. 175.

STUCK, FRANZ VON (1863–1928), German painter. Among his mainly allegorical and symbolic illustrations there is an impressive painting of the final Nibelungen catastrophe, *Der Nibelunge Not* (ca. 1920).
[UM]

Bibliography
Kastner, Jörg. *Das Nibelungenlied in den Augen der Künstler vom Mittelalter bis zur Gegenwart.* Exhibition catalog. Passau: Passavia Universitätsverlag, 1986, pp. 77–78.
Schulte-Wülwer, Ulrich. *Das Nibelungenlied in der deutschen Kunst des 19. und 20. Jahrhunderts.* Gießen: Anabas, 1979, pp. 168–169.
Storch, Wolfgang, ed. *Die Nibelungen: Bilder von Liebe, Verrat und Untergang.* Munich: Prestel, 1987, pp. 228–229, 239, 315.

TÀPIES, ANTONI (b. 1923), Spanish Catalan painter, draftsman, printer, and sculptor. Probably inspired by Wagner's *Ring des Nibelungen,* Tàpies created two paintings in 1950, *L'escamoteix de Wotan* (The trick to make Wodan disappear), and *El dolor de Brunhilda* (The sorrow of Brünnhilde), the scenic backdrop for which is painted mostly in red.
[UM]

Bibliography
Storch, Wolfgang, ed. *Die Nibelungen: Bilder von Liebe, Verrat und Untergang.* Munich: Prestel, 1987, pp. 278–279, 315.

THOMA, HANS (1839–1924), probably the most popular German painter of his time. There are many Wagner illustrations among his approximately nine hundred drawings and paintings, most of them taken from the *Ring des Nibelungen.* Five Nibelungen paintings (1876–1880) were commissioned by Otto Eisner of Frankfurt and five Nibelungen frescoes (as well as some others based on *Tannhäuser* and *Parsifal*) were created as decoration for the staircase in Frankfurt architect Simon Ravenstein's mansion (1884). Thoma used himself as the model for the god Wotan in several pictures (1876–1916), and he was also asked by Cosima Wagner to design costumes for the *Ring* at the Bayreuth Festival.
[UM]

Bibliography
Kastner, Jörg. *Das Nibelungenlied in den Augen der Künstler vom Mittelalter bis zur Gegenwart.* Exhibition catalog. Passau: Passavia Universitätsverlag, 1986, pp. 73–74.
Schulte-Wülwer, Ulrich. *Das Nibelungenlied in der deutschen Kunst des 19. und 20. Jahrhunderts.* Gießen: Anabas, 1979, pp. 147–150.

Storch, Wolfgang, ed. *Die Nibelungen: Bilder von Liebe, Verrat und Untergang.* Munich: Prestel, 1987, pp. 7, 87, 178–179, 203–205, 292, 315.

TIECK, FRIEDRICH (1776–1851), German sculptor. In 1809 he designed for his sick brother, the romantic poet Ludwig Tieck, sixty-two playing cards displaying heroes from the Arthurian legends, the Nibelungs, the Amelungs, and the Charlemagne tradition. More than ten years later they were published by Friedrich Heinrich von der Hagen (1821–1823). The pictures, fashioned in a theatrical style, became the object of considerable ridicule, and their detractors included the Grimm brothers.

[UM]

Bibliography
Schulte-Wülwer, Ulrich. *Das Nibelungenlied in der deutschen Kunst des 19. und 20. Jahrhunderts.* Gießen: Anabas, 1979, pp. 20–24.

TRILLHAASE, ADALBERT (1858–1936), German artist. He painted a farcical version of *Siegfrieds Tod* (before 1925).

[UM]

Bibliography
Storch, Wolfgang, ed. *Die Nibelungen: Bilder von Liebe, Verrat und Untergang.* Munich: Prestel, 1987, pp. 255, 315.

WAGNER, FERDINAND (1847–1927), German *Historienmaler.* Not only did he, together with Frank Kirchbach, decorate the Nibelungenzimmer (Nibelungen room) at Schloß Drachenburg on the Rhine, he also produced monumental paintings, including two between 1888 and 1894 for a room in the Passau city hall (Große Rathaussaal) that depicted scenes from the *Nibelungenlied: Einzug Chriemhilts an der Seite ihres Oheims, des Bischof Pilgrin* (Entrance of Kriemhild at the side of her uncle, Bishop Pilgrin) and *Donaunixen prophezeien Hagen den Untergang im Hunnenland* (Danubian water sprites prophesy to Hagen the catastrophe in the land of the Huns).

[UM]

Bibliography
Wappenschmidt, Heinz-Toni. "Nibelungenlied und Historienmalerei im 19. Jahrhundert." In *Die Nibelungen: Ein deutscher Wahn, ein deutscher Alptraum,* edited by Joachim Heinzle and Anneliese Waldschmidt. Frankfurt a. M.: Suhrkamp, 1991, 219–250; 239–244.

WARTBURG. The Wartburg castle near Eisenach (Thuringia), residence of the Landgraves of Thuringia since the thirteenth century, has no apparent connection with the Nibelungen legend. It was the site of the legendary Sängerkrieg auf der Wartburg (Song contest on the Wartburg). It was also here that Martin Luther wrote his German translation of the Bible, and in 1817 progressive professors and students met at the Wartburg to call for freedom and the unity of the German people. In 1847 Grand Duke Carl Alexander von Sachsen-Weimar commissioned the restoration of the castle, which was supervised by architect Hugo von Ritgen of Darmstadt. Plans for Moritz von Schwind's Nibelungen frescoes could not be realized during the restoration, but Ritgen arranged for other Nibelungen decorations to be provided, including thematic paintings by Rudolf Hofmann and images of legendary German heroes on the column capitals.

[UM]

Bibliography
Schulte-Wülwer, Ulrich. *Das Nibelungenlied in der deutschen Kunst des 19. und 20. Jahrhunderts.* Gießen: Anabas, 1979, pp. 122–128.

WRUBEL, MICHAIL (1856–1901), Russian artist. He painted a portrait of Princess Marjia Tenischewa in 1899, depicting her as a Wagnerian Valkyrie.

[UM]

Bibliography
Storch, Wolfgang, ed. *Die Nibelungen: Bilder von Liebe, Verrat und Untergang.* Munich: Prestel, 1987, pp. 75, 315.

PART X

Miscellaneous: Historians, Clerics, Politics, the Military, Propaganda, Psychology, Education, Iconography, and Geography

CALLIMACHUS EXPERIENS, the nom de plume of Filippo Buonoccorsi (1437–1496). Forced to flee from Venice for political reasons, he traveled all over Europe, ending up in the service of the king of Poland. In 1486 he wrote an account of the life of Attila, hoping thereby to encourage an alliance between Austria, Poland, and Venice against Hungary. This account tells how Attila, on his way to attack Gaul, took away both the life and the army of Gundicarius, king of the Burgundians.

[JVM]

CARLYLE, THOMAS (1795–1881), the Scottish writer Thomas Carlyle is remembered for his vivid accounts of historical events (e.g., "The French Revolution," 1837), his powerful commentaries on contemporary issues ("Chartism," 1839; "Past and Present," 1843) and his prolific collections of letters. His *History of Frederick the Great* (1858–1865) occupied him for a decade and a half and reflects his lifelong association with Germany and in particular with German literature. His *Life of Schiller* (1823–1824) and his translations of Goethe's *Wilhelm Meister* (1824–1827) are early evidence of this, but his essays and lectures on a wide variety of subjects demonstrate the breadth of his interest, and his knowledge of early German literature. His essay on the *Nibelungenlied* appeared in the *Westmin-ster Review* in 1831. Its occasion was the appearance in 1827 of Karl Simrock's translation, but Carlyle uses the opportunity for a wide-ranging assessment of the poem, its origins, and its qualities. He includes substantial extracts in his own reasonably faithful, if mannered, translation. The whole essay is inevitably very much a product of its day, but it contains some astute observations on the nature of the work, and it provides a unique insight into Britain's acquaintance with early German literature in the first half of the nineteenth century. Almost contemporary with it are Carlyle's "Early German Literature" and his "Historic Survey of German Poetry." His more widely known, very long lecture, "On Heroes, Hero-Worship and the Heroic in History," appeared in 1841.

[MEG]

Bibliography

Carlyle, Thomas. *Critical and Miscellaneous Essays, collected and republished.* London: Chapman and Hall 1888.

———. *On Heroes, Hero-Worship and the Heroic in History.* London: Chapman, 1872.

COMPACT DISCS—GERMANY. For a number of years the production of CDs in Germany and Austria that recreate such Middle High German epics and romances as the *Nibelungenlied,*

Parzival, and *Tristan* has proven quite popular. The state-run broadcasting companies have taken the lead in this regard. The German medievalist Peter Wapnewski has introduced and interpreted the romances of Wolfram von Eschenbach and Gottfried von Strassburg, as well as the *Nibelungenlied.* Franz Fühmann's version of the *Nibelungenlied* is read by the actor Peter Fitz (b. 1931). The Austrian author Michael Köhlmeier known for his retelling of classical legends, was less successful in his endeavor to reproduce the *Nibelungenlied* as oral performance. Rolf Vatke (born 1922), a medical doctor and also an expert in "Schüttelreime" (humorous poems that interchange rhyming syllables), produced a successful rendition of the *Nibelungenlied* in this genre which was effectively presented on a CD by the songwriter and singer Hanns-Dieter Hüsch. The Viennese musician and singer Eberhard Kummer, produced a CD using the medieval *Hildebrandston,* which contained five *âventiuren* of the *Nibelungenlied,* five stanzas from the poetry of Der von Kürenberg, and a so-called elegy by Walther von der Vogelweide.

[UM]

Bibliography

Die Nibelungen. Narrated by Michael Kühlmeier. ORF Edition Radio Literatur, 1998. Compact disc.

Fühmann, Franz. *Das Nibelungenlied.* Narrated by Peter Fitz. Deutsche Grammophon, 1993. Compact disc.

Hanns-Dieter Hüsch spricht: Das Nibelungenlied. Aus dem Sagenhorn geschütte(l)t von Rolf Vatke. Merkton, 1996.

Kummer, Eberhard. *Das Nibelungenlied, Kürenberger, Walther von der Vogelweide im "Hildebrandston."* Preisser Records, 1999.

Wapnewski, Peter. *Nibelungenlied.* DerHörVerlag, 1996. Compact disc.

DER LINDELBRUNNEN DER GEMEINDE MOSSAUTAL. Not far from Grasellenbach on the Nibelungen- und Siegfriedstraße (Bundesstraße 460) near Hüttental, about 25 kilometers east of Heppenheim, is the "Lindelbrunnen," a spring also associated with Siegfried. A plaque states that, according to tradition, Siegfried was slain there. In many tales about the spring a knight was supposed to have been killed there by his own gang of robbers. The knight had "charmed" himself with fat and had only one spot on his back without fat since he could not reach it, a scenario reminiscent of that of Siegfried and the dragon's blood (see also ODENHEIM).

[SMJ]

Bibliography

Huber, Werner. *Auf der Suche nach den Nibelungen. Städte und Stätten, die der Dichter des Nibelungenliedes beschrieb.* With photographs by Michael Gööck. Gütersloh: Präsentverlag, 1981, pp. 40–41.

DOLCHSTOSSLEGENDE ("Stab-in-the-back-theory"). *Dolchstoß* was the term used by many Germans after World War I to explain how Germany had lost the war. The origins of this interpretation are to be found in comments on the armistice by Erich von Ludendorff (1865–1937), chief of the German General Staff. He declared that the army, still undefeated, had been "stabbed in the back" by traitors at home, a sentiment that was echoed on December 17, 1918, by the *Neue Zürcher Zeitung.* The German expression is derived from the French "coup de poignard dans le dos," to be found in political statements made after the French capitulation in the Franco-Prussian War of 1870–1871. Both Adolf Hitler in *Mein Kampf* (1925) and the former general and Reich president Paul von Hindenburg in his political testament compared the German army to Siegfried, who like the frontline soldier had fallen victim to a treacherous blow from behind.

[WW]

Bibliography

Endres, Fritz, ed. *Paul von Hindenburg: Briefe, Reden, Berichte.* Munich: Langewiesche-Brandt, 1934, p. 188.

Hitler, Adolf. *Mein Kampf.* Munich: Eher, 1925, p. 707.

Münkler, Herfried, and Wolfgang Storch. *Siegfrieden: Politik mit einem deutschen Mythos.* Berlin: Rotbuch, 1988, pp. 86–94.

FAEROE ISLANDS, a group of eighteen islands with an impressive number of cliffs enclosed by Scotland, Iceland, and Norway. An autonomous part of Denmark since 1948, they are inhabited today by approximately 50,000 people who enjoy the same high standard of living as the rest of the Scandinavians. An unbroken tradition of ballad singing and dancing rooted in the late Middle Ages and still vividly alive makes these islands of special interest to literary scholars as well as musicians. The lyrics of some 250 ballads have been recorded here since the eighteenth century and the melodies have come down to us orally. The ballads, partly Faeroese and partly Danish, have various contents: history, heroic legends, love, magic, social criticism and medieval motifs. Ballads dealing with Sigurd and the Nibelungs, Charlemagne and Roland, Dietrich von Bern, and with Tristan exist in popular tradition even into the present. The Faeroese ballads were kept alive by the geographical isolation of the islands and through the ballads' important function in saving the identity of the small Faeroese people during the Danish occupation (i.e., since the Reformation). The texts of comparable ballads exist in Norway, Iceland, and Denmark, but the original manuscripts of such ballads have vanished along with the tunes. Three Nibelung dance ballads have survived on the Faeroes Islands: *Sjurð-ar kvaeð-i* (*Regin smið-ur*), *Brynhildar táttur,* and *Høgna táttur.* The ballads recount the Nibelungen legend according to the Norse tradition, beginning with Sjurð-a's (Sigurd's) youth and ending with the disaster at Artala's (Atli's) court. The performance of all three ballads takes approximately three hours. During the performance men and women alternately play the role of lead singers and dancers, and others join them. They perform in a huge circle, utilizing the same basic steps: two steps to the left, one to the right. The circle dance continues for hours without major changes in pace, only expression. This kind of "square dancing" presumably originated in medieval France, spread over all of Europe, but survived only in marginal regions. Outside of the Germanic language family, for example, it is known only in the Balkans or in Greece.

[UM/AE]

Bibliography
Djurhuss, N., and Matras C., eds. *Føroya kvaeði. Corpus Carminum Faeroensium.* 6 vols. Copenhagen: Munksgaard and Akademisk forlag, 1941–1972.

Lockwood, W. N. *Die Färöischen Sigurdlieder nach der 'Sandoyarbók.'* Mit Grammatik und Glossar. Torshavn: Føroya Fróðskaparfelag, 1983.

Debes, Hans J. "Faroe Islands." In *Medieval Scandinavia: An Encyclopedia,* edited by Philipp Pulsiano. New York: Garland, 1993, pp. 184–187.

de Boor, Helmut. *Die Färöischen Lieder des Nibelungenzyklus.* Heidelberg: Winter, 1918.

Müller, Ulrich. "Die färöischen Tanzballaden: Ihr 'Sitz im Leben' 1985." In vol. 2 of *Die färöischen Nibelungen-Balladen: Texte und Übersetzung,* edited by Klaus Fuss. Göppingen: Kümmerle, 1985.

Smith-Dampier, E. M. *Sigurd the Dragon-Slayer: A Faroese Ballad Cycle.* Oxford: Blackwell, 1934.

Syndergaard, Larry E. *English Translations of the Scandinavian Medieval Ballads: An Analytical Guide and Bibliography.* Turku: Nordic Institute of Folklore, 1995.

Wylie, Jonathan, and Margolin, David. *The Ring of Dancers: Images of Faroese Culture.* Philadelphia: University of Pennsylvania Press, 1981.

FREDEGAR(IUS). The name of this seventh-century Frankish writer is now applied to a set of much-copied Latin chronicles by several hands and continued into Carolingian times (eventually under the patronage of a Count Nibelung). The earliest part contains the story of the vendettas of Chilperic and Brunhild, based on Gregory of Tours.

[BOM]

Bibliography
Wallace-Hadrill, J. M. *The Long-Haired Kings.* London: Methuen, 1962, pp. 71–94.

GÖRING, HERMANN (1893–1946), commander-in-chief of the German air force and Reichsmarschall of Nazi Germany. On January 30, 1943, two days before the capitulation of Field Marshal Friedrich von Paulus's Sixth Army at Stalingrad, Göring addressed the Wehrmacht and compared the Battle of Stalingrad to the last stand of the Nibelungs in Etzel's Great Hall, where the beleaguered heroes had accepted their fate. He extolled the virtues of the Nibelung warriors, who were willing to make the supreme sacrifice and perform their duty unswervingly to the bitter end, as fitting examples for the soldiers in Stalingrad, as well as representative of the German struggle for life.

[WW]

Bibliography
Göring, Hermann. "Stalingrad: Der größte Hero-
enkampf unserer Geschichte." *Völkischer
Beobachter,* February 3, 1943, no. 34, pp. 3f.
Brackert, Helmut. "Nibelungenlied und Na-
tionalgedanke: Zur Geschichte einer deutschen
Ideologie." In *Mediaevalia litteraria,* edited by
Ursula Hennig and Herbert Kolb. Munich: Beck,
1971, pp. 343–364.
Krüger, Peter. "Etzels Halle und Stalingrad: Die Rede
Görings vom 30. 1. 43." In *Die Nibelungen: Ein
deutscher Wahn, ein deutscher Alptraum. Studien
und Dokumente zur Rezeption des Nibelun-
enstoffs im 19. und 20. Jahrhundert,* edited by
Joachim Heinzle and Anneliese Waldschmidt.
Suhrkamp Taschenbuch Materialien 2110.
Frankfurt a. M.: Suhrkamp, 1991, pp. 151–190.

GRASELLENBACH, a resort town located
about 28 kilometers northeast of Heidelberg and
less than 30 kilometers due east of Worms. Although not mentioned by name in the *Nibelungenlied,* the town claims to have a spring that has
been traditionally known as the "Siegfried Brunnen." A tall cross has been erected next to the
spring, bearing at its base a quotation from stanza
981 of the *Nibelungenlied* (MS **B**): "Da der herre
Sifrit ob dem brunnen tranch,/er schoz in durch
daz cruce, daz von den wunden spranch/daz blut
im von dem hercen vaste an Hagenen wat./so
groze missewende ein helt nimmer mer begat"
("Then, as Siegfried bent over and drank from
the spring, he [Hagen] shot him through the
lower back, so that his heart's blood leapt from
the wound and splashed against Hagen's clothes.
No warrior will ever do a darker deed"). Crosses
are traditionally erected in memory of a murder,
and farmers in the area have always said that a
mighty knight had been killed at that spring. This
is one of three "Siegfried Springs" (see also
ODENHEIM and DER LINDELBRUNNEN).

[SMJ]

Bibliography
Huber, Werner. *Auf der Suche nach den Nibelungen:
Städte und Stätten, die der Dichter des Nibe-
lungenliedes beschrieb.* With photographs by
Michael Gööck. Gütersloh: Präsentverlag, 1981,
pp. 38–39.

GREGORY OF TOURS (ca. 539–594), the
principal historian of the Merovingian Franks
and bishop of Tours from 573. In book IV of his
10-book *Historia Francorum* (History of the
Franks) he presents the political vendettas between Sigibert and Chilperic, and the intrigues of
their wives.

[BOM]

Bibliography
Gregory of Tours. *History of the Franks,* translated by
Lewis Thorpe. Harmondsworth: Penguin, 1974.
Latin text in the *MGH Scriptores rerum Mero-
vingicarum* I, edited by W. Arndt and Bruno
Krusch. Hanover: MGH, 1885. Reprint, 1961.

HAGEN OFFENSIVE, the name given to the
World War I German offensive planned on the
Western Front in July 1918, in accordance with
which the army group called the "Deutscher
Kronprinz" (German Crown Prince) was to attack along the French front from Moreuil to the
Marne. The offensive eventually broke down,
most likely as a result of the splitting of forces to
accommodate a simultaneous German attack
east of Reims (Reims-Marneschutz Offensive).

[WM]

HOHENEMS, originally Embs, is a town located in the valley of the Upper Rhine in the
Austrian province of Vorarlberg. In the Middle
Ages Ems was massively fortified and served as
the residence of the lords of Embs and of the
imperial counts of Hohenems from 1560 on. In
1765 control of Hohenems passed to the House
of Habsburg. It was in the palace library at
Hohenems where, on June 28, 1755, Jacob Hermann Obereit, a physician from Linz, acting on a
suggestion of the Zurich scholar Johann Jacob
Bodmer, discovered a manuscript of the *Nibelungenlied* that is now referred to as manuscript
C. He was hardly aware of the significance of his
find, which he reported to Bodmer the next day.
In the following month the manuscript was sent
to Bodmer, who made the discovery known on
March 24, 1756, in the "Freymütigen Nach-
richten von Neuen Büchern und anderen zur
Gelehrtheit gehörigen Sachen," as though he had
made the find himself. The following year
Bodmer published a partial edition of the second
part of the work under the title *Chriemhilden
Rache.* Almost a quarter century later, in 1779,

another *Nibelungenlied* manuscript was located there and came to be catalogued as manuscript **A**.

[WW]

IRISH SIEGFRIED, the term used by biographer Tim Pat Coogan to describe the Irish patriot and revolutionary leader Michael Collins (1890–1922). The association of Collins with Siegfried appears to have been originally made by a contemporary of Collins, Kathleen Napoli MacKenna, who referred to him in her unpublished memoirs as "Siegfried, the personification of joyous, powerful youth." Collins also shared Siegfried's penchant for bringing disorder to the establishment and like his Germanic counterpart met an untimely end through assassination by forces with whom he had formerly been allied.

[WM]

Bibliography

Coogan, Tim Pat. *The Man Who Made Ireland: The Life and Times of Michael Collins.* Niwot, CO: Roberts Rinehart Publishers, 1992, pp. xiv, 109.

JORDANES (Iordanes), a Gothic historian, whose book *De origine actibusque Getarum* (551 A.D.), is a summary of a comprehensive but lost history by Cassiodorus (490–585). Although badly written and unreliable, Jordanes's *Getica* are a unique historiographic source, especially for the fifth and sixth centuries. Jordanes's import for the *Nibelungenlied* lies mostly in his passages about Attila, which were based through Cassiodorus on otherwise lost accounts by Priscus, an eyewitness at Attila's court. In particular Jordanes/Cassiodorus/Priscus report that Attila died after a wedding banquet, suffocating from a nose bleed, that he was found with his Germanic bride Ildico weeping at his side, and that he was buried with elaborate rituals. The name (H)Ildico has usually been related to the name Kriemhilt but may also appear in the name of Helche (see *Chronica Hungarorum*). In general the account by Jordanes/Cassiodorus/Priscus, especially the remarkable funeral song that it includes, attests to a very positive view of Attila in the Southeast, diametrically opposed to his negative image in the North.

[WLH]

Bibliography

Jordanes. *De origine actibusque Getarum,* edited by Theodor Mommsen. Monumenta Germaniae Historica, Auctores Antiquissimi. Vol. V,1, Berlin: Weidmann, 1882, pp. 53–138.

Mierow, Christopher, ed. *The Gothic History of Jordanes in English Version.* Princeton: Princeton University Press, 1908.

JUNG, CARL GUSTAV (1875–1961), Swiss psychologist/psychiatrist, known as the father of analytical psychology. Jung recorded a dream he experienced on December 18, 1913, in which, with the assistance of a "brown-skinned man, a savage," he kills Siegfried with rifle shots as the hero rushes in a chariot made of the bones of the dead down a mountainside. In the dream Jung was appalled by his action, although his fear of discovery was alleviated by a heavy downpour which he believed would wipe out all traces of the deed. He was, nonetheless, filled with terrible feelings of guilt. Jung interpreted Siegfried as the personification of the will of the Germans, the desire to have their own way, and also of his personal attempt to assert himself in a similar manner. The dream demonstrated to him, through the death of Siegfried, that such a course was no longer appropriate.

Jung refers repeatedly to figures from the Nibelungen tradition throughout his psychological works. In *Symbols of Transformation* he points to parallels between the Judas legend and the betrayal of Siegfried by Hagen. He sees in Wagner's treatment of the Siegfried figure the longing of the archetypal hero for the "mother-imago," while Hagen is representative of Father Wotan, whom Siegfried had previously conquered.

[WM]

Bibliography

Jung, Carl Gustav. *Memories, Dreams, Reflections.* Recorded and edited by Aniela Jaffé. Rev. ed., translated by Richard and Clara Winston. New York: Vintage, 1965, p. 180.

———. *Symbols of Transformation.* 2nd ed., translated by R. F. C. Hull. Bollingen Series XX. Princeton: Princeton University Press, 1976, pp. 30, 358–364, 385–390.

Wehr, Gerhard. *Jung: A Biography.* Translated by David M. Weeks. Boston: Shambhala, 1987, pp. 179–181.

KÉZA, SIMON, a Hungarian cleric, author of *Gesta Hungarorum.* This book, written between 1282 and 1285 and dedicated to King Ladislaus IV, traces the Hungarian people back to Hunor and Magor, the sons of the giant Menroth, builder of the tower of Babel. The early parts of Keza's account are more legendary than historical. He believed that the Huns were Hungarians, placed the career of Attila (whom he called Ethela) sometime after the year 700, and thought that the battle of the Catalaunian fields was fought in Catalonia. He took over Jordanes's version of Attila's death by suffocation due to a nosebleed on his wedding night, but changed the bride's name from Ildico to Micolt.

[JVM]

Bibliography
Kéza. Simon. *Gesta Hungarorum.* The Deeds of the Hungarians. Central European Medieval Texts. [N.p]: European University Press, 1999.

NIBELUNGEN-BRÜCKE (Nibelungen Bridge), the name given to the former Adolf-Hitler-Brücke in Regensburg over the Danube. The bridge was blown up at the end of April 1945, but rebuilt and renamed after the war. At the entrance to the bridge is a large stone monument with the designation "Nibelungen Bruecke" and crested by a monumental eagle.

[WM]

NIBELUNGEN DIVISION was the official designation of 38th SS (Panzer) Grenadier Division, the last division formed in the elite Waffen-SS (Combat SS) of the German armed forces in World War II. A division in name only, it does not appear to have exceeded regimental strength (veterans occasionally refer to it as the Niegelungene Division: "the division that never made it to divisional strength"). The combat formations designated as comprising the German Nineteenth Army on the Upper Rhine on April 7, 1945, refer only to an SS brigade named "Nibelungen," although an American military report dated April 27, 1945, refers to three grenadier regiments of the SS Division as "Nibelungen." Waffen-SS divisions wore cuffbands with the names of their respective units on the lower left arm of their uniforms, and while a cuffband with the designation "Nibelungen" may occasionally crop up in a collection of SS regalia, it is most assuredly a postwar fake, as no official cuffbands were ever issued to the unit, given its formation late in the war. The Nibelungen Division was established in March/April 1945, chiefly from officer candidates of the SS-Junkerschule Bad Tölz (and was also designated for a period as the "SS-Grenadier-Division-Junkerschule Tölz"). It was undoubtedly accorded the designation "Nibelungen" because of the connotations of absolute loyalty associated with the name, although given the ultimate fate of the fictitious Nibelungs/Burgundians and the historical circumstances surrounding the division's genesis, the significance of the designation took on a wider dimension. Its first commander was SS-Obersturmbannführer (lieutenant colonel) Richard Schulze-Kossens (March/April 1945), former adjutant to Adolf Hitler and in postwar years a frequent lecturer at West Point. According to Klietmann, the unit saw action in the Danube basin in the area of Vohburg-Neustadt-Kehlheim, ironically through part of what has been designated the "Nibelungenstraße." The Nibelungen Division fought a final defensive action around Landshut/Bavaria and surrendered to the Americans on May 8, 1945, in Reit/Winkel. Although on the surface it might seem that this was the unit that formed the basis for the division commanded by the notorious General Wilhelm Tanz in the novel *Die Nacht der Generäle* (The Night of the Generals) by the German author Hans Hellmut Kirst, the activities of the division in Kirst's novel (as well as in the 1967 film of the same name), in which the unit is miraculously transformed from a Wehrmacht into a Waffen-SS division when it is moved from the eastern front to Paris, are as fictitious as Kirst's major protagonist and have no relationship whatsoever to the combat record of the historical Nibelungen division.

[WM]

Bibliography
Klietmann, K.-G. *Die Waffen-SS:. Eine Dokumentation.* Osnabrück: Verlag "Der Freiwillige" G.m.b.H., 1965, pp. 305–306.
Mehner, Kurt. *Die Waffen-SS und Polizei 1939–1945.* Norderstedt: Militär-Verlag, 1995, pp. 263–264.
Schneider, Klaus. *Spuren der "Nibelungen" 1945: Dokumentation über Soldaten der 38. Grenadier-*

Division "Nibelungen" der Waffen-SS. Berg: Vowinckel, 1999.

Tessin, Georg. *Verbände und Truppen der deutschen Wehrmacht und Waffen SS im Zweiten Weltkrieg 1939–1945,* edited by Bundesarchiv-Militärarchiv with the support of the Arbeitskreis für Wehrforschung. Vol. 5: *Die Landstreitkräfte 31–70.* Frankfurt a. M.: Mittler, [n.d.], p. 77.

NIBELUNGENGAU, an area covered by present-day Wachau, between Persenbeug and Weitenegg. Pöchlarn is located in the center. The term "Nibelungengau" is used as a tourist slogan.

[SSch]

NIBELUNGENHALLE (Nibelung Hall), a modern auditorium complex and conference center in Passau, Germany, built in 1935 and known as the "Ostmark-Halle" (East March Hall) during the National Socialist period. Located in the heart of the city that figures so prominently in the *Nibelungenlied,* the hall draws its name directly from the epic. Because of its relatively large capacity (3,500 persons seated, 5,100 standing) the Nibelungenhalle is the year-round site of various concerts, sports events, and exhibits in Passau, most notably the annual Ash Wednesday assembly of the Christian Social Union, a conservative political party based in Bavaria. Two more recent Nibelungen exhibitions can be seen in the City Hall of Passau. In the large Barock room there are two wall paintings done in Barock style by Ferdinand Wagner, who specialized in historical scenes (1886), namely, Kriemhild's entry into Passau and Hagen's meeting with the three water sprites.

[MR/UM]

NIBELUNGENLIED POSTAGE STAMPS, a set of six postage stamps, a charity series, issued in Austria on March 8, 1926, depicting scenes from the *Nibelungenlied,* including Siegfried's slaying of the dragon, the journey of the Burgundians to Iceland, the quarrel of the queens, Hagen and the water sprites, and Rüdiger welcoming the Burgundians/Nibelungs to Bechelarn.

[WM]

NIBELUNGENSTÄDTE (Nibelungen Cities). Numerous cities in Germany and Austria with ties, however tenuous, to the *Nibelungenlied* frequently like to call themselves "Nibelun-

genstädte" (e.g., "Nibelungenstadt Pöchlarn.") Naturally most of these cities are located on the so-called Nibelungenstraße. In Pöchlarn there is a monument, erected in 1987, with the coats of arms of sixteen Nibelungenstädte (see map, p. 312).

[SMJ]

NIBELUNGENSTRASSE, literally, the Nibelung Road, or the route traveled (five different times, all in the second half of the *Nibelungenlied*) between the realm of the Burgundians and that of King Etzel. Because the *Nibelungenlied* generates so many actual geographic place-names between the Rhineland and Hungary, this route can be traced with some precision. On a present-day map the Nibelungenstraße begins in Germany at Worms and moves eastward via the Odenwald through Lorsch and Miltenberg, to Großmehring and Pförring, where it meets the Danube and then goes on to Passau. Once within Bavaria and Austria the geographic detail becomes richer, reflecting the likelihood that the poet was native to this region. East of Passau the route is basically that of the Danube itself: Eferding, Enns, into the Nibelungengau through Pöchlarn, on to Melk and then through the Wachau to Traismauer and to Vienna. The exact site of Etzelnburg, the residence of King Etzel and the eastern-most point along the Nibelungenstraße, is less certain, though it has been associated with several different locales north of Budapest. In their advertising campaign the Deutsche Zentrale für Tourismus (German Central Office for Tourism) issued an attractive brochure on "The Nibelungen Route," which included the Hagen monument in Worms among the stations to visit as well as the Odenwald, where the kings of Burgundy had gone hunting (see map, p. 312).

[MR]

NIBELUNGENTREUE (Nibelungen loyalty), the term used by Reich Chancellor Bernhard von Bülow in a speech to the Reichstag on March 29, 1909, during the pre-World War I crisis in Bosnia. It was intended to characterize the German alliance with the Austro-Hungarian Empire. In 1914, at the outbreak of World War I, Franz von Liszt equated Hagen with Germany and Völ-

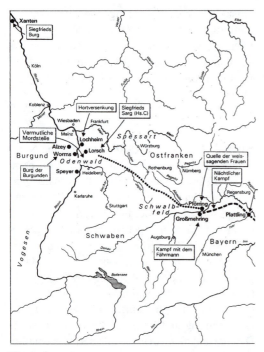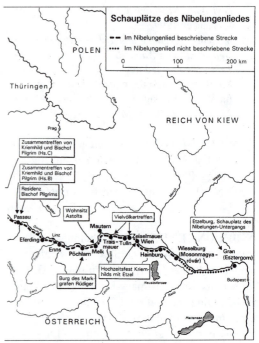

Figure 2

ker with Austria. Professors of German, such as Gustav Roethe, glorified Nibelungentreue as a German virtue. The concept also found application as a political slogan both during World War I and in the Weimar Republic. Even the seventh volume of *Trübners Deutsches Wörterbuch,* published in 1956, referred to the Nibelungentreue displayed by the (second) German Reich when it came to the assistance of a beleagured Austria in 1914. For the most part it is used nowadays for ironic effect.

[WW]

Bibliography
Fürst Bülows Reden. Vol. 5, *1907–1914.* Leipzig: Reclam, 1914, pp. 127ff.
Härd, John Evert. *Das Nibelungenepos: Wertung und Wirkung von der Romantik bis zur Gegenwart.* Tübingen, Basel: Francke, 1996, pp. 156ff.
Liszt, Franz von. *Von der Nibelungentreue.* Berlin: Heymann, 1914, pp. 7ff.
Roethe, Gustav. *Von deutscher Art und Kultur.* Berlin: Weidmann, 1915, p. 36.
Trübners Deutsches Wörterbuch. Vol. 7, edited by Alfred Goetze. Berlin: de Gruyter, 1956, cols. 113b/114a.

NIBELUNGEN-VERLAG (Nibelungen Publishing Company). Established in both Berlin and Leipzig on August 4, 1934 by Joseph Goebbels' Propaganda Ministry, the Nibelungen-Verlag published literally millions of anti-Bolshevik and anti-Jewish diatribes between 1938 and 1944. Its Director was Eberhard Taubert. The majority of the books produced by the company were written by former Russian and German communists who had "seen the light" and were eager to report on the disappointment they had experienced in the "workers' paradise."

[WM/OP]

NIBELUNGENWERKE. The name given to the tank-building factory established in St. Valentin, Austria, just prior to World War II. It was here that all of the tanks designed by Ferdinand Porsche were built, including the formidable Tigers and the sixty-five-ton tank destroyer *Elefant.*

[WM]

Bibliography
Schneider, Wolfgang. *Elefant, Jagdtiger, Sturmtiger. Rarities of the Tiger Family.* Translated by Edward Force. Schiffer Military History. Vol. 18. West Chester, PA.: Schiffer, 1990.

NORDIC STONES. Among the stones from medieval Scandinavia that contain runes or various images, there are some that depict scenes from the Nordic sagas of gods and heroes, including the Nibelungen myth. Such stones include the Stone of Tanberg (Norway, eleventh century), the Rock Carving of Ramsundsberg (Sweden, early eleventh century), a few other stone carvings in Sweden (e.g., "Sigurdristningar"), the stone set up by Vikings on the Isle of Man around 1000 that belong to the group of so-called Manx Crosses, and stone crosses in England. The interpretation of the images, which are often in poor condition, is occasionally controversial. Individual scenes from the Nibelungen myth are depicted or alluded to in very abbreviated and stylized form, particularly the story of Sigurd's fight with the dragon and Gunnar in the snakepit. The images at Ramsundsberg (about 100 kilometers west of Stockholm) are particularly impressive. Spread over almost five meters on a rock projection are the well preserved carvings of a whole series of Sigurd images. Ploss, von See, and others interpret these scenes and those in the Norwegian churches as the Christian interpretation of old myths. Thus, Sigurd the dragon slayer has been associated with St. George, the Christian dragon slayer. The works by Ploss and von See contain illustrations as well as interpretations.

[UM]

Bibliography

Althaus, Sylvia. *Die gotländischen Bildsteine: Ein Programm.* Göppingen: Kümmerle, 1993.

Ploss, Emil. *Sigurd, der Drachenkämpfer. Untersuchungen zur germanisch-deutschen Heldensage.* Cologne: Böhlau, 1966. Contains illustrations of almost all extant monuments.

See, Klaus von. "Sigurd der Drachentöter: Mittelalterliche Bilddenkmäler in Skandinavien." In *Die Nibelungen: Bilder von Liebe, Verrat und Untergang,* edited by Wolfgang Storch. Munich: Prestel, 1987, pp. 119–123.

NORWEGIAN CHURCHES. Various scenes from the Nibelungen myth that are similar to the images found on Nordic stones are found in medieval Norwegian churches, namely, Sigurd the dragon slayer and Gunnar in the snakepit. These scenes appear as reliefs in wood and are found on two church chairs from Blaker (ca. 1200: Sigurd?) and Heddal (ca. 1200: Gunnar), and especially on portal boards made from oak or elm in the stave churches in Hylestad (Gunnar; Sigurd), Austad (Gunnar and Sigurd), Vegusdal (Sigurd), and Lundeval (Sigurd). They all date from about the year 1200 or later in the thirteenth century. Illustrations and interpretations of the scenes can be found in both Ploss and von See, who believe that, as with the Nibelungen carvings on medieval Nordic stones, the images deal with the Christian interpretation of old myths. Compare as well the similar Sigurd scenes in the stone church portal in SANGUESA, Spain.

[UM]

Bibliography

Ploss, Emil. *Sigurd, der Drachenkämpfer: Untersuchungen zur germanisch-deutschen Heldensage.* Cologne: Böhlau, 1966. Contains illustrations of almost all extant monuments.

See, Klaus von. "Sigurd der Drachentöter: Mittelalterliche Bilddenkmäler in Skandinavien." In *Die Nibelungen. Bilder von Liebe, Verrat und Untergang,* edited by Wolfgang Storch. Munich: Prestel, 1987, pp. 119–123.

OLAH, NICOLAUS (1493–1568), Hungarian cleric, chaplain to Maria of Hungary while she was viceroy of the Netherlands, friend of Erasmus and other humanists, eventually archbishop of Esztergom and chancellor to Ferdinand I. He introduced the Jesuits into Hungary and suppressed the Reformation there while urging reforms within the church. Olah wrote *Hungaria,* a history of Hungary, and in 1537 *Athila,* an account of the life of Attila. In the account he reports that Attila became king of the Huns in 401 and that there is great uncertainty among the chroniclers concerning how long he lived. He makes Dietrich of Verona a contemporary and suffragan of Attila, and reports that Attila killed Gundicarius, king of the Burgundians, in personal combat, after which his Huns annihilated the Burgundian army. He accepts Jordanes's story of Attila's death from suffocation by a nosebleed on his wedding night but says that the bride was named Mycoltha, a princess of Bactria, not the Germanic Ildico in Jordanes account.

[JVM]

PEDAGOGY. The *Nibelungenlied* became a part of the curriculum in German schools at the time of the Wars of Liberation fought against

Napoleon under the leadership of Prussia. Tracing its reception as a pedagogical tool throughout the nineteenth and twentieth centuries, one notes the manner in which noble ideals and heroic virtues dating from the Hohenstaufen period about 1200 were transformed, sometimes in rather irrational and inconsistent ways, into national symbols and models for the middle class. August Wilhelm Schlegel's comparison of the *Nibelungenlied* with Homer's *Iliad* lent legitimacy to the idea propagated in the schools that the former reflected the true character of the Germans just as the classical epic had mirrored the character of the Greeks. Through the writings of Friedrich Heinrich von der Hagen, August Wilhelm and Friedrich Schlegel, as well as Friedrich de la Motte Fouqué, the *Nibelungenlied* soon came to be regarded as a national myth. Around 1815 it served as a platform for the presentation of a political and nationalist viewpoint in the German school system with the aim of engendering patriotic fervor among the young. The first editions of the epic were produced after educators such as Franz Josef Mone (1818) and Johann August Zeune (1815) promoted curricula that included topics from old German literature, including readings from the *Nibelungenlied*. Following the Congress of Vienna, the conference of European powers held after the first exile of Napoleon (1814–1815), the forces of reaction demonstrated no interest in the ideal of German unity or the national sentiment of the middle class. Consequently the school curricula in German states such as Prussia, Bavaria, Saxony, or Hessen-Nassau were dominated by Greek and Latin texts with respect to literature classes. Not until 1848 and the unsuccessful revolution that occurred in Germany in that year did the *Nibelungenlied* again become a subject for study in literature classes. The work was readily available in editions, such as that by Philipp Wackernagel, which were specifically designed for use in new secondary schools that deviated from the traditional classical model. Such new schoolbooks contained subjects that could serve as models of German spirit and national character. More cautious scholars, including Georg Gottfried Gervinus, Karl Lachmann, and Wilhelm Wilmanns, warned against pseudohistoric interpretation and the superficial treatment of the subject matter in schools, but their influence remained insignificant. Such other prominent philologists as Karl Müllenhoff or August Lübben strongly supported the use of the *Nibelungenlied* in schools, as they considered it to be just as important as classical literature.

After the founding of the German Empire and throughout the Wilhelminian era, Germanists such as Konrad Burdach and Otto Lyon emphasized the educational value of the *Nibelungenlied* for illustrating the heroic German character. More and more school editions of the medieval epic then appeared, along with other readings from German heroic poetry. In the 1890s the curricula of most German secondary schools (which were determined by the German federal states), as well as those of Austria, prescribed the *Nibelungenlied* or the Nibelungen theme as compulsory reading. In the years before and during the First World War, many commentaries used in the schools praised the Nibelungs as models for Germanic ideals worthy of emulation, such as loyalty, glory, honor, strength, courage, and, above all, contempt of death. Siegfried, who in the epic is treacherously killed by Hagen, became the true German national hero. The number of school texts dealing with the Nibelungs increased during the Weimar Republic. Most of those texts underscore the significance of the Nibelungs as the embodiment of the German "way of life," as models of patriotism, and as the natural way for Germans to behave. Editions and translations of the *Nibelungenlied* were seen as a means of guaranteeing the continuity of national and racial identity following Germany's defeat in World War I and the imposition of the Treaty of Versailles. Hagen was then no longer seen as a murderer, but rather as a model for loyalty and defiance in the face of unrelenting fate. The central control of the educational system under National Socialism (1933–1945) sought to propagate the totalitarian principles of fascist leadership and absolute obedience to superiors. The popular pedagogue of the time, Severin Rüttgers, recommended that the *Nibelungenlied* be used to teach pupils the importance of unswerving loyalty and the acceptance of one's destiny. He believed that the lesson of the Nibelungs would help prepare the young for their own life struggle. Siegfried and Hagen were portrayed as Nordic supermen, while the Huns were depicted as subhuman creatures. The consequence of such harnessing of the *Nibelungenlied* to political aims was the nonhistorical treatment of the work that dominated after the Second World War. In the 1950s and 1960s the emphasis was on the aesthetic significance of the work, with attention devoted to the tragic nature of this tale of passion and destiny. In virtually all of the states of the Federal Republic of Germany, the *Nibelungenlied* was included among the required readings in the upper classes of the secondary schools. Since the late 1960s, however, medieval literature has been purged from the schools. The *Nibelungenlied* was not deemed suitable for curricula that emphasized such things as social responsibility, social criticism, and modern literature. The study of the *Nibelungenlied* within its historical context and the reception of the epic over the centuries are topics that are now covered exclusively in seminars at the university level.

[WW]

Bibliography

Ehrismann, Otfrid. *Nibelungenlied. Epoche, Werk, Wirkung.* Munich: Beck, 1987, pp. 262–277.

Wunderlich, Werner. "'Ein Hauptbuch bey der Erziehung der deutschen Jugend . . .': Zur pädagogischen Indienstnahme des Nibelungenliedes für Schule und Unterricht im 19. und 20. Jahrhundert." In *Die Nibelungen: Ein deutscher Wahn, ein deutscher Alptraum. Studien und Dokumente zur Rezeption des Nibelungenstoffs im 19. und 20. Jahrhundert,* edited by Joachim Heinzle and Anneliese Waldschmidt, Frankfurt a.M.: Suhrkamp, 1991, pp. 119–150.

POETA SAXO. An unnamed Saxon monk in Corvey who wrote a five-book poetic history of Charlemagne towards the end of the ninth century, based largely on earlier chroniclers. A reference in the fifth book to popular songs (presumably in German) on the Merovingian Frankish kings is perhaps evidence of earlier stages of the poetic tradition.

[BOM]

PRISCUS OF PANIUM, a fifth-century Greek historian and a major source on the Huns and Attila. His work is lost, but extracts were copied and used by later writers such as Cassiodorus and Jordanes.

[BOM]

Bibliography

Gordon, C. D. *The Age of Attila.* Ann Arbor: University of Michigan Press. 1960. Reprint, New York: Dorset, 1992, with most of the fragments in translation.

PSYCHOLOGY. A psychological approach to the *Nibelungenlied* is possible if the figures are understood as individuals acting like real persons and whose motives for their actions are expressed in the poem. Marianne Wahl-Armstrong considered the extent to which the characters in the *Nibelungenlied* may be considered as individuals whose personalities can be identified by their behavior, or whether they must be seen merely as figures with specific functions within the narrative. She thus sees the figures, especially Kriemhild, as personalities, contrary to the common opinion that fate determines their actions and that heroic poetry is interested only in action, not in motivation. In the interim, attempts have been made to interpret the behavior and actions of the figures as characters changing and developing in the course of time. Kriemhild's story could be read as a novel: from her decision as a young girl to avoid a lover's grief by renouncing love, and then as a loving young woman, a sister defending her hereditary rights against a patriarchal system in which only her brothers count, as a widow unable to take revenge without abandoning her female role, the resulting *marriage of convenience,* the aging woman unable to forget and pursuing her revenge without regard as to the number of innocent victims, and finally to her acting as a virago, leaving the limits of female and human behavior and provoking her own destruction. To some degree other figures also display individual characteristics; not only central figures like Hagen, the firm defender of patriarchy, as well as Siegfried, Brünhild, and Gunther, but even such secondary ones as Volker. The strictly psychological approach is used in popular interpretations, where it is exaggerated to an extent certainly not intended by the author. The *Nibelungenlied* offers as well the possibility of seeing the actions of the figures determined by an inevitable fate emanating from beyond the human world. A novelistic element in the *Nibelungenlied* is the fact that the motivations of the various figures are not at odds with those we would expect from human beings. At the same time, being a heroic epic, the *Nibelungenlied* neither emphasizes the psychological motivations nor does it encourage us to seek a possible motivation behind each action of a figure. The Old Norse texts show a heroic ideal of bravery, defiance of death and fearlessness (especially *Atlakviða*), in contrast to Greek heroes, who do show fear. The main male characters must meet this ideal; their opponents are avaricious, cowardly, and treacherous. The portrayal of Gunther as a weak king, as occurs in some scenes of the *Nibelungenlied,* has no counterpart in the Norse analogues. Gunnar acts in *Atlakviða* "sem konungr scyldi" (as a king ought to). Female figures, in particular, are bearers of wisdom (prophecies and warnings), express their grief, incite men to revenge, and occasionally take an active part in revenge (e.g., Guðrún; Signy in *Volsunga saga*).

[HR]

Bibliography

Boyer, Regis. *Meurs et Psychologie des Anciens Islandais.* Paris: Editions du Porte-glaive, 1986.

Clover, Carol. "Hildigunnr's Lament." In *Structure and Meaning in Old Norse Literature,* edited by J. Lindow et al. Odense: Odense University Press, 1986, pp. 141–183.

Jung, Carl Gustav. *Symbolik des Geistes.* Zurich: Rascher, 1948.

Malinowski, B. *Myth in Primitive Psychology.* London: Paul, Trench, Trubner & Co., 1926.

McConnell, Winder. *The Nibelungenlied.* Boston: Twayne, 1984.

McNeely, J. Trevor. "Norse Heroic Psychology and the Niflung Lays." *Discourse* 9 (1966): 439ff.

Wahl-Armstrong, Marianne. *Rolle und Charakter: Studien zur Menschendarstellung im Nibelungenlied.* GAG 221. Göppingen: Kümmerle, 1979.

Weber, Gerd W. "Sem konungr scyldi. Heldendichtung und Semiotik." In *Helden und Heldensage. Festschrift für Otto Gschwantler,* edited by H. Reichert and G. Zimmermann. Philologica Germanica 11. Vienna: Fassbaender, 1990, pp. 447–481.

ROSENBERG, ALFRED (1893–1946), National Socialist ideologue and author of *Der Mythus des 20. Jahrhunderts* (The Myth of the 20th Century), in which Rosenberg proclaimed the advent of a new (or the rejuvenation of an ancient) myth based on blood (race). This "Blut-mythus" (blood myth) came to form the basis of a new consciousness on the part of the Germans regarding their unity, their strength, and their future potential as a people. Rosenberg regarded the *Nibelungenlied* as one of the greatest expressions of occidental artistic creativity. He rejected the view that the German epic was not on the same aesthetic level as the *Iliad* and emphasized, in particular, the greatness of the inner forces motivating the main characters. His judgment of Siegfried is uncritical ("shining in eternal glory") and devoid of any real understanding of the hero's darker side. Hagen, on the other hand, is seen as a remarkable combination of greed and unbending loyalty. Rosenberg's final comment on the Nibelungen theme is to compare the Siegfried (Baldur) myth with the very essence of the German soldier of 1914, at the outbreak of the First World War.

[WM]

Bibliography

Rosenberg, Alfred. *Der Mythus des 20. Jahrhunderts: Eine Wertung der seelisch-geistigen Gestaltenkämpfe unserer Zeit.* 129th–132nd ed. Munich: Hoheneichen, 1938.

SACHBÜCHER (Nonfictional works). The *Nibelungenlied* is not only the subject of scholarly research. It also generates interest among the general public. Helmut Berndt has stated that books dealing with Nibelungen themes that are intended for the layman include, besides literary perspectives, references to history, culture, and geography. Readers are interested in learning about the background of these stories and the geographical areas in which they flourished. The *Sachbücher* take up these topics, elucidating the historical and literary roots of the story and its figures and also dealing with the geographical places in the *Nibelungenlied*. These books are often handsomely illustrated. They may include bibliographies with scholarly literature on the subject, but the quality of the works cited varies from case to case.

[SSch]

Bibliography

Auf den Spuren der Nibelungen und Bergisches Land. Farbige Abbildungen und topographisch genaue Karten der Wanderwege des Sauerländischen Gebirgs-Vereins. Sauerland, [1980].

Berndt, Helmut. *Die Nibelungen: Auf den Spuren eines sagenhaften Volkes.* 2nd ed. Oldenburg: Lubbe, 1988.

————. *Das 40. Abenteuer: Auf den Spuren des Nibelungenlieds* Oldenburg: Stalling, 1968

Böckmann, Walter. *Der Nibelungen Tod in Soest: Neue Erkenntnisse zur historischen Wahrheit.* Düsseldorf: Econ, 1981.

Dworschak, Fritz. *Wachau und Nibelungengau.* Munich: Schnell & Steiner, 1961.

Hansen, Walter. *Die Spur des Sängers: Das Nibelungenlied und sein Dichter.* With color photographs by Eberhard Grames. Bergisch-Gladbach: Lübbe, 1987.

Huber, Werner. *Auf der Suche nach den Nibelungen: Städte und Stätten, die der Dichter des Nibelungenliedes beschrieb. (In search of the Nibelungen; A la Découverte des Nibelungen.)* With photographs by Michael Göock. Gütersloh: Bertelsmann, 1981 [German/English/French edition].

Kolb, Julius. *Vom Rhein zur Donau: Auf den Spuren der Nibelungen.* Munich: Herbig, 1989.

Storch, Wolfgang, ed. *Das Buch der Nibelungen: Eine repräsentative Sammlung vom mittelalterlichen Nibelungenlied bis zu Bertolt Brecht.* Munich: Heyne, 1988.

SANGUESA, a city in Northern Spain at the *camino de Santiago* near Pamplona. Some sculptures around the main entrance of the Santa María la Real Church appear to depict scenes from the Nordic Sigurd legend (twelfth century).

[UM]

Bibliography

Müller, Ulrich. "Nibelungen-Rezeption am Pilgerweg nach Santiago? Das Portal von 'Santa María la Real' im nordspanischen Sangüesa." In *3. Pöchlarner Heldenliedgespräch: Die Rezeption des Nibelungenliedes,* edited by Klaus Zatloukal. Vienna: Fassbaender, 1995, pp. 146–155.

SAXO GRAMMATICUS, a Danish cleric and historian. He was born in about 1145, probably in Zeeland, and earned the name Grammaticus in the fourteenth century for his perceived Latin eloquence. Saxo's major work, the *Gesta Danorum* (or *Historia Danica*), was completed about 1210. The work was written at the request of Archbishop Absalon, under whom Saxo served from 1178 to 1201. It is the first significant Danish literary work and the first important account of Danish history. In it Saxo shows the influence of a number of classical and medieval Latin historians, and he employed Icelandic sources and Danish tradition as well.

The *Gesta Danorum* is contained in sixteen volumes; the first nine are a compendium of the myths of Danish gods/kings, the stories of foreign heroes, and old Norse and Icelandic lays and sagas. Saxo's story of Amleth the Dane (Book III) is usually taken as Shakespeare's source for *Hamlet.* The last seven books of the *Gesta* are Saxo's account of historical times and end with Canute's conquest of Pomerania in 1185.

Although the *Gesta Danorum* does not tell a Sigurd/Volsung story, there are clear connections with it: Saxo's account of how Frode, son of Haldanus (Half-Dane), slew the dragon parallels the legend of Sigurd and Fafnir in that the instructions Frode receives mirror those given Sigurd. The *Volsunga saga* version of the deaths of Svanhild and her brothers at the hands of Jormunrek are told as well by Saxo, though Saxo's Gudrun is a helpful sorceress rather than the mother of the slain. Much of Book IX of the *Gesta* is devoted to the deeds of Ragnar Loðbrók as found in the saga bearing his name, although he is not married to a daughter of Sigurd and thus no connection is made to the events of the *Volsunga saga.* The presence of such stories, without a Volsung connection, support the notion that the relationship between a Sigurd legend and other Scandinavian tales, as well as the attempt to place Sigurd's adventures in actual history, first appeared in the *Ragnarssaga Loðbrokar.*

[JKW]

Bibliography

Fisher, Peter, trans., and Hilda Ellis Davidson, ed. *The History of the Danes: Saxo Grammaticus.* Cambridge: Brewer, 1979.

SIEGFRIED ICONOGRAPHY. Siegfried/Sigurd as dragon slayer was depicted in stone (Nordic Stones) and in wood (Norwegian churches) in medieval Scandinavia. Ploss, von See, and others see these images of the hero as Christian interpretations of the old myth, whereby Sigurd is compared to the Christian dragon slayer St. George. Also to be considered in this regard is the Archangel Michael, who is also a Christian dragon slayer. Another favorite motif among the images is Gunnar in the snakepit, a type of "Germanic martyr." Since the more recent "rediscovery" of the *Nibelungenlied* and the Nibelungen saga, Siegfried has been the subject of countless paintings and sketches and almost always depicted as a giant figure with blond and curly hair. The aesthetic worth of many of these portrayals is very much tied to the time in which they were produced, and some are quite modest. This stereotypical Siegfried also appears in dramatic works, in opera, and in film. A thorough study of the phenomenon remains to be written. Many illustrations are to be found in Schulte-Wülwer as well as in the exhibition catalogs from Passau and Munich.

[UM]

Bibliography

Kastner, Jörg. *Das Nibelungenlied in den Augen der Künstler vom Mittelalter bis zur Gegenwart.* Exhibition catalog. Passau: Passavia Universitätsverlag, 1986.

Ploss, Emil. *Sigurd, der Drachenkämpfer: Untersuchungen zur germanisch-deutschen Heldensage.* Cologne: Böhlau, 1966. Contains illustrations of almost all extant monuments.

Schulte-Wülwer, Ulrich. *Das Nibelungenlied in der deutschen Kunst des 19. Jahrhunderts.* Gießen: Anabas, 1979.

See, Klaus von. "Sigurd der Drachentöter: Mittelalterliche Bilddenkmäler in Skandinavien." In *Die Nibelungen: Bilder von Liebe, Verrat und Untergang,* edited by Wolfgang Storch. Munich: Prestel, 1987, pp. 119–123.

SIEGFRIED LINE. The name given by the Germans to a line of fortifications dating from World War I (1917) and ranging along Germany's western borders with France, Belgium, Luxembourg, and the Netherlands. It was called the "Hindenburg Line" by the Allies. It was breached by British tanks in late November 1917, although the attack could not be pressed home owing to the lack of infantry following the severe losses in the Battle of Ypres. During the Second World War the Germans referred to the fortifications as the "Westwall," while the British continued to refer to them as the "Siegfried Line," even composing the satirical song "We're going to hang out the washing on the Siegfried Line" (Jimmy Kennedy and Michael Carr, 1939).

[WM]

SPIELREIN, SABINA (SIEGFRIED FANTASY). The Siegfried fantasy is a recurring motif in the diary and works of Sabina Spielrein in the years 1911 to 1918. Spielrein, who became a psychoanalyst in Switzerland and Russia, where she was murdered by the fascists in 1944, was at the time of this fantasy a patient of Carl Gustav Jung. In her dream Spielrein gave birth to Siegfried. This dream represents more than an erotic fantasy directed at Jung. Her Germanic hero was the personification of two of her desires (1) to establish a union between Christianity and Judaism; and (2) to effect a reconciliation between Jungian and Freudian psychoanalysis. The Siegfried fantasy involves both union and self-annihilation and points to Spielrein's ambivalent position as a woman and a Jew. The reactions of both Freud and Jung to the Siegfried fantasy are extremely problematic; both psychologists have used it not only to further their personal rivalry, but also to support fundamental political differences.

[IS]

Bibliography

Carotenuto, Aldo, ed. *Tagebuch einer heimlichen Symmetrie. Sabina Spielrein zwischen Jung und Freud.* Freiburg: Kore, 1986.

Spielrein, Sabina. *Sämtliche Schriften.* Freiburg: Kore, 1987.

Stephan, Inge. "Judentum, Weiblichkeit, Psychoanalyse: Das Beispiel Sabina Spielrein." In *Jüdische Kultur und Weiblichkeit in der Moderne,* edited by Inge Stephan et al. Cologne: Böhlau, 1994, pp. 51–72.

UNTERNEHMEN NIBELUNGEN (Operation Nibelungen) was the name given to the tactical assault operation carried out against English and Canadian troops on January 17, 1945, at 5:00 p.m. by the Ninth Company, Third Battalion, Thirty-sixth Regiment of the Sixteenth SS-Panzergrenadierdivision "Reichsführer-SS." The Allied forces had taken up position in farm buildings (Casa Rasponi) located along the Senio Canal near Fusignano, Italy. The panzer grenadiers, sometimes forced to engage in hand-to-hand fighting against the enemy, were unsuccessful in their bid to dislodge the English and Canadians. After sustaining heavy casualties, the Germans called off the assault during the evening of the same day.

[WM]

Bibliography

"Im gleichen Schritt und Tritt." Dokumentation der 16. SS-Panzergrenadierdivision "Reichsführer-SS," edited by Divisionsgeschichtliche Arbeitsgemeinschaft der Truppenkameradschaft der 16. SS-Panzergrenadier- Division "Reichsführer-SS." Munich: Schild, 1998, pp. 660–661.

UNTERNEHMEN WALKÜRE (Operation Valkyrie). This designation is often associated solely with the major German resistance movement (Count von Stauffenberg, Admiral Canaris, et al.) and their plans to eliminate Hitler in July 1944, seize control of the military chain of command, and essentially take over the government in Germany. "Unternehmen Walküre" was actually the name of the plan drawn up much earlier in the war by General Fritz Fromm, in charge of the Ersatz Heer, the "Home" or "Replacement" Army. (Fromm was later executed as a member of the July 20th conspirators.) The aim of "Walküre" was to prepare for the eventuality of an uprising among the increasing numbers of foreign workers and prisoners of war being held in Germany. "When the bomb plotters carried out their attempt to kill Hitler, they activated an amended version of 'Valkyrie,' and it was the unusual features in the amended version which aroused the suspicion that the actions which were being ordered were not intended to quell a foreign uprising but to carry out a *coup d'etat* by the generals against the elected government" (Lucas, p. 30).

[WM]

Bibliography

Lucas, James. *The Last Year of the German Army. May 1944–May 1946.* London: Arms and Armour Press, 1995.

Translations of the Nibelungenlied and the Klage Other than German

The following bibliography lists known translations of the *Nibelungenlied* into twenty-three languages other than German (for translations into German see p. 327 "Bibliographies," Grosse/ Rautenberg). Some major language groups, including languages of the African continent, the Middle East, and many Asian languages, are not represented; the compilers were unable to locate any editions, although they may well exist.

Citations were identified by searching major computerized databases, existing print bibliographies and catalogs, references found in secondary literature, and by inquiry among scholarly sources. Some less reliable sources, such as book lists, dealers' catalogs, and footnotes, were also consulted.

Entries are listed alphabetically by language and within language by date of publication. With few exceptions, entries are in the original language. Inconsistencies in orthography, special symbols and diacritics were unavoidable, due to the multiplicity of sources used. While citations strive to include all basic elements (author, translator, title, imprint, and date), pragmatic reasons, such as unavailability of items for inspection, did not always allow for confirmation of bibliographic information. Without having the book in hand, it was not always possible to differentiate a reprint from a new edition, or a scholarly translation from a popular rendition, or to determine whether the text was complete or partial. In the interest of comprehensiveness, we choose to include even incomplete information.

In the 1856 edition of *Das Nibelungenlied* (Leipzig: Wiegand's) German scholar Friedrich Zarncke mentions the single early translation of which there is any trace: a thirteenth-century Dutch translation which survives as two fragments of a single parchment. The 1875 and 1887 editions of Zarncke's book contain further discussions of early translations, including some by notable poets. A short excerpt in English, attributed to Sir Walter Scott, was published in Edinburgh in 1814 (*Illustrations of Northern Antiquities;* see entry below), and Thomas Carlyle's metrical translation of a few strophes was published in an essay in the *Westminster Review,* Nr. 29 (1831). Paul Piper also lists translations from 1767 to 1889 in *Die Nibelungen. Erster Teil: Einleitung und die Klage.* Deutsche National-Litteratur, Bd. 6, 2. Berlin/Stuttgart, 1889. [BC, OP]

Armenian

Nibelungnerun ergê; t'argmanets' Arsēn Gh. Ghazikean. Venetik: Mkhit'arean tpagrut'iwn, 1925.

Chinese

Ni-pei-lung-ken chih ko. Ch'ien Ch'un-ch'i i. Pei-ching ti 1 pan. Pei-ching: Jen min wen hsueh ch'u pan she, 1994.

Czech

Píseño Nibelunzich. Ze staronemeckého originalu přelozil Frantisek V. Autrata: Praha, 1941.

Píseño Nibelunzich; Nárêk nad hrdiny Písnê. Ze stredohornonemeckého orig. přel. a pozn. k textu napsal Jindrich Pokorný; Doslov Pavel Trost; Ilustr. Miloslav Troup; Typografie Jan Solpera. 2., přeprac. a dopl. vyd. Praha: Odeon, 1989 (Pardubice: Východoces. tiskárny).

Nibelungy. Staronemecky original novocesky reprodukuje prof. Jan Kamenar. (unpublished)

Píseň o Nibelunzich. Prêlozil Jindrîch Pokorný. Praha: 1974.

Danish

Nibelungekvadet, i Dansk oversattelse (noget forkortet) ved Chr. Fledelius. Med understottelse af Carlsbergfondet. Kjøbenhavn og Kristiania: Gyldendalske boghandel, Nordisk forlag, 1912.

Dutch

1. and 2. Aventiure. Trans. by H. van de Hove. In: *De Broederhand. Tijdschrift voor neder- en hoogduitsche Letterkunde,* Wetenschap, Kunst en openbaar Leven. Opgesteld door Dr. J. W. Wolf. Brussel: 1845, S. 362–366.

Der Nevelingen Nood door Max Rooses. Brussel: J. Nijs, 1866.

Der Nevelingen Nood door Max Rooses. Dendermonde: E. Ducaju Zoon, 1867.

Het Nibelungenlied. Vertaald en ingeleid door Jan de Vries. Amsterdam: Wereldbibliotheek, 1954.

English

Illustrations of Northern Antiquities, from the earlier Teutonic and Scandinavian Romances, being an abstract of the Book of Heroes and Nibelungen Lay; with Translations of Metrical Tales from the old German, Danish, Swedish, and Icelandic Languages, with Notes and Dissertations. By Mr. Weber and Mr Jamieson. Edinburgh: 1814, pp. 167–213.

The Nibelungen Lied; or, Lay of the last Nibelungers. Translated into English verse after Carl Lachmann's collated and corrected text by Jonathan Birch. Berlin: Duncker, 1848. (Munich, 3rd ed. 1887; 4th ed. 1895)

The Fall of the Nibelungers: otherwise the Book of Kriemhild. A Translation of The Nibelunge Not, or Nibelungenlied by William Nanson. Lettsom. London: Williams and Norgate, 1850. (2nd ed.1873; London & New York, 3rd ed. 1890; New York, 4th ed. 1903, ⁵1908)

Echoes from mist-land, or, The Nibelungen lay: revealed to lovers of romance and chivalry by Auber Forestier. Chicago: S. C. Griggs; London: Trubner, 1877. (Chicago & London, 2nd ed. 1889, c. 1887)

Golden Threads from an ancient Loom; Das Nibelungen Lied, adapted to the use of Young readers. L. Hands. London: 1880.

The lay of the Nibelungs. Translated from the German by Alfred C. Foster-Barham. London & New York: Macmillan, 1887. Also Routledge: London, 1887[?], 1893.

The Fall of the Nibelungs done into English by Margaret Armour; illustrated and decorated by W. B. Macdougall. London: J. M. Dent, 1897. Also New York. (Repr. London: J. M. Dent, 1907; New York: E. P. Dutton, 1908; Repr. 1913, 1923, 1934, 1939, 1952)

The lay of the Nibelungs metrically translated from the Old German text by Alice Horton, and edition by Edward Bell, M.A.; to which is prefixed the essay on the Nibelungen lied by Thomas Carlyle. London: G. Bell, 1898. (2nd ed. 1901, 3rd ed. 1909)

Volsunga saga: The story of the Volsungs and Nibelungs, with certain songs from the Elder Edda. Translated from the Icelandic by Eirikr Magnusson and William Morris. London: Chiswick Press, 1901.

The Nibelungenlied, translated by William Nanson Lettsom; with a special introduction by William H. Carpenter. Editors and artists edition; Revised edition. New York: Colonial Press, 1901. Also Collier Press, Co-operative Publication Society. (Repr. 1977 Folcroft, Pa.: Folcroft Library Editions)

The Nibelungenlied translated into rhymed English verse in the metre of the original by George Henry Needler. New York: H. Holt, 1904. Also 1905, 1906.

Stories of the Nibelungen for young people, arranged by Gertrude R. Schottenfels. Chicago: A. Flanagan, [c1905].

The Nibelungs. Translated by George P. Upton. 2nd ed. Chicago: McClurg, 1906, 1911.

The Nibelungenlied. Translated by John Storer Cobb. Boston: Small, Maynard, 1906.

The Linden Leaf; or the Story of Siegfried retold from the Nibelungen Lied. London: [s.l.], 1907.

The Nibelungenlied translated from the Middle High German, with an introductory sketch and notes by Daniel Bussier Shumway. Boston: Houghton Mifflin, 1909. (Repr. Boston/New York, 1937)

The lay of the Nibelung men translated from the Old German text by Arthur S. Way. Cambridge: Cambridge University Press, 1911.

The Nibelungenlied: a prose translation, [translated by Margaret Armour]. London: J. M. Dent; New York: E. P. Dutton, 1939. (Repr. 1949, 1952)

Song of the Volsungs and the Nibelungs, translated by William Morris. Chicago: Published by Henry Regnery for the Great Books Foundation, 1949. (Repr. 1956)

The Nibelungenlied. Translated from the German by Margaret Armour, with an introduction by Franz Schoenberner. Illustrated by Edy Legrand. New York: Printed for the members of the Limited Editions Club by John Enschede en Zonen, 1960; Heritage Press ed., 1961. (Repr. 1995)

The tale of the Nibelungs, retold by E. F. Dodd. Macmillan, 1960.

The Song of the Nibelungs. A verse translation from the Middle High German *Nibelungenlied* by Frank G. Ryder. Detroit: Wayne State University Press, 1962. (Repr. 1982; repr. Francis G. Gentry and James K. Walter, eds. *German Epic Poetry: The Nibelungenlied, the older Lay of Hildebrand, and other Works* (*German Library,* vol. 1). New York: Continuum, 1995.)

The Nibelungenlied. Translated with an introduction and notes by D. G. Mowatt. London: Dent; New York: Dutton, 1962. (Repr. 1963, 1965)

Medieval Epics. Beowulf, The Nibelungenlied, The Song of Roland, The Cid. Standard translations by W. S. Merwin, Helen Mustard, and William Alfred. New York: Modern Library, 1963. (Repr. 1998)

The Nibelungenlied, a new translation by A. T. Hatto. Baltimore: Penguin Books, 1965. (Repr. 1966, rev. ed. Harmondsworth, 1969, 1970, 1972, 1973, 1975, 1976, 1978, 1979, 1981, 1982)

Grimes, Heilan Yvette. *The Legend of the Nibelungenlied (Scandinavian Saga Literature Series,* vol. 2). Wolfeboro, NH: Longwood Academic, 1989.

The Nibelungenlied. Translated from the Germanic and with an introduction by Robert Lichtenstein. Lewiston: Edwin Mellen Press, 1991.

The Lament of the Nibelungen. Translated and with an introduction by Winder McConnell. Columbia, S.C.: Camden House, 1994.

French

Le Nibelungenlied; traduction nouvelle, avec une introduction et des notes par F. Piquet. Paris: La Renaissance du livre, [n.d.].

Les Nibelungen: ou, Les Bourguignons chez Attila, Roi des Huns. Poème traduit de l'ancien idiome Teuton avec des notes historiques et littéraires par Mme. Ch. Moreau de la Meltiere; publié par Francis Riaux. Paris: Charpentier, 1837.

La fin tragique des Nibelons: ou, Les Bourguignons a la cour d'Attila. Poème traduit du Thyois ou vieux Allemand et mis en lumière par J.L. Bourdillon. Paris: J. Cherbuliez, 1852.

Les Nibelungen. Traduction nouvelle, précédée d'une étude sur la formation de l'épopée par Emile de Laveleye. Paris: Hachette; Bruxelles: A. Lacroix, van Meenen, 1866.

La saga des Nibelungen dans les Eddas et dans le Nord Scandinave. Traduction précédée d'une étude sur la formation des épopées nationales par E. de Laveleye. Bruxelles: A. Lacroix, Verboeckhoven et cie, 1866. Paris: Librairie Internationale, 1866.

Les Nibelungen; poème traduit de l'allemand par E. de Laveleye. Nouvelle édition. Paris: C. Marpon et E. Flammarion, 1879. (Repr. 1895)

La chanson des Nibelunge, traduite du moyen-haut-allemand avec une introduction et des notes par J. Firmery. Paris: A. Colin, 1909.

La légende des Nibelungen. A. Ehrhard. Paris: H. Piazza, 1929. (Repr. 1966, 1982)

La chanson des Nibelungen. Traduction intégrale avec introduction et notes par Maurice Colleville et Ernest Tonnelat. Paris: Aubier, Editions Montaigne, 1944. (Repr. 1958, 1971)

La chanson des Nibelungen. Traduction nouvelle par Maurice Betz, illustrée par Ed. Bendemann et J. Hubner. Paris: A l'enseigne du pot cassé, 1944.

Le Nibelungenlied. Édition partielle, avec introduction, notes et glossaire par Maurice Colleville et Ernest Tonnelat. Paris: Aubier, 1948.

Les Nibelungen. Traduction et préface de Raymond d'Haleine. Paris: Aubier, 1949.

La légende des Nibelungen: chanson de geste du XIII siècle. Texte de G. Bourdoncle, bois originaux d'Y. Lanore. Paris: F. Lanore, 1956.

Légendes des Nibelungen. Transcrites en allemand moderne par Edmund Mudrak; traduites en français par Robert Rezette. Paris: Nouvelles Éditions Latines, 1965.

La chanson des Nibelungen. Claude Mettra; présentation de Michel Cazenave. Paris: A. Michel, 1984.

La chanson des Nibelungs. Traduite du moyen haut allemand, présentée et annotée par Jean Amsler. [Paris]: Fayard, 1992.

Frisian

De Nibelungen. Walter A. Kreye. 1. Aufl. Leer: Schuster, 1970.

Greek

[*Das Nibelungenlied*]. [s.n.]: Tessaloniki, 1987.

Hebrew

ha-Nibelungim : ve-sipurim aherim, tirgem mi-Germanit ve-'ibed Shelomoh Tan'i. Tel Aviv: 'Am 'oved, 748, 1988.

Shirat ha-Nibelungim, me-et mehaber alum-shem; targum le-'Ivrit (mi-Germanit—'al- pi targumehem shel Zimrok ve-Yunghans) divre mavo, he'arot be-guf ha-tekst, maftehot, likut ve-shiluv iyurim, . . . Tel Aviv: Yaron Golan, 1996.

Italian

Il Canto dei Nibelongi, antico poema tedesco. Prima traduzione Italiana di Carlo Gernezzi. Milano: presso Pirotta E.C. tipografi-libraj, 1847.

I Nibelunghi; poema epico germanico; traduzione in versi italiani di Italo Pizzi. Milano: U. Hoepli [1889].

Alcuni episodi scelti dal poema dei Nibelunghi e pubblicata con una grammatica e un vocabolario da Giuseppe Ciardi-Dupr'e. Firenze: Libreria editrice fiorentina, 1905.

Ferrea gente, la saga dei Nibelunghi, narrata in prosa per Salvino Chiereghin. Torino: Societa Editrice Internazionale, 1953.

I Nibelunghi, a cura di L. di Sangiusto, prefazione e note di G.V. Amoretti. Nuova ed. Torino: Unione Tipografico Editrice Trinese, 1962.

I Nibelunghi, ed. Laura Mancinelli. Torino: [s.n.], 1972. 4th ed. 1984. (Repr. 1995)

I Nibelunghi, a cura di Giovanni Vittorio Amoretti. 1. ed. Milano: Editori Associati, 1988.

Japanese

Nibelungen no uta. 1. Yukiyama Toshio yaku. Tōkyō: Iwanami shoten, 1939.

Nibelungen no uta. Yukiyama Toshio yaku. Tōkyō: Iwanami shoten, Showa 14-[1939].

Nibelungen no uta. 3. Yukiyama Toshio yaku. Tōkyō: Iwanami shoten, 1942.

Nibelungen no uta. 1. Sagara Morio yaku. Tōkyō: Iwanami shoten, 1975.

Nibelungen no uta. Sagara Morio yaku. Kaihan. Tōkyō: Iwanami shoten, 1975.

Nibelungen no uta. 3. Sagara Morio yaku. Tōkyō: Iwanami shoten, 1975.

Nibelungen no uta: nīberunkuzoku no yakunan zen'yaku jojishi. Hattori Masaki yaku. Tōkyō: Toyo shuppan, 1977.

Nibelungen no uta. Sagara Morio yaku. Tōkyō: Iwanami shoten, 1981.

Nibelungen no Uta. 1. Okazaki Tadahiro yaku. Hiroshima: Keisuis ha, 1989.

Korean

Nibellunggen ŭi norae. H Ch'ang-un omgim. Ch'op'an. Sul-si: Pmusa, 1990.

Latin

Das Nibelungenlied, XX.–XXXIX, Aventiure: Nach der Handschrift B. Herausgegeben von Elfriede Stutz. Heidelberg:Winter, 1946

Lithuanian

Nibelungu giesme. Krištopaitė, Danutė.Vilnius: Vaga, 1980.

Polish

Pisn o Nibelungach w przekladzie A. J. Szabranskiego. Warschau: [s.n.], (1881/82). [Cited in Zarncke as "erscheint (1881/82) bogenweise in der Biblioteka najaclniejszych utworow"]

Nidola Nibelungow, (1–264). L. German, przeklad z jezyka sredniowiecznego gorno- niemieckego (wedlug wydania K. Bartscha). Krakau: Programm der Oberrealschule, 1881.

Romanian

Cîntecul Nibelungilor. Repovestit de Adrian Maniu, ilustraţii de A. Demian. Bucureşti: Editura de Stat pentru literaturăşi artă, 1958.

Russian

Pesn' o Nibelungakh. [Per. so sredneverkhnenem. i primech. IU. B. Korneeva]. Izd. podgot. V. G. Admoni [i dr. Poslesl. V. G. Admoni, s. 305–335]. Leningrad, "Nauka," Leningr. otd-nie, 1972.

Beovul'f. Starshaia edda. Pesn' o nibelungakh. Vstupit. stat ia, A. Gurevicha. Moskva: Khudozh. Literatura, 1975.

Serbo-Croatian

Pesma o Nibelunzima. Prevod i komentar Ivan Pudić. Beograd : Srpska književna zadruga, 1973.

Spanish

Los Nibelungos: poema aleman. Versión castellana en prosa de D. A. Fernandez Merino. Barcelona: C. Verdaguer, 1883.

Cantar de los Nibelungos. [Traducción al español de Mariano y Agustin Santiago Luque]. La Habana: Direccion Nacional de Educacion General, MINED, 1927.

Los nibelungos. Por Antonio Espina. Madrid: Aguilar, c1956.

Los Nibelungos. Traducción del aleman por Mariano y Agustin Santiago Luque. Madrid: Aguilar, 1963.

Los Nibelungos. Leyendas. Buenos Aires: Editorial Mundi, 1967.

El cantar de los Nibelungos. Traducción al español e introducción de Marianne Oeste de Bopp. Mexico: Porrua, 1975, [2]1978, [7]1995.

Los Nibelungos y otros textos. [Traducción, adaptación e introducciones, Elisabet [sic] Siefer; revisón de textos, Ma. Angeles González S.] México: SEP/Trillas, 1982.

La leyenda de los Nibelungas. Prólogo de Claude Mettra; ilustraciones de Grégoire Soberski; cubierta de Philippe Fix; traducción Alberto Villaba Rodríguez. Madrid: Altea, 1983.

Cantar de los Nibelungos. Edición de Emilio Lorenzo. 1a. ed. Madrid: Swan y Visor, 1983.

Cantar de los Nibelungos. Versión de Esther Tusquets; dibujos de José Bellalta. Barcelona: Lumen, 1984.

Cant dels Nibelungs. Versió d'Esther Tusquets. Ill. per Josep Bellalta. [Trad. al català de: Monserrat Gispert].—1. ed. [Barcelona]: Ed. Lumen, 1991.

Swedish

Nibelungen sangen: tolkad fran medelhogtyskan och med inledning av John Everet Härd. Stockholm: Natur och kultur, 1993.

Selected Bibliography

The following bibliography is selective and brief. It is intended to serve as an introduction to research on the Nibelungen theme and to act as a stimulus for further reading. Not taken into account are primary works of reception or writings about Richard Wagner. For guidance on the entire Wagnerian tradition the reader is referred to the *Wagner Handbook* of Ulrich Müller and Peter Wapnewski, listed below in Part VI, Reception. Of course, the more extensive bibliographies appended to individual entries should also be consulted.

I BIBLIOGRAPHIES

Abeling, Theodor. *Das Nibelungenlied und seine Literatur: Eine Bibliographie (Burt Franklin: Bibliography and Reference Series,* vol. 363). Reprint New York: Franklin, 1970.

Grosse, Siegfried, and Ursula Rautenberg. *Die Rezeption mittelalterlicher deutscher Dichtung: Eine Bibliographie ihrer Übersetzungen und Bearbeitungen seit der Mitte des 18. Jahrhunderts.* Tübingen: Niemeyer, 1989, 166–230.

Krogmann, Willy, and Ulrich Pretzel. *Bibliographie zum Nibelungenlied und zur Klage (Bibliographien zur deutschen Literatur des Mittelalters,* vol. 1). 4th ed. Berlin: Schmidt, 1966.

Überschlag, Doris. "Nibelungen-Bibliographie seit 1980." Wunderlich, Werner, and Müller, Ulrich. *"Waz sider da geschach." American-German Studies on the Nibelungenlied: Text and Reception (Göppinger Arbeiten zur Germanistik,* vol. 564). Göppingen: Kümmerle, 1992. 293–350.

II EDITIONS OF THE MEDIEVAL TRADITION
Nibelungenlied
A:

Lachmann, Karl, ed. *Der Nibelunge Noth und die Klage.* (Reprint of 5th edition [1878], Ulrich Pretzel, ed.) Hamburg: Robert Mölich Verlag, 1848.

Laistner, Ludwig, ed. *Das Nibelungenlied nach der Höhenems-Münchener Handschrift (A) in phototypischer Nachbildung, nebst Proben der Handschriften B und C.* Munich: Verlagsanstalt für Kunst und Wissenschaft, 1886.

Pretzel, Ulrich, ed. *Das Nibelungenlied: Kritisch herausgegeben und übertragen.* Stuttgart: Hirzel, 1973.

B:

Das Nibelungenlied und die Klage: Handschrift B (Cod. Sangall. 857). Fotomechanischer Nachdruck der Original-Handschrift (Deutsche

Texte in Handschriften, vol. 1). Cologne and Graz: Böhlau, 1962.

Wisniewski, Roswitha, ed. *Das Nibelungenlied.* 22nd ed. Reprint, Mannheim: Brockhaus, 1988.

C and Other Manuscripts:

Batts, Michael S., ed. *Das Nibelungenlied: Ein Paralleldruck der Handschriften A, B, und C nebst Lesarten der übrigen Handschriften.* Tübingen: Niemeyer, 1971.

Brackert, Helmut, ed. *Das Nibelungenlied: Mittelhochdeutscher Text und Übertragung. Übersetzt und mit einem Anhang versehen,* 2 vols. (Fischer Taschenbücher, vols. 6038, 6039). Frankfurt: Fischer Taschenbuch Verlag, 1981

Brackert, Helmut, ed. *Die Nibelungen: In der Wiedergabe von Frank Keim. Illustrationen von Karl 0. Czeschka* (Insel-Taschenbuch, vol. 14). Frankfurt: Insel, 1972.

de Boor, Helmut, ed. *Das Nibelungenlied. Zweisprachig. Herausgegeben und übersetzt* (Sammlung Dieterich, vol. 250). 3rd ed. Leipzig: Dieterich 1989.

Ehrismann, Otfrid, ed. *Das Nibelungenlied: Abbildungen, Transkriptionen, und Materialien zur gesamten handschriftlichen Überlieferung der I. und XXX. Aventiure* (Litterae, vol. 23). Göppingen: Kümmerle, 1973.

Engels, Heinz, ed. *Das Nibelungenlied: A Complete Transcription in Modern German Type of the Text of Manuscript C from the Fürstenberg Court Library, Donaueschingen. With an Essay on the Manuscript and Its Provenance by Erna Huber.* New York: Praeger, 1969.

Glaßner, Christine. "Ein Fragment einer neuen Handschrift des Nibelungenliedes in Melk." *Beiträge zur Geschichte der deutschen Sprache und Literatur* 120 (1998): 376–394.

Heinzle, Joachim, and Klaus Klein. "Zu den Melker Fragmenten des Nibelungenlieds." *Zeitschrift für deutsches Altertum* 127 (1998): 373–380.

Henning, Ursula, ed. *Das Nibelungenlied nach der Handschrift C* (Altdeutsche Textbibliothek, vol. 81). Tübingen: Niemeyer, 1977.

Hoffmann, Werner, ed. *Das Nibelungenlied: Text, Nacherzählung, Wort- und Begriffserklärungen.* Darmstadt: Wissenschaftliche Buchgesellschaft, 1972.

Hornung, Hans, and Günther Schweikle, eds. *Das Nibelungenlied in spätmittelalterlichen Illustrationen: Die 37 Bildseiten des Hundeshagenschen Kodex der Staatsbibliothek Preussischer Kulturbesitz Berlin.* 2nd ed. Bozen: Athesia, 1983.

Keller, Adelberg von, ed. *Das Nibelungenlied nach der Piaristenhandschrift herausgegeben* (Biblio-

thek des Litterarischen Vereins in Stuttgart, vol. 142). Tübingen: Litterarischer Verein in Stuttgart, 1879.

Rosenfeld, Hans-Friedrich. "Nibelungenfragmente aus Rosenheim und München." *Beiträge zur Geschichte der deutschen Sprache und Literatur* (Tübingen) 109 (1987): 14.

Schröder, Werner, ed. *Der Nibelunge Liet und Diu Klage: Die Donaueschinger Handschrift 63 [Laßberg 174]. Mit einem forschungsgeschichtlichen Beitrag zu ihrer Bedeutung für Überlieferung und Textgeschichte des Epos* (Deutsche Texte in Handschriften, vol. 3). Cologne, Vienna: Böhlau, 1969.

Springeth, Margarete. "Beobachtungen zur Nibelungenrezeption in der Wiener Piaristenhandschrift (k)." In *3. Pöchlarner Heldenliedgespräch. Die Rezeption des Nibelungenliedes,* edited by Klaus Zatloukal. Philologica Germanica 16. Vienna: Fassbaender, 1995, pp. 173–185.

Lament

Bartsch, Karl, ed. *Diu Klage.* Reprint ed. Leipzig, 1875. Darmstadt: Wissenschaftliche Buchgesellschaft, 1964.

McConnell, Winder. *The Lament of the Nibelungen.* Columbia, SC: Camden House, 1994.

Volsunga Saga

Anderson, George K., ed. and trans. *The Saga of the Volsungs, Together with Excerpts from the Nornageststhattr and Three Chapters from the Prose Edda.* Newark: University of Delaware, 1982.

Byock, Jesse L., ed. and trans. *The Saga of the Volsungs: The Norse Epic of Sigurd the Dragon Slayer.* Berkeley: University of California, 1990.

Diederichs, Ulf, ed. *Nordische Nibelungen: Die Sagas der Völsungen, von Ragnar Lodbrok und von Hrolf Kraki. Aus dem Altnordischen übertragen von Paul Hermann.* Neuausgabe. Reprint der Texte nach der Sammlung Thule, vol. 21: *Isländische Heldenromane,* Jena 1923 (Diederich's Gelbe Reihe, vol. 54). Cologne: Diederichs, 1985.

Finch, R. G., ed. *The Saga of the Volsungs: Edited and Translated with Introduction, Notes, and Appendices (Icelandic Texts).* London and Edinburgh: Nelson, 1965.

Magnússon, Eirikr, and William Morris, eds. *Volsunga Saga: The Story of the Volsungs and Nibelungs with Certain Songs from the Elder Edda. With an Introduction and Notes by H. Halliday Sparling (Camelot Series).* London and New York: Walter Scott Publishing, 1888.

Schlauch, Margaret, trans. *The Saga of the Volsungs: The Saga of Ragnar Lodbrok, Together with The Lay of Kraka.* 2nd ed. New York: American-Scandinavian Foundation, 1949.

Thidrekssaga

Bertelsen, Henrik, ed. *Thidriks saga af Bern,* 2 vols. (Samfund til Udgivelse af gammel nordisk Litteratur, vol. 34). Copenhagen: 1905–11, 1908–11.

Erichsen, Finne. *Die Geschichte Thidreks von Bern* (Thule: Altnordische Dichtung und Prosa, vol. 22). 3rd ed. Dusseldorf, Cologne: Diederichs, 1967.

Haymes, Edward, trans. *The Saga of Thidrek of Bern* (Garland Library of Medieval Literature, vol. 56). New York: Garland, 1988.

Hyltén-Cavallius, Gunnar Olof, ed. *Sagan om Didrik af Bern: Efter svenska handskrifter* (Samlinger utgifna af Svenska Fornskrift-Sällskapet, vol. 5.1, 11). Stockholm: Norstedt, 1850–1854.

Edda

Faraday, Winifred, ed. *The Edda.* New York: AMS Press, 1972. Reprint of 1st ed. 1902.

Genzmer, Felix. *Die Edda: Götterdichtung, Spruchweisheit und Heldengesänge der Germanen.* Eingeleitet von Kurt Schier. 3rd ed. Munich: Diederichs, 1995.

Hollander, Lee M., ed. and trans. *The Poetic Edda.* 2nd ed. Austin: University of Texas, 1962

Larrington, Carolyne, ed. *The Poetic Edda: Translated with an introduction and notes* (World's Classics). Oxford and New York: Oxford University Press, 1996.

Neckel, Gustav, ed. *Die Lieder des Codex Regius nebst verwandten Denkmälern.* 4th ed. Hans Kuhn (Germanische Bibliothek). Heidelberg: Winter, 1968.

Taylor, Paul B., W[ynstan] H[ugh] Auden, trans. *The Elder Edda: A Selection.* New York: Vintage, 1970 [recte. 1969].

Terry, Patricia, trans. *Poems of the Vikings: The Elder Edda.* Indianapolis: Bobbs-Merrill, 1969.

Hürnen Seyfried

Golther, Wolfgang, ed. *Das Lied vom Hürnen Seyfrid nach der Druckredaktion des 16. Jahrhunderts. Mit einem Anhange: das Volksbuch vom gehörnten Siegfried nach der ältesten Ausgabe (1726).* 2nd edition. Halle: Niemeyer, 1911.

King, Kenneth C., ed., *Das Lied vom Hürnen Seyfrid: Critical Edition with Introduction and Notes.* Manchester: Manchester University Press, 1959.

Anthology

Storch, Wolfgang, ed. *Das Buch der Nibelungen: Eine repräsentative Sammlung vom mittelalterlichen Nibelungenlied bis zu Bertolt Brecht* (Heyne-Bücher: Heyne Allgemeine Reihe, vol. 6983) Munich: Heyne, 1988.

III   HISTORY OF RESEARCH

Ehrismann, Otfrid. *Nibelungenlied 1755–1920: Regesten und Kommentare zu Forschung und Rezeption* (Beiträge zur deutschen Philologie, vol. 15). Gießen: Schmitz, 1986.

Fleet, Mary. "The Recent Study of the Nibelungenlied." *Journal of English and Germanic Philology* 52 (1953): 32–49.

Gentry, Francis G. "Trends in 'Nibelungenlied' Research since 1949: A Critical Review." *Amsterdamer Beiträge zur Älteren Germanistik* 7 (1974): 125–135.

Hoffmann, Werner. "Die englische und amerikanische Nibelungenforschung. " *Zeitschrift für deutsche Philologie* 84 (1965): 267–278.

———. *Das Siegfriedbild in der Forschung* (Erträge der Forschung, vol. 127). Darmstadt: Wissenschaftliche Buchgesellschaft, 1979.

Körner, Josef. *Nibelungenforschungen der deutschen Romantik.* Darmstadt: Wissenschaftliche Buchgesellschaft, 1968.

McConnell, Winder. "The *Nibelungenlied.* Some Comments on Recent Research." *Res Publica Litterarum* 13 (1990): 155–178.

Moelleken, Wolfgang W. "Methodik der Nibelungenliedinterpretation," *German Quarterly* 39 (1966): 289–298.

Sperberg-MacQueen, Christopher M. *An Analysis of Recent Work on Nibelungenlied Poetics.* Stanford: Stanford University Press, 1985.

Thorp, Mary. *The Study of the Nibelungenlied: Being the History of the Study of the Epic and Legend from 1755 to 1937.* Oxford: Oxford University Press, 1940.

IV   GENERAL

Andersson, Theodore M. *A Preface to the 'Nibelungenlied.'* Stanford: Stanford University Press, 1987.

———. *The Legend of Brynhild* (Islandica, vol. 63). Ithaca, London: Cornell University Press, 1980.

———. "Why does Siegfried Die?" In *Germanic Studies in Honor of Otto Springer,* edited by Stephen J. Kaplowitt. Pittsburgh: K & S Enterprises, 1978. 29–39.

Bartels, Hildegard. *Epos, die Gattung in der Geschichte: Eine Begriffsbestimmung vor dem Hintergrund der Hegelschen 'Ästhetik' anhand* von *'Nibelungenlied' und 'Chanson de Roland'* (Frankfurter Beiträge zur Germanistik, vol. 22). Heidelberg: Winter, 1982.

Batts, Michael. *Die Form der Aventiuren im Nibelungenlied* (Beiträge zur deutschen Philologie, vol. 29).Gießen: Schmitz, 1961.

Bäuml, Franz H., and Donald J. Ward. "Zur mündlichen Überlieferung des Nibelungenliedes." *Deutsche Vierteljahresschrift für Literaturwissenschaft und Geistesgeschichte* 41 (1967): 351–390.

———and Edda Spielmann. "From Illiteracy to Literacy: Prolegomena to a Study of the Nibelungenlied." *Forum for Modern Language Studies* 10 (1974): 248–259.

———and Eva-Maria Fallone. *A Concordance to the Nibelungenlied: Bartsch-de Boor Text. With Structural Pattern Index, Frequency Ranking List, and Reverse Index* (Compendia, vol. 7). Leeds: Maney, 1976.

Bekker, Hugo. *The Nibelungenlied: A Literary Analysis.* Toronto: Toronto University Press, 1971.

Bernreuther, Marie-Luise. *Motivationsstruktur und Erzählstrategie im 'Nibelungenlied' und in der 'Klage'* (Wodan, vol. 41). Greifswald: Reineke-Verlag, 1994.

Boklund-Schlagbauer, Ragnhild. *Studien zu Erzählstrukturen im Nibelungenlied und in nordischen Fassungen des Nibelungenstoffes* (Göppinger Arbeiten zur Germanistik, vol. 626). Göppingen: Kümmerle, 1996.

Bönnen, Gerold and Volker Gallé, eds. *Ein Lied von gestern? Wormser Symposium zur Rezeptionsgeschichte des Nibelungenliedes.* Worms: Stadtarchiv, 1999 (Der Wormsgau, Beiheft 35).

Borghart, Kees Hermann Rudi. *Das Nibelungenlied: Die Spuren mündlichen Ursprungs in schriftlicher Überlieferung* (Amsterdamer Publikationen zur Sprache und Literatur, vol. 31). Amsterdam: Rodopi, 1977.

Brackert, Helmut. *Beiträge zur Handschriftenkritik des Nibelungenliedes* (Quellen und Forschungen zur Sprach- und Kulturgeschichte der germanischen Völker. N.F., vol. 11). Berlin: Schmidt, 1963.

Breuer, Dieter, and Jürgen Breuer. *Mit spaeher rede: Politische Geschichte im Nibelungenlied.* 2nd ed. Munich: Fink, 1996.

Bumke, Joachim. *Die vier Fassungen der Nibelungenklage: Untersuchungen zur Überlieferungsgeschichte und Textkritik der höfischen Epik im 13. Jahrhundert.* Berlin, New York: de Gruyter, 1996.

Burger, Bernhard. *Die Grundlegung des Unter-gangsgeschehens im Nibelungenlied.* Freiburg: Hochschulverlag, 1985.

Buschinger, Danielle, and Wolfgang Spiewok, eds. *La chanson des Nibelungen hier et aujourd'hui: Actes du colloque, Amiens, 12 et 13 janvier 1991* (Wodan, vol. 7). Amiens: Université de Picardie, 1991.

Curschmann, Michael. "'Nibelungenlied' und 'Nibelungenklage': Über Mündlichkeit und Schriftlichkeit im Prozeß der Episierung." In *Deutsche Literatur im Mittelalter. Kontakte und Perspektiven. Hugo Kuhn zum Gedenken,* edited by Christoph Cormeau. Stuttgart: Metzler, 1979, 85–119.

———. "'Nibelungenlied' und 'Klage.'" *Die deutsche Literatur des Mittelalters: Verfasserlexikon.* 2nd ed., vol. 6. Berlin, New York: de Gruyter, 1987, 926–969.

Czerwinski, Peter. "*Das Nibelungenlied:* Widersprüche höfischer Gewaltreglementierung." Frey, Winfried, Raitz, Walter, and Seitz, Dieter, eds. *Einführung in die deutsche Literatur des 12. bis 16. Jahrhunderts,* vol. 1: *Adel und Hof—12/13. Jahrhundert* (Grundkurs Literaturgeschichte). Opladen: Westdeutscher Verlag, 1979, 49–87.

Dürrenmatt, Nelly. *Das Nibelungenlied im Kreis der höfischen Dichtung.* Bern: Lang, 1945.

Ehrismann, Otfrid. *Das Nibelungenlied: Epoche—Werk—Wirkung* (Arbeitsbücher zur Literaturgeschichte). Munich: C. H. Beck, 1987.

Falk, Walter. *Das Nibelungenlied in seiner Epoche: Revision eines romantischen Mythos* (Germanische Bibliothek, vol. 3). Heidelberg: Winter, 1971.

Fechter, Werner. *Siegfrieds Schuld und das Weltbild des Nibelungenliedes.* Hamburg: Toth, 1948.

Fenik, Bernard. *Homer and the Nibelungenlied: Comparative Studies in Epic Style.* Cambridge [et al.]: Harvard University Press, 1986.

Frakes, Jerold C. *Brides and Doom: Gender, Property, and Power in Medieval German Women's Epic* (Middle Ages Series). Philadelphia: University of Pennsylvania Press, 1994.

Fromm, Hans. "Der oder die Dichter des Nibelungenliedes." *Colloquio italo-germanisco sul thema I Nibelunghi. Organizzato d'intesa con la Bayerische Akademie der Wissenschaften (Roma, 14–15 maggio 1973).* Rome: Accademia nazionale dei Lincei, 1974, 63–74.

Gentry, Francis G. *Triuwe and Vriunt in the Nibelungenlied* (Amsterdamer Publikationen zur Sprache und Literatur, vol. 19). Amsterdam: Rodopi, 1975.

Göhler, Peter. *Das Nibelungenlied: Erzählweise, Figuren, Weltanschauung, literaturgeschichtliches Umfeld* (Literatur und Gesellschaft). Berlin: Akademie-Verlag, 1989.

Gotzmann, Carola L. *Heldendichtung des 13. Jahrhunderts: Siegfried, Dietrich, Ortnit* (Information und Interpretation, vol. 4). Frankfurt [et al.]: Lang, 1987.

Hansen, Hilde E. *'Das ist Hartnäckigkeit in einer verwerflichen Sache; sie selbst nennen es Treue:' Literatursoziologische Untersuchungen zum Nibelungenlied* (Europäische Hochschulschriften, Reihe 1: Deutsche Sprache und Literatur, vol. 1195). Frankfurt [et al.]: Lang, 1990.

Haug, Walter. "Höfische Idealität und heroische Tradition im Nibelungenlied." *Colloquio italogermanisco sul thema I Nibelunghi. Organizzato d'intesa con la Bayerische Akademie der Wissenschaften (Roma, 14–15 maggio 1973).* Rome: Accademia nazionale dei Lincei, 1974, 35–50.

Haymes, Edward R. *The Nibelungenlied: History and Interpretation* (Illinois Medieval Monographs, vol. 2). Urbana, Chicago: University of Illinois Press, 1986.

Heinzle, Joachim. *Mittelhochdeutsche Dietrichepik: Untersuchungen zur Tradierung, Überlieferungskritik und Gattungsgeschichte später Heldenepik* (Münchner Untersuchungen und Texte zur deutschen Literatur des Mittelalters, vol. 62). Zurich, Munich: Artemis, 1978.

———. *Das Nibelungenlied: Eine Einführung* (Fischer Taschenbuch, vol. 11843). Frankfurt: Fischer Taschenbuch Verlag, 1994.

Hoffmann, Werner. *Das Nibelungenlied* (Sammlung Metzler, vol. 7). 6th ed. Stuttgart: Metzler, 1992.

Höfler, Otto. "Die Anonymität des Nibelungenlieds." Hauck, Karl, ed. *Zur germanisch-deutschen Heldensage* (Wege der Forschung, vol. 14). Darmstadt: Wissenschaftliche Buchgesellschaft, 1965, 330–392. (Originally in *Deutsche Vierteljahresschrift für Literaturwissenschaft und Geistesgeschichte* 29 (1955): 167–213.)

Janota, Johannes, and Jürgen Kühnel. "'Uns ist in niuwen mæren wunders vil geseit': Zu Ritter-Schaumburgs 'Die Nibelungen zogen nordwärts.'" *Soester Zeitschrift* 97 (1985): 13–25.

Ihlenburg, Karl Heinz. *Das Nibelungenlied: Problem und Gehalt.* Berlin: AkademieVerlag, 1969.

Kaiser, Gert. "Deutsche Heldenepik." In *Europäisches Hochmittelalter* (Neues Handbuch der Literaturwissenschaft, vol. 7), edited by Henning Krauss. Wiesbaden: Athenaion, 1981, 181–216.

Knapp, Fritz Peter, ed. *Nibelungenlied und Klage:*

Sage und Geschichte, Struktur und Gattung. Passauer Nibelungengespräche 1985. Heidelberg: Winter, 1987.

Körner, Josef. *Das Nibelungenlied* (Aus Natur und Geisteswelt, vol. 591). Leipzig: Teubner, 1921.

Kralik, Dietrich. *Die Sigfridtrilogie im Nibelungenlied und in der Thidrekssaga.* Halle: Niemeyer, 1941.

Kunstmann, Heinrich: *Vorläufige Untersuchungen über den bairischen Bulgarenmord von 631/632: Der Tatbestand* (Slavistische Beiträge, vol. 159). Munich: Sanger, 1982.

Mackensen, Lutz. *Die Nibelungen: Sage, Geschichte, ihr Lied und sein Dichter* (Schriften zur Literatur- und Geistesgeschichte, vol. 1). Stuttgart: Hauswedell, 1984.

Mancinelli, Laura. *La canzone dei Nibelunghi: Problemi e valori.* Torino: Giappichelli, 1969.

Masser, Achim, ed. *Hohenemser Studien zum Nibelungenlied.* (Montfont: Vierteljahrsschrift für Geschichte und Gegenwart Vorarlbergs, 32, no. 3–4). Dornbirn: Vorarlberger Verlagsanstalt, 1981.

McConnell, Winder. *The Nibelungenlied* (Twayne's World Authors Series: German Literature). Boston: Twayne, 1984.

———, ed. *A Companion to the Nibelungenlied* (Studies in German Literature, Linguistics, and Culture). Columbia: Camden House, 1998.

Moser, Dietz Rüdiger, and Marianne Sammer. *Nibelungenlied und Klage. Symposion Kloster Andechs 1955, mit Nachträgen bis 1998.* Munich: Universität München Institut für Bayerische Literaturgeschichte, 1988.

Mowatt, D.G., and Hugh D. Sacker. *The Nibelungenlied. An Interpretative Commentary.* Toronto: University of Toronto Press, 1967.

Müller, Jan-Dirk. "'Sivrit: künec—man—eigenholt'. Zur sozialen Problematik des Nibelungenliedes." *Amsterdamer Beiträge zur Älteren Germanistik* 7 (1974): 85–124.

———. "Das Nibelungenlied." In *Mittelhochdeutsche Romane und Heldenepen: Interpretationen* (Universal-Bibliothek, 8914). Stuttgart: Reclam, 1993, 146–172.

———. *Spielregeln für den Untergang. Neue Lektüren des Nibelungenliedes.* Tübingen: Niemeyer, 1998.

Müller, Reinhard. "Nibelungenlied." In *Deutsches Literatur-Lexikon: Biographisch-bibliographisches Handbuch,* edited by Wilhelm Kosch. 3rd edition, vol 11, edited by Heinz Rupp and Carl Ludwig Land. Bern/Stuttgart: Francke, 1988, 235–251.

Mueller, Werner A. *The Nibelungenlied Today: Its*

Substance, Essence, and Significance (University of North Carolina Studies in the Germanic Languages and Literatures, vol. 34). Chapel Hill: University of North Carolina Press, 1962. Reprint, New York: AMS, 1966.

Nagel, Bert. *Das Nibelungenlied: Stoff—Form—Ethos.* 2nd ed. Frankfurt: Hirschgraben, 1970.

Neumann, Friedrich. *Das Nibelungenlied in seiner Zeit* (Kleine Vandenhoeck-Reihe, vol. 253). Göttingen: Vandenhoeck & Ruprecht, 1967.

Oergel, Maike. *The Return of King Arthur and the Nibelungen. National Myth in Nineteenth-Century English and German Literature* (European Cultures: Studies in Literatur and the Arts, vol. 10). Berlin/ New York: de Gruyter, 1998.

Panzer, Friedrich. *Studien zum Nibelungenlied.* Frankfurt: Diesterweg, 1945.

———. *Das Nibelungenlied: Entstehung und Gestalt.* Stuttgart: Kohlhammer, 1955.

Reichert, Hermann. *Nibelungenlied und Nibelungensage* (Böhlau Studien-Bücher). Vienna and Cologne: Böhlau, 1985.

Reuter, Otto Sigfrid. *Gestalten und Gedanken im Nibelungenliede* (Forschungsreihe historische Faksimiles). Reprint Bremen: Faksimile-Verlag, 1986.

Rupp, Heinz, ed. *Nibelungenlied und Kudrun* (Wege der Forschung, vol. 54). Darmstadt: Wissenschaftliche Buchgesellschaft, 1976.

Schulze, Ursula. "Nibelungenlied." In *Deutsche Dichter I: Mittelalter,* edited by Gunter E. Grimm and Frank Rainer Max (Universal-Bibliothek 8611). Stuttgart: Reclam, 1989, 142–163.

———. *Das Nibelungenlied* (Universal-Bibliothek, vol. 17604). Stuttgart: Reclam, 1997.

Schröder, Walter J. *Das Nibelungenlied: Versuch einer Deutung.* Halle: Niemeyer, 1954.

Schröder, Werner. *Nibelungenlied-Studien.* Stuttgart: Hirzel, 1968.

Seitter, Walter. *Das politische Wissen im Nibelungenlied: Vorlesungen* (Internationaler Merve-Diskurs, vol. 141). Berlin: Merve, 1987.

———. *Versprechen, versagen: Frauenmacht und Frauenästhetik in der Kriemhild Diskussion des 13. Jahrhunderts* (Internationaler Merve-Diskurs, vol. 154). Berlin: Merve, 1990.

———. *Distante Siegfried-Paraphrasen: Jesus, Helmbrecht, Dietrich* (Internationaler Merve-Diskurs, vol. 179). Berlin: Merve, 1993.

Simon, Elisabeth. *Höfisch-ritterliche Elemente im Nibelungenlied. Ein Beitrag zur Frage nach der sozialen Herkunft des Verfassers.* Duisburg: Lange, 1927.

Sklenar, Hans. "Die literarische Gattung der Nibelungenklage und das Ende 'alter mære.'" *Poetica* 9 (1977): 41–61.

Splett, Jochen. *Rüdiger von Bechelaren: Studien zum 2. Teil des Nibelungenliedes* (Germanische Bibliothek, Reihe 3). Heidelberg: Winter, 1968.

Stech, Julian. *Das Nibelungenlied: Appellstrukturen und Mythosthematik in der mittelhochdeutschen Dichtung* (Europäische Hochschulschriften, Reihe 1: Deutsche Sprache und Literatur, vol. 1410). Frankfurt [et al.]: Lang, 1993.

Tally, Joyce A. *The Dragon's Progress: The Significance of the Dragon in 'Beowulf,' the 'Volsunga Saga,' 'Das Nibelungenlied,' and 'Der Ring des Nibelungen,'* Denver: University of Colorado Press, 1983.

Wachinger, Burghart. *Studien zum Nibelungenlied: Vorausdeutungen, Aufbau, Motivierung.* Tübingen: Niemeyer, 1960.

Wailes, Stephen. "The *Nibelungenlied* as Heroic Epic." In *Heroic Epic and Saga: An Introduction to the World's Great Folk Epics,* edited by Felix J. Oinas. Bloomington: Indiana University Press, 1978, 120–143.

Wakefield, Ray M. *Nibelungen Prosody* (De proprietatibus litterarum, Seria practica, vol. 112). The Hague: Mouton, 1976.

Wapnewski, Peter. "Rüdigers Schild: Zur 37. Aventiure des 'Nibelungenliedes'." *Euphorion* 54 (1960): 380–410.

Weber, Gottfried. *Das Nibelungenlied: Problem und Idee.* Stuttgart: Metzler, 1963.

Wenzel, Horst. "'Ze hove und ze holze—offenlich und tougen': Zur Darstellung und Deutung des Unhöfischen in der höfischen Epik und im Nibelungenlied." In *Höfische Literatur, Hofgesellschaft, Höfische Lebensform um 1200,* edited by Gert Kaiser and Jan-Dirk Müler. Dusseldorf: Droste, 1986, 277–300.

Wisniewski, Roswitha. *Die Darstellung des Nibelungenuntergangs in der Thidreksaga: Eine quellenkritische Untersuchung* (Hermea, NF vol. 9). Tübingen: Niemeyer, 1961.

———. *Mittelalterliche Dietrichdichtung* (Sammlung Metzer, vol. 205). Stuttgart: Metzler, 1986.

Wunderlich, Werner, and Ulrich Müller, eds. *"Waz sider da geschach." American-German Studies on the Nibelungenlied. Text and Reception* (Göppinger Arbeiten zur Germanistik, vol. 564). Göppingen: Kümmerle, 1992.

Zatloukal, Klaus, ed. *Pöchlarner Heldenliedgespräch: Das Nibelungenlied und der mittlere Donauraum* (Philologica Germanica, vol. 12). Vienna: Fassbaender, 1990.

V HISTORY AND HEROIC LEGEND

Berndt, Helmut. *Die Nibelungen: Auf den Spuren eines sagenhaften Volkes* (Bastei-Lübbe Taschenbuch; vol. 44109). Bergisch Gladbach: Lübbe, 1992.

Hansen, Walter. *Die Spur der Helden: Die Gestalten des Nibelungenliedes in Sage und Geschichte. Mit Illustrationen aus der Hundeshagener Handschrift.* Bergisch Gladbach: Lübbe, 1988.

Haymes, Edward R., and Susann T. Samples. *Heroic Legends of the North: An Introduction to the Nibelung and Dietrich Cycles* (Garland Reference Library of the Humanities, vol. 1403). New York, London: Garland, 1996.

Haug, Walter. "Andreas Heuslers Heldensagenmodell: Prämissen, Kritik und Gegenentwurf. " *Zeitschrift für deutsches Altertum* 104 (1975): 273–292.

Heusler, Andreas. *Nibelungensage und Nibelungenlied. Die Stoffgeschichte des deutschen Heldenepos.* Reprint 6th ed. Darmstadt: Wissenschaftliche Buchgesellschaft, 1991.

Huber, Werner. *Auf der Suche nach den Nibelungen.* Gütersloh: Präsentverlag, 1981.

Kolb, Julius. *Vom Rhein zur Donau: Auf den Spuren der Nibelungen.* Munich: Droemer Knaur, 1989.

Murdoch, Brian. *The Germanic Hero: Politics and Pragmatism in Early Medieval Poetry.* London, Rio Grande: Hambledon, 1996.

Reyl, Gerhard. *Spuren im Wind: Das Nibelungenlied als Geschichtsquelle.* Limburg: Schaub, 1995.

Uecker, Heiko. *Germanische Heldensage* (Sammlung Metzler, vol. 106). Stuttgart: Metzler, 1972.

von See, Klaus. *Germanische Heldensage: Stoffe, Probleme, Methoden. Eine Einführung.* 2nd ed. Frankfurt: Athenäum, 1981.

Wahl Armstrong, Marianne. *Rolle und Charakter. Studien zur Menschendarstellung im Nibelungenlied* (Göppinger Arbeiten zur Germanistik, vol. 221). Göppingen: Kümmerle, 1979.

VI RECEPTION

Bartsch, Karl. "Die dichterische Gestaltung der Nibelungensage." Bartsch, Karl. *Gesammelte Vorträge und Aufsätze.* Freiburg i. Br., Tübingen: Mohr, 1883, 86–108.

Brackert, Helmut. "Nibelungenlied und Nationalgedanke: Zur Geschichte einer deutschen Ideologie." In *Mediaevalia litteraria: Festschrift für Helmut de Boor,* edited by Helmut Kolb and Ursula Hennig. Munich: Beck, 1971, 343–364.

Bunge, Eldo F. "Siegfried in German Literature." *Philological Quarterly* 19 (1940): 29–65.

Das Nibelungenlied in der deutschen Kunst des 19. und 20. Jahrhunderts: Ausstellung der Stadtbibliothek Worms 31. Mai—15. August 1991. Worms: Stadtbibliothek Worms, 1981.

Ehrismann, Otfrid. *Das Nibelungenlied in Deutschland. Studien zur Rezeption des Nibelungenliedes von der Mitte des 18. Jahrhunderts bis zum Ersten Weltkrieg* (Münchner Germanistische Beiträge 14). Munich: Fink, 1975.

Frenzel, Elisabeth. *Stoffe der Weltliteratur. Ein Lexikon dichtungsgeschichtlicher Längsschnitte* (Kröners Taschenausgabe, vol. 300). 7th ed. Stuttgart: Kröner, 1988, 549–557.

Gentry, Francis G. "Die Rezeption des Nibelungenliedes in der Weimarer Republik." In *Das Weiterleben des mittelalters in der deutschen Literatur,* edited by James F. Poag and Gerhild Scholz-Williams. Königstein: Athenäum, 1983, 142–156.

Gruener, G. "The *Nibelungenlied* and Sage in modern Poetry." *Publications of the Modern Language Association of America* 11 (1896): 220–257.

Härd, John Evert. *Das Nibelungenepos: Wertung und Wirkung von der Romantik bis zur Gegenwart.* Tübingen, Basel: Francke, 1996.

Heinzle, Joachim, and Waldschmidt, Anneliese, eds. *Die Nibelungen: Ein deutscher Wahn, ein deutscher Alptraum. Studien und Dokumente zur Rezeption des Nibelungenstoffes im 19. und 20. Jahrhundert* (Suhrkamp Taschenbuch, vol. 2110) Frankfurt: Suhrkamp, 1991.

Hess, Günter. "Siegfrieds Wiederkehr: Zur Geschichte einer deutschen Mythologie in der Weimarer Republik." *Internationales Archiv für Sozialgeschichte der deutschen Literatur* 6 (1981): 112–144.

Hoffmann, Werner. "Nibelungenromane." In *Helden und Heldensage: Otto Gschwantler zum 60. Geburtstag* (Philologica Germanica, vol. 11). Vienna: Fassbaender, 1990, 113–142.

Kastner, Jörg. *Das Nibelungenlied in den Augen der Künstler vom Mittelalter bis zur Gegenwart: Ausstellung in der Staatlichen Bibliothek Passau vom 2. Mai 1986 bis 12. Juni 1986.* Passau: Passavia-Universitätsverlag, 1986.

Kolk, Rainer. *Berlin oder Leipzig? Eine Studie zur sozialen Organisation der Germanistik im 'Nibelungenstreit'* (Studien und Texte zur Sozialgeschichte der Literatur, vol. 30). Tübingen: Niemeyer, 1990.

Martin, Bernhard R. *Nibelungen-Metamorphosen: Die Geschichte eines Mythos.* Munich: Iudicium, 1992.

Müller, Ulrich, and Peter Wapnewski, eds. *Wagner Handbook.* Deathridge, John, trans. and ed. Cambridge, Mass. and London: Harvard University Press, 1992 (Originally *Richard Wagner-Handbuch*. Stuttgart: Kröner, 1986).

Münkler, Herfried, and Wolfgang Storch, eds. *Siegfrieden: Politik mit einem deutschen Mythos* (Rotbuch, vol. 330). Berlin: Rotbuch Verlag, 1988.

Müller, Ulrich. "Die Auferstehung der Nibelungen: Beobachtungen zur Rezeption des Nibelungen-Mythos in den Achtziger Jahren." In *Festschrift für Rudolf Große zum 65. Geburtstag,* edited by Sabine Heimann et al. Stuttgart: Heinz, 1989, 495–506.

Rehorn, Karl. *Die deutsche Sage von den Nibelungen in der deutschen Poesie.* Frankfurt: 1877.

Schulte-Wülwer, Ulrich. *Das Nibelungenlied in der deutschen Kunst des 19. und 20. Jahrhunderts* (Kunstwissenschaftliche Untersuchungen des Ulmer Vereins, Verband für Kunst- und Kulturwissenschaften, vol. 9). Gießen: Anabas, 1980.

Storch, Wolfgang, ed. *Die Nibelungen: Bilder von Liebe, Verrat und Untergang.* Munich: Prestel, 1987.

Thomas, Neil, ed. *The Nibelungenlied and the Third Reich: Celtic and Germanic themes in European Literature.* Lewiston, NY: Mellen, 1994.

Vollmer, Hans. *Das Nibelungenlied, erläutert und gewürdigt, mit einem Überblick über die Sage und die neuere Nibelungendichtung.* 4th ed. Leipzig: Bredt, 1915.

[Vonbank, Elmar, ed.] *Nibelungenlied: Ausstellung zur Erinnerung an die Auffindung der Handschrift A des Nibelungenliedes im Jahre 1779 im Palast zu Hohenems.* Bregenz: Vorarlberger Landesmuseum, 1979.

Wilmanns, Wilhelm. *Der Untergang der Nibelunge in alter Sage und Dichtung* (Abhandlungen der Gesellschaft der Wissenschaften Göttingen, Philologisch-Historische Klasse, N.F., vol. 7,2). Berlin: Weidmann, 1903

Wolzogen, Hans von. *Der Nibelungenmythos in Sage und Literatur.* Berlin: Weber, 1876.

Wunderlich, Werner. *Der Schatz des Drachentödters: Materialien zur Wirkungsgeschichte des Nibelungenliedes zusammengestellt und kommentiert* (Literaturwissenschaft-Gesellschaftswissenschaft, vol. 30). Stuttgart: Klett-Cotta, 1977.

Wunderlich, Werner. "'Total krasse Helden.'" In *Sammlung, Deutung, Wertung: Ergebnisse, Probleme, Tendenzen und Perspektiven philologischer Arbeit: Mélanges de littérature médiévale et linguistique allemande, offerts à Wolfgang Spiewok à lóccasion de son soixantième anniversaire,* edited by Danielle Buschinger. Amiens: Université de Picardie. Centre d'Etudes Médiévales, 1988. 369–383.

Zatloukal, Klaus, ed. *3. Pöchlarner Heldenliedgespräch: Die Rezeption des Nibelungenliedes* (Philologica Germanica, vol. 16). Vienna: Fassbaender, 1995.

Index

Boldface numbers denote main articles.

A

"Abend am Rhein" (Evening by the Rhine) (Grill), 241

abstrakta konkreta, 265

Adam of Bremen, 34

Adelind, **49**
of *Klage,* 49, 59

adelvrî (noble and free), **141**

Adolf Hitler-Brücke, 310

Aesir, **49**

Aetius, Flavius, **49**
historical information, 49, 54, 60, 77

Ageidius Tschudi of Glarus, 197

Agnar/Auðabrodir, **49**
of *Helreið Brynhildar* (Brynhild's Ride to Hel), 20
of *Ragnars saga Loðbrókar,* 34
of *Sigrdrífumál* (The Lay of Sigrdrifa), 39
of *Volsunga Saga,* 49, 54

Aladarius, 184

Alberich/Albrich, **49–50**
cloak of invisibility of, 23, 50, 155, 162
as guardian of hoard, 23, 49–50, 147
Nibelungenlied, action in, 23, 49–50, 147
in *Ortnit,* 50
in *Ring* cycle, 50

Albrecht, Paul, 52

Albrecht von Kemenaten, of Dietrich epics, 6

Aldrian (1), **50**
king of Niflungaland, *Þiðreks Saga,* 42, 50

Aldrian (2), **50**
son of Atli, *Þiðreks Saga,* 50

Aldrian (3), **50**
son of Hogni, *Þiðreks Saga,* 50

Alexander (Rudolf von Ems), 225

Alf, of *Volsunga saga,* 45

Alf laila walaila, 189

Alfrik/Alpris, **50–51**
of *Thiðreks saga,* 50–51

Alibrand, of *Þiðreks saga,* 42

Almanzor, 183

Alphart, of Dietrich epics, 6

Alpharts Tod, 63
conflict in, 6
events of, 6, 84
as heroic epic, 201

Alphonse VI, king of Spain, 188

Alsvid (1), **51**
horse of *Volsunga saga,* 51

Alsvid (2), **51**
son of Heimir, *Volsunga saga,* 51, 84

"Ältere Nibelungenôt" (Elder Nibelungenôt), **191– 192**
epic dimensions of, 27, 191, 192

Alzei/Alzeye, **51**
historical information, 51
reference in *Klage,* 51
reference in *Nibelungenlied,* 51

"Am Rheine" (On the Rhine) (Schlegel), 260

Amals, 66